Origen: *On First Principles*

Origen: *On First Principles*

A Reader's Edition

TRANSLATED BY

JOHN BEHR

BASED ON THE EDITION OF
'ORIGEN: *ON FIRST PRINCIPLES*'
IN THE OXFORD EARLY CHRISTIAN TEXTS SERIES

OXFORD

UNIVERSITY PRESS

OXFORD

UNIVERSITY PRESS

Great Clarendon Street, Oxford, OX2 6DP,
United Kingdom

Oxford University Press is a department of the University of Oxford.
It furthers the University's objective of excellence in research, scholarship,
and education by publishing worldwide. Oxford is a registered trade mark of
Oxford University Press in the UK and in certain other countries

Published in the United States of America by Oxford University Press
198 Madison Avenue, New York, NY 10016, United States of America

British Library Cataloguing in Publication Data
Data available

Library of Congress Control Number: 2019952272

ISBN 978-0-19-884531-7

Printed and bound in Great Britain by
CPI Group (UK) Ltd, Croydon, CR0 4YY

For Fr Andrew
Ecclesiasticus sub fide Christi vivens et in medio ecclesiae positus

Preface

Several years ago now I interrupted the series of books I was writing to prepare the ground for the next volume in the sequence by undertaking an edition, translation, and study of the fragments of Diodore of Tarsus and Theodore of Mopsuestia. I had thought that, having completed that task, I would be able to return to the series. However, as I continued to study the period concerned, I became convinced that, in order to understand Evagrius and the sixth-century Origenist controversy properly, I would have to go back to take a closer look at the work here edited and translated, Origen's *On First Principles*. That, together with my increasing dissatisfaction with the standard English translation, based on Koetschau's edition of the text—representing as it does a curious byway of earlier Origen scholarship, yet remaining the translation and layout of the text that we are forced to use in the classroom—compelled me to undertake this new edition and translation, together with the extensive study that precedes it. It might be possible, now, to continue my series on the formation of Christian theology, but I suspect that there is more work to be done on the early stages of the formation of Christian theology, especially on the Gospel of John and a new edition and translation of *Against the Heresies* by Irenaeus of Lyons.

I have come to the conclusions presented here in the introduction over the course of repeatedly teaching a seminar class on Origen, grappling almost every year for the last decade with the difficult task of trying to make sense of this text, which lies, in so many ways, at the heart of subsequent theological reflection. I am deeply grateful to my students, who were prepared to grapple with the text with me. In particular I would like to thank Ignatius Green, my teaching assistant during the semester when this work finally came together, for carefully reading through what I had prepared and making numerous helpful suggestions. I would also like to thank Fr Khaled Anatolios, Paul Blowers, Conor Cunningham, Christina Gschwandtner, Tracy Gustilo, Fr John McGuckin, and Paul Saieg, for allowing me to talk through my interpretation of this work with them, and for making valuable suggestions. I would like to thank Tom Perridge and Karen Raith for their encouragement and forbearance, and especially the copyeditor, Malcolm Todd, and proofreader, Helen Hughes, for their sharp eyes, meticulous attention to detail, and comprehensive understanding of how the different elements of the work fit together, and all those involved in the final stages of production. Finally, this work is dedicated to Fr Andrew Louth, a long-time mentor in the ways of the Fathers.

Contents

Origen: *On First Principles*

PART ONE: THEOLOGY
I: The Apostolic Preaching

Abbreviations

Abbreviations for classical and Patristic texts are those found in the following:

The SBL Handbook of Style for Ancient Near Eastern, Biblical and Early Christian Studies, ed. P. H. Alexander et al. (Peabody, MA: Hendrickson, 1999).

For texts not listed in this handbook, the following have been used:

H. G. Liddell and R. Scott, *A Greek–English Lexicon,* rev. H. S. Jones with R. McKenzie. 9th edn with revised supplement (Oxford: Clarendon Press, 1996).

G. W. Lampe, *A Patristic Greek Lexicon* (Oxford: Clarendon Press, 1961).

Scriptural references have been given according to the LXX; this principally affects the numeration of the Psalms and the naming of 1 & 2 Samuel and 1 & 2 Kings as 1–4 Reigns.

ACO	*Acta Conciliorum Oecumenicorum*
ACW	Ancient Christian Writers
ANF	Ante-Nicene Fathers
BLE	*Bulletin de littérature ecclésiastique*
CCSA	Corpus Christianorum Series Apocryphorum
CCSL	Corpus Christianorum: Series Latina
CSEL	Corpus Scriptorum Ecclesiasticorum Latinorum
FC	Fathers of the Church
GCS	Die griechische christliche Schriftsteller der ersten [drei] Jarhunderte
GNO	Gregorii Nysseni Opera
JR	*Journal of Religion*
JTS	*Journal of Theological Studies*
LCL	Loeb Classical Library
Mansi	J. D. Mansi, ed., *Sacrorum conciliorum nova et amplissima collectio* (Florence, 1759–98)
NPNF	Nicene and Post Nicene Fathers
OAF	Oxford Apostolic Fathers
OCP	*Orientalia Christiana periodica*
OECS	Oxford Early Christian Studies

OECT	Oxford Early Christian Texts
PG	Patrologia Graeca
PL	Patrologia Latina
PO	Patrologia Orientalis
PPS	Popular Patristic Series
PTS	Patristiche Texte und Studien
RAug	*Recherches Augustiniennes et Patristiques*
RB	*Revue Biblique*
RSR	*Recherches de Science Religieuse*
SBL	Society of Biblical Literature
SC	Sources chrétiennes
StP	*Studia Patristica*
SVF	*Stoicorum Veterum Fragmenta*
SVTQ	*Saint Vladimir's Orthodox Theological Quarterly*
TU	Texte und Untersuchungen
ZNTW	*Zeitschrift für die neutestamentliche Wissenschaft und die Kunde der älteren Kirche.*

Introduction

1 ORIGEN AND HIS *ON FIRST PRINCIPLES*

Origen of Alexandria (*c*.185–*c*.254) was the greatest theological luminary of his age.[1] He was the most prolific Christian writer, or perhaps any writer, of the ancient world; Epiphanius (no friend of Origen) claimed that Origen's literary output amounted to six thousand works, while Jerome derides that number as impossible yet still asserts that Eusebius' list amounted to at most two thousand works, still an impressive number by any reckoning.[2] They include his monumental *Hexapla* (an edition of the Scriptures in six versions: Hebrew, the Septuagint, and other Greek translations), texts on Scriptural interpretation in various genres (commentaries, homilies, and scholia), treatises on martyrdom, prayer, and the Pascha, and one of the greatest apologetic works of early Christianity. He travelled extensively, visiting Rome to hear the great Christian teachers there, made visits to the Holy Land to explore the geography of the Scriptures, and was called to various councils of bishops around the Mediterranean to expound the faith and to examine the faith of others, even bishops. A transcript of an actual dialogue that took place at just such a meeting was discovered in the middle of the last century: in it Origen is described as 'teaching' those, including bishops, gathered together.[3] In the following

---

[1] The primary source for Origen's life is Eusebius, *Eccl. hist.* 6.1–39. On this text, see Robert M. Grant, 'Eusebius and his Lives of Origen', in *Forma Futuri: Studi in Onore del Cardinale Michele Pellegrino* (Turin: Bottega d'Erasmo, 1975), 635–49. The most important and comprehensive study is Pierre Nautin, *Origène: Sa vie et son œuvre* (Paris: Beauchesne, 1977). See also Henri Crouzel, *Origen*, trans. A. S. Worrall (Edinburgh: T. & T. Clark, 1989), 1–58 and John A. McGuckin, 'The life of Origen', in idem, ed., *The Westminster Handbook to Origen* (Louisville: Westminster John Knox Press, 2004), 1–23.

[2] Epiphanius, *Pan.* 64.63.8; Jerome, *Ruf.* 2.22.

[3] This is the *Dialogue of Origen with Heraclides and his Fellow Bishops on the Father, the Son, and the Soul*, discovered only in 1941. In *Dial.* 25, when Bishop Philip enters, Bishop Demetrius comments 'Our brother Origen is teaching (διδάσκει) that the soul is immortal.' The practice of bringing in 'theological experts' to examine the faith of those under question continues through the third century, as is seen in the case of Paul of Samosata, who was 'unmasked' at the Council of Antioch in 268/9, by the inquisition of Malchion, the learned head of a Rhetorical School in the city. See J. Behr, *Way to Nicaea*, Formation of Christian Theology, 1 (Crestwood, NY: St Vladimir's Seminary Press, 2001), 208–12. By the middle of the following century, the situation had changed: the bishops assembled in Antioch in 341 repudiated the charge of 'Arianism' by

century he would be appealed to by Athanasius as 'the labour-loving Origen' who had defended the consubstantiality of the Son with the Father, and lauded by Gregory the Theologian as 'the whetstone of us all'.[4]

Yet, when the Second Council of Constantinople met in 553 it condemned Origen and his 'impious writings'.[5] At the heart of this condemnation—going right back to Origen's conflict with Demetrius of Alexandria; the polemic begun against him by the turncoat Origenist, Methodius of Olympus, in the last decade of the third century; and a few decades later in the crisis that prompted Pamphilus, with the assistance of Eusebius, to write his *Apology for Origen;* followed later in the fourth century when Epiphanius, in his zeal to expose all heresies, precipitated a train of events that would bring about the spectacular falling-out of the former friends Rufinus and Jerome, causing a tsunami across the Christian world from the capital city of Rome to the heart-lands of Egyptian monasticism; and, finally, lurking behind the more daring speculations of the sixth-century 'Origenists' that were a significant part of his condemnation—lay the book here presented and translated, *On First Principles*.[6] It was, moreover, its translation that was the reason why, Jerome says, he took it upon himself to attack Rufinus, and it was the controversy that this caused which ultimately resulted in the original Greek text being lost to the ravages of history.

---

asking indignantly how they, as bishops, could be thought to be following a presbyter, that is, Arius. Athanasius, *Syn.* 22.3 (ed. Opitz, 248.29–30).

[4] Athanasius, *Decr.* 27; Gregory the Theologian as recorded in the *Suidae Lexicon,* ed. Adler, 3.619.

[5] Origen was condemned by name in the eleventh anathema of its closing session. For the relation of this condemnation to the two lists of anti-Origenist anathemas drawn up in 543 and 553, see Richard Price, *The Acts of the Council of Constantinople of 553 with Related Texts on the Three Chapters Controversy,* Translated Texts for Historians, 51, vol. 2 (Liverpool: Liverpool University Press, 2009), 270–99.

[6] On Methodius of Olympus, see John Behr, *The Nicene Faith,* Formation of Christian Theology, 2 (Crestwood, NY: St Vladimir's Seminary Press, 2004), 38–48; the sole surviving contemporary reference to Methodius comes from the *Apology for Origen* written by Pamphilus and Eusebius in the early fourth century, though this line is only preserved by Jerome: 'How can Methodius, who said this and that from the doctrines of Origen, now have the audacity to write against him?' (Jerome, *Ruf.* 1.11). For the situation that caused Pamphilus and Eusebius to write their *Apology for Origen,* see Rowan Williams, '*Damnosa haereditas*: Pamphilus' *Apology* and the Reputation of Origen', in H. C. Brennecke, E. L. Grasmuck, and C. Markschies, eds., *Logos: Festschrift für Luise Abramowski zum 8 Juli 1993* (Berlin: De Gruyter, 1993), 151–69, and Behr, *Nicene Faith,* 53–9. For the late fourth-century controversy, see especially Elizabeth A. Clark, *The Origenist Controversy: The Cultural Construction of an Early Christian Debate* (Princeton: Princeton University Press, 1992). And for the sixth-century controversy and condemnation, see Antoine Guillaumont, *Les 'Képhalia gnostica' d'Évagre le Pontique et l'histoire de l'origénisme chez les Grecs et chez les Syriens,* Patristica Sorbonensia, 5 (Paris: Seuil, 1962), and Daniel Hombergen, *The Second Origenist Controversy: A New Perspective on Cyril of Scythopolis' Monastic Biographies as Historical Sources for Sixth-Century Origenism,* Studia Anselmiana, 132 (Rome: S. Anselmo, 2001). For the relationship between the condemnation of 'Origenism' and the 'Three Chapters', see John Behr, *The Case against Diodore and Theodore: Texts and their Contexts,* OECT (Oxford: Oxford University Press, 2011), 108–29.

I Origen in Alexandria

Origen wrote *On First Principles* in Alexandria sometime around AD 229/30, by which time he had already come into conflict with Demetrius.[7] To set the work in proper context, it is necessary to describe both earlier events in his life and the situation of Christianity in Alexandria. Origen had been brought up as a devout Christian by his parents, with his father, Leonidas, a teacher of literature, training him in the divine Scriptures. Eusebius mentions that when Leonidas looked at his son asleep, 'he uncovered his breast as if the divine Spirit were enshrined within it, and kissed it reverently, considering himself blessed in his goodly offspring'.[8] The young Origen was also zealously impetuous: his mother had to hide his clothes so that he couldn't follow his father to martyrdom, although the story about his self-castration should probably be rejected.[9] After the martyrdom of Leonidas during the time of the prefect Laetus (199/200–3), leaving his family destitute, a wealthy lady gave refuge to Origen in her house and made it possible for him to continue his studies until he was able to support himself by teaching. She also treated as her 'adopted son' a certain heretic from Antioch called Paul, whose teaching had attracted 'a multitude not only of heretics but also of our people', though Eusebius underscores that Origen never joined Paul in prayer.[10] To all appearances, this group did not gather for prayer (or not, in Origen's case) in the house of their patroness in addition to, or instead of gathering elsewhere in an otherwise constituted church. The impression given by Eusebius is that even in the early third century there were a number of such communities coexisting in Alexandria, and that the relationships, and boundaries, between these house churches were somewhat hazy.[11]

When persecutions began again, under the prefect Aquila (206–10/11), all the teachers of Christianity in Alexandria fled the city, leaving Origen alone to

---

[7] Cf. Nautin, *Origène,* 370–1.   [8] Eusebius, *Eccl. hist.* 6.2.11.

[9] Eusebius, *Eccl. hist.* 6.2.5. It is at a slightly later period, when he had begun his work of instructing Christians, that Eusebius places Origen's self-castration (*Eccl. hist.* 6.8), suggesting that he did this in order to avoid charges of misconduct from pagans regarding his dealings with women (though Eusebius also claims that he kept it a secret) and that it had resulted from an over-literal interpretation of Matt. 19. Epiphanius, on the other hand, records a tradition that attributed Origen's renowned chastity to the use of drugs (*Panarion,* 64.3.12). Henry Chadwick suggests that both stories are 'malicious gossip', *Early Christian Thought and the Classical Tradition* (Oxford: Clarendon Press, 1987 [1966]), 68. Origen, routinely criticized for his allegorical interpretation, derides those who would take that scriptural passage literally (*Comm. Matt.* 15.1–5).

[10] Eusebius, *Eccl. hist.* 6.2.2–14.

[11] See also Eusebius' somewhat embarrassed report of a situation that happened later, during the time of Dionysius in *Eccl. hist.* 7.9, and the comments of Rowan Williams, 'Origen: Between Orthodoxy and Heresy', in W. A. Bienert and U. Kühneweg, *Origeniana Septima* (Leuven: Peeters, 1999), 3–14, at p. 6.

instruct those who turned to him 'to hear the Word of God'.[12] It is, notably, only after the persecutions ceased that Demetrius begins to play any role in Eusebius' narrative. Upon his return to the city, Demetrius was clearly obliged to praise Origen's valiant work, but also seems to have wanted to appropriate Origen's activity under his own authority. According to Eusebius, 'when he saw yet more coming to him [Origen] for instruction', Demetrius 'entrusted to him alone the school of catechesis' while he himself 'presided over the church', and in turn Origen gave up the teaching of grammar by which he had supported himself, as not 'consonant with divine training', and even sold his cherished volumes of literature in exchange for a meagre fixed income to support himself in his new position.[13] What we see here, I would suggest, is the first attempt at the establishment of monepiscopacy in the city of Alexandria, roughly contemporaneous with the establishment of monepiscopacy in Rome. It is really only from this point, when the activity of previously independent teachers (and leaders of Christian communities) was placed at the service of a newly-emerging monarchical style of episcopal leadership, that we can begin to speak of the 'Catechetical School' of Alexandria.[14] The establishment of monepiscopacy was not an easy development, nor a quick one. We should recall that even into the fourth century, the bishop of Alexandria had more authority over the regions outside Alexandria than he did over the strong presbyters in the city, an uneasy situation that is certainly part of the background for the eruption of the controversy between the presbyter Arius and the bishop Alexander.[15]

That Origen was not quite happy with the new configuration is shown by the letter he wrote after his final departure from Alexandria, in which he defends the propriety of studying philosophy and investigating heretical

[12] Eusebius, *Eccl. hist.* 6.3.1. On Eusebius' conflation of the two phases of the persecutions, see Nautin, *Origène*, 363–5. Eusebius states that it was 'some of the heathen' who came to Origen, though he assumes that Origen, and Pantaenus and Clement before him, were only ever involved in catechesis in the 'catechetical school'. In *Hom. Jer.* 4.3, Origen describes how during the times of martyrdom 'we came to the gathering, and the entire Church was present' (ἐπὶ τὰς συναγωγάς, καὶ ὅλη ἡ ἐκκλησία... παρεγίνετο). Nautin refers this to the persecution under Aquila; his conclusion, however, that some priests must have remained in the city, seems unnecessary (*Origène*, 416, fn. 11). See also n.25 below on the question of Origen's later 'ordination'.
[13] Eusebius, *Eccl. hist.* 6.3.8–9.
[14] Cf. Annewies van den Hoek, 'The Catechetical School of Early Christian Alexandria and Its Philonic Heritage', *HTR* 90 (1997), 59–87.
[15] Cf. Rowan Williams, *Arius: History and Tradition,* 2nd edn (London: SCM Press, 2001 [1987]), 42: 'The bishop of Alexandria occupied at this date what may seem a highly paradoxical position in the Egyptian church: on the one hand...he more closely resembled an archbishop or even a patriarch than any other prelate in Christendom....On the other hand, within Alexandria itself the bishop was surrounded by powerful and independent presbyters, supervising their own congregations.' On the development of the episcopacy in Alexandria, see Alistair C. Stewart, *The Original Bishops: Office and Order in the First Christian Communities* (Grand Rapids, MI: Baker Academic, 2014), 188–99.

doctrines.[16] He continues his letter by pointedly reminding his readers that Heraclas, 'who is now a member of the presbytery of Alexandria', had attended the lectures of the famous philosopher Ammonius Saccas for five years longer than he had himself and that, although Heraclas had previously worn common apparel, he has now laid it aside to adopt the philosopher's mantle and continues in his study of the books of the Greeks. Clearly there were other dimensions to Origen's tense relations with Demetrius. It is probably at this period that Origen visited Rome, perhaps to look for a more congenial milieu in which to pursue his studies and teaching, as had many others before him.[17] According to Eusebius, when Origen returned from Rome, he entrusted 'his pupil' Heraclas with 'the preliminary studies of those just learning the elements', so that he himself could have the time necessary for 'the deeper study of divine things and for the investigation and interpretation of the holy Scriptures' and teach only the more advanced.[18] It is more likely, however, that Demetrius was more directly involved in this reconfiguration, ousting Origen from his previous position.[19]

Supported by his wealthy patron Ambrose, whom he had converted from Valentinianism, and who in turn provided Origen with seven stenographers, and as many copyists, 'skilled in elegant writing', Origen set to the task of literary production, beginning with his *Commentary on the Psalms* and works concerned with more speculative and philosophical issues.[20] When the first few books of his *Commentary on Genesis* appeared, the tension between Origen and Demetrius increased, only to be exacerbated further with the work *On First Principles*. Eusebius speaks of Origen departing Alexandria for Palestine 'when no small warfare broke out in the city'.[21] Some have attempted to date this 'warfare' to an earlier period, perhaps referring to the violence unleashed by the Emperor Caracalla when he visited the city in the autumn and winter of 215–16, in retribution for the mockery made of him by students there. But as Origen previously did not leave the city during times of persecution, even when every other Christian leader did so, and as he went to Palestine, taking refuge with Alexander in Jerusalem (no friend of Demetrius), and as he returned to Alexandria only when urged to do so by deacons sent by Demetrius,

---

[16] An extract from the letter is preserved in Eusebius, *Eccl. hist.* 6.19.12–14.
[17] Nautin, *Origène*, 365, 418, would place this trip around 215; McGuckin, 'The Life of Origen', places it in 212.
[18] Eusebius, *Eccl. hist.* 6.15.
[19] Robert L. Wilken speaks of Origen being 'relieved of his duties by the bishop'. 'Alexandria: A School for Training in Virtue', in P. Henry, ed., *Schools of Thought in the Christian Tradition* (Philadelphia: Fortress, 1984), 15–30, at 17.
[20] For Ambrose, see Eusebius, *Eccl. hist.* 6.19 and 23.
[21] Eusebius, *Eccl. hist.* 6.19.16.

it is much more plausible to see the 'warfare' that erupted in Alexandria as the final breakdown in relations between Demetrius and Origen.[22]

While he was taking shelter in Jerusalem, the bishops of that region invited Origen to preach and expound the Scriptures in public and before bishops. What was normal in Palestine, however, ran counter to Demetrius' developing sense of the episcopacy, and Demetrius protested vociferously that it was unheard of for a layman to preach in the presence of bishops. Alexander, nonplussed, simply replied: 'I know not how he [Demetrius] comes to say what is plainly untrue,' and gave precedents for this practice.[23] Origen did eventually return to Alexandria, but his and Demetrius' respective visions of the Church were too different for any lasting peace. Back in Alexandria, Origen opened his new work, his magisterial *Commentary on John,* with the assertion that the true Levites, the priests and high priests, are 'those who devote themselves to the divine Word and truly exist by the service of God alone', words which Origen later used to describe himself and a piety which infuses the whole of Eusebius' description of him.[24]

Origen left Alexandria for good probably in 231, to settle in Palestine, where, according to Eusebius, 'he received the laying-on of hands for the presbyterate at Caesarea from the bishops there'.[25] Here he continued teaching, preaching, and writing, and undertook various trips, such as his visit to Arabia at the invitation of the bishops there to investigate the teachings of Beryllus. During the pogroms against Christians launched by Decius (250–1), Origen, then in his sixties, suffered extreme torture, being stretched on the rack, to no less than 'four spaces', Eusebius recounts with horror, only to be denied the martyrdom he had sought in his youth. He spent his final days, as a broken man, writing letters 'full of comfort to those in need' until his death a few years later.[26]

---

[22] Nautin, *Origène,* 366.   [23] Eusebius, *Eccl. hist.* 6.19.17–18.
[24] Origen, *Comm. Jo.* 1.10–11; cf. Eusebius, *Eccl. hist.* 6.19.12.
[25] Eusebius, *Eccl. hist.* 6.23.4. The plural 'bishops' is rather odd here, for in later times it became a firmly established practice that a single bishop lays his hands on the one he is ordaining as his presbyter, while the laying-on of hands by many bishops is reserved for elevation to the episcopacy. Here, as in other contexts and on other matters, Eusebius, as a fourth-century bishop, cannot envision any other practice than that to which he is accustomed. Eusebius' words, I would suggest, indicate a transitional phase in the development of the ordination practices, and should probably be taken as indicating the reception of Origen as an elder of the church of Caesarea, though perhaps without any oversight (ἐπισκοπή) of a particular community but free to continue his work as a teacher and writer. On the terms ἐπίσκοπος and πρεσβύτερος, see Stewart, *Original Bishops,* 11–53.
[26] Eusebius, *Eccl. hist.* 6.39.5.

II *On First Principles*

On First Principles was a controversial book from the beginning. And it still is, perhaps even more so, as we no longer have the original Greek text. It is routinely described as being the first attempt at a systematic theology, laying out the theological points that are universally held as certain and speculatively developing those that remain. But before we can consider the work further, we have to deal with the fact that we only have the complete work as it exists in the Latin translation of Rufinus—or rather the only extant version of the work is that of Rufinus' translation, for he readily admits in his prefaces that he has omitted some parts of the work and developed others.

Rufinus' translation

Rufinus began his translation of *On First Principles* at the request of the Roman nobleman Macarius in the summer of 398.[27] However, even by this stage he had already become embroiled in a bitter controversy with Jerome. A few years earlier, Epiphanius of Salamas had launched an attack against John of Jerusalem for his 'Origenism' and had uncanonically ordained Jerome's brother, Paulinian, to the priesthood, so that the monastery in which they resided at Bethlehem might be independent of John. Rufinus had sided with John and appealed to Theophilus of Alexandria, who had not yet become an opponent of Origenism. Jerome, on the other hand, supported Epiphanius and translated his letter to John.[28] Jerome claims that he had intended it only for a private readership, but that friends of Rufinus had bribed someone for a copy of it and were now using it to inflame the controversy further, also charging Jerome with having falsified the original.[29] Jerome then began a full-scale literary attack against John of Jerusalem, though he seems to have abandoned the project once he and Rufinus made peace, just before Rufinus departed for Rome in 397.[30]

Once in Rome, and prevailed upon by Macarius, Rufinus set about the task of translating *On First Principles* into Latin. Jerome's friends in Rome, Pammachius and Oceanus, managed to acquire a copy of the translation and sent it to Jerome, with a letter saying that they found many things in it which

---

[27] See Karl Holl, 'Die Zeitfolge des ersten origenistischen Streits' (1916), reprinted in idem, *Gesammelte Aufsätze zur Kirchengeschichte. II Der Osten* (Tübingen: J.C.B. Mohr [Paul Siebeck], 1928), 310–50, at 324. For the many different, and often intensely personal, dimensions to the controversy which erupted at this stage, see Clark, *Origenist Controversy,* 11–42.

[28] This letter is now counted as Jerome, *Ep.* 51.   [29] Jerome, *Ep.* 57.2–4.

[30] Jerome, *Ruf.* 3.33. Here he recalls how 'I had joined hands with you over the slain Lamb in the Church of the Resurrection.'

appeared to be unorthodox and that it seemed to them that Rufinus had omitted many passages that would have proved the heretical character of Origen. They asked Jerome to produce his own translation and make evident the falsifications and interpolations, and they further mention that Rufinus, in his preface to the work, made a subtle allusion to Jerome, to the effect that he was doing nothing other than completing the work of translating Origen begun by Jerome himself.[31] Now under attack in Rome, Rufinus defended his own theological orthodoxy in a written statement to Pope Anastasius and began an *Apology against Jerome.* Jerome, in turn, set about writing his own *Apology against Rufinus,* the first two books of which were written only on the basis of verbal reports about the contents of Rufinus' *Apology,* and the third after he had finally received a copy of the work.

Despite much bluster, aimed at Rufinus himself, Jerome's *Apologies* are, it has to be said, remarkably lacking in detail regarding the alleged errors in Rufinus' translations. For example, after stating that

> I find among the many bad things written by Origen the following most distinctly heretical: that the Son of God is a creature, that the Holy Spirit is a servant; that there are innumerable worlds succeeding one another in eternal ages; that angels have been turned into human souls…that our bodies themselves will grow aerial and spirit-like, and gradually vanish and disperse into thin air and into nothing; that in the restitution of all things…[all beings, including the devil] will be of one condition and degree…then will begin a new world from a new origin…[in which] one who is now a virgin may chance then to be a prostitute.

Jerome then continues rather lamely: 'These are the things I point out as heresies in the books of Origen; it is for you to point out in which of his books you have found them contradicted.'[32] Only in Jerome's letter to Avitus, written some ten years later, do we have not only paraphrases of Origen's reported teaching but substantial passages in which he claims to be quoting Origen in his own words as accurately translated by Jerome himself.[33]

Such, briefly, is the context in which Rufinus translated *On First Principles* and composed his two prefaces, the first after completing the first two books, and the second a little later after completing the third and fourth. In his first preface, Rufinus mentions that Origen's books, and especially *On First Principles,* 'have been corrupted in many places by heretics and malevolent persons', and that his writings are often 'for other reasons most obscure and very difficult', discussing as they do subjects which philosophers spend their whole lives investigating to no avail. As such, he continues,

---

[31] The letter of Pammachius and Oceanus is counted as Jerome, *Ep.* 83. See also Jerome's reply in *Ep.* 84.
[32] Jerome, *Ruf.* 2.12.   [33] Jerome, *Ep.* 124.

Wherever, therefore, we found in his writings anything contrary to that which he had himself elsewhere piously laid down regarding the Trinity, we have either omitted it, as being corrupt or interpolated, or we have rendered it according to that rule which we frequently find affirmed by him. If, however, as speaking now to persons of skill and knowledge, he has expressed himself obscurely while wanting to proceed quickly, we have, to make the passage clearer, added what we have read more fully on the same subject in his other works, seeking [to provide] explanation. We have said nothing of our own, however, but simply returned to him his own statements, though said in other places.   (1 Pr.3)

In the second preface, he repeats that he has 'taken care not to translate such passages as appear to be contrary to the rest of Origen's teaching and to our faith, but to omit them as being interpolations and forgeries of others', and then further specifies that,

If he appeared to have uttered any novelties about rational beings, since the chief point of the faith does not consist in this, for the sake of knowledge and exercise (since perhaps by necessity we must reply to certain heresies in such a manner) I have neither omitted them in these nor in the preceding books, except when perhaps he wished to repeat in the subsequent books what he had already said in those previous ones and, for the sake of brevity, I thought it convenient to cut out some of these repetitions.   (2 Pr.)

It is important to note Rufinus' precision: it is only with regard to matters pertaining to the Trinity that, if he found anything in the work that seemed to him contrary to what Origen says elsewhere, he omitted it as either corrupt or an interpolation; whereas if it is something unusual relating to rational beings, he has no problem in retaining the passages, apart from removing repetitions. While on the other hand, if something is particularly difficult or obscure, he has expanded the text by including passages from other works of Origen. It has, it should also be noted, proven impossible to identify such interpolated passages in Rufinus' translation of *On First Principles*. The most that even Jerome can claim is that Rufinus has inserted a passage of scholia composed by Didymus into *Princ.* 1.1.8.[34]

That Origen's works were subject to corruption and interpolation is certain; it even led to Pamphilus writing a short text on this very topic, *On the Falsification of the Books of Origen,* which also only survives in the Latin translation of Rufinus. It is also something that happened during Origen's own lifetime. In his work, Pamphilus includes a passage from a letter of Origen written to close friends in Alexandria, portions of which are also included by Jerome in his *Apology against Rufinus,* translated from the Greek by Jerome himself, and thus beyond suspicion. In this letter, after mentioning how the Apostle

---

[34] Cf. Jerome, *Ruf.* 2.11.

Paul also had to deal with falsified material alleging to come from himself (cf. 2 Thess. 2.1–3), Origen recounts the following incident:

> I see, then, that something like this is also happening to us. For a certain author of a heresy, when a discussion was held between us in the presence of many persons and was recorded, took the document from those who had written it down. He added what he wanted to it, removed what he wanted, and changed what seemed good to him. Then he carried it around as if it were from me, pouring scorn conspicuously on the things that he himself had composed. The brethren who are in Palestine were indignant over this. They sent a man to me at Athens who was to receive from me the authentic copy. Prior to this I had not even re-read or revised the work, but it was lying there in such a neglected state that it could hardly be found. But I sent it, and I say with God as my witness that, when I met the man who had falsified the work, [and asked him] why he had done this, he answered, as if he were giving me satisfaction: 'Because I wanted to adorn and purify that discussion.' Behold with what kind of 'purification' he 'purified' my discussion: with that kind of 'purification' by which Marcion 'purified' the Gospels or the Apostle![35]

Jerome also provides evidence that works, or rather a specific work, of Origen had been corrupted. After complaining about Rufinus' bad translation of this letter ('turning it into Latin, or rather overturning it'), so masking its real intent of assailing Demetrius of Alexandria and inveighing against bishops worldwide, Jerome mentions a written dialogue between Origen and a Valentinian called Candidus on the topics of the Son's relation to the Father and whether the Devil can be saved. Origen, according to Jerome, 'rightly' taught that the Devil is not of a substance doomed to perish, but fell by his own will, and so can be saved, which Candidus then changed into the calumny that Origen held that the diabolical nature itself can be saved.[36] But, Jerome adds, it is only with respect to this particular dialogue that Origen claims his words have been falsified.

Although Jerome excoriates Rufinus for his translation, modern assessments are more favourable. In the case of *On First Principles,* we are able to compare a good portion of the work, *Princ.* 3.1 and 4.1–3, with the Greek text as it has been preserved for us in the *Philocalia,* the compilation of extracts from Origen's writings prepared by Basil of Caesarea and Gregory the Theologian in the mid fourth century. It is indeed true that Rufinus often expands the text, bringing in further extended imagery or additional scriptural quotations, though it is also the case that the editors of the *Philocalia* have omitted other passages (e.g. *Princ.* 3.1.23) for no clear reason. But when

---

[35] Pamphilus, *Fals.* 7; cf. Jerome, *Ruf.* 2.18.   [36] Jerome, *Ruf.* 2.19.

Rufinus does so, it is never to distort the sense deliberately. As John Rist concludes from a detailed comparison of passages from *Princ.* 3.1:

> What we have just been looking at are no obvious deformations of the text due to a desire to save Origen from accusations of heresy, but the more subtle and often unconscious changes which arise from Rufinus being a product of Latin rather than Greek culture, from his Latin desire for rhetorical embellishment and Vergilian echoes, and from his emphasis on law and the judiciary, rather than on philosophical enquiry and the quarrels of the schools. Of the world in which Origen himself moved and thought it appears from our study that Rufinus was largely ignorant.[37]

For better or worse, the Latin translation of Rufinus, with his own forthright admission about his translation practices, remains the text of *On First Principles* as we have it.

Modern Editions

However, the problems surrounding this seminal work of Origen were exacerbated in modern times by the edition of the text produced by Paul Koetschau in 1913, and then by the translation into English of this edition by G. W. Butterworth in 1936, which thereafter became the standard translation for English-speaking scholarship, replacing the earlier translation of Frederick Crombie for the Ante-Nicene Christian Library series (included later in the Ante-Nicene Fathers series).[38] Every prior editor, from Jacques Merlin (1512) to Charles Delarue (1733; later incorporated into PG 11), had presented Rufinus' translation intact, with Delarue also incorporating, for the first time, parallel passages from the *Philocalia*, Jerome, and Justinian, alongside Rufinus' text. Koetschau, on the other hand, taking his lead from Rufinus' own admission of having omitted certain passages, determined that Rufinus cannot be trusted at all and, convinced that the accounts of Origen's teaching given by his opponents, especially the letter of Jerome to Avitus, the reports of Justinian, and even the anathemas of 553, do in fact represent Origen's authentic teaching, set about the task not only of putting passages from others in parallel, but

---

[37] John M. Rist, 'The Greek and Latin Texts of the Discussion on Free Will in *De Principiis*, Book III', in Henri Crouzel, Gennaro Lomiento, and Joseph Rius-Camps, eds., *Origeniana: Premier colloque international des études origéniennes (Monserrat, 18–21 septembre 1973)*, Quaderni di 'Vetera Christianorum', 21 (Bari: Istituto di Letteratura Cristiana Antica– Università di Bari, 1975), 97–111 at 111. See also, in the same volume, Henri Crouzel, 'Comparisons précises entre les fragments du *Peri Archon* selon la *Philocalie* et la traduction de Rufin', *Origeniana*, 113–21.

[38] Paul Koetschau, *De principiis*, Origenes Werke 5, GCS (Leipzig: Hinrichs, 1913); G. W. Butterworth, *Origen: On First Principles* (London: SPCK, 1936).

breaking up Rufinus' translation, wherever he thought he could discern a lacuna, and interpolating into its flow passages supplied from elsewhere.[39]

At some points, the passages so inserted clearly twist what Origen said. For instance, at the beginning of *Princ.* 2.9.1, Rufinus has Origen saying: 'In that beginning it must be supposed that God created so great a number of rational or intellectual creatures, or whatever the intellects mentioned above are to be called, as he foresaw would be sufficient.' Koetschau inserts into the body of his text a couple of sentences from Justinian's *Epistle to Menas* saying: 'In the beginning under consideration, God, by his will, caused to subsist as large a number of intellectual beings as he was able to control; for it must be admitted that the power of God is finite and its circumscription must not be done away with under the pretext of praise.'[40] Origen, as we will consider in more detail later on, contemplates the beginning of things by looking to their end (cf. *Princ.* 1.6.1); and with the certainty of the apostolic affirmation that in the end all things will be subject to God, who in turn will be 'all in all' (1 Cor. 15:28), describes the beginning in similar terms. Rather than an affirmation based on a definitive eschatological end, it has become, in the hands of his opponents, an affirmation of the limited power of a finite God. Alternatively, as it is put in *On Faith*, ascribed to Rufinus the Presbyter of Palestine, in a sentence given by Koetschau in his critical apparatus, 'Origen says, "God did not make all those whom he wished, but only those whom he could hold together and grasp."'[41]

Rufinus readily states, as we have seen, that he has omitted or reworked parts of the text that pertain to the Trinity, and, indeed, many of the passages supplied by Koetschau to *Princ.* 1 have a stronger 'subordinationist' flavour to them than Rufinus' translation, as for instance, the passage from Justinian's *Epistle to Menas* placed by Koetschau in the middle of *Princ.* 1.2.13.[42] Here Origen is expounding how Christ is said to be 'the image of his goodness' (Wis. 7:26), describing the Father as the 'primal goodness from which the Son is born', such that the Son is 'the image of his goodness', for 'there is no other second goodness existing in the Son, besides that which is in the Father'. It is for this reason, Origen says, that Christ rightly says 'No one is good but one, the God and Father.'[43] In Justinian's report, this becomes the assertion that:

---

[39] The problems with Koetschau's edition (and thereby Butterworth's translation) have, of course, been noted before. See, most recently, Ronnie J. Rombs, 'A Note on the Status of Origen's *De Principiis* in English', *VC* 61 (2007), 21–9.

[40] Justinian, *Ep. ad Menam* (ed. Schwartz, 190.8–14, two sentences of which are repeated at 209.3–6).

[41] Rufinus of Palestine, *De fide*, PL 21, 1131b.

[42] Justinian, *Ep. ad Menam* (ed. Schwartz, 210.1–6).

[43] Matt. 19:17; Mark 10:18; Luke 18:19. Origen habitually adds the word 'Father' to this saying of Christ.

Perhaps also the Son is good, but yet not good simply, and that just as *he is the image of the invisible God* and, in this respect, God, but not the one of whom Christ himself says *that they may know you the only true God,* so also he is the image of the goodness, but not, as the Father, invariably good.

The possible negative implications are drawn out of Origen's position and attributed to him, though with the qualifier 'perhaps'.

At other times, Jerome's paraphrases of what Origen wrote are inserted by Koetschau into the body of the text for no apparent reason. For instance, in *Princ.* 1.7.4, Koetschau interpolates a passage from Jerome's letter to Avitus beginning, 'the sun also and the moon and the rest of the stars are animated . . .'. As Origen has indeed been discussing how Scripture presents the celestial bodies as living beings, there is no need for this addition, especially as it is only a paraphrase given by Jerome, who continues a few lines later in the letter by saying, 'that no one should suppose that what I say is ours, let us quote his actual words'.[44] That Koetschau should prefer Jerome's paraphrase over Rufinus' translation clearly demonstrates the level of distrust he had for Rufinus.[45]

However, most serious is the fact that, although Rufinus carefully specified that even when Origen 'appeared to have uttered any novelties about rational beings' he has not omitted these because the substance of the faith is not affected, the largest interpolations introduced by Koetschau, especially the infamous 'Fragments' 15 and 17a inserted into *Princ.* 1.8, concern precisely the 'Origenist' teachings about eternally existing intellects and their fall into bodies. These are, moreover, passages which Koetschau literally 'made up', by stitching together sentences from various anti-Origenist writers.[46] Likewise many of the anathemas from 553 are included within the text of Rufinus, as if Origen himself could have written them. The effect of all of this—especially when these texts are presented, in Butterworth's translation, under the capitalized heading 'GREEK' (and the details relegated to small print in the footnotes), to give the impression to the unwary reader that this is the authentic text of Origen himself—is to seriously distort the text that we have, beyond any hope of comprehension. It is not Rufinus who produced a 'garbled version of Origen's work', as Butterworth charges him, but Koetschau and Butterworth himself.[47]

---

[44] Jerome, *Ep.* 124.4.

[45] Butterworth, who in his introduction lambasts Rufinus even more than does Jerome for the inadequacies of his translation, lamely comments here: 'The passage is clearly meant to give a true representation of the original, though not perhaps in a strict translation' (*On First Principles,* p. 62, n.8).

[46] These 'fragments' are included in the Appendix as items 10 and 12.

[47] Butterworth, *On First Principles,* xli.

Fortunately scholarship has moved on. It no longer looks upon Origen as a platonizing Christian, indulging in speculative flights of fancy based upon an arbitrary allegorical reading of Scripture.[48] It has also become universally accepted that the anathemas of the sixth century and the reports of Justinian were directed primarily against Evagrius and sixth-century 'Origenism', rather than Origen himself.[49] In this changed climate, more recent editors and translators of the text have proceeded, rightly, from the assumption that we should begin, as we always must, not with the alleged teaching of a writer, by which we then reconstruct the text, but with the text itself, however we have it, on the basis of which we then try to understand his teaching. Thus the French translation of Marguerite Harl, Gilles Dorival, and Alain Le Boulluec, published in 1976, consigned every reported fragment of Origen's text to an appendix, presenting them in a chronological order, to map the developing reports of Origen's teaching, rather than in accordance with their supposed place within the text itself.[50] In the same year, a new German edition and translation, prepared by Herwig Görgemanns and Heinrich Karpp, places most (but not all) of the extracts in the space between the text and the critical apparatus, and relegates the anathemas to an appendix.[51] Two years later, these were followed by the first instalment of a new edition and French translation undertaken by Henri Crouzel and Manlio Simonetti for the *Sources chrétiennes* series; they relegated all the fragments and parallels to separate volumes, accompanied by extensive and detailed notes.[52] The most recent edition, that of Samuel Fernandez, places the Greek texts that are genuine parallels to Rufinus' text alongside the Latin text and places other extracts, as did Görgemanns and Karpp, between the text and the critical apparatus. None of these recent editors and translators have considered it to be of any value to reproduce Koetschau's Fragments 15 and 17a, and understandably so.

The object of this edition and translation is to present again (especially for an English-speaking readership, which has so far been deprived of a translation of *On First Principles* representing the advances in scholarship on Origen made since Koetschau and Butterworth) Rufinus' Latin text and its translation, as an unbroken whole. I have followed other recent editors and translators in placing material which is genuinely in parallel with Rufinus' texts between the Latin text and the critical apparatus. I have relegated all other material, including Koetschau's Fragments 15 and 17a, to an appendix; they are a historical curiosity which should be retained, even if only as a reminder of the byways

---

[48] See especially Mark Julian Edwards, *Origen Against Plato*, Ashgate Studies in Philosophy and Theology in Late Antiquity (Aldershot: Ashgate, 2002).

[49] See especially Guillaumont, *Les 'Képhalia gnostica'*, 124–70.

[50] *Origène. Traité des Principes (Peri Archon)*, Études Augustiniennes (Paris, 1976).

[51] *Origenes vier Bücher von den Prinzipien* (Darmstadt, 1976; 3rd edn 1992).

[52] *Origène: Traité des Principes*, SC 252, 253, 268, 269, 312 (Paris: Cerf, 1978, 1980, 1984).

of earlier scholarship on Origen. I have also taken the step, for the sake of consistency, of placing the Greek texts from the *Philocalia* (i.e. *Princ.* 3.1 and 4.1–3) below the Latin text of Rufinus. There is no real doubt about their authenticity; but this is primarily an edition of Rufinus' Latin translation of Origen's *On First Principles,* and, it should always be recalled, the compilers of the *Philocalia* also omitted sections from what they reproduced.

2 THE STRUCTURE OF *ON FIRST PRINCIPLES*

Even having accepted that we must at least begin with Rufinus' text, there nevertheless remain further, and perhaps the most perplexing, problems requiring attention. As Brian Daley comments: 'Few subjects have puzzled and challenged interpreters of Origen more than the structure, the purpose, and even the title of his treatise *Περὶ ἀρχῶν.*'[53] Any attempt to understand Origen, in part or in whole, must address these questions, beginning with the structure.

The text as it has come down to us, in the eight manuscripts dating from the ninth to the thirteenth century used by modern editors, all present the text as divided into four books and further supply a variety of chapter headings.[54]

The division of the work into four books seems to go back to Origen himself, for at the end of *Princ.* 3 he signs off: 'we here bring the third book to end'. It is possible, of course, but unlikely, that these are Rufinus' words; Pamphilus, working with the Greek text, also knew of the division of *On First Principles* into four books, specifying, in his *Apology,* from which book it was that he drew particular passages. The division of the work into four books, however, is not a thematic division.[55] As Basilius Steidle pointed out, back in 1941, the work is in fact divided into three parts, *Princ.* 1.1–2.3, 2.4–4.3, 4.4, with each part dealing with a threefold series of similar subjects: the Father, Son, and Holy Spirit; the nature and freedom of created intellectual beings; and the material world, with its beginning and end, in which their salvation is worked

---

[53] Brian E. Daley, 'Origen's *De Principiis:* A Guide to the Principles of Christian Scriptural Interpretation', in John Petruccione ed., *Nova et Vetera: Patristic Studies in Honor of Patrick Halton* (Washington, DC: Catholic University of America Press, 1998), 3–21, at 3.

[54] For further details on the manuscripts and chapter headings, see John Behr, ed. and trans. *Origen: On First Principles, OECT* (Oxford: Oxford University Press, 2017), xc and the Appendix.

[55] Crouzel's assertion, that 'Un tome c'est la quantité de texte que contient un rouleau de papyrus', made originally in the introduction to his edition of the work (SC 252, p. 16) and repeated in his study on the Alexandrian (*Origen,* 46) and by many others since, though appealing, suffers, as Charles Kannengiesser points out, from the fact that no evidence is ever given for this assertion, and, moreover, as the books are of different lengths, one would have to accept that the rolls were cut accordingly and so 'the argument becomes circular'; 'Origen, Systematician in *De Principiis*', in R. J. Daly, ed., *Origeniana Quinta* (Leuven: University Press–Peeters, 1992), 395–405, at 395.

out.[56] Once pointed out, the basic lines of this structure are indeed obvious and have been adopted in various ways in most recent editions.

The further division into chapters is, however, more problematic. As Marguerite Harl notes, despite being 'extremely audacious' in his handling of Rufinus' text, Koetschau was, ironically, very conservative with respect to the chapter headings, reproducing the chapter headings (though only some) from the same particular manuscripts as had Delarue before him.[57] Yet the manuscripts differ greatly in regard to the chapter headings. In his introduction, Koetschau lists the complete series of headings found in the two manuscripts he used for his headings, *Codex Bambergensis* Msc. Part. 113 (B IV, 27 = B) and *Codex Casinensis* 343 (= C).[58] Yet these manuscripts give many more headings than have been used by editors. For instance, for *Princ.* 1.2, on Christ, they have no less than seven separate headings. Other manuscripts, on the other hand, have no headings at all, such as *Codex Abricensis* 66 and *Codex Sorbonicus* lat. 16322, which merely differentiate chapters by means of an enlarged capital letter. Besides the article of Harl, it is striking how little attention has been devoted to the question of the chapter headings; only in the most recent edition, that of Fernandez (2015), do all these variants appear in the critical apparatus for the first time.[59] Koetschau held that it was 'very likely' that the basis for the division into chapters, and some of the chapter headings themselves, go back to Rufinus, and that their increase resulted from scribal additions over the course of time, a position now generally held, though the implications of this have not yet been fully assimilated and acted upon.[60]

There are two other important points of reference for trying to understand the structure of *On First Principles*. The first is Origen's own Preface to the work, in which he gives a long list of items pertaining in various ways to the apostolic and ecclesiastical preaching; we will consider this in detail below. The other is an external point of reference, and important because it

---

[56] 'Neue Untersuchungen zu Origenes Περὶ Ἀρχῶν', *ZNTW* 40 (1941), 236–43. On the structure of *On First Principles*, see also Manlio Simonetti, 'Osservazioni sulla struttura del *De Principiis* di Origene', *Rivista di filologia e di istruzione classica*, n.s. 40 (1962), 273–90, 372–93; Paul Kübel, 'Zum Aufbau von Origenes De Principiis', *VC* 25 (1971), 31–9; Marguerite Harl, 'Structure et coheréce du *Peri Archôn*', in Crouzel et al., eds, *Origeniana*, 11–32; Gilles Dorival, 'Remarque sur la forme du *Peri Archon*', in Crouzel et al., eds, *Origeniana*, 33–45; Henri Crouzel, 'Qu'a voulu faire Origène en composant le *Traité des Principes*', *BLE* 76 (1975), 161–86, 241–60; Gilles Dorival, 'Nouvelles remarques sur la forme du *Traité des Principes*', *RAug* 22 (1987), 67–108; and Daley, 'Origen's *De Principiis*'.

[57] 'Recherches sur le περὶ ἀρχῶν d'Origène en vue d'une nouvelle édition: La division en chapitres', *StP* 3, TU 78 (Berlin 1961), 57–67, at 57–8.

[58] Koetschau, *De Principiis*, CXLIII–CXLVIII.

[59] Even Gustave Bardy, in his otherwise painstaking study, *Recherches sur l'histoire du texte et des versions latines du* De Principiis *d'Origène*, Mémoires et Travaux des Facultés catholiques de Lille, 25 (Paris: Édouard Champion, 1923), completely neglects the topic.

[60] Koetschau, *De Principiis*, CXLI.

bears witness to the Greek text now no longer extant. This is the report that Photius provides of the work in his *Myriobiblios* or *Bibliotheca*.[61] In his brief account of the work, Photius does indeed speak of four books, and provides brief summaries of the topics covered, which often match the Latin titles found in the manuscripts, though these are typically shorter, and, for some inexplicable reason, what we know as *Princ.* 3.6, 'On the End or Consummation', is found, according to Photius, at the beginning of Book 4.

I The Two Cycles

On the basis of various manuscript headings, Origen's Preface, and Photius' report, Crouzel and Simonetti, in their edition, further refined the division of the work into the two main 'cycles', by differentiating nine 'treatises'. It will be helpful at this stage to set in parallel Photius' account, the chapter headings used by Koetschau/Butterworth (those most familiar to the English reader) and schema adopted by Crouzel and Simonetti (see pp. xxx–xxxii).[62]

What seems a rather random progression of themes in Koetschau and Butterworth is brought into greater clarity by the division of the work into two 'cycles'. But what is the relation between the two cycles, and the topics treated in each?

Steidle himself, building upon Hal Koch's *Pronoia und Paideusis*, had suggested that there were parallels between Origen's work and the contemporary 'school philosophy', in which the basic 'principles' were developed in similar, repeated patterns, building up cycles of teaching.[63] Also important in developing a better understanding of the structure of *On First Principles* were the works of classicists in the early twentieth century, especially the study on Horace's *Ars poetica* by Eduard Norden, in which he explored how introductory handbooks (the εἰσαγωγαί) for fields such as poetics, rhetoric, philosophy, and physics developed in the Hellenistic period, originating in Stoic circles and extending to middle and late Platonism, and also showed how they often had a bipartite structure, in which the first part provided a summary of the

---

[61] Photius, *Bibliotheca*, 8.

[62] The translation produced by Harl, Dorival, and Le Boulluec is structured slightly differently, dividing each cycle into nine treatises; neither Görgemanns/Karpp nor Fernandez format their editions according to a larger scheme, though both recognize that the work is divided into two 'cycles' and a summary. The variations between the most recent editions do not affect the points that I will make below.

[63] Steidle, 'Neue Untersuchungen', 240. Hal Koch, *Pronoia und Paideusis. Studien über Origenes und sein Verhältnis zum Platonismus* (Berlin: De Gruyter, 1932), 251ff.

Photius	Koetschau/Butterworth	Crouzel/Simonetti
		First Cycle of Treatises (1.1–2.3) **Expounding all of the Three Archai (in a large sense)**
		First Treatise *On the Father, Son and Holy Spirit (1.1–4)*
The first deals with the Father, the Son, and the Holy Spirit; in this his statements are often blasphemous, saying that the Son was made by the Father, the Holy Spirit by the Son; and that the Father pervades all existing things, the Son only the rational being, the Holy Spirit only those being saved.	1.1: God 1.2: Christ 1.3: The Holy Spirit 1.4: Loss, or falling away	(I) 1.1: On God (II) 1.2: On Christ (III) 1.3.1–4: On the Holy Spirit (IV) 1.3.5–4.2: On the particular action of each Person (Appendix) 1.4.3–5: The Father is the Creator of the whole eternity of the intelligible world contained in his Son
He also says other irrational things full of impiety; he babbles about metempsychosis, and the stars being alive, and other similar things.		
His first book mythologize about the Father, and Christ (as he calls him),		
and the Holy Spirit,		
and also rational beings.	1.5: Rational natures	*Second Treatise* *On Rational Creatures (1.5–8)* (I) 1.5–6: On rational creatures in general (A) 1.5.3–5: The accidental character of rational creatures
	1.6: The end or consummation 1.7: Things corporeal and incorporeal	(B) 1.6: The beginning and the end (II) 1.7–8. The different orders of rational creatures (A) 1.7.2–5: The Stars
Second book is about the world and the created things in it,	1.8: The angels 2.1: The world 2.2: The perpetuity of bodily nature 2.3: The beginning of the world and its causes	(B) 1.8: Angels (demons and human beings) *Third Treatise* *On the World and the creatures found in it (2.1–3)*

Photius	Koetschau/Butterworth	Crouzel/Simonetti
		Second Cycle of Treatises (2.4–4.3) **Corresponding to diverse points in the Preface** *First Treatise* *That the God of the Law and the Prophets and of the Gospels is one and the same God for the Old and New Testaments (2.4–5)*
and that there is one God of the Law and the prophets, and the same God is of the Old and the New Testament;	2.4: That the God of the Law and the Prophets, and the Father of our Lord Jesus Christ, is one	(A) 2.4: First section
	2.5: The just and the good	(B) 2.5: On the Just and the Good
and about the incarnation of the Saviour,	2.6: The Incarnation of Christ	*Second Treatise* *On the Incarnation of the Saviour* (2.6)
and that the same Spirit is in Moses and the rest of the prophets and the holy apostles;	2.7: The Holy Spirit	*Third Treatise* *That the same Spirit was in Moses and in the other prophets and in the apostles (2.7)*
and also about the soul,	2.8: The soul	*Fourth Treatise* *On the Soul (2.8–9)*
	2.9: The world and the movements of rational creatures, both good and evil and the causes of these movements	(I) 2.8: On the soul in general (II) 2.9: On the world, the movements of rational creatures, good or bad, and their causes
		Fifth Treatise *On the resurrection, punishments, and promises (2.10–11)*
resurrection, the punishment, and the promises.	2.10: The resurrection and the judgement	(I) 2.10: On resurrection (II) 2.10.4: On punishments (III) 2.11: On the promises
	2.11: The promises	
The third book is about self-determination;	3.1: Free will	*Sixth Treatise* *On Free Will* 3.1: On Free Will
how the devil and opposing powers, according to the Scriptures, waged war against the human race;		*Seventh Treatise* *How the Devil and adverse powers fight the human race according to the Scriptures (3.2–4)*

Photius	Koetschau/Butterworth	Crouzel/Simonetti
	3.2: The opposing powers	(I) 3.2: On the adverse powers
		(II) 3.3: On the three forms of wisdom
	3.3: The threefold wisdom	(III) 3.4: Is it true, as some say, that everyone possesses two souls?
	3.4: Whether the statement made by some is true, that each individual has two souls	
that the world was created and is perishable, having had a beginning in time.	3.5: That the world took its beginning in time	*Eighth Treatise (3.5–6)* (I) 3.5: That the world is made and perishable, having begun in time
The fourth book is about the end;	3.6: The consummation of the world	(II) 3.6: On the subject of the end
		Ninth Treatise (4.1–3) *That the Scriptures are divine and how they are to be read*
that the Scriptures are divine;	4.1: The divine inspiration of the Scriptures	(I) 4.1: That the Scriptures are inspired by God
the end is on how one ought to read and understand the Scriptures.	4.2: Many not understanding the Scriptures spiritually and interpreting them erroneously, have fallen into heresies	(II) 4.2–3: That many do not understand the spiritual meaning of Scripture, and misunderstanding fall into heresy
	4.3: Illustrations from the Scriptures of the method in which Scripture should be understood	
	4.4: Summary of the doctrine concerning the Father, the Son, and the Holy Spirit, and of the other matters discussed in the foregoing chapters	4.4: Recapitulation on the Father, the Son, and the Holy Spirit, and the other points treated above

important points, whereas the second part would develop these points from a different perspective.[64]

Building upon such earlier work, Harl and Dorival argued that *On First Principles* should best be understood in the company of those handbooks that offer a systematic presentation of philosophy, such as Alcinous' *Epitome*.[65] Here, after discussing the nature of philosophy itself and its modes of knowing and judging, Alcinous turns 'to a discussion of first principles [περὶ τῶν ἀρχῶν] and doctrines of theology, taking our start from the primary elements [ἀπὸ τῶν πρώτων] and then descending from these to examine, first, the origin of the world, and finally the origin and nature of the human being'; the three first principles for Alcinous, are, working upwards, matter, the intelligible forms, and God.[66] The parallels to the range of topics covered by Origen are indeed striking. And there was at least one work from this period that was called *On First Principles,* written by Longinus, a student of Ammonius Saccas and a contemporary of Plotinus and Origen.[67] Regarding the two main parts of the work, Harl suggests that the first part is more global, general, complete, and integrated, whereas the second part takes up particular questions for discussion. In her estimation, moreover, the second part is the principal focus of the work, for it corresponds to the programme set out by Origen himself in his Preface.[68] Origen has, in their telling, taken a brave new step in the development of Christian theology, by composing a Christian 'physics', a treatment of the origin, composition, and end, of the world and the human being, drawing upon Scripture, tradition, and human reason.

---

[64] Eduard Norden, 'Die Composition und Litteraturgattung der horazischen Epistula ad Pisones', *Hermes*, 40 (1905), 481–528, which remains one of the most important studies on the topic. Manfred Fuhrman, *Das systematische Lehrbuch: Ein Beitrag zur Geschichte der Wissenschaften in der Antike* (Göttingen: Vandenhoeck and Ruprecht, 1960), 122–31, argued that the bipartite structure has a Sophistic origin. A further important work is the extensive analysis of the *De mundo* attributed to Aristotle by A.-J. Festugière in his *La révélation d'Hermès Trismégiste*, vol. 2 (Paris: Cabalda, 1949), 460–518. The works they identify as so structured are quite extensive, including: Horace, *Ars poetica* (*Ep. ad Pisones*), before 4 BC; Quintillian, *Institutio oratoria*, before AD 96; the *De mundo* attributed to Aristotle, dated variously between 50 BC and AD 180; Alexander of Aphrodisias, *De fato,* AD 198–209; Iamblichus, *De mysteriis,* third century AD; and Sallustius' *De Diis et mundo,* fourth century AD.

[65] Harl, 'Structure et cohérence', 21; Dorival, 'Remarques', 34–6.

[66] Alcinous, *Epit.* 8.1; the forms are dealt with in *Epit.* 9, and God, 'the third principle', in *Epit.* 10. See also Apuleius, *Dogm. Plat.* 5, another second-century 'handbook' on Platonic philosophy, which also presents the 'three principles': God, matter, and forms.

[67] Porphyry, *Vit. Plot.,* 14; the work of Longinus is now lost; Justin Martyr also might well be referring to another work with the same title when he writes, *2 Apol.* 6.8: 'The Stoic philosophers themselves place a high value on these things in their discussion of [or: treatise on] ethics, so that it is shown that in their discussion of [or: treatise on] first principles and bodies (ἐν τῷ περὶ ἀρχῶν καὶ σωμάτων λόγῳ) they are not good guides.' Daley, 'Origen's De Principiis', 4, fn. 8, would translate λόγος here as 'treatise'; Denis Minns and Paul Parvis (ed. and trans. OECT [Oxford: Oxford University Press, 2009]) translate it as 'discussion'.

[68] Harl, 'Structure et cohérence', 16–17.

Crouzel and Simonetti, as indicated in the synoptic table above, follow Harl in their description of the two 'cycles': the first cycle deals with the three 'principles' 'au sense large'—the Trinity, rational creatures, the world—while the second corresponds to diverse points set out in the Preface. Charles Kannengiesser, on the other hand, is a bit more sceptical, both of the analogies drawn by Dorival from works either beyond Origen's reach or after his time, and of the way in which the bipartite structure has been used, for once it has been 'imposed on *Peri Archon* as it is', it cannot help but elicit 'a distinctive evaluation of the "first" and "second" exposition'.[69] Kannengiesser's own suggestion is that in fact the first exposition is the work *On First Principles* 'proper', corresponding tightly to the series of items listed in the Preface, and that to this original work Origen subsequently added a series of lectures, strongly coloured by an anti-Marcionite polemic.[70] Perhaps more interestingly, Kannengiesser also suggests that rather than looking to philosophical handbooks, a bipartite structure can be discerned in many writings much closer to home for Origen, not least in several letters of Paul, and 'explicitly' in many treatises of Philo, Justin's *First Apology* as well as the *Dialogue*, Irenaeus' *Demonstration,* as well as Clement of Alexandria's *Paedagogue,* though all this without any serious or sustained analysis. But he makes a valid point in conclusion: 'It would probably be a rewarding task to analyze Origen's double exposition in *Peri Archon* proper…with a closer look at its patristic, Alexandrian, and scriptural models', though any such analysis must surely be of the whole book, rather than only '*Peri Archon* proper' (i.e. the first cycle).[71]

II The Division into Chapters

However, before we attempt to take any such analysis further, we must return to the question of the division into chapters, for only once we have reached as

---

[69] Kannengiesser, 'Origen, Systematician in *De Principiis*', 396.   [70] Ibid. 402.

[71] Ibid. 402. For a full examination, using many of the studies mentioned above, of the bipartite structure of Irenaeus' *Demonstration,* see Susan L. Graham, 'Structure and Purpose of Irenaeus' *Epideixis*', StP 36 (Leuven: Peeters, 2001), 210–21, though this has recently been challenged by James B. Wiegel, 'The Trinitarian Structure of Irenaeus' *Demonstration of the Apostolic Preaching*', SVTQ 58.1 (2014), 113–39, who argues persuasively for a threefold structure. A bipartite structure is evident at the heart of Athanasius, *On the Incarnation,* where, between the introductory paragraphs and the concluding refutations of the Jews and Gentiles, the main part of the heart of the work is given over to examining the work of Christ in the Passion, in two different perspectives, the 'divine dilemma' regarding life and death, in an 'existential' perspective, and the same dilemma regarding knowledge and ignorance, an 'epistemological' perspective; the transition from one to the other is clearly indicated by Athanasius himself: 'This, therefore, is the first cause of the Incarnation of the Saviour. One might also recognize that his gracious advent consistently occurred from the following' (*Inc.* 10). It should also be noted that *On the Incarnation* itself is the second part of a diptych, the first being *Against the Gentiles.* See Athanasius, *On the Incarnation,* ed. and trans. John Behr (Crestwood, NY: St Vladimir's Seminary Press, 2011), 38–9.

secure a conclusion about them as we can, can we then turn to the question of structure. Even a cursory look at the chapter headings provided by Koetschau and Butterworth should raise some eyebrows. For instance, where do the headings for *Princ.* 3.3, 'The threefold wisdom', and *Princ.* 3.4, 'Whether the statement made by some is true, that each individual has two souls', come from and how do they fit into any coherent sequence of reflection? The fact is that the heading for *Princ.* 3.3, and its placement at this point, is not found in any manuscript at all; it was inserted by Merlin in his edition, and has been included by all subsequent editors. The two manuscripts containing the most headings, B and C, have the heading, 'That there is a difference between the Wisdom of God and the wisdom of this world and the wisdom of the rulers of this world, or how one might be entrapped through that wisdom which is the wisdom of the rulers of this world', inserted a sentence before the place where Merlin put his heading. The very length of this heading clearly indicates that it is a scribal note, not a chapter heading going back to Origen himself, as also does the brevity of this supposed 'chapter'. Moreover, as Origen makes clear, although turning at this point to the question of knowledge, the subject of his treatment continues to be the work of the opposing powers, as the first sentence of *Princ.* 3.3.2 indicates, and it remains so until the conclusion of *Princ.* 3.3.6, as the final statement affirms: 'But let these points, expounded by us according to our strength, suffice regarding those powers which are opposed to the human race'. *Princ.* 3.2–3 is one complete block, treating 'the opposing powers'.

In the case of *Princ.* 3.4, although Origen does indeed turn, from *Princ.* 3.4.2 onwards, to the question of the statement made by some to the effect that there are 'two souls' in each human being, the opening statement of *Princ.* 3.4.1 makes clear the overarching topic of his intended discussion: 'And now, I think, we must not pass over in silence the subject of human temptations, which are engendered sometimes from flesh and blood, or from the shrewdness of flesh and blood, which is said to be hostile to God.' This simple observation makes clear the sequence of his exposition: having treated, in *Princ.* 3.2–3, the temptations that arise from 'the opposing powers', Origen now turns to those that derive from our human nature, flesh and blood.

Similar points must be made with regard to the divisions between *Princ.* 1.3–4, 1.5–6, 2.1–3, and the headings given to *Princ.* 1.7 and 2.10. *Princ.* 1.4, given the heading 'Loss or falling away' by Koetschau and Butterworth, is in fact a continuation of the discussion about the Holy Spirit in *Princ.* 1.3. This is seen clearly from the opening line of *Princ.* 1.5: 'After the discussion concerning the Father and the Son and the Holy Spirit, which we have briefly treated, as far as we are able, it follows that we should also say a few words about the rational beings.' Origen does indeed discuss what it means to fall away in *Princ.* 1.4, but this is a continuation of *Princ.* 1.3.8, where he had been discussing how rational beings might participate in the sanctifying power of the Holy Spirit, unless they slacken in their piety, in which case they will fall away from that participation. *Princ.* 1.4 is not a separate chapter, oddly positioned between a chapter on the Holy Spirit and one on rational beings, but a continuation of the discussion already begun in *Princ.* 1.3.8, tying together the work of the Trinity and the life of rational beings in ways which will be important for us later on.

Princ. 1.6, although turning to the question of 'the end or consummation', is likewise not a separate chapter. When Origen opens *Princ.* 1.7, he speaks of having treated the topic of rational beings after having spoken of the Father, Son, and Holy Spirit. The 'end or consummation' that he brings into his discussion at *Princ.* 1.6 continues the discussion in *Princ.* 1.5.3 about whether the variety of rational beings results from their choices and actions or from God himself, and he turns to the end in order to understand the beginning, as is made clear in *Princ.* 1.6.2. Origen treats the end itself in a preliminary way in *Princ.* 1.6.4, and more fully in *Princ.* 3.6. *Princ.* 1.5–6 is thus a complete block. Origen opens *Princ.* 1.5.1 by saying that after having discussed the Father, Son, and Holy Spirit, 'it follows that we should also say a few words about the rational beings, their species and orders and functions', for Scripture provides us with many names of different orders of rational beings: the holy angels (treated briefly in the second paragraph of *Princ.* 1.5.1, and more fully in *Princ.* 1.8), the opposite kind, who have turned aside (treated in the first paragraph of *Princ.* 1.5.2), and then human beings, the 'rational animals' (second paragraph of *Princ.* 1.5.2). Origen then continues by showing that God did not cause rational beings to be in these positions, as is proved by further examples from Scripture, to conclude that it lies within ourselves whether to be holy or become an opposing power (*Princ.* 1.5.3–5), and ends the chapter by turning to the 'end', when God will be 'all in all', in order to understand the beginning. The organization of the whole of this chapter, and the development of its argument, is both coherent and tight.

The final misleading division of chapters is *Princ.* 2.1, 2, 3. 'The perpetuity of bodily nature' is not arbitrarily juxtaposed between a treatment of 'the world' and 'the beginning of the world and its causes'. Origen specifies in the opening lines of *Princ.* 2.1 that he will not only treat the beginning and the end of the world, but also the arrangement of events between these two points. By the term 'world' Origen understands more than simply the created world in general or materiality and corporeality in particular (which are indeed treated in *Princ.* 2.1.4–2.2); it also includes the 'arrangement' (the cosmos in the sense of the Greek term; see *Princ.* 2.3.6) of rational creatures in all their variety and diversity, held together by providence as one harmonious body tending towards unity in God (*Princ.* 2.1.2–3). Again, *Princ.* 2.1–3 is a complete block, treating 'the world' in all senses of that term.

Finally, we have the headings given to two other chapters. It is incorrect to title *Princ.* 1.7 'Things corporeal and things incorporeal'. This would again be an odd topic to juxtapose between a discussion about rational beings and one on the angels. Although Origen does indeed begin with a discussion about bodily and bodiless things, things visible and things invisible, he opens *Princ.* 1.7.2, with the clear statement: 'We have made these preliminary remarks wanting to come, in order, to the investigation of the sun and moon and stars'. This chapter should thus be so titled, or, as he puts it more briefly later on, 'The celestial beings'. Once again, this clarifies the sequence of topics treated by Origen: rational beings, then celestial beings (for the Scriptures do indeed speak of the sun, moon, and stars as being animated and rational), and finally the angels, before turning to a discussion about how all these rational beings fit together as one world. Similarly for *Princ.* 2.10, the resurrection is only discussed, as the opening lines make clear, in order that Origen might come in proper order to a treatment of the judgement, and then, in the following chapter, the promises.

III Theology and Economy

Let us now return to the question of the relationship between the two cycles of exposition. It is clear that the second is longer than the first, and also is often more directed towards erroneous teaching. However, there is a much more significant difference between the two cycles that should be noted. This can be seen by the way in which Origen opens the discussion of the same topic in each, most clearly in treatments of Christ. In the first cycle, Origen begins:

> In the first place, we must know that in Christ the nature of his divinity, as he is the only-begotten Son of God, is one thing, and another is the human nature, which in the last times he took on account of the economy.   (*Princ.* 1.2.1)

He opens up the treatment of Christ in the second cycle in the following way:

> It is time, now that these points have been discussed, for us to return to the Incarnation of our Lord and Saviour, how he became human and dwelt among human beings. The divine nature having been considered, to the best of our feeble ability,…it remains that we should seek the medium between all these created things and God, that is, the *Mediator,* whom the Apostle Paul calls *the first-born of all creation.*   (*Princ.* 2.6.1, referring to 1 Tim. 2:5 and Col. 1:15)

The correlation between the two chapters could not be clearer, and the most appropriate terms to describe the respective treatments in the two cycles are 'theology' (a term not actually used here, but certainly implied by his reference to his previous consideration of the divine nature) and 'economy'. This differentiation also seems evident in the parallel treatments of other topics. In the first cycle God is treated rather abstractly, focusing primarily on his being bodiless; in the second cycle it is specified that this one God is the God of the

Law and the Prophets and the Father of our Lord Jesus Christ. In the first cycle the Holy Spirit is considered together with the Father and Christ, and discussed primarily in terms of the power of sanctification; in the second, he affirms that it is the same Spirit who was in both the prophets and apostles, and his treatment then discusses the pouring out of the Holy Spirit upon all flesh and his role as another paraclete, as a consoler rather than advocate, for to advocate is Christ's work. In the first cycle, rational beings are discussed in terms of their arrangement; in the second, the focus is much more on the struggles in which they find themselves.

IV The Apostolic and the Ecclesiastical Preaching

Having clarified these chapter divisions and headings, we can now turn back to Origen's Preface to his work and see, not only just how precisely he has laid out its overarching structure, but also a further differentiation that has significant implications for our understanding of *On First Principles* and Origen's theology as a whole. While it is routinely stated that in the Preface Origen differentiates between those theological points that are established and those that remain open for further reflection, this is not quite exact. Origen begins his Preface by quoting John 1:17, 'grace and truth came through Jesus Christ', and further specifies that by the words of Christ he means not only 'those which he spoke when he became human and dwelt in the flesh; for even before this, Christ, the Word of God, was in Moses and the prophets', and still is in those such as Paul who have Christ speaking in them (Pr.1; 2 Cor. 13:3). However, as differences of teaching have arisen, it is necessary to 'guard the ecclesiastical preaching, handed down from the apostles through the order of succession and remaining in the churches to the present: that alone is to be believed to be the truth which differs in no way from the ecclesiastical and apostolic tradition' (Pr.2). Moreover, the apostles 'delivered with utmost clarity...certain points that they believed to be necessary, leaving, however, the grounds of their statements to be inquired into' by those who excel in the gifts of the Spirit, language, wisdom, and knowledge; while on other points they simply asserted things to be so, 'keeping silence about how or whence they are' so that those who have proved themselves worthy of receiving wisdom might 'have an exercise on which they might display the fruit of their ability' (Pr.3).
Origen then continues (my underlined emphasis):

> [Pr.4.] The particular points, which are clearly handed down by <u>the preaching of the apostles</u> are as follows:
> First, that there is one God, who created and arranged all things,...This just and good God, the Father of our Lord Jesus Christ, himself gave the law and the

prophets and the Gospels, who is also the God of the apostles and of the Old and New Testaments.

Then, again, that Jesus Christ himself, who came, was born of the Father before all creatures. After ministering to the Father in the foundation of all things, for *by him were all things made,* in the last times, emptying himself, he became human and was incarnate…

Then, again, they handed down that the Holy Spirit is associated in honour and dignity with the Father and the Son. But in this case it is not yet clearly discerned whether he is born or not-born, or whether he is to be considered as himself Son of God or not: but these are points which are yet to be inquired into, to the best of our ability, from holy Scripture, and investigated with the requisite wisdom. That this Holy Spirit inspired each one of the saints, both the prophets and the apostles, and that there was not one Spirit in those of old but another in those who were inspired at the coming of Christ, is indeed most clearly taught throughout the churches.

[Pr.5] After these points, also, that the soul, having its own substance and life, shall, after it departs from this world, obtain an inheritance of eternal life and blessedness, if its actions shall have excelled, or be delivered up to eternal fire and torments, if the sin of its wicked deeds shall so direct it: and also, that there is to be a time of resurrection from the dead, when this body, which now *is sown in corruption, shall rise in incorruptibility,* and that which *is sown in dishonour, will rise in glory.*

This also is defined in the ecclesiastical preaching, that every rational soul possesses free-will and volition; that it is in conflict against the devil and his angels, and opposing powers, because they strive to burden it with sins; but if we live rightly and carefully, we should endeavour to shake off such a burden….

[Pr.6] Regarding the devil and his angels and the opposing powers, the ecclesiastical preaching has taught that they indeed exist, but what they are, or how they exist, it has not explained sufficiently clearly….

[Pr.7] This also is part of the ecclesiastical preaching, that this world was made and began at a certain time and, because it is corruptible, will be dissolved. But what existed before this world, or what will exist after it, has not yet become known openly to many, for no clear statement on this is set forth in the ecclesiastical preaching.

[Pr.8] Then, finally, that the Scriptures were written by the Spirit of God, and that they have not only the meaning which is obvious, but also another which escapes the notice of most….

[Pr.9] This is also in the ecclesiastical preaching, that there are certain angels of God and good powers, who minister to him in accomplishing the salvation of human beings; but when these were created, or of what kind of being, or how they exist, is not explained with sufficient clarity. Regarding the sun, moon, and stars, whether they are animated beings or inanimate is not clearly handed down.

The first point to note is that for each of the four primary items (God, Christ, the Spirit, and rational beings) Origen already makes a twofold statement relating to the two cycles of the work, theology and economy. Second, although

Origen speaks, in Pr.2, of 'the ecclesiastical and apostolic tradition' in the singular, 'preserved through the order of succession' and present in the churches to his day, he does in fact make a distinction, between those things which the apostles 'delivered with utmost clarity' and those that they merely asserted, leaving the grounds of their statements for further reflection. This distinction is, moreover, parsed out by Origen in the list given above in terms of what belongs to the apostolic preaching and what to the ecclesiastical preaching. The tradition is indeed singular, but it is comprised of both the apostolic preaching and the ecclesiastical preaching.

This distinction between the apostolic preaching and the ecclesiastical preaching is, furthermore, maintained throughout the course of *On First Principles*. Thus, after discussing the apostolic preaching (that is, God, Christ, the Spirit, and rational beings) in *Princ.* 1.1–6, Origen begins his next chapter with these words:

> The matters, then, which we have examined above, were considered by us in a more general manner, treating and discussing rational natures, more through discernment of inference than by dogmatic definition, after the place where we spoke, to the best of our ability, of the Father and the Son and the Holy Spirit. Let us now, therefore, consider those matters that it is appropriate to discuss in the following pages, according to our teaching, that is, according to the faith of the Church. (*Princ.* 1.7.1)

The reference to having treated some matters 'more through discernment of inference than by dogmatic definition' only applies to the latter part of the preceding chapter (*Princ.* 1.5–6). As we have seen above, *Princ.* 1.5–6 begins by describing what Scripture asserts to be the case: amongst the rational beings, there are holy angels, opposing powers, and the 'rational animals' in between. It is when examining the causes for this variation, and understanding the beginning in terms of the end, a discussion which is now already described as 'the ecclesiastical faith', that Origen changes the mode of his argumentation: 'These things are indeed spoken about by us with great fear and caution, discussing and investigating rather than establishing as fixed and certain' (*Princ.* 1.6.1). Just as in *Princ.* 1.3–4, the chapter on the Holy Spirit, where Origen already discusses rational beings in its latter part, before turning to the rational beings themselves in the following chapter, to sort out what Scripture says about these beings, so also, in *Princ.* 1.5–6, Origen cannot stop himself from also beginning to speak about matters pertaining to 'the ecclesiastical faith' by attempting to provide an explanation for the cause of their differences. But it is only in *Princ.* 1.7.1 that he definitively turns to 'our teaching, that is, according to the faith of the Church'. Thus, although in the opening sentence he says that 'it has been pointed out by us above what are those points that must be clearly determined by dogma, which, I think, we have done to the best of our ability when we spoke about the Trinity', the scriptural affirmations regarding rational beings also belong to what is given as apostolic preaching, even though already in *Princ.* 1.6.1, he has begun treating 'matters of a kind needing discussion rather than definition'.

Similarly in the second cycle, after treating the apostolic preaching (*Princ.* 2.2–9), he opens the next chapter by saying:

> But since our discourse has reminded us of the judgement to come and of the retribution and punishment of sinners, in accordance with the things threatened by holy Scripture and contained in the ecclesiastical preaching…let us also see what ought to be thought about these points.   (*Princ.* 2.10.1)

As with the transition in the first cycle, Origen has already prepared the way for the further, more speculative, subjects which he is about to treat, and which he again describes as 'the ecclesiastical preaching'. There are three further references, in the appropriate sections, to 'the ecclesiastical faith' (*Princ.* 1.7.1; 3.1.1, preserved also in Greek; 3.5.1), but these two key transitional points, and their conformity to the Preface, are sufficient to establish this further level of division within *On First Principles*. The differentiation between the apostolic and the ecclesiastical preaching would seem to be that the apostolic proclamation concerns the basic elements of the Gospel preaching—God, through Christ, in the Spirit, acting to save rational creatures, bringing them into life in himself—while the ecclesiastical preaching deals with corollaries of this apostolic preaching: that, if we are able to be saved, or not, in Christ, we must have self-determination, in the exercise of which we find ourselves in conflict with opposing powers and with ourselves, and that although our end is in the eternity of God, we have nevertheless come into being in time.

The final item from the list of topics given in the Preface is Scripture and its divine character and two levels of meaning. Scripture is not treated at all in the first cycle, and so, I would suggest, *Princ.* 4.1–3 should not be thought of as part of the second cycle, but instead, following Daley's insightful essay, that it be seen as a distinct section and, in fact, the real purpose of the whole work.[72] We will consider this further below, once we have concluded our analysis of the structure of the two cycles that precede it. Based on the above reflections, I would propose, and have adopted for the layout of the text and translation, the following structure for *On First Principles*.

Preface

Part One: Theology

I: The Apostolic Preaching
    God (1.1)
    Christ (1.2)

---

[72] Daley, 'Origen's *De Principiis*'.

The most important implication of taking *On First Principles* as structured in this manner is that the basic division is *not* between God, on the one hand, and creation (rational and otherwise) on the other, as it would come to be in later theology when the distinction between uncreated and created reality takes precedence, and as it is in the structuring of the opening chapters in other editions of this work. Rather, rational beings are taken together *with* God, Christ, the Holy Spirit as the four elements of the apostolic preaching (and how indeed could it be otherwise, given that it is *preaching*—there must be hearers ready to hear the good news) and reflected upon first on a theological level and then an economic level. The distinction between uncreated and created reality perhaps became the fundamental distinction in the following century, as a result of the

'Arian' controversy, in which both sides could claim precedence in Origen; but, in another sense, it only became primary as theological reflection later on (perhaps only in more recent times) became detached from the liturgical worship of the Church. It is striking, for instance, how even in the last third of the fourth century, and in his work written specifically against Eunomius, Gregory of Nyssa begins the 'exposition of our own conception of the truth' by dividing up reality in a way much more akin to Origen, both of them following the Apostle Paul's distinction between things that are seen and transient and those that are unseen and eternal (2 Cor. 4:18). Gregory's words will be important for our later discussion, and so we will quote part of them here:

> Now, the ultimate division of all being is into the intellectual and the perceptible [Πάντων τῶν ὄντων ἡ ἀνωτάτω διαίρεσις εἴς τε τὸ νοητὸν καὶ τὸ αἰσθητὸν τὴν τομὴν ἔχει]; the perceptible nature is called by the Apostle *that which is seen*. For as all body has colour, and the sight apprehends this, he calls this world by the rough and ready name of *that which is seen*...The common term, again for the intellectual world, is with the apostle, *that which is not seen:* by withdrawing all idea of comprehension by the senses he leads the mind [διάνοιαν] on to the immaterial and intellectual. Reason [ὁ λόγος] again divides this *which is not seen* into the uncreated and the created, inferentially comprehending it: the uncreated being that which effects the creation, the creation that which owes its origin and its force to the uncreated. In the sensible world, then, is found everything that we comprehend by our organs of bodily sense, and in which the differences of qualities involve the idea of more or less...But in the intelligible world—that part of it, I mean, which is created—the idea of such differences as are perceived in the perceptible cannot find a place; another method, then, is devised for discovering the degrees of greater and less.[73]

The distinction between the uncreated and the created finds its place within the overarching apostolic distinction between the seen and transient, on the one hand, and the unseen and eternal, on the other. Rational beings, as intellects, clearly fall within the latter, along with the Father, Son, and Holy Spirit. We will return later to what all this might mean for Origen's understanding of creation, time, and eternity.

Origen's monotheism, then, is not that of later philosophical deism (not even a Trinitarian deism), with God considered in or by himself (or as three), prior to and independent of rational beings. It is rather a biblical monarchical monotheism, in which God is seen as presiding over the heavenly court, in the celebration of the heavenly liturgy: 'God is in the congregation of gods' (Ps. 82:1). This is the vision of God that pervades the Scriptures, throughout the Old Testament, and even increasing in the literature of Second Temple

---

[73] Gregory of Nyssa, *Eun.* 1.270–3; the discussion continues for several more sections before beginning his response to Eunomius on its basis (1.282).

Judaism and apocalyptic works, to the New Testament proclamation that the crucified and risen Christ has been exalted to sit at the right hand of the Majesty on high (Heb. 1:3), in the throne room beheld by John in his Apocalypse, in which the One who sits on the throne and the slain Lamb are offered 'blessing and honour and glory and might unto the ages of ages' (Rev. 5:13).[74]

It is also the vision of God experienced by Christians in their worship upon earth, where the heavenly and earthly liturgy coincide. It is captured most concisely in the preface to the anaphora of Basil the Great:

> Master, the One who is, Lord, God, Father, Almighty, who are to be worshipped, it is truly right and proper and fitting the majesty of your holiness to praise you, to hymn you, to bless you, and to worship you, to thank you, to glorify you, the only God who truly exists; to offer you with a broken heart and a spirit of humility, this our reasonable worship. For it is you who have granted us the knowledge of your truth. And who is able to tell of all your acts of power? To make all your praises heard or to recount all your wonders at every moment? Master of all things, Lord of heaven and earth and all creation, seen and unseen, who are seated on a throne of glory and look upon the deeps, without beginning invisible, unsearchable, uncircumscribed, unchangeable,

> the Father of our Lord Jesus Christ, the great God and Saviour, our hope, who is the image of your goodness, perfect seal of your likeness, revealing you the Father in himself, living Word, true God, pre-eternal Wisdom, Life, Sanctification, Power, the true Light,

---

[74] The literature for this has, over the past decades, become immense. For this theme in the Old Testament and its context, see: William Albright, *Yahweh and the Gods of Canaan: A Historical Analysis of Two Contrasting Faiths* (Garden City: Doubleday, 1968); E. Theodore Mullen, *The Assembly of Gods: The Divine Council and Early Hebrew Literature*, Harvard Semitic Monographs, 24 (Chico: Scholars Press, 1986); Mark S. Smith, *The Early History of God: Yahweh and the Other Deities in Ancient Israel* (San Francisco: Harper, 1990); also useful are the two essays by Patrick D. Miller, 'The Divine World and the Human World', chap. 1 in idem, *Genesis 1–11: Studies in Structure and them*, JSOT Supplement 8 (Sheffield: JSOT Press, 1978), 9–26; idem, 'The Sovereignty of God', in Doug Miller, ed., *The Hermeneutical Quest* (Allison Park, PA: Pickwick, 1986), 129–44. For the Second Temple Judaism, Christianity, and early apocalyptic, see John J. Collins, *The Apocalyptic Imagination: An Introduction to the Jewish Matrix of Christianity*, 2nd edn (Grand Rapids, MI: Eerdmans, 1998); David M. Hay, *Glory at the Right Hand: Psalm 110 in Early Christianity*, SBL Monograph Series, 18 (Nashville: Abingdon, 1973); Larry Hurtado, *One God, One Lord: Early Christian Devotion and Ancient Jewish Monotheism* (Philadelphia: Fortress, 1988), and idem, *Lord Jesus Christ: Devotion to Jesus in Earliest Christianity* (Grand Rapids, MI: Eerdmans, 2003); Christopher Rowland, *The Open Heaven: A Study of Apocalyptic in Judaism and Early Christianity* (New York: Crossroad, 1982); Alan F. Segal, *Two Powers in Heaven: Early Rabbinic Reports about Christianity and Gnosticism*, Studies in Late Antiquity (Leiden: Brill, 1977; reprinted Waco: Baylor University Press, 2012). A full and excellent survey of the primary literature, from ancient Canaan to the New Testament and apocalyptic literature, together with many further references to modern studies, can be found in Paul B. Sumner, 'Visions of the Divine Council in the Hebrew Bible' (PhD thesis, Malibu, CA: Pepperdine University, 1991), several revised chapters of which can be found online at http://www.hebrew-streams.org/works/hebrew/council.html (accessed 19 December 2015).

through whom the Holy Spirit was made manifest, the Spirit of truth, the grace of sonship, the pledge of the inheritance to come, the first-fruits of the eternal good things, the life-giving power, the source of sanctification,

through whom every rational and intelligent being is empowered, worships you and ascribes to you the everlasting [ἀΐδιον] hymn of glory, because all things are your servants.[75]

In this tapestry of Scriptural allusions, the God and Father, Christ, his Son and our great God and Saviour, the Holy Spirit, and all rational and intellectual beings are held together in the flow of one continuous sentence, expressing one movement from God, through Christ, through the Spirit, through whom all rational beings, in return, send forth praise to God. It is, moreover, an 'everlasting', or more strictly timeless, hymn that the servants of God—creatures, who have come into being in time, distinct from the uncreated God—offer to their Lord.

The distinction between the apostolic and the ecclesiastical preaching, with its placement of rational beings together with God, Christ, and the Spirit, brings us into some of the thorniest problems of interpreting Origen's theology: the idea that he taught that rational beings exist eternally, before and outside of creation, and that, through satiety or sloth, they fell into the various ranks of increasingly dense bodies—ideas that were (rightly!) anathematized in the sixth century. Before we turn to these matters, however, we must first consider what is the place of his treatment of Scripture in *On First Principles*, and, indeed, what might be meant by the title itself.

V Scripture, Book Four, and the Purpose of *On First Principles*

We will deal with the difficulties of understanding the place of *Princ.* 4, its treatment of Scripture and the Recapitulation, quite extensively, as doing so will also prepare the groundwork for the following sections of this Introduction. Much of the problem with the title derives from the ambiguity of the term 'principle' (ἀρχή), an ambiguity noted by Rufinus in his first preface: he suggests that it can be translated either by 'principle' (*principium*) or by 'principality' (*principatus*). Daley points out that the word ἀρχή, which basically means 'source' or 'beginning', was used in ancient philosophy to mean either 'the root assumption of a theoretical system, a principle in a logical sense or the ultimate underlying cause for the existence of some actual thing, a principle in a causal or ontological sense'.[76] While nineteenth- and early twentieth-century

---

[75] For the Greek text, see F. E. Brightman, *Eastern Liturgies* (Oxford: Clarendon Press, 1896), 321–3; the translation is that of Archimandrite Ephrem Lash.

[76] Daley, 'Origen's *De Principiis*', 6.

scholars took the title of Origen's work in the first sense, as providing the fundamental axioms of a theological system, some clearly stated, others to be worked out, more recent scholars, as we have seen, took the title in the second sense, so that the work is understood, in the company of other introductory handbooks, as treating the primary realities of God and beings. Daley help-fully suggests, instead, that the title 'bears an ambiguity of reference Origen may well have intended: constructing a cohesive survey of the ontological principles of the world's beings, as Christian faith perceives them, also brings together for him, the logical principles for an understanding of the content of revelation that is both the anchor and the starting point of authentic and cre-ative biblical interpretation.'[77] The advantage of this approach is that it enables us to understand the place of Origen's treatment of Scripture *(Princ.* 4.1–3), following the two cycles of theological and economic interpretation of the content of the apostolic and the ecclesiastical preaching.

Origen ends his Preface, after enumerating the topics for consideration, by briefly discussing the (non-Scriptural) term 'incorporeal' and concludes by saying that

> everyone who desires to construct a certain structure and a body of all these things, in accordance with reason, must make use of elements and foundations [probably: στοιχείοις καὶ ἀρχαῖς] of this sort...that by clear and cogent argu-ments the truth about each particular point may be discovered, and he may form, as we have said, one body, by means of illustrations and assertions, either those which he came upon in the holy Scriptures or those which he discovered to fol-low by investigation and right reason.   (Pr.10)

As Daley observes, Origen clearly sees himself as building, out of what he has found in Scripture and what follows on from this, 'the kind of integrated, demonstrative, logically coherent system of knowledge that in the Aristotelian tradition was called a science (ἐπιστήμη)'.[78] The most important characteristic of such knowledge was that it was built upon premises or axioms that were proper to the knowledge itself. According to Aristotle, such 'hypotheses' are the starting points or first principles (ἀρχαί) of demonstration.[79] They cannot be proved, otherwise they would be dependent upon something prior to them, and we would be led into an infinite regression.[80] They are simply grasped by the intellect (νοῦς), through the course of its lived experience in the world, and as such are grounded in sense-perception and held together by the memory.[81]

---

[77] Ibid.   [78] Ibid. 10.   [79] Cf. Aristotle, *Metaph.* 5.1.2 (1013a17).
[80] Cf. Ibid. 4.4.2 (1006a6–12).
[81] Cf. Aristotle, *An. post.* 2.19 (99b17–100b17). Jonathan Barnes, in a passage used by Daley, points out that in describing the characteristics of scientific knowledge, Aristotle is not prescrib-ing a particular method of inquiry, but 'is concerned with the organization and presentation of results of research: its aim is to say how we may collect into an intelligible whole the scientist's various discoveries—how we may so arrange the facts that their interrelations, and in particular

Aristotle's account of knowledge (ἐπιστήμη) was largely appropriated by later philosophy and incorporated into the handbooks of philosophy, contemporary with Origen. In the face of the Sceptics, it also became a matter of necessity to begin any systematic presentation of philosophy with an account of the 'criterion' or 'canon', which, as we have seen above, is what Alcinous does; Origen also appeals to the canon in his Preface. Without a criterion or canon, knowledge is simply not possible, for all inquiry will be drawn helplessly into an infinite regression. Epicurus' *Canon* seems to have been the first work devoted to establishing 'the criteria of truth'.[82] In Hellenistic philosophy, it was generally held that it is preconceptions (πρόληψεις—generic notions synthesized out of repeated sense perceptions, later held to be innate) that facilitate knowledge and act as criteria.[83] The self-evidence (ἐνάργεια) of the sense perceptions, for the Epicureans, and the clarity of cognitive impressions, for the Stoics, provide the infallible criterion for examining what truly exists, though, as Clement of Alexandria points out, even Epicurus accepted that this 'preconception of the intellect' is 'faith', and that without it, neither inquiry nor judgement is possible.[84]

Returning to Aristotle, the knowledge he is speaking about is also connected to wisdom. Daley highlights a passage from the *Magna Moralia* attributed to Aristotle (expanding a point made briefly in the *Nichomachean Ethics*) explaining how wisdom combines both intellect or intuitive knowledge and knowledge (ἐπιστήμη). While the intellect deals with the first principles of things intelligible and existent, knowledge (ἐπιστήμη) deals with what can be demonstrated, as the first principles themselves are indemonstrable. Wisdom, however,

> is compounded of both knowledge and intellect, for wisdom is concerned both with the first principles and with what is already demonstrated from the first principles, those things that are the concern of knowledge. So far, then, as it is

their explanations, may best be revealed and grasped.' *Aristotle's Posterior Analytics*, 2nd edn (Oxford: Clarendon, 1993), xii.

[82] Cf. Diogenes Laertius, *Vita*, 10.31.
[83] See the texts gathered together by A. A. Long and D. N. Sedley, together with their comments, in *The Hellenistic Philosophers*, vol. 1, *Translations of the Principal Sources, with Philosophical Commentary*, and vol. 2, *Greek and Latin Texts with Notes and Bibliography* (Cambridge: Cambridge University Press, 1987), vol. 1, 78–90 (Epicureanism); 236–59 (Stoicism); vol. 2, 83–93 (Epicureanism); 238–59 (Stoicism). See also G. Striker, 'Κριτήριον τῆς ἀληθείας', *Nachrichten der Akademie der Wissenschaften in Göttingen*, Phil.-hist. Kl. (1974), 2:47–110; and the essays gathered in the following: M. Schofield, M. Burnyeat, and J. Barnes, eds., *Doubt and Dogmatism: Studies in Hellenistic Epistemology* (Oxford: Oxford University Press, 1980); P. Huby and G. Neals, eds., *The Criterion of Truth* (Liverpool: Liverpool University Press, 1989).
[84] Clement, *Strom.* 2.5.16.3.

concerned with first principles, [wisdom] partakes of intellect; so far as it is concerned with what can thereafter be demonstrated, it partakes of knowledge.[85]

This is exactly the kind of wisdom that Origen wants to present, the Wisdom that is Christ himself, whose primary title is the Wisdom of God, for Wisdom is 'the beginning [ἀρχή] of [God's] ways for his works' (Prov. 8:22; *Princ.* 1.2.1–3). And, as Origen makes clear in the opening and concluding lines of the Preface, the Christian knowledge he intends to expound as a coherent structure is the teaching of Christ, the Word of God who spoke in Moses and the prophets and also in the apostles.

But it is only after having expounded, twice over, the first principles of this system of knowledge, and the primary elements that it contains, that Origen turns to the Scriptures themselves. He begins by noting how to this point his discussion has been based on 'the common conceptions [ταῖς κοιναῖς ἐννοίαις] and the evidence [τῇ ἐναργείᾳ] of things that are seen' (those things that for Aristotle serve as the principles for knowledge, ἐπιστήμη) and has also used the testimonies from the Scriptures, but that it is now time to turn to the Scriptures themselves, to show that they are indeed divine by demonstrating how they speak of Christ (*Princ.* 4.1.1). The connection between understanding the divine character of the Scriptures and their speaking of Christ is particularly highlighted by Origen: it was not possible to show the divine inspiration of the ancient Scriptures before the sojourn of Christ; but the sojourn of Jesus led to the clear conviction that they were composed by heavenly grace. 'The light contained in the Law of Moses, but hidden by a veil, shone forth at the sojourn of Jesus, when the veil was taken away and the good things, of which the letter had a shadow, came gradually to be known' (*Princ.* 4.1.6).

However surprising this might be to a modern reader, it was a commonly acknowledged point to early Christians. Irenaeus makes exactly the same point: Christ was hidden in the Scriptures, which could not be understood until the time when the things that they had spoken of had come to fulfilment; the book had been 'shut up' and 'sealed, until the consummation' (cf. Dan. 12.4) and so is full of enigmas and ambiguities; those who read it without possessing the proper explanation only find a myth, for the truth that it contains is only brought to light by the cross of Christ, and only reading it in this way do we find our way into the Wisdom of God and ourselves come to shine with

---

[85] Aristotle, *Mag. mor.* 1.34.13–14 (1197a21–29): Ὁ δὲ νοῦς ἐστι περὶ τὰς ἀρχὰς τῶν νοητῶν καὶ τῶν ὄντων· ἡ μὲν γὰρ ἐπιστήμη τῶν μετ' ἀποδείξεως ὄντων ἐστίν, αἱ δ' ἀρχαὶ ἀναπόδεικτοι, ὥστ' οὐκ ἂν εἴη περὶ τὰς ἀρχὰς ἡ ἐπιστήμη, ἀλλ' ὁ νοῦς. Ἡ δὲ σοφία ἐστὶν ἐξ ἐπιστήμης καὶ νοῦσυγκειμένη. ἔστιν γὰρ ἡ σοφία καὶ περὶ τὰς ἀρχὰς καὶ τὰ ἐκ τῶν ἀρχῶν ἤδη δεικνύμενα, περὶ ἃ ἡ ἐπιστήμη. ᾗ μὲν οὖν περὶ τὰς ἀρχάς, τοὐνοῦαὐτὴ μετέχει, ᾗ δὲ περὶ τὰ μετὰ τὰς ἀρχὰς μετ'ἀποδείξεως ὄντα, τῆς ἐπιστήμης μετέχει· See also Aristotle, *Eth. nic.* 6.7.3 (1141a17–20).

his light as did Moses.[86] The same point, as J. Louis Martyn has made clear, is evident in the Gospel of John and the writings of Paul: 'the fundamental arrow in the link joining scripture and gospel points from the gospel story to the scripture and not from scripture to the gospel story. In a word, with Jesus' glorification, belief in scripture *comes into being* by acquiring an indelible link to belief in Jesus' words and deeds.'[87] For Christians to read Scripture *as Scripture* is to read it in an apocalyptic key. Even if we are not prepared to do so ourselves, it is still essential to recognize that when we read the writings of the early Christian Fathers, they, nevertheless, are reading Scripture in this way.

Despite the fact that the meaning of Scripture often eludes us, that it does indeed contain a divine sense is not disproved by our lack of comprehension, just as God's providential ordering of the world and its affairs, which also often eludes us, is not refuted by our inability to comprehend it (*Princ.* 4.1.7). And so, Origen urges us, using the words of Paul, to '[leave] behind the teaching of the first principles of Christ, which are but the elementary principles of knowledge, [and] press on to perfection' (ibid.; Heb. 6:1), so that we might receive the wisdom that Paul says he speaks to the perfect (1 Cor. 2:6). He concludes, putting together various passages from Paul: 'this wisdom will be stamped upon us distinctly, according to the revelation of the mystery [κατὰ ἀποκάλυψιν μυστηρίου] which was kept secret through times eternal, but now made manifest through the prophetic Scriptures and the appearance of our Lord and Saviour Jesus Christ, to whom be glory for all ages. Amen.'[88]

What follows, in *Princ.* 4.2–3, are indications about how to read and understand Scripture, based upon 'the rule of the heavenly Church of Jesus Christ [handed down] through succession from the apostles'.[89] It is here that he suggests that there are three levels of meaning in Scripture, corresponding to the body, soul, and spirit in a human being (*Princ.* 4.2.4–6), though, as this is

---

[86] Irenaeus, *Haer.* 4.26.1. See John Behr, *Irenaeus of Lyons*, CTIC (Oxford; Oxford University Press, 2013), 124–40. And more fully for Origen, Behr, *Way to Nicaea*, 169–84.

[87] J. Louis Martyn, 'John and Paul on the Subject of Gospel and Scripture', in idem, *Theological Issues in the Letters of Paul*, Studies of the New Testament and its World (Edinburgh: T & T Clark, 1997), 209–30, at 216, his emphasis. See also the other essays in his volume: 'Epistemology at the Turn of the Ages', 89–110; 'Apocalyptic Antinomies', 111–23; and 'Christ and the Elements of the Cosmos', 125–40. For further discussion, see the stimulating collection of essays edited by Joshua B. Davis and Douglas Harink, *Apocalyptic and the Future of Theology: With and Beyond J. Louis Martyn* (Eugene, OR: Cascade, 2012).

[88] *Princ.* 4.1.7; Rom. 16:25–7; 2 Tim. 1:10 (cf. 1 Tim. 6:14). It is worth noting that the only other place where Origen concludes a section with a doxology and 'Amen' is *Princ.* 3.5.8.

[89] *Princ.* 4.2.2 (Greek). Is he here making a contrast with the rule and succession of the church on earth, as appealed to in the Preface, perhaps now having come into greater conflict with Demetrius? This might explain the concluding doxology and 'Amen' at the end of *Princ.* 4.1.7, making *Princ.* 4.2–3 an expansion of his hermeneutic in a more strained context. Is it perhaps even possible that a previous 'edition' concluded with the doxology and 'Amen' at the end of *Princ.* 3.5?

rarely carried out by Origen himself in his commentaries and homilies, it is far
from being intended as a methodological procedure; it is rather the simple
observation that the meaning of any given passage is not always self-evident.[90]
More important are the three aims that the Spirit had in inspiring the
Scriptures: first, to instruct human beings about themselves and their situation
(*Princ.* 4.2.7); second, to conceal these points, from those not prepared to
undertake the toil of discovering matters of such importance, within the narratives of Scripture and yet make this 'body' of Scripture beneficial to the
multitude through an abundance of moral examples (*Princ.* 4.2.8); and third,
to weave into the narrative enough 'stumbling blocks' and 'obstacles and
impossibilities' so that we become aware that there is a deeper meaning to be
found rather than remaining merely at the level of the letter (*Princ.* 4.2.8). The
principal aim in all of this was to make known the connection ($\epsilon\hat{\iota}\rho\mu\acute{o}s$) amongst
the spiritual events and the sequence ($\dot{\alpha}\kappa o\lambda o\upsilon\theta\acute{\iota}\alpha$) of intellectual realities,
harmonizing things that happened, according to the narrative, to the more
mystical meanings, but sometimes interweaving things that did not happen.[91]
After giving various examples of such things—either things that could not
have happened or prescriptions that are impossible to fulfil—both in the Old
Testament and in the New, Origen reiterates, 'our position is that with respect
to the whole of the divine Scripture all of it has a spiritual meaning, but not all
of it has a bodily meaning' (*Princ.* 4.3.5).

Origen gives us his assurance that just because he asserts that some passages
do not have a 'bodily meaning' this does not at all mean that he holds that
none of it happened or that most precepts are not meant to be fulfilled literally.
But, as we have been directed by Christ himself to 'search the Scriptures', he
knows that he must also give a positive account of how to read Scripture, at
least in outline: 'the manner of understanding of which seems to us to be such
as follows' (end of 4.3.5, Greek). On the surface level, Scripture does indeed
give an account of how God chooses a certain nation, Israel, also called Jacob,
which was divided into twelve tribes during the times of Jeroboam, with the
ten tribes subject to him being named Israel, and the remaining two, the tribe
of Levi and the one ruled over by the seed of David, being called Judah, the
metropolis of which is Jerusalem (*Princ.* 4.3.6). But, when Paul speaks of 'Israel
according to the flesh' (1 Cor. 10:18), and says that 'not all who are descended
from Israel belong to Israel' (Rom. 9:6), Origen takes him to mean that there is

---

[90] Cf. Karen Jo Torjesen, *Hermeneutical Procedure and Theological Method in Origen's Exegesis*
(Berlin: De Gruyter, 1986), 35–43, and *passim*.
[91] Origen, *Princ.* 4.2.9. Irenaeus also appeals to the 'order and sequence' of the Scriptures,
when complaining about how his opponents rearrange the tiles of the mosaic of Scripture to
produce an image of a dog or fox (*Haer.* 1.8.1); but, he continues a little later, those, who know
the 'canon of truth' are able to restore the tiles to the proper place (*Haer.* 1.9.4) and restore the
image of the king.

also an 'Israel according to the Spirit', made up of Jews who are so, not openly, with circumcision in the flesh, for 'he is a Jew who is one in secret, and circumcision is of the heart, in spirit not in letter' (Rom. 2:28–9). So, Origen concludes, while Scripture provides a narrative (the bulk of which is indeed true according to the letter) of the bodily Israelites descending from Adam, if truth be told, 'Adam is Christ', from whom all the spiritual Israelites descend, and Eve likewise is the Church, 'the Jerusalem which is above', 'our mother', 'the city of the living God', to which we are called, 'to the festal gathering and the church of the first-born who are enrolled in heaven'.[92]

Likewise, also, for Egypt and the Egyptians, Tyre and the Tyrians, for no one, Origen points out, takes what is said in Ezekiel about Pharaoh or the ruler of Tyre as referring to a human being, nor in Isaiah about Nebuchadnezzar.[93] In what follows, Origen uses this differentiation to seek out 'the dark and invisible and hidden treasures' (Isa. 45:3), hidden in the Scriptures, alluding back to many of the topics that he has covered in the first three books.[94] Having opened up a world of unseen mysteries, Origen concludes by returning to the other item mentioned in the Preface, the existence of things bodiless, affirming, as he has done at several points throughout the work, that though bodiless in themselves, they never exist without a body, for the Trinity alone is, strictly speaking, bodiless.[95]

This discussion about bodiless reality at the end of his treatment of Scripture also resurfaces in the final part of Book 4, the 'Recapitulation' (*Princ.* 4.4). In fact, it dominates the whole last half of this concluding chapter (*Princ.* 4.4.5–10), forming an *inclusio* with the concluding paragraphs of the Preface. After summarizing many of the points he has made during the course of the work, Origen turns to the question of matter, devoting several pages to showing just how difficult a philosophical concept it is. He claims to have found no instance in Scripture where the word 'matter' is used to refer to a substance underlying bodies; when Isaiah says, 'And he shall devour matter [ὕλη] like hay' (Isa. 10:17), the word refers to 'sins'. If the bodiless God is said to be a 'consuming fire', as Origen had explained in the opening paragraphs of *Princ.* 1.1, it is not

---

[92] *Princ.* 4.3.7–8; Gal. 4:26; Heb. 12:22–3. On the eternal and heavenly Church, see F. Ledegang, *Mysterium Ecclesiae: Images of the Church and Its Members in Origen,* Bibliotheca Ephemeridum Theologicarum Lovaniensium, 156 (Leuven: Leuven University Press–Peeters, 2001), 141–51, 196–200.

[93] *Princ.* 4.3.9; cf. Ezek. 29:1–9; 28; Isa. 14:12. These figures and passages are treated at length in *Princ.* 1.5.

[94] *Princ.* 4.3.11–15. See also *Princ.* 2.11.5, 'The Promises', which discusses what we will come to know when we depart and are with Christ (Phil. 1:23). The items mentioned by Origen have much in common with the apocalyptic texts. Cf. Michael E. Stone, 'List of Revealed Things in the Apocalyptic Literature', in Frank Moore Cross et al., eds., *Magnalia Dei: The Mighty Acts of God* (New York, 1976), 414–52.

[95] *Princ.* 4.3.15; cf. 1.7.1; 2.2.2; 4.4.8; see also *Cels.* 6.71; 7.32.

because he consumes bodily matter, but rather our evil thoughts, wicked actions, and desire for sin, so that he makes us capable of receiving his Word and Wisdom, as Christ himself had promised, saying 'I and the Father shall come and make our abode in him': 'he makes them, after all their vices and passions have been consumed, into a temple pure and worthy of himself' (*Princ.* 1.1.2; John 14:23).

For Origen, matter is certainly not itself a first principle, as some philosophers postulated (*Princ.* 4.4.6). But it is possible, Origen suggests, by way of a verse from First Enoch, 'My eyes have seen your imperfection', to differentiate between matter and its properties or qualities, so that 'the mind of the prophet, examining and discussing every single visible thing, walked until it arrived at the first principle in which it beheld imperfect matter without qualities; for it is written in the same book, with Enoch himself speaking, "I beheld the whole of matter"', which Origen takes to mean the divisions of matter into everything in this world.[96]

God alone, Origen continues, is uncreated, and, being good by nature, he wants to benefit others, those, that is, who are able to receive him and be begotten as sons. Moreover, as God makes all things 'by number and measure' (Wis. 11:20), he alone being without end or measure, all created things are distinguished by number, in the case of intellectual beings, and by measure, in the case of matter. Intellectual beings necessarily use bodies, for God alone is bodiless, but, as we can differentiate, in thought alone, between matter itself and its properties, the properties of the body can change, by the will of the Creator, as the case demands. And just as our physical eyes are able to partake of light, and are thus of one nature, so also every intellect that partakes of the intellectual light of the divine nature is also of one nature and substance with each other. And sharing in the light of the Father, Son, and Holy Spirit, it is necessary that we should become incorruptible and eternal, 'so that the eternity of divine goodness may be understood in this respect as well, that those who obtain its benefits are also eternal' (*Princ.* 4.4.9). Even if we fall away from this, we retain within ourselves 'some seeds, as it were, of being restored and recalled to a better understanding, when *the inner human being,* who is also called the "rational" human being, is renewed *according to the image and likeness* of God who created him'.

If, then, the human being is made 'in the image and likeness' of God, this is not seen in the form of the body, in or through matter subject to corruption, but through the acquisition of virtue, as the human being learns to be merciful

---

[96] *Princ.* 4.4.8; 1 Enoch 21:1 (GCS 5, p. 50.4), which uses the word ἀκατασκεύαστος, no doubt taken from Gen. 1:2; and 1 Enoch 19:3 (GCS 5, p. 48.18f), which speaks of Enoch seeing the 'extremities of all things' (πέρατα πάντων). The text is found in Clement of Alexandria, *Ecl. proph.* 2.1 (Stählin, 3.137.16–17): καὶ εἶδον τὰς ὕλας πάσας. Cf. 2 Enoch 40:1.

as the Father is and so become perfect as he is (Luke 6:36; Matt. 5:48). We are therefore called to advance from bodily things, perceptible to the senses, to bodiless and intellectual realities, which are not perceptible to the senses, yet nevertheless seen through that which Solomon, the teacher of wisdom, calls 'a divine sense' (*Princ.* 4.4.10; Prov. 2:5). It is with this sense that we will perceive rational beings, and with this sense Origen asks that what he has said and written be understood. Finally Origen concludes his work by referring to the distinction between first principles and the demonstrations that they enable: 'And concerning those points about which we have spoken, or others which follow on from them, we must think in accordance with the pattern we have laid out above.'

In the acquisition of divine virtues and a divine sense we do not shed our bodies or become bodiless, as Origen was repeatedly charged with having taught. Rather, the properties and qualities of our bodies, which are distinct from matter itself, are transformed, as those of iron are when placed in fire, to use the analogy that Origen applies to Christ himself, which we will consider more fully later; iron placed in fire becomes wholly fire, so that no other property is perceived in it. Our bodies now are certainly corruptible; when we die, they will disintegrate and be dissolved back into the earth. But, as Origen expounds at length in *Princ.* 3.6, the last chapter of his second cycle of teaching, when what is sown in corruption and weakness, as an animated body, rises in the consummation, it will do so in power and glory, as a spiritual body (cf. 1 Cor. 15:42–4). In this, God 'has the service of matter in every way, so that he can transform and apply it in whatever forms and species he desires' (*Princ.* 3.6.7). It is of this transformed, spiritual body that Paul further says, 'we have a house not made by hands, eternal in the heavens' (2 Cor. 5:1; *Princ.* 3.6.4). Moreover, in this eschatological consummation, 'God will be all in all' and so we too will become 'one' as the Father and Son 'are one'.[97] It is with this discussion of 'the principle of bodily nature, or of the spiritual body' that Origen brings his second cycle to a close. As created beings, then, differentiated by number and always embodied in matter, we are nevertheless called to become one, eternal, and, purged of our vices and passions by the consuming fire that God is, to become the temple of God himself. In other words, we are called to embody the bodiless God, not in matter as we presently experience it, but in matter transformed by the power of God: 'God…makes and transforms all things' (Amos 5:8; *Princ.* 3.6.7).

---

[97] 1 Cor 15:28; John 17:24, as cited by Origen in *Princ.* 3.6.1; his exposition of God being 'all in all' is strikingly similar to that of the human soul of Christ in the Word, as iron in the fire: the rational being 'will think God, see God, hold God; God will be the mode and measure of its every movement; and thus *God* will be *all* to it'.

VI Conclusion and the Context of *On First Principles*

As this rather lengthy survey of *Princ.* 4 (which was necessary in order to prepare the ground for the following sections of this Introduction) demonstrates,
Princ. 4.1–3 is not merely yet another treatise added on, with a number of
others, to an already existing work, as Kannengiesser claimed, nor, as Harl
maintained, a separate treatise on hermeneutics, which, while not an after-
thought, as it is already mentioned in the Preface, is a change of direction
nevertheless, moving from 'physics' to a theory of spiritual knowledge.[98]
Rather, as Daley argued, it is 'its real goal: the introduction to a deeper way of
reading Scripture that will be possible for him and plausible to his readers only
after they have mastered the doctrinal structure he has been presenting in
books one through three'.[99] The work as a whole is remarkably well organized
and structured, from the laying out of the structure in the Preface, through the
two treatments, theological and economic, of the apostolic preaching and the
ecclesiastical preaching, organizing a coherent body of theological knowledge,
whose first principles, or axioms, regarding the first principles of God, Christ,
the Holy Spirit, and rational beings, have been established and their implications demonstrated, which then serve as a hermeneutical grounding for the
studious reader to return to the Scriptures, with a divine sensibility, to be
nourished by them so as to become as merciful and perfect as is God, and to
realize their rightful place in the heavenly worship and as the temple of God.

   If this, then, is the structure and the purpose of *On First Principles,* we are
better able to understand the context in which it was written. As mentioned
earlier, it was almost certainly written in 229/30. According to Nautin, by this
time Origen had already completed his *Hexapla,* a *Commentary on Psalms 1–25,*
his *Stromata,* a work *On the Resurrection,* and his *Commentary on Lamentations.*
It was after completing the first few books of his *Commentary on Genesis* that
Origen wrote *On First Principles.*[100] As Nautin suggests, the most likely reason
why Origen switched from completing his *Commentary on Genesis* to writing
On First Principles was criticism directed against his exegesis of the opening
verses of Genesis.[101] The work was intended to demonstrate the grounding of
his hermeneutic in a coherently presented account of the scientific knowledge
of the ecclesial faith, which in turn would lead his readers into the deeper
mysteries of theology and cosmogony. But far from reassuring his critics, 'no
small warfare broke out in the city', as we saw earlier described obliquely by
Eusebius, almost certainly alluding to the breakdown in relations between

---

[98] Kannengiesser, 'Origen, Systematician in *De Principiis*', 402; Harl, 'Structure et coherénce', 24.
[99] Daley, 'Origen's *De Principiis*', 13.
[100] For these works and their dates, see Nautin, *Origène,* 368–72.   [101] Ibid. 370, 423–5.

Origen and Demetrius, which, again almost certainly, as we have seen, involved more than theological and exegetical differences alone.

3 THEOLOGY

Now that we have examined, in detail, the structure and purpose of *On First Principles*, we are in a position to reconsider some of the more difficult theological problems it presents, especially those that gave rise to the charges raised against Origen for having taught that there was an eternal realm of intellects, all of whom, apart from the one united to the Word, fell away into a diversity of ranks and bodies, but that after innumerable cycles of rising and falling, all will be restored to unity in God. As it happens, two of the key passages upon which these assertions are based lie within the two chapters on Christ, which thereby provide us with further material for exploring, respectively, his treatment of theology and then the economy.

I An Eternal Creation?

That Origen held creation to be in some sense eternal is based primarily on his argument in *Princ.* 1.2.10. This chapter deals with the titles of Christ expressing his divinity, especially and primarily Wisdom, who says of herself that God 'created me as the beginning of his ways' (Prov. 8:22). Origen's teaching on creation is notoriously complex and has been the subject of controversy almost from the beginning. Earlier on in *Princ.* 1.2, Origen had explained this verse in terms that recall both the Platonic 'ideas' and the Stoic 'reasons', suggesting that as,

> within this very subsistence of Wisdom was every capacity and form of the creation that would come to be—both of those things which exist primarily and of those which occur in consequence, having been formed beforehand and arranged by the power of foreknowledge regarding these very created things, which had been as it were outlined and prefigured in Wisdom herself—Wisdom herself says through Solomon that she was *created the beginning of the ways* of God, that is, containing within herself the beginning and the reasons and the species of the entire creation.[102]

---

[102] *Princ.* 1.2.2. See also *Princ.* 1.4.4: 'In this Wisdom, therefore, who ever was with the Father, was creation always delineated and shaped, and there never was a moment when the prefiguration of those things, which were to be thereafter, was not in Wisdom.'

At that stage in his argument, then, if creation can be said to be eternal, it is only in a prefigurative sense.

However, when Origen turns, in *Princ.* 1.2.10, to consider the verse in which Wisdom is said to be 'the emanation of the purest glory of the Almighty' (Wis. 7:25), he seems to imply a more concrete content to the eternal existence of creation. He begins by examining what might be meant by 'the glory of the Almighty' to then be able to understand what its 'emanation' is, and does so by way of an analogy to the correlation, used earlier in the chapter, between the existence of a father and that of a son, to demonstrate that the Son is eternal (*Princ.* 1.2.2). As it is impossible to be a father without a son, so also it is impossible for God to be almighty 'if there are not those over whom he can exercise his power', and, as it is clearly better for God to be almighty than not, those things by virtue of which he is almighty must always have existed: 'if there never is a "when" when he was not almighty, by necessity those things must also subsist by which he is called the *Almighty,* and he must always have had those over whom he exercised power and which were governed by him as king or prince' and of these things, he adds, he will speak more fully in the proper place, when discussing the subject of his creatures (*Princ.* 1.2.10). Pared down to the bare bones of the logical structure of the analogy, as was done by Methodius of Olympus,[103] and those who follow in his wake, this opening passage does indeed seem to suggest that creation must in some sense be eternally actualized for God to be eternally the Almighty. Stated in such a manner, as Williams suggests, it rests upon the premise that true statements about God must hold eternally, and the mistaken inference from this that anything standing in relation to God must also exist eternally.[104]

However, as we have seen when considering the structure of the work, and as Origen himself reminds us in the last lines of the opening paragraph of this section, he is not here concerned with created beings themselves, but with the various titles of Christ and how they correlate amongst themselves and with the Father. So much is the analogy open to misunderstanding that he continues with a warning:

> But even now, although briefly, I think it necessary to give a warning, since the question before us concerning Wisdom is how Wisdom is *the* ἀπόρροια *(or the emanation) of the purest glory of the Almighty,* lest anyone should consider that the title of *Almighty* is anterior in God to the birth of Wisdom, through whom he is called Father, since it is said that [Wisdom] is the *emanation of the purest glory of the Almighty.* Let him who would think like this hear what the Scriptures

---

[103] See the account given by Methodius of Olympus (in a work entitled περὶ τῶν γενητῶν, 'On creatures'), as preserved by Photius *Bibl. cod.* 235 (Henry 5, 302a30–302b4); the passage is given in the footnotes to the text at *Princ.* 1.2.10.

[104] Williams, *Arius*, 138.

clearly proclaim, saying, *In Wisdom have you made all things,* and the Gospel teaches, that *All things were made by him and without him nothing was made,* and let him understand from this that the title of *Almighty* cannot be older in God than that of Father, for it is through the Son that the Father is almighty.[105]

In other words, Origen's concern is not so much the status of creation itself, but to work out the hierarchy of the scriptural titles for God and Christ. If Wisdom is said to be 'the ἀπόρροια *(or the emanation) of the purest* glory of the Almighty', it is nevertheless 'in Wisdom' that God has made all things and by the Word that 'all things were made', so that 'the title of *Almighty* cannot be older in God than that of Father, for it is through the Son that the Father is almighty'. In doing this, Origen establishes a fundamental theological point: the creative activity of God must be understood in terms of his existence already as Father.[106] This is, in fact, the opening affirmation of almost every subsequent creed: I believe in One God Father Almighty. God's creative act is thus grounded in the eternal relationship between Father and Son.

Origen continues his examination of the verse in question by pointing out that, as an 'emanation', Wisdom also shares in 'the glory of the Almighty', as is shown by the fact that Christ, the coming one, is also called 'the Almighty' in Scripture (Rev. 1:8). Moreover, since Scripture calls Christ 'God' (John 20:28), we should not hesitate to also call the Son of God 'Almighty'. And so:

> in this way will that saying be true, which he himself says to the Father, *All mine are yours and yours mine, and I am glorified in them.* Now, if all things which are the Father's are also Christ's, and, among all that the Father is, he is also *Almighty,* then without doubt the only-begotten Son ought to be *Almighty,* so that the Son might have all that the Father has. *And I am glorified,* he says, *in them.* For, *at the name of Jesus every knee shall bow, of things in heaven, and things on earth, and things under the earth, and every tongue shall confess that Jesus is Lord in the glory of God the Father.* So, in this way is God's Wisdom herself the pure and clear *emanation of the glory of God,* in respect of his being *Almighty,* glorified as the *emanation* of omnipotence or of glory.[107]

That is, not only does Scripture confer the title 'Almighty' upon both God and Christ, but the truth of their omnipotence is demonstrated by Paul's words in Philippians, that, as a result of the Passion, every knee bows at the name of Jesus. The dominion which the Father holds over all things, and by virtue of which he is called 'the Almighty', is exercised through his Son, who is thus also called 'Almighty', for 'at the name of Jesus every knee bows'. So, Origen concludes: 'if every knee bows to Jesus, then, without doubt, it is Jesus to whom all

---

[105] *Princ.* 1.2.10; Ps. 103:24; John 1:3.

[106] Cf. Peter Widdicombe, *The Fatherhood of God from Origen to Athanasius* (Oxford: Clarendon, 1994), 76, and *passim.*

[107] *Princ.* 1.2.10; John 17:10; Phil. 2:10–11.

things have been subjected, and he it is who exercised power over all things, and through whom all things have been subjected to the Father'.

To make his point even clearer, Origen continues by explaining just what the glory of this omnipotence is:

> And we add this, so that it may be more clearly understood what the *glory* of omnipotence is. The God and Father is *Almighty* because he has power over all things, that is, over heaven and earth, sun and moon, and all things in them. And he exercises power over them through his Word, for *at the name of Jesus every knee bows, of things in heaven, and things on earth, and things under the earth.* And, if *every knee bows* to Jesus, then, without doubt, it is Jesus to whom *all things have been subjected*, and he it is who exercised power over all things, and through whom *all things have been subjected* to the Father; for it is through Wisdom, that is by Word and Reason, not by force and necessity, that they have been subjected. And therefore his glory is in the very fact that he possesses all things, and this is the *purest and most clear glory* of omnipotence, that by Reason and Wisdom, not by force and necessity, all things have been subjected. Now the *purest and most clear glory* of Wisdom is a convenient designation to distinguish it from that glory which is not called pure or genuine.[108]

Christ's glory is 'pure or genuine', unlike that of every being that is created, for, as created and thus alterable, they can only possess righteousness or wisdom as an accidental property, and so they can also always fall away, whereas, as Origen concludes his treatment of this verse from Wisdom in *Princ.* 1.2.10, 'since the Wisdom of God, who is his only-begotten Son, is in all respects unalterable and unchangeable, and every good quality is in her essentially, such that it can never be changed or altered, therefore her glory is declared to be pure and genuine'.

For Origen, then, in *Princ.* 1.2.10, not only does the attribute of omnipotence which calls creation into being derive from the relationship between the Father and the Son, but the 'glory of omnipotence' is found nowhere else but on the cross, as the reference to the Philippians hymn makes clear. If we do not strip away from his argument the scriptural verses that he is in fact discussing, to treat it merely as a logical argument, but instead pay attention to the scriptural verses he uses to develop his argument, we see a very different picture emerge.

We will consider the relationship between Christ and the Cross more fully later, in the next section of the Introduction when we turn to the economy, but for now it is sufficient to note that Origen consistently connects Christ's lordship with his exaltation on the cross: 'the Son became king through suffering the cross'.[109] In other words, the 'omnipotence' Origen is speaking about when

---

[108] *Princ.* 1.2.10; Phil. 2:10–11; 1 Cor. 15:27–8.
[109] *Comm. Jo.* 1.278: ἐβασίλευσε γὰρ διὰ τοῦ πεπονθέναι τὸν σταυρόν.

using the analogy with the relationship between Father and Son is the power revealed through the weakness of the cross. And likewise the 'creation' that is brought into being by this omnipotence of God is not simply that of lifeless, inanimate, and irrational matter, over which a workman might exercise his power, but the creation brought into existence through his Word, 'by word and reason, not by force and necessity', that is, through persuasion upon rational, self-determining beings, who through God's long economy of creative activity come, in the end, to bow their knees in subjection to Christ, through whose own subjection to the Father God comes to be 'all in all'.[110]

To understand what is going on here, it is important to note that the word 'creation', even in modern English, can be used in various ways. It can refer, for instance, to God's initial act of creation, creating the world *ex nihilo,* or it can refer to what which is thus brought into being, the creation, in which we now live and breathe. However, there is another sense in which the word can be used. Williams, in discussing how Origen spoke about the Son with reference to Proverbs 8:22, suggestively comments that for Origen 'creation, *ktisis,* is strictly only the unimpeded expression of God's rational will'.[111] In this sense, following Proverbs 8:22, where Wisdom says of herself 'the Lord created me', Origen can perhaps even speak of Wisdom, the Son of God, as being a 'creature', though by this Origen clearly means something other than what was later understood as 'creation'.[112] The 'creation' of God, everything brought into subjection to him such that he is 'all in all', is the reality brought into existence at the end, not the beginning, it is eschatological, not protological. And it is only by looking to the end that Origen, as we will see further below, tries to get some idea of the beginning.

Later tradition, with roots already in Isaiah (esp. 65:17–24), would of course speak of this as a 'new creation', or creation renewed, but that this eschatological reality can simply be called 'the creation' is also evidenced by the New Testament. It is seen most clearly in the opening self-identification that the risen Christ speaks to the church of Laodicea: 'The words of the Amen, the faithful and true witness [ὁ μάρτυς], the beginning of God's creation [ἡ ἀρχὴ

---

[110] 1 Cor. 15:27–8; treated most fully in *Princ.* 3.6.   [111] Williams, *Arius,* 141.

[112] *Princ.* 4.4.1; the Greek text of the passage in question is preserved by Justinian (Schwartz, 209.11–15), said to be from *Princ.* 4 and numbered by Koetschau as Fragment 32; it is included in the Appendix as item no. 24a. Given what we are seeing, it is not unlikely at all that Origen would be prepared to speak in this way; it is after all what is implied by Prov. 8:22. Likewise in Preface 4, where Rufinus has Origen saying that 'Jesus Christ himself, who came, was born of the Father before all creatures', Jerome (*Ep.* 124.2.1) claims that Origen asserted that 'Christ, the Son of God, was not begotten but made' (*non natum esse, sed factum*). Origen almost certainly wrote γενητός (from γίγνομαι, 'to come into being' or 'to happen') rather than γεννητός (from γεννάω, 'to be born'), two words which could be used equivalently in certain circumstances but which did not become firmly distinguished until the controversies of the fourth century; but to leave the explanation at that rather misses the fuller picture of Origen's understanding of creation.

τῆς κτίσεως τοῦΘεοῦ]' (Rev. 3:14). The Christ of the Apocalypse, the apocalyptic Christ, is the 'beginning' of God's creation. That 'the beginning of God's creation' is an 'Amen' is significant: God's 'creation' requires a response, an 'Amen'. It is, moreover, as the reference to 'faithful and true martyr' indicates, something that comes about through death. As the verse from the Psalm puts it: 'You take away their breath, they die and return to the dust, you send forth your Spirit and they will be created [κτισθήσονται]' (Ps. 103:29–30). The movement of the work of God is always, in Scripture, from death to life: 'I kill and I make alive' (Deut. 32:39). The 'Amen' which completes the creative work of God, making it his creation, is that given by the martyr.[113]

In an important passage in his *Commentary on John,* Origen differentiates between creating and fashioning or moulding:

> Because, therefore, the first human being fell away from the superior things and desired a life different from the better life, he deserved to be a beginning [ἀρχὴν] neither of something created nor made [οὔτε κτίσματος οὔτε ποιήματος], but *of something moulded [πλάσματος] by the Lord, made [πεποιημένον] to be mocked by the angels.* Now, our superior being [ἡ προηγουμένη ὑπόστασις] is in our being made [κτίσαντος] *according to the image* of the Creator, but that resulting from a cause [ἡ ἐξ αἰτίας] is in the thing moulded [ἐν τῷ...πλάσματι], which was received from the dust of the earth.[114]

Here Origen, ever keen to discern the proper ordering of scriptural terminology, is working out, as Harl suggested, a hierarchy of terms describing the different aspects of 'creation': a descending gradation of 'create' (κτίζειν), 'make' (ποιεῖν), and 'mould' (πλάσσειν).[115] He does this by noting the different verbs used in the two creation accounts in the opening chapters of Genesis, by way of a verse from Job: our 'προηγουμένη being' is not simply a 'superior' existence, as created in the image of God, an intellectual reality superior to bodily matter, but also, more immediately, our primary or primordial existence: Gen 1:26 comes, literally, before Gen 2:7, when God takes dust from the

---

[113] This is perhaps also connected to the fact that whereas everything else in Gen. 1 is simply spoken into existence by a divine 'fiat', 'Let there be', the only thing said to be God's own work, that for which he takes counsel and is, as such, his own project, to make human beings in his image, is given in the subjunctive, 'Let us make' (Gen. 1:26–7). As we have seen, for Origen, the 'image' character of the human being is not seen in the body itself, but rather in the acquisition of virtue by a human being, their 'Amen'. This 'project' is only completed on the cross, as described in the Gospel of John, with Christ's final word, 'it is finished' or 'it is perfected' (John 19:30), and before which Pilate says 'Behold the human being' (John 19:5), and then by the martyrs, such as Ignatius, who on his way to martyrdom asks that the Romans be silent about him so that he can follow Christ in martyrdom and so 'become human' (*Rom.* 6). See further John Behr, *Becoming Human: Meditations on Christian Anthropology in Word and Image* (Crestwood, NY: St Vladimir's Seminary Press, 2013).

[114] *Comm. Jo.* 20.182, citing Job 40:19 and Gen. 1:26.

[115] Marguerite Harl, 'La préexistence des âmes dans l'oeuvre d'Origène', in Lothar Lies, ed., *Origeniana Quarta* (Innsbruck: Tyrolia Verlag, 1987), 238–58, at 244.

earth and 'moulds' the human being. That which comes from the earth is neither simply 'created nor made', though, because resulting 'from a cause', it has 'been made to be mocked by the angels'. Though this might seem like a superior intellectual being mocking a lower earthly one, it cannot but help recall the 'mocking' of Christ, on his way to becoming 'the beginning of God's creation'. Moreover, as Adam was the father of all human beings descended from him, for those who discern the spiritual meaning of Scripture, as we have seen when discussing *Princ.* 4, 'Adam is Christ', from whom are descended all those who have the Church as their heavenly mother (*Princ.* 4.3.7). So when Origen asks, in the opening of his *Homilies on Genesis,* what is 'the beginning' (ἀρχή) in which God made heaven and earth? He answers, who else can it be 'except our Lord and *Saviour of all,* Jesus Christ, *the first-born of every creature*?'[116] Although the first account of Genesis comes first, literally, scripturally, and therefore theologically, yet for us, in our own experience of existence, the second account is first: we come into this world in Adam, until we too learn to give our 'amen' to God in Christ.[117]

II The 'Foundation' of the World

A further important term for Origen's understanding of creation is καταβολή, usually translated in the Scriptural translations as 'foundation', but which, as Origen makes clear in a very dense passage, signifies rather a casting downwards. *Princ.* 3.5.4 occurs, as we have seen, in Origen's treatment of the 'economic' dimensions of the principles of the faith, that is, in terms of the actual working out, or the arrangement, of God's plans and activity. He beings by appealing to various scriptural verses in which the term 'foundation' appears (though some of this may well be Rufinus' additions, together with explanatory

---

[116] Origen, *Hom. Gen.* 1.1, citing 1 Tim. 4:10 and Col. 1:15. He continues: '*In* this *beginning, therefore, that is in his Word, God made heaven and earth,* as the evangelist John also says at the beginning of his Gospel: *In the beginning was the Word and the Word was with God and the Word was God. This same was in the beginning with God. All things were made by him and without him nothing was made* [John 1:1–3]. Scripture is not speaking here of any temporal beginning [Non *ergo hic temporale aliquod principium dicit*], but it says that the heaven and the earth and all things which were made were made *in the beginning*, that is, in the Saviour.'

[117] The same idea is found in Irenaeus, Gregory of Nyssa, and Maximus the Confessor, and, indeed, all the way through the end of the Byzantine era. It is very clearly stated, for example, by Nicholas Cabasilas, *Life in Christ* 6.91–4 (6.12 Eng.): 'It was for the new human being that human nature was created at the beginning, and for him mind and desire were prepared. ... It was not the old Adam who was the model for the new, but the new Adam for the old. ... For those who have known him first, the old Adam is the archetype because of our fallen nature. But for him who sees all things before they exist, the first Adam is the imitation of the second. To sum it up: the Savior first and alone showed to us the true human being, who is perfect on account of both character and life and in all other respects.'

comments for his Roman readers). Especially important is Ephesians 1:4, which speaks of how God 'has chosen us before the foundation of the world'. Origen attempts to explain what is implied by this term:

> I am of the opinion that as the end and the consummation of the saints will be in those [worlds] that are *not seen* and *eternal* [2 Cor. 4:18] it must be supposed, from a contemplation of that very end, as we have frequently pointed out above, that rational creatures have also had a similar beginning. And if they had a beginning such as the end for which they hope, they were undoubtedly from the beginning in those [worlds] that are *not seen* and *eternal*. And if this is so, then there has been a descent from the higher conditions to the lower, not only on the part of those souls who have by the variety of their own movements deserved it, but also on that of those who, to serve the whole world, were brought down from the higher and invisible conditions to these lower and visible ones, even against their will. *Because the creation was subjected to futility, not willingly, but by the one who subjected it in hope* [Rom. 8:20], so that both the sun and the moon and the stars and the angels of God might fulfil an obedient service for the world; and for those souls which, because of their excessive spiritual defects needed these denser and more solid bodies, and because of those for whom this was necessary, this visible world was founded. From this, therefore, a descent of everyone alike would seem to be indicated by the meaning of the word, that is, of καταβολή. The whole creation indeed entertains the hope of freedom, of being *set free from the bondage of corruption* when *the children of God* [Rom. 8:21], who either fell away or were scattered abroad, shall be gathered together into one, or when they shall have fulfilled their other duties in this world, which are known to God alone, the Artificer of all things.[118]

There are several things in this dense passage that must be noted clearly. First, it is by a contemplation of the end that Origen speculates about the beginning. This is clearly an important point for him; he says he has pointed it out repeatedly (treated most fully in *Princ.* 1.6.1), and we will turn to it again later in this Introduction. As we have seen, when discussing the 'Recapitulation', he holds that those who come to share in the immortality and incorruptibility of God also share in his eternity—they 'are also eternal' (*Princ.* 4.4.9). If our end is to enter into the eternity of God, being purged by him as a consuming fire, and so coming to share in his properties (as does the iron in the fire), then we too, while still embodied, material, creatures, will be in a world 'not seen' and 'eternal', with 'a house not made by hands, eternal in the heavens' (2 Cor. 4:18–5:1; *Princ.* 2.3.6; 3.6.4). This being so, then our beginning in this world and its time can only be thought of as a falling away from that eternal and heavenly reality.

The second point to note is that Origen does not speak about the falling away of all rational beings from their end as being caused by sinful move-

---

[118] *Princ.* 3.5.4. On the 'foundation' as a 'throwing-down', see also Origen, *Comm. Jo.* 19.149, and Jerome, *Comm. Eph.* 1.4 (especially when he reports what 'another says', presumably Origen).

ments, satiety, or boredom. While some, certainly, have fallen away because of their own movements, in all their variety, others have descended to minister to those who have fallen. This is something Origen returns to frequently throughout his works. 'Not everyone who is a captive', Origen begins his first homily on Ezekiel, 'endures captivity on account of his sins'.[119] Or as he puts it in his *Commentary on John,* in reference to a scriptural verse we have already seen: 'it is possible that the dragon is not the beginning of the work of the Lord in general, but is the beginning of the many made with a body *to be mocked by his angels*, since some can exist with a body in another manner'. And likewise, he continues, Paul, 'not willing, but of hope' wishes 'to remain in the flesh', for he preferred 'to depart and be with Christ', yet he remained in the state he is in for the benefit of others.[120]

Third, Origen does not describe this falling away in terms of taking a body or becoming embodied, but rather as resulting in those who fall away having 'denser and more solid bodies'. In his chapter treating, economically, the soul, Origen suggests, through the supposed etymology of the word 'soul' (taking ψυχή to come from ψυχόω, which, as a passive verb, can mean 'to become cold'), that the intellect becomes a soul through cooling down. As he notes, as God is 'a consuming fire', whenever Scripture speaks of the manifestation of God in creation, it is in fiery terms (the burning bush, for instance), whereas whenever it speaks of the work of the adverse powers, and these powers themselves, it is always as 'cold' (*Princ.* 2.8.3). Christ, he continues, has come 'to cast fire upon the earth', and so sets Simon and Cleopas' hearts aflame on the road to Emmaus.[121] If our end is to be in the consuming fire that is God, transformed by incorporeal fire, and coming to share in the properties of that fire, while the matter of our bodies remains what it is, our cooling down by descending from that fire results in our bodies becoming 'denser'.

The fourth point is that it is this descent, of all, in various ways and for various purposes, that is indicated by the scriptural expression 'the foundation of the world'. But, fifth, and perhaps most important, is that, by starting with the end to speculate about the beginning, our 'election', which happens 'before the foundation of the world', is, in a very real sense, the call that brings us into being, prior to being 'fashioned' in 'the foundation of the world', and prior also to our being 'created', which only properly happens at the end.

Finally, as we have 'descended' or rather, in fact, been 'thrown down' from our high calling into this world, which results from a 'cause' that required our being 'fashioned' from the dust of this earth, then our coming into being in the

---

[119] *Hom. Ezech.* 1.1; see also the first five chapters, expanding on this theme.
[120] *Comm. Jo.* 1.98–100, referring to Job 40:19 and Phil. 1:23–4; see also *Comm. Jo.* 2.175–92, examining the figure of John the Baptist, 'a man sent by God' (John 1:6).
[121] Luke 12:49; 24:32; brought together by Origen in *Hom. Jer.* 20.8 and *Hom. Ex.* 13.14.

time of this world, and our being 'fashioned' to become, in the end, 'created', means that our subjection to decay, not by our own will, 'but by the one who subjected it in hope', are the 'birth-pangs' of creation (an apocalyptic theme if there ever was one), as it labours in travail until the revelation, the *apokalypsis*, of the sons of God (Rom 8:19–22).

Our 'election', then, is in a real sense in God, prior to our being fashioned from the dust of the earth and the foundation of the world: we are primarily and primordially called to participate in the heavenly liturgy, and to enter into that eschatological and apocalyptic reality is to be created. But, because of certain causes, our being created (only realized in the end) is by way of our being fashioned or moulded from the dust of the earth, the earth which has itself been 'thrown down', to be mocked by the angels.

What was the cause of this falling away? In a word, as we will see in the next section, it was the scandal of 'the lamb slain from the foundation of the world' (Rev. 13:8). While happening in the time of the world at a particular moment, it is an eternal reality in God, and so is always spoken of in the past tense. As difficult as this might be for us to understand, with our modern preoccupation with history and chronology, it is the presupposition of Christians from the time that the risen Christ opened the books to show how Moses and all the prophets spoke of how it was necessary for the Son of Man to suffer to enter into his glory (cf. Luke 24:24–6). As Irenaeus had put it a few decades before Origen, when Isaiah says, 'I have seen with my eyes the King, the Lord of hosts', and the other prophets similarly in their words, visions, and mode of life, they 'see the Son of God as a human being, conversing with human beings, while prophesying what was to happen, saying that he who was not come as yet was present, proclaiming also the impassible as subject to suffering, and declaring that he who was then in heaven had descended [*descendisse*] into the dust of death' (*Haer.* 4.20.8). Or, almost a millennium later, as Anselm put it: 'When God does anything, once it is done it is impossible for it not to have been done, but it is always true that it has been done' (*Cur* 17). To see what it might mean that the Passion has an eternal bearing, we must turn to the treatment of Christ in the economic section of the work.

4 ECONOMY

So far we have considered, in *Princ.* 1.2, the 'theology' regarding Christ, examining the titles found in Scripture expressive of his divine nature, and we have followed the reflections contained therein about creation, omnipotence, and the glory of omnipotence, which, by way of Philippians 2 and the exaltation of

Christ in his subjection, results in all creation bowing their knee in adoration of the one upon whom the most exalted name is bestowed. To see further how this is actually worked out on an 'economic' level, and perhaps also to give insight into the falling away of those called to participate in the eternal liturgy celebrated in the heavens, let us turn to the chapter on Christ in the second, 'economic', cycle.

I The Incarnation

Origen opens the chapter with these words: 'It is time, now that these points have been discussed, for us to return to the Incarnation of our Lord and Saviour, how he became human and dwelt among human beings' (*Princ.* 2.6.1). Note that he does not say that we will now turn to the topic of the Incarnation, but rather will resume discussing it. That is, his presentation of the divine titles of Christ in *Princ.* 1.2, expressive of his divine nature, was not a treatment of the 'pre-incarnate' Word, who subsequently, at a certain point in the economy, becomes 'incarnate'. As Rowan Williams strikingly puts it, and as we will have cause to consider more deeply later, 'the existence of Jesus is not an episode in the biography of the Word'.[122]

Having considered Christ's divine names, Origen now turns to how the same Christ is spoken of as 'the Mediator' (*Princ.* 2.6.1; 1 Tim. 2:5). He begins by praising highly the lofty pre-eminence of Christ, as being above all things. Yet this is only done to heighten even more the fact that this one has been revealed in the lowliest terms possible:

> But of all the marvellous and magnificent things about him, this altogether sur-
> passes the astonishment of the human intellect, and the frailty of mortal intelli-
> gence does not discover in what way it can think or understand how that mighty
> Power of divine majesty, that very Word of the Father and that very Wisdom of
> God, *in whom were created all things visible and invisible* [Col. 1:16], can be
> believed to have been within the compass of that man who appeared in Judea;
> and indeed that the Wisdom of God entered into the womb of a woman, to be
> born an infant and to utter cries like the wailing of infants; then, afterwards, that
> he was also reported to be troubled in death, as even he himself acknowledges,

---

[122] *Arius*, 244. The full passage is worth quoting: 'Rather paradoxically, the denial of a "history" of transactions in God focuses attention on the history of God with us in the world: God
has no *story* but that of Jesus of Nazareth and the covenant of which he is the seal. It is a matter
of historical fact at least that the Nicene *verus Deus* was the stimulus to a clarification of the *verus
homo* in the century and a half after the council: the Word of God is the condition of there being
a human identity which is the ministering, crucified and risen saviour, Jesus Christ; but the existence of Jesus is not an episode in the biography of the Word. It remains obstinately—and cru-
cially—a fact of our world and our world's limits.'

saying, *My soul is sorrowful even unto death* [Matt. 26:38]; and that, at the end, he was brought to that death which is accounted by human beings the most shameful, although he rose again on the third day. When, then, we see in him some things so human that they appear to differ in no respect from the common frailty of mortals, and some things so divine, that they are appropriate to nothing else but that primal and ineffable nature of divinity, the narrowness of human understanding is bewildered and, struck with amazement at so great a wonder, it knows not which way to turn, what to hold to, or whither to take itself. If it thinks of God, it sees a mortal being; if it thinks of a human being, it perceives him returning from the dead with spoils after conquering the kingdom of death.

(*Princ.* 2.6.2)

Only in this way, he continues, is 'the truth of both natures…shown to be in one and the same being'. But he fears that 'the explanation of that mystery may perhaps even be beyond the reach of the whole creation of heavenly powers', so he will speak 'in the fewest words possible'.

We then have one of the most intriguing and extraordinarily dense and rich passages in the whole of *On First Principles,* which must be quoted in full:

The only-begotten Son of God, therefore, through whom, as the previous course of discussion has shown, *all things were made, visible and invisible* [Col. 1:16], according to the mind of Scripture both made all things and loves what he made [cf. Wis. 11:24]. For as he is himself *the* invisible *image of the invisible God* [Col. 1:15], he invisibly bestowed upon all rational creatures a participation in himself, in such a way that each one received from him a degree of participation to the extent of the loving affection by which they adhered to him. But whereas, because of the faculty of free will, a variety and diversity had taken hold of individual souls, so that one was attached to its Creator by a more ardent, and another by a feebler and weaker, love, that soul, of which Jesus said, *No one takes my soul from me* [John 10:18], adhering, from *the beginning of creation* [Rev. 3:14] and ever after, inseparably and indissolubly, to him, as to the Wisdom and the Word of God, and the Truth and the true Light, and receiving him wholly and passing itself into his light and splendour, was made with him in a pre-eminent degree *one spirit,* just as the Apostle promises to those who ought to imitate him, that *He who is joined to the Lord is one spirit* [1 Cor. 6:17]. With this substance of the soul mediating between God and the flesh (for it was not possible for the nature of God to be mingled with a body without a mediator) there is born, as we said, the God-man, the medium being that substance for which it was certainly not con-trary to nature to assume a body. Yet neither, on the other hand, was it contrary to nature for that soul, as a rational substance, to receive God, into whom, as we said above, as into the Word and the Wisdom and the Truth, it had already wholly passed. And therefore, either because it was wholly in the Son of God or because it received the Son of God wholly into itself, deservedly it is called, along with the flesh which it had assumed, the Son of God and the Power of God, the Christ and the Wisdom of God; and, on the other hand, the Son of God, through whom all things were created, is named Jesus Christ and the Son of Man.[123] And, moreover, the Son of God is said to have died, that is, in virtue of that nature which could accept death; and he, who is proclaimed as coming in the glory of God the Father with the holy angels, is called the Son of Man. And for this reason, throughout the whole of Scripture, the divine nature is spoken of in human terms as much as human nature is adorned with marks indicative of the divine. For of this, more than anything else, can that which is written be said, that *They shall both be in one flesh, and they are no longer two, but one flesh* [Matt. 19:5–6; Gen. 2:24]. For the Word of God is thought to be more *in one flesh* with the soul than a man with his wife. And, moreover, to whom is it more fitting to be one spirit with God than to this soul, which has so joined itself to God through love that it may deservedly be said to be one spirit with him?   (*Princ.* 2.6.3)

This passage does indeed seem to suggest classic 'Origenist' teaching: there was a pre-existing realm of intellects, all united to the Word, but, because of their varying love for him, they subsequently fell away in various degrees.[124] However, the Scriptural verse given—No man takes my soul from me...(I lay it down of myself)—indicates that Origen is thinking of a different, and scriptural rather than mythological, scene altogether. The most concrete passage in Scripture, where all who had, with varying degrees of love, adhered to their Creator, fell away, except one, is the crucifixion (at least in the Synoptic Gospels, we will return to John later), though, of course, seen apocalyptically in the light of the cross, the whole of Scripture is read as speaking about the continuing falling away from God, from the beginning. When Jesus lays down his soul of his own accord, Origen says—adhering, inseparably and indissolubly, from 'the beginning of creation', to the Word and Wisdom of God, the Truth and the Light—he receives him wholly and passes into his light, to be made 'one spirit' with him, as the apostle promises to those who imitate him, so that, with the soul mediating between the Word and the flesh (by laying down the soul), the *theanthropos,* the God-man, is born, so that the soul, along with the flesh, is called the Son of God, and the Son of God is called not simply Jesus, but Jesus Christ and the Son of Man.

Reading this passage this way, which is, admittedly, novel (as was our reading of *Princ.* 1.2.10 above), flies in the face of the standard interpretation of Origen, which itself goes back to the polemics raised against him. It also flies in the face of what we think we know about the 'Logos Christology' and 'incarnational theology' of the early Church that we expect to find in Origen. Instead it might seem to present Origen as some kind of adoptionist. But it is, nevertheless, how Origen speaks concretely and explicitly in his *Commentary on*

---

[123] The title 'Son of Man' here is not simply a statement about Christ's humanity, but an apocalyptic term (cf. Dan. 7:13), as is made clear in its use in the next sentence.

[124] Cf. Crouzel, *Origen*, 192–4.

John, which, as it survives in Greek, is undisputedly his own words. In the last section of the last book of this commentary, and appealing to the same verse from Paul, Origen writes:

> Now I think God also highly exalted this man when he became obedient *unto death, and the death of a cross.* For the Word in the beginning with God, God the Word, was not capable of being highly exalted. But the high exaltation of the Son of Man which occurred when he glorified God in his own death consisted in the fact that he was no longer different from the Word but was the same with him [ἡ δὲ ὑπερύψωσις τοῦ υἱοῦ τοῦ ἀνθρώπου, γενομένη αὐτῷ δοξάσαντι τὸν θεὸν ἐν τῷ ἑαυτοῦ θανάτῳ, αὕτη ἦν, τὸ μηκέτι ἕτερον αὐτὸν εἶναι τοῦ λόγου ἀλλὰ τὸν αὐτὸν αὐτῷ]. For if *he who is joined to the Lord is one spirit,* so that it is no longer said that *they are two,* even in the case of this man and the spirit, might we not much more say that the humanity of Jesus became one with the Word when he who did not consider *equality with God* something to be grasped was highly exalted? [Phil. 2:6] The Word, however, remained in his own grandeur, or was even restored to it, when he was again with God, God the Word being man.
>
> (*Comm. Jo.* 32.324–6)

The unity of the God-man is again effected upon the Cross, for after it, and in its light, we can no longer differentiate between human and divine properties: we no longer know Christ by a set of fleshly properties, but we now only know him as the Word of God. The abasement of the Cross is not a concealment of his divinity, but rather its fullest revelation: 'We must dare say that the goodness of Christ appeared greater and more divine and truly in accordance with the image of the Father *when he humbled himself and became obedient unto death, even death on a Cross*' (*Comm. Jo.* 1.231). It is here, on the Cross, that we finally see the true form and divinity of the Son of God, and from this moment on we no longer 'see' Jesus with our bodily perception, for 'even though we once knew Christ according to the flesh, we know him thus no longer'.[125]

These claims might sound rather 'adoptionist' and even seem to anticipate Diodore of Tarsus and Theodore of Mopsuestia.[126] But it is, nevertheless, what we are given to see in the Synoptic Gospel (again, we will return to John later),

---

[125] 2 Cor. 5:16. It is important to recognize, especially given Paul's words in 1 Cor. 2:6–16, that the contrast to knowing 'according to the flesh' is not, now, while still in this passing age, some kind of ecstatic spiritual experience of 'seeing' God directly, 'face to face': it is his opponents, the spiritual enthusiasts in Corinth, who were claiming this. Paul had resorted to such an appeal in his first letter to the Corinthians, but now realized that he could not do so again. He appeals to the new creation, but, as Martyn points out, 'he is careful...to imply that the opposite of the old-age way of knowing is not that of the new age—this point must be emphasized—but rather the way of knowing which is granted at the juncture of the ages'. He does not speak of seeing the face of God, nor of knowing by the Spirit, for he, as everyone else, does not yet live in the new age. As Martyn puts it, 'the implied opposite of knowing by the norm of the flesh is not knowing by the norm of the Spirit, but rather knowing *kata stauron* ("by the cross")'. J. Louis Martyn, 'Epistemology at the Turn of the Ages,' in idem, *Theological Issues,* 89–110, here at 107 and 108.

[126] See Behr, *The Case against Diodore and Theodore,* 42–7; see the passages of Theodore preserved by Leontius (LT 2–6, *Case,* 284–91).

and especially in the Letter to the Hebrews and Revelation. It is also something that is found not only in earlier writers, but also in the later Orthodox tradition. Ignatius of Antioch, for instance, speaks of 'the one physician...Jesus Christ' as 'first passible and then impassible' (*Eph.* 7.2). He also speaks of his impending martyrdom in similar terms to Origen's description of the birth of the God-man: 'Birth-pangs are upon me. Suffer me, my brethren; hinder me not from living, do not wish me to die....Suffer me to receive the pure light; when I shall have arrived there, I shall become a human being. Suffer me to follow the example of the Passion of my God' (*Rom.* 6).

But it is with Gregory of Nyssa, to whom we already have had recourse, that we find the most striking similarities; Gregory is often held to be the most 'Origenist' of the Cappadocian Fathers, yet nevertheless was recognized, at the Seventh Ecumenical Council, as 'being called by all the father of the fathers'.[127] As we have seen, Gregory opens his *Contra Eunomium* by saying that the most universal division is between the seen and the unseen, and that the distinction between uncreated and created falls within the latter realm. In *Contra Eunomium* 3.3, Gregory provides an account of Peter's statement in Acts, that 'God made [ἐποίησεν] him both Lord and Christ, this Jesus whom you crucified' (Acts 2:36), in terms of the distinction between uncreated and created.[128] Whereas Eunomius would see the Son's suffering upon the Cross as a mark of distinction between him and the impassible Father, for Gregory it instead reveals 'the supreme exercise of his power' rather than 'an indication of weakness', showing that 'the God made manifest through the Cross ought to be honoured just as the Father is honoured' (*Eun.* 3.3.30–4). Moreover, he continues, 'we say that the body also, in which he accepted the Passion, being combined with the divine nature, was by that commingling made into that which the assuming nature is'. With regard to Peter's words, Gregory points out that it is not as though there are two subjects here; rather, 'Scripture says that two things have been done to a single person, the Passion by the Jews, the honour by God, not as though there was one who suffered and another who was honoured by the exaltation' (*Eun.* 3.3.42). This is shown even more clearly, for Gregory, when Peter says he was 'exalted by the Right Hand of God'.[129] So, Gregory says, 'the Apostle said that the humanity [τὸ ἀνθρώπινον] was exalted, being exalted by becoming Lord and Christ; and this took place after the Passion' (*Eun.* 3.3.43). He then continues in even stronger terms:

> He who says *exalted by the Right Hand of God* clearly reveals the unspeakable economy of the mystery, that the Right Hand of God, who made all things that are, who is the Lord by whom all things were made and without whom nothing

---

[127] *Acta*, sixth session, vol. 5; Mansi, 13.293e.

[128] For a full exposition of this text, see Behr, *Nicene Faith,* 436–45.

[129] Acts 2:33, reading the dative as expressing agency, rather than 'to the right hand' as most modern translations do.

that is subsists, himself raised to his own height the human being [τὸν ... ἄνθρωπον] united to him, making him also, by the commixture, to be what he is by nature: he is Lord and King, and the King is called Christ; these things he made him too.... And this we are plainly taught by the voice of Peter in his mystic discourse, that the lowliness of the one crucified in weakness (and weakness, as we have heard from the Lord, indicates the flesh [Mt 26:41]), that, by virtue of its mingling with the infinite and boundless [nature] of the Good, remained no longer in its own measures and properties, but by the Right Hand of God was raised up together, and became Lord instead of servant, Christ the King instead of a subject, highest instead of lowly, God instead of man.   (*Eun.* 3.3.44)

This might also sound like some kind of adoptionism, but it is not. Rather, to paraphrase Gregory's argument here and throughout *Against Eunomius* 3.3: through the Passion, Christ, as human, becomes that which as God he always is. The cross is our lens and prism for understanding the revelation of God in Christ; it brings into focus 'the God revealed through the Cross' and allows us to see the whole of creation and the economy as refracted into its diverse aspects. We cannot begin with an understanding of God, or the Son of God in whom he is revealed, apart from the Cross. If we attempt to theologize apart from the Cross, to see God revealed in Christ apart from the Passion (after which we no longer know him in the flesh) we will end up defining divinity in human terms. This is Gregory's chief complaint about Apollinarius: he 'defines the divine by means of the perceptible appearance, rather than by intellectual contemplation', for 'the true account', according to Gregory, is that Christ 'is human and God, by what is seen human, by what is understood God'.[130] In perhaps his most startling comment, Gregory puts it this way:

Christ [is] always, both before the economy and after it; [the] human being, however, [is] neither before it nor after it, but only during the time of the economy. Neither [is] the human being before the Virgin, nor, after the ascent into heaven, [is] the flesh still in its own properties.[131]

What he seems to be pointing to is that although 'Moses and all the prophets' had always spoken about how the Son of Man enters his glory by suffering, and this is also the content of the apostolic preaching, yet during the time when Jesus walked the earth, seen in the flesh by fleshly eyes, the glory and divinity of the Son of Man was not in fact seen, not until the exaltation on the Cross.

---

[130] *Antirrheticus* (GNO 3.1, p. 191.24–7): οὐκοῦν κατὰ τὸν ἀληθῆ λόγον καὶ ἄνθρωπος ἐστι καὶ θεός, τῷ ὁρωμένῳ ἄνθρωπος, τῷ νοουμένῳ θεός. ὁ δὲ οὐ τοῦτό φησιν, ἐν τῷ συμπεράσματι τῷ φαινομένῳ τὸ θεῖον, οὐ τῷ νοητῷ ὁριζόμενος.

[131] *Antirrheticus* (GNO 3.1, p. 222.25–9): ἀλλὰ πάντοτε μὲν ὁ Χριστὸς καὶ πρὸ τῆς οἰκονομίας καὶ μετὰ τοῦτο· ἄνθρωπος δὲ οὔτε πρὸ τούτου οὔτε μετὰ ταῦτα, ἀλλ' ἐν μόνῳ τῷ τῆς οἰκονομίας καιρῷ. οὔτε γὰρ πρὸ τῆς παρθένου ὁ ἄνθρωπος οὔτε μετὰ τὴν εἰς οὐρανοὺς ἄνοδον ἔτι ἡ σὰρξ ἐν τοῖς ἑαυτῆς ἰδιώμασιν.

For Origen, likewise, the identity of Christ, the Son of God, is shown through the Passion, hanging upon the Cross. The very last line of *Philocalia* 15, which discusses the apparently poor quality of scriptural language and the apparently poor aspect of Jesus, and the various forms in which both Scripture and Jesus appear, concludes:

> But how can Celsus, and the enemies of the divine Word, and such as do not investigate Christianity with a love of truth, know the meaning of the different appearances of Jesus? I refer to the different periods of his life, to anything he did before the Passion and whatever happened after his Resurrection from the dead.[132]

The unchanging identity of Christ is fixed upon the Cross, which as lens and prism enables us to see everything as patterned upon it. If we, for instance, attempt to look behind the Cross to see the human being Jesus before the Passion, as if the Passion had never happened (rather unhistorical in its attempt to be historical), we will end up seeing Jesus as he appears in his human properties, as the son of the carpenter from Nazareth; we will not 'see', or rather intellectually contemplate the Word of God, and so will not be doing theology. If, on the other hand, we look *through* the Cross, we see the unchanging identity of the crucified one throughout his life, from his birth from the Virgin and throughout his ministry. And this is, of course, the same hermeneutic needed to read Scripture and encounter the Word of God: the Word of God 'eternally takes flesh in the Scriptures' ($\dot{\alpha}\epsilon\grave{\iota}$ $\gamma\grave{\alpha}\rho$ $\dot{\epsilon}\nu$ $\tau\alpha\hat{\iota}\varsigma$ $\gamma\rho\alpha\varphi\alpha\hat{\iota}\varsigma$ $\dot{o}$ $\lambda\acute{o}\gamma o\varsigma$ $\sigma\grave{\alpha}\rho\xi$ $\dot{\epsilon}\gamma\acute{\epsilon}\nu\epsilon\tau o$) so that he might tabernacle amongst us, but only if we recline on his breast, as did John, do we come to know the Word.[133] We must ascend the mountain, to see him transfigured, speaking with Moses and Elijah, the Law and the Prophets, about his 'exodus' in Jerusalem.[134] If we stay at the level of the flesh, the letters, we will never come to contemplate the Word.

Returning to *Princ.* 2.6, Origen continues his economic account of Christ by examining further what is meant by the title 'Christ', bestowed upon this one, and does so by bringing in the verse from the Psalms, 'You loved righteousness and hated iniquity. Therefore God, your God, anointed you with the oil of gladness beyond your fellows' (Ps. 44:7–8, *Princ.* 2.6.4). It is, he comments, 'by the merit of its love [that] it is anointed with the oil of gladness, that is, the soul with the Word of God is made Christ'. And as the Psalm verse also speaks of

---

[132] *Philoc.* 15.20, a text coming from *Cels.* 6.77. The two main parts of *Philoc.* 15.20 are not 'two unrelated topics' put together by 'an inky-fingered drudge, who knew his Origen very well, but did not know much else' working in the library of Caesarea, as Neil McLynn, 'What was the *Philocalia* of Origen?' puts it. *Meddelanden från Collegium Patristicum Lundense* 19 (2004), 32–43, at 34 and 40. It instead shows a remarkable grasp of Origen's understanding of the interrelation between Scripture, and its exegesis, and Christology.
[133] Origen, *Philoc.* 15.19.   [134] Luke 9:31; cf. Behr, *Way to Nicaea*, 169–81.

being anointed 'beyond your fellows', the anointing in this case indicates that the grace of the Spirit was given to him not as it had been given to the prophets, 'but that the essential fullness of the Word of God himself was in it', for, as the Apostle says, 'in him the fullness of divinity dwelt bodily' (Col. 2:9). It is for this reason that Isaiah can say that 'he did no sin' (Isa. 53:9), and Hebrews, that 'he was tempted in all things as we are, yet without sin' (Heb. 4:15), and, even more, 'before the child know how to call father or mother, he turned himself away from iniquity' (Isa. 8:4 and 7:16). Having come to this conclusion, Origen then attempts to answer those who, accepting that Christ did not sin, ask how he can possess a rational soul, since it is in the nature of such souls to be capable of both good and evil (*Princ.* 2.6.5). While it cannot be doubted that the nature of Christ's soul was the same as that of all other human beings, 'otherwise it could not be called a soul', yet, he continues:

> this soul, which is Christ's, so chose to love righteousness that, in accordance with the immensity of its love, it adhered to it unchangeably and inseparably, so that the firmness of purpose and immensity of affection and inextinguishable warmth of love destroyed all thought of alteration or change, such that what was dependent upon the will is now changed into nature by the exertion of long usage; and so it is to be believed that there is in Christ a human and rational soul, and yet not be supposed that it had any thought or possibility of sin.
>
> (*Princ.* 2.6.5)

It is here, in explaining how this might be so, that Origen brings in the analogy of iron placed in a fire 'receiving the fire throughout all its pores and veins and becoming wholly fire'.[135] Could we say, Origen asks, that, while it remains in the fire and incessantly burning, the iron is ever capable of becoming cold? So also, he continues, bringing back in the idea of the anointing:

> In this way, then, that soul which, like iron in the fire, was placed in the Word forever, in Wisdom forever, in God forever, is God in all that it does, feels, and understands; and therefore it can be called neither alterable or changeable, since, being ceaselessly kindled, it came to possess immutability from its union with the Word of God. To all the saints some warmth of the Word of God must indeed be supposed to have passed; but in this soul it must be believed that the divine fire itself essentially rested, from which some warmth may have passed to others. Finally, the fact that it says, *God, your God, anointed you with the oil of gladness above your fellows,* shows that that soul is anointed in one way, with the oil of gladness, that is, with the Word of God and Wisdom, and his fellows, that is, the holy prophets and apostles, in another way. For they are said to have *run in the*

---

[135] The background for this idea is the theory of mixture developed by the Stoics. See esp. Alexander of Aphrodisias, *Mixt.* 3, 218.1–2 (*SVF* 2.473), reporting Chrysippus' teaching: 'fire as a whole passes through iron as a whole, while each of them preserves its own substance' (τὸ πῦρ ὅλον δι᾽ ὅλου χωρεῖν τοῦσιδήρου λέγουσι, σώζοντος αὐτῶν ἑκατέρου τὴν οἰκείαν οὐσίαν).

fragrance of his ointment [Song 1:4], while that soul was the vessel containing the ointment itself, of whose glowing heat all the prophets and apostles are made worthy partakers. Therefore, as the fragrance of the ointment is one thing, and the substance of the ointment another, so also Christ is one thing and his fellows another. And just as the vessel itself, which contains the substance of the ointment, can in no way accept any foul smell, yet it is possible that those who participate in its fragrance, if they move a little way from its glowing heat, may accept any foul smell that comes upon them, so also, in the same way, it was impossible that Christ, being as it were the very vessel in which was the substance of the ointment, should accept an odour of an opposite kind, while his fellows, in proportion to their proximity to the vessel, will be partakers and receivers of his fragrance.   (*Princ.* 2.6.6)

Just as a piece of iron, identified by certain properties (cold and hard), when placed in a fire loses all those properties, while yet remaining the iron that it is, to become identified by the properties of the fire (hot and fluid), so also, the human nature of Jesus (identified by certain sense-perceptible human properties), is no longer known by these properties, but rather by the properties of God, being beyond space and time, revealed, as we have seen, in and through the cross, known by intellectual contemplation. Through the Passion, Christ, as human, becomes that which, as God, he always is.

Extremely important in *Princ.* 2.6.4–6 is that by being anointed 'beyond his fellows' Christ enables his fellows to share in his unction, to be themselves anointed of God; it is a ministry exercised towards them. This ministerial character of Christ's activity, and, indeed, identity, is extended by Origen, in his *Commentary on John*, to include his, and our, being God and gods. Answering those who fear to call Christ 'God', lest it imply ditheism, Origen writes:

Their problem can be resolved in this way. We must say to them that at one time God, with the article, is very God, wherefore also the Saviour says in his prayer to the Father, *That they may know you the only true God* [John 17:3]. On the other hand, everything besides the very God, which is made God by participation in his divinity, would more properly not be said to be the God, but god [πᾶν δὲ τὸ παρὰ τὸ αὐτόθεος μετοχῇ τῆς ἐκείνου θεότητος θεοποιούμενον οὐχ ὁ θεὸς ἀλλὰ θεὸς κυριώτερον ἂν λέγοιτο]. To be sure, his *firstborn of every creature* [Col. 1:15], inasmuch as he was the first to be with God and has drawn divinity into himself, is more honoured than any other gods besides him (of whom God is God as it is said, *The God of gods, the Lord has spoken, and he has called the earth* [Ps. 49:1]). It was by his ministry that they became gods, for he drew from God that they might be deified, sharing ungrudgingly also with them according to his goodness. *The* God, therefore, is the true God. The others are gods formed according to him as images of the prototype. But again, the archetypal image of the many images is *the Word with the* God, who was *in the beginning* [John 1:1]. By being *with the God* he always continues to be *God*. But he would not have this if he were not *with God*, and he would not remain *God* if he did not continue in unceasing contemplation of the depth of the Father.   (*Comm. Jo.* 2.17–18)

It is through his entry into God, by his unceasing contemplation of the depths of the Father, that the Lord is God and ministers this divinity to others, who thereby also become gods. The 'firstborn of every creature', by being the first to be with God and drawing divinity into himself, also enable us to become gods in him, by sharing in his anointing, and also to be born of God as the martyrs are, as we have seen, in following him in his Passion, so that Christ becomes 'the firstborn of many brethren'.[136] Not only that, but for Origen, we come to be so eternally:

The Saviour is eternally begotten by the Father, so also, if you possess the *Spirit of adoption* [Rom. 8:15] God eternally begets you in him according to each of your works, each of your thoughts. And being begotten you thereby become an eternally begotten son of God in Christ Jesus.[137]

Becoming an eternally begotten son of God in Christ Jesus, we in fact put on the identity of Jesus. We can now return to the Gospel of John, where, unlike the Synoptics, in which all the disciples fall away at the Passion, the beloved disciple, who had reclined on the breast of Jesus at the table, now remains at the foot of the Cross, along with the Virgin, to hear words only spoken in the Gospel of John:

We might dare say, then, that the Gospels are the firstfruits of all Scriptures, but that the firstfruits of the Gospels is that according to John, whose meaning no one can understand who has not leaned on Jesus' breast nor received Mary from Jesus to be his mother also. But he who would be another John must also become such as John, to be shown to be Jesus, so to speak. For if Mary had no son except Jesus, in accordance with those who hold a sound opinion of her, and Jesus says

---

[136] Rom. 8:29. Another striking passage describing the birth of the martyrs is in the 'Letter of the Churches of Vienne and Lyon to Asia and Phrygia' (preserved in Eusebius 5.1.45–6), describing the death of Blandina and Attalus, which recalls those who had fallen away back to life: 'Through their continued life the dead were made alive, and the martyrs showed favour to those who had failed to witness. And there was great joy for the Virgin Mother in receiving back alive those whom she had miscarried as dead. For through them the majority of those who had denied were again brought to birth and again conceived and again brought to life and learned to confess; and now living and strengthened, they went to the judgment seat.' See Behr, *Irenaeus*, 198–203. The identity of the Virgin Mother, whose womb is made pure by Christ so that we too can be born of it, is strikingly put by Irenaeus, commenting on Isa. 7:14, 8:3, and 9:6: these verses speak of 'the union of the Word of God with his own handiwork, that the Word would become flesh, and the Son of God the Son of Man, the pure one opening purely that pure womb which regenerates human beings unto God and which he himself made pure, having become that which we are, he is *God Almighty* and has a generation which cannot be declared' (*Haer.* 4.33.11).

[137] *Hom. Jer.* 9.4: καὶ ἀεὶ γεννᾶται ὁ σωτὴρ ὑπὸ τοῦ πατρός, οὕτως καὶ σὺ ἐὰν ἔχῃς "τὸ τῆς υἱοθεσίας," ἀεὶ γεννᾷ σε ἐν αὐτῷ ὁ θεὸς καθ' ἕκαστον ἔργον, καθ' ἕκαστον διανόημα, καὶ γεννώμενος οὕτως γίνῃ ἀεὶ γεννώμενος υἱὸς θεοῦ ἐν Χριστῷ Ἰησοῦ·

to his mother, *Behold your son* [John 19:26], and not, 'Behold, this man also is your son', he has said equally, 'Behold, this is Jesus whom you bore'. For indeed everyone who has been perfected *no longer lives, but Christ lives in him* [Gal. 2:20], and since *Christ lives in him,* it is said of him to Mary, *Behold your son,* the Christ.[138]

Putting on the identity of Jesus, as an eternally begotten son of God, although we come into being in time, our end, through death and resurrection in Christ, is to be a participant in the eternal liturgy in the heavenly court. Yet, as the eternity of God is strictly speaking outside of time, non-temporal, entering into that reality is not entering into an eternity conceived in a temporal fashion, to enter, as it were, at a given moment in that eternity, taken as an endless chronological duration, as a continuation of our present temporal life. It is rather to enter into a non-temporal and non-spatial eternal reality, again as iron in the fire.[139] And so, in a sense, we must always already be there, even though we have not yet, within the chronology of this world, arrived there. As such, our life on earth is, in a real sense, a shadow of that reality, stretched out upon the earth; our true reality is 'hidden with Christ in God' (Col. 3:3).

And so Origen completes his account of 'the Incarnation', that is, the account of Christ as unfolded in the economy, with this passage:

I think that Jeremiah the prophet also, understanding what was the nature of the Wisdom of God in him, which was also the same which he had assumed for the salvation of the world, said, *The breath of our face, Christ the Lord, of whom we said that under his shadow we shall live among the nations* [Lam. 4:20]. For just as the shadow of our body is inseparable from the body, and assumes and performs the movements and gestures of our body without deviation, so I think that the prophet, wishing to indicate the work and movement of Christ's soul, which was inseparably attached to him and accomplished everything according to his movement and will, called this the shadow of Christ the Lord, under whose shadow we were to live among the nations. For in the mystery of this assumption live the nations, who, imitating that soul through faith, come to salvation. Moreover David, when saying, *Remember, O Lord, my reproach, with which they have reproached me in exchange for your Christ* [Ps. 88:51–2], seems to me to indicate

---

[138] *Comm. Jo.* 1.23. See the fascinating study of Jeffrey F. Hamburger, *St. John the Divine: The Deified Evangelist in Medieval Art and Theology* (Berkeley: University of California Press, 2002).

[139] The later tradition would even assert that we become 'uncreated', thus emphasizing that the primary distinction, as we saw with Gregory of Nyssa, is between the unseen and seen realms, for the distinction in the former realm, between uncreated and created, is thus overcome. Cf. Gregory Palamas, *Triad* 3.1.31: 'But as we have shown above, the saints clearly state that this adoption and deifying gift, actualized by faith, is real. . . . The divine Maximus has not only taught that it is real, but also that it is unoriginate (and not only uncreated), uncircumscribed and supratemporal, so that those attaining it are thereby perfected as uncreated, unoriginate, and uncircumscribed, although in their own nature they derive from nothing' (ὡς καὶ τοὺς αὐτῆς εὐμοιρηκότας δι᾽αὐτὴν ἀκτίστους, ἀνάρχους, καὶ ἀπεριγράπτους τελέσαι, καίτοι διὰ τὴν οἰκείαν φύσιν ἐξ οὐκ ὄντων γεγονότας).

the same. And what else does Paul mean when he says, *Your life is hidden with Christ in God* [Col. 3:3], and, again, in another place, *Do you seek a proof of him who speaks in me, that is, Christ?* [2 Cor. 13:3] And now he says that Christ was hidden in God.[140] The meaning of this, unless it be shown to be something like that which was signified by the prophet with the shadow of Christ, as we said above, probably exceeds the apprehension of the human mind. But we also see many other statements in the divine Scriptures regarding the significance of the word 'shadow', such as that in the Gospel according to Luke, where Gabriel says to Mary, *The Spirit of the Lord will come upon you, and the power of the Most High will overshadow you* [Luke 1:35]. And the Apostle says of the law that those who have circumcision in the flesh *serve a copy and shadow of the heavenly things* [Heb. 8:5]. And elsewhere it is said, *Is not our life upon the earth a shadow?* [Job 8:9] If then, both the Law which is upon the earth is a shadow, and our whole life which is upon the earth is a shadow, and we live among the nations under the shadow of Christ, it must be considered whether the truth of all these shadows may not come to be known in that revelation, when no longer *through a mirror and in a riddle, but face to face* [1 Cor. 13:12] all the saints shall be counted worthy to behold the glory of God and the causes and truth of things. The pledge of this truth already being received through the Holy Spirit, the Apostle said, *Even if we had formerly known Christ according to the flesh, we know him thus no longer* [2 Cor. 5:16].   (*Princ.* 2.6.7)

Origen then finishes the chapter with a typical statement of humility: this is what he has in mind to say, but 'if there is anyone who is able to discover something better and to confirm what he says by clearer statements from the holy Scriptures, let those accounts be received rather than mine'. Our true identity is 'hidden with Christ in God' and it is under his shadow that our lives are lived out in this world, such that our whole life is but a shadow, yet a shadow that is cast, as upon the Virgin, by the power of the Most High. The truth of all these things will only be known when we no longer see through a mirror, but face to face, beholding 'the glory of God and the causes and truth of things'. Yet even now a pledge of the truth is given to us in Christ, whom, as we have repeatedly seen, we no longer know, or should seek to know, according to the flesh.

II The 'Pre-existence' and Incarnation of Christ

If this chapter, *Princ.* 2.6, which we have traced in detail, supplementing it with other texts from Origen himself, and the wider tradition, is what Origen understands by 'the Incarnation of Christ', it is clearly something other than, in Rowan Williams' arresting words, 'an episode in the biography of the Word', as

---

[140] Perhaps alluding to 2 Cor. 5:16, cited at the end of the paragraph.

if the task of theology were to narrate an account of a pre-existent, preincarnate divine person called the Word, who, at a certain point in time, becomes flesh, by being born as a human being, to return to the Father thirty-three years later. The incoherence of such an approach, which it has to be said, is rather common in theological works, was pointed out by Herbert McCabe, in his insightful essay 'The Involvement of God'.[141]

'It is part of my thesis', McCabe argues, 'that there is no such thing as the preexistent Christ.' It was 'invented', he suggests, in the nineteenth century, 'as a way of distinguishing the eternal procession of the Son from the incarnation of the Son', that is, to affirm that 'Jesus did not become Son of God in virtue of the incarnation. He was already Son of God before that.'[142] McCabe rejects the notion from two points of view. First, 'to speak of the pre-existent Christ is to imply that God has a life-story, a divine story, other than the story of the incarnation... *First* the Son of God pre-existed as just the Son of God and *then* later he was the Son of God made man.' This is incoherent, and 'incompatible at least with the traditional doctrine of God', for as he points out: 'There can be no succession in the eternal God, no change. Eternity is not, of course, a very long time; it is not time at all... Eternity is not timeless in the sense that an instant is timeless.... No: eternity is timeless because it totally transcends time.'[143] Speaking of the Son of God 'becoming man' or 'coming down from heaven', McCabe writes, 'makes a perfectly good metaphor, but could not literally be true'. 'From the point of view of God, then, *sub specie eternitatis,* no sense can be given to the idea that at some point in God's life-story, the Son became incarnate.'[144]

Yet, from our point of view, in history, McCabe continues, 'there was certainly a time when Jesus had not yet been born'. And so, as McCabe puts it, 'Moses could have said with perfect truth "Jesus of Nazareth is not yet" or "Jesus does not exist" because, of course, the future does not exist; this is what makes it future.'[145] Yet while saying 'Jesus does not exist', Moses could also have simultaneously said truthfully 'The Son of God does exist'. This, McCabe concedes, might be called the 'pre-existence of Christ',

> meaning that at an earlier time in our history (and there isn't any time except in history) these propositions would both have been true: 'Jesus does not exist', 'The Son of God does exist', thus apparently making a distinction between the

[141] First printed in *New Blackfriars* (November 1985), reprinted in Herbert McCabe, *God Matters* (London: Geoffrey Chapman, 1987; Continuum, 2012), 39–51.

[142] Ibid. 49. See also Karl-Josef Kuschel, *Born Before All Time? The Dispute over Christ's Origin* (New York: Crossroad, 1992).

[143] McCabe, 'Involvement', 49, his emphasis. See now Ilaria Ramelli and David Konstan, *Terms for Eternity: Aiônios and Aïdios in Classical and Christian Texts* (Piscataway, NJ: Gorgias Press, 2011).

[144] McCabe, 'Involvement', 50.   [145] Ibid.

existence of Jesus and the existence of the Son of God. But the phrase 'pre-existent Christ' seems to imply not just that in the time of Moses 'The Son of God exists' would be true, but also that the proposition 'The Son of God exists *now*' would be true. And this would be a mistake. Moses could certainly have said, 'It is true now that the Son of God exists' but he could not have truly said 'The Son of God exists now'. *That* proposition, which attributes *temporal* existence ('now') to the Son of God, is the one that became true when Jesus was conceived in the womb of Mary. The simple truth is that apart from incarnation the Son of God exists at no time at all, at no 'now', but in eternity, in which he acts upon all time but is not himself 'measured by it', as Aquinas would say. 'Before Abraham was, I am'.[146]

Grappling with the intersection of time and eternity does indeed, and necessarily, stretch the limits of human thought, acting as it must do within time. It is difficult to know what to make of the phrase 'the pre-existent Christ'. It is not clear how it would have been rendered in Greek; there the typical expression, which 'pre-existent' is presumably meant to translate, is προαιώνιος, which simply means 'eternal', outside time, not a 'prior existence', the 'pre' prefix being added to emphasize the point. McCabe's point might have been clearer if instead of speaking about 'the pre-existent Christ', he had spoken of the 'pre-incarnate Word', a phrase I have yet to find in patristic literature, though it abounds in secondary scholarship. Indeed, although the creeds do speak of how the Son 'came down from heaven and was incarnate', which as McCabe suggests is a good metaphor, the subject of the second article of the Creeds of Nicaea and Constantinople, the one who came down from heaven to be incarnate, is not a 'pre-incarnate Word' (the term 'Word' does not even appear in the Creeds), but rather the one subject, the one Lord Jesus Christ. The intersection between time and eternity is naturally correlated to the relationship between 'theology' and 'economy', the two levels on which Origen expounds his first principles: in the first, we speak of Christ as divine, in the second we speak of the same Christ as the mediator; but this does not provide a narrative in which a divine subject later becomes human.[147]

When McCabe writes that it would be true for Moses, as indeed it would be, to say 'Jesus does not exist' or 'is not yet', although it would also be true for Moses to say 'It is true now that the Son of God exists', without splitting Jesus and the Son into two different subjects (for it would not be true for Moses to say 'The Son of God exists *now*'), he seems to be pointing towards the same idea that we saw Origen, and Gregory of Nyssa, trying to articulate, that is, that Jesus, as a human being, through the Passion, becomes that which, as God, he always is, *outside of time*. Their way of expressing this point, however, focuses

---

[146] Ibid. His emphasis.

[147] As Frances M. Young: 'There is no possibility of "narrative" in *theologia*, but narrative constitutes *oikonomia;* one is in time, the other beyond time.' *Biblical Exegesis and the Formation of Christian Culture* (Cambridge: Cambridge University Press, 1997), 143.

our attention much more strictly upon the Cross, seeing the life of Jesus always in that light, and, indeed, the whole of creation and its history, seen from the final end-point. The Incarnation, therefore, should perhaps be thought of as the enfleshing of the eternal heavenly reality in the assumption of flesh by the eternal Word, which simultaneously (as iron in the fire) transforms the earthly properties of the flesh, through the fire of the Passion, into the very properties of the Word (so that they are no longer seen), as Jesus goes to the Father, preparing the way for others to follow him and in so doing ministering divinity and the anointing to them, so that the eternal reality of the heavenly court and its liturgy is enfleshed in those who follow him. Understood in such a way, we can perhaps better understand the next great Alexandrian theologian, Athanasius, whose work *On the Incarnation,* the first to be so titled, does not focus on the birth of the Word, in the sense of a biographical 'episode', conflating the infancy narratives of Matthew and Luke (who do not mention the Word of God) with John 1:14 (which doesn't speak of a birth), but shows rather how the one on the Cross is in fact the Word of God, who through the Passion demonstrates his resurrection *in* those who follow him by taking up the Cross.[148]

5 'IN MY END IS MY BEGINNING'

The surprise that will no doubt be caused by the claim that the idea of a 'pre-existent' or, better, 'pre-incarnate' divine Word is incoherent, or perhaps rather, mythological, is likely to be matched by the surprise that, despite all the discussion about Origen's teaching on 'the pre-existence of souls' or 'preexistent souls' (or, for that matter, 'pre-existent intellects'), these phrases do not, as Harl points out, actually occur in the writings of Origen.[149] In *Contra Celsum,* Origen emphatically maintains that he is not teaching some kind of Platonic transmigration of souls, 'but a different and more sublime view' (*Cels.* 4.17). That this is not some kind of later retraction is made clear by a similar statement in his *Commentary on John,* where he contrasts the idea of souls transmigrating from one body to another (μετενσωμάτωσις) with 'embodiment' (ἐνσωμάτωσις).[150]

---

[148] Cf. Behr, introduction, *St Athanasius: On the Incarnation,* 36–40.

[149] Harl, 'Préexistence des âmes', p. 257, n.2. The quotation in the heading for this section is from T. S. Eliot, *The Four Quartets,* East Coker, last line, in *Collected Poems 1909–1962* (Orlando: Harcourt, 1963); used with permission.

[150] *Comm. Jo.* 6.86; see also 6.66–71; *Cels.* 1.13; 1:20; 4.40; 5.29; 7.32; 8:30; *Comm. Matt.* 11.17; 13.1. On the whole question of divine embodiment, see now Benjamin D. Sommer, *The Bodies of God and the World of Ancient Israel* (Cambridge: Cambridge University Press, 2009).

What gave rise to this incorrect shorthand is likely Origen's repeated references to 'antecedent causes' that result in the different position of intellectual beings within the cosmos. Before we tackle this question, however, we would do well to remind ourselves that Origen consistently begins any discussion about the beginning of things by looking towards the end. The fullest statement of this is given in *Princ.* 1.6.2:

> Seeing, then, that such is the end, when all enemies will be subjected to Christ, and when the last enemy, death, will be destroyed and when the kingdom shall be delivered to the God and Father by Christ, to whom all things have been sub-jected [cf. 1 Cor 15:24–7], let us, I say, from such an end as this contemplate the beginning of things. For the end is always like the beginning, and, therefore, as there is one end of all things, so ought there to be understood one beginning of all things, and as there is one end of many things, so also from one beginning there are many differences and varieties, which, in turn, through the goodness of God and by subjection to Christ and through the unity of the Holy Spirit, are recalled to one end which is like the beginning: that is, all those who *bending the knee at the name of Jesus* have displayed by this the proof of their subjection to him, those who are *of the heavens and of the earth and of the regions under the earth* [Phil. 2:10]—the entire universe being indicated by the three terms—those, that is, who from that one beginning, each one variously led by his own impulse, were arranged in different orders according to their merit, for goodness does not exist in them essentially, as it does in God and his Christ and the Holy Spirit.

Although he does indeed claim that 'the end is always like the beginning', he does not start from 'the beginning', but rather looks to the end, when all things are brought into subjection to God, in order to search for some idea of the beginning. If the end is to be this unity of all in God and as God (for God will indeed be all in all), now 'enfleshed' by the assumption of flesh into this heavenly reality (as iron in fire), then the beginning of all things is also to be understood as a unity.

There is, of course, an anti-Gnostic thrust to what Origen repeatedly says throughout *On First Principles:* God is not an arbitrary despot who wilfully creates different beings of diverse natures.[151] But, if God is not the cause of the variety (and much suffering and misery), then the cause must result from ourselves, while God is the one who is able to arrange all things, as vessels of honour and vessels of dishonour, in the same house, such that each is able to purge itself from dishonourable things to become 'a vessel unto honour, sanctified and useful to the master, prepared for every good work' (1 Tim. 2:20–1, *Princ.* 3.1.21). With this assertion from Paul, Origen continues, 'it does not seem absurd, when we are discussing antecedent causes in the same order and by the same method, to think in the same manner regarding souls, that this is

---

[151] Cf. esp. *Princ.* 2.9.6 and 3.1.22–4.

the reason why Jacob was loved even before he was born into this world and Esau hated while he was still held in the womb of his mother' (*Princ.* 3.1.22).

P. Tzamalikos' treatment of Origen's understanding of the relationship between time and eternity, in his own re-reading of Origen, can help us greatly in understanding these 'antecedent causes'.[152] Tzamalikos points out that, for Origen: 'The view of time as the continuum where divine and creaturely will encounter each other proves the finiteness of the world. If the world were infinite, there would be no foreknowledge.' This is not because, as we noted earlier had become the charge against Origen, he holds that 'God cannot *comprehend* the infinite, but because in that case "foreknowledge" would make no sense. If the world is beginningless and endless, any notion of *before* (hence of fore-knowledge) is meaningless. Consequently, if there is no foreknowledge, *prophecy* makes no sense either, since no *end* of the world makes sense.'[153]

If Origen begins by contemplating the end, that is because there is an end, and this end makes a beginning possible, as well as giving coherence and purpose to what happens. 'Action is meaningful, since this is subject to judgement and has an eschatological perspective.'[154] But this means, as Tzamalikos points out later, 'though odd as it may appear, the prospective fulfilment of certain prophecy is the *cause*, whereas the utterance of prophecy is the *result*, although it temporally precedes the event itself....it is the future that determines the past.'[155] As Origen put it in *Contra Celsum*,

> We say that the one who made the prediction was not the cause of the future event, because he foretold that it would happen; but we hold that the future event, which would have taken place even if it had not been prophesied, constitutes the cause of its prediction by the one with foreknowledge. (*Cels.* 2.20)

It is because Christ died on the cross that the prophets spoke about this, not because they spoke about it that he then died, and, in fact, when they spoke about it, they did so, as we noted earlier, as a past event, and, given that its happening is the 'cause' of the prophecy, Christ himself speaks of it as an eternal 'necessity' (cf. Luke 24:26). How is this possible? Tzamalikos answers:

> The answer to this question is that this causality, although manifest in history, is in fact a causality between time and timelessness. Prophecy is uttered by a prophet, who 'looks to the future' [*Comm. Rom.* 7.19.2], yet it is God who speaks *through* the prophet. What is uttered originates in God's own foreknowledge. Prophecy as a *result*, although manifested in time, actually springs from timelessness.[156]

---

[152] P. Tzamalikos, *Origen: Philosophy of History and Eschatology*, Supplements to *VC*, 85 (Leiden: Brill, 2007). It should be noted that Tzamalikos deliberately does not work from *On First Principles*, except as a last resort, for he regards Rufinus' translation as a 'chimerical version' (*Origen*, 9).

[153] Ibid. 52.   [154] Ibid. 53.   [155] Ibid. 119.   [156] Ibid. 121.

Tzamalikos' analysis of the function of foreknowledge and prophecy, within the framework of a definite time-frame, with a beginning and end, is readily applicable to the 'antecedent causes' spoken about by Origen: their anteriority is not simply chronological, but always related to the timelessness of God's foreknowledge. Rather than imagining a host of eternally existing intellects who through some pre-cosmic fall descend into bodies, it seems more probable that the 'antecedent causes' invoked by Origen to reconcile the inequality of human fate with an affirmation of the justice of God refers to the anteriority of the foreknowledge of God, who knows all things for each from their womb.[157] Or as Origen puts it, when discussing Paul's description of his own 'election' before his birth (Rom. 1:1 and Gal. 1:15), 'any one who is predestined through the foreknowledge of God is the cause of the events known', rather than being 'saved by nature' as he charges his opponents with teaching (*Philoc.* 25).

However, as Paul speaks about being 'called' from before his birth, we should perhaps revisit the sophisticated understanding, and vocabulary, that Origen has for describing the different aspects of God's creation. To summarize (and extrapolate) what we saw earlier: God has called or elected all to existence in the heavenly court from before the foundation of the world. Seeing to what they are called is a cause for scandal and falling away, with the result that we come to be in temporal existence: the world itself is 'thrown down', and we come into existence in time, fashioned or moulded from the dust of the earth. As this happens, the lamb is also 'slain from the foundation of the world'.[158]

---

[157] As argued by Harl, 'Préexistence des âmes'.

[158] The historical and trans-historical, or eternal, significance of the single event of the crucifixion should be underscored. Origen did not teach that there was a crucifixion in the heavens before that on earth, as Jerome alleges (*Ruf.* 1.20): 'Your Origen allows himself to treat of *metempsychosis,* to introduce an innumerable number of worlds, to clothe rational creatures in one body after another, and to say that Christ has often suffered, and will suffer again, it being always profitable to undertake what has once been profitable.' See also the texts cited in the Appendix, item no. 23. Origen does indeed speak of the sacrifice of Christ being offered for the salvation of those on earth and those in heaven, and of the crucifixion being both invisible and visible, but it is always the single sacrifice of the cross. Cf. Origen, *Princ.* 2.3.5; *Or.* 27.15; *Comm. Jo.* 1.255; *Hom. Lev.* 1.3–4; *Hom. Jes. Nav.* 8.3; *Hom. Luc.* 10.3. It is only 'from' the foundation of the world, not 'before', that the Lamb is slain (Heb. 13:8); yet, I would suggest, it is the same reality, constituting divine life, but seen from a different perspective. Seeing what divine life looks like— voluntary self-sacrificial love—those called to enter into this react in various ways, falling away or taking it upon themselves to serve those who fall away, and, in this way, the voluntary self-sacrificial love takes on the character of the Passion. These two perspectives are there in Peter's speech (Acts 2:23): 'this Jesus, delivered up according to the definite plan and foreknowledge of God, you crucified and killed by the hands of lawless men'. It happens, bloodily, at our hands, but is nevertheless the eternal economy of God. The same double-perspective is seen right through the Scriptures, most clearly with Joseph, who was sold into slavery, but yet was sent into Egypt by God 'to preserve life' (Gen. 45:5); and again in liturgy, where we celebrate the one 'who was given up, no, rather, gave himself up for the life of the world' (John Chrysostom, Preface to the Anaphora). We, in time, begin with the 'given up', but learn to think theologically in terms of 'gave himself up'. The 'giving himself up', on the other hand, is primary in God, but takes on the

Yet, at the same time, through the slaying of the Lamb within time at the Passion, at which all fall away (with the notable exception of the beloved disciple in the Gospel of John the Theologian), we are, in fact, brought to participate in the heavenly liturgy through, and requiring, our own taking up the cross. Thus the cause both for diversification as well as unification, in a movement that gives flesh to the heavenly reality (and transforms that flesh into an eternal state) is the self-sacrificial love that is divine life, celebrated eternally in the heavens, but taking on the character of the slaying of the Lamb as those called to the feast fall away, both eternally in the heavens and in time on earth. Yet at the same time this sacrifice is also the means by which the final unity of God's creation is achieved, when God is indeed 'all in all', enfleshed, and the marriage of the Lamb is consummated. In all of this, one must bear in mind, however, that Origen is differentiating between different aspects (as with the different titles of God and Christ, and the different words for creation) of one and the same eternal reality, not narrating a mythology.

Origen's predecessor in Alexandria, Clement, had already appealed to the paradoxical intersection between time and eternity to explain what happens sacramentally in the life and being of the newly baptized and those who have grown to become mature in their faith.[159] 'Being baptized, we are illumined; illumined we become sons; being made sons, we are perfected; being perfected we are made immortal. "I have said", he says, "that you are gods, sons of the Most High"' (*Paed.* 1.6.26.1; Ps. 81:6). Christians are, he says, already, here and now (ἐνθένδε ἤδη), practising the heavenly life by which they are deified (*Paed.* 1.12.98.3). Answering those who do not understand how one can speak of a neophyte as already perfect, Clement explains:

> There is nothing intermediate between light and darkness. But the end is reserved till the resurrection of those who believe, and it is not the reception of some other thing, but the obtaining of the promise previously made. For we do not say that both take place at the same time—both the arrival at the end and the anticipation of that arrival. For eternity and time are not the same, neither is the attempt and the final result; but both have reference to the same thing, and one and the same person is concerned in both. Faith, so to speak, is the attempt generated in time; the final result is the attainment of the promise secured for eternity.... having in anticipation grasped by faith that which is future, after the resurrection we receive it as present.[160]

character of 'was given up' because of our reaction, so that the lamb is indeed 'slain from the foundation of the world'.

---

[159] Cf. John Behr, *Asceticism and Anthropology in Irenaeus and Clement*, OECS (Oxford: Oxford University Press, 2000), 152–9, for the newly baptized, and 185–207, though I would now soften my criticism of Clement.

[160] *Paed.* 1.6.28.3–29.3: Μὴ γὰρ κατὰ τὸν αὐτὸν χρόνον ἅμα ἄμφω συνίστασθαί φαμεν, τήν τε πρὸς τὸ πέρας ἄφιξιν καὶ τῆς ἀφίξεως τὴν πρόληψιν· οὐ γάρ ἐστι ταὐτὸν αἰὼν καὶ χρόνος οὐδὲ μὴν

The word for this 'anticipation' of our eschatological reality, already real in faith, is the same term, προλήψις, that, as we saw earlier when considering Aristotelian and Hellenistic epistemology, was used, as it is by Clement himself (especially in *Strom.* 2), to refer to the generic notions, 'presuppositions', synthesized out of repeated sense-perceptions, which alone make knowledge possible. Its use here, in a sacramental context, gives further substance to what that might be for the baptized: 'faith is the substance of things hoped for, the conviction of things not seen' (Heb. 11:1). Without undermining this perfection of the newly baptized, Clement insists that it must still be worked upon, to make this perfection actual already now. 'As gnosis is not born with human beings, but is acquired, and the learning of its elements demands application, training and growth; and then from incessant practice it passes into a habit; so, when perfected in the mystic habit, it abides, being made infallible through love' (*Strom.* 6.9.78.4). Indeed for such a one, Clement says, habit 'becomes nature'.[161] The mature, perfected Christian, the 'Gnostic', 'is already in the midst of that which will be, anticipating hope by gnosis', for 'through love the future is already present for him'.[162] For such Gnostics, their whole life is one unceasing festival: 'Holding festival, then, in our whole life, persuaded that God is altogether on every side present, we cultivate our fields praising; we sail the sea, hymning; in all the rest of our conversation we conduct ourselves according to the rule' (*Strom.* 7.7.35.6). Finally, in the most striking terms:

> This is the activity of the perfected Gnostic, to have converse with God through the great High Priest, being made like the Lord, as far as may be, by means of the whole service [θεραπεία] towards God, [a service] which tends to the salvation of human beings, through care of the goodness towards us, and on the other side, through liturgy, through teaching and through beneficence in deeds. Being assimilated to God, the Gnostic even creates and fashions himself [ἑαυτὸν κτίζει καὶ δημιουργεῖ], and adorns those who hear him; assimilating, as far as possible, by an ascesis that tends to apatheia, to him who is by nature impassible; and this is uninterrupted converse and communion with the Lord.   (*Strom.* 7.2.13.2–3)

With the future already present for him, when he will be deified (or rather already is, though it is always difficult to know to what extent Clement is describing an idealized portrait), the mature, perfected Christian shares in the

---

ὁρμὴ καὶ τέλος, οὐκ ἔστιν· περὶ ἓν δὲ ἄμφω καὶ περὶ ἄμφω ὁ εἷς καταγίνεται. Ἔστι γοῦν, ὡς εἰπεῖν, ὁρμὴ μὲν ἡ πίστις ἐν χρόνῳ γεννωμένη, τέλος δὲ τὸ τυχεῖν τῆς ἐπαγγελίας εἰς αἰῶνας βεβαιούμενον....ἐκεῖνο δὲ τῷ πιστεῦσᾳ ἤδη προειληφότες ἐσόμενον, μετὰ τὴν ἀνάστασιν ἀπολαμβάνομεν γενόμενον

[161]   *Strom.* 7.7.46.9; see also 4.22.138.3.
[162]   *Strom.* 6.9.73.4: ὃ δ'ἐν οἷς ἔσται, δι᾽ ἀγάπης ἤδη γενόμενος, τὴν ἐλπίδα προειληφὼς διὰ τῆς γνώσεως and 6.9.77.1: κἄστιν αὐτῷ δι᾽ ἀγάπην ἐνεστὸς ἤδη τὸ μέλλον.

activity of God, even to the point of 'creating himself'. The whole life of such a perfected human being is one of festival and thanksgiving.

It is, then, in the earthly liturgy that we most closely approximate, are 'images' or 'icons' of our eternal reality, 'mystically imaging [μυστικῶς εἰκονίζοντες] the Cherubim' as the 'Cherubic hymn' in the Liturgies of John Chrysostom and Basil (referred to earlier) puts it. Speaking of Christians in worship as 'icons' of the cherubim is not meant to imply that our end is to become angels (it is rather to become created human beings), but just as when iron and bronze, to extend Origen's analogy, are placed in a fire, they become indistinguishable from the fire and from each other, so too there are no distinctions in Christ: we remain male and female (and do not become angels), but indistinguishably human in Christ, in whom 'there is neither male nor female' (Gal. 3:28). Instead, what we have is, as in the preface to Basil's anaphora (and Origen's preferred way of speaking), the whole assembly of rational beings, where 'rational' is defined by relation to the Word of God,[163] praising God together eternally in the heavenly court. We do not have many details about what liturgy was like in the time of Origen, but it does seem to be the case that the introduction of the Sanctus in the liturgy goes back to the period just after Origen, while the idea of participation in the heavenly liturgy is intimated by various writers before him, picking up on apocalyptic themes from Second Temple Judaism.[164] As Bryan Spinks says of this dimension of Christian worship:

> In Christ the space of heaven and the region of earth are united. In the eucharist the worshipper enters heaven through Christ, and is represented by the High Priest. Here time and eternity intersect and become one, and this world and the world to come elide.[165]

I have intimated, sometimes overtly, throughout this Introduction, that there are apocalyptic dimensions to Origen's theology and his *On First Principles*. Now that we have come to the end of the Introduction, it might be helpful to lay out more fully these apocalyptic dimensions. The best context for understanding the apocalyptic framework is the 'correspondence' and 'two-level drama' that John Ashton, in his work on the Gospel of John, describes as being one of the four key elements of apocalyptic: two of which are temporal, two

---

[163] Cf. Origen, *Comm. Jo.* 2.114: 'we could also say that the saint alone is rational'.

[164] Robert Taft, 'The Interpolation of the Sanctus into the Anaphora: When and Where? A review of the Dossier', *OCP* 57 (1991), 281–308; 58 (1992), 83–121. For apocalyptic themes in the approach to the liturgy by earlier writers, see now Sverre Elgvin Lied, 'Participation in Heavenly Worship: The Pre-Nicene Growth of a Concept' (PhD thesis, VID Specialized University, Stavanger, 2016).

[165] Bryan D. Spinks, *The Sanctus in the Eucharistic Prayer* (Cambridge: Cambridge University Press, 1991), 206.

ages (mystery) and two stages (dream or vision), and two are spatial, insiders/ outsiders (riddle) and above/below (correspondence).

According to Ashton, the effect of Christ's riddling discourse and the Messianic Secret, whereby the readers of the Gospel know, and therefore see, more than the disciples within the narrative, is to set up a two-level drama in a framework of correspondence. This element of correspondence is found in most apocalyptic literature, especially clearly in the 'Similitudes' of the Enochic material. Although there is some debate about how to translate the Hebrew, Aramaic, and Ethiopic terms, Ashton is probably right to suggest that 'correspondence' is the best rendering, not least because it brings out a further element of the riddling discourse of Christ: παραβολή literally means a 'juxtaposition', with a consequent 'comparison' or 'analogy', so entailing a 'correspondence'.[166] In the Enochic material, the term 'correspondence' is used to compare and liken things on earth and things in heaven, establishing connections between the realm above and the realm below (cf. esp. 1 Enoch 43:4). Or, as it is put in the *Ascension of Isaiah*: 'as it is on high, so also is it on earth; what happens in the vault of heaven happens similarly here on earth.'[167] It is important to note, as Ashton points out, that:

> For Enoch, and for apocalyptic writers generally, there are not two worlds but one: or rather the whole of reality is split into matching pairs (rather like the biological theory of DNA) in which one half, the lower, is the mirror-image (albeit in this case a distorting mirror) of the higher. That is why a revelation of what is above is not just relevant or related to what happens or is about to happen on earth: rather what happens on earth is a re-enactment in earthly terms of what has happened in heaven: a correspondence![168]

There is one reality, as we emphasized when looking at different verbs Origen used for 'creation', which are but aspects of the singular work of God.

In his investigation of the context of the relationship between the community around John and others, both the Jewish community and other Christian communities, J. Louis Martyn came to a very similar insight into the dynamics of what he calls the 'stereoptic vision' of John:

> John did not create the literary form of the two-level drama. It was at home in the thought-world of Jewish apocalypticism: the dicta most basic to the apocalyptic thinker are these: God created both heaven and earth. There are dramas taking place both on the heavenly stage and on the earthly stage. Yet these dramas are not really two, but rather one drama.... One might say that events on the

---

[166] John Ashton, *Understanding the Fourth Gospel*, New Edition (Oxford: Oxford University Press, 2007), 325.

[167] *Ascension of Isaiah* 7:10, trans. R. H. Charles, revised by J. M. T. Barton in H. F. D. Sparks, *Apocryphal Old Testament* (Oxford: Clarendon Press, 1984), 797.

[168] Ashton, *Fourth Gospel*, 327.

heavenly stage not only correspond to events on the earthly stage, but also slightly precede them in time, leading them into existence, so to speak. What transpires on the heavenly stage is often called 'things to come'. For that reason events seen on the earthly stage are entirely enigmatic to the man who sees only the earthly stage. Stereoptic vision is necessary, and it is precisely stereoptic vision which causes a man to write an apocalypse: 'After this I looked, and lo, in heaven an *open door!* And the first voice, which I had heard...said, 'Come up hither and I will show you what must take place after this'.[169]

In his analysis of how this stereoptic vision is enacted in the Gospel of John, Martyn points to three modifications from the correspondence found in apocalyptic literature. First, both levels of the drama are enacted on earth, between the life of Christ and the life of the Johannine community. Second, the temporal extension does not parallel the heavenly with the earthly, but, again, the two stages or times of Christ's own life and that of his body, the community. And third, 'John does not in any overt way indicate to his reader a distinction between the two stages'.[170] Moreover, Martyn points out that although John obviously does not write an apocalypse but a Gospel, yet 'the relation of his Gospel to the Apocalypse should probably be reexamined in the light of the way in which he presents his two levels'.[171]

Martyn and Ashton are concerned with the narrativity of the Gospel of John: how a drama is unfolded over time and the correlation of the two stages of understanding with the history of the community in which the Gospel was written. However, as we attempt to understand Origen, what is important is the idea of correspondence, for Origen, between the end and the beginning, the above and the below, heaven and earth, that which is unseen and that which is seen (the fundamental distinction, according to Gregory of Nyssa, prior even to the difference between created and uncreated)—two realms which, as different as they are in our present experience, are ultimately, eschatologically, one and the same, for 'God will be all in all'. To see this, we need 'stereoptic vision', or 'a divine sense', in the words of Solomon used by Origen. We are participants in both simultaneously, through the paradoxical intersection of (non-temporal) eternity and time. This is not, Origen insists, a realm of Platonic 'forms', nor a bodiless world that only exists in our imagination; and neither is it a Platonic 'myth of transmigration, in which the soul falls from the vaults of heaven', but 'a different and more sublime view'.[172] It is, I would suggest, an apocalyptic vision created by the intersection of eternity and time, with the former opened up to us in and through the Passion of Christ, while we yet remain in the latter. We are, simultaneously, in both; and

---

[169] J. Louis Martyn, *History and Theology in the Fourth Gospel*, 3rd edn (Louisville: Westminster John Knox Press, 2003 [1968]), 130, quoting Rev. 4:1, emphasis Martyn's.
[170] Martyn, *History and Theology*, 130–1.   [171] Ibid. 130, fn. 198.
[172] Origen, *Princ.* 2.3.6; *Cels.* 1.20; 4.17.

we are brought into close approximation with our true being, now 'hidden with Christ in God', in the earthly liturgy, which is an image of the heavenly liturgy. Our end, in Christ, is to be a participant in the heavenly court, celebrating the heavenly liturgy in the eternity of God; and although this will only be a 'present reality', as it were, for us after our sojourn (and being fashioned) upon earth, yet as an eternal reality, we are always already there, and have always been so. For our election or calling by God precedes our formation and our eventual creation. Moreover, our 'place' in the heavenly court is determined by our choices in this life. Yet that is a reality that nevertheless 'precedes' our place in this life in this world, and so, in Origen's terms, it determines our place in this life as an 'antecedent cause', enabling us, through this life governed by the economy of God, to be perfected in the end in him.

Origen: *On First Principles*

Rufinus' Preface

1. I know that very many of the brethren, driven by a desire for knowledge of the Scriptures, have requested of some scholars, experts in Greek letters, that they should make a Roman of Origen and present him to Latin ears.[1] To this end also, when our brother and colleague, at the entreaty of Bishop Damasus, had translated two of the *Homilies on the Song of Songs* from Greek into Latin, he composed so elegant and splendid a preface to that work as to inspire a desire in everyone to read and avidly study Origen, saying that one could apply to his soul the saying, *The King has brought me into his chamber*,[2] asserting that while he 'in other works surpassed all other writers, in the Song of Songs he had surpassed even himself'.[3] He promises, indeed, in that same preface, that he himself will present the books on the Song of Songs and numerous others of Origen to Roman ears. But he, I see, finding greater pleasure in his own pen, pursues an end with greater glory, that he may be a 'father of the word'[4] rather than a translator. Accordingly we take up the work that was begun and approved of by him, although we are not able to provide such eloquent words as that great man. Therefore I am afraid lest, through my fault, that man, whom he has deservedly acknowledged as the other teacher of knowledge and wisdom in the Church after the apostles, should, through our own poverty of language, appear far inferior to what he is.

2. Continually thinking of this, I kept silent and did not yield to the brethren frequently entreating me to undertake this work. But your influence, most faithful brother Macarius, is so persuasive that not even lack of skill is able to withstand it. Because of this, that I might not find you too severe in your demands, I gave way, even against my resolution, yet on the agreement and arrangement, however, that in translating I would follow as far as possible the rule observed by my predecessors, and especially by that distinguished man whom I mentioned above. He, when translating into Latin more than seventy treatises, called *Homilies*, of Origen, and also a number of tomes on the writings of the Apostle, in which are found in the Greek a good many stumbling-blocks, so smoothed over and purified them all in his translation that a Latin reader would find in them nothing that differs from our faith. His example, then, we follow to the best of our ability, if not with the same power of eloquence yet at least with the same rules of method, taking care not to reproduce

---

[1] Rufinus here, and at the end of the paragraph, is alluding to the opening sentence of Jerome's preface to his translation (undertaken ca. 379–81) of Origen's *Hom. Ezech.*: 'It is indeed a great thing that you are asking, my friend, that I make Origen a Latin and give to Roman ears the man who in the opinion of Didymus the Seer was the second teacher of the churches after the Apostle.'

[2] Song 1:4.   [3] Jerome, Preface to Origen, *Hom. Cant.*   [4] Cf. Plato, *Symp.* 177d.

those passages in the books of Origen which are found to be inconsistent or contrary to himself.

3. The cause of these variations we have explained more fully in the *Apology,* which Pamphilus wrote in defence of the works of the same Origen, to which I added a brief tract, in which we showed, I think, by clear proofs that his books have been corrupted in many places by heretics and malevolent persons, and especially those which you now request me to translate, that is *Peri Archon,* which may be rendered either *On First Principles* or *On Principalities,* and which are indeed for other reasons most obscure and very difficult. For here he discusses subjects concerning which philosophers, after spending their whole lives upon them, have been able to discover nothing. But our author strives, as far as he possibly can, to turn to piety the faith in a Creator and the knowledge of creatures, which they had dragged down to impiety. Wherever, therefore, we found in his writings anything contrary to that which he had himself elsewhere piously laid down regarding the Trinity, we have either omitted it, as being corrupt and interpolated, or we have rendered it according to that rule which we frequently find affirmed by him. If, however, as speaking now to persons of skill and knowledge, he has expressed himself obscurely while wanting to proceed quickly, we have, to make the passage clearer, added what we have read more fully on the same subject in his other works, seeking [to provide] explanation.[5] We have said nothing of our own, however, but simply returned to him his own statements, though said in other places.[6]

4. I have made these remarks in the preface, therefore, by way of precaution, lest slanderers should perhaps think that they have again discovered a pretext for accusation. For you have seen what perverse and contentious men will do. In the meantime, however, we have undertaken this heavy labour, with the aid of God by your prayers, not to shut the mouths of slanderers (for this is not possible, unless perhaps God should do it), but to provide material to those who desire to advance in the knowledge of realities. I adjure and request everyone who copies or reads these books, in the presence of God the Father and of the Son and of the Holy Spirit, and by his belief in the kingdom to come, the mystery of the resurrection from the dead, and by that *everlasting fire which is prepared for the devil and his angels,*[7] that, if he would not have for an eternal inheritance that place where there is *weeping and gnashing of teeth,*[8] and where *their fire is not quenched and their worm does not die,*[9] he neither add anything to this writing, nor take anything from it,[10] nor insert anything, nor alter

---

[5] It is difficult to identify these passages. Jerome (*Ruf.* 2.11) claims that Rufinus inserted a passage of scholia composed by Didymus into *Princ.* 1.1.8.

[6] Cf. Jerome, *Ruf.* 3 (= *Ep. adv. Ruf.*) 39.   [7] Matt. 25:41.

[8] Matt. 8:12; Luke 13:28.   [9] Isa. 66:24; Mark 9:48.

[10] Cf. Deut. 4:2; Rev. 22:18–19.

anything, but that he shall compare his copy with the exemplar from which he transcribed it and shall correct it to the letter and punctuate it, and not have an incorrect or unpunctuated manuscript, lest the difficulty of ascertaining the sense, if the manuscript is not punctuated, should cause greater difficulties to the readers.

Origen's Preface

Pr.1. All[1] who believe and are assured that *grace and truth came through Jesus Christ,*[2] and who know Christ to be the truth, according to his saying, *I am the truth,*[3] derive the knowledge which leads human beings to live a good and blessed life from no other source than from the very words and teaching of Christ. And by the words of Christ we mean not only those which he spoke when he became human and dwelt in the flesh; for even before this, Christ, the Word of God, was in Moses and the prophets.[4] For without the Word of God how could they have been able to prophesy of Christ? In proof of this, it would not be difficult to show from the divine Scriptures how Moses or the prophets were filled with the Spirit of Christ in what they said and all that they did, were it not our purpose to confine the present work within the briefest possible limits. And therefore I think it sufficient to quote this one testimony of Paul from the epistle which he writes to the Hebrews, in which he says as follows, *By faith Moses, when grown up, refused to be called the son of Pharaoh's daughter, choosing rather to be afflicted with the people of God, than to enjoy the pleasures of sin for a season, considering abuse suffered for Christ greater riches than the treasures of the Egyptians.*[5] And that he also spoke, after his ascension into heaven, in his apostles, is shown by Paul in this way, *Or do you seek a proof of Christ who speaks in me?*[6]

Pr.2. Since, however, many of those who profess to believe in Christ differ not only in small and trivial matters, but even on great and important matters— such as concerning God or the Lord Jesus Christ or the Holy Spirit, and not only regarding these but also regarding matters concerning created beings, that is, the dominions and the holy powers—because of this it seems necessary first of all to lay down a definite line and clear rule regarding each one of these

---

[1] These opening lines have been preserved in Greek by Eusebius of Caesarea, *C. Marc.* 1.4.26, numbered by Koetschau as Fragment 1. Marcellus points to Plato, *Gorgias* 454e, for a parallel to the opening words.

[2] John 1:17.   [3] John 14:6.

[4] Cf. Origen, *Comm. ser. Matt.* 28; *Hom. Isa.* 1.5; *Hom. Lev.* 1.1; *Hom. Jer.* 9.1; *Cels.* 6.5, 21.

[5] Heb. 11:24.   [6] 2 Cor. 13:3.

matters, and then thereafter to investigate other matters.[7] For just as, although many Greeks and barbarians promise the truth, we gave up seeking it from all who claimed it for false opinions after we had come to believe that Christ was the Son of God and were persuaded that we must learn it from him, so also, although there are many who think that they know what are the teachings of Christ, and not a few of them think differently from those before them, one must guard the ecclesiastical preaching, handed down from the apostles through the order of succession and remaining in the churches to the present: that alone is to be believed to be the truth which differs in no way from the ecclesiastical and apostolic tradition.[8]

Pr.3. Now it ought to be known that the holy apostles, in preaching the faith of Christ, delivered with utmost clarity to all believers, even to those who seemed somewhat dull in the investigation of divine knowledge, certain points that they believed to be necessary, leaving, however, the grounds of their statements to be inquired into by those who should merit the excellent gifts of the Spirit and especially by those who should receive from the Holy Spirit himself the grace of language, wisdom, and knowledge;[9] while on other points they stated that things were so, keeping silence about how or whence they are, certainly so that the more diligent of their successors, being lovers of wisdom, those, I mean, who should prepare themselves to be worthy and capable of receiving wisdom, might have an exercise on which they might display the fruit of their ability.

Pr.4. The particular points, which are clearly handed down by the preaching of the apostles are as follows:[10] First, that 'there is one God, who created and arranged all things', and who, when nothing existed, made all things;[11] he is God from the first creation and foundation of the world, the God of all the just, of Adam, Abel, Seth, Enosh, Enoch, Noah, Sem, Abraham, Isaac, Jacob, the twelve patriarchs, Moses, and the prophets; and that this God in the last days,[12] as he had announced beforehand by his prophets, sent our Lord Jesus Christ to

---

[7] On the 'rule' (κανών), see Gal. 6:16; Irenaeus, *Haer.* 1.9.4–10.1; Tertullian, *Praescr.* 13–14; Clement of Alexandria, *Strom.* 6.15.125.3; 7.15–17; Origen, *Princ.* 1.7.1; 4.2.2; 4.3.14; *Comm. Jo.* 13.98.

[8] Cf. Origen, *Comm. ser. Matt.* 46. On 'tradition' more generally, see Irenaeus, *Haer.* 3.2–3; Tertullian, *Praescr.* 21–37; Clement, *Strom.* 7.16–17.

[9] Cf. 1 Cor. 12:7–8.

[10] For other lists of the articles of belief, see Origen, *Comm. ser. Matt.* 33; *Comm. Jo.* 32.187–93; *Fr. Tit.* (PG 14, 1303).

[11] Hermas, *Mand.* 1.1, cited also in Origen, *Princ.* 1.3.3; *Comm. Jo.* 32.187; cf. *Comm. Jo.* 1.103.

[12] Cf. Heb. 1:1.

call first Israel to himself and second the Gentiles,[13] after the unfaithfulness of the people of Israel. This just and good God, the Father of our Lord Jesus Christ,[14] himself gave the law and the prophets and the Gospels, who is also the God of the apostles and of the Old and New Testaments.

Then, again, that Jesus Christ himself, who came, was born of the Father before all creatures.[15] After ministering to the Father in the foundation of all things, for *by him were all things made*,[16] in the last times, emptying himself, he became human and was incarnate;[17] being God, when made human he remained what he was, God. He assumed a body like to our own, differing in this respect only, that it was born of a virgin and of the Holy Spirit.[18] And that this Jesus Christ was born and did suffer in truth, and not in appearance,[19] and truly died our common death,[20] and did truly rise from the dead, and after the resurrection, having sojourned a while with his disciples, was taken up.

Then, again, they handed down that the Holy Spirit is associated in honour and dignity with the Father and the Son. But in this case it is not yet clearly discerned whether he is born or not-born,[21] or whether he is to be considered as himself Son of God or not: but these are points which are yet to be inquired into, to the best of our ability, from holy Scripture, and investigated with the requisite wisdom.[22] That this Holy Spirit inspired each one of the saints, both the prophets and the apostles, and that there was not one Spirit in those of old but another in those who were inspired at the coming of Christ, is indeed most clearly taught throughout the churches.

Pr.5. After these points, also, that the soul, having its own substance and life, after it departs from this world shall, according to its merits, either obtain an

---

[13] Cf. Matt. 15:24; 28:19. [14] Cf. Rom. 15:26 etc.

[15] Cf. Jerome, *Ep.* 124.2.1 (ed. Hilberg 3, 97.9), who claims that, at the beginning of the first book, Origen asserts: 'Christ, the Son of God, was not begotten but made' (*Christum, filium dei, non natum esse, sed factum*). Origen almost certainly wrote γενητός (from γίγνομαι, 'to come into being' or 'to happen') rather than γεννητός (from γεννάω, 'to be born'), two words which could be used equivalently in certain circumstances but which did not become firmly distinguished until the controversies of the fourth century. In a passage preserved by Justinian (see the Appendix, item no. 5), Origen is reported to have said that everything apart from the God and Father of all is γενητός. However Origen also states emphatically that Christ is 'eternally begotten': cf. esp. *Hom. Jer.* 9.4; *Princ.* 1.2.2. See also the comments in the Introduction, sections 3 and 5, regarding Origen's understanding of 'creation'.

[16] John 1:3. [17] Cf. Heb. 1:2; Phil. 2:7; John 1:14.

[18] Cf. Origen, *Comm. Jo.* 32.191; *Hom. Luc.* 17.4; *Cels.* 1.66, 69; 2.23, 31.

[19] Cf. Origen, *Fr. Jo.* 53 (GCS 4, pp. 526–7); *Cels.* 2.16.

[20] Cf. Origen, *Dial.* 25–7; *Mart.* 39.

[21] Cf. Jerome, *Ep.* 124.2.3 (ed. Hilberg 3, 97.24–98.1): 'And while he declares that he does not know whether the Holy Spirit is created or uncreated [*utrum factus sit an infactus*], he has later on given his own opinion that except God the Father alone there is nothing uncreated [*infactum*]', referring to *Princ.* 1.2.6. See comments above in n.15.

[22] Cf. Origen, *Comm. Jo.* 2.75–6.

inheritance of eternal life and blessedness, if its actions shall have excelled, or be delivered up to eternal fire and torments, if the sin of its wicked deeds shall so direct it:[23] and also, that there is to be a time of resurrection of the dead, when this body, which now *is sown in corruption, shall rise in incorruptibility,* and what *is sown in dishonour, will rise in glory.*[24]

This also is defined in the ecclesiastical preaching, that every rational soul possesses free will and volition;[25] that it is in conflict against the devil and his angels, and opposing powers, because they strive to burden it with sins;[26] but if we live rightly and carefully, we should endeavour to shake off such a burden. From which it follows, also, that we understand ourselves not to be subject to necessity, so as to be altogether compelled, even against our will, to do either good or evil.[27] For if we possess free will, some powers perhaps may be able to urge us to sin, and others to help us to salvation;[28] we are not, however, compelled by necessity to act either rightly or wrongly, as those think who say that the course and movement of the stars are the cause of human actions, not only of those which take place outside the realm of free will, but also of those which are placed within our own power.

But with respect to the soul, whether it is derived from the seed being transferred, so that the principle or substance of it may be held to be in the seminal particles of the body itself, or whether it has any other beginning, and this beginning itself, whether it is begotten or not begotten, or whether it is imparted to the body from without or not, is not explained with sufficient clarity in the preaching.[29]

Pr.6. Regarding the devil and his angels and the opposing powers, the ecclesiastical preaching has taught that they indeed exist, but what they are, or how they exist, it has not explained sufficiently clearly. This opinion, however, is held by most, that this devil was an angel, but having become an apostate he persuaded as many angels as possible to fall away with himself, and even until now these are called his angels.[30]

Pr.7. This also is part of the ecclesiastical preaching, that this world was made and began at a certain time and, because it is corruptible, will be dissolved.[31] But what existed before this world, or what will exist after it, has not yet become

---

[23] Cf. Origen, *Cels.* 3.31; 8.48, 52.   [24] 1 Cor. 15:42–3.

[25] Cf. Origen, *Cels.* 3.69; 4.83; *Fr. Tit.* (PG 14, 1305a).

[26] Cf. Origen, *Comm. Jo.* 20.378.

[27] Cf. Origen, *Hom. Jer.* 20.2; *Comm. Jo.* 32.189; *Fr. Jo.* 53 (GCS 4, pp. 526–7).

[28] Cf. Origen, *Or.* 27.12.

[29] Cf. Origen, *Princ.* 3.4.2; *Comm. Jo.* 2.182; *Comm. Cant.* 2; *Cels.* 3.80; 4.30; *Fr. Tit.* (PG 14, 1306b).

[30] Cf. Irenaeus, *Dem.* 16; Athenagoras, *Leg.* 24; Origen, *Princ.* 1.5.4–5; *Cels.* 6.44–5.

[31] Cf. Origen, *Cels.* 1.37; 4.9, 21; *Comm. Jo.* 1.178.

known openly to many, for no clear statement on this is set forth in the ecclesiastical preaching.

Pr.8. Then, finally, that the Scriptures were written by the Spirit of God, and that they have not only the meaning which is obvious, but also another which escapes the notice of most. For the things that are described [therein] are the forms of certain mysteries and images of divine things. There is one mind throughout the entire church about this, that *the* whole *law is* indeed *spiritual*,[32] yet that which the law conveys is not known by all but only by those on whom the grace of the Holy Spirit is bestowed in the word of wisdom and knowledge.

The term ἀσώματος (that is, 'bodiless'[33]) is unused and unknown not only in many other writings, but also in our own Scriptures. If anyone should quote it to us out of that pamphlet called *The Teaching of Peter*, where the Saviour is seen to say to his disciples, 'I am not a bodiless daemon,'[34] he must be answered, in the first place, that this work is not itself included among the ecclesiastical books, and it can be shown that it is not a writing of Peter nor of anyone else who was inspired by the Spirit of God. But even if the point were conceded, the sense of the word ἀσώματος there does not indicate the same as that intended by Greek and pagan authors, when philosophers discuss bodiless nature. For in that pamphlet, he used the words 'bodiless daemon' to indicate that the form or outline of the daemonical body, whatever it is, is not like this dense and visible body of ours; rather what he said must be understood according to the intention of the author of the pamphlet, that is, that he did not have such a body as the daemons have (which is naturally fine and thin like air, and because of this is considered or called 'bodiless' by many[35]), but that he had a solid and palpable body. Now, according to human custom, everything that is not such is called bodiless by the simple or uneducated, just as one says that the air we breathe is bodiless, because it is not a body that can be grasped and held or resist pressure.

Pr.9. We shall inquire, however, whether the actual thing which Greek philosophers call ἀσώματος (that is, 'bodiless') is found in the holy Scriptures

---

[32] Rom. 7:14.

[33] These explanatory words come of course from Rufinus.

[34] Perhaps *The Preaching of Peter*. The same quotation is given by Ignatius of Antioch (*Smyrn.* 3.2), without mentioning its source. Eusebius (*Hist. eccl.* 3.36.11) repeats these words from Ignatius, as does Jerome (*Vir. Ill.* 16), who elsewhere (*Comm. Isa.* 18.1) describes them as coming from the Gospel of the Hebrews. The closest canonical parallel would be Luke 24:39.

[35] Cf. Tertullian, *Apol.* 22.5. In *Comm. Matt.* 17.30, Origen says that our present 'lowly body' (Phil. 3:21) will, in the resurrection, be transformed into one like those of the angels, 'ethereal and brilliant light' (αἰθέρια καὶ αὐγοειδὲς φῶς). See also *Princ.* 3.6.4–6 on the character of the 'spiritual body' mentioned by Paul. On the other hand, Origen is emphatic that only the Trinity is bodiless: *Princ.* 1.6.4; 2.2.2; 4.3.15.

under another name. For it is also to be investigated how God himself is to be understood, whether as bodily and formed according to some shape,[36] or of a different nature than bodies, a point which is not clearly indicated in our preaching. The same is also to be investigated even regarding Christ and the Holy Spirit, and indeed it is to be investigated no less of every soul and every rational nature.

Pr.10. This[37] is also in the ecclesiastical preaching, that there are certain angels of God and good powers, who minister to him in accomplishing the salvation of human beings; but when these were created, or of what kind of being, or how they exist, is not explained with sufficient clarity. Regarding the sun, moon, and stars, whether they are animated beings or inanimate is not clearly handed down.[38]

Everyone, therefore, who desires to construct a certain structure and body of all these things, in accordance with reason, must make use of elements and foundations of this sort, according to the precept which says, *Enlighten yourselves with the light of knowledge,*[39] that by clear and cogent arguments the truth about each particular point may be discovered, and he may form, as we have said, one body, by means of illustrations and assertions, either those which he came upon in the holy Scriptures or those which he discovered followed from investigation and right reason.

---

[36] Cf. Origen, *Cels.* 6.64; 7.27, 38, 66; 8.49; *Sel. Gen.* 1:26 (PG 12, 93).
[37] The first sentence is preserved in Greek by Antipater of Bostra as reported in John of Damascus, Sacra Parallela (PG 96, 501c); it is numbered by Koetschau as Fragment 3.
[38] Cf. Plato, *Tim.* 38e; Origen, *Princ.* 1.7; *Cels* 5.10–11; *Hom. Jer.* 10.6.
[39] Hos. 10:12.

PART ONE: THEOLOGY

I: The Apostolic Preaching

God

1.1.1.[1] I know that some will try to say that even according to our Scriptures God is a body, since they find it said in the writings of Moses, *God is a consuming fire,*[2] and in the Gospel according to John, *God is spirit, and those who worship him must worship him in spirit and truth.*[3] Fire and spirit, according to them, will be reckoned to be nothing other than a body. I would like to ask them what they have to say about the saying, *God is light,* as John says in his epistle, *God is light and in him there is no darkness.*[4] He, indeed, is that light which illumines the whole understanding of those who are capable of receiving truth, as it is said in the thirty-fifth Psalm, *In your light shall we see light.*[5] For what other light of God is being spoken of, in which one sees light, except the power of God by which someone, being illumined, either sees clearly the truth of all things or comes to know God himself, who is called the truth?[6] Such, therefore, is the saying, *In your light shall we see light,* that is, in your Word and Wisdom, who is your Son, in him we shall see you, the Father. Can it possibly be that, because he is called *light,* he shall be supposed to be like the light of the sun? Or how can there be even the slightest ground for thinking that from bodily light anyone could grasp the cause of knowledge and come to the understanding of truth?

1.1.2. If, then, they accept this assertion of ours, which is proved by reason itself, regarding the nature of light, and acknowledge that God cannot be understood to be a body in the sense that light is, similar reasoning will hold for the phrase, *a consuming fire.*[7] For what does God *consume* in respect of the fact that he is *fire*? Can he possibly be thought to consume bodily matter, *wood or hay or stubble?*[8] And what, in this, would be worthy of the praise of God, if God is a fire consuming materials of that kind? Let us rather consider that God does indeed consume and destroy, but that he consumes evil thoughts, he consumes wicked actions, he consumes the desires for sin, when they enter the minds of believers, and that, inhabiting with his Son those souls which are rendered capable of receiving his Word and Wisdom, according to the saying,

---

[1] According to Photius, *Bibl. cod.* 8 (ed. Henry 1, 3b36–7), the first book of *Princ.* 'concerns the Father and the Son and the Holy Spirit'. The Latin manuscripts, however, have 'On God'. The title 'Father' is used in *Princ.* 2.4, which opens part two of *Princ.* with the heading, 'That the God of the Law and the Prophets, and the Father of our Lord Jesus Christ, is One'.

[2] Deut. 4:24.

[3] John 4:24. Origen, *Sel. Gen.* 1:26 (PG 12, 93) mentions Melito as one who spoke of the 'body' of God.

[4] 1 John 1:5.   [5] Ps. 35:15.

[6] Cf. John 14:6; Origen, *Comm. Jo.* 13.132–7.

[7] Cf. Origen, *Princ.* 2.8.3; *Comm. Jo.* 13.138–9; *Hom. Lev.* 1.4; *Hom. Ezech.* 1.3.

[8] 1 Cor. 3:12.

I and the Father shall come and make our abode with him,[9] he makes them, after all their vices and passions have been consumed, into a temple pure and worthy of himself.[10]

Those, moreover, who, because of the statement that *God is spirit,* think that he is a body, must be answered in this way. It is the custom of holy Scripture, when it wishes to designate anything of a contrary nature to this dense and solid body, to call it 'spirit', as when it says, *The letter kills, but the spirit gives life.*[11] Here there is no doubt that by 'letter' is meant bodily things, and by 'spirit' intellectual things, which we also call 'spiritual'. The Apostle also says, moreover, that, *Even to this day, when Moses is read, a veil lies over their hearts; but when someone turns to the Lord the veil is removed; and where the Spirit of the Lord is, there is freedom.*[12] For so long as someone has not turned to a spiritual understanding, *a veil lies over his heart,* by which veil, that is, a duller understanding, Scripture itself is said or thought to be veiled; and this is what is meant by the veil placed over the countenance of Moses when he spoke to the people,[13] that is, when the Law was publicly read aloud. But if we *turn to the Lord,* where also is the Word of God, and where the Holy Spirit reveals spiritual knowledge, then *the veil is removed,* and thus with an *unveiled face we shall behold the glory of the Lord* in the holy Scriptures.[14]

1.1.3. And although many saints participate in the Holy Spirit, the Holy Spirit cannot on that account be thought of as a kind of body that, divided into bodily parts, is partaken of by each one of the saints; but he is rather a sanctifying power, in which all, who have deserved to be sanctified by his grace, are said to have a share.[15] And so that what we say may be more easily understood, let us take an illustration from things very dissimilar. There are many who take part in the sciences and art of medicine: are we to suppose that all those who participate in medicine have some body, called medicine, placed before them and remove particles [of it] for themselves and thus take a share in it? Must we not rather understand that all who with a quick and trained mind grasp the art and science itself may be said to participate in medicine? But these illustrations from medicine are not to be reckoned similar in every way when compared with the Holy Spirit; they establish only this, that that, of which a share is had by many, is not immediately to be considered a body. For the Holy Spirit differs widely from the system or science of medicine, in that the Holy Spirit is an

---

[9] John 14:23. Cf. Origen, *Or.* 20.2; 23.1; 25.1; *Hom. Jer.* 8.1; *Hom. Jes. Nav.* 20.1, 24.3; *Cels.* 8.18.
[10] Cf. Origen, *Cels.* 8.18–19.   [11] 2 Cor. 3:6.
[12] 2 Cor. 3:15–17.   [13] Cf. Exod. 34:33, 35.
[14] 2 Cor. 3:16–18. Cf. Origen, *Hom. Gen.* 6.1; *Hom. Jer.* 5.8; *Hom. Ezech.* 14.2; *Cels.* 5.60.
[15] Cf. Origen, *Hom. Num.* 6.2; *Cels.* 6.70.

intellectual being and subsists and exists distinctly,[16] whereas medicine is nothing of the sort.

1.1.4. We must now pass on to the word of the Gospel, where it is written that *God is spirit*,[17] and must show that this is to be understood in conformity with what we have said. Let us inquire when our Saviour spoke these words, to whom, and what was being sought. We find, without any doubt, that he uttered them to the Samaritan woman, saying to her, who thought according to the belief of the Samaritans that God ought to be worshipped on Mount Gerizim, that *God is spirit*. For the Samaritan woman, supposing him to be a Jew, was asking of him whether God ought to be worshipped in Jerusalem or *on this mountain*; she spoke thus: *All our fathers worshipped on this mountain, and you say that in Jerusalem is the place where one ought to worship.*[18] To this belief, then, of the Samaritan woman, who thought that because of the privileges of material places, God was less rightly or rightly worshipped either by the Jews in Jerusalem or by the Samaritans on Mount Gerizim, the Saviour answered that one who would follow God must refrain from all preference for material places, and spoke thus: *The hour is coming when neither in Jerusalem nor on this mountain shall true worshippers worship the Father. God is spirit, and those who worship him must worship him in spirit and truth.*[19] See also how appropriately he has associated truth with spirit: he called [God] *spirit* to distinguish him from bodies, and *truth* to distinguish him from a shadow or an image. For those who worshipped in Jerusalem, *serving a shadow and image of heavenly things*,[20] worshipped God neither in truth nor spirit; similarly also those who worshipped on Mount Gerizim.[21]

1.1.5. Having refuted, then, as best we could, every notion which suggests that God be thought of in any bodily way, we assert that, according indeed to truth, God is incomprehensible and immeasurable. For whatever it is that we are able to sense or know of God, it is necessarily to be believed that he is by many degrees far better than what we perceive him to be. Just as, if we were to see someone scarcely able to bear a spark of light, or the light of a very small lamp, and if we wish to acquaint such a one, whose eyesight is not strong enough to

---

[16] The word translated 'being' here is *subsistentia*, almost certainly rendering ὑπόστασις; see also *Comm. Jo.* 2.75–6. Schnitzer (*Origenes,* 15, note) suggests ὑπόστασις ἐστὴ νοητὴ καὶ ὑφίσταται ἰδίως καὶ ὑπάρχει, but as Crouzel and Simonetti (SC 253, p. 23) point out, the 'subsists and exists distinctly' could be Rufinus' explanatory addition.

[17] John 4:24.   [18] John 4:20.

[19] John 4:21, 23–4.   [20] Heb. 8:5.

[21] While Origen here seems to treat both those in Jerusalem and those in Gerizim as equally worshipping 'neither in truth nor spirit', elsewhere (*Comm. Jo.* 13.80–5) he differentiates between them, with Jerusalem being a shadow of worship 'in spirit and truth', while Gerizim is a heterodox cult.

bear more light than what we have said, with the brightness and splendour of the sun, would it not be necessary for us to tell him that the splendour of the sun is unspeakably and immeasurably better and more glorious than all this light which he saw? So also our mind, when shut in by the fetters of flesh and blood and rendered, by its participation in such materials, duller and more obtuse, although it is regarded as far more excellent in comparison with bodily nature, yet when it strives after bodiless things and searches for a glimpse of them, it scarcely has room for some spark or small lamp. For what, among all intellectual, that is, bodiless beings, is so superior to all others, so unspeakably and immeasurably superior, as God, whose nature assuredly the vision of the human intellect is not able to grasp or see, however exceptionally pure or clear that intellect may be?

1.1.6. It will not seem absurd if we use another illustration to make the matter clearer still. Our eyes frequently cannot look at the nature of the light itself, that is, upon the substance of the sun; but when we see its brightness and rays pouring in through windows, perhaps, or any small opening for light, we can reflect about how great is the source and fountain of bodily light. So too the works of divine providence and the art of this universe are as if rays of the nature of God, in comparison with his own substance and being. Therefore because our own intellect is not able to behold God as he is, it understands the father of the universe from the beauty of his works and the comeliness of his creatures.[22]

God, therefore, is not to be thought to be either a body or existing in a body, but to be a simple intellectual being, accepting in himself no addition whatever; so that he cannot be believed to have in himself a more or a less, but is, in all things, μονάς [unity], or, if I may say, ἑνάς [oneness],[23] and the intellect[24] and source from which all intellectual being and intellect takes its beginning. Now an intellect, to move and operate, needs no bodily space, nor sensible magnitude, nor bodily shape or colour, nor does it need anything else whatever of things proper to bodies or matter. Wherefore that simple and wholly

---

[22] For seeing God through creation, and especially the beauty of creation, see Wis. 13:1–9, esp. v. 5; Rom. 1:20. For the description of God as 'father' (*parentem*) of the world, see: Plato, *Tim.* 28c; Alcinous, *Epit.* 10.3; Philo, *Decal.* 107, 134; *Corp. Herm.* 1.12, 1.13; Eph. 4:6; *1 Clem.* 19.2; Justin, *1 Apol.* 63; Tatian, *Or.* 4; Clement of Alexandria, *Protr.* 5.66; *Paed.* 1.5.21; 1.6.42; *Strom.* 1.28.178; 5.1.6; 5.11.71; Origen, *Comm. Jo.* 1.57; *Cels.* 8.53.

[23] The term μονάς has a Pythagorean background and the term ἑνάς a Platonic one; the former emphasizes more the unity that gave rise to multiplicity, and the latter the singularity considered in itself, unrelated to anything else. Cf. Plato, *Parm.* 137c; *Soph.* 245a; Alcinous, *Epit.* 10.8; Clement of Alexandria, *Paed.* 1.8.71; 2.8.75; *Strom.* 5.11.71.2; 5.12.81.4–82.3.

[24] Elsewhere Origen says that God transcends 'intellect' and 'being': *Cels.* 7.38; see also *Mart.* 47 and *Comm. Jo.* 19.37. For the Aristotelian background of describing God as 'intellect', see esp. *Metaph.* 12.9 (esp. 1074b34–5); for Plotinus, Origen's contemporary, the 'intellect' is the first production of 'the one' (*Enn.* 5.1).

intellectual being can have no delay or hesitation in its movements or operations, lest the simplicity of the divine nature should appear to be circumscribed or impeded somewhat by such an addition, and lest that which is the first principle of all things should be found to be composite and diverse, and to be many, not one; since the sole species of divinity, if I may speak thus, necessarily exists free from all bodily admixture.

Moreover, it is certain, even from the observation of our own intellect, that intellect does not need space to move according to its own nature. For if it abides within its own sphere, and nothing from any cause occurs to obstruct it, it will never be slowed down at all, by reason of difference in place, from performing its own movements; nor, on the other hand, does it gain any addition or increase of mobility from the quality of [particular] places. If anyone were to object, for example, that among those who sail and are tossed by the waves of the sea the intellect is somewhat less vigorous than is usual on land, it is believed that they suffer this not from the difference of place, but from the commotion or disturbance of the body to which the intellect is joined or attached. For it seems contrary to nature, as it were, for a human body to live at sea, and, because of this, as if unequal to the task, the body appears to sustain the movements of the intellect in an irregular and disordered manner and to carry out its quick movements with a slower delivery, not less than those on land when they are in the grip of a fever, of whom it is certain that if the intellect fulfils its functions less effectively because of the strength of the fever, the cause is not to be found in any fault of place, but in the illness of the body, on account of which the body, disturbed and disordered, in no way renders to the intellect services customary under well-known and natural conditions, since we human beings are animals composed from a concurrence of body and soul, and in this way [alone] did it become possible for us to live upon the earth. But God, who is the beginning of all things, is not to be regarded as a composite being, lest perchance there be found, prior to the first principle itself, elements, out of which whatever is called composite has been composed.[25]

Neither does the intellect require bodily magnitude to perform any act or movement, as does an eye which, for the purpose of seeing, expands when looking at large bodies, but narrows and contracts when looking at small ones. The intellect indeed requires intellectual magnitude, because it grows, not in a bodily manner, but an intellectual manner. For the intellect does not increase by bodily increments together with the body, up to the twentieth or thirtieth year of age, but, by applying instructions and exercises, a certain sharpening of its faculties is honed and the powers implanted within are roused to intelligence, and it is rendered capable of greater intellectual efforts, not increased by bodily increments but by being honed through exercises in

---

[25] Cf. Aristotle *Phys.* 8.10 (266a10–267b26); *Metaph.* 12.7.12–13 (1073a4–13).

learning. Yet it cannot receive these immediately from boyhood or from birth, because the framework of limbs, which the intellect uses as instruments for its own exercises, is as yet weak and feeble, being neither able to bear the force of the mind's working nor sufficiently developed to exhibit a capacity for receiving education.

1.1.7. But if there are any who consider the intellect itself and the soul to be a body, I wish they would tell me how it can receive reasons and arguments on matters of such great importance, of such difficulty and of such subtlety. Whence does the power of memory come to it, whence the contemplation of invisible things, and whence does the understanding of bodiless things reside in the body? How does a bodily nature investigate the disciplines of the arts and the meanings and reasons of things? Whence also is it able to perceive and understand the divine doctrines, which are manifestly bodiless? Unless, perhaps, someone should think that as the very bodily form and condition of the ears or eyes contributes something to hearing and seeing, and as the individual members of the body, formed by God, have some adaptation, even from the very quality of their form, for doing that for which they were naturally appointed, so also it is supposed that the condition of the soul or intellect must be understood as if fitly and suitably formed for the purpose of perceiving and understanding individual things and of being set in motion by vital movements. I do not know, however, who could describe or say what sort of appearance the intellect has, inasmuch as it is an intellect and moves in an intellectual manner.

Moreover, in confirmation and explanation of what we have said regarding the intellect or soul, that it is superior to all bodily nature, the following remarks may be added. Appropriately connected to each bodily sense is a sensible substance, towards which the bodily sense is directed. For example, sight is connected with colour, shape, and size; hearing with voice and sound; smell with odours, good or bad; taste with flavours; touch with heat or cold, hard or soft, rough or smooth. But it is clear to all that the sense of the intellect is far superior to the senses mentioned above.[26] How, then, would it not appear absurd if to these inferior senses should be connected substances to which they are directed, but that to this superior power, that is, the sense of the intellect, there should be nothing substantial at all connected with it, but that the faculty of an intellectual being should be an accident or corollary to bodies? Those who assert this, without a doubt speak in disparagement of that substance which is the better part in them; even more, in doing so they even do wrong to God himself, when they suppose that he may be understood by means of bodily nature, since according to them that which may be understood

---

[26] Cf. Origen, *Dial.* 16–24; *Hom. Luc.* 16.7–8.

or perceived by means of a body is also itself a body; and they are unwilling for it to be understood that there is a certain affinity between the intellect and God,[27] of whom the intellect itself is an intellectual image, and that by means of this it is able to know to some degree the nature of divinity, especially if it is purified and separated from bodily matter.

1.1.8. But perhaps these assertions may seem to have less authority with those who wish to be instructed in divine things from the holy Scriptures, and who seek to have it proved to them from that source how the nature of God surpasses the nature of bodies. See, then, if the Apostle also does not say the same thing when, speaking of Christ, he says, *Who is the image of the invisible God, the firstborn of every creature.*[28] Not, as some suppose, that the nature of God is visible to some and invisible to others; for the Apostle does not say 'the image of God who is invisible to men' or 'invisible to sinners', but pronounces, with absolute constancy, on the very nature of God, saying *the image of the invisible God.* And John, also, saying in the Gospel, *No one has seen God at any time,*[29] clearly declares to all who are able to understand that there is no being to which God is visible; not as if he were a being visible by nature and yet eludes and escapes the gaze of the frailer creatures, but because by nature it is impossible for him to be seen.

If you should ask of me what is my opinion regarding the only-begotten himself, whether I would say that the nature of God, which is naturally invisible, is not even visible to him, do not let this question immediately seem to you impious or absurd, for we shall of course give a reasonable answer.[30] It is one thing to see, and another to know; to see and to be seen is a property of bodies; to know and to be known is a property of intellectual beings. Whatever, therefore, is a property of bodies cannot be predicated either of the Father or of the Son; but what pertains to the nature of divinity is common to the Father and the Son. Precisely, then, he himself, in the Gospel, did not say that no one has seen the Father except the Son, nor anyone the Son except the Father, but said, *No one knows the Son except the Father, nor anyone the Father except the Son.*[31] From this it is clearly shown that whatever it is among bodily beings that is called 'seeing' and 'being seen', is called, between the Father and the Son, 'knowing' and 'being known', through the faculty of knowledge not by the frailness of sight. Because, then, neither 'seeing' nor 'being seen' can properly be applied to a bodiless and invisible being, neither is the Father, in the Gospel, said to be seen by the Son, nor the Son by the Father, but to be known.

---

[27] Cf. Origen, *Princ.* 4.4.10.   [28] Col. 1:15.   [29] John 1:18.

[30] Here Koetschau inserts a sentence from Jerome, *Jo. Hier.* 7 (PL 23, 360); it is included in the Appendix as item no. 1.

[31] Matt. 11:27.

1.1.9. But if someone lays before us the question why it was said, *Blessed are the pure in heart, for they shall see God,*[32] from that very passage, in my opinion, will our argument be much more firmly established; for what else is seeing God in the heart than, as we have explained above, to understand and to know him with the intellect?[33] For the names of the organs of sense are frequently applied to the soul, so that it may be said to see with the eyes of the heart, that is, to infer some intellectual conclusion by means of the faculty of intelligence.[34] So also it is said to hear with the ears when it perceives the deeper meaning. So also we say that it is able to use teeth, when it eats and consumes *the bread of life* which *comes down from heaven.*[35] In a similar way it is said to use the services of the other members which are transferred from their bodily significance and applied to the faculties of the soul, just as Solomon says, *You will find a divine sense.*[36] For he knew that there were within us two kinds of senses: one kind of sense being mortal, corruptible, human, the other kind being immortal and intellectual, which he here calls *divine*. By this divine sense, therefore, not of the eyes, but of a pure heart, which is the intellect, God may be seen by those who are worthy. That the intellect, that is, the intellectual faculty is indeed called *heart*, you will find abundantly in all the Scriptures, both old and new.

Having understood, therefore, the nature of God, in a manner greatly inferior to what is fitting, because of the weakness of human intelligence, let us now see what is meant by the name of Christ.

---

[32] Matt. 5:8.

[33] For a similar treatment of this verse, see *Fr. Jo.* 13 (GCS 4, p. 495); *Cels.* 7.33, and more generally *Cels.* 6.69; 7.34, 44; *Comm. Jo.* 28.23–38; *Comm. ser. Matt.* 85; *Or.* 13.4.

[34] Cf. Origen, *Dial.* 16–24; *Hom. Luc.* 16.7–8.   [35] John 6: 35, 33.

[36] Prov. 2:5. Origen's reading of this text (which we have in Greek in *Cels.* 7.34) is: αἴσθησιν θείαν εὑρήσεις, whereas the usual LXX reading is: ἐπίγνωσιν θεοῦ εὑρήσεις.

Christ

1.2.1.[1] In the first place, we must know that in Christ the nature of his divinity, as he is the only-begotten Son of God, is one thing, and another is the human nature, which in the last times he took on account of the economy. As such, we must first see what the only-begotten Son of God is, who is called by many and diverse names according to the circumstances and beliefs of those speaking.[2] For he is called *Wisdom*, as Solomon said, speaking in the person of Wisdom: *The Lord created me the beginning of his ways for his works; before he made anything, before the ages, he established me. In the beginning, before he made the earth, before the springs of water came forth, before the mountains were made firm, before all the hills, he begets me.*[3] He is also called the *First-born*, as the Apostle Paul says, *Who is the First-born of all creation.*[4] The *First-born* is not, however, by nature another than *Wisdom*, but is one and the same. Finally, the Apostle Paul says, *Christ the Power of God and the Wisdom of God.*[5]

1.2.2. Let no one, however, suppose that when we call him *the Wisdom of God*, we mean something unsubstantial;[6] that is, to take an example, that we understand him to be not, as it were, some wise living being, but rather a certain thing which makes [others] wise, offering and implanting itself in the intellects of those who are made capable of receiving his virtues and intelligence. If, then, once it is rightly understood that the only-begotten Son of God is his Wisdom subsisting substantially,[7] I do not think that our mind now ought to stray beyond this to the suspicion that his very ὑπόστασις (that is, subsistence[8]) might have something bodily, since everything that is bodily is distinguished by shape or colour or size. And who in his sound mind ever sought for shape or colour or measurable size in wisdom, inasmuch as it is wisdom? And how can one, who has learnt to know and think piously about God, think or believe that the God and Father ever existed, even for a single moment, without begetting this Wisdom? For he would either say that God was unable to beget Wisdom before he begot her, so that afterwards he begot into being her

---

[1] Photius, *Bibl. cod.* 8 (ed. Henry 1, 4a1–4), begins by saying that the first book of *Princ.* concerns 'the Father, the Son, and the Holy Spirit', but continues by saying: 'The first book is full of fables about the Father, and (as that one says) Christ, and the Holy Spirit, and rational beings' (Ἔστι δ᾽ ὁ μὲν πρῶτος αὐτῷ λόγος μεμυθολογημένος περὶ πατρὸς καὶ (ὡς ἐκεῖνός φησι) περὶ Χριστοῦ καὶ περὶ ἁγίου πνεύματος, ἔτι καὶ περὶ λογικῶν φύσεων). In *Princ.* 1.2.6, Origen speaks of others who have fallen into 'absurd fables'.
[2] For the names or aspects (ἐπίνοιαι) of Christ, see *Comm. Jo.* 1.90–292, esp. 119, 123, 136.
[3] Prov. 8:22–5. On the present tense of 'begets', see esp. *Hom. Jer.* 9.4 and *Comm. Jo.* 1.204, and below, *Princ.* 1.2.2, 4. On 'Wisdom' being the 'oldest' aspect of Christ, see *Comm. Jo.* 1.118.
[4] Col. 1:15.   [5] 1 Cor. 1:24.
[6] Cf. Origen, *Comm. Jo.* 1.151–2; 10.264; *Or.* 15.1; *Dial.* 4; *Fr. Tit.* (PG 14, 1304d).
[7] Cf. Origen, *Comm. Jo.* 6.188; *Or.* 27.12; *Cels.* 8.12.
[8] These are clearly Rufinus' words.

who formerly did not exist, or else that he was able but, what is impious even to say about God, unwilling to beget; both alternatives, as is patent to all, are absurd and impious, that is, either that God advanced from a condition of being unable to being able, or that, while being able, he hid this and delayed the begetting of Wisdom.

Therefore we acknowledge that God is always the Father of his only-begotten Son, who was indeed born of him, and derives from him what he is, but without, however, any beginning, not only that which may be distinguished by periods of time, but even that which intellect alone is accustomed to contemplate within itself or to contemplate, if we may thus speak, with the bare intellect and reason. Wisdom is thus believed to be begotten beyond the limits of any beginning that we can speak of or understand. And since within this very subsistence of Wisdom was every capacity and form of the creation that would come to be—both of those things which exist primarily and of those which occur in consequence, having been formed beforehand and arranged by the power of foreknowledge regarding these very created things, which had been as it were outlined and prefigured in Wisdom herself—Wisdom herself says through Solomon that she was *created the beginning of the ways* of God, that is, containing within herself the beginning and the reasons and the species of the entire creation.[9]

1.2.3. Now, in the same way in which we have understood that Wisdom is *the beginning of the ways* of God, and is said to be *created*, that is, forming beforehand and containing within herself the species and reasons of the whole creation, in the same manner must she be understood to be the Word of God, as she discloses to all other beings, that is, to the entire creation, the reason of the mysteries and secrets which are contained within the Wisdom of God, and so she is called the Word, because she is, as it were, the interpreter of the secrets of the intellect. Whence the saying, written in the Acts of Paul, seems right to me, that 'he is the Word, a living being'.[10] John, however, speaks more sublimely and brilliantly at the beginning of his Gospel, defining the Word, by an appropriate definition, to be God, saying, *And the Word was God and he was in the beginning with God.*[11] Let the one, then, who assigns a beginning to the Word of God or to the Wisdom of God consider with care lest his impiety is cast upon the unbegotten Father himself, denying that he was always father

---

[9] For the ideas in this paragraph, see *Princ* 1.4.4–5; 2.3.6; *Comm. Jo.* 1.111, 113–15; 19.146–50; *Cels.* 5.22, 39; 6.64; *Comm. Cant.* 3 (GCS 8, p. 208).

[10] The Acts of Paul are mentioned by Eusebius, *Hist. eccl.* 3.3.5, but are not extant; they are other than the Acts of Paul and Thecla. Origen also cites from these Acts in *Comm. Jo.* 20.91. The saying quoted here is echoed in Origen's *Hom. Jer.* 20.1, where the Word is described as being ζῷον. It is possible that this goes back to Heb. 4:12: ζῶν γὰρ ὁ λόγος.

[11] John 1:1–2.

and that he begot the Word and possessed Wisdom in all previous times or ages, or whatever else one can call them.

1.2.4. This Son, therefore, is also *the truth* and *the life* of all things which exist,[12] and rightly so. For how could things that were created live, except by life?[13] Or how could those things that are truly exist, unless they were derived from the truth? Or how could rational beings exist, unless the Word or Reason preceded them?[14] Or how could they be wise, unless there was Wisdom? But since it was to come to pass that some should also fall away from life, and bring death upon themselves by this very act of falling away from life (for death is nothing else than a departure from life), and since it was not to follow that those, who had once been created by God to live,[15] should utterly perish, it was necessary that, before death, there should be such a power that would destroy the death that was to come and be *the resurrection*,[16] the figure of which is in our Lord and Saviour, which resurrection exists in the Wisdom and Word and Life of God. Then, in next place, since it was to come to pass that some of those who were created, possessing the good not by nature, that is, substantially, but by accident, would not be able to remain unchangeable and unalterable and to abide always in the same blessings with equilibrium and moderate measure, but, turning and changing, would fall away from their condition, the Word and Wisdom of God became *the way*.[17] She is called *the way* because she leads to the Father those who walk along her. Whatever, therefore, we have said of the Wisdom of God will appropriately be applied and understood also in the case of saying that the Son of God is *the life* and that he is *the word* and that he is *the way* and that he is *the truth*, and that he is *the resurrection*; for all these titles are named from his works and his powers, and in none of them is there the slightest ground for understanding anything bodily, which might seem to designate size or form or colour.

But whereas the offspring of humans or of other animals, whom we see around us, correspond to the seed of those of whose seed they are or of those in whose wombs they are formed and nourished, having from these whatever it is that they have taken and bring into the light of day when they are born, it is abominable and unlawful to equate the God and Father, in the begetting of his only-begotten Son and in his giving [him] subsistence, with any generation of humans or other animals; but it must be something exceptional and worthy of God, for which can be found no comparison at all, not merely in things, but even in thought or imagination, such that a human mind could apprehend

---

[12] John 14:6. [13] Cf. Origen, *Comm. Jo.* 1.126, 188, 267; 2.112–32.
[14] Cf. Origen, *Comm. Jo.* 1.266–75; 2.21–33; 6.188; *Or.* 27.2.
[15] Cf. Wis. 1:14. [16] John 11:25. Cf. Origen, *Comm. Jo.* 1.181–2, 268.
[17] John 14:6. Cf. Origen, *Comm. Jo.* 1.183–4; 6.103–7; 32.80–2, 400.

how the unbegotten God becomes Father of the only-begotten Son. For this is an eternal and everlasting begetting, just as brightness is begotten from light.[18] For he does not become Son, in an external manner, through adoption in the Spirit,[19] but is Son by nature.

1.2.5. Let us now see how what we have said is also supported by the authority of the divine Scripture. The Apostle Paul says that the only-begotten Son is *the image of the invisible God* and *the first-born of all creation;*[20] and when writing to the Hebrews, he says of him that he is *the splendour of the glory and the express figure of his substance.*[21] Nevertheless, we also find in the book of Wisdom, which is said to be Solomon's,[22] a certain description of the Wisdom of God written in this way, *For she is the breath of the power of God, and the* ἀπόρροια (that is, *emanation*) *of the purest glory of the Almighty; for that reason, therefore nothing defiled can enter into her. For she is the radiance of eternal life and the flawless mirror of the working of God and the image of his goodness.*[23] Now we hold, as we said above, that the Wisdom of God has her subsistence nowhere else but in him who is the beginning of all things, from whom also she is born. Since this Wisdom is the one who alone is Son by nature, she is therefore called *the only-begotten.*

1.2.6. Let us now see what ought to be understood when he is called the *image of the invisible God*, so that by this we might perceive how God is rightly called the Father of his Son; and let us first of all consider things which are customarily called 'images' by human beings. That which is painted or sculpted on some material, such as wood or stone, is sometimes called an image; and sometimes a child is called the image of its parent, when the likeness of the features of the parent are in no way distorted in the child. Now I think that the first of these examples may be applied to that man who was made *in the image and likeness* of God, whom we will consider more precisely, God willing, when we come to expound this passage in Genesis.[24]

However, the image [aspect] of the Son of God might be compared to the second example, even in respect of the fact that he is *the* invisible *image of the*

---

[18] Cf. Wis. 7:26; Heb. 1:3. See also Justin, *Dial.* 61, 128; Tatian, *Orat.* 5; Tertullian, *Prax.* 8.5; Origen, *Comm. Jo.* 32.353.

[19] Cf. Rom. 8:15.   [20] Col. 1:15.   [21] Heb. 1:3.

[22] Cf. Origen, *Princ.* 4.4.6, where he notes that it is 'a book not held in authority by all'.

[23] Wis. 7:25–6.

[24] Gen. 1:26. In *Princ.* 1.3.3 and 2.3.6, Origen refers to an already complete work on Gen. 1–2; Origen's *Commentary on Genesis* must have been written together with *Princ.*, but it is no longer extant. His treatment of Gen. 1:26 can be found in *Hom. Gen.* 1.13 and *Sel. Gen.* 1:26 (PG 12, 93).

invisible God,[25] just as, according to the narrative, we say the image of Adam is his son Seth. For it is written thus, *And Adam begot Seth in his own image and in his own form.*[26] This image preserves the unity of nature and substance of a father and of a son. For if *all that the Father does, the Son also does likewise,*[27] then by the fact that the Son does all things like the Father, the image of the Father is formed in the Son, who is assuredly born of him, as an act of his will proceeding from the intellect.[28] And therefore I consider that the will of the Father ought to be sufficient for the subsistence of what he wills; for in willing he uses no other means than that which is produced by the counsel of his will. In this way, then, the subsistence of the Son is also begotten by him.

This point must, above all, be upheld by those who acknowledge nothing to be unbegotten, that is, unborn, except the God and Father.[29] One must, moreover, be careful not to fall into the absurd fables of those who depict for themselves certain emanations, so as to divide the divine nature into parts and divide the God and Father as far as they can, since even to entertain the slightest suspicion of this regarding a bodiless being is not only of extreme impiety but also of ultimate folly, and neither does it in any way accord with intelligence to think that a substantial division of a bodiless nature is possible. Rather, then, as an act of the will proceeds from the intellect, and neither cuts off any part nor is separated or divided from it, so, in some similar fashion, is the Father to be supposed to have begotten the Son, that is, his own image, so that just as he is himself invisible by nature, so also he has begotten an image that is invisible.

For the Son is the Word, and therefore it is understood that nothing in him is perceptible to the senses; he is Wisdom, and in Wisdom there is no suspicion of anything bodily; *he is the true light, which enlightens every human being coming into this world,*[30] but he has nothing in common with the light of this sun. Our[31] Saviour, therefore, is the *image of the invisible God* and Father; in

---

[25] Col. 1:15. For Irenaeus, the image of God in the human being is inscribed in the flesh (*Haer.* 5.6.1); as he argues against his opponents, an image must have form, and form can only exist in matter (*Haer.* 2.7, 19.6).

[26] Gen. 5:3.   [27] John 5:19.   [28] Cf. Origen, *Comm. Jo.* 13.228–34.

[29] According to Jerome, *Ep.* 124.2.3 (ed. Hilberg 3, 97.26), Origen asserted that the Father alone was 'uncreated' (*infactum*). Fernandez would place in parallel here a sentence from Justinian, *Ep. ad Menam* (ed. Schwartz, 210.9–10), which Koetschau would insert into *Princ.* 1.3.3; it is given in the Appendix as item no. 5. See above, *Princ.* Pr.4, n.15.

[30] John 1:9.

[31] For what follows, see Jerome, *Ep.* 124.2.1 (ed. Hilberg 3, 97.10–13), who reports Origen as asserting that: 'The Son, who is the image of the invisible Father, compared to the Father is not the truth, but compared with us, who cannot receive the truth of the almighty Father, he seems a simulacrum of the truth' (*Filium, qui sit imago inuisibilis patris, conparatum patri non esse ueritatem; apud nos autem, qui dei omnipotentis non possumus recipere ueritatem, imaginariam ueritatem uideri*). The Synodal Letter of the Council of Alexandria in 400 (= Jerome, *Ep.* 92.2.1; ed. Hilberg 2, 148.26–149.1), presided over by Theophilus of Alexandria, reports Origen's teaching in a more extreme form: 'For when the volume περὶ ἀρχῶν, which we call *On First Principles,*

relation to the Father himself, the truth, and in relation to us, to whom he revealed the Father, the image,[32] by which we come to the knowledge of *the Father*, whom *no one* else *knows except the Son and he to whom the Son has willed to reveal him.*[33] And he reveals him by being himself understood.[34] For to the one who has understood the Son himself, the Father is also understood, according to his own words, *He that has seen me, has seen the Father also.*[35]

1.2.7. But since we quoted the saying of Paul regarding Christ, in which he says of him that he is *the splendour of the glory of God and the express figure of his substance,*[36] let us see what we are to learn from this. *God is light,* according to John.[37] The only-begotten Son, therefore, is *the splendour* of this light, proceeding from him inseparably, as does splendour from light, and enlightening the whole creation.[38] For following what we have already explained— regarding how he is *the way* and leads to the Father, and how he is *the word*, interpreting and making known to the rational creation the secrets of wisdom and the mysteries of knowledge, and is also *the truth* and *the life* and *the resurrection*—in the same way ought we to understand also the action of *the splendour*: it is by splendour that we understand and perceive what light itself is. This *splendour*, presenting itself softly and gently to the frail and weak eyes of mortals, and gradually training, as it were, and accustoming them to bear the brightness of the light, when it has removed from them everything that clouds and impedes vision, according to the Lord's saying, Cast out the *beam from your own eye,*[39] renders them capable of receiving *the splendour* of the light, even becoming in this respect a kind of mediator between human beings and the light.[40]

---

was read, in which it is written that the Son compared with us is truth, but compared with the Father is falsehood…' (*Nam cum legeretur uolumen* περὶ ἀρχῶν, *quae nos 'de principiis' possumus dicere, in quibus scriptum est, quod filius nobis conparatus est ueritas et patri conlatus mendacium…*). According to a work by an anonymous defender of Origen, as reported by Photius, *Bibl. cod.* 117 (ed. Henry 2, 92a33–5), Origen was accused of teaching 'that the image of God, considered in relation to God, whose image he is, in so far as he is the image, is not truth (ὅτι ἡ εἰκὼν τοῦ θεοῦ ὡς πρὸς ἐκεῖνον οὗ ἐστιν εἰκών, καθὸ εἰκών, οὐκ ἔστιν ἀλήθεια).

[32] Koetschau inserts here, as Fragment 4, a sentence from Justinian, *Ep. ad Menam* (ed. Schwartz, 209.25–7) which is said to be from *Princ.* 1; the text is included in the Appendix as item no. 2.

[33] Matt. 11:27.

[34] Cf. Origen, *Comm. Jo.* 13.35; 32.359; *Cels.* 7.43–4.

[35] John 14:9. Koetschau suspects a further omission at this point, perhaps to be filled with either of the following passages: Jerome *Ep.* 124.2.1 (ed. Hilberg 3, 97.14–17) or Theophilus' Synodal Letter for AD 400 (= Jerome, *Ep.* 92.2.1; ed. Hilberg 2, 149.2–3); these texts are included in the Appendix as item no. 3.

[36] Heb. 1:3.   [37] 1 John 1:5.

[38] Cf. Origen, *Comm. Rom.* 2.5; *Comm. Jo.* 13.153.

[39] Matt. 7:5.   [40] Cf. 1 Tim. 2:5.

1.2.8. But since he is called by the Apostle not only the *splendour of the glory* but also the *express figure of his substance* or *subsistence*, it doesn't seem to me idle to turn our intellect to the issue of how there can be said to be, besides the substance or subsistence of God himself, whatever that substance or subsistence means, another *figure of his substance*. Consider, then, whether the Son of God—who is also called his Word and Wisdom and alone knows the Father and *reveals him to whom he will*, to those, that is, who become capable of receiving his Word and Wisdom—may not, in regard to this very point of making God to be understood and known, be called *the figure of his substance* or *subsistence*; that is, when Wisdom outlines in herself, first of all, the things which she wishes to reveal to others, by which God may be known and understood by them, then she may also be called *the express figure of the substance* of God.

In order, however, that it may be more fully understood in what way the Saviour is *the figure of the substance* or *subsistence* of God, let us use an example, which, although it does not fully or properly represent the subject we are treating, may yet be taken, solely so that it may be seen that when the Son, *who was in the form of God, emptied himself,*[41] he desires to demonstrate, by this very emptying, *the fullness of divinity.*[42] For example,[43] suppose there were a statue of such magnitude as to fill the whole world and on that account could be seen by no one; but that another statue was made similar to it in every respect, in the shape of limbs and outline of countenance, in form and matter, but not in its immensity of size, so that those who were unable to perceive and behold the immense one, on seeing the latter could be assured that they had seen the former, because it preserved every outline of limb and countenance, and even the form and matter, with an absolutely indistinguishable similarity; by some such likeness, the Son of God emptying himself of equality with the Father and showing us the way by which we may know him, becomes *the express figure of his substance*, so that we, who were unable to look upon the glory of the pure light while it remained in the magnitude of his divinity, may, by his becoming for us *the splendour*, obtain the way of beholding the divine light through looking upon *the splendour*. This comparison with statues, of course, although belonging to material things, is to be allowed for no other purpose than to show that the Son of God, though placed within the very small confines of a human body, yet through the likeness of his works and power demonstrated that the immense and invisible greatness of the God and Father was in him, as he said to his disciples, that *He who sees me, sees the Father also*, and, *I and the*

---

[41] Phil. 2:6–7.   [42] Col. 2:9.

[43] Cf. Jerome, *Ep.* 124.2.2: 'He gives an illustration of two statues, a larger one and a small: the first fills the world and is somehow invisible through its size, the latter is perceptible to our eyes; the former he compares to the Father, the second to the Son.'

Father are one, with which is also to be understood the similar saying, that *The Father is in me, and I in the Father.*[44]

1.2.9. Let us now see what is the meaning of the passage we find written in the Wisdom of Solomon, where it is said of Wisdom that, *She is a breath of the power of God, and the* ἀπόρροια (that is, the *emanation*[45]) *of the purest glory of the Almighty and the splendour of eternal light and the flawless mirror of the working of God and the image of his goodness.*[46] Determining here, then, five points regarding God, from each of them he points out a certain characteristic of the Wisdom of God: for he speaks of *the power,* and *the glory,* and *the eternal light,* and *the working,* and *the goodness of God.* He says, however, that Wisdom is *a breath* not *of the glory of the Almighty,* nor *of the eternal light,* nor *of the working* of the Father, nor *of his goodness,* for it was not appropriate that breath should be ascribed to any of these; but, with all propriety, he says that Wisdom *is a breath of the power of God.*[47] Now, *the power of God* must be understood as that by which he is strong, that by which he establishes, preserves, and governs all things visible and invisible, and that by which he is sufficient for all things, for whom he exercises his providence and with whom he is present, as if united with them. *The breath,* then, or if I may speak thus, the vigour of all this great and so immense *power* itself comes to have its own subsistence, for although it proceeds from the power itself as will from the intellect, nevertheless even the will of God itself becomes the power of God. Another power, therefore, comes to be, subsisting in its own properties, a kind of *breath,* as the passage of Scripture affirms, of the first and unbegotten *power of God,* drawing from him whatever it is.[48]

There is no 'when' when it did not exist.[49] For if anyone wished to assert that it did not formerly exist, but came into subsistence afterwards, let him say why the Father who caused him to subsist did not do so before. And if he has conceded that there was a single beginning, in which beginning that *breath* proceeded from *the power of God,* we shall ask again why not even before the beginning of which he has spoken; and in this way, always seeking earlier and ascending with our questions, we shall arrive at this conclusion, that, as God was always able and willing, it was never becoming, nor could there be any other reason, such that he would not always have this good thing that he desired.[50] From this it is demonstrated that that *breath of the power of God* has always existed, having no beginning but God himself. Nor indeed was it fitting

---

[44] John 14:9; 10:30, 38. Cf. Origen, *Comm. Jo.* 20.153–9.
[45] These explanatory words are of course from Rufinus.
[46] Wis. 7:25–6.   [47] Cf. Origen, *Comm. Jo.* 13.153.
[48] Cf. Origen, *Cels.* 8.12.   [49] Cf. Origen, *Princ.* 4.4.1; *Comm. Rom.* 1.5.
[50] This argument, that God is both able and willing, has already been used above (*Princ.* 1.2.2), regarding the begetting of Wisdom. See also Clement of Alexandria, *Strom.* 5.14.141.

that there should be any other beginning, but God himself, from whom it is and is born. According to the saying of the Apostle, that *Christ is the power of God*, it should be called not only *the breath of the power of God*, but power from power.

1.2.10. Let us now examine the saying that [Wisdom] *is the ἀπόρροια (that is, the emanation) of the purest glory of the Almighty*, and let us first consider what the *glory of the Almighty* is, and then we shall understand what is its *emanation*. In[51] the same way that no one can be a father if there is no son, nor can one be a lord if he owns neither possessions nor a slave, so even God cannot be called 'Almighty' if there are not those over whom he can exercise his power; and, therefore, that God may be shown to be almighty, it is necessary that all things exist. For if anyone would have it that some ages or periods, or whatever else he likes to call them, passed away, ages when those things that have been made had not yet been made, he would undoubtedly prove that during those ages or periods God was not almighty but became almighty afterwards, from the time when he began to have those over whom he could exercise power; and in this way he will appear to have received a certain increase and to have come from a lower to a higher state, since it is not doubted that it is better for him to be almighty than not to be so. And how would it not seem absurd that God, not having something of those things fitting for him to have, should afterwards, by a kind of progress, come to have it? But if there never is a 'when' when he was not almighty, by necessity those things must also subsist by which he is called the *Almighty*, and he must always have had those over whom he exercised power and which were governed by him as king or prince; of which

---

[51] What follows can be compared to the account given by Methodius of Olympus (in a work entitled περὶ τῶν γενητῶν, 'On creatures'), as preserved by Photius *Bibl. cod.* 235 (ed. Henry 5, 302a30–302b4): 'Origen, whom he calls the Centaur, said that the universe is co-eternal with the only wise and independent God. For he says, if there is neither a workman without products, nor maker without things made, neither is there an Almighty without those under his power (for the workman must be so called from the products, and the maker from the things made, and the Almighty from those things under his power); it is necessary, then, that it is from the beginning that these things were made by God, and that there was no time in which they did not exist. For if there was a time when the things made did not exist, then, as there were no made things, so there was no maker; you see what sort of impiety follows. Rather the unchangeable and unalterable God will undergo alteration and transition; for if he made the universe later, it is clear that he transitioned from not making to making. But this is absurd, given what has been said. It is not possible, therefore, to say that the universe is not beginningless and co-eternal with God.' Note, however, that the argument of *Princ.* 1.2.10 is that the title 'Father' is 'older' than 'Almighty', for it is in Wisdom and by the Word that God has made all things; and that the subjection of all things to God, by virtue of which he is 'Almighty', is not exercised through force, but through Wisdom, for it is at the name of Jesus, the crucified and exalted Lord, that all knees bow. The implications of this for Origen's understanding of creation, and its 'eternity', are explored in the Introduction, sections 3 and 5.

we shall speak more fully in the proper place, when we come to discuss the subject of his creatures.

But even now, although briefly, I think it necessary to give a warning, since the question before us concerning Wisdom is how Wisdom is *the ἀπόρροια* (or *the emanation*) *of the purest glory of the Almighty*, lest anyone should consider that the title of *Almighty* is anterior in God to the birth of Wisdom, through whom he is called Father, since it is said that Wisdom, who is the Son of God, is the *emanation of the purest glory of the Almighty*. Let him who would think like this hear what the Scriptures clearly proclaim, saying, *In Wisdom have you made all things,*[52] and the Gospel teaches, that *All things were made by him and without him nothing was made,*[53] and let him understand from this that the title of *Almighty* cannot be older in God than that of Father, for it is through the Son that the Father is almighty.[54]

But since it says that the *glory* is *of the Almighty*, of which *glory* Wisdom is the *emanation*, this is given to be understood, that Wisdom, through which God is called *Almighty,* has a share even in the glory of omnipotence. For through Wisdom, who is Christ, God holds power over all things, not only by the authority of having dominion, but also the voluntary obedience of his subjects. And that you may understand that the omnipotence of the Father and the Son is one and the same, just as God and the Lord are one and the same with the Father, listen to the way in which John speaks in the Apocalypse: *These things says the Lord God, who is and who was and who is to come, the Almighty.*[55] For he *who is to come*, who else is that than Christ? And just as no one ought to be offended that, while the Father is God, the Saviour also is *God,*[56] so also, since the Father is called *Almighty*, no one ought to be offended that the Son of God is also called *Almighty*.

For in this way will that saying be true, which he himself says to the Father, *All mine are yours and yours mine, and I am glorified in them.*[57] Now, if all things which are the Father's are also Christ's, and, among all that the Father is, he is also *Almighty,* then without doubt the only-begotten Son ought to be *Almighty,* so that the Son might have all that the Father has. *And I am glorified,* he says, *in them.* For, *at the name of Jesus every knee shall bow, of things in heaven, and things on earth, and things under the earth, and every tongue shall confess that Jesus is Lord in the glory of God the Father.*[58] So, in this way is God's Wisdom herself the pure and clear *emanation of the glory of God*, in respect of his being *Almighty,* glorified as the *emanation* of omnipotence or of glory.

[52] Ps. 103:24.   [53] John 1:3.
[54] 'Older', clearly, in a logical, rather than chronological, sense; a point affirmed in the first article of later creeds: 'We believe in one God Father Almighty...'
[55] Rev. 1:8.   [56] John 20:28.
[57] John 17:10.   [58] Phil. 2:10–11.

And we add this, so that it may be more clearly understood what the *glory* of omnipotence is. The God and Father is *Almighty* because he has power over all things, that is, over heaven and earth, sun and moon, and all things in them. And he exercises power over them through his Word, for *at the name of Jesus every knee bows, of things in heaven, and things on earth, and things under the earth*. And, if *every knee bows* to Jesus, then, without doubt, it is Jesus to whom *all things have been subjected,* and he it is who exercised power over all things, and through whom *all things have been subjected* to the Father;[59] for it is through Wisdom, that is by Word and Reason, not by force and necessity, that they have been subjected. And therefore his glory is in the very fact that he possesses all things, and this is the *purest and most clear glory* of omnipotence, that by Reason and Wisdom, not by force and necessity, all things have been subjected. Now the *purest and most clear glory* of Wisdom is a convenient designation to distinguish it from that glory which is not called pure or genuine.

Every being that is alterable and changeable, although it may be glorified in works of righteousness or wisdom, because it has righteousness or wisdom as accidents, and because what is accidental can also fall away, its glory cannot be called genuine and pure. But since the Wisdom of God, who is his only-begotten Son, is in all respects unalterable and unchangeable, and every good quality is in him essentially, such that it can never be changed or altered, therefore his glory is declared to be pure and genuine.

1.2.11. In the third place, Wisdom is said to be the *splendour of eternal light*; the force of this expression we have explained in the preceding pages, when we introduced the illustration of the sun and the splendour of its rays, and showed, to the best of our power, how this should be understood. We shall add, however, this one point. That which neither had a beginning of existence, nor can ever cease to be what it is, is properly called everlasting or eternal. And this is pointed out by John when he says, *God is light*.[60] Now his Wisdom is the *splendour* of that light, not only in respect of its being light, but also in respect of its being everlasting light, so that his Wisdom is eternal and everlasting splendour. If this be fully understood, it clearly shows that the subsistence of the Son derives from the Father himself, yet not temporally nor from any other beginning except, as we have said, from God himself.

1.2.12. But Wisdom is also termed *the flawless mirror of the ἐνεργεία (that is, the working) of God*. It must first be understood, then, what the *working* of the power of God is. It is a kind of strength, if we may speak thus, by which the Father works, either when he creates or when he acts in providence, or judges, or when he arranges and orders individual things, each in its own time. For as

---

[59] Cf. 1 Cor. 15:27–8.   [60] 1 John 1:5.

in a mirror the image formed in the mirror moves along or acts with all the same motions and actions with which the one who looks into the mirror moves or acts, and deviates from them in absolutely nothing, even so Wisdom is to be understood concerning herself, when she names herself the *flawless mirror* of the paternal power and working; just as the Lord Jesus Christ, who is the Wisdom of God, declares about himself when he says, *The works which the Father does, these the Son does likewise.*[61] And again he says, *the Son can do nothing of himself except what he sees the Father doing.*[62]

As, then, the Son in no respect is separated or differs from the Father in the power of his works, nor is the work of the Son anything other than the Father's, but one and the same movement, so to speak, is in all things, he therefore called him a *flawless mirror*, that by this expression it might be understood that there is no dissimilarity whatsoever between the Son and the Father.[63] How, indeed, are the things done by a pupil, in likeness and imitation of the teacher, as some have said, to be compared to [the idea] that those things are made by the Son in bodily matter which were first formed by the Father in a spiritual substance, when in the Gospel the Son is said to do not similar things, but the same things *likewise?*

1.2.13. It remains to inquire what *the image of his goodness* is. In this, I think, the same thing must be understood as we expressed above in regard to the image formed by the mirror. For the Father is, without doubt, the primal goodness, from which the Son is born, who, being in every respect the image of the Father, may doubtless be properly called *the image of his goodness.*[64] For there is no other second goodness existing in the Son, besides that which is in the Father. And therefore the Saviour himself rightly says in the Gospel, *No one is good but one, the God* and Father,[65] that by this it may be understood that the Son is not of some other *goodness*, but of that only which is in the Father, of whom he is rightly called the *image*, because neither is he of any other source but from that primal goodness, so that there is not seen in the Son another goodness than that which is in the Father, nor is there any dissimilarity or difference of goodness in the Son. And therefore it is not to be imagined that there is some kind of blasphemy, as it were, in the words, *No one is good but one, the God* and Father, as if, on that account, it be supposed to be denied that either Christ or the Holy Spirit is *good*; but, as we have said above, the primal goodness is recognized in the God and Father, from whom both the Son, being

---

[61] John 5:19.   [62] *Ibid.*

[63] Cf. Origen, *Princ.* 1.2.6; *Comm. Jo.* 13.228–34; *Cels.* 8.12; *Hom. Lev.* 13.4.

[64] Koetschau and Fernandez insert here, as Fragment 6, a passage from Justinian, *Ep. ad Menam* (ed. Schwartz, 210.1–6), said to come from *Princ.* 1; the text is included in the Appendix as item no. 4.

[65] Matt. 19:17; Mark 10:18; Luke 18:19. Origen adds the word '[and] Father'.

begotten, and the Holy Spirit, proceeding,[66] without doubt draw into themselves the nature of that goodness, which exists in the source, from whom the Son is born and the Spirit proceeds. But if there are any other things called good in the Scriptures, whether angel, or human, or servant, or treasure, or a good heart, or a good tree, all these are called thus inexactly, having in them an accidental, not an essential, goodness.

But it would be a large undertaking, for another work and another time, to collect all the titles of the Son of God, for example, how he is *the true light*,[67] or *the door*,[68] or *the righteousness,* or *the sanctification,* or *the redemption*,[69] and numerous others, and to explain for what reasons, either pertaining to powers or virtues, he is termed each one of these.[70] But, content with those we have advanced above, let us now examine the remaining points in order.

---

[66] It is perhaps, as Crouzel and Simonetti suggest, Rufinus who adds the term 'proceeding', for Origen does not appeal to this word or John 15:26 in his chapters on the Holy Spirit.
[67] John 1:9.   [68] John 10:7, 9.   [69] 1 Cor. 1:30.
[70] See esp. Origen, *Comm. Jo.* 1.125–288; the first books of Origen's *Commentary on John* were written in Alexandria, probably soon after *Princ.*

The Holy Spirit

1.3.1. Following on, then, we must now investigate as briefly as we are able the subject of the Holy Spirit. All who perceive, in whatever way, the existence of providence, confess that God, who created and arranged all things, is unbegotten and confess him as the Father of the universe.[1] That he has a Son is not only declared by us; although this may seem sufficiently strange and incredible to those considered philosophers among the Greeks and barbarians, yet the belief in him seems to have been held by some even of them, in their acknowledging that all things were created by the word or reason of God.[2] We, however, by faith in that teaching which we hold for certain to be divinely inspired, believe that it is possible in no other way to explain and to bring to human knowledge a higher and more divine teaching regarding the Son than by means of those Scriptures alone which were inspired by the Holy Spirit, that is, the evangelical and apostolic Scriptures and also, according to the statement of Christ himself, those of the law and the prophets.[3] But of the subsistence of the Holy Spirit, no one could have even a suspicion, except those who were familiar with the law and the prophets, or those who profess a belief in Christ. For although no one is able to speak worthily of God the Father, it is nevertheless possible to gain some notion of him from the fact of the visible creation and from those things which the human mind naturally perceives;[4] and it is possible, moreover, for this to be confirmed from the holy Scriptures.[5] But regarding the Son of God, although *no one knows the Son except the Father*,[6] however it is again from the holy Scriptures that the human mind is taught how it ought to think of him too; not only from the New, but also from the Old Testament, through those things which, though done by the saints, are figuratively referred to Christ, and from which it is possible to perceive both his divine nature and also the human nature assumed by him.

1.3.2. Many passages of the Scriptures have taught us that there is the Holy Spirit, as when David, in the fiftieth Psalm, says *And take not your Holy Spirit from me*,[7] and in Daniel, where it is said, *The Holy Spirit which is in you*.[8] And in the New Testament we are taught by abundant testimonies, as when the

---

[1] For the description of God as 'father of the universe', see above, *Princ.* 1.1.6, and the material cited in n.22 there.

[2] Cf. Plato, *Ep.* 2.312e–313a, cited in Origen, *Cels.* 6.18, and Plato *Ep.* 6.323d cited in *Cels* 6.8. See also Plato, *Tim.* 34b, alluded to by Justin Martyr, *1 Apol.* 60.

[3] Cf. Luke 24:25–7; John 5:39, 46.

[4] Cf. Origen, *Comm. Rom.* 1.16; *Comm. Cant.* 3 (GCS 8, p. 208); *Hom. Lev.* 5.1; Sel. Ex. 12:43–4 (PG 12, 285d).

[5] E.g. Wis. 13:1–9, esp. v. 5; Rom. 1:20.   [6] Matt. 11:27.   [7] Ps. 50:13.

[8] Dan. 4:6(9) Θ.

Holy Spirit is related to have descended upon Christ,[9] and when the Lord himself breathed upon the apostles after the resurrection, saying, *Receive the Holy Spirit,*[10] and to Mary it is said by the angel, *The Holy Spirit shall come upon you,*[11] and Paul teaches that *No one can say that Jesus is the Lord except in the Holy Spirit,*[12] and, in the Acts of the Apostles, *through the laying on of the apostles' hands the Holy Spirit was given* in baptism.[13] From all of which we learn that the substance of the Holy Spirit was of such authority and dignity that saving baptism is not complete except by the authority of the most excellent of all, the Trinity,[14] that is, by the naming of the Father, Son, and Holy Spirit,[15] and that the name of the Holy Spirit is also joined to the unbegotten God the Father and to his only-begotten Son. Who, then, is not amazed at the greatness of the majesty of the Holy Spirit, when he hears that *he who shall speak a word against the Son of man* may hope for forgiveness, but *he who shall blaspheme the Holy Spirit shall have no forgiveness, neither in the present world nor in that to come?*[16]

1.3.3. That all things were created by God and that there is no being that exists which has not received its existence from him is established from many declarations throughout the whole of Scripture, while those claims falsely advanced by some regarding matter coeternal with God or unbegotten souls, in which they would have it that God implanted not so much existence but quality and order of life, are refuted and rejected. For even in that little book called *The Shepherd* or *The Angel of Repentance,* composed by Hermas, it is thus written: 'First of all, believe that there is one God who has created and arranged all things; who, when nothing existed before, caused all things to be; and who contains all things, but himself is contained by none.'[17] And in the book of Enoch similar things are transcribed.[18] But up to the present time we have been able to find no passage in the holy Scriptures in which the Holy Spirit is said to be made or created,[19] not even in the way that we have shown above that Solomon speaks of Wisdom, or the way in which expressions such as Life or Word or the other titles of the Son of God, which we have treated, are to be

---

[9] Matt. 3:16 *et par.*   [10] John 20:22.
[11] Luke 1:35.   [12] 1 Cor. 12:3.   [13] Acts 8:18.
[14] The Greek word τριάς is found in Origen, *Comm. Jo.* 6.166; 10.270; *Comm. Matt.* 15.31; *Fr. Jo.* 20 and 36 (GCS 4, pp. 500, 512).
[15] Cf. Matt. 28:19.   [16] Matt. 12:32.
[17] Hermas, *Mand.* 1.1, cited also in Origen, *Princ.* 1.Pr.4.
[18] Enoch is cited by Origen in *Princ.* 4.4.8; *Hom. Num.* 28.2; *Comm. Jo.* 6.217; and *Cels.* 5.55, where he states that it is not generally held to be divine by the churches.
[19] That Rufinus has faithfully rendered Origen at this point is demonstrated by Rufinus, *Adult.* 1 and Jerome, *Ruf.* 2.15; in *Comm. Jo.* 2.73, Origen, on the basis of John 1:3, calls the Spirit γενητόν. See above, *Princ.* Pr.4, n.15.

understood.[20] *The Spirit of God*, therefore, who *moved upon the waters*,[21] as it is written, in the beginning of the creation of the world, I think to be none other than the Holy Spirit, so far as I am able to understand; just as, indeed, we have shown in our exposition of the passages themselves, not according to the narrative, but according to the spiritual understanding.[22]

1.3.4. Some of our predecessors have observed that in the New Testament, whenever the Spirit is named without that adjective, which designates the quality of the Spirit, the Holy Spirit is to be understood, as, for instance, *Now the fruit of the Spirit is love, joy, peace,* and the rest.[23] And again here, *Having begun in the Spirit, are you now concluding in the flesh?*[24] We, however, think that this distinction may also be preserved in the Old Testament, as when it says, *Who gives Spirit to the people who are upon the earth and Spirit to those who walk on it.*[25] For, without doubt, everyone who walks upon the earth, that is terrestrial and bodily things, participates also in the Holy Spirit, receiving it from God.[26] And my Hebrew master used to say that those two seraphim, which are described in Isaiah as six-winged, crying one to another, and saying, *Holy, holy, holy, Lord of Sabbaoth,*[27] were to be understood of the only-begotten Son of God and of the Holy Spirit.[28] And we think that that expression also, which is in the song of Habakkuk, *In the midst of the two living creatures* (or *of the two lives*), *you will be known,*[29] ought to be understood of Christ and of the Holy Spirit. For all knowledge of the Father is acquired through the revelation of the Son in the Holy Spirit, so that both of these, who are called *living beings* or *lives* by the prophet, exist as the cause of the knowledge of God the Father. For as it is said of the Son, that *no one knows the Father except the*

---

[20] Here Koetschau inserts, as Fragment 7, a sentence from Justinian, *Ep. ad Menam* (ed. Schwartz, 210.9–10); Fernandez would place this sentence in *Princ.* 1.2.6. It is included in the Appendix as item no. 5.

[21] Gen. 1:2.   [22] This work is no longer extant.

[23] Gal. 5:22.   [24] Gal. 3:3.   [25] Isa. 42:5.

[26] Given that Origen later (*Princ.* 1.3.5–8) holds that the Holy Spirit is given only to those who are thereby sanctified, it is probable that here Origen, following Isa. 42:5 LXX, made a distinction between breath (πνοή) and spirit (πνεῦμα), lost in Rufinus' translation of both terms by *spiritus*. Cf. Irenaeus, *Haer.* 5.12.2, commenting on the same passage of Isa.: 'thus telling us that breath is indeed given in common to all people upon earth, but that the Spirit is theirs alone who tread down earthly desires'.

[27] Isa. 6:2–3.

[28] This interpretation, again attributed to his Hebrew teacher, in *Princ.* 4.3.14, and *Hom. Isa.* 1.2; 4.1. According to Rufinus (*Apol. Hier.* 2.31, 50), Jerome inserted a statement ('Let no one think that there is a difference of nature in the Trinity when the offices of the persons are distinguished') when translating Origen's *Homilies on Isaiah*. This interpretation, of Jewish-Christian background (its origin is not identifiable), became a routine point of objection against Origen. See Jerome, *Epp.* 18A.7 (not mentioning Origen); 61.2; 84.3; the comments of Antipater of Bostra, *apud* John of Damascus, *Sacra Parallela* (PG 96, 505); and Justinian, *Ep. ad Menam* (ed. Schwartz, 210.7–14).

[29] Hab. 3:1.

Son, and he to whom the Son chooses to reveal him,[30] the same again does the Apostle say of the Holy Spirit, when he states, *God has revealed to us by his Spirit, for the Spirit searches out everything, even the deep things of God.*[31] And again in the Gospel, when the Saviour, mentioning the divine and profounder teachings, which his disciples were not yet able to receive, spoke thus to the apostles: *I have yet many things to say to you, but you cannot bear them now; when the Comforter, the Holy Spirit is come, who proceeds from the Father, he will teach you all things, and will bring to your remembrance all things that I have said to you.*[32] And one must understand, therefore, that as the Son, who alone knows the Father, reveals him to whom he will, so the Holy Spirit, who alone *searches even the deep things of God*, reveals God to whom he will. *For the Spirit breathes where it wills.*[33]

It is not to be supposed, however, that the Spirit also knows through the Son's revelation. For if the Holy Spirit knows the Father through the Son's revelation, he passes from ignorance to knowledge; and it is both equally impious and foolish to confess the Holy Spirit and yet to ascribe ignorance to him. For even if something else existed before the Holy Spirit, it was not by progression that he came to be the Holy Spirit, as if someone should dare to say that at the time when he was not yet the Holy Spirit he was ignorant of the Father, but that after he had received knowledge, he became the Holy Spirit; for if this were the case, the Holy Spirit would never have himself been in the unity of the Trinity,[34] that is, along with God, the unchangeable Father, and his Son, unless he had always been the Holy Spirit. To be sure, when we speak these words, such as 'always' or 'was' or adopt any similar word with temporal significance, they are to be taken simply and with due allowance, since the significations of these terms are temporal, but the things of which we speak, though spoken of by a stretch of language in a temporal mode, yet surpass in their nature every idea of a sense of time.[35]

1.3.5. Nevertheless it seems proper to inquire what is the reason why he *who is born again by God*[36] unto salvation has need of both the Father and the Son and the Holy Spirit, and will not obtain salvation apart from the entire Trinity, and why it is impossible to become a partaker of the Father or the Son without the Holy Spirit. In discussing these things it will undoubtedly be necessary to describe the working particular to the Holy Spirit, and that which is particular to the Father and the Son.[37] I am of the opinion, then, that the working of the

---

[30] Matt. 11:27.   [31] 1 Cor. 2:10.
[32] John 16:12–13; 14:26; 15:26.   [33] John 3:8.
[34] Cf. Origen, *Princ.* 1.8.3; *Hom. Num.* 11.8. On the word 'Trinity', see above, n.14.
[35] Cf. *Princ.* 4.4.1; *Fr. Jo.* 1 (GCS 4).   [36] 1 Pet. 1:3.
[37] Koetschau inserts here, as Fragment 9, a passage from Justinian, *Ep. ad Menam* (ed. Schwartz, 208.26–32); it is included in the Appendix as item no. 6.

Father and of the Son takes place in both saints and sinners, in rational human beings and in dumb animals, and even in things which are without life, and in absolutely everything that exists; but that the working of the Holy Spirit does not at all extend into those things which are without life, or into those which though living yet are dumb; nor is it even found in those who, though rational, still *lie in wickedness*,[38] not having converted to better things. In those alone, I think, who already turn to better things and walk in the ways of Jesus Christ,[39] that is, who are engaged in good actions and abide in God,[40] is there the work of the Holy Spirit.

1.3.6. That the working of the Father and the Son is both in saints and sinners is clear from this, that all who are rational beings are partakers of the Word of God, that is, Reason, and in this way, as it were, bear certain seeds, implanted within them, of Wisdom and Justice, which is Christ.[41] And in him who truly exists, who said by Moses, *I am who I am*,[42] all things that are have participation, which participation in the God and Father extends to all, the righteous and sinners, rational and irrational beings, and absolutely everything that exists. The Apostle Paul also certainly shows that all have participation in Christ, saying, *Do not say in your heart, 'Who will ascend into heaven?', that is, to bring Christ down, or 'Who will descend into the abyss?', that is, to bring Christ up from the dead. But what does Scripture say? The Word is near you, on your lips and in your heart.*[43] By this he indicates that Christ is in the hearts of all in respect of his being the Word or Reason, participating in which they are rational beings. That saying also, in the Gospel, *If I had not come and spoken to them, they would not have sin; but now they have no excuse for their sin*,[44] is clearly about those who have reached the age of reason, up to which time a human being does not *have sin* and from which age he is responsible for sin, and reveals how, by participation in the Word or Reason, human beings are said to *have sin*; evidently from the time they become capable of understanding and knowledge, when the reason implanted within them has suggested to them the difference between good and evil, and when they have already begun to know what evil is, if they do it they render themselves responsible for sin. And this is the meaning of the saying, that human beings *have no excuse for their sin*, that, from the time when the divine Word or reason has begun to show within the heart the difference between good and evil, they ought to avoid and guard against that which is evil; and also when it says, *Whoever knows to do good, but does not do it, it is sin*.[45] Moreover, that all human beings

---

[38] 1 John 5:19.   [39] Cf. 1 Cor. 4:17.   [40] Cf. Eph. 2:10; 1 John 4:13.
[41] Cf. Justin Martyr, *1 Apol.* 46; *2 Apol.* 10, 13; Origen, *Comm. Jo.* 1.243–6, 267–75; 2.15, 105–11; 6.188–90; *Hom. Jer.* 14.10.
[42] Exod. 3:14.   [43] Rom. 10:6–8; Deut. 30:14.
[44] John 15:22.   [45] Jas. 4:17.

are not without communion with God is taught in the Gospel in this way, with the Saviour saying, *The kingdom is not coming with observation; neither will they say, 'Lo, here it is!' or 'There!', but the kingdom of God is within you.*[46] But we must also see whether perhaps the same thing is meant by what is written in Genesis, when it says, *And he breathed into his face the breath of life, and the human being became a living soul.*[47] For if this is to be understood as applying generally to all human beings, then all human beings have a participation in God. But if it is understood as spoken of the Spirit of God, since Adam also is found to have prophesied some things,[48] then it may be accepted as given not generally but to whoever is holy.

1.3.7. Finally, also, at the time of the flood, when *all flesh had corrupted the way of God,*[49] it is written that God said, of the unworthy and sinners, *My Spirit shall not abide with those human beings for ever, for they are flesh.*[50] In this it is clearly shown that the Spirit of God is taken away from whoever is unworthy. In the Psalms, also, it is written, *You will take away their spirit, and they will die and return to the earth. You will send forth your Spirit, and they will be created and you will renew the face of the earth,*[51] which is clearly intended of the Holy Spirit, who, after sinners and the unworthy have been taken away and destroyed, creates for himself a new people and renews the face of the earth, when, through the grace of the Spirit, *laying aside the old human being with his actions,* they begin to *walk in the newness of life.*[52] And therefore what is said fitly applies to the Holy Spirit, because he will not dwell in all, nor in those who are flesh, but in those whose earth has been renewed. Finally, for this reason the Holy Spirit was handed over *through the laying-on of the apostles' hands* after baptism.[53] Our Saviour, also, after the resurrection, when *the old things had passed away and all things had become new,*[54] being himself *the new human being,*[55] and *firstborn from the dead,*[56] his apostles also being renewed by faith in his resurrection, said, *Receive the Holy Spirit.*[57] This is doubtless what the saving Lord himself meant in the Gospel, when he said that *new wine cannot be put into old wineskins,*[58] and commanded that new wineskins be made, that is, that human beings should *walk in the newness of life,*[59] that they might receive the new wine, that is, the newness of the grace of the Holy Spirit.

---

[46] Luke 17:20–1.   [47] Gen. 2:7.

[48] For Adam as a prophet, on the basis of Gen. 2:24 and Eph. 5:31–2, see Theophilus of Antioch, *Autol.* 2.28; Clement of Alexandria, *Strom.* 1.21.135; Origen, *Comm. Cant.* 2 (GCS 8, pp. 157–8).

[49] Gen. 6:12.   [50] Gen. 6:3.   [51] Ps. 103:29–30.

[52] Col. 3:9; Rom. 6:4.   [53] Acts 8:18.   [54] 2 Cor. 5:17.

[55] Eph. 2:15.   [56] Col. 1:18.   [57] John 20:22.

[58] Matt. 9:19, *et par.*   [59] Rom. 6:4.

In this way, then, is the working of the power of God the Father and of the Son extended without distinction over every creature, but participation in the Holy Spirit is possessed, we find, only by the holy ones. Accordingly it is said, *No one can say that Jesus is Lord except in the Holy Spirit.*[60] Even the apostles themselves are only just once deemed worthy to hear, *You shall receive power when the Holy Spirit has come upon you.*[61] For this reason, also, I think it follows that he who has sinned against the Son of man is worthy of forgiveness,[62] because he who is a participant in the Word or Reason, if he ceases to live reasonably, seems to have fallen into ignorance or folly and therefore to deserve forgiveness; whereas he who has once been deemed worthy of participation in the Holy Spirit, and turned back again, is, by this very fact and deed, said to have blasphemed against the Holy Spirit.[63]

Let no one indeed suppose that we, from having said that the Holy Spirit is bestowed only upon the holy ones, but that the benefits or workings of the Father and of the Son extend to the good and to the bad, to the just and to the unjust, by so doing exalt the Holy Spirit over the Father and the Son, or assert that his dignity is greater; this would assuredly not follow at all. For it is the particularity of his grace and actions that we have been describing. Moreover, nothing in the Trinity can be called greater or less, for one fount of divinity upholds the universe by his Word or Reason and by the Spirit of his mouth sanctifies all things worthy of sanctification, as it is written in the Psalm, *By the Word of the Lord were the heavens established and by the Spirit of his mouth all their power.*[64] There is also a certain particular working of the God and Father, besides that which he bestowed upon all things so that they should by nature exist. And there is also a certain particular ministry of the Lord Jesus Christ to those upon whom he grants that they should be, by nature, rational; by this ministry it is given that they, in addition to being, might be good. And there is again another grace of the Holy Spirit, which is bestowed upon the deserving, through the ministry of Christ and the working of the Father, in proportion to the merits of those who have become capable of receiving it.[65] This is most clearly pointed out by the Apostle Paul, when explaining that the power of the Trinity is one and the same, in the passage where he says, *There are varieties of gifts, but the same Spirit; and there are varieties of ministries, but the same Lord; and varieties of workings, but it is the same God who works all in all. But to each is given the manifestation of the Spirit as is profitable.*[66] From which is most clearly shown that there is no separation in the Trinity, but that this, which is

---

[60] 1 Cor. 12:3.   [61] Acts 1:8.   [62] Cf. Matt. 12:32.
[63] Cf. Origen, *Comm. Jo.* 2.80; 28.124–5.   [64] Ps. 32:6.
[65] On the particular workings of the Father, Son, and Holy Spirit, see also Origen, *Comm. Jo.* 2.77; *Or.* 2.6; *Princ.* 2.7.3.
[66] 1 Cor. 12:4–7.

called the gift of the Spirit, is ministered through the Son and worked by the God and Father. *All these are worked by one and the same Spirit, dividing to each as he wills.*[67]

1.3.8. Having, then, made these declarations regarding the unity of the Father and of the Son and of the Holy Spirit, let us return to the order in which we began the discussion. The God and Father bestows upon all that they should be; and participation in Christ, in respect of the fact that he is the Word or Reason, renders them as rational beings. From which it follows that they are deserving either of praise or blame, because they are capable of virtue and vice. For this reason, consequently, there is present the grace of the Holy Spirit, that those who are not essentially holy may be made holy by participating in it. When, then, they have, firstly, from the God and Father, that they should be; secondly, from the Word, that they should be rational beings; thirdly, from the Holy Spirit, that they should be holy—they become capable of Christ anew, in respect of his being the Righteousness of God, those, that is, who have previously been sanctified by the Holy Spirit; and those who have been deemed worthy to progress to this level by the sanctification of the Holy Spirit will attain, no less, to the gift of wisdom according to the power and working of the Spirit of God. This is what I think Paul means when he says that, *to some is given the word of wisdom, to others the word of knowledge, according to the same Spirit.*[68] And, while pointing out each distinction of gifts, he refers them all to the fount of the universe and says, *there are varieties of workings, but one God who works all in all.*[69] Whence also the working of the Father, which confers existence upon all things, is found to be more glorious and magnificent, while each one, by participation in Christ, as wisdom and knowledge and sanctification, makes progress and comes to a higher level of perfection; and when one who is sanctified by this participation in the Holy Spirit is made purer and cleaner, he more worthily receives the grace of wisdom and knowledge so that, when all stains of pollution and ignorance are removed and cleansed, he may receive so great an advance in cleanliness and purity that what he received from God—that he should be such—is such as to be worthy of God, of him who gave it indeed to be pure and perfect; so that the one who is thus may be as worthy as he who made him be this. For in this way he, who is such as the one who made him wished him to be, will receive from God the power always to be and to abide forever. That this may come to pass and that those who were created by him may unceasingly and inseparably be present with He Who Is— this is the work of wisdom, to instruct and to train them and to lead them on to perfection by the strengthening and unceasing sanctification of the Holy Spirit, by which alone they are able to attain God.

[67] 1 Cor. 12:11.   [68] 1 Cor. 12:8.   [69] 1 Cor. 12:6.

In this way, then, through the ceaseless working of the Father and of the Son and of the Holy Spirit on our behalf, exercised at each stage of progress, we may just, if firm, at the last behold the holy and blessed life,[70] in which, when after many struggles we are able to enter it, we ought so to continue that no satiety of that good should ever seize us,[71] but the more we perceive of its blessedness, the more the desire for it in us should be expanded and extended, while with ever more zeal and capacity we attain and hold fast the Father and the Son and the Holy Spirit.

But if satiety should ever take hold of any one of those who stand on the highest and perfect stage, I do not think such a one would be removed and fall all at once, but he must descend gradually and by degrees (so that it may sometimes happen that if a brief lapse takes place, the person quickly recovers and returns to himself), not come crashing down utterly, but retrace his steps and return to his former state and be able to re-establish that which had been lost through negligence.

1.4.1.[72] That we might show what is this decrease or fall of those who live negligently,[73] it will not seem out of place to employ a comparison for illustration. Suppose, then, someone who has gradually become experienced in practical or theoretical knowledge, for example of geometry or medicine, until he had reached perfection, having trained himself for a long time in its principles and practice, so as to acquire a complete mastery of the aforesaid art—it could never happen to such a one that, having fallen asleep skilled, he should wake up unskilled. It is not to our purpose now to adduce or note those accidents occasioned by some injury or weakness, for they do not apply to the proposed comparison or illustration. According, then, to what we have proposed, so long as that geometrician or doctor exercises himself in the study and the rational principles of his art, the knowledge of his discipline will remain with him; but if he is indifferent to the exercises and neglects its practice, then gradually, by his negligence, a few details will at first drop off, then next even more, until, over a length of time, everything departs into oblivion and is utterly effaced from the memory. It is certainly possible, when he has first begun to fall away and the corrupting negligence is still small, that he might, if aroused and returned speedily to himself, recover those things which had but recently

---

[70] Cf. Origen, *Or.* 25.1–2; *Mart.* 39; *Comm. Jo.* 20.288–93.

[71] On 'satiety' (κόρος), see Philo, *Her.* 240; *Post.* 145; *Abr.* 134; Origen, *Princ.* 3.1.13; 3.4.3.

[72] The Latin manuscripts here have the heading: 'On the Loss or Fall [of Rational Beings]'. What follows, however, is not a separate chapter, as is made clear in the opening words of *Princ.* 1.5.1, where a new chapter begins, and also by *Princ.* 1.7.1, which refers back to the preceding discussion (i.e. *Princ.* 1.5–6) as having treated rational beings.

[73] On negligence, see Origen, *Princ.* 1.6.2; 2.9.2; 2.9.6; 3.1.12; 4.4.9; *Comm. Jo.* 20.363; *Hom. Ezech.* 9.5; *Cels.* 6.45; 7.69.

been lost and cultivate anew those things which had been to that point only slightly abolished. Let us now apply this to those who have devoted themselves to the knowledge and wisdom of God, about whom the study and practice surpasses all disciplines in incomparable ways, and let us contemplate, according to the form of the comparison proposed, what is the acquisition of knowledge or what is its disappearance, especially when we hear from the Apostle what is said of those who are perfected, that they shall behold *face to face* the glory of the Lord *by the revelation of the mysteries*.[74]

1.4.2. But wanting to show the divine benefits bestowed upon us by the Father and the Son and the Holy Spirit, that Trinity which is the fount of all holiness,[75] we have spoken of these things by way of a digression and we have considered touching the subject of the soul, which came up, although cursorily, as we were discussing the related topic concerning rational beings. However, we shall more conveniently consider the whole subject of rational beings, which is divided into three genera and species, in the proper place, with our God through Jesus Christ and the Holy Spirit so allowing.[76]

1.4.3.[77] Therefore we call this blessed and ἀρχική (that is, sovereign, sustaining all things) <power>the Trinity.[78] This is the good God and benevolent Father of the universe, the δύναμις both εὐεργετική and δημιουργική,[79] that is, the power that does good and creates and provides. It is both absurd and impious to suppose that these powers have been idle at any time even for a moment. Indeed, it is unlawful to entertain the slightest suspicion that these powers, through which primarily God is worthily known, should at any time

---

[74] Cf. 1 Cor. 13:12; Rom. 16:25; Origen, *Princ.* 2.6.7; *Comm. Jo.* 1.93; 2.229; *Hom. Num.* 21.1; *Comm. Cant.* 3 (GCS 8, p. 183). At this point, Koetschau inserts into the text two sentences from Jerome, the first from *Jo. Hier.* 16 (PL 32, 368), the second from *Ep.* 124.3.1 (ed. Hilberg 3, 98.7–12); they are included in the Appendix as item no. 7. But, as Görgemanns and Karpp note (p. 187, n.2), the last sentence of *Princ.* 1.4.1, beginning 'Let us now apply this', functions not as an introduction to a new discussion, but as the conclusion to the preceding.

[75] Cf. *Comm. Jo.* 6.166.

[76] The division of rational beings into three genera and species is taken up in *Princ.* 1.5.1, where he discusses the holy and the wicked powers, and those who are in between, in a position of trial and struggle. A similar threefold classification is found in *Princ.* 1.8.4, in terms of the angelic orders, the opposing powers, and human beings.

[77] *Princ.* 1.4.3–5 is not found in one group of manuscripts (γ), and seems to have the character of a recapitulation; the other manuscripts have here the heading 'On things created and made', which is preserved, in parentheses, by Koetschau (but was not followed in this by Butterworth) and Crouzel and Simonetti, and by Görgemanns and Karpp as a sub-heading. *Princ.* 1.4.3 continues the subject matter of the opening words of *Princ.* 1.4.2, relegating the remainder of that paragraph to be picked up in the next section.

[78] The words in parenthesis, and following 'that is' in the next sentence, are clearly Rufinus' attempt to explicate the Greek terms. For the term ἀρχικός applied to the Trinity, see Origen, *Comm. Matt.* 15.31, and to teachings, *Comm. Jo.* 10.160.

[79] Cf. Origen, *Cels.* 5.15; *Fr. Jo.* 1 (GCS 4).

have ceased from workings worthy of him and have become inactive. For neither can it be supposed that these powers which are in God, more, which are God, could have been hindered from without, nor, on the other hand, with nothing obstructing them, can it be believed that they were reluctant or neglected to act and work things worthy of themselves. It is therefore not possible to imagine any moment whatsoever when that beneficent power did not work good. Whence it follows that there always were those for whom it worked good, that is, his works or creatures, and that, doing good by order and desert, God dispensed, in the power of this providence, his benefits upon them. And by this it seems to follow that at no moment was God not creator, nor benefactor, nor provident.

1.4.4. Yet, again, human intelligence is dulled and constrained regarding this point: in what way it is possible to understand that, from the fact that God is, his creatures have always existed and that they have subsisted, if we may so say, without a beginning, those things, that is, that must undoubtedly be believed by us to be created and made by God. Since, then, there is this conflict amongst human thoughts and reasonings, the strongest arguments on both sides presenting themselves and opposing each other, and each bending the intellect of the theorist in its own direction, because of the poor and small capacity of our intellects, this occurs to us, which can be confessed without any risk to piety: that God always has been Father, always having the only-begotten Son, who at the same time, as we explained above, is called Wisdom. This is that very Wisdom in whom God always delighted when the world was finished, that, by this, God might be understood to rejoice always.[80] In this Wisdom, therefore, who ever was with the Father, was creation always delineated and shaped, and there never was a moment when the prefiguration of those things, which were to be thereafter, was not in Wisdom.[81]

1.4.5. It is probably in this way, because of our weakness, that we will seem to hold a reverent belief about God, saying neither that creatures are uncreated and coeternal with God,[82] nor, on the other hand, that God did no good before, changing so that he might do so; for true is that text, *In Wisdom did you make all things*.[83] And assuredly if all things were made in Wisdom, since Wisdom always was, there always were in Wisdom, according to prefiguration and pre-formation, those things which afterwards were made substantially. This is, I think, the thought and meaning of Solomon, saying in Ecclesiastes: *What is that which has been made? The same as that which will be; and what is that*

---

[80] Cf. Prov. 8:30–1; Origen, *Comm. Jo.* 1.55.
[81] Cf. Origen, *Princ.* 1.2.2, 10; 2.3.6; *Comm. Jo.* 1.111, 113–15; 19.146–50; *Cels.* 5.22, 39; 6.64.
[82] Cf. Origen, *Princ.* 1.3.3; 2.9.2.   [83] Ps. 103:24.

which has been created? The same as that which will be created! There is nothing new under the sun. If anyone should speak of something and say, 'Look, this is new!', it has already been, in the ages that were before us.[84] If, therefore, particular things which are under the sun were already in the ages, which were before us, for *there is nothing new under the sun,* then[85] without doubt all genera and species always were, and perhaps even individual things. Nevertheless, either way the fact is made clear that God did not begin at a certain time to create, when he had not done so before.

[84] Eccles. 1:9–10.
[85] Cf. Justinian *Ep. ad Menam* (ed. Schwartz, 210.25–7), an extract said to come from *Princ.* 1 and numbered as Fragment 10 by Koetschau: 'All genera and species always were, but another says even that which is numerically unique; either way it is clear that God did not begin to create, having been idle before.'

Rational Beings

1.5.1. After the discussion concerning the Father and the Son and the Holy Spirit, which we have briefly treated, as far as we are able, it follows that we should also say a few words about the rational beings, their species and orders and functions, of the holy and also the wicked powers, and also about those who are between them, that is, the good and evil powers, who are, moreover, as yet placed in struggle and trial. For we find in the holy Scriptures very many names of certain orders and functions of holy beings, as well as of the opposite kind, which we shall first lay out, and then we shall attempt, to the best of our ability, to ascertain the meaning of them.

There are certain holy angels of God, whom Paul calls *ministering spirits, appointed to serve those who shall receive the inheritance of salvation.*[1] Also, in the writings of the same saint Paul we find him giving the names, from whence they are I know not, of certain *thrones and dominions and principalities and authorities,*[2] and after the enumeration of these, as if knowing that there are still other rational offices and orders beyond those which he named, he says of the Saviour, *Who is above every principality and authority and power and dominion, and every name that is named, not only in this age but also in that which is to come.*[3] From which he evidently shows that there are certain others besides those which he had mentioned, which may indeed be named in this age, but were not however named by him now, and perhaps were not known by anyone else; and that there are others, which may not be named in this age, but will be named in the age to come.

1.5.2.[4] Then, in the next place, one should know that every rational being that turns aside from the measures and ordinances of reason is undoubtedly involved in sin by this departure from what is right and just. Every rational being, therefore, is capable of praise and censure: of praise, if, in conformity to that reason which he has in himself, he advance to better things; of censure, if he depart from the order and course of what is right, for which he is rightly subject to pains and penalties.[5] And this is also thought to apply to the devil himself and those who are with him and are called *his angels.*[6] The titles of

---

[1] Heb. 1:14.   [2] Col. 1:16.

[3] Eph. 1:21. Cf. Origen, *Comm. Jo.* 1.215.

[4] Here the manuscripts contain the heading 'On the Opposing Powers'. The opening paragraph of this chapter specifies that it will deal with 'rational beings' in terms of their species, orders, and functions, beginning with the holy powers (the second paragraph of *Princ.* 1.5.1), then the wicked powers (*Princ.* 1.5.2), and then those in between (*Princ.* 1.5.2, third paragraph, on human beings, 'rational animals'); *Princ.* 1.5 then continues by discussing whether the first two categories were already made either holy or wicked, and as such are so by nature.

[5] Cf. Origen, *Princ.* 1.6.1; 2.10.4–5; *Cels.* 4.99; *Hom. Jer.* 20.2.

[6] Matt. 25:41; Rev. 12:7, 9.

these beings, however, have to be explained, that we may know who they are with whom our discussion must deal.

The name, then, of *Devil,* and *Satan,* and *Wicked One,* who is also described as being *the Enemy* of God,[7] is mentioned in many places of Scripture. Moreover, certain *angels of the devil* are mentioned,[8] and also a *ruler of this world,*[9] who, whether the devil himself or someone else, is not yet clearly manifest. There are also certain *rulers of this world* mentioned, possessing a kind of *wisdom* which is *to be destroyed;*[10] but whether these are those rulers, who are also those *principalities against whom we wrestle,*[11] or others, is not easily decided, it seems to me, by anyone. After the *principalities,* certain *powers* are also named, *against whom we wrestle* and maintain a struggle, as also *against the rulers of this world* and *the governors of this darkness;* and certain *spiritual hosts of wickedness in the heavenly places* are also mentioned by Paul himself.[12] And what is to be said of the *evil spirits* and *impure demons* who are mentioned in the Gospels?[13] Then, again, there are those called by a similar name, *things heavenly,* who are said to *bend,* or will bend, *the knee at the name of Jesus,* as well as *things earthly* and *things under the earth,* which Paul enumerates in order.[14]

And, in this context where we have been discussing rational beings, it would not be right to be silent regarding ourselves, human beings, for we are certainly said to be 'rational animals'[15]; this, indeed, is not to be idly passed over, that even of us human beings certain different orders are named, as when it is said, *The portion of the Lord is his people Jacob; Israel is the line of his inheritance,* whereas other nations are called a portion of the angels, since *when the Most High divided the nations and scattered the sons of Adam, he fixed the boundaries of the nations according to the number of the angels of God.*[16] And therefore, along with the other rational beings, we must examine the account of the human soul.

1.5.3. Since, then, so many and so important names of orders and offices have been mentioned, behind which it is certain that there are substantial beings, it must be inquired whether God, the Author and Creator of all things, made some of them holy and blessed, so that they could receive nothing at all of the

---

[7] Matt. 13:39.   [8] Matt. 25:41; Rev. 12:9.
[9] John 12:31; 14:30; 16:11.   [10] 1 Cor. 2:6.   [11] Eph. 6:12.
[12] Eph. 6:12.   [13] Luke 7:21; 4:33.   [14] Phil. 2:10.
[15] Cf. Aristotle, *Eth. nic.* 1.12.9–15. See also Porphyry, *Exp. Cat.* 60.18–19: λέγομεν γὰρ ἄνθρωπον εἶναι ζῷον λογικὸν θνητὸν νοῦ καὶ ἐπιστήμης δεκτικόν· and Gregory of Nyssa, *Hom. op.* 8: λογικόν τι ζῷον ἐστιν ὁ ἄνθρωπος.
[16] Deut. 32:9, 8. On the idea of the nations being assigned angels, see Sir. 17:17; *T. Naph.* 8; *Jub.* 15:31–2; Philo, *Post.* 91–3; Irenaeus, *Haer.* 3.12.9; Clement of Alexandria, *Strom.* 6.17.157.5; 7.2.6.4; Origen, *Princ.* 1.8.1; 3.3.2–3; *Hom. Jes. Nav.* 23.3; *Hom. Num.* 11.4; *Hom. Luc.* 12.3; *Cels.* 5:30.

contrary,[17] and made others in such a way that they were made capable of virtue as much as wickedness; or whether it should be supposed that he created some in such a way as to be altogether incapable of virtue and others able to receive no wickedness whatsoever, able only to remain in blessedness, and others again who can receive either. But, in order that our first inquiry may begin with the names themselves, let us consider whether the holy angels, from the point at which they exist, have always been holy, and are holy, and will be holy, and neither have ever received nor were able to receive an occasion of sin. Then, in the next place, let us consider whether those who are called holy *principalities* began, from the point they were created by God, to exercise power over others who were made subject to them, and whether these latter were created such and for this purpose, that they might be subordinate and subject.[18] Similarly, whether those who are called *authorities* were created such and for this purpose, that they might exercise authority, or whether this is some prize or reward for their virtue, by which they advanced to this authority and dignity. Moreover, also, whether those who are called *thrones* (or seats) acquired that seat and stability of blessedness simultaneously with the bringing forth of their substance, so that they possess this solely by the will of the Creator; and whether those who are called *dominions* did not have their dominion added to them as a reward for their progress, but given as a privilege of their creation, so that it is in some way inseparable from them and natural.

Now, if we accept the view that the holy angels and holy powers and the blessed seats and the glorious powers and the magnificent dominions possess those powers and dignities and glories by essence, it will doubtless appear to follow that those which have been mentioned with contrary functions must be regarded in the same manner; so that those principalities with whom is our struggle must themselves be supposed not to have received this determination of opposition and resistance to every good after falling from the good through the freedom of the will, but to have come into existence with it essentially in them. Similarly, also, with the authorities and powers: [it must be supposed that] the wickedness that is in them is not subsequent and posterior to their essence. Those, again, whom he called *governors and rulers of the darkness of the world*: [it must be supposed] that they rule and occupy the darkness not from the perversity of determination but from the necessity of their creation. Consequential reasoning itself forces the same thing to be thought regarding spirits of wickedness and evil spirits and unclean demons.

But if to think this regarding the wicked and opposing powers seems to be absurd—and it certainly is absurd that the cause of their wickedness should be separated from the determination of their own will and ascribed of necessity

---

[17] Cf. Clement of Alexandria, *Exc.* 12, on the 'protoctistes'.
[18] On the naming of angels according to their activity, see Origen, *Cels.* 5.4; *Comm. Jo.* 2.145.

to their Creator—are we not forced to acknowledge the same thing regarding the good and holy powers, that is, that it is not by essence that goodness is in them, which we have clearly shown to be the case with Christ and the Holy Spirit alone,[19] as also, undoubtedly, with the Father? For the nature of the Trinity has been shown to have nothing that is compound, lest these properties might seem to come to apply subsequently. From which it remains that, in the case of every creature, it is by its works and its movements that those powers, who appear to hold sway over others or to exercise authority or dominion, are set above and placed over those whom they are said to rule or on whom they exercise their authority, from their merits and not by a privilege of creation.[20]

1.5.4. But that we might not appear to be making assertions about such important and difficult matters solely on the basis of inference or to compel the assent of our hearers by conjectures alone, let us see whether we can obtain any statements from the holy Scriptures, by the authority of which these positions may be more credibly maintained. First we shall adduce what the holy Scriptures contain regarding wicked powers; then we shall next investigate the others, as the Lord shall be pleased to enlighten us, that in matters of such difficulty we may arrive at what is closest to the truth or what should be our belief according to the rule of piety.[21]

Now, we find in the prophet Ezekiel two prophecies addressed to *the prince of Tyre*, the first of which might appear to anyone, before he heard the second also, to be spoken of some man who was the prince of the Tyrians. For the meantime, then, we shall take nothing from that first prophecy. But as the second is most clearly of such a kind that nothing may be understood as relating to a human being, but of some superior power who had fallen away from the superior things and been cast down into inferior and worse things, we shall take from it an illustration, by which it may be demonstrated most clearly that those opposing and wicked powers were not formed and created such by nature, but from what is better they came into what is worse, and were turned to what is worse;[22] and that those blessed powers, also, were not of such a nature as to be unable to receive the opposite, should one so choose and be negligent and not guard with all care the blessedness of its condition. For if it is related that he, who is called *the prince of Tyre*, was amongst the saints and

---

[19] Cf. Origen, *Princ.* 1.2.13; 1.6.2; 1.8.3.

[20] Görgemanns and Karpp (p. 203, n.15) suggest that here is a more appropriate place for the material from Jerome that Koetschau placed within the text at the end of *Princ.* 1.4.1; for this material, see the Appendix, item no. 7.

[21] On 'rule' ($\kappa\alpha\nu\dot{\omega}\nu$), see above, *Princ.* Pr.2, n.7.

[22] On this point, and what follows regarding the Prince of Tyre, see Origen, *Princ.* 3.2.1; *Comm. Rom.* 5.10; *Hom. Ezech.* 13; *Cels.* 6.44.

was *blameless* and was placed *in the paradise of God*, adorned with *a crown of comeliness and beauty,* how, I ask, is it to be supposed that such a one was inferior in any way to any of the holy ones? For he is described as having been himself *a crown of comeliness and beauty* and as having walked blameless *in the paradise of God*; and how can anyone suppose that such a being was not one of those holy and blessed powers which, as assuredly placed in blessedness, one must believe to be endowed with no other honour than this?

But let us now see what we are taught by the words of the prophecy themselves. *The Word of the Lord,* he says, *came to me, saying: Son of man, take up a lament over the prince of Tyre, and say to him, Thus says the Lord God: You were a signet of likeness and a crown of beauty among the delights of the paradise of God; you were adorned with every fine stone or gem, and were clothed with carnelian and topaz and emerald and carbuncle and sapphire and jasper, set in gold and silver and agate and amethyst and chrysolite and beryl and onyx; you filled your treasuries with gold and your storehouses among you. From the day <you> were created with the cherubim, I placed you in the holy mountain of God. You were in the midst of the fiery stones; you were blameless in your days, from the day you were created until iniquities were found in you; from the abundance of your commerce you did fill your storehouses with iniquity and you sinned and were wounded from the mountain of God. And a cherub drove you from the midst of the fiery stones; your heart was elated because of your comeliness, and your knowledge was corrupted with your beauty; on account of the multitude of your sins, I cast you down upon the earth in the presence of kings; I have given you, because of your sins and your iniquities, to be an exhibition and laughing-stock; by your commerce you have polluted your holy places. And I shall bring forth fire from your midst, and it shall devour you, and I shall render you as ashes and cinders on the earth, in the sight of all who see you; and all who knew you among the nations, shall mourn over you. You shall become destruction, and shall exist no longer for ever.*[23]

These, then, being the words of the prophet, who is there who on hearing, *You were a signet of likeness and a crown of beauty among the delights of the paradise of God,* or on hearing that *From the day you were created with the cherubim, I placed you in the holy mountain of God,* could so weaken their meaning as to suppose that these things were said of some human being or saint, not to mention the prince of Tyre? Or what fiery stones will he imagine, in the midst of which any human being could have lived? Or who could be supposed to have been *blameless* from the very day he was created, yet when acts of wickedness were found in him some time later, it is said that he was cast down upon the earth? This certainly means that it is said of one who, not being upon earth, was cast down upon it, whose holy places are also said to be polluted.

---

[23] Ezek. 28:11–19.

We have shown, then, that these statements from the prophet Ezekiel regarding the prince of Tyre refer to an adverse power, by which it is most clearly demonstrated that that power was formerly holy and blessed, from which blessedness he fell, from the point when iniquity was found in him, and was cast upon the earth, and was not such by nature or creation. We think, therefore, that these words were spoken of a certain angel who had been appointed to the office of governing the Tyrian people, and to whose care their souls also seem to have been entrusted. But what Tyre, or what souls of Tyrians, we ought to understand, whether that Tyre situated within the region of the province of Phoenicia, or some other of which this one we know on earth is a figure, and whether the souls of the Tyrians are those of the former or those of the inhabitants of that Tyre which is spiritually understood, does not seem to need investigation here, lest perhaps we should appear to investigate in passing matters of such importance and so great obscurity that they demand a work and treatment of their own.[24]

1.5.5. Again, we are taught such things by the prophet Isaiah about another opposing power. He says, *How did the Day Star, who used to arise in the morning, fall from heaven? He who assailed all nations has been crushed and beaten to the earth. You said in your heart, 'I will ascend into heaven, above the stars of heaven shall I place my throne; I will sit upon a lofty mountain, above the lofty mountains which are towards the north; I will ascend above the clouds; I will be like the Most High.' But now you will be brought down to the lower world and to the foundations of the earth. Those who see you will be amazed at you, and will say, 'This is the human being who used to trouble the whole earth, who shook kings, who made the whole world a desert, who destroyed cities, who did not loose those who were in chains.' All the kings of the earth have slept in honour, each one in his own house; but you shall be cast out on the mountains, like an execrable corpse among the many corpses who have been pierced through with swords, and have descended to the lower world. As a garment clotted and stained with blood will not be clean, so too you shall not be clean, because you have destroyed my land and killed my people: you shall not remain for ever, most wicked seed. Prepare your sons for death because of the sins of your father,*[25] *lest they rise again and possess the earth as an inheritance and fill the earth with wars. I will rise up against them, says the Lord of Sabaoth, and cause their name and their remnant and their seed to perish.*[26]

---

[24] On the question of the 'Tyrians', especially in light of Matt. 11:21, see Origen, *Princ.* 3.1.17; 4.3.9; *Comm. Jo.* 10.286; *Hom. Ezech.* 13.1.

[25] All the manuscripts of *Princ.* have 'your father'; Crouzel and Simonetti translate as 'their father' following the LXX reading as given in Codex Marchalianus.

[26] Isa. 14:12–22.

Most clearly by these words is he, who formerly was the Day Star and used to arise in the morning, shown to have fallen from heaven.[27] For if, as some think, he was a being of darkness, how is he said to have formerly been the Day Star? Or how could he, who had nothing of the light in himself, arise in the morning? Moreover, the Saviour himself also teaches us, saying of the devil, *Behold, I see Satan fallen like lightning from heaven,*[28] for he once was light. Furthermore, our Lord, who is the truth, compared even the power of his own glorious advent to lightning, saying, *For as the lightning shines from one end of heaven to the other, so will be the coming of the Son of Man.*[29] Yet he neverthe-less compares Satan to lightning and says that he fell from heaven in order that, by this, he might show him to have been in heaven, to have had a place among the holy ones, and to have participated in that light in which all the holy ones participate, by which they are made *angels of light*[30] and the apostles are said, by the Lord, to be *the light of the world.*[31] In this manner, then, even this one was once light, before he went astray and fell to this place and had his glory turned into dust, which is the particular mark of the wicked, as the prophet also says, from which too he was called the *ruler of this world,*[32] that is, of an earthly habitation, for he ruled over those who were obedient to his wicked-ness, since *the whole of this world* (I now call 'world' this earthly place[33]) *lies in the evil* one,[34] that is, in this apostate. That he is an apostate (that is, fugitive[35]), the Lord also, in Job, says, *You will catch, with a fish hook, the apostate* (that is, a fugitive) *dragon.*[36] It is certain that by the dragon is understood the devil himself.[37]

If, therefore, the opposing powers are called apostates, and are said to have once been *blameless*, while to be *blameless* exists essentially in none except the Father and the Son and the Holy Spirit, but holiness is an accidental quality in every created being (for what is accidental is able also to fall away[38]), and those opposing powers were once *blameless* and were once amongst those who still remain *blameless*,[39] from this it is evident that no one is either essentially or

---

[27] Cf. Origen, *Princ.* 4.3.9; *Comm. Jo.* 10.286; *Hom. Ezech.* 13.1.   [28] Luke 10:18.
[29] Matt. 24:27.   [30] 2 Cor. 11:14.
[31] Matt. 5:14.   [32] John 12:31; 16:11.
[33] Cf. Origen, *Comm. Gen.* 3 (= *Philoc.* 14); *Comm. Jo.* 19.129; *Comm. Rom.* 3.1; *Cels.* 6.59; *Hom. Ps. 36,* 2.4; *Princ.* 4.3.10–12.
[34] 1 John 5:19.   [35] These are of course Rufinus' explanatory words.
[36] Job 40:25; 26:13.   [37] Cf. Origen, *Comm. Jo.* 20.182; *Or.* 26.5.
[38] Cf. Origen, *Princ.* 1.3.8; 1.5.3; 1.8.3.
[39] Note that there are some rational beings who have remained 'blameless', those, that is, who presumably exercise their given ministry for the benefit of others who have fallen away from their calling. Cf. Origen, *Princ.* 1.6.2; 1.8.4; 2.9; 4.2.7; 4.3.12; *Hom. Ezech.* 1.1–5; *Hom. Luc.* 34.4. In *Comm. Jo.* 2.175–92, Origen describes how John the Baptist and Isaiah were 'sent' for such ministry, and refers to the Hebrew document called 'The Prayer of Joseph', where this teaching is 'stated outright', 'namely that those better than other souls have descended to human nature from being angels' (*Comm. Jo.* 2.188).

naturally *blameless*, nor essentially polluted. And[40] it follows from this that it lies within ourselves and in our own actions whether we be blessed and holy, or, through sloth and negligence, we fall from blessedness into wickedness and ruin to such a degree that, through too great an advance, so to speak, in wickedness, one may descend even to that state (if one shall have neglected himself to such an extent) that he may become what is called an opposing power.

1.6.1.[41] An end or consummation would seem to be an indication that things are perfected and consummated.[42] Which now reminds us that, regarding these things which are so hard and difficult to understand, if anyone cherishes a desire to read them and to understand such things he ought to apply a perfect and instructed understanding, lest, perchance, if he has no experience in investigations of this kind, they may appear to him as vain and superfluous, or if, by other investigations, his mind is already prejudiced and closed, he may reckon these to be heretical and opposed to the ecclesiastical faith, not so much convincing by reason but determining by the prejudice of his own mind. These things are indeed spoken about by us with great fear and caution, discussing and investigating rather than establishing as fixed and certain. For it has been pointed out by us above what are those points that must be clearly determined by dogma, which, I think, we have done to the best of our ability when we spoke about the Trinity;[43] but now, however, we are occupied, as best we can, in matters of a kind needing discussion rather than definition.

There will be, then, an end and consummation of the world, when every one shall be subjected to punishments on account of sins; this time, when he will render to each one what is deserved, is known to God alone.[44] We think, indeed, that the goodness of God through Christ may recall his whole creation

---

[40] Cf. Jerome *Ep.* 124.3.2 (ed. Hilberg 3, 98.13–18): 'And, in a subsequent passage: moved, he said, by these reasonings we suppose that by their own free act some are numbered with the saints and servants of God, and others, through their own faults, departing from holiness fell into such negligence that they were changed into opposing powers.'

[41] Most manuscripts have the heading 'On the End or Consummation' here, though, as noted by Görgemanns and Karpp (p. 215, n.1), Origen does not in fact make a chapter division, as is seen by the fact that at the beginning of the next chapter, he refers back to the preceding pages as having discussed rational beings (i.e. *Princ.* 1.5–6). Although it might seem that here he begins a new topic, 'the end', as part of the 'ecclesiastical faith' (mentioned for the first time since the Preface), he looks to the 'end' *in order* to understand the beginning (see *Princ.* 1.6.2), and so continue the discussion begun in *Princ.* 1.5.3, on the question of whether the variety of rational beings results from their choices and actions or from God himself. Origen turns to 'the end', in a preliminary manner, in *Princ.* 1.6.4, and more fully in *Princ.* 3.6.

[42] On the different senses of the word 'end' ($\tau \acute{\epsilon} \lambda o s$), see Origen, *Sel. Ps.* (PG 12, 1053).

[43] Cf. Origen, *Princ.* 1.1–4.   [44] Cf. Origen, *Princ.* 1.5.2; *Cels.* 4.99; *Hom. Jer.* 20.2.

to one end, with even his enemies being overcome and subdued.[45] For thus says holy Scripture, *The Lord said to my Lord: Sit at my right hand, until I make your enemies a footstool for your feet.*[46] And if what the prophetic language means here is less than clear to us, we may learn from the Apostle Paul, saying more openly that, *For Christ must reign until he has put all his enemies under his feet.*[47] But if even that plain statement of the Apostle has not sufficiently informed us what is meant by *enemies being placed under [his] feet*, listen to him in what follows, *For all things must be subjected to him.*[48] What then is this *subjection* by which all things must be made subject to Christ? I am of the opinion that it is the same subjection by which we also wish to be subject to him, by which the apostles, and all the saints who have followed Christ, were also subject to him. For the word 'subjection', as to how we are subject to Christ, indicates the salvation, which is of Christ, of those who are subject; as David said, *Shall not my soul be subject to God? For from him comes my salvation.*[49]

1.6.2. Seeing, then, that such is the end, when all enemies will be subjected to Christ, and when the last enemy, death, will be destroyed and when the kingdom shall be delivered to the God and Father by Christ, to whom all things have been subjected,[50] let us, I say, from such an end as this contemplate the beginning of things.[51] For the end is always like the beginning, and, therefore, as there is one end of all things, so ought there to be understood one beginning of all things, and as there is one end of many things, so also from one beginning there are many differences and varieties, which, in turn, through the goodness of God and by subjection to Christ and through the unity of the Holy Spirit, are recalled to one end which is like the beginning: that is, all those who *bending the knee at the name of Jesus* have displayed by this the proof of their subjection to him, those who are *of the heavens and of the earth and of the regions under the earth*[52]—the entire universe being indicated by the three terms—those, that is, who from that one beginning, each one variously led by his own impulse, were arranged in different orders according to their merit, for goodness did not exist in them essentially, as it does in God and his Christ and the Holy Spirit. For in this Trinity alone, which is the author of all things, does goodness exist essentially; others possess it as an accident and something

---

    [45] On the final subjection of all things to God, see Origen, *Princ.* 1.2.10; 3.5.6–8; 3.6; *Comm. Jo.* 6.295–6; *Comm. Matt.* 16.8; *Comm. ser. Matt.* 8; *Hom. Ps. 36,* 2.1; *Hom. Lev.* 7.2. See also the comments in the Introduction, sections 3 and 5, regarding Origen's eschatology.
    [46] Ps. 109:1.   [47] 1 Cor. 15:25.   [48] 1 Cor. 15:27, 28.
    [49] Ps. 61:1.   [50] Cf. 1 Cor. 15:24–7.
    [51] On the relation between the beginning and the end, see *Barn.* 6.13; Origen, *Princ.* 2.1.1; 2.1.3; 3.6.3; *Comm. Jo.* 13.244; *Cels.* 8.72. See also the comments in the Introduction, sections 3 and 5, regarding creation and its completion.
    [52] Phil. 2:10.

that can be lost;[53] and only then are they in blessedness, when they participate in holiness and wisdom and in divinity itself.[54]

But,[55] if they are negligent and careless about such participation, then each one, by fault of his own slothfulness,[56] becomes—one more quickly, another more slowly, one to a greater extent, another to a lesser—the cause of his own lapse or fall. And since, as we have said, this fall or lapse, by which each one departs from his original state, has in itself the greatest diversity, according to the impulse of the intellect or intention, one falls slightly, another more seriously, to the lower things: in this is the just judgement of the providence of God, that it should happen to everyone according to the diversity of his conduct, in proportion to the merit of his declension and revolt. Certain of those, indeed, who have remained in that beginning, which we have described as being similar to the end which is to come, are allocated, in the ordering and arranging of the world, the rank of angels, others that of powers, others of principalities, others of authorities (clearly that they may exercise authority over those who need to have authority over their head[57]), others the rank of thrones (that is, having the office of judging or ruling those who need this), others dominion (doubtless over slaves); all of which divine providence bestows upon them, in fair and just judgement, according to their merit and the progress by which they advanced in the participation and imitation of God.[58] Those,[59] however, who have been removed from their state of primal blessedness, yet not removed irremediably, have been made subject to the governance and rule of those holy and blessed orders, which we have described above; availing themselves of their help, and being reformed by their instruction and salutary discipline, they may be able to return and be restored to their

---

[53] Cf. Origen, *Princ.* 1.4.3; 1.5.5; 1.8.3.

[54] Cf. Origen, *Princ.* 1.3.8; 3.6.1; *Mart.* 47; *Cels.* 3.47.

[55] Cf. Justinian *Ep. ad Menam* (ed. Schwartz, 210.29–211.7), an extract identified as coming from *Princ.* 1 and numbered by Koetschau as Fragment 11: 'For those who do not pay vigilant attention to themselves, changes of condition take place, from their own fault, either quicker or slower, greater or lesser, so that from this fault, by a divine judgement corresponding to the better or worse movements of each and according to merit, one will have an angelic rank in the future arrangement, or ruling power, or authority over certain beings, or a throne over subjects, or lordship over slaves; while those not completely falling away will have the oversight and aid of those mentioned. And thus for the most part it is from those set under the rulers and the authorities and thrones and dominions, and perhaps sometimes even from these, that the race of human beings will be constituted in the world in unity.'

[56] Cf. Origen, *Princ.* 3.3.6; *Frag. Lam.* 23 (GCS 3, p. 245).   [57] Cf. 1 Cor. 11:10.

[58] Cf. Origen, *Princ.* 1.8.4; 2.9.6; 3.6.1; *Hom. Ezech.* 1.3.

[59] Cf. Jerome, *Ep.* 124.3.3 (ed. Hilberg 3, 98.23–99.4), recounting the teaching of Origen, but not given as a direct quotation: 'Those who have wavered and faltered, but have not completely fallen down, shall be subjected to the care and rule and governance of better things, of principalities, powers, thrones, dominions; and perhaps of these the human race will be formed in one of the worlds when, according to Isaiah, there shall be a *new heaven and earth*.' Jerome's account continues at the beginning of *Princ.* 1.6.3.

former state of blessedness. It is from these, I suggest, as far as I am able to understand, that this order of the human race has been established, which, in the future age or in the coming ages, when there shall be a *new heaven and new earth*, according to Isaiah,[60] will certainly be restored to that unity promised by the Lord Jesus, praying to the God and Father on behalf of his disciples, *I do not pray for these alone, but for all who shall believe in me through their word, that all may be one, as I, Father, am in you, and you in me, that they also may be one in us;* and again, where he says, *That they may be one, even as we are one, I in them and you in me, that they may be perfected in one;*[61] and just as the Apostle Paul also confirms, saying, *Until we all attain to the unity of the faith in the perfect man, to the measure of the stature of the fullness of Christ;*[62] and just as the same Apostle now exhorts us, who even in the present life are placed in the Church, in which is the figure of the kingdom to come, to this same image of unity, saying, *That you all say the same thing, and that there be no divisions among you, but that you be perfected in one and the same mind and in one and the same judgement.*[63]

1.6.3. It[64] should be known, however, that some of those who fell away from that one beginning, which we have spoken about above, have given themselves to such unworthiness and wickedness that they have become undeserving of that instruction and training by which the human race, through the flesh, with the aid of the heavenly powers, is being instructed and trained, but, on the contrary, they are adversaries and opponents of those who are being trained and formed. And thus it is that this whole life of mortals is full of conflicts and struggles, for opposing and attacking us are those who have fallen from a better condition without any looking back, who are called *the devil and his angels*[65] and the other orders of wickedness, which the Apostle names amongst the opposing powers.[66]

But[67] whether any of these orders, which live under the rule of the devil and obey his malice, will be able in some future age to be converted to goodness,

---

[60] Isa. 65:17.   [61] John 17:20–3.

[62] Eph. 4:13.   [63] 1 Cor. 1:10.

[64] Cf. Jerome, *Ep.* 124.3.4 (ed. Hilberg 3, 99.4–9), continuing to recount Origen's teaching: 'Those, however, who have not become worthy, that they should return through the human race to their former state, shall become *the devil and his angels* and the worst kind of demons, and will be allocated, according to their varying merits, diverse offices in one of the worlds.'

[65] Matt. 25:31.   [66] Cf. Origen, *Princ.* 3.2.

[67] Cf. Justinian, *Ep. ad Menam* (ed. Schwartz, 211.10–12), an extract said to be from *Princ.* 1: 'But I think that of those subjected to the worst rulers and authorities and world-powers, in each world or certain worlds, some are perhaps able, through doing good deeds and wanting to transfer from these powers, to attain sometime to humanity.' Jerome's account (*Ep.* 124.3.5; ed. Hilberg 3, 99.9–14), continuing from the passages given in previous footnotes, runs as follows: 'The demons themselves and the rulers of darkness in any world or worlds, if they desire

through the faculty of free will which is in them, or whether persistent and inveterate wickedness might be changed, by habit, into a kind of nature,[68] you, reader,[69] must judge, that is, if in any way, both in these *seen and temporal* ages and in those *unseen and eternal* ages,[70] that portion will be wholly discordant from that final unity and harmony. In the meantime, however, both in these *seen and temporal* ages and in those that are *unseen and eternal,* all those beings are arranged in order, by reason, according to the measure and dignity of their merits, so that some at first, others second, some even in the last times and through heavier and severer punishments endured for long duration and, so to speak, for many ages, are renewed by these harsh correctives and restored, at first by the instruction of the angels, and then by the powers of a higher rank, that, advancing thus through each stage to better things, they arrive even at those things which are *unseen and eternal,* having traversed, by some form of instruction, every single office of the heavenly powers.[71] From[72] which, so I think, this consequence appears to be demonstrated, that every rational being is able, passing from one order to another, to go from each order to all and from all to each, while it continues, through its faculty of free will, susceptible of promotions and demotions according to its own actions and efforts.[73]

1.6.4. Now, since Paul says that some things are *seen and temporal,* and others, besides these, *unseen and eternal,*[74] we ask how those things which are seen are

to turn to better things, become human beings and thus revert to their original beginning, in order that, being disciplined in human bodies through punishments and torments, whether they bear them for a long or short time, they may reach again the exalted heights of the angels.' See also Jerome, *Jo. Hier.* 16 (PL 23, 368).

---

[68] On the idea of action being changed by habit into nature, see Origen, *Comm. Jo.* 20.174, and, in the case of the human soul of Christ, *Princ.* 2.6.5–6; see also *Hom. Jer.* 18.1, a propos of Jer. 18:1–16. For Aristotle, *Eth. nic.* 7.10.4 (1152a30–3), habit 'is like nature'. Clement of Alexandria also speaks of habit 'becoming nature', see *Strom.* 7.7.46.9; see also 4.22.138.3.

[69] Origen addresses his readers also in *Princ.* 2.3.7; 2.8.4, 5; 3.6.9.

[70] Cf. 2 Cor. 4:18.

[71] Cf. Origen, *Princ.* 1.6.2; 2.5.3; 2.10.6; 3.1.23; 3.6.6; *Cels.* 4.99; 5.31; *Hom. Exod.* 3.3.

[72] Cf. Jerome *Ep.* 124.3.6 (ed. Hilberg 3, 99.14–18), continuing his account of Origen's teaching: 'From which, by rational inference, it is shown that any rational creature can come to be out of any other, not once or suddenly but repeatedly: we may become angels and, if we live negligently, demons, and, in turn, demons, if they desire to possess virtues, may attain to the angelic dignity.' The following is also preserved in the Scholia on Dionysius the Areopagite's Ecclesiastical *Hierarchy* (PG 4, 173a): 'as Origen says in the first book of *On First Principles*: every argument shows, then, I think, that every rational being is able to come to be out of any other rational being whatsoever'.

[73] Görgemanns and Karpp add the following sentence from the Scholia on Dionysius the Areopagite's *Ecclesiastical Hierarchy* (PG 4, 173a), which follows immediately from the sentence quoted in the previous footnote: 'And after a little he adds, saying: after the end comes upon all, an emission and a fall take place again.'

[74] Cf. 2 Cor. 4:18.

transient—whether because there will be nothing at all after this [world], in all those periods or ages to come in which the dispersion and division from the one beginning is restored to one and the same end and likeness, or because while the form of the things that are seen passes away, their substance, however, is in no way corrupted.[75] And Paul seems to confirm the latter view, when he says, *The form of this world passes away.*[76] David, also, seems to indicate the same thing, when he says, *The heavens will perish, but you will endure; and they will all become old like a garment, and you will change them like clothing, like a garment they will be changed.*[77] For if the heavens are to be changed, assuredly that which is changed does not perish; and if the form of the world passes away, it is not, by any means, an annihilation or destruction of the material substance that is indicated, but a kind of change of quality and transformation of form takes place. Isaiah, also, when he says prophetically that *there will be a new heaven and a new earth,*[78] undoubtedly suggests something similar. For this renewal of heaven and earth, and the transmutation of *the form of this world,* and the changing of the heavens will undoubtedly be prepared for those who, travelling along the way which we have indicated above, are stretching out towards that end of blessedness, to which even the enemies themselves are said to be subjected, in which end God is said to be *all and in all.*[79] And if anyone thinks that in that end material, that is, bodily, nature will perish utterly, he cannot in any respect meet my argument, how beings so numerous and powerful are able to live and exist without bodies, since it is thought to be a property of God alone, that is, of the Father and of the Son and of the Holy Spirit, to exist without any material substance and apart from any association of a bodily addition.[80] Another, perhaps, might say that in that end every bodily substance will be so pure and refined that it must be thought of as the aether,[81] in a way, and of a heavenly purity and clearness. Just how it will be, however, God alone knows with certainty, and those who are his friends[82] through Christ and the Holy Spirit.

---

[75] On the issue of the transience, and permanence, of matter and corporeality, see *Princ.* 2.1–3; 3.6; 4.4.8.

[76] 1 Cor. 7:31.   [77] Ps. 101:27.   [78] Isa. 65:17.

[79] 1 Cor. 15:28. Cf. Origen, *Princ.* 3.6, for a full treatment of this verse.

[80] A point repeated at *Princ.* 2.2.2; 4.3.15.

[81] Origen rejects the idea of 'aether' as a fifth element, as was probably advocated in Aristotle's lost work *On Philosophy*; see Cicero, *Acad.* 1.7.26; Origen, *Princ.* 3.6.6; *Comm. Jo.* 13.126; *Cels.* 4.60.

[82] Cf. John 15:15; Jas. 2:23.

II: The Church's Preaching

The Celestial Beings

1.7.1.[1] The matters, then, which we have examined above, were considered by us in a more general manner, treating and discussing rational beings, more through discernment of inference than by dogmatic definition, after the place where we spoke, to the best of our ability, of the Father and the Son and the Holy Spirit. Let us now, therefore, in the following pages consider those matters that it is appropriate to discuss according to our teaching, that is, according to the faith of the Church.[2]

All souls and all rational beings, whether they are holy or wicked, were made or created. They are all, according to their proper nature, bodiless;[3] even despite this fact, that they are bodiless, they are nonetheless created, because all things were made by God through Christ, as John teaches, in a comprehensive way, in the Gospel, saying: *In the beginning was the Word, and the Word was with God, and the Word was God. The same was in the beginning with God. All things were made by him and without him was nothing made.*[4] Moreover, when describing created things by species, and numbers, and orders, the Apostle Paul, who shows that all things were made through Christ, speaks in this way, saying: *And in him were all things created, things in heaven and things on earth, whether visible or invisible, whether thrones or dominions, or principalities, or authorities: all things were created by him and in him, and he is before all things, and he is the head.*[5] Clearly therefore he declares that *in* Christ and *through* Christ were all things made and created, whether *visible*, which are bodily, or *invisible*, which I judge to be none other than the bodiless and spiritual powers. But then, it seems to me, he enumerates, in what follows, the species of those things that he had called, in a comprehensive manner, bodily or bodiless: thrones, dominions, principalities, authorities.

1.7.2. We have made these preliminary remarks wanting to come, in order, to the investigation of the sun and moon and stars, through the method of

---

[1] Here the manuscripts have the heading 'On Things Bodiless and Bodily'. However, as *Princ.* 1.7.2 makes clear, the discussion of things bodiless and bodily in *Princ.* 1.7.1 is meant as a preliminary discussion to the subject matter of this chapter, that is, the sun, moon, and stars (which Koetschau, in his apparatus, suggests as a title), referred to collectively in this chapter as 'celestial beings'.

[2] Görgemanns and Karpp (p. 233, n.2), following Franz Heinrich Kettler (*Der ursprüngliche Sinn der Dogmatik des Origenes*, Beiheft 31 zur ZNW (Berlin: Töplemann, 1966), 31–2), would have the words 'according to our teaching, that is, according to the faith of the Church' begin the next paragraph; Crouzel and Simonetti, and Fernandez, keep this phrase with the preceding sentence. Cf. Manlio Simonetti, 'Osservazioni sulla struttura del De Principiis di Origene', *Rivista di filologia e d'istruzione classica*, N.S. 40 (1962), 273–90, 372–93, at 388–9.

[3] Although souls and rational beings are 'bodiless' in themselves, Origen is emphatic that they never exist without a body. Cf. *Princ.* 1.6.4; 2.2.2; 4.3.15; 4.4.8.

[4] John 1:1–3.   [5] Col. 1:16–18.

inference: [to ask] whether they also ought to be reckoned among the principalities, on account of their being said to be *made in* ἀρχάς (that is, *for rulership) of the day and of the night,*[6] or whether they are to be supposed to have only that rulership of the day and of the night which they accomplish in the office of illuminating them, but are not however of the order and office of principalities? Now, when it is said that *all things were made through him* and *in him were created all things, whether things in heaven or things on earth,* there can be no doubt that also those things which are in the firmament, which is called heaven[7] and in which *the lights* are said *to have been placed,* are to be numbered among the celestial beings. And, then, since the course of the discussion has clearly found that all things were made or created, and that among those things which were made there is nothing which may not accept good or evil, and be capable of either, how shall we reckon as consistent the opinion held even by some of our own people about the sun and moon and stars, that they are unchangeable and incapable of becoming the opposite of what they are? Not a few have thought such even about the holy angels, and certain heretics [have thought the same] even of souls, which they call spiritual beings.

First, then, let us see what reason itself can discover about the sun and moon and stars, whether what some suppose is right, that they are foreign to changeability; and, as far as possible, let the statement of the holy Scriptures be first adduced.[8] For Job appears to show that not only may the stars be subject to sins, but even that they are not clean from the contagion of sin. For it is written thus: *The stars also are not clean in his sight.*[9] This is certainly not to be understood of the splendour of their body, as if one were to say, for example, that a garment is not clean; if it were thus understood, then the injustice would without doubt rebound to the Creator, as if accused of the uncleanness in the splendour of their body. For if they are not able, by their own diligence, to assume for themselves a brighter body, or, through sloth, one less pure, why are *the stars* reproached for being *not clean,* since they would not be praised even if they were clean?

---

[6] Gen. 1:16. Rufinus' Latin text has kept the Greek word ἀρχάς, and explained it parenthetically; the word connection between Gen. 1:16 and Col. 1:16 is impossible to render in English: what is translated as 'rulership' is the same noun, in Latin and Greek, as what had previously been rendered as 'principality', one of the heavenly ranks.

[7] In *Princ.* 2.9.1, Origen differentiates between the 'heaven' and the 'firmament'.

[8] That the celestial bodies are animated and rational beings was a common place in antiquity (e.g. Plato, *Tim.* 40b; *Leg.* 10.898a and 899a; Alcinous, *Epit.* 14.7), and provided many occasions for criticism of astrology, fatalism, or worship of heavenly bodies (e.g. Origen, *Cels.* 5.8–11). As the following paragraphs make clear, however, Origen develops his cosmology by taking the language of Scripture at its word, literally.

[9] Job 25:5. In *Comm. Jo.* 1.257, Origen accepts that this might have been said 'hyperbolically'.

1.7.3. But to make this point more clearly understood, we ought to inquire, first, whether it is right to think that they are living and rational beings; then, next, whether their souls came into existence along with their bodies or whether they are discerned to be before the bodies; and, also, whether it is to be understood that, after the consummation of the age, they are to be released from their bodies and, just as we cease from this life, so they too will cease from illuminating the world. Although to inquire into these things may seem somewhat audacious, yet, roused as we are by the desire to ascertain the truth, it does not seem absurd to examine and to test, by the grace of the Holy Spirit, all that is possible for us.

We think, therefore, that they may be designated as living beings, because they are said to receive commandments from God, for that does not normally happen except to rational living beings. He speaks, thus, a commandment:[10] *I have commanded all the stars.*[11] What are these commandments? Clearly that each star, in its order and course, should supply the world with splendour to the extent entrusted to it. Those called 'planets' move in one kind of course, and those called ἀπλανεῖς [that is, 'fixed'] in another. It is most clearly shown from this, that no movement can take place in any body without a soul nor can living beings be at any time without movement.[12] With stars, then, moving with such order and regularity, such that their courses do not appear at any time ever to be derailed, how would it not be the height of obtuseness to say that such order and such observance of rule and plan is carried out or accomplished by irrational beings? In Jeremiah, indeed, the moon is even called *the queen of heaven.*[13] But if the stars are living and rational beings, without doubt there will appear among them both some progress and regress. For that which Job said, *And the stars are not clean in his sight*, seems to me to indicate some such idea.

1.7.4. It is now to be ascertained whether those beings, which the course of the discussion has found to be living and rational, appear to have received their soul together with their bodies, at the time when Scripture says that *God made two great lights, the greater light to rule the day and the lesser light to rule the night and the stars also,*[14] or whether the spirit was implanted not with [the creation of] their bodies but from without, once the bodies were made.[15]

---

[10] Koetschau supposes that there is an omission here, which would have included a citation of Ps. 103:19; however, see note by Crouzel and Simonetti, SC 253, p. 107, n.17.
[11] Isa. 45:12.   [12] Cf. Origen, *Princ.* 2.8.1; 2.9.2; 3.1.2; *Cels.* 6.48.
[13] Jer. 44:17–19, 25.
[14] Gen. 1:16. On the stars being commanded by God, see also Origen, *Cels.* 5.11; *Hom. Jer.* 10.6.
[15] Crouzel and Simonetti, SC 253, p. 108, n.23, suggest that the term translated by Rufinus as *spiritus* in this sentence and the next was νοῦς, 'intellect.' On the terminology of 'spirit' and 'soul,' see esp. *Princ.* 2.8.3–4.

I suspect, in fact, that the spirit was implanted from without, but it seems to be a valuable task to demonstrate this from the Scriptures. To make the assertion through inference will be seen to be easy, but assuredly more difficult for it to be established by the testimonies of the Scriptures. Now it may be shown to be possible by inference thus: if the soul of a human being, which, while it remains the soul of a human being, is certainly inferior, is proved to have not been made with the body but separately and implanted from without,[16] much more is this the case with those living beings which are called celestial. Now, with regard to the human being, how will the soul of him who supplanted his brother in the womb, that is, Jacob,[17] appear to be formed together with the body? Or how could the soul of him who, while lying in his mother's womb, was filled with the Holy Spirit, be formed or fashioned together with the body? I mean John, leaping in his mother's womb and jumping with great joy because the sound of the salutation of Mary had come to the ears of his mother Elizabeth.[18] How could that soul who, *before he was fashioned in the womb,* is said to be known by God, and, *before he came from the womb,* was sanctified by him, be formed or fashioned together with the body?[19] Otherwise it would seem that God fills some with the Holy Spirit neither by judgement nor according to merits, and sanctifies [them] undeservedly. And how shall we avoid that word which says, *Is there unrighteousness with God? By no means!*[20] Or this, *Is there no respect of persons with God?*[21] For this is the consequence of that defence which holds that souls come to exist together with bodies. Therefore,[22] so far as it is possible to adduce from a comparison with the condition of the human being, I think it follows that whatever reason itself and the authority of Scripture appear to show in the case of human beings, such ought much more to be held regarding celestial beings.

1.7.5. But[23] let us see whether we can find in holy Scripture any indications properly applicable to the celestial beings themselves. The Apostle Paul speaks

---

[16] The idea that the soul pre-exists its entrance, 'from without', into the body, is found in Platonism (e.g. Plato, *Phaed.* 76–7; Alcinous, *Epit.* 16.2; Philo, *Gig.* 12); however, as is clear, Origen develops his position by trying to take account of the particularity of the language of Scripture. See also Origen, *Princ.* 2.8.3–4; 2.9.6–7; 3.3.5; *Comm. Jo.* 13.327; 20.162; 20.182–3; *Cels.* 4.40; 5.29; 7.32; and the comments in the Introduction, sections 3 and 5, about creation.

[17] Cf. Gen. 25:22–6.

[18] Cf. Luke 1:41, 44; Origen, *Comm. Jo.* 6.252–6; *Hom. Luc.* 7–9.

[19] Cf. Jer. 1:5. These examples recur frequently in Origen in an anti-Gnostic and antideterminist context; see esp. *Comm. Jo.* 2.174–92; *Princ.* 2.9.7; 3.3.5.

[20] Rom. 9:14.   [21] Rom. 2:11.

[22] In place of this sentence, Koetschau substitutes a passage from Jerome, *Ep.* 124.4.1 (ed. Hilberg 3, 99.22–7), followed by a sentence from Justinian, *Ep. ad Menam* (ed. Schwartz, 212.20–3), said to come from *Princ.* 1, and numbered by Koetschau as Fragment 13; both texts are included in the Appendix as item no. 8.

[23] This passage echoed in Jerome, *Jo. Hier.* 17.

thus: *For,* he says, *the creation was subjected to vanity, not willingly but by reason of him who subjected it in hope, because creation itself shall be set free from the bondage of corruption into the glorious liberty of the sons of God.*[24] To what *vanity,* pray, was *the creation subject,* or what *creation,* or how is it *not willingly,* or *in* what *hope?* And how is the creation itself *to be set free from the bondage of corruption?* Moreover, the same Apostle also says in another place, *For the expectation of the creation waits for the revelation of the sons of God.*[25] And again elsewhere he says, *And not only we, but also creation itself groans and is in travail until now.*[26] Hence it must be asked what are its groans and what are the pains?

Let us first see, then, what is the *vanity* to which the creation is subject. I reckon that the *vanity* is nothing other than the body;[27] for although the body of the stars is ethereal,[28] it is nevertheless material. Whence also Solomon, it seems to me, arraigns the whole of bodily nature as somehow burdensome and impeding the vigour of spirits[29] this way: *Vanity of vanities, all is vanity, says the Preacher; all is vanity. I have looked,* he says, *and have seen all things that are under the sun, and, behold, all is vanity.*[30] To this, then, was creation subjected, especially that creation which assuredly possesses, by virtue of its function, the greatest and most eminent authority in this world; that is, the sun and the moon and the stars are said to be subject to *vanity* because they were clothed with bodies and allotted the task of giving light to the human race.

And this creation, he says, *was subjected to vanity not willingly.*[31] For it did not by will undertake rendering service to *vanity,* but because he who subjected it willed it, on account of the one who subjects it, promising those who were being subjected to *vanity* unwillingly that when the service of their distinguished work should be complete they would be set free from this bondage of corruption and vanity, when the time of the glorious redemption of the sons of God should have arrived. Having received this hope and hoping for the fulfilment of this promise, *the whole creation* now, in the meantime, *groans together,* as even suffering for those whom it serves, and patiently labours in pain, hoping for what has been promised.

---

[24] Rom. 8:20–1.   [25] Rom. 8:19.   [26] Rom. 8:23, 22.

[27] Cf. Origen, *Princ.* 2.8.3; 2.9.7; 3.5.4; *Comm. Jo.* 1.95–102; 1.173; *Cels.* 7.65; *Comm. Rom.* 7.4.

[28] By this, Origen means that the matter of stars is very refined, not that they (along with the intellect) are composed out of a fifth element, as was probably advocated in Aristotle's lost work *On Philosophy.* See Cicero, *Acad.* 1.7.26, and Origen, *Princ.* 3.6.6; *Comm. Jo.* 13.126; *Cels.* 4.60.

[29] Probably again translating the term νοῦς, 'mind' or 'intellect'; see above, n.15.

[30] Eccl. 1:2, 14.

[31] Rom. 8:20. It is important to note that in all this discussion about being subjected to vanity, despite many allegations from the time of Jerome to the present day, there is no mention of a prior sin nor of this as being punitive: it is a subjection to vanity, taken as embodiment, with a view to the revelation of the sons of God. For further discussion, see the Introduction, section 5.

Consider also that passage—whether perhaps this saying of Paul can also be applied to those who, although not willingly, yet by the will of him who subjected them and in hope of the promises, are made subject to vanity—where he says: *I would wish to be dissolved* (or *return*) *and be with Christ; for it is far better.*[32] For I think that the sun too might say likewise, '*I would wish to be dissolved (or return) and be with Christ; for it is far better.*' And whereas Paul adds, *But to remain in the flesh is more necessary on your account,*[33] the sun might say, 'To abide in this celestial and shining body is more necessary on account of *the revelation of the sons of God.*' One might well think and say the same regarding the moon and the stars.

Let us now consider what is *the freedom of the creation* and its *deliverance from bondage.*[34] When *Christ shall have delivered up the kingdom to the God and Father,*[35] then those living things, when they shall have first been made the kingdom of Christ, shall also be delivered up, together with the whole of that kingdom, to the rule of the Father; so that when *God shall be all in all,*[36] they also, since they are a part of the all, may have God in themselves, as he is in all things.

---

[32] Phil. 1:23. The connection between Rom. 8 and Phil. 1:23–4 is also made in *Comm. Jo.* 1.99–100 and *Comm. Rom.* 7.4.

[33] Phil. 1:24.

[34] Cf. Rom. 8:21. Koetschau here inserts a passage from Jerome *Ep.* 124.4.1–3 (ed. Hilberg 3, 100.2–17); it is included in the Appendix as item no. 9. Something is perhaps missing at this point, for Origen does not in fact go on to a lengthy discussion about *the freedom of the creation* and its *deliverance from bondage*; although, as he understands this to be the Christ's delivery of all to God, so that God might finally be *all in all*, which has already been treated in *Princ.* 1.6, there is not much more that needs to be said at this point.

[35] 1 Cor. 15:24.   [36] 1 Cor. 15:28.

Angels

1.8.1. A similar method or reasoning must be used in regard to the angels, it seems to me, not supposing that it happens accidentally that a particular office is assigned to a particular angel, curing and healing, for example, to Rafael, supervising wars to Gabriel, attending to the prayers and supplications of mortals to Michael.[1] It should be supposed that they deserve these offices in no other way than by their own merits and receive them on account of the zeal and virtue which they displayed before the construction of this world; then, afterwards, this or that kind of office was assigned to each in the order of archangels, while others deserved to be enrolled in the order of angels and to act under this or that archangel, or under that leader or ruler of his order.[2] All these things, as we have said, were arranged not accidentally nor indiscriminately, but by the most appropriate and righteous judgement of God and were disposed by merit, with God himself judging and approving: so that to one angel the Church of the Ephesians would be entrusted, to another the Church of the Smyrnaeans;[3] one angel was to be Peter's, another Paul's;[4] and then such and such angels, who *daily behold the face of God,* would be entrusted to each of *the little ones,* who are in the Church;[5] and there would also be some angel who *encamps round about them that fear God.*[6]

All of these [functions], assuredly, it is to be supposed, are not performed by accident or chance, nor because they [the angels] were made such by nature, lest in doing this God be charged with partiality; but it is to be believed that they were conferred by God, the most just and impartial ruler of all things, according to the merits and virtues and according to the activity and ability of each,[7] **1.8.2.** lest we fall into the silly and impious myths of those who imagine a diversity of spiritual natures, both among the heavenly beings and also between human souls, and on this basis [imagine] that they were established by different creators, for while it seems absurd, and really is absurd, that to one and the same creator should be ascribed diverse natures of rational beings, they are

---

[1] Cf. Tob. 3:17; *1 Enoch* 40:9; *III Bar.* 11–15; Origen, *Hom. Num.* 14.2; *Cels.* 1.25; *Hom. Jes. Nav.* 23.4.

[2] Cf. Origen, *Comm. Jo.* 1.216.   [3] Cf. Rev. 2:1, 8.

[4] Cf. Acts 12:15; Origen, *Hom. Luc.* 23; *Hom. Num.* 11.4.

[5] Matt. 18:10. On the 'guardian angels', see Origen, *Princ.* 2.10.7; 3.2.4; *Hom. Num.* 14.2; 20.3. *Hom. Jes. Nav.* 23.3; *Hom. Ezech.* 1.7; *Comm. Matt.* 18.10; *Hom. Luc.* 23.

[6] Ps. 33:8.

[7] At this point some manuscripts have the heading 'Concerning those who maintain that spiritual natures are of different kinds', which in other manuscripts appear as part of the text. Koetschau places these words as a heading in parentheses; Görgemanns and Karpp have relocated these words as a heading at the beginning of the paragraph (after the quotation from Ps. 33:8); Crouzel and Simonetti and Fernandez relegate these words to the text-critical apparatus. At this point Koetschau inserts a lengthy passage, as Fragment 15, which he composed out of various tendentious accounts of Origen's teaching; this is included in the Appendix as item no. 10.

nevertheless ignorant of the cause of that diversity.[8] They say that it does not seem logical that one and the same creator, with there being no grounds for merits, should confer upon some the power of domination and subject others to domination, that he should bestow principalities on some and make others subject to principalities. All such opinions, indeed, as I would reckon, are refuted and confuted by thinking through that reasoning which we developed above, by which the cause of the diversity and variety between each creature was shown to derive from their own conduct—whether more zealous or more sluggish, according to virtue or malice—and not to an unfairness on the part of the Arranger.

But, that this may be more easily understood to be the case with heavenly beings, let us borrow an example from what has been done or is done among human beings, in order that from visible things we may, by inference, behold things invisible too. They [our opponents] will affirm that Paul and Peter were without doubt of a spiritual nature.[9] When, therefore, Paul is found to have done much that is contrary to religion, in having persecuted the Church of God,[10] and Peter to have committed so grave a sin as, when questioned by the maid who kept the door, to have asserted with an oath that he did not know who Christ was,[11] how is it possible that these—who, according to them, were spiritual—should have fallen into sins like this, especially as they are in the habit of frequently asserting and saying that *it is not possible for a good tree to produce evil fruit?*[12] And if a good tree cannot produce evil fruit, yet according to them Paul and Peter were from the root of a good tree, how should they be considered to have brought forth fruits so wicked? And if they should give the answer which they generally fabricate—that it was not Paul who persecuted but some other, I know not whom, who was in Paul, and that it was not Peter who denied, but some other who denied in Peter—why did Paul say, if he had not sinned, that *I am not worthy to be called an apostle, because I persecuted the Church of God?*[13] And why did Peter weep most bitterly, if another sinned? From this, all their fooleries are shown.

1.8.3. According to us, however, there is nothing amongst all rational creation that is not capable of both good and evil. But it does not follow that, because we say there is no nature which is not able to allow evil in, we therefore affirm that every being has allowed evil in, that is, has become evil; but just as one may say that the nature of every human being has the possibility of sailing, but

---

[8] For accounts of such teachings, see Irenaeus, *Haer.* 1.6–7.
[9] Cf. 1 Cor. 2:12–16.   [10] Cf. 1 Cor. 15.9; Gal. 1:13.
[11] Cf. Matt. 26:69–74; John 18:17.
[12] Matt. 7:18; Luke 6:43; for the use of this verse, see also Clement of Alexandria, *Strom.* 3.5.44; Origen, *Princ.* 2.5.4; 3.1.18; *Comm. Jo.* 13.73; *Comm. Rom.* 8.11.
[13] 1 Cor. 15:9.

from that, however, it does not follow that every human being will sail; or, again, it is possible for every human being to learn the art of grammar or medicine, but it is not therefore proved that every human being is either a doctor or a grammarian; so, if we say that there is no nature which is not able to allow evil in, it has not necessarily been shown, however, [that every being] has allowed evil in.[14] For, in our view, not even the devil himself was incapable of good; but although able to allow the good in, he does not, however, also desire it or make any effort towards virtue.[15] For as we are taught by those quotations we cited from the prophets, he was at one time good, when he dwelt *in the paradise of God, among the cherubim*.[16] Just[17] as he had in himself the capacity of allowing in either virtue or evil, and falling away from virtue he turned with his whole mind towards evil, so also other creatures, having the capacity for either, by avoiding evil by their will, they cleave to the good.

There is no nature, therefore, which does not allow in good or evil except the nature of God, which is the fountain of all good things, and of Christ: for he is wisdom, and wisdom assuredly is not able to allow folly in; and he is righteousness, and righteousness will certainly never allow unrighteousness in; and he is word and reason, which indeed cannot be made irrational; moreover, he is also light, and it is certain that *darkness does not overcome* the light.[18] Similarly, also, the nature of the Holy Spirit, being holy, does not admit of pollution, for it is naturally or substantially holy. If any other nature is holy, it is so as sanctified by the reception or the inspiration of the Holy Spirit, not having this by nature, but as an accidental addition to it, for which reason, as an accidental addition, it may also be lost.[19] So too it is possible for a person to possess an accidental righteousness, whence also it is possible for the same one to fall away. And even the wisdom which a person has is still accidental, yet it is within our power, through our endeavour and worthiness of life, if we devote

---

[14] The text as preserved in Pamphilus' *Apology* (68) contains this extra sentence, which does not appear in any of the manuscripts of *Princ.*: 'and, on the other hand, there is no nature which may not allow good in, but neither, however, will it be proved thereby that every being has allowed in what is good'.

[15] A teaching of Origen also reported by Jerome, *Ep.* 124.4.4 (ed. Hilberg 3, 100.17–19), 'maintaining that while not incapable of virtue the devil has not chosen to be virtuous' (*adserens diabolum non incapacem esse uirtutis et tamen necdum uelle capere uirtutem*). Of Origen's dialogue with Candidus, Jerome (*Ruf.* 2.19) reports: 'Candidus asserted that the devil is of a nature wholly evil that can never be saved. Against this Origen rightly replied (*recte Origenes respondit*) that he is not of a substance destined for destruction, but that it is by his own will that he fell and can be saved. This Candidus falsely turned into a reproach against Origen, as if he has said that the diabolical nature could be saved'.

[16] Cf. Ezek. 28:13–14; Origen, *Princ.* 1.5.4–5.

[17] In place of this sentence, Koetschau substitutes, as Fragment 16, a sentence taken from Antipater of Bostra as quoted by John of Damascus, *Sacra Parallela* (PG 96, 505); it is included in the Appendix as item no. 11.

[18] John 1:5.   [19] Cf. Origen, *Princ.* 1.3.5–8.

ourselves to the work of wisdom, to become wise; and if we always demonstrate zeal for it, we shall always participate in wisdom, and that will happen to us to a greater or lesser extent, depending upon the worthiness of our life and the degree of our zeal. For the goodness of God, as is befitting to him, incites and attracts all to that blessed end, where *all pain and sorrow and sighing have fled away*[20] and disappear.

1.8.4. As far as it seems to me, I think that the preceding discussion has sufficiently proved that it is not from any random or chance occurrence that the principalities hold their princedoms or the other orders are assigned their respective offices, but they have obtained the degree of their dignity in proportion to their merits, although it is not for us to know or inquire what those acts were through which they deserved to come into a particular order. It is sufficient to know this much, to demonstrate the impartiality and righteousness of God, that, according to the statement of the Apostle Paul, *there is no respect of persons with God,*[21] who rather dispenses everything in accordance with the merit and progress of each. No angelic office, therefore, exists except by merit, neither do powers exercise their power except as a result of their progress, nor do those called thrones, that is, the judging and ruling powers, administer except by merits, nor do dominions exercise dominion otherwise than by merit, and this is the first order, supreme and most eminent, of rational creatures in the heavenly places, arranged in a glorious variety of offices.[22]

One should think in the same way of the opposing powers, who have given themselves over to such places and offices so as to be *principalities* or *powers* or *world rulers of darkness* or *spiritual hosts of wickedness*[23] or *malignant spirits* or *unclean demons,*[24] not holding this substantially, nor because they were created such, but having been assigned these degrees in malice in proportion to their conduct and the progress which they made in wickedness. And this is the other order of rational creatures, who have devoted themselves to wickedness so precipitously that they are unwilling rather than unable to recall themselves, as the frenzy for wicked deeds is now a passion and gives delight.

The third order of rational creatures is that of those spirits who are judged fit by God to replenish the human race, that is, the souls of human beings, some of whom, because of their progress, we see assumed into the order of angels,[25]

---

[20] Isa. 35:10.   [21] Rom. 2:11.

[22] Note again (as in *Princ.* 1.5.5, at n.39) that the angelic ranks, and their glorious arrangement, is not the result of a fall, but rather of their merit and progress, in service of others. Cf. Origen, *Princ.* 1.6.2; 2.9; 4.2.7; *Hom. Ezech.* 1.1–5.

[23] Eph. 6:12.   [24] Luke 7:21, 4:33. Cf. Origen, *Princ.* 1.5.2.

[25] Perhaps alluding to Matt. 22:30. Cf. Clement of Alexandria, *Paed.* 1.6.36; 2.10.110; *Strom.* 6.13.105; 7.14.84; Origen, *Comm. Jo.* 1.9; 13.41; *Hom. Lev.* 9.11; *Comm. Matt.* 17.30.

those, that is, who have been made *sons of God* or *sons of the resurrection*,[26] or who, forsaking the darkness, have loved the light and been made *sons of the light*,[27] or who, after winning every battle and being made peaceable, become *sons of peace*[28] or *sons of God*, or those who, mortifying their members on earth and rising above not only their bodily nature but even the ambiguous and fragile movements of the soul itself, have *united themselves to the Lord*, being made altogether spiritual that they may always be *one spirit* with him,[29] discerning every single thing with him, until they arrive at the point that they become perfected *spiritual beings* who *judge all things* by a mind illuminated in all sanctity by the Word and Wisdom of God, while they are utterly incapable of being judged by anyone.[30]

We[31] think that those views are by no means to be admitted which some are unnecessarily accustomed to inquire into or to advance, that is, that souls come to such a degree of abasement that, forgetting their rational nature and dignity, they descend even into the condition of irrational beings, either animals or beasts; in support of these claims they are accustomed to quote certain alleged proofs from Scripture: the fact, for instance, that a beast to which a woman has unnaturally given herself shall be deemed equally guilty with the woman and it shall be ordered to be stoned with her;[32] or that it is commanded to stone a bull that gores;[33] or even that Balaam's ass spoke, when *God opened its mouth*, and *the dumb beast of burden, answering with a human voice, reproved the madness of the prophet*.[34] All[35] these assertions, we not only do not

---

[26] Luke 20:36; Rom. 8:14.   [27] Luke 16:8.

[28] Matt. 5:9; Luke 10:6.   [29] 1 Cor. 6:17.

[30] 1 Cor. 2:15. At this point, Koetschau inserts his Fragment 17a, comprised of various tendentious accounts of Origen's teaching; it is included in the Appendix as item no. 12.

[31] In place of this sentence, Koetschau substitutes a passage from Justinian, *Ep. ad Menam* (ed. Schwartz, 211.19–23), said to be from *Princ.* 2 and numbered by Koetschau as Fragment 17b; the text is included in the Appendix as item no. 13.

[32] Cf. Lev. 20:16.   [33] Cf. Exod. 21:29.   [34] 2 Peter 2:16; cf. Num. 22:28–30.

[35] In the concluding lines of this paragraph, Origen, according to Rufinus, explicitly rejects the teaching that souls might descend to the level of irrational animals. Jerome, in *Ep.* 124.4.4–5 (ed. Hilberg 3, 100.19–101.4), claims that this in fact was the teaching of Origen: after claiming to quote Origen's very words (given in the Appendix as item no. 9), Jerome asserts that Origen, 'at the end' of his book, 'argues at great length that an angel, or a human soul, or a demon, which he asserts are of a single nature though of diverse wills, may through exceeding negligence or folly become a beast of burden, and that, to avoid the pain of punishment and burning of fire, it may choose rather to become a dumb animal or dwell in seas or rivers, or to take the body of this or that animal, so that we should fear not only the body of a quadruped but even a fish'. But then Jerome continues: 'And, at the end, not to be accused of the teachings of the Pythagoreans, who assert *metempsychosis*, after this wicked discussion, in which he has wounded the soul of his reader, he says, "These, in our mind, are not dogmas, but as inquiries and conjectures, so that they might not seem to be completely untouched" (*Haec inquit iuxta nostram sententiam non sint dogmata sed quaesita tantum atque proiecta, ne penitus intractata uiderentur*).' This version of the conclusion of this chapter is similar to Rufinus' other rendering, in his translation of Pamphilus' *Apology* (175): 'But these things, insofar as they concern us,

accept, but, running contrary to our faith, we refute and reject. After refuting and rejecting this perverse teaching, however, at the proper time and place, we shall show how those passages which they quote from the holy Scriptures ought to be understood.

are not dogmas, but have been said for the sake of discussion and are rejected. They have only been said lest it seem that a question that had been raised has gone unanswered' (*Sed haec quantum ad nos pertinet non sint dogmata sed discussionis gratia dicta sint et abiciantur. Pro eo autem solo dicta sunt ne uideatur quaestio mota non esse discussa*). The similarity between these passages of Jerome and Pamphilus/Rufinus is enough to establish that Origen did indeed conclude *Princ.* 1.8.4 this way, despite Jerome's attempt to suggest otherwise. For further discussion see Crouzel and Simonetti (SC 253, pp. 119–25). Origen consistently rejects the idea of *metempsychosis* or rather *metensomatosis*: see *Comm. Jo.* 6.66–71, 86 (which contrasts μετενσωμάτωσις with ἐνσωμάτωσις); *Cels.* 1.13; 5.29; 7.32; *Comm. Matt.* 11.17; 13.1.

The World

2.1.1.[1] Although everything that has been discussed in the preceding book has had reference to the world and its arrangement,[2] it now seems reasonable, however, to revisit a few particular points concerning the world, that is, about its beginning and end, and those events between its beginning and the end, which were arranged by divine providence, and about those which are supposed to have occurred before the world or after the world.

In this investigation, the first point which clearly appears is that its entire constitution, which is various and diverse,[3] consists of rational and more divine natures and of a diversity of bodies, and also of dumb animals, that is, wild beasts and farm animals and birds, and of all things which live in the waters; then, secondly, of places, that is of the heaven or heavens and earth and water, and also of the air, which is in the middle, which they call 'aether', and of everything which proceeds from, or is born of, the earth.[4] There[5] being, then, so great a variety in the world, and so great a diversity even among rational beings themselves, on account of which every other variety and diversity is thought to have come about, what other cause ought to be given for the existence of the world, especially if we consider that end, discussed in the preceding book, by which all things are to be restored to their original state? And if what was said there seems to be sound, what other cause, as we have said, can we imagine for the great diversity of this world, except the diversity and variety of the movements and declensions of those who fell away from that original

---

[1] Most manuscripts simply have here a capital letter demarcating the beginning of a chapter; one (Ab) has 'On the beginning and end of the world', and two others (B C) speak more broadly of the reasons and causes of the world and what is thought to be before and after the world. According to Photius, *Bibl.* 8 (ed. Henry 1, 4a5–6), the second book begins by treating 'the cosmos and created things in it' (περί κόσμου καὶ τῶν ἐν αὐτῷ κτισμάτων). As Origen specifies in the opening lines that he will not only treat of the beginning and the end of the world, but the arrangement of events between these two points, I have followed previous editors in entitling this chapter simply 'The World'; it must be borne in mind, however, that the subject of the 'world' is broader than the created world in general or materiality and embodiment in particular (though this is treated in *Princ.* 2.1.4–2.2); it includes also the arrangement (the *cosmos* in the sense of the Greek term. cf. *Princ.* 2.3.6) of rational creatures in all their variety and diversity, held together by providence as one harmonious body tending towards unity in God (*Princ.* 2.1.2–3).

[2] Although Origen says that 'everything that has been discussed in the preceding book' was concerned with 'the world and its arrangement', he clearly has in mind only *Princ.* 1.7–8, thus indicating more firmly that *Princ.* 1.7–8 is a continuous discussion distinct from *Princ.* 1.1–6.

[3] Cf. Origen, *Princ.* 2.9.2, 5.

[4] On the earth, see Origen, *Comm. Jo.* 19.130–42; *Cels.* 6.59; on the heavens, *Comm. Jo.* 19.143–50.

[5] Cf. Justinian, *Ep. ad Menam* (ed. Schwartz, 211.14–16), an extract numbered as Fragment 18 by Koetschau: 'Since the cosmos is so greatly varied and comprises so great a diversity of rational beings, what else can be said to be the cause of its existence, except the variety of the falling away of those declining dissimilarly from unity?'

unity and harmony in which they were at first created by God, and who, being disturbed and torn away from that state of goodness, and then being driven about by the diverse motions and desires of their souls, have drawn aside the single and undivided goodness of their nature, by the diversity of their inclinations, into the various qualities of minds?

2.1.2. But God, by the ineffable art of his wisdom, transforming and restoring all things, in whatever state they are, to some useful purpose and to the common advantage of all, recalls those very creatures, which differed from each other in the variety of so many souls, into one unanimity of work and endeavour, so that, although the motions of the souls may be diverse, they nevertheless bring to completion the fullness and perfection of one world, and the very variety of intellects tends towards the one end of perfection. For it is one power which grasps and holds together all the diversity of the world, and leads the various movements towards one work, lest such an immense work as that of the world should be dissolved by the dissensions of souls.[6] And for this reason we think that God, the father of all,[7] for the salvation of all his creatures through the ineffable plan of his Word and Wisdom, so arranged each thing, that every spirit[8] or soul, or whatever else the rational beings ought to be called, should not be compelled by force, against the freedom of its will, to anything other than that which the movements of its mind directs—for in that case the faculty of free will would seem to be taken away, which would certainly change the quality of the nature itself—and that the diverse movements of their wills would be suitably and usefully adapted to the harmony of one world, with some of them needing assistance and others being able to assist, some again providing struggles and conflicts for those who are making progress, whose diligence would be esteemed as more worthy of approval and the place of rank obtained after victory would be held more surely, as it has been established through the difficulties of the endeavours.

2.1.3. Therefore, although arranged into diverse functions, the condition of the whole world is nevertheless not to be thought of as being dissonant or discordant; but just as our one body is fitted with many members, and is held together by one soul, so also, I think, the whole world ought to be regarded as

---

   [6] Origen has a very strong conception of the providence of God. E.g. *Hom. Gen.* 3.2; *Cels.* 3.38; 4.74; 6.71; 7.68; 8.70. The apparently discordant and unequal variety and diversity of rational beings in the world, resulting from their differing movements in their freedom and self-determination, is simultaneously harmoniously arranged by God in such a way that what has been subjected to corruption is brought, through that corruption, into subjection to God so that God might be all in all. See *Princ.* 1.5–6; 1.7.5; 2.9.6–8; 3.1.21–4; 3.6.
   [7] Cf. Origen, *Princ.* 1.1.6, and n.22 there.
   [8] Perhaps 'intellect'; see above *Princ.* 1.7.4, n.15.

some immense and enormous animal, which is held together by the Power and Reason of God, as by one soul.[9] This, I reckon, is also indicated by holy Scripture by that passage, spoken through the prophet, *Do I not fill the heaven and the earth? says the Lord;*[10] and again, *Heaven is my throne, and the earth my footstool;*[11] and by what the Saviour said, when he tells us, *Do not swear, neither by heaven, for it is the throne of God, nor by earth, for it is his footstool;*[12] and further in what Paul affirms, when he addressed the assembly of Athenians, saying, *In him we live and move and have our being.*[13] For how do we *live and move and have our being* in God, except by the fact that he binds and holds together the whole world by his power? And how is the *heaven the throne of God* and *the earth his footstool*, as the Saviour himself declares, except by the fact that his power fills all things in heaven and in earth, as he says, *Do I not fill the heaven and the earth? says the Lord?* I do not think, therefore, from the passages which we have pointed out, that anyone will find it difficult to grant that God, the father of all, fills and holds together the world with the fullness of his power.

And now, since the argument of the preceding discussion has shown the diverse movements and varying opinions of rational creatures to have been the cause of the diversity that is in this world, it must be seen whether it is appropriate for this world to have an end similar to the beginning.[14] For there is no doubt that its end must be sought amidst much diversity and variety; and this variety, when found at the end of this world, will in turn provide causes and occasions for the diversities of the other world which is to come after this one; for clearly the end of this world is the beginning of the one to come.

2.1.4. If the course of the discussion has found this to be so, it now seems reasonable, since the diversity of the world cannot exist without bodies, to discuss the subject of bodily nature. It is evident from things themselves that bodily nature accepts diverse and various changes, such that it is able to be transformed from everything to everything, as, for example, the conversion of wood into fire, and of fire into smoke, and of smoke into air; and even oil, a liquid, is changed into fire. Does not food itself, whether of humans or of animals, show the same fact of change? For whatever it is that we take as food is

---

[9] An idea going back to Plato, *Tim.* 30b. For Alcinous, *Epit.* 14.3–4, the world was endowed with both a soul and an intellect. For Origen, it is Christ as the Power of God who permeates all: *Comm. Jo.* 6.154, 188–9; *Hom. Ps. 36*, 2.1. Cf. Justin Martyr, *1 Apol.* 60; *2 Apol.* 6.

[10] Jer. 23:24.   [11] Isa. 66:1.   [12] Matt. 5:34–5.

[13] Acts 17:28. Paul is quoting words often attributed to Epimenides, the seventh–sixth century BC Cretan philosopher.

[14] Cf. Origen, *Princ.* 1.6.2, where the end in question is the subjection of all things to God, whereas here the focus is on the origin of *this* world or arrangement of variety and diversity, which, when it comes to an end, still provides an occasion for further worlds or arrangements, a question picked up in *Princ.* 2.3.1 below.

converted into the substance of our body. But, although the way water is changed into earth or into air and air in turn into fire or fire into air, or air into water, is not difficult to explain, yet on the present occasion it is enough merely to call them to mind, as it is the subject of bodily matter that we want to discuss. By matter, then, we understand that which underlies bodies, that is, that from which, with the inclusion and insertion of qualities, bodies exist. We speak of four qualities: heat, cold, dryness, and wetness. These four qualities, being implanted in ὕλη, that is, matter (for matter is found to exist on its own definition, apart from those qualities we have mentioned above), produce the different kinds of bodies. Yet, although this matter, as we have said above, exists according to its own proper definition without qualities, it is however never found without qualities.[15]

This matter, then, which is so great, and such that it is able to suffice for all bodies in the world that God willed to exist and to attend upon and serve the Creator for whatever forms and species he wished in all things, receiving into itself whatever qualities he wished to bestow upon it—I do not understand how so many and such distinguished men have held it to be uncreated, that is, not made by God himself, the creator of all things, but that its nature and power were the result of chance. And I am astonished that they should find fault with those who deny that God is the maker of the universe or his providential administration of it, and accuse of impiety those who think that such a great work as the world could exist without a maker or overseer, while they themselves incur a similar charge for saying that matter is uncreated and coeternal with the uncreated God. According to their account, then, if we suppose, for example, that matter did not exist, as they maintain, saying that God could not create anything when nothing existed, without doubt he was idle, not having matter on which to work, matter which, they think, was available to him not by his own provision but by chance; and it seems to them that this, which was discovered by chance, was able to suffice for him for the immensity of such a work and for the exercise of the might of his power, that, receiving the plan of all his Wisdom, it might be separated and formed into a world. This seems to me to be very absurd and proper to human beings who are altogether ignorant of the power and intelligence of uncreated nature. But in order that we may look into the plan of things more carefully, let it be granted for a little while that matter did not exist and that God, when nothing existed before, caused to exist those things which he wished to exist: what are we to suppose? That God would have created matter either better or greater or of another kind

---

[15] For the background of this account of matter and qualities, resulting in bodies, see: Plato, *Tim.* 50b–51c; Alcinous, *Epit.* 8; Plutarch, *Comm. not.* 34, 48; Sextus Empiricus, *Adv. math.* 10.312. For Origen, see also: *Princ.* 3.6.6–7; 4.4.6–8; *Comm. Jo.* 13.127, 262–7, 429; *Cels.* 3.41; 4.54–7; 6.77.

than that which he produced from his own Power and Wisdom, in order that that might exist which formerly did not, or would he have created it inferior and worse, or similar to and the same as that which they call uncreated? Now, I think it will very easily be understood by anyone that neither a better nor inferior matter could have assumed the forms and species of the world, if it had not been such as that which did assume them. And, therefore, how will it not seem impious to call 'uncreated' that which, if believed to have been made by God, is found without doubt to be such as that which is called 'uncreated'?

2.1.5. But that we may believe on the authority of the Scriptures that this is so, hear how, in the book of Maccabees, where the mother of seven martyrs exhorts one of her sons to endure torture, this dogma is confirmed: *I implore you, my son, to look at the heaven and the earth and at all things which are in them, and, beholding these, to know that God made them when they did not exist.*[16] In the book of *The Shepherd* also, in the first Mandate, it says as follows: 'First of all believe that there is one God who created and arranged all things, and from that which was not made all things to exist.'[17] Perhaps also that passage in the Psalms refers to this, which says, *He spoke and they were made; he commanded and they were created.*[18] For when it says *he spoke and they were made*, it seems to be said to indicate the substance of things that exist; while when it says *he commanded and they were created*, it seems to be said of the qualities by which the substance itself has been formed.

2.2.1.[19] At this point, some are accustomed to inquire whether, just as the Father begets an only-begotten Son, and brings forth the Holy Spirit, not as if not previously being, but because the Father is the origin and source of the Son or the Holy Spirit, and no before or after can be understood in respect of them, so also a similar kind of association or relationship can be understood between rational beings and bodily matter. That they may examine this question more fully and attentively, they are accustomed to divert the beginning of the discussion elsewhere, in order to ask whether this very bodily nature, which bears the lives, and contains the movements, of spiritual and rational intellects, will, like them, endure eternally, or will absolutely perish and pass away. That this may be determined more precisely, it seems it must first be asked if it is possible

---

[16] 2 Macc. 7:28.
[17] Hermas, *Mand.* 1.1. The appeal to 2 Macc. and Hermas recurs in Origen, *Comm. Jo.* 1.103 in defence of the doctrine of creation *ex nihilo.*
[18] Ps. 32:9 and 148:5; this verse is also quoted in *Cels.* 2.9 and 6.60, though without a similar interpretation.
[19] The manuscripts have a separate heading at this point, 'On the Perpetuity of Bodily Nature', which is included as a separate chapter by Koetschau (and followed by Butterworth) and Görgemanns and Karpp; however, it is clear that Origen is continuing the discussion begun in *Princ.* 2.1, and which continues until the end of *Princ.* 2.3.

for rational beings to continue, completely bodiless, when they have reached the summit of holiness and blessedness (something which seems to me to be most difficult and almost impossible), or whether they must necessarily always be united to bodies. If, then, anyone is able to show a reason whereby it would be possible for them to be wholly without bodies, it would appear logical that as a bodily nature, created out of nothing after intervals of time, was thus produced when it did not exist, so also it would cease to exist when the need of its services had passed away.

2.2.2. If it is impossible for this point in any way to be maintained, that is, that any other being, apart from the Father, the Son, and the Holy Spirit, can live without a body, then the necessity of logic and reason compels one to understand that principally, indeed, rational beings were created, yet that material substance is to be separated from them only in thought and understanding and that it seems to have been formed either for them or after them, but that they never have lived nor live without it; for a bodiless life will rightly be considered only of the Trinity.[20] Now, that material substance of this world, as we have said above, having such a nature that accepts every kind of transformation, when it is dragged down to lower beings is moulded into the denser and more solid condition of body, so as to distinguish those visible and various forms of the world; but when it serves the more perfect and blessed beings, it shines in the splendour of *celestial bodies*[21] and adorns either the angels of God or the *sons of the resurrection*[22] with the garment of a *spiritual body*,[23] from all of which is composed the diverse and various conditions of the one world.[24]

But if one should desire to discuss these things more fully, it will be necessary to examine the holy Scriptures with greater attention and diligence, with all fear of God and reverence, to see if perhaps there can be found in them a secret and hidden meaning about these things, if there is anything in things

---

[20] Cf. Origen, *Princ.* 1.6.4; 1.7.1; 2.9.1; 4.3.15; 4.4.8. That rational beings are 'principally' created as such, yet united to material bodies that can only be separated 'in thought', see esp. *Comm. Jo.* 20.182: 'Because, therefore, the first human being fell away from the superior things and desired a life different from the better life, he deserved to be a beginning neither of something created nor made, but of *something moulded by the Lord, made to be mocked by the angels* [Job 40:19]. Now, our superior being is our being made *according to the image* [Gen. 1:26] of the Creator, but that resulting from a cause is in the thing moulded, which was received from the dust of the earth' (καὶ ἡμῶν δὲ ἡ προηγουμένη ὑπόστασις ἐστιν ἐν τῷ κατ᾽ εἰκόνα τοῦ κτίσαντος· ἡ δὲ ἐξ αἰτίας ἐν τῷ ληφθέντι ἀπὸ τοῦ χοῦ τῆς γῆς πλάσματι.) For the different words used to describe these different aspects of creation, and how they correlate, see the Introduction, section 3.

[21] 1 Cor. 15:40; cf. Origen, *Comm. Matt.* 17.30.

[22] Luke 20:36; Matt. 22:30.   [23] 1 Cor. 15:44.

[24] The life of the resurrection, in which there will still be differences (as Origen asserts, following 1 Cor. 15:41–2; e.g. *Princ.* 2.3.7), forming the diversity of that age and world, is thus not yet the final consummation, when, according to 1 Cor. 15:28, God will be 'all in all' (treated in *Princ.* 3.6).

abstruse and concealed (the Holy Spirit explaining the meaning to those who are worthy) about such matters, after many testimonies have been collected on this very idea.

2.3.1.[25] It remains, after these matters, to inquire whether there was any other world before this world which is now, and if so whether it was such as this one which is now, or slightly different or inferior; or whether there was no world at all, but something like that which we understand will be after the end of all things, *when the kingdom shall be delivered up to the God and Father,*[26] which, nonetheless, may have been the end of another world, of that, namely, after which this world began; and whether the various lapses of intellectual beings provoked God to this varied and diverse condition of the world. This point also, I think, must similarly be investigated, that is, whether after this world there will be any healing or improvement[27]—severe indeed and full of pain for those who were unwilling to obey the Word of God—through instruction and rational training, by which those may arrive at a fuller understanding of the truth who have devoted themselves in this present world to these pursuits and, being made more purified in intellect, they have advanced to be, here and now, capable of divine Wisdom; and whether after this the end of all things follows immediately, or whether, for the correction and improvement of those who need it, there will be again another world, either similar to this which now is, or better than it, or greatly inferior; and how long that world, whatever kind it is after this one, shall exist or whether it will exist at all; and whether there will be a time when there is no world anywhere, or whether there has been a time when there was no world at all; or whether there have been, or will be, many, or whether it shall ever happen that there will be one equivalent to another and like it in every respect and indistinguishable from it.[28]

---

[25] Most manuscripts have a separate heading at this point, 'The Beginning of the World and its Causes', included by Koetschau (followed by Butterworth) and Görgemanns and Karpp; however, again, as with *Princ.* 2.2, it is clear that there is no real break here, but that Origen is continuing the discussion begun in *Princ.* 2.1, which continues until the end of *Princ.* 2.3. Jerome, *Ep.* 124.5.1 (ed. Hilberg 3, 101.5–12), paraphrases Origen's discussion here in this manner: 'In his second book he asserts that there are innumerable worlds, not, as Epicurus, with many and similar ones existing at once, but that after the end of one world comes the beginning of another, and there was a world before this world of ours, and another will exist in turn after it, and another after that, another after another. He is in doubt whether there will ever be one world similar in every respect to another, so that they would appear to differ in no respect, or whether it is certain that there will never be one world totally indistinguishable and similar to another.'

[26] 1 Cor. 15:24.

[27] Cf. Origen, *Princ.* 1.6.3; 2.10.4–8. For an eschatological 'baptism of fire' or purification, see Origen, *Hom. Jer.* 2.3; *Hom. Lev.* 8.4; 14.3; *Comm. Matt.* 15.23; *Comm. Jo.* 2.57.

[28] This last possibility is refuted by Origen below in *Princ.* 2.3.4, and more fully in *Cels.* 5.20–3, where it is attributed to the Stoics.

2.3.2. That it may appear more clearly, then, whether the matter of bodies can subsist for periods of time and, just as it did not exist before it was made, so it may again be reduced such that it is not, let us first see whether it can possibly happen that someone lives without a body. For[29] if it is possible for someone to live without a body, then all things are able to be without a body, for all things, as our former treatise has shown, tend towards one end.[30] Now, if all things are able to dispense with bodies, there will undoubtedly be no bodily substance, for which there is no purpose. But how shall we understand that statement made by the Apostle in the places where he discusses the resurrection of the dead, when he says, *This corruptible [body] must put on incorruptibility and this mortal [body] must put on immortality. When this corruptible [body] shall put on incorruptibility and this mortal [body] shall put on immortality, then shall come to pass what is written: Death is swallowed up in victory'. 'O death, where is your victory? O death, where is your sting?' For the sting of death is sin, and the power of sin is the law.*[31] The Apostle, then, seems to suggest some such meaning: when he says, *this corruptible [body]* and *this mortal [body]*, with the gesture, as it were, of touching or pointing out, to what else does it apply except bodily matter? Therefore, this matter of the body, which is now corruptible, shall put on incorruptibility, when a perfected soul, instructed with the teachings of incorruptibility, shall have begun to use it.

And I would not have you surprised if we call a perfected soul the clothing of a body, for it, on account of the Word of God and his Wisdom, is now named *incorruptibility*; for, indeed, Jesus Christ himself, who is the Lord and the Creator of the soul, is said to be the clothing of the saints, as the Apostle says, *Put you on the Lord Jesus Christ.*[32] As Christ, then is the clothing of the soul, so by an intelligible kind of reason is the soul said to be the clothing of the body. For it is its ornament, covering and concealing its mortal nature.[33] The saying, *The corruptible must put on incorruptibility,* is, then, such as if he had said: 'this corruptible nature of the body must receive the clothing of incorruptibility, a soul possessing in itself incorruptibility, because, clearly, it has put on Christ who is the Wisdom and Word of God.' But when this body, which someday we shall have in a more glorious state, shall have become a partaker in life, it then accedes to what is immortal, such that it also becomes incorruptible. For whatever is mortal is, by consequence, also corruptible; but we cannot say, however, that what is corruptible is also mortal. Thus we call a stone or

---

[29] Cf. Jerome, *Ep.* 124.5.2 (ed. Hilberg 3, 101.13–18): 'And again a little further on he writes: If, he says, as the course of the discussion itself makes necessary, all things have lived without bodies, then all bodily nature will be swallowed up and what was once made out of nothing will be reduced into nothing, and there will be a time when its use is again necessary.'

[30] Cf. *Princ.* 2.1.2, and further back at *Princ.* 1.6.2.

[31] 1 Cor. 15:53–6; Isa. 25:8; Hos. 13:14.   [32] Rom. 13:14.

[33] Cf. Origen, *Comm. Jo.* 13.430; *Cels.* 5.19; 7.32; *Or.* 25.3.

piece of wood corruptible, but we do not, however, consequently call them mortal. But since the body participates in life, as life can be separated and is separated from it, we consequently call it mortal and, according to another sense, we also speak of it as corruptible.

With remarkable insight, therefore, the holy Apostle, first referring to the general cause of bodily matter—of which matter the soul always makes use, whatever the qualities are with which it is endowed, now, indeed, fleshly, but after a while more refined and pure, which are called spiritual—says, *This corruptible [body] must put on incorruptibility;* and second, referring to the special cause of the body, says, *This mortal [body] must put on immortality.* Now what else can this *incorruptibility* and *immortality* be except the Wisdom and the Word and the Righteousness of God, which mould and clothe and adorn the soul? And thus it comes about that it is said that the corruptible puts on incorruptibility and the mortal immortality. For, although we now may make great progress, as yet *we know in part and prophesy in part,* and *see through a glass darkly*[34] those very things which we seem to understand, *this corruptible [body]* does not yet *put on incorruptibility* nor is *this mortal [body]* encompassed with *immortality*; and since without a doubt this training of ours in the body is drawn out to a very long period,[35] that is, up to the time when our very bodies, with which we are encompassed, may, on account of the Word and Wisdom and perfect Righteousness of God, be worthy of *incorruptibility* and *immortality*, therefore it is said, *This corruptible [body] must put on incorruptibility and this mortal [body] must put on immortality.*

2.3.3. Nevertheless, those who think that rational creatures are able at any time to lead a life outside the body, may here raise such questions as the following. If[36] it is true that *this corruptible [body] shall put on incorruptibility and this mortal [body] shall put on immortality,* and that *death* shall be *swallowed up* at the end, this demonstrates nothing other than that material nature, upon which death could work, is to be destroyed, while those who are in the body seem to have the acumen of intellect dulled by the nature of bodily matter. If, however, they are outside the body, then they will escape all the vexation of this kind of disturbance. But since they would not be able to escape immediately all bodily clothing, they are first to be considered as lingering in more refined and purer bodies, which are stronger, beyond being conquered by death or pierced by *the sting of death*, so that, by the gradual cessation of material

---

[34] Cf. 1 Cor. 13:9, 12.   [35] Cf. Origen, *Princ.* 2.11.4–7.

[36] Jerome continues his account of Origen's words in *Ep.* 124.5.3 (ed. Hilberg 3, 101.18–25) in this way: 'And in the following: If, as has been demonstrated by reason and the authority of Scripture, *this corruptible [body] shall put on incorruptibility and this mortal [body] shall put on immortality,* and *death* shall be *swallowed up* in victory, then, perhaps, all bodily nature will be removed from the midst, for it is only in this that death can operate.'

nature, death may be *swallowed up* and, in the end, be destroyed, and all its *sting* completely blunted by divine grace, of which the soul has become capable and has thus deserved to attain incorruptibility and immortality. And then it will worthily be said by all, *Where, O death, is your victory? Where, O death, is your sting? The sting of death is sin.* If,[37] therefore, these conclusions seem to be logical, it follows that it must be believed that our condition will at some future point be bodiless; and if this is admitted, and all are said to be subjected to Christ, it is necessary that this [bodiless condition] be conferred on all to whom subjection to Christ extends, since[38] all who are subject to Christ will in the end be subject to the God and Father, to whom Christ is said to deliver up the kingdom; and thus it appears that the use of bodies will then cease. And if it ceases, it returns to nothing just as it also did not exist before.

But let us see what happens to those who thus assert these things. For it will be seen to be a necessity that, if bodily nature be destroyed, it must be restored again and created,[39] since it seems possible that rational natures, from whom the faculty of free will is never taken away, may again be subjected to certain movements, granted this by God, lest, if they should always hold an unchangeable condition, they would be ignorant that it is by the grace of God and not by their own virtue that they have been placed in that final state of blessedness;[40] and these movements undoubtedly will again be accompanied by a variety and diversity of bodies, by which the world is always adorned, nor will the world ever be able to exist except from variety and diversity, which can in no way be effected without bodily matter.

---

[37] Cf. Jerome, *Ep.* 124.5.4 (ed. Hilberg 3, 101.25–102.4) continues his account of Origen's words thus: 'And a little further on: If these things are not contrary to the faith, perhaps one day we shall live without bodies. And if he who is perfectly subject to Christ is understood to be without body, and all are to be subjected to Christ, we also shall be without body when we have become perfectly subjected to him.'

[38] Cf. Justinian, *Ep. ad Menam* (ed. Schwartz, 211.25–7), an extract said to come from *Princ.* 2 and numbered by Koetschau as Fragment 19: 'But if those subject to Christ shall in the end be subject to God, then all will lay aside their bodies, and I think that then there will be a dissolution of bodily natures into non-being, to be restored a second time, if rational beings should fall again.' See also Jerome, *Ep.* 124.5.5 (ed. Hilberg 3, 102.4–16), continuing the above quotations: 'And in the same passage: When all things will be subjected to God, all bodies will have been laid aside; and then the entire nature of bodily things will be dissolved into nothing; but which, if necessity should demand it a second time, on account of a fall of rational creatures, it would come to exist again. For God has given souls over to struggle and conflict, in order that they may understand that the complete and final victory has been attained not by their own strength but by the grace of God. And, therefore, I think that on account of a variety of causes worlds become diverse and that the errors of those who contend that worlds are alike are shattered.'

[39] Cf. Origen, *Princ.* 3.6.3; 4.4.8.

[40] On the necessity of grace, see Origen, *Princ.* 3.1.15, 17, 24; *Com. Ps.* 4.6 (= *Philoc.* 26.7); *Cels.* 7.33; *Hom. Ps. 36,* 4.1.

2.3.4. Now, as for those who assert that worlds similar to each other and in all respects alike sometimes come into existence, I do not understand by what proofs they can defend this.[41] For if there is said to be a world similar in all respects to this world, then it will come to pass that Adam and Eve will do the same things as they did before, again the same flood, and the same Moses would again lead a people numbering six hundred thousand out of Egypt, Judas will also betray the Lord twice, Paul will a second time keep the clothes of those who stoned Stephen, and everything which has been done in this life will be said to be repeated: I do not think that this can be established by any reasoning, if souls are driven by freedom of will and maintain their progression or regression by the power of their will. For souls are not driven on in some cycle which revolves again to the same cycle after many ages, so as either to do or desire this or that, but at whatever the freedom of their own disposition aims, to that they direct the course of their actions.

For what is said by these persons is much the same as if one were to assert that if a bushel of corn were poured out on the ground it could happen that the way the grain fell would be identical and utterly indistinguishable the second time [as the first], such that every individual grain would lie, on the second time, close to that grain where it had been thrown before, and scattered in the same order and with the same marks as happened in the first pouring; which, with the innumerable grains in the bushel, is certainly an impossible thing to happen, even if they were to be poured out incessantly and continually for countless ages. Thus, it therefore seems to me impossible that the world could be restored for a second time, with the same order and with the same amount of births and deaths and actions; but that diverse worlds, with non-negligible variations, are able to exist, so that for certain clear causes the condition of one world may be better, while for other causes another worse, and for other causes another an intermediate condition. But what may be the number or the measure of this, I confess myself ignorant. If anyone is able to demonstrate it, I would gladly learn.

2.3.5. This world, however, which is itself called an *age*,[42] is said to be the end of many ages. Now the holy Apostle teaches that in that age which was before

---

[41] A Stoic position countered most fully by Origen in *Cels.* 4.67–8 and 5.20–1, where it is also attributed to the Platonists and Pythagoreans; in this passage of *Princ.* Origen takes scriptural figures for examples, in *Cels.* he takes figures from Greek history, especially Socrates.

[42] Perhaps Wis. 13:9. Cf. Origen, *Sel. Ps.* 5 (PG 12, 1172d): 'Aeon is a natural system containing different principles from various bodies on account of the knowledge of God' (Αἰών ἐστι σύστημα φυσικὸν, ἐκ σωμάτων ποικίλων λογικὰς διαφορὰς περιέχων τῆς τοῦ θεοῦ γνώσεως ἕνεκεν). P. Tzamalikos, *Origen: Philosophy of History and Eschatology* (Leiden: Brill, 2007), 190, suggests thinking of 'aeon' as 'space-time': 'The "world" is a reality which is made of two agents interwoven with each other: "the structure of the world" (the *spatial* element of space-time) and "time" (the *temporal* element of space-time).'

this Christ did not suffer, nor even in the age which was before that; and
I know that I am not able to enumerate the number of anterior ages in which
he did not suffer. I will quote, however, from what statements of Paul I have
come to this understanding. He says, *But now he has appeared, once for all, at
the consummation of the ages to take away sin by the sacrifice of himself.*[43] For
he says that he was *once for all* made a *sacrifice* and *he has appeared at the
consummation of the ages to take away sin.*[44] Now, that after this age, which is
said to have been made *for the consummation of* other *ages,* there will be yet
other coming ages, we have clearly learnt from Paul himself, who says, *That in
the coming ages he might show the immeasurable riches of his grace in kindness
towards us.*[45] He did not say, 'in the coming age,' nor 'in two ages,' but *in the
coming ages,* whence I infer, by his language, that many ages are indicated.

If, however, there is something greater than the ages—so that, among created beings certain ages may be understood, but among those which exceed
and surpass visible created beings [something greater than the ages], which
perhaps will take place in *the restitution of all things,*[46] when the universe will
come to a perfect end—then possibly that period in which the consummation
of all things will take place is to be understood as something more than an age.
In regard to this the authority of holy Scripture prompts me, which says, *For
an age and further;*[47] for when it says *further,* it undoubtedly wishes that something greater than an age be understood. And see if that which the Saviour
says, *I desire that where I am these also may be with me,* and, *as I and you are
one, so also these may be one in us,*[48] does not seem to point to something more
than an age or ages, perhaps even more than the *ages of ages,*[49] that is to say,
that period when all things are no longer in an age, but when *God is all in all.*[50]

2.3.6. Having discussed, according to our ability, these points regarding the
subject of the world, it does not seem inappropriate to inquire what the very
term 'world' means, which term in holy Scripture is shown frequently to have
different significations. For what we call in Latin 'world,' is termed in Greek

---

[43] Heb. 9:26.

[44] The same affirmation is found in Origen, *Or.* 27.15 and *Comm. Jo.* 1.255. Jerome (*Ruf.*
1.20), on the other hand, asserts: 'Your Origen allows himself to treat of *metempsychosis,* to
introduce an innumerable number of worlds, to clothe rational creatures in one body after
another, and to say that Christ has often suffered, and will suffer again, it being always profitable to undertake what has once been profitable.' See also the texts cited in the Appendix, item
no. 23. Origen does indeed speak of the sacrifice of Christ being offered for the salvation of
those on earth and those in heaven, and of the crucifixion being both invisible and visible, but
it is always the single sacrifice of the cross. Cf. Origen, *Hom. Lev.* 1.3–4; *Hom. Jes. Nav.* 8.3;
Hom. Luc. 10.3.

[45] Eph. 2:7. Cf. Origen, *Comm. Jo.* 13.351.   [46] Acts. 3:21.

[47] Cf. Ps. 113:26, 125:8, 124:2.   [48] John 17:24,21.

[49] Cf. Gal. 1:5; 1 Tim. 1:17.   [50] 1 Cor. 15:28. Cf. Origen, *Princ.* 3.6.

κόσμος; and κόσμος signifies not only 'world' but also 'ornament'.[51] Consequently, in Isaiah, where a reproving speech is directed to *the ruling daughters of Sion,* and he says, *instead of a head ornament of gold, you will have baldness because of your works,*[52] he uses for *ornament* there the same word as for world, that is, κόσμος. It is even said that the clothing of the high priest contained a plan of the world, as we find in the Wisdom of Solomon, when it says that *Upon the long robe was the whole world.*[53] This earthly sphere of ours, with its inhabitants, is also called *world,* as when Scripture says, *The whole world lies in wickedness.*[54] Indeed, Clement, a disciple of the apostles, mentions those whom the Greeks call ἀντίχθονας,[55] and other parts of the earthly sphere, to which no one of our people is able to approach, nor can any of those who are there cross over to us, which he also termed 'worlds', when he says, 'The ocean is impassable to human beings and the worlds which are beyond it, which are governed by these same ordinances of the ruler God'.[56]

That universe, which consists of heaven and earth, is also called a world, as Paul says, *For the form of this world will pass* away.[57] Our Lord and Saviour indeed points out a certain other world besides this visible one, which it is difficult to describe and point out, for he says, *I am not of this world.*[58] For he thus says, *I am not of this world,* as if he were of a certain other world. As we have already said, an exposition of this world is difficult for us, lest we afford to any an occasion for the supposition by which they think that we affirm the existence of certain 'images' which the Greeks call ἰδέας; for it is certainly foreign to our ways of thinking, to speak of a bodiless world that exists only in the imagination or in the unsteady realm of thoughts; and how they can affirm either that the Saviour is from thence, or that the saints will go thence, I do not see. There is no doubt, however, that something more glorious and splendid than this present world is pointed out by the Saviour, to which he invites and exhorts believers in him to aim. But whether that world, which he desires to be known, is far separated and divided from this either by space and nature and glory, or whether it is superior in glory and quality but confined within the limits of this world, which seems to me more probable, is nevertheless uncertain and, I think, an unsuitable subject for the thoughts and minds of human beings. But from what Clement seems to indicate when he says, 'The ocean is impassable to human beings and the worlds <which> are beyond it', naming in

---

[51] The following explanatory words are clearly written by Rufinus. Origen expounds the various meanings of the word 'cosmos' similarly in *Comm. Jo.* 6.301–5 and *Comm. Matt.* 13.20.
[52] Isa. 3:17, 24.   [53] Wis. 18:24.   [54] 1 John 5:19.
[55] Lit. people 'of the opposite earth', i.e. of the southern hemisphere. The idea of a 'counterearth' (ἀντίχθων) was invented by the Pythagoreans, according to Aristotle (*Cael.* 293a20–4); Stobaeus, 1.15.7, reports the teachings of Philolaus about this idea. The Latin geographer Pomponius Mela adopted the concept in the first century AD.
[56] *1 Clem.* 20.8.   [57] 1 Cor. 7:31.   [58] John 17:14, 16.

the plural the worlds beyond it, which he also indicates are directed and governed by the same providence of the most high God, he would seem to throw out to us some seeds of that understanding by which it might be supposed that the entire universe of things that exist, celestial and super-celestial, earthly and infernal, is called, generally, a single and perfect 'world,' within which, or by which, other worlds, if there are any, must be supposed to be contained.

Accordingly, some wish the sphere of the sun or moon, and of the other celestial bodies, which they call πλανήτας [literally 'wanderers,' that is, planets], to each be called 'world'; and also that the uppermost [sphere], which they call ἀπλανῆ ['non-wandering'], they nevertheless wish to be properly called 'world'. Finally they appeal to the book of Baruch the prophet as a witness to this asser-tion, because in it the seven worlds or heavens are more clearly indicated.[59] Nevertheless, above that σφαῖραν ['sphere'], which they call ἀπλανῆ ['non-wandering'], they would have another, which, just as our heaven contains all things under the heaven, so that one, they say, by its immense size and ineffable span encloses all the spheres within its more magnificent circumference, so that all things are within it, just as this earth of ours is under the heaven. This is also believed to be called in Scripture the *good land* and the *land of the living*,[60] having its own heaven, which we have spoken of before, in which heaven the names of the saints are said to be written or to have been written by the Saviour; by which heaven that earth is embraced and enclosed which the Saviour in the Gospel promises to the meek and gentle.[61] Furthermore they would have it that this earth of ours, which was formerly called *the dry land*, has been called by the name of that earth, just as *the firmament* was called *heaven* from the name of that heaven.[62] But we have treated such opinions more fully in the place where we had to inquire into what the meaning is of *In the beginning God created the heaven and the earth*.[63] For another heaven and another earth are shown to exist besides that *firmament* which is said to have been made after the second day, or that *dry land* which was afterwards called *earth*.

---

[59] This must be *Third Baruch* (the *Greek Apocalypse of Baruch*), though in the text as we now have it, which is probably incomplete, Baruch travels through only five heavens. Irenaeus (*Dem.* 9), commenting on the seven spirits named by Isa. 11:2–3, had also spoken of seven heavens; as does *Ascen. Isa.* 7–9, which describes a journey through the firmament and the seven heavens though only six heavens and the firmament are mentioned in *Ascen. Isa.* 10. Aristo of Pella is also reported to have taught seven heavens (cf. PG 4, 421bc).

[60] Cf. Exod. 3:8; Jer. 11:19; Ps. 26:13, 141:6.   [61] Cf. Matt. 5:4.

[62] Cf. Gen. 1:10, 8. See Origen, *Sel. Ps. 36*, 2 (PG 12, 1332–3): 'There is also that other earth, of which the Scripture speaks, *flowing with milk and honey*, which the Saviour in the Gospels promises to the meek, when he says, *Blessed are the meek, for they shall possess the earth*. This earth of ours, which we inhabit, is in its proper designation called the *dry land*, just as the heaven which we behold is properly called the *firmament*. But the firmament takes the name of heaven from the name of that other heaven, as the Scripture teaches in Genesis.' See also *Hom. Ps. 36*, 2.4, 5.4; *Cels.* 7.28–9, 31.

[63] Gen. 1:1. This is not, however, treated in Origen's *Homilies on Genesis*.

Certainly what some say of this world—that it is corruptible because of the fact that it was made, and yet it is not corrupted, because the will of God, who made it and holds it together lest it should be mastered by corruption, is stronger and more powerful than corruption—may more correctly be supposed of that world, which we have above called ἀπλανῆ ['non-wandering'], since, by the will of God, it is not at all subject to corruption,[64] because it has not admitted any causes of corruption. For it is obviously the world of saints and of those purified to resplendence, and not of the wicked like that world of ours. We must see if it is not perhaps in reference to that world that the Apostle said, *We look not to the things that are seen, but to the things that are unseen; for the things that are seen are temporal, but the things that are unseen are eternal. For we know that if our earthly house of this tabernacle were destroyed, we have a building from God, a house not made by hands, eternal in the heavens.*[65] And when it says elsewhere, *Because I have seen the heavens, the work of your fingers,*[66] and when God said, through the prophet, about all things visible, that *My hand has made all things,*[67] he declares that that *eternal house* which he promises to the saints in heaven was not *made with hands,* undoubtedly demonstrating the difference of creation between those things that are seen and those that are not seen. When it says *those things that are not seen* it does not mean the same as 'those things that are invisible.' For those things which are invisible are not only not seen, but do not even possess a nature that is able to be seen, which the Greeks have called ἀσώματα, that is bodiless; whereas the things of which Paul says, *they are not seen,* possess a nature that is able to be seen, but, he explains, they have however not yet been seen by those to whom they are promised.[68]

2.3.7. Having[69] sketched, then so far as we have been able to understand, these three opinions about the end of all things and the supreme blessedness, let each one of our readers judge for himself, with all care and diligence,

---

[64] Cf. Rom. 8:20–1.   [65] 2 Cor. 4:18–5:1.

[66] Ps. 8:4.   [67] Isa. 66:2.

[68] Cf. Origen, *Frag. Jo.* 13 (GCS 4, pp. 494–5); *Cels.* 7.46; on the identity between the bodiless and invisible, see *Princ.* Pr.8–9; 1.7.1; 4.3.15.

[69] Cf. Jerome, *Ep.* 124.5.6 (ed. Hilberg 3, 102.16–103.6): 'And again: three conjectures of the end are suggested to us, from which the reader is invited to discover the truest and best. Either we shall live without a body, when, being made subject to Christ, we shall be made subject to God and God shall be *all in all*; or as things made subject to Christ shall be, with Christ himself, made subject to God and joined into one compact union, so every substance shall be refined into highest quality and rarefied into aether, which is of a purer and simpler nature; or else that sphere, which we have above called ἀπλανῆ [non-wandering] and whatsoever is contained within its span, will be dissolved into nothing, but that further sphere, by which the ἀντιζώνη [lower-zone] is held together and bounded, will be called the good land, while that other sphere, which revolves around this same land and is called *heaven*, will serve as a dwelling place for the saints.'

whether one of them can be approved and adopted.[70] It has been said that it
must be supposed either that it is possible to lead a bodiless life, after all things
have become subject to Christ and through Christ to the God and Father,
when *God will be all in all*.[71] Or that when all things have been made subject to
Christ, and through Christ to God, with whom they become *one spirit*,[72] by
virtue of the fact that rational beings are spirits, then the bodily substance
itself, being united to the best and most pure spirits and being changed, according to the quality or merits of those who assume it, into an ethereal character—
as the Apostle says, *and we shall be changed*[73]—and will shine with light. Or
else that when the *form* of those things which are seen *passes away*,[74] and all
corruptibility has been shaken off and cleansed away, and the entire condition
of this world, in which the spheres of the planets are said to be, has been super-
seded or transcended, there is established the abode, above that sphere which
is called 'non-wandering,' of the pious and the blessed, as it were, in a *good land*
and *the land of the living*,[75] which will be inherited by the meek and the gentle,
to which belongs that heaven (which, with its more magnificent circumference, surrounds and contains that land itself) which is truly and principally
called heaven; in this heaven and earth, the end and perfection of all things can
safely and most surely take place, where, that is to say, those who, after the
rebuke of punishments which they have endured, by way of purgation, for
their offences, fulfilling and discharging every obligation, may deserve a habitation in that land; while those who have been obedient to the Word of God
and, being compliant, have proved themselves already capable of receiving his
Wisdom, are said to be deserving of the kingdom of that heaven or heavens,
and thus the saying is more worthily fulfilled, *Blessed are the meek, for they
shall inherit the earth*, and *Blessed are the poor in spirit, for they shall inherit the
kingdom of heaven*, and what is said in the Psalm, *He shall exalt you and you
shall inherit the land*.[76] For it is called a descent to this earth, but an exaltation
to that which is on high. In this way, therefore, a sort of road seems to be
opened up for the progress of the saints, from that earth to those heavens, so
that they would appear not so much to remain in that land but to dwell there,
that is, to pass on, when they will have made progress in it, to the inheritance
of the *kingdom of heaven*.

---

[70] Origen addresses his readers also in *Princ.* 1.6.3; 2.8.4, 5; 3.6.9.
[71] 1 Cor. 15:28.   [72] 1 Cor. 6:17.   [73] 1 Cor. 15:51.
[74] Cf. 1 Cor. 7:31; 2 Cor. 4:18.   [75] Cf. Exod. 3:8; Jer. 11:19; Ps. 26:13, 141:6.
[76] Matt. 5:5, 3; Ps. 36:34.

PART TWO: ECONOMY

I: The Apostolic Preaching

That the God of the Law and the Prophets and the Father of our Lord Jesus Christ is One

2.4.1.[1] These matters having been discussed in order as best as we have been able, it follows, according to what we proposed at the beginning, that we refute those who think that the Father of our Lord Jesus Christ is a different God than him who gave Moses the sayings of the Law or sent the prophets, who is the God of the fathers Abraham, Isaac, and Jacob. For it is necessary, first of all, to be firm in this article of our faith. That expression, therefore, must be considered which is frequently uttered in the Gospels and is adjoined to every single act of our Lord and Saviour, *That it might be fulfilled what was spoken by this or that prophet,*[2] it being evident that the prophets are those of the God who made the world. From this, therefore, it is logically concluded that he who sent the prophets himself foretold what was to be foretold of Christ. And there is no doubt that the Father himself, and not another than him, foretold these things. The fact, moreover, that illustrations from the Old Testament are frequently given by the Saviour or his apostles indicates nothing other than the authority attributed by the Saviour and his apostles to the ancients. The fact, furthermore, that the Saviour, when urging his disciples to the exercise of kindness, says, *Be you perfect, as your heavenly Father is perfect, who bids his sun to rise on the good and on the evil, and sends rain on the just and on the unjust,*[3] suggests even to a man of the meanest intelligence the most obvious meaning, that he is putting before his disciples for imitation no other God than the maker of heaven and the giver of rain.

Again, when he says that those who pray ought to say, *Our Father who art in heaven,*[4] what else does it seem to indicate except that God is to be sought in the better parts of the world, that is, of his creation? And when, again, laying down those excellent principles regarding oaths, he says that one ought not to swear *neither by heaven, for it is the throne of God, nor by earth, for it is his footstool,*[5] does he not appear most openly to be in harmony with the words of the prophet, *Heaven is my throne and the earth is my footstool.*[6] And, yet again, when casting out of the temple those who sold sheep and oxen and doves, overturning the tables of the moneychangers, and saying, *Take these things away, and do not make my Father's house a house of trade,*[7] he undoubtedly called *Father* that God to whose name Solomon had raised up a magnificent temple. And, again, that passage which says, *Have you not read what was said*

---

[1] Photius, *Bibl.* 8 (ed. Henry 1, 4a6–8), describes this section as showing ὅτι εἷς θεὸς νόμου καὶ προφητῶν καὶ ὅτι ὁ αὐτὸς παλαιᾶς καὶ καινῆς διαθήκης θεός (that the God of the Law and the Prophets is one and that the same is God of the Old and New Testaments).

[2] Cf. Matt. 2:15; 4:14; etc. [3] Matt. 5:48, 45.

[4] Matt. 6:9. This text is cited to make a similar point by Clement of Alexandria, *Paed.* 1.8.72.

[5] Matt. 5:34–5. [6] Isa. 66:1. Cf. Origen, *Comm. Jo.* 6.201–2. [7] John 2:14–16.

by God to Moses: I am the God of Abraham and the God of Isaac and the God of Jacob; he is not the God of the dead but of the living,[8] most clearly teaches us that he called the God of the patriarchs, because they were holy and living, the God of the living, the same one, that is, who said in the prophets, *I am God and there is no God besides me.*[9] For if the Saviour, knowing that he who is written [of] in the law is *the God of Abraham,* and that it is the same one who says, *I am God and there is no God besides me,* confesses that this very one, who does not know of the existence of any other God above himself as the heretics suppose, is the Father, he absurdly declares that one to be the Father, who does not know of a higher God. If, on the other hand, it is not because he does not know, but he is deceitful in saying there is no other God than himself, then it is even more absurd that he should acknowledge his Father to be a liar. From all these points, the mind is led to this conclusion, that he knows of no other Father than God the maker and creator of all things.

2.4.2. It would be tedious if we were to collect out of all the passages in the Gospels the proofs by which the God of the Law and the Gospels is proved to be one and the same. Let us, however, touch briefly on the Acts of the Apostles, where Stephen and the apostles address their prayers to that God who made heaven and earth and who spoke by the mouth of his holy prophets, calling him the God of Abraham, Isaac, and Jacob, the God who led his people out of the land of Egypt.[10] These expressions undoubtedly direct our minds to faith in the Creator and implant an affection for him in those who have piously and faithfully learnt this about him, just as also the Saviour himself, when asked what was the greatest commandment in the Law, replied saying, *You shall love the Lord your God with all your heart and with all your soul and with all your mind. And the second is like unto it: You shall love your neighbour as yourself.* And to these he added, *On these two commandments hang all the law and the prophets.*[11] How, then, is it that he commends to him whom he was instructing and leading into discipleship this commandment above all other commandments, by which undoubtedly affection for the God of that Law was kindled, since these things had been said by the Law in these very words?[12]

But let it be granted, in the face of all these most evident proofs, that it is of some other unknown God that the Saviour says, *You shall love the Lord your God with all your heart,* and the rest of what was said. Now how, if the Law and the Prophets are from the Creator, as they say,[13] that is, from another God than him whom they call good, shall what he adds seem to be said logically, that, *On these two commandments hang the Law and the Prophets?* For how shall that

---

[8] Matt. 22:31–2.   [9] Isa. 46:9.   [10] Cf. Acts 4:24; 3:13, 18; 7:32, 34, 40, etc.
[11] Matt. 22:36–7, 39–40.   [12] Cf. Lev. 19:18; Deut. 6:5.
[13] Cf. Ptolemy, *Flor.* 7.2–4; Heracleon in Origen, *Comm. Jo.* 6.108–9.

which is strange and foreign to God depend upon God? And when Paul says, *I thank my God, whom I serve from my forefathers with a pure conscience,*[14] he transparently shows that he came to Christ not as to some new God. For what other forefathers of Paul are meant to be intended except those of whom he says, *Are they Hebrews? So am I. Are they Israelites? So am I.*[15] Does not the very preface of his Epistle to the Romans carefully demonstrate the very same point, to those who know how to understand the letters of Paul, that is, what God Paul preaches? For he says, *Paul, a servant of Jesus Christ, called to be an apostle, set apart for the Gospel of God, which he promised beforehand through his prophets in the holy Scriptures concerning his Son, who was made of the seed of David according to the flesh, but designated Son of God in power according to the Spirit of holiness by the resurrection from the dead of Jesus Christ our Lord,* and the rest.[16] And also the passage that says, '*You shall not muzzle the mouth of an ox when it is threshing the grain.' Is it for the oxen that God is concerned? Or does he speak altogether for our sake? For our sake it was written so that he that ploughs should plough in hope and he that threshes, in the hope of partaking.*[17] Here he clearly points out that God, who gave the Law for our sake, that is, for the sake of the apostles, says, *You shall not muzzle the mouth of an ox when it is threshing the grain*, and that his concern was not for oxen but for the apostles, who were preaching the Gospel of Christ. In other passages also, Paul himself, embracing the promises of the Law, speaks thus: *Honour your father and your mother, which is the first commandment, with a promise, that it may be well with you, and that you may live long upon the land, the good land, which the Lord your God will give you.*[18] By this, he undoubtedly makes known that the Law and the God of the Law and his promises are pleasing to him.

2.4.3. But since the advocates of this heresy are sometimes wont to ensnare the hearts of the simple by certain deceptive sophistries, I think it not unreasonable to bring forward the assertions they are accustomed to make, so that we can refute their deceit and lies. They say, then, that it is written that *No one has seen God at any time;*[19] but that God, whom Moses proclaims, was seen both by Moses himself and by his fathers before him, whereas the one who is announced by the Saviour has been seen by no one at all. Let us therefore also ask them whether the one whom they acknowledge as God and who, they say, is other than God the creator, is visible or invisible? If they should say that he is visible, besides being proved to go against that passage of Scripture which says of the Saviour that *He is the image of the invisible God, the first-born of all creation,*[20] they will also fall into the absurdity of saying that God is bodily. For

---

[14] 2 Tim. 1:3.   [15] 2 Cor. 11:22.   [16] Rom. 1:1–4.
[17] 1 Cor. 9:9–11; Deut. 25:4.   [18] Eph. 6:2–3; Exod. 20:12.
[19] John 1:18.   [20] Col. 1:15.

in no other way can anything be seen except through shape and size and colour, which are the properties of bodies. And if God is declared to be a body, then, since every body is made of matter, God will also be found to be made of matter; but if he is made of matter, and matter is undoubtedly corruptible, then God, according to them, will be corruptible. We will ask them again: is matter made or uncreated, that is, not made? If they shall say that it is not made, that is, uncreated, we shall ask them if one part of matter is God and another part the world? But if they shall say of matter that it is made, it will undoubtedly follow that they acknowledge that he, whom they call God, is made, which certainly neither their reason nor ours can accept.

But they will say: God[21] is invisible. And what will you do? If you say that he is invisible by nature, then neither ought he to be visible to the Saviour. But, on the contrary, God, the Father of Christ, is said to be seen, since *he who sees the Son,* he says, *sees also the Father.*[22] This certainly presses you very hard, but is understood by us more correctly not of seeing but of understanding. For he who has understood the Son has understood the Father also. In this way, then, Moses also must be supposed to have seen God, not seeing him with bodily eyes, but understanding him with the vision of the heart and the perception of the mind, and this only in part. For it is clear that he, that is, the one who gave the oracles to Moses, says, *You shall not see my face, but my back.*[23] These words are of course to be understood in that mystical sense which befits the understanding of divine sayings, with those old wives' fables, which are fabricated by the ignorant regarding the front and back parts of God, being utterly rejected and spurned. Let no one indeed suppose that we have entertained any impiety when we said that the Father is not visible even to the Saviour, but consider the distinction used in dealing with the heretics. For we have said that it is one thing to see and to be seen, and another to know and to be known or to understand and to be understood. To see, then, and to be seen is a property of bodies, which it would certainly not be right to apply either to the Father or to the Son or to the Holy Spirit in relation to each other. For the nature of the Trinity exceeds the limit of sight, yet it grants to those who are in the body, that is, to all other creatures, the property of sight in relation to each other; but to bodiless and, especially, intellectual beings, nothing else is appropriate except to know and to be known, as the Saviour himself declares, saying, *No one knows the Son except the Father, nor does any one know the Father, except the Son and any one to whom the Son will reveal him.*[24] It is clear, therefore, that he did not say, 'No one has seen, except the Son', but, *No one knows except the Son.*

---

[21] Cf. Jerome, *Ep.* 124.6.1 (ed. Hilberg 3, 103.9-11): 'In the same book he writes: Grant that God is invisible. If he is invisible by nature, neither will he be visible to the Saviour.'

[22] John 14:9.

[23] Exod. 33:23. Cf. Origen, *Hom. Jer.* 17.2; *Comm. Cant.* 3 (GCS 8, p. 231).

[24] Matt. 11:27. Cf. Origen, *Princ.* 1.1.8.

2.4.4. If, however, on account of those statements which are made in the Old Testament, as when God is angry or repents or is said to suffer any other human affection, they think that they are provided with material for refuting us who affirm that God must be believed to be altogether impassible and free from all these affections, then it must be shown to them that similar statements are found even in the parables of the Gospel: as when it says that he who planted a vineyard and let it out to husbandmen—which husbandmen killed the servants who were sent to them, and at last even put to death the son sent to them—is said, having become angry, to have taken away the vineyard from them and to have delivered over the wretched husbandmen to a wretched destruction and to have handed over the vineyard to other husbandmen who would render him the fruit in its season.[25] So also with those citizens who, when a nobleman[26] had set out to receive for himself a kingdom, sent messengers after him, saying, 'we *do not want this man to reign over us*'; on his return, having received the kingdom, the nobleman, becoming angry, commanded them to be slain before him and their city to be burnt by fire.[27] But we, when we read of the anger of God, either in the Old or the New Testament, we do not take the things said according to the letter, but seek in them a spiritual meaning, that we may think in a manner worthy for understanding God. On these points, we showed, according to our poor ability, when expounding as best we could that verse in the second Psalm which says, *Then shall he speak to them in his anger and trouble them in his fury*, in what way it ought to be understood.[28]

2.5.1.[29] But, since this fact disturbs some, that the leaders of that heresy appear to have made for themselves a distinction, as they have said that the just is one thing and the good another, and have applied this distinction even to divinity, maintaining that the Father of our Lord Jesus Christ is indeed a good God but not just, while the God of the Law and Prophets is just but not good, I think it necessary to respond to this question with as much brevity as possible.

They reckon, then, goodness to be some such disposition which is bound to do good to all, even when the one given the benefit is unworthy and does not deserve to obtain good; but, it seems to me, they have not correctly applied this

---

[25] Cf. Matt. 21:33–41.
[26] Rufinus has *pater familias*, presumably translating ἄνθρωπός τις εὐγενής as in Luke 19:12.
[27] Cf. Luke 19:12–27.
[28] Ps. 2:5. The explanatory passage referred to here no longer exists. Cf. Origen, *Hom. Jer.* 18.6: 'If you hear of the anger of God and his wrath, do not suppose that anger and wrath are passions of God. The purposes of using this way of speaking are for converting and bettering the infant, since we also use a fearful expression with children, not from an actual state of mind but because of a purpose to cause fear....So then it states that God is also said to be angry and wrathful in order that you can convert and become better.' See also *Hom. Jer.* 20.1.
[29] The manuscripts here have the title 'On the Just and the Good [God β]', included by Koetschau (followed by Butterworth) and by Görgemanns and Karpp.

definition, thinking that no good is done to the one who is visited with anything severe or harsh. Justice, on the other hand, they suppose to be some such disposition that renders to each one in proportion to what they deserve. But here, again, they do not correctly interpret the meaning of their own defin-ition. For they think that it is just to do evil to the evil and good to the good, that is, that, according to their view, one who is just does not appear to wish good for the evil, but to bear a kind of hatred against them; and they collect together the narratives they find anywhere in the Scriptures of the Old Testament recounting, for example, the punishment of the flood and of those who are reported to have perished in it, or how Sodom and Gomorrah were destroyed by a shower of fire and brimstone, or how all died in the desert because of their sins, so that none of those who had left Egypt were found to enter the promised land except Joshua and Caleb. From the New Testament, however, they gather sayings of mercy and compassion, by which the disciples are trained by the Saviour, and by which it seems to be declared that *No one is good but one, God the Father*,[30] and on this basis they have dared to name the Father of our Saviour Jesus Christ a good God, but they say that the God of the world is another, whom they are pleased to term just, but not also good.

2.5.2. Now, in the first place, I think, they must be required to show, if they can, according to their own definition, that the Creator is just in punishing according to their merits either those who perished at the time of the flood, or the inhabitants of Sodom, or those who had left Egypt, when we sometimes see much more wicked and heinous crimes committed than those for which the above mentioned were destroyed, while we do not yet see every sinner pay-ing the penalty of his deserts; or will they say that he who at one time was just has now become good? Or will they rather reckon that now he is just, but patiently bears human offences, whereas then he was not even just, when he exterminated innocent children and suckling babes along with monstrous and ungodly giants?[31] Now, they think such things because they know not how to heed anything beyond the letter; otherwise they would show how it is just, according to the letter, for the sins of the parents to be visited upon the heads of the children to the third and fourth generation, and on the children's chil-dren after them.[32] By us, however, such things are not understood according to the letter, but as Ezekiel taught, when speaking that parable, we inquire what the parable itself inwardly signifies.[33] Moreover, they ought to explain this also, how he is just and rewards everyone according to his merits,[34] he who

---

[30] Cf. Mark 10:18; Luke 18:19; neither text includes 'the Father'.
[31] Cf. Gen. 6:4; 7:1–3.   [32] Cf. Exod. 20:5, 34:7; Deut. 5:9.
[33] Cf. Ezek. 18:2–3. Cf. Origen, *Sel. Ex.* (PG 12, 289c); *Hom. Ex.* 8.6.
[34] Cf. Ps. 61:13.

punishes the earthly-minded and the devil when they have done nothing worthy of punishment; for they were not able to do any good if, according to them, they were of a wicked and ruined nature. And as for them calling him a judge, he appears to be a judge not so much of acts as of natures, and if, naturally, an evil nature cannot do good, neither can a good nature do evil.

Then, in next place, if he whom they call good is good to all, he is undoubtedly good also to those who are destined to perish; why then does he not save them? If he does not wish to, he will no longer be good; if he wishes to, and is not able, he will not be omnipotent. Let them rather hear, in the Gospels, of the Father of our Lord Jesus Christ preparing fire for *the devil and his angels*.[35] And how shall that work, as punitive as sorrowful, befit, according to their view, a good God? Even the Saviour himself, the Son of the good God, protests in the Gospels and declares that *if signs and wonders had been done in Tyre and Sidon, they would have repented long ago, sitting in sackcloth and ashes*.[36] Yet when he had come near to those very cities and had entered their borders,[37] why, pray, does he decline to enter those territories and to show them an abundance of *signs and wonders*, if it were certain that by such actions they would *repent in sackcloth and ashes*? As he does not indeed do this, he undoubtedly abandons to destruction those whom the very language of the Gospel shows not to be of a wicked or ruined nature, for it indicates that they were able to repent. Moreover, in a certain parable of the Gospel, *when the king came in to see the guests*, who had been invited, *he sees a certain person not clothed with a wedding garment and says to him: 'Friend, how did you get in here not having a wedding garment?'* Then he says to the servants: '*Bind him hand and foot, and cast him into the outer darkness; there will be weeping and gnashing of teeth.*'[38] Let them tell us who is that king who entered in to see the guests and finding among them one with unclean garments, ordered him to be bound by his servants and cast into outer darkness: is he indeed the one whom they call just? How then had he commanded good and bad to be invited, yet had not directed their merits to be investigated by his servants? This certainly indicates not the disposition of one who is just, as they say, and who rewards according to merits, but of an indiscriminate benevolence to all. If, on the other hand, this parable must be understood of the good God, that is, either of Christ or the Father of Christ, what else is it that they object to in the just God, nay, rather, what accusation can they bring against the God of the Law comparable to this, that he ordered the one who had been invited by his servants, whom he had sent to call good and bad, to be bound hand and foot and to be cast into the outer darkness because of his unclean garments?

---

[35] Matt. 25:41.   [36] Matt. 11:21.   [37] Cf. Matt. 15:21–2.   [38] Matt. 22:11–13.

2.5.3. These points, which we have drawn from the authority of Scripture, ought to be sufficient to refute the arguments that the heretics are accustomed to bring forward. It will not seem improper, however, if we discuss the matter with them in a few words from the perspective of logical reasoning.[39] We would ask them, then, whether they know what account of virtue and wickedness is held by men, and whether it appears to follow that we can speak of virtues in God,[40] or, as it seems to them, in these two gods. Let them also answer this: if they consider goodness to be a virtue, which I think they will undoubtedly admit, what then will they say of justice? They will surely never, it seems to me, be so foolish as to deny that justice is a virtue. If, therefore, virtue is a good and justice is a virtue, then justice is indubitably goodness. But if they say that justice is not something good, it only remains that it is either an evil or something indifferent. Now I think it folly to respond to those who say that justice is an evil, for I will seem to be replying either to senseless words or to men with disturbed minds. How can that appear an evil, which is able to render good to those who are good, just as they themselves admit? But if they say that it is something indifferent, it follows that, since justice is something indifferent, so also temperance and prudence and all the other virtues will be held as things indifferent.[41] What then shall we reply to Paul, when he says, *If there be any virtue, if there be any praise, think on these things, which you have learned and received and heard and seen in me*?[42]

Let them, then, by searching the holy Scriptures, tell us what the various virtues are, and let them not hide behind what they say—that the God who rewards everyone according to their merits renders ill to the evil out of hatred towards the wicked, and not because those who have sinned need to be treated with harsher remedies and because he applies to them those remedies which, though aiming at improvement, seem at the present to inflict a sense of pain.[43] They do not read what is written concerning the hope of those who were

---

[39] The 'logical reasoning' (*ex ratione ipsius consequentiae*) in question here is the connection (ἀντακολουθία) which unites the virtues, a teaching going back to the Stoics (e.g. *SVF* 1.49; 3.72) and found in Clement of Alexandria, *Strom.* 2.9.45; 2.18.80.

[40] The idea of virtues in God, accepted by Plato and the Stoics, was denied by Aristotle (*Eth. nic.* 10.8), but reasserted by Plotinus (*Enn.* 1.2), for whom the divinities, rather than possessing virtues as human beings do, have instead the principles from which our virtues derive. Origen, likewise, speaks of the Father as being the origin of virtues, which are seen in the titles of Christ, to be participated in by rational beings.

[41] This Stoic distinction between good, bad, and things indifferent (μέσον or ἀδιάφορον) is frequently used by Origen, e.g. *Princ.* 3.1.18; 3.2.7.

[42] Phil. 4:8–9.

[43] The idea that suffering has pedagogic or therapeutic value goes back to Plato: *Gorg.* 525b; *Resp.* 2.380bc; *Leg.* 11.934a. It is found repeatedly in Scripture, and in many earlier Christian writers: *1 Clem.* 56.16; Irenaeus, *Haer.* 4.37–9; Clement of Alexandria, *Ped.* 1.8.64; *Strom.* 4.24.153–4. For Origen, see also: *Princ.* 1.6.3; 2.10.6; *Hom. Ezech.* 1.2; *Hom. Ex.* 8.5; *Hom. Jer.* 6.2; 12.5; *Cels.* 3.75; 4.72; 6.56; *Frag. Ex.* 10.27 (= *Philoc.* 27.1–8). For Origen, as for Irenaeus (e.g. *Haer.* 3.20), this also includes the experience of death: *Comm. Matt.* 15.15; *Hom. Lev.* 14.4.

destroyed in the flood, of which hope Peter says this in his first Epistle: *For Christ died in the flesh, but was made alive by the Spirit, by which he went and preached to the spirits who were held in prison, who were once unbelievers, while the patience of God waited in the days of Noah, during the building of the ark, in which a few, that is eight souls, were saved through water, as also, by a like figure, baptism now saves you.*[44] And concerning Sodom and Gomorrah, let them tell us whether they believe that the prophetic words were from the creator God, of him, that is, who is related to have rained upon them a shower of fire and brimstone. What does the prophet Ezekiel say of them? *Sodom,* he says, *shall be restored to her former estate.*[45] And, in afflicting those who are deserving of punishment, how does he not afflict for the good? He also says to the Chaldeans, *You have coals of fire: sit on them; these will be a help to you.*[46] And regarding those who fell in the desert, let them hear what is related in the seventy-seventh Psalm, which bears the superscription of Asaph: for he says, *When he was killing them, then they would seek him out.*[47] He does not say that some sought him after others had been slain, but he says that those who were killed perished in such a manner that, when put to death, they sought God. From all of which it is established that the just and good God, of the Law and of the Gospels, is one and the same, and that he does good with justice and punishes with goodness; since neither goodness without justice, nor justice without goodness, can convey the dignity of the divine nature.

Compelled by their subtleties, we shall add the following remarks. If the just is different from the good, then, since the wicked is the opposite of the good and the unjust of the just, the unjust will doubtless be something other than wicked; and since, according to you, the just is not good, so neither will the unjust be wicked; and, in turn, as the good is not just, so the wicked will not be unjust. But how can it not seem absurd that to a good God there should be a wicked opposite, while to a just God, whom they say is inferior to the good, there should be no opposite! For there is no other who can be called unjust, as there is Satan, who is called wicked. What then? Let us return to the point from which we began. They will not be able to say that the wicked is not also unjust and the unjust not also wicked. And if in these opposites, injustice is inseparably inherent in wickedness and wickedness in injustice, then indubitably the good will be inseparable from the just, and the just from the good, so that, as we can say that the vice of wickedness and of injustice is one and the same, so also we should hold that the virtue of goodness and justice is one and the same.

2.5.4. But again they recall us to the words of Scripture, bringing forward that famous question of theirs. For, they say, it is written that *A good tree cannot*

---

[44] 1 Pet. 3:18–21.   [45] Ezek. 16:55.   [46] Isa. 47:14–15.   [47] Ps. 77:34.

bear evil fruit, nor can an evil tree bear good fruit; for the tree is known by its fruit.[48] What then, they say? What sort of a tree the Law is, is shown by its fruits, that is, by the words of its precepts. For if the Law is found to be good, then undoubtedly he who gave it is believed to be a good God; but if it is found to be just rather than good, then God will also be considered a just legislator. The Apostle Paul speaks in no roundabout way: *The Law is good, and the commandment is holy and just and good.*[49] From which it is clear that Paul had not learned the language of those who separate the just from the good, but had been instructed by God and enlightened by the Spirit of his God, who is at the same time both *holy and good and just,* and speaking by his Spirit he declared that the commandment of the Law was *holy and just and good.* And that he might show even more clearly that goodness was in the commandment to a greater degree than justice and holiness, repeating his words, he mentions goodness alone, instead of the three, saying, *Did that which is good, then, become death to me? God forbid!*[50] Knowing, naturally, that goodness is the genus of virtues, and that justice and holiness are species of the genus, and therefore having named both the genus and the species together in the preceding verses, he fell back, when repeating his words, to the genus alone. But in those that follow, he says, *Sin wrought death in me through what is good.*[51] Here he includes by means of the genus that which he had earlier set out through the species. In this way also is to be understood that statement, *A good man, out of the treasure of his heart, brings forth good things; and an evil man out of his evil treasure brings forth evil.*[52] For here also it used the genus of good or evil, showing, without doubt, that in a good man there were both justice and temperance and prudence and piety and everything that can either be called or be understood to be good. Similarly, it spoke of an evil man, who undoubtedly also is unjust and impure and impious and everything that in its own way disfigures an evil man; for just as no one considers a man evil, nor indeed can he be evil without these marks of wickedness, so also it is certain that without these virtues no one will be reckoned good.

There still remains to them that passage, which they think is given specially to them as a shield, where the Lord said in the Gospel, *No one is good but one, God the Father,*[53] claiming that this word is particular to the Father of Christ, who, however, is other than God the creator of all things, to which creator he gave no title of goodness. Let us therefore see if in the Old Testament the God of the prophets and creator of the world and legislator is not called good. What is that which is said in the Psalms? *How good is God to Israel, to the upright in*

---

[48]   Matt. 7:18; 12:33. Cf. Origen, *Princ.* 1.8.2; *Comm. Jo.* 13.73.
[49]   Rom. 7:12.   [50]   Rom. 7:13.   [51]   Rom. 7:13.   [52]   Luke 6:45.
[53]   Cf. Mark 10:18; Luke 18:19; neither text includes 'the Father'.

heart![54] and, *Let Israel now say that he is good, and that his mercy endures forever.*[55] And in the Lamentations of Jeremiah it is written, *The Lord is good to those who wait for him, to the soul that seeks him.*[56] As, therefore, God is frequently called good in the Old Testament, so also the Father of our Lord Jesus Christ is termed just in the Gospels. In fact, in the Gospel according to John, our Lord himself, praying to the Father, says, *O just Father, the world has not known you.*[57] And lest perhaps they should say that he called the Creator of the world *Father* and named him *just* because of the assumption of flesh, they are prevented by the phrase that immediately follows, for he says, *the world has not known you.* According to them, however, the world is ignorant of the good God alone; for it most certainly recognizes its own creator, as the Lord himself says, *the world loves what is its own.*[58] Clearly, then, he whom they consider to be the good God is called *just* in the Gospels. With leisure, indeed, it would be possible to gather a great many testimonies where, in the New Testament, the Father of our Lord Jesus Christ is called *just* and where, in the Old Testament, the Creator of heaven and earth is called *good*, so that the heretics, convicted by numerous testimonies, may at last perhaps be put to shame.

---

[54] Ps. 72:1.   [55] Ps. 117:2.   [56] Lam. 3:25.
[57] John 17:25.   [58] John 15:19.

The Incarnation of Christ

2.6.1. It is time, now that these points have been discussed, for us to return to the Incarnation of our Lord and Saviour, how he became human and dwelt among human beings. The divine nature having been considered, to the best of our feeble ability, by the contemplation of his own works rather than from our own understanding, and his visible creation having been observed while the invisible was contemplated by faith, since human frailty can neither see everything by the eye nor comprehend everything by reason, as we human beings are weaker and frailer than all other rational beings (for those held to be in heaven or above the heavens are superior), it remains that we should seek the medium between all these created things and God, that is, *the Mediator*,[1] whom the Apostle Paul calls *the firstborn of all creation*.[2] For seeing what is related in holy Scripture of his majesty, and observing that he is called *the image of the invisible God,* and *the firstborn of all creation,* and that *in him all things were created, visible and invisible, whether thrones or dominions or principalities or powers; all things were created through him and in him, and he is before all things, and in him all things hold together,*[3] who is the head of all things, alone having as his head God the Father, as it is written, *the head of Christ is God;*[4] seeing, also, that it is written, *No one knows the Father except the Son, nor does anyone know the Son except the Father*[5] (for who is able to know what Wisdom is, except he who begot her; or who knows clearly what Truth is, except the Father of Truth; or who indeed is able to investigate the universal nature of his Word, and of that God who is from God except God alone, with whom the Word was?[6]), we ought to hold it for certain that none, except the Father alone, knows this Word (or Reason, if he is to be so called), this Wisdom, this Truth, of whom it is written, *I suppose that even the world itself could not hold the books which would be written,*[7] that is to say, regarding the glory and the majesty of the Son of God. For it is impossible to commit to writing that which concerns the glory of the Saviour.

After consideration of such great and marvellous things concerning the nature of the Son of God, we are lost in deepest amazement that such a being, pre-eminent above all others, should have emptied himself of his condition of majesty,[8] and become a human being, and dwelt among human beings,[9] as is

---

[1] 1 Tim. 2:5. Cf. Irenaeus, *Haer.* 3.18.7; 5.17.1; Tertullian, *Prax.* 27.15; *Carn. Chr.* 15.1.
[2] Col. 1:15.   [3] Col. 1:15–17.   [4] 1 Cor. 11:3.
[5] Matt. 11:27.   [6] Cf. John 1:1.
[7] John 21:25. Cf. Origen, *Princ.* 4.3.14; *Comm. Jo.* 1.24; 13.26–32; 19.59; 20.304; *Comm. Matt.* 14.12.
[8] Cf. Phil. 2:7.   [9] Cf. John 1:14.

evidenced by the grace poured upon his lips,[10] and by the witness that the Father of heaven bore him,[11] and as is confirmed by the various signs and wonders and mighty deeds done by him; who also, before that presence of his which he manifested in the body, sent the prophets as his forerunners and messengers of his coming, and after his ascension into heaven made his holy apostles, ignorant and unlearned men from the tax-gatherers and fishermen but filled with his divine power, to journey throughout the world, that they might gather together, out of every nation and every population, a people of devout believers in him.

2.6.2. But of all the marvellous and magnificent things about him, this altogether surpasses the astonishment of the human intellect, and the frailty of mortal intelligence does not discover in what way it can think or understand how that mighty Power of divine majesty, that very Word of the Father and that very Wisdom of God, *in whom were created all things visible and invisible,*[12] can be believed to have been within the compass of that man who appeared in Judea; and indeed that the Wisdom of God entered into the womb of a woman, to be born an infant and to utter cries like the wailing of infants; then, afterwards, that he was also reported to be troubled by death, as even he himself acknowledges, saying, *My soul is sorrowful even unto death;*[13] and that, at the end, he was brought to that death which is accounted by human beings the most shameful, although he rose again on the third day. When, then, we see in him some things so human that they appear to differ in no respect from the common frailty of mortals, and some things so divine, that they are appropriate to nothing else but that primal and ineffable nature of divinity, the narrowness of human understanding is bewildered and, struck with amazement at so great a wonder, it knows not which way to turn, what to hold to, or whither to take itself. If it thinks of God, it sees a mortal being; if it thinks of a human being, it perceives him returning from the dead with spoils after conquering the kingdom of death. This, therefore, must be contemplated with all fear and reverence, that the truth of both natures may be shown to be in one and the same being, so that nothing unworthy or unbecoming should be perceived in that divine and ineffable substance, nor on the other hand that the things done should be supposed to be fantasies of deceptive appearances.[14] To utter these things in human ears and to explain them in words far exceeds the powers either of our worthiness or of our talent and speech. I think indeed that it surpasses the capacity even of the holy apostles; indeed, rather, the explanation of

---

[10] Cf. Ps. 44:3; Origen, *Sel. Ps.* 44.3 (PG 12, 1428–9).
[11] Cf. Matt. 3:17; Mark 1:11; Luke 3:22.   [12] Col. 1:16.
[13] Matt. 26:38; Mark 14:34.
[14] Cf. Origen, *Comm. Jo.* 19.6–11; 20.268–75; 32.188.

that mystery may perhaps even be beyond the reach of the whole creation of heavenly powers. Concerning him, then, not by some rashness but because the order of the arrangement demands, we will mention, in the fewest words possible, the points that our faith contains, rather than those that the assertion of human reason is accustomed to claim, laying before you our suspicions rather than any clear affirmations.[15]

2.6.3. The only-begotten Son of God, therefore, through whom, as the previous course of discussion has shown, *all things were made, visible and invisible,*[16] according to the mind of Scripture both made all things and loves what he made.[17] For as he is himself *the* invisible *image of the invisible God,*[18] he invisibly bestowed upon all rational creatures a participation in himself, in such a way that each one received from him a degree of participation to the extent of the loving affection by which they adhered to him. But whereas, because of the faculty of free will, a variety and diversity had taken hold of individual souls, so that one was attached to its Creator by a more ardent, and another by a feebler and weaker, love, that soul, of which Jesus said, *No one takes my soul from me,*[19] adhering, from *the beginning of creation*[20] and ever after, inseparably and indissolubly, to him, as to the Wisdom and the Word of God, and the Truth and the true Light, and receiving him wholly and passing itself into his light and splendour, was made with him in a pre-eminent degree *one spirit,* just as the Apostle promises to those who ought to imitate him, that *He who is joined to the Lord is one spirit.*[21] With this substance of the soul mediating between God and the flesh (for it was not possible for the nature of God to be mingled with a body without a mediator) there is born, as we said, the God-man,[22] the medium being that substance for which it was certainly not contrary to nature to assume a body.[23] Yet neither, on the other hand, was it contrary to nature for that soul, as a rational substance, to receive God, into whom, as we said above, as into the Word and the Wisdom and the Truth, it had already wholly passed. And therefore, either because it was wholly in the Son of God or because it received the Son of God wholly into itself, deservedly it is called, along with

---

[15] For similar caution, see Origen, *Princ.* 1.6.1; 2.3.7; *Comm. Jo.* 32.291, 294; *Comm. Matt.* 14.22; *Hom. Num.* 14.1.

[16] Col. 1:16.   [17] Cf. Wis. 11:24.   [18] Col. 1:15.

[19] John 10:18. Cf. Jerome, *Ep.* 124.6.2 (ed. Hilberg 3, 103.11–16): 'And lower down he says: no other soul which has descended into a human body has portrayed in itself so pure and genuine a likeness to its former condition, as that of which the Saviour says, *No man takes my soul from me, but I lay it down of myself.*'

[20] Rev. 3:14.   [21] 1 Cor. 6:17. Cf. Origen, *Comm. Jo.* 32.326; *Cels.* 6.47.

[22] This term *Deus-homo* is also found in Origen, *Hom. Ezech.* 3.3, translated by Jerome, and undoubtedly represents an original θεάνθρωπος. The Greek term was found in a fragment in M. Rauer's first edition of the *Comm. Luc.* (GCS, Origenes Werke 91, p. 48) but was removed in the second edition after suspicion was cast upon it by R. Devreesse, though others have since accepted it. Cf. Crouzel and Simonetti, SC 253, p. 175, n.18.

[23] Cf. Origen, *Comm. Rom.* 3.8.

the flesh which it had assumed, the Son of God and the Power of God, the Christ and the Wisdom of God; and, on the other hand, the Son of God, through whom all things were created, is named Jesus Christ and the Son of Man.[24] And, moreover, the Son of God is said to have died, that is, in virtue of that nature which could accept death; and he, who is proclaimed as coming in the glory of God the Father with the holy angels, is called the Son of Man.[25] And for this reason, throughout the whole of Scripture, the divine nature is spoken of in human terms as much as human nature is adorned with marks indicative of the divine. For of this, more than anything else, can that which is written be said, that *They shall both be in one flesh, and they are no longer two, but one flesh.*[26] For the Word of God is thought to be more *in one flesh* with the soul than a man with his wife. And, moreover, to whom is it more fitting to be one spirit with God than to this soul, which has so joined itself to God through love that it may deservedly be said to be one spirit with him?

2.6.4. That[27] the perfection of love and the sincerity of his genuine affection produced this inseparable union with God, so that the assumption of his soul happened neither accidentally nor from partiality towards persons, but was conferred upon it by the merit of its virtues, listen to the prophet speaking to it: *You loved righteousness and hated iniquity. Therefore God, your God, anointed you with the oil of gladness beyond your fellows.*[28] By the merit of its love, therefore, it is anointed with the oil of gladness, that is, the soul with the Word of God is made Christ; for to be anointed with the oil of gladness means nothing else than to be filled with the Holy Spirit.[29] And when he said, *beyond your fellows*, he indicates that the grace of the Spirit was not given as to the prophets, but that the essential fullness of the Word of God himself was in it, as the

---

[24] Cf. Origen, *Comm. Rom.* 1.6, commenting on Rom. 1:4, 'from the resurrection from the dead, Jesus Christ our Lord'. It is important to note that the unity spoken of here turns upon the Passion; as Origen puts it elsewhere (*Comm. Jo.* 32.325): 'The high exaltation of the Son of Man which occurred when he glorified God in his own death consisted in the fact that he was no longer different from the Word but was the same with him' (ἡ δὲ ὑπερύψωσις τοῦ υἱοῦ τοῦ ἀνθρώπου, γενομένη αὐτῷ δοξάσαντι τὸν θεὸν ἐν τῷ ἑαυτοῦ θανάτῳ, αὕτη ἦν, τὸ μηκέτι ἕτερον αὐτὸν εἶναι τοῦ λόγου ἀλλὰ τὸν αὐτὸν αὐτῷ). See the Introduction, section 4.

[25] The term 'Son of Man' is for Origen, as for Dan. 7:13, an eschatological term.

[26] Cf. Matt. 19:5–6; Gen. 2:24. This verse is also used for the Christological union in Origen, *Cels.* 6.47. See also *Comm. Jo.* 32.326.

[27] Cf. Justinian, *Ep. ad Menam* (ed. Schwartz, 210.16–20), an extract said to come from *Princ.* 2 and to show that 'the Lord was a mere human being'; it is numbered by Koetschau as Fragment 20: 'For this reason the human being became Christ, becoming so from his goodness, as the Prophet bears witness, saying *You loved righteousness and hated iniquity. Therefore God, your God, anointed you with the oil of gladness beyond your fellows.* It was fitting for him who had never been separated from the Only-begotten to share the name of Only-begotten and to be glorified with him.'

[28] Ps. 44:7–8.

[29] 'Christ', of course, meaning the 'Anointed'. Cf. Irenaeus, *Haer.* 3.9.3; 3.17.1; Origen, *Comm. Jo.* 1.191–7.

Apostle says, *In whom the fullness of divinity dwelt bodily.*[30] Finally, on this account he not only said, *You loved righteousness,* but added, *and hated iniquity.* For to have *hated iniquity* is the same as what the Scripture says of him, that *He did no sin, neither was there any guile found in his mouth,*[31] and, *He was tempted in all things as we are, yet without sin.*[32] Moreover the Lord himself says, *Which of you convicts me of sin?*[33] And again he says of himself, *Behold, the ruler of this world is coming, and finds nothing in me.*[34] All of which show that in him there was no sense of sin. And that he might show more clearly that no sense of sin had ever entered into him, the Prophet says, *Before the child could know how to call father or mother, he turned himself away from iniquity.*[35]

2.6.5. But if the fact, as we have shown above, that there is in Christ a rational soul, should seem a difficulty to anyone, because we have frequently shown throughout all our discussions that the nature of souls is capable of both good and evil,[36] the difficulty will be explained in the following way. It cannot be doubted that the nature of that soul was the same as all others, otherwise it could not be called a soul, if it was not truly a soul. But since the ability of choosing good or evil is present to all, this soul, which is Christ's, so chose to love righteousness that, in accordance with the immensity of its love, it adhered to it unchangeably and inseparably, so that the firmness of purpose and immensity of affection and inextinguishable warmth of love destroyed all thought of alteration or change, such that what was dependent upon the will is now changed into nature by the exertion of long usage;[37] and so it is to be believed that there is in Christ a human and rational soul, and yet not be supposed that it had any thought or possibility of sin.

2.6.6. For a fuller explanation of the matter, however, it will not seem absurd if we use an illustration, although on a subject so hard and so difficult there is not an abundance of suitable illustrations to be used. However, if we may speak without any prejudice: the metal iron is capable of cold and heat; if, then, a lump of iron is placed in a fire forever, receiving the fire throughout all its pores

---

[30] Col. 2:9.   [31] Isa. 53:9; 1 Pet. 2:22.   [32] Heb. 4:15.
[33] John 8:46.   [34] John 14:30.   [35] Combining Isa. 8:4 and 7:16.
[36] Cf. Origen, *Princ.* Pr.5; 1.3.6; 1.7.2; 1.8.3, etc.

[37] In *Princ.* 1.6.3, Origen asks whether wickedness might also be changed by habit into a kind of nature. On the idea of freely chosen actions being changed, by habit, into a kind of nature, see also Origen, *Comm. Jo.* 20.174, and *Hom. Jer.* 18.1, a propos of Jer. 18:1–16. On the background of this idea, see Aristotle, *Eth. nic.* 7.10.4 (1152a30–3), for whom habit 'is like nature'; and Clement of Alexandria's description of the perfected 'Gnostic', for whom habit has 'become nature', in *Strom.* 7.7.46.9, and 4.22.138.3.

and veins and becoming wholly fire,[38] provided that the fire is never removed from it and it itself is not separated from the fire, could we at all say that this, which is by nature a lump of iron, when placed in the fire and incessantly burning, is ever capable of accepting cold? On the contrary, rather, which is truer, we say that, as we often observe by the eye happening in furnaces, it has become wholly fire, since nothing else is discerned in it except fire; and if anyone were to attempt to touch or handle it, he would feel the power not of iron but of fire. In this way, then, that soul which, like iron in the fire, was placed in the Word forever, in Wisdom forever, in God forever, is God in all that it does, feels, and understands;[39] and therefore it can be called neither alterable nor changeable, since, being ceaselessly kindled, it came to possess immutability from its union with the Word of God. To all the saints some warmth of the Word of God must indeed be supposed to have passed; but in this soul it must be believed that the divine fire itself essentially rested, from which some warmth may have passed to others.[40] Finally, the fact that it says, *God, your God, anointed you with the oil of gladness above your fellows,* shows that that soul is anointed in one way, with the oil of gladness, that is, with the Word of God and Wisdom,[41] and his fellows, that is, the holy prophets and apostles, in another way. For they are said to have *run in the fragrance of his ointment,*[42] while that soul was the vessel containing the ointment itself, of whose glowing heat all the prophets and apostles are made worthy partakers. Therefore, as the fragrance of the ointment is one thing, and the substance of the ointment another, so also Christ is one thing and his fellows another. And just as the vessel itself, which contains the substance of the ointment, can in no way accept any foul smell, yet it is possible that those who participate in its fragrance, if they move a little way from its glowing heat, may accept any foul smell that comes upon them, so also, in the same way, it was impossible that Christ, being as it were the very vessel in which was the substance of the ointment, should accept an odour of an opposite kind, while his fellows, in proportion to their proximity to the vessel, will be partakers and receivers of his fragrance.

2.6.7. I think that Jeremiah the prophet also, understanding what was the nature of the Wisdom of God in him, which was also the same which he had

---

[38] An image found with the Stoics. See esp. Alexander of Aphrodisias, *Mixt.* 3, 218.1–2 (*SVF* 2.473), reporting Chrysippus' teaching: 'fire as a whole passes through iron as a whole, while each of them preserves its own substance' (τὸ πῦρ ὅλον δι᾽ ὅλου χωρεῖν τοῦ σιδήρου λέγουσι, σώζοντος αὐτῶν ἑκατέρου τὴν οἰκείαν οὐσίαν).

[39] Cf. Origen, *Princ.* 3.6.3, where similar claims are made for perfected rational beings in the eschatological state when 'God is all in all' (1 Cor. 15:28).

[40] Cf. Origen, *Comm. Jo.* 2.17.

[41] Note that here, as in *Princ.* 4.4.4, the 'oil' is the Word and Wisdom of God, while in *Princ.* 2.6.4 it is the Holy Spirit.

[42] Song 1:4.

assumed for the salvation of the world, said, *The breath of our face, Christ the Lord, of whom we said that under his shadow we shall live among the nations.*[43] For just as the shadow of our body is inseparable from the body, and assumes and performs the movements and gestures of our body without deviation, so I think that the Prophet, wishing to indicate the work and movement of Christ's soul, which was inseparably attached to him and accomplished everything according to his movement and will, called this the shadow of Christ the Lord, under whose shadow we were to live among the nations. For in the mystery of this assumption live the nations, who, imitating that soul through faith, come to salvation. Moreover David, when saying, *Remember, O Lord, my reproach, with which they have reproached me in exchange for your Christ,*[44] seems to me to indicate the same. And what else does Paul mean when he says, *Our life is hidden with Christ in God,*[45] and, again, in another place, *Do you seek a proof of him who speaks in me, that is, Christ?*[46] And now he says that Christ was hidden in God.[47] The meaning of this, unless it be shown to be something like that which was signified by the Prophet with the shadow of Christ, as we said above, probably exceeds the apprehension of the human mind. But we also see many other statements in the divine Scriptures regarding the significance of the word 'shadow', such as that in the Gospel according to Luke, where Gabriel says to Mary, *The Spirit of the Lord will come upon you, and the power of the Most High will overshadow you.*[48] And the Apostle says of the Law that those who have circumcision in the flesh *serve a copy and shadow of the heavenly things.*[49] And elsewhere it is said, *Is not our life upon the earth a shadow?*[50] If then, both the Law which is upon the earth is a shadow, and our whole life which is upon the earth is a shadow, and we live among the nations under the shadow of Christ, it must be considered whether the truth of all these shadows may not come to be known in that revelation, when no longer *through a mirror and in a riddle, but face to face,*[51] all the saints shall be counted worthy to behold the glory of God and the causes and truth of things.[52] The pledge of this truth already being received through the Holy Spirit, the Apostle said, *Even if we had formerly known Christ according to the flesh, we know him thus no longer.*[53]

Meanwhile, these are the thoughts that have occurred to us at the moment, regarding subjects of such difficulty as the incarnation and divinity of Christ. If there is anyone who is able to discover something better and to confirm what he says by clearer statements from the holy Scriptures, let those accounts be received rather than mine.

---

[43] Lam. 4:20. Cf. Irenaeus, *Dem.* 71.   [44] Ps. 88:51–2.   [45] Col. 3:3.
[46] 2 Cor. 13:3.   [47] Perhaps alluding to 2 Cor. 5:16, cited at the end of the paragraph.
[48] Luke 1:35.   [49] Heb. 8:5.   [50] Job 8:9.   [51] 1 Cor. 13:12.
[52] Cf. Origen, *Princ.* 2.11.7; *Comm. Jo.* 1.39–40; *Comm. Cant.* 2 and 3 (GCS 8, pp. 121, 160, 173, 211).
[53] 2 Cor. 5:16.

The Holy Spirit

2.7.1.[1] Since, then, after those first discussions, which, as the subject demanded, we set out at the beginning regarding the Father and the Son and the Holy Spirit, it seemed that we ought to go back again and show that the same God was both the creator and founder of the world and the Father of our Lord Jesus Christ, that is, that the God of the Law and the Prophets and of the Gospels is one and the same; and, then, regarding Christ, who had previously been shown to be the Word and Wisdom of God, it needed to be shown, in the subsequent chapters, how he became human; it remains that we now also return, as briefly as we can, to the subject of the Holy Spirit.

It is time, therefore, to discuss to the best of our ability a few points regarding the Holy Spirit, whom our Lord and Saviour in the Gospel according to John, called *the Paraclete*.[2] Now just as it is the same God himself and the same Christ himself, so also it is the same Holy Spirit himself who was in the prophets and in the apostles, that is, both in those who believed in God before the coming of Christ and in those who have sought refuge in God through Christ. We have heard, indeed, that certain heretics have dared to say that there are two Gods and two Christs, but we have never known of two Holy Spirits being preached by any one.[3] For how would they be able to affirm this from the Scripture, or what distinction would they be able to give between Holy Spirit and Holy Spirit, if indeed any definition or description of the Holy Spirit could possibly be found out. For even if we grant to Marcion or Valentinus that it is possible to draw distinctions regarding divinity, and to describe the nature of the good as one, and that of the just as another, what will he contrive or what will he invent so that he can introduce a distinction in the Holy Spirit? I consider, then, that they are able to find nothing which points to any distinction of whatever kind.

2.7.2. Now we reckon that every rational creature, without distinction, receives participation in him in the same way as [they do] in the Wisdom of God and in the Word of God. I observe, however, that the principal coming of the Holy Spirit to human beings is declared after the ascension of Christ to heaven rather than before his coming. For before that, the gift of the Holy Spirit was conferred upon only the prophets and upon a few others, if there happened to be any

---

[1] Photius, *Bibl.* 8 (ed. Henry 1, 4a8–10), describes this section of *Princ.* 2 as demonstrating 'that there was the same Spirit in Moses and the other prophets and the holy apostles' (ὅτι τὸ αὐτὸ πνεῦμα ἐν Μωϋσῇ καὶ τοῖς ἄλλοις προφήταις καὶ ἁγίοις ἀποστόλοις·).

[2] John 14:16 etc.

[3] See also *Fr. Tit.* (PG 14, 1304d–1305a): 'Moreover if there are any [*Sed et si qui sunt*] who say that it was one Holy Spirit who was in the prophets, but another who was in the apostles of our Lord Jesus Christ, they commit one and the same offence of impiety as those who, so far as in them lies, cut and rend the nature of the divinity by saying there is one God of the Law and another of the Gospels.'

among the people deserving of it; but after the coming of the Saviour, it is written that that was fulfilled *which was spoken by the prophet Joel, 'And in the last days it shall be that I will pour out my Spirit upon all flesh, and they shall prophesy';*[4] which indeed is similar to that passage which says, *All nations shall serve him.*[5] Through the grace of the Holy Spirit, therefore, along with numerous other results, this most magnificent fact is demonstrated, that, regarding those things which were written in the Prophets or in the Law of Moses, there were at that time only a few, that is, the prophets themselves, and scarcely any other anywhere out of the whole people, who were able to transcend the bodily meaning and to perceive something greater, that is, who were able to understand something spiritual in the Law or the Prophets; but now there are innumerable multitudes of believers who, although not all are able to explain in order and with clarity the logic of spiritual understanding, are all, nevertheless, firmly persuaded that neither ought circumcision to be understood in a bodily manner, nor the rest of the Sabbath, nor the pouring out of the blood of an animal, nor that on these points oracles were given by God to Moses; there is assuredly no doubt that this understanding is suggested to all by the power of the Holy Spirit.[6]

2.7.3. And just as there are many ways of understanding Christ,[7] who, although he is Wisdom, does not, however, exercise or assume the power of wisdom in all, but only in those who apply themselves to wisdom in him (nor, although he is called a physician,[8] does he act towards all as a physician, but only towards those who having understood their feeble and sick condition flee to his compassion that they may obtain health), so also, I think, is it with regard to the Holy Spirit, in whom is every manner of gift.[9] For, *To some is bestowed by the Spirit the word of wisdom, to others the word of knowledge, to others faith;*[10] and so to each person who is able to receive him, the same Spirit becomes that and is understood to be that which the person, who is worthy to partake of him, needs. These divisions and differences not being heeded by those who hear him called *the Paraclete* in the Gospel,[11] and not considering by what work or operation he is called *Paraclete*, they have compared him to some common spirit or other, and by this have tried to disturb the churches of Christ, so that they cause no small dissensions among the brethren. But the Gospel shows him to be of such power and majesty that it says the apostles

---

[4] Acts 2:16–17, Joel 2:28.   [5] Ps. 71:11.
[6] For the Spirit providing inspiration in the reading of Scripture, see also Origen, *Princ.* Pr.8; *Hom. Gen.* 9.1; *Hom. Lev.* 6.1; *Hom. Num.* 26.3; *Comm. Cant.* Prol. (GCS 8, p. 77); *Comm. ser. Matt.* 40; *Comm. Jo.* 10.172–3.
[7] On the 'aspects' of Christ, see Origen, *Princ.* 1.2; *Comm. Jo.* 1.90–292, esp. 119, 123, 136.
[8] Cf. Matt. 9:12; Ignatius, *Eph.* 7.2; *Diogn.* 9.6; Clement of Alexandria, *Protr.* 1.8; *Ped.* 1.1.1; 1.2.6; 1.9.83; Origen, *Princ.* 2.10.6; 3.1.13–15; *Comm. Jo.* 1.124; *Cels.* 3.62; *Hom. Lev.* 8.1; *Hom. Jer.* 12.5.
[9] Cf. Origen, *Princ.* 1.3.7; *Comm. Jo.* 2.77.
[10] 1 Cor. 12:8–9.   [11] Cf. John 14:16 etc.

were not able to receive those things that the Saviour wanted to teach them until the Holy Spirit should come,[12] who, pouring himself into their souls, would be able to enlighten them regarding the nature and faith of the Trinity. But these people, because of the ignorance of their understanding, are not only themselves unable to expound coherently what is true, but they are not even able to pay attention to what is said by us; entertaining lowly thoughts, unworthy of his divinity, they have delivered themselves over to errors and deceits, being depraved by a spirit of error rather than instructed by the precepts of the Holy Spirit, according to the saying of the Apostle, *Following the doctrine of demon spirits, who prohibit marriage* to the destruction and ruin of many, and [enjoin] unsuitable *abstinence from food*,[13] that by a display of stricter observance they may seduce the souls of the innocent.

2.7.4. We must therefore know that the Paraclete is the Holy Spirit, teaching things greater than can be uttered by the voice, and, if I may so speak, which are unutterable and *which it is not lawful for a human being to utter*,[14] that is, which cannot be indicated by human language. For the phrase *it is not lawful* is, we think, said by the Apostle instead of 'it is not possible', just as also in the place where he said, *All things are lawful but not all things are helpful; all things are lawful, but not all things build up.*[15] Those things which are within our power, because we can have them, he says are lawful for us. But the Paraclete, who is called the Holy Spirit, is so called from his consolation (for παράκλησις is termed *consolatio* in Latin[16]); for anyone who has deserved to participate in the Holy Spirit, by the knowledge of ineffable mysteries, undoubtedly obtains consolation and gladness of heart. When he has come to know, by the direction of the Spirit, the reasons for all things that happen—why and how they happen—his soul can in no respect be troubled or accept any feeling of sadness; nor is he alarmed by anything, as, clinging to the Word of God and his Wisdom, he calls *Jesus 'Lord' in the Holy Spirit.*[17]

And, since we have made mention of the Paraclete, and have explained to the best of our ability how he ought to be regarded, and as our Saviour is also called a *paraclete* in the Epistle of John, when he says, *If any of us sin, we have a paraclete with the Father, Jesus Christ the righteous; and he is the expiation for our sins*,[18] let us consider whether this term 'paraclete' should signify one thing regarding the Saviour, and another regarding the Holy Spirit. Now, 'paraclete', when spoken of the Saviour, seems to mean intercessor, for in Greek 'paraclete' signifies both consoler and intercessor.[19] Because, then, of the

---

[12] Cf. John 16:12–13; Origen, *Princ.* 1.3.4.

[13] 1 Tim. 4:1, 3.   [14] 2 Cor. 12:4.   [15] 1 Cor. 10:23.

[16] These are clearly Rufinus' explanatory words.

[17] 1 Cor. 12:3.   [18] 1 John 2:1–2.

[19] On Christ as expiation and intercessor, see Origen, *Hom. Lev.* 7.2; *Or.* 15.4; *Cels.* 3.49; 4.28.

phrase which follows, where he says that *He is the expiation for our sins*, the name 'paraclete' seems to be understood of our Saviour as meaning rather intercessor; for he is said to intercede with the Father *for our sins*. Regarding the Holy Spirit, however, 'paraclete' must be understood as consoler, because he provides consolation for the souls to whom he opens and reveals the sense of spiritual knowledge.

The Soul

2.8.1. After this, the order [of our discussion] now requires us to investigate the soul in a general manner, and beginning with the lower beings to ascend to the higher ones.[1] Now, that there are souls in every single living creature, even those that abide in the waters, is, I suppose, doubted by no one. For this is supported by the general opinion of all, and receives confirmation by the authority of holy Scripture, when it is said that, *God created the great sea monsters and every soul of animated beings that move, which the waters brought forth according to their kind.*[2] It is confirmed also from the common understanding of reason, by those who establish a definition of 'soul' in exact terms. For 'soul' is defined in this way, as a φανταστική and ὁρμητική substance (which may be expressed in Latin, though not so precisely, as capable of perception and movement).[3] It is certainly appropriate for this to be said of all animated beings, even those that abide in the water; and the same definition of soul may be shown to hold for winged creatures too. Scripture also adds its authority to another opinion, when it says, *You shall not eat the blood, because the soul of all flesh is its blood, and you shall not eat the soul with the flesh;* in which it most clearly indicates that the blood of every animated being is its 'soul'.[4] But, since it is said that *the soul of all flesh is its blood,* if anyone were now to ask about bees and wasps and ants and those other things which are in the waters, oysters and cockles, and all others which are without blood, and yet are most clearly shown to be animated beings, it must be replied that in animated beings of this kind, the same force which in others is exerted by the power of red blood is exerted in them by that fluid which is within them, although it be of a different colour, for it does not matter what colour it is, provided the substance is endowed with life. There is no doubt, even in common opinion, that beasts of burden or cattle are animated beings. Moreover, the teaching of divine Scripture is also clear, when God says, *Let the earth bring forth the living soul according to kind: four-footed beasts and creeping things and beasts of the earth according to kind.*[5] And then, with respect to the human being, although there is no doubt, nor could anyone ask the question, yet divine Scripture declares that *God breathed into his face the breath of life and the human being became a living soul.*[6]

---

[1] In *Comm. Jo.* 6.85–7, written after he had arrived in Caesarea, and thus after *Princ.*, Origen commences an investigation into the soul in similar terms.

[2] Gen. 1:21.

[3] These words in parentheses are clearly Rufinus' attempt to explain the Greek terms. For the background for this definition of 'soul', see Aristotle, *De an.* 3.9; Philo, *Alleg. Int.* 2.23; *Deus* 41; Tertullian, *An.* 14–16; and elsewhere in Origen: *Princ.* 3.1.2–3; *Cels.* 6.48.

[4] Lev. 17:14. Cf. Clement of Alexandria, *Paed.* 1.6.9; Origen, *Dial.* 10.

[5] Gen. 1:24.   [6] Gen. 2:7.

It remains for us to inquire about the angelic order, whether they also have souls or are souls; and also of the other divine and celestial powers, as well as the opposing powers. We nowhere, indeed, find any attestation in divine Scripture where angels or any other divine spirits, who are *ministers of God*,[7] are said to have or be souls; and yet they are supposed by very many to be animated beings. But with regard to God, we find it written as follows, *And I will set my soul against that soul which has eaten blood, and I will eradicate him from among his people*,[8] and also elsewhere, *Your new moons and Sabbaths and great days, I will not accept; your fasts and holidays and festal days, my soul hates.*[9] And in the twenty-first Psalm it is said thus about Christ (for it is certain that this psalm is spoken in his person, as the Gospel bears witness[10]): *You, O Lord, do not put your help far from me; attend to my support; deliver my soul from the sword, and my only-one from the hand of the dog;*[11] there are, however, many other testimonies regarding the soul of Christ when he dwelt in the flesh.

2.8.2. Concerning the soul of Christ, considering the rationale of the incarnation will obviate for us every question. For just as he truly possessed flesh, so also he truly possessed a soul. As for that, indeed, which is called in Scripture *the soul of God*,[12] it is difficult to think or to say how it ought to be understood; for we acknowledge at the same time that nature to be simple and without any addition by mixture; nevertheless, however it is to be understood, it seems, meanwhile, to be called *the soul of God*, whereas regarding Christ it is not doubted. And therefore, if that definition of soul appears to apply also to them, it does not seem to me to be absurd to say or to think some such thing even regarding the holy angels and the other heavenly powers. For who can rationally deny that they are capable of perception and movement? If that definition appears to be correct—that a substance rationally capable of perception and movement is called 'soul'—then the same definition would seem also to apply to angels. For what else is in them other than rational perception and movement? Things for which there is one definition undoubtedly have the same substance. Paul indeed indicates that there is a kind of *animated human being*, who, he says, *is not able to receive the things of the Spirit of God*, but says that the teaching of the Holy Spirit seems *to him to be foolish*, and *he is not able to understand it because it is spiritually discerned.*[13] In another place he says that *it is sown an animated body and rises a spiritual body*,[14] showing that in the resurrection of the just there will be nothing of the animated in those who

---

[7] Heb. 1:4.

[8] Lev. 17:10. The Göttingen edition of the LXX has here: 'I will set my face [πρόσωπον] against the soul who eats blood,' with 'soul' as a variant reading in the eighth-century Codex Venetus.

[9] Isa. 1:13–14.   [10] Cf. Mark 15:34 etc.   [11] Ps. 21:20–1.

[12] Isa. 1:14; 42.1, etc. The meaning of this phrase is treated below, in *Princ.* 2.8.5.

[13] 1 Cor. 2:14.   [14] 1 Cor. 15:44.

have been accounted worthy of the life of the blessed. And therefore we ask whether there is not some substance which, in so far as it is soul, is imperfect? But whether it be imperfect because it falls away from perfection, or because it was created such by God, we shall investigate when each point begins to be discussed in order.[15] For if *the animated human being does not receive the things of the Spirit of God* and, because of the fact that he is animated, is unable to receive an understanding of a better nature, that is, of the divine, it is perhaps for this reason that Paul, wishing to teach us more plainly what it is through which we are able to understand the things of the Spirit, that is, spiritual things, joins and associates the intellect, rather than the soul, with the Holy Spirit. For this, I think, he indicates when he says, *I will pray with the Spirit and I will pray with the intellect also; I will sing a psalm with the Spirit and I will sing a psalm with the intellect also.*[16] He does not say that 'I will pray with the soul', but 'with the Spirit and intellect'; nor does he say, 'I will sing with the soul' but 'I will sing with the Spirit and intellect'.

2.8.3. But perhaps it will be asked: if it is the intellect which with the Spirit prays and sings, and the same which receives both perfection and salvation, how does Peter say, *Receiving the outcome of our faith, the salvation of our souls?*[17] If the soul neither prays nor sings with the Spirit, how shall it hope for salvation? Or,[18] if it should attain to blessedness, shall it no longer be called a soul? Let us see if perhaps it is possible for an answer to be given in this way: that,[19] just as the Saviour *came to save what was lost,*[20] and then, once it is saved, that which was formerly said to be lost is not lost, so also perhaps that which is being saved is called 'soul', but when it has been saved it will be called by the name of its more perfect part. But it appears to some that this also can be added: that, just as that which was lost undoubtedly existed before it was lost, when it was something—I know not what—other than lost, and just as

---

[15] This question is taken up in *Princ.* 2.9. [16] 1 Cor. 14:14. [17] 1 Pet. 1:9.

[18] Cf. Jerome, *Ep.* 124.6.3–4 (ed. Hilberg 3, 103.16–104.1): 'And in another place: Wherefore with infinite caution it must be considered whether souls, when they will have become saved and will have attained to the blessed life, may not perhaps cease to be souls. For just as the Lord and Saviour *came to* seek and *save that which was lost,* that it might cease to be lost, so also the soul, which was lost and which the Lord came to save, when saved, will cease to be a soul. It must likewise be asked whether, just as the lost was once not lost and there will be a time when it will not be lost, so also the soul may once not have been a soul, and there will be a time when it might not remain a soul.'

[19] Cf. Justinian *Ep. ad Menam* (ed. Schwartz, 212.10–14), an extract said to come from *Princ.* 2 and numbered by Koetschau as Fragment 21: 'Just as the Saviour *came to save the lost,* but when the lost is saved, it is no longer lost; so also it was when he came to save the soul, as to save the lost, that saved soul no longer remains a soul [neither does the lost remain lost]. It must also be considered if, just as there was a "when" when the lost was not lost and there will be a "when" when it will not be lost, so also there was a "when" when the soul was not a soul and will be a "when" when it will not be a soul.'

[20] Matt. 18:11.

there will assuredly be a 'when' when it is not lost, so also the soul, which is said to have become lost, will appear to have been something at that 'when' when it had not as yet become lost, and on account of this [i.e. becoming lost] may have been called a 'soul', but, in turn, when delivered from being lost it may once again be that which it was before it became lost and was called a 'soul'.

But from the very signification of the name 'soul', as indicated in Greek, it seems to several careful investigators that a meaning of no small importance may be suggested. For the divine word calls God a fire, when it says, *Our God is a consuming fire.*[21] And concerning the substance of angels, it says as follows, *Who makes his angels spirits and his ministers burning fire,*[22] and in another place, *The angel of the Lord appeared in a flame of fire in the bush.*[23] We have, moreover, received a command to be *aglow with the Spirit,*[24] by which without doubt the Word of God is shown to be fiery and hot. The prophet Jeremiah also hears from him who gave him the oracles, *Behold I have given my words into your mouth as a fire.*[25] As God therefore *is fire,* and the angels *a flame of fire,* and the saints are all *aglow with the Spirit,* so, on the contrary, those who have fallen away from the love of God are undoubtedly said to have cooled in their love for him and to have become cold. For the Lord also says that *because iniquity has multiplied, the love of many will grow cold.*[26] And all things, whatever they are, which are likened in the holy Scriptures to the adverse power, you always find to be cold.[27] For the devil is called a *serpent* and a *dragon:* what can be found colder than these? For the dragon—which certainly is referred to as one of the wicked spirits—is said to reign in the waters, and the prophet states that he lives in the sea;[28] and elsewhere the Prophet says, *I will bring my holy sword against the dragon, the fleeing serpent, against the dragon, the crooked serpent, and it will slay him;*[29] and again he says, *Even if they sink from my eyes and descend to the depths of the sea, there I will command the dragon and it shall bite them.*[30] In Job also, he is said to be *king over all that are in the waters.*[31] The prophet threatens that, *From the north evils shall flare up against all who inhabit the earth.*[32] Now the north wind is described in the Scriptures as cold,

---

[21] Deut. 4:24, 9:3; Heb. 12:29. Often (as in e.g. *Princ.* 1.1.1–2), the image of God as a 'consuming fire' is understood in terms of God purging evil and sin; here it is taken as God setting his saints aflame with the Spirit. In *Hom. Jer.* 20.8 and in *Hom. Ex.* 13.4, Origen contrasts these two functions of 'fire', explaining the second by bringing together the 'fire' that Christ came to cast on the earth with the burning of Simon's and Cleopas' hearts on the road to Emmaus (Luke 12:49, 24.32); see also *Frag. Luc.* 256.

[22] Ps. 103:4; Heb. 2:7. Cf. Origen, *Sel. Ps.* 27.1 (PG 12, 1284).

[23] Exod. 3:2.   [24] Rom. 12:11.

[25] Jer. 5:14. Cf. Origen, *Hom. Jer.* 20.8–9. In *Cels.* 4.1, Origen cites Jer. 1:9–10, adding the words 'as fire' to the first clause; these words are not given in the LXX, but appear in Jer. 5:14.

[26] Matt. 24:12.   [27] Cf. Origen, *Sel. Ps.* 27.1 (PG 12, 1284).

[28] Cf. Ezek. 29:3; 32:2.   [29] Isa. 27:1.   [30] Amos 9:3.

[31] Job 41:26.   [32] Jer. 1:14.

according to the text in Wisdom, *The cold north wind.*[33] The same things must without doubt be understood of the devil. If, then, those things which are holy are termed *fire* and *light* and *aglow,* while those which are contrary are termed cold, and if the love of sinners is said to grow cold, it must be asked whether perhaps even the word 'soul' (which in Greek is ψυχή[34]) is so called from a cooling down from a more divine or better condition,[35] and has been transplanted, that is, it is seen to have cooled down from that natural and divine warmth, and therefore to have been placed in its present position with its present designation.[36]

Finally, see if you can easily find in the holy Scriptures a place where the soul is properly described in terms of praise; for it frequently occurs in terms of blame, as here, *An evil soul destroys him who possesses it,*[37] and, *The soul which sins, it shall die.*[38] For after it has been said, *All souls are mine; as the soul of the father, so also the soul of the son is mine,* it seemed to follow that he would say, 'the soul that does righteousness, it shall be saved' as well as *the soul which sins, it shall die.* But here we see that he has associated with the soul what is blameworthy, but has been silent regarding what was deserving of praise. It must be considered, therefore, if perhaps, as we have said is shown by the name itself, it was called ψυχή, that is, soul, from the fact that it has cooled down from the glow of the righteous and participation in the divine fire, and yet has not lost the power of restoring itself to that condition of fervour in which it was at the beginning. Whence the prophet also appears to point out some such idea, when he says, *Return, O my soul, unto your rest.*[39] From all these things, this appears to be shown, that the intellect, falling away from its status or dignity, was made or named soul; and if restored and corrected, it returns to being an intellect.[40]

---

[33] Sirach 43:20. Origen also refers to Sirach as 'Wisdom' in *Frag. Jo.* 74 and 136 (GCS 4, pp. 541 and 573).

[34] Rufinus' explanatory words.

[35] Cf. Plato, *Crat.* 399; Aristotle, *De an.* 1.2.405b; *SVF* 2.222; Philo, *Somn.* 1.31; Tertullian, *An.* 25.6 and 27.5.

[36] At this point, Koetschau places, as Fragment 22, a passage from Epiphanius, *Panarion* 64.4.7–8 (Holl 2, 412.5–11), which is paralleled by a passage from Jerome, *Jo. Hier.* 7 (PL 23, 360). These passages are in the Appendix, as item no. 14.

[37] Sirach 6:4.   [38] Ezek. 18:4.   [39] Ps. 114:7.

[40] Cf. Origen, *Princ.* 2.11.7; *Or.* 9.2; *Mart.* 12, a propos of Luke 9:23–5 and Mark 8:34–7, and Gal. 2:20: 'If we wish to save our soul in order to get it back better than a soul, let us lose it by our martyrdom.' After this paragraph, Koetschau places the following material: as Fragment 23a, the anathemas (2 to 6a) from the Second Council of Constantinople, with an extra sentence from Justinian, *Ep. ad Menam* (ed. Schwartz, 202.13–14) appended to anathema 4; two sentences from Justinian, *Ep. ad Menam* (ed. Schwartz, 190.19–24); and then, as Fragment 23b, a passage from Justinian, *Ep. ad Menam* (ed. Schwartz, 212.5–8), said to be from *Princ.* 2, and a passage from Jerome's *Ep.* 124.6.5–6 (ed. Hilberg 3, 104.2–16). These passages are in the Appendix as item no. 15.

2.8.4. Now, if it is thus, it seems to me that this departure and falling away of the intellect is not to be thought of as equal in all, but as a greater or lesser change into soul, and that some intellects even retain something of their former vigour, and others, on the other hand, retain either nothing or a very small amount. And so it is that some are found immediately from the beginning to be of a more fervent sharpness of intellect, while others duller, and some are born wholly obtuse and altogether intractable. Our statement, however, that the intellect is changed into a soul, or anything else that seems to look towards this, the reader must carefully consider and explore for himself; the points advanced by us must not be thought of as dogmas, but discussed in the manner of exploration and discussion.[41]

Let the reader also take this into consideration, that of those things that are written in the Gospel regarding the soul of the Saviour, it is noticeable that some are ascribed to it under the name of soul, and others are considered under the name of 'spirit'. For when it wishes to indicate any suffering or disquiet affecting him, it indicates it under the name of soul, as when it says, *Now is my soul troubled,*[42] and, *My soul is sorrowful, even unto death,*[43] and, *No one takes my soul but I lay it down of myself.*[44] Into the hands of his Father [however] he commends not his soul but his spirit,[45] and when he says that *the flesh is weak,* he does not say that the soul is willing, but the spirit;[46] whence it appears that the soul is a kind of medium between the weak flesh and the willing spirit.[47]

2.8.5. But perhaps someone may meet us with one of those objections, of which we have given warning in our own arguments, and may say: 'How then is mention made of a soul of God?' To which we shall reply in this way: just as all things which are said of God in bodily terms—such as fingers or hands or arms or eyes or feet or mouth—we say they are not to be understood as these human members, but that certain of his powers are indicated by these names of bodily members; so also it must be supposed that it is something else which is indicated by this phrase, *the soul of God.* And if it is allowable for us to venture to say anything further on such a subject, *the soul of God* may perhaps be understood of his only-begotten Son. For just as the soul, planted throughout the whole body, moves all things and drives and activates everything, so also the only-begotten Son of God, who is his Word and Wisdom, extends and

---

[41] For similar expressions, see Origen, *Princ.* 1.6.1; 1.8.4; 2.3.7; 2.6.7. Origen addresses his readers three times in the concluding paragraphs of this chapter, and also in *Princ.* 1.6.1; 2.3.7; 3.6.9.

[42] John 12:27.   [43] Matt. 26:38 etc.   [44] John 10:18.

[45] Cf. Luke 23:46.   [46] Cf. Matt. 26:41 etc.

[47] John 13:21, however, states that Jesus was 'troubled in spirit'; for Origen's attempt to clarify the distinction between 'soul' and 'spirit' to explain this verse, see *Comm. Jo.* 32.218–28.

stretches to every power of God, being implanted in him.[48] And, perhaps as an indication of this mystery, in the Scriptures God is spoken of or described as a body.[49] It must indeed be considered whether it is not perhaps also on this account that the soul of God may be understood of his only-begotten, because he himself came into this place of affliction and descended into the valley of tears and into this place of our humiliation, as it says in the Psalm, *Because you humbled us in the place of affliction.*[50] Finally, I know some who, expounding that saying which is spoken by the Saviour in the Gospel, *My soul is sorrowful, even unto death,*[51] have interpreted it of the apostles, whom, as being better than the rest of the body, he called his soul. For as the multitude of believers is called his body,[52] they say that the apostles, as being better than the remaining multitude, ought to be understood as his soul.

We have brought forward as best we could these points regarding the rational soul, as points of discussion for our readers, rather than as fixed and defined. And with regard to the souls of animals and other dumb creatures, let what we have said in general terms above suffice.

---

[48] Cf. Origen, *Princ.* 1.3.5–6. [49] Cf. Origen, *Or.* 23.3, citing Gen. 3.8–9.
[50] Ps. 43:20, 83:7. [51] Matt. 26:38 etc.
[52] Cf. 1 Cor. 10: 17; 12:27; Eph. 4:12; 5:30.

The World and Movements of Rational Creatures

2.9.1.[1] But now let us return to the order of the proposed discussion, and contemplate the beginning of creation,[2] insofar as the intellect is able to contemplate the beginning of the creative working of God. In[3] that beginning,

[1] According to Photius, *Bibl.* 8 (ed. Henry 1, 4a), after treating the Father, Son, and Holy Spirit, *Princ.* 2 concludes with discussion 'again about the soul, the resurrection, the punishments, the promises' (ἔτι περὶ ψυχῆς, περὶ ἀναστάσεως, περὶ κολάσεως, περὶ ἐπαγγελιῶν); the last three items are clearly dealt with in *Princ.* 2.10 and 2.11. The subject matter treated in this chapter is not mentioned by Photius, and could conceivably be included with the previous chapter, for the discussion here is not about the created world in general (e.g. its materiality and temporality), but the 'world' (the *cosmos* in the sense of the Greek term) of rational creatures, how they are arranged in all their variety and diversity and for what reasons, as is also the case in *Princ.* 2.1.1 (see n.1 there). Most of the manuscripts have a longer title here: 'On the world, movements of rational creatures, good or bad, and their causes.' Although their movements and their causes are mentioned briefly in *Princ.* 2.9.2 (and are treated much more fully in *Princ.* 3), the last sentence of *Princ.* 2.9.2 makes it clear that this is subordinate to the question of the purpose of the variety and diversity of souls and the order underlying it, in particular the pedagogic and salvific purpose of this arrangement as embraced in God's providence.

[2] It is important to bear in mind that the word translated in these opening sentences as 'beginning' (*initium*, certainly translating ἀρχή), following the pattern set by the usual translations of Gen. 1:1 and John 1:1 (both of which Origen cites below), undoubtedly has a wider range of meanings than the English 'beginning', especially for Origen (this book itself is entitled Περὶ Ἀρχῶν, rendered in Latin as *De Principiis*, but not translated into English as *On Beginnings*). It is not with the initial chronological moments of creation that Origen is here concerned or what happened before this age (as he is, say, in *Princ.* 2.1–3), but with the 'principle' of the arrangement of souls and the pedagogic and salvific purpose of the variety and diversity that is to be found in the cosmos, though this principle of arrangement cannot of course be separated from the origin of their coming to be in this way. As Origen comments elsewhere (*Hom. Gen.* 1.1): '*In the beginning, God made heaven and earth*. What is the beginning of all things, except our Lord and *Saviour of all*, Jesus Christ *the firstborn of every creature* [1 Tim. 4:10; Col. 1:15]? *In this beginning*, therefore, that is in his Word, *God made heaven and earth*, as the evangelist John also says at the beginning of his Gospel: *In the beginning was the Word and the Word was with God and the Word was God. This same was in the beginning with God. All things were made by him and without him nothing was made* [John 1:1–3]. Scripture is not speaking here of any temporal beginning [*Non ergo hic temporale aliquod principium dicit*], but it says that the heaven and the earth and all things which were made were made *in the beginning*, that is, in the Saviour.' On the term ἀρχή see also Origen, *Comm. Jo.* 1.90–108 and *Hom. Ps. 77*, 2.2 (GCS 13, p. 437.1–3).

[3] Cf. Justinian, *Ep. ad Menam* (ed. Schwartz, 190.8–14), an extract said to come from *Princ.* 2 and numbered by Koetschau as Fragment 24: 'In the beginning under consideration, God, by his will, caused to subsist as large a number of intellectual beings as he was able to control; for it must be admitted that the power of God is finite and its circumscription must not be done away with under the pretext of praise. For if the divine power were infinite, of necessity it could not even understand itself, for the infinite is by nature incomprehensible. He made, then, just as many as he was able to grasp and to hold them in hand and hold them together under his providence, just as he prepared as much matter as he was able to bring to order.' See also Theophilus of Alexandria, *Ep. Pasch.* 2 (= Jerome, *Ep.* 98.17; ed. Hilberg 2, 202.16–18): [Origen says:] 'God made as many beings as he could grasp and hold in subjection to himself and govern by his providence'; and Rufinus Palaest. *De fide* 17 (PL 21, 1131b): [Origen says:] 'God did not make all those whom he wished, but only those whom he could hold together and grasp.' The impossibility of comprehending the infinite is repeated in *Princ.* 3.5.1 and 4.4.8. Origen's thought here, as elsewhere, is eschatological, that is, he begins from the givenness of a definitive end, when all rational beings are brought to subjection to God so that 'God will be all in all' (1 Cor. 15:28); as their number is therefore fixed at the end, it must likewise be so from the beginnning. See especially *Princ.* 1.6.1–2 and the Introduction, section 3.

then, it must be supposed that God created so great a number of rational or intellectual creatures, or whatever the intellects mentioned above are to be called, as he foresaw would be sufficient. It is certain that he made them according to some definite number, predetermined by himself; for it is not to be supposed, as some would, that created beings have no limit, because where there is no limit, neither can there be any comprehension or circumscription. But if it were thus, then indeed created things could neither be held together nor provided for by God. For, naturally, whatever is infinite will also be incomprehensible. Moreover, as Scripture says, God *has ordered all things in number and measure,*[4] and therefore *number* will rightly be applied to rational creatures or intellects, that they be as many as may be arranged, governed, and held together by the providence of God. But *measure* will appropriately be applied to bodily matter, which, it is to be believed, was created by God in such quantity as he knew would be sufficient for the ordering of the world. These, then, are what are held to be created by God in the beginning, that is, before all things. And this, we think, is indicated even in that *beginning* which Moses introduces somewhat obscurely when he says, *In the beginning God made the heaven and the earth.*[5] For it is certain that it is not said of the firmament or the dry land, but of that heaven and earth from which this heaven and earth, which we see, subsequently borrowed their names.[6]

2.9.2. But since these rational natures, which as we have said above were made in the beginning, were made when they did not previously exist, by this very fact—that they were not, and then they began to exist—they are necessarily changeable and mutable, since whatever power existed in their substance was not in it by nature but was the result of the beneficence of their Maker. What they are, therefore, is neither their own nor eternal, but given by God. For it did not always exist, and everything that is given can also be taken away and withdrawn. The cause for withdrawal would be this, that the movements of the souls are not directed rightly and commendably. For the Creator granted to the intellects created by him the power of voluntary and free movement,[7] that the good that was in them might become their own,[8] being preserved by their own free will; but sloth and weariness of the labour of preserving the good, and an aversion to and a neglect of better things, supplied the beginning of withdrawal from the good.[9] But to withdraw from the good is nothing else than to come to be in evil. For it is certain that to lack good is to be evil. Whence it happens that, by whatever measure one falls away from the good, by

---

[4] Wis. 11:20.   [5] Gen. 1:1.

[6] Cf. Gen. 1:6–10; Origen, *Princ.* 2.3.6 (and the passage from *Sel. Ps. 36*, 2, cited in n.62 there); *Cels.* 6.59.

[7] Cf. Origen, *Princ.* 1.3.6; 1.5.2; 1.7.2; 1.8.3; 3.1.2–6.

[8] Cf. Origen, *Princ.* 1.3.8; 2.6.3; 3.6.1.

[9] On 'satiety', see Origen, *Princ.* 1.3.8–4.1 (and the material cited in n.71 there); *Comm. Matt.* 11.17; *Cels.* 6.44; *Or.* 29.13. On 'negligence', see Origen, *Princ.* 1.4.1 and the material cited in n.73 there.

the same measure one arrives in wickedness. In which condition, according to its own movements, each intellect, neglecting the good either to a greater or lesser extent, was drawn into the opposite of good, which undoubtedly is evil.[10] From which it appears that the Creator of all things accepted certain seeds and causes of variety and diversity in order that, according to the diversity of intellects, that is, of rational creatures (which diversity they must be supposed to have engendered from the causes which we have mentioned above), he might create a world various and diverse.[11] And what we mean by various and diverse is what we now wish to explain.

2.9.3. Now, we call 'world' everything which is above the heavens or in the heavens or upon the earth or in those places which are called the lower regions,[12] or any places whatever that anywhere exist, together with those who are said to dwell in them: all this is therefore called 'world'. In this world some beings are said to be super-celestial, that is, placed in the more blessed abodes and clothed with heavenly and resplendent bodies, and among these many differences are revealed, as, for instance, when the Apostle said that *The glory of the sun is one, another the glory of the moon, another the glory of the stars, for star differs from star in glory.*[13] Some beings, on the other hand, are called *earthly*,[14] and among them, that is, among human beings, there is no small difference; for some of them are barbarians, others Greeks, and of the barbarians some are wilder and fierce, and others are more gentle. Some of them use laws that are most highly approved, others more common and severe, and yet others have inhuman and savage customs rather than laws. Some of them, from the initial moment of their birth, are immediately in a position of humiliation and are in subjection and brought up as slaves, being placed under the dominion either of masters or princes or tyrants, while others are brought up with more freedom and more reasonably; some with healthy bodies, others in sickness from their earliest years, some defective in sight, others in hearing and speech, some born thus, others deprived of such senses immediately after birth, or else suffer such misfortune when fully grown. And what need is there for me to repeat and enumerate all the misfortunes of human miseries, from which some are free while others are afflicted, when every single person can weigh and consider them each for themselves? There are also certain invisible powers, to whom is entrusted the administration of things upon the earth, and among them no small difference must be believed to exist,[15] as is also found to be the case among human beings. The Apostle Paul indeed intimates that

---

[10] Cf. Origen, *Princ.* 2.6.3. Elsewhere Origen states that some rational beings have voluntarily accepted a lower state, for service to others, while yet remaining blameless; see esp. *Princ.* 1.5.5, and the material cited there in n.39, and 2.9.7 below.
[11] Cf. Origen, *Princ.* 2.1.   [12] Cf. Origen, *Princ.* 4.3.10.
[13] 1 Cor. 15:41.   [14] 1 Cor. 15:40.   [15] Cf. Origen, *Princ.* 1.8.1.

there are also certain 'lower [powers]',[16] and that among them, in like manner, must undoubtedly be sought a condition of variety. It seems superfluous to inquire about dumb animals and birds and those creatures which live in the waters, as it is certain that these ought to be regarded not as ruling beings but subordinate ones.

2.9.4. Therefore, since all things which have been created are said to have been made through Christ and in Christ—as the Apostle Paul most clearly indicates, saying, *For in him and through him were all things created, whether things in heaven or things on earth, visible or invisible, whether thrones or dominions or principalities or authorities: all things were created through him and in him,*[17] and also John, in the Gospel, indicates the same thing, saying, *In the beginning was the Word and the Word was with God and the Word was God; the same was in the beginning with God. All things were made through him, and without him was nothing made,*[18] and also in the Psalms it is written, *In Wisdom you made them all,*[19]—[and] since, therefore, Christ, as he is the Word and the Wisdom, is also the Righteousness,[20] it will undoubtedly follow that those things which were created in the Word and Wisdom are said to be created also in that Righteousness, which is Christ; whereby, clearly, it may be seen that in created things there was nothing unrighteous or accidental, but all may be shown to be such as the rule of equity and righteousness demands. How, then, this great variety of things and such great diversity can be understood as most righteous and equitable, I am sure cannot be explained by human intelligence or speech, unless as prostrate supplicants we beseech the Word and Wisdom and Righteousness himself, who is the only-begotten Son of God, that he, pouring himself through his grace into our minds, may deign to illuminate what is obscure, to open what is shut, and to unveil what is secret, if, indeed, we should be found either to seek or to ask or to knock so worthily such that we deserve when seeking to receive, or when asking to find, or when knocking that it be commanded to be opened.[21] Not relying, then, on our own intelligence but on the help of that Wisdom which made all things and of that Righteousness which we believe to be in all created things, even though we are meanwhile not able to assert how, we shall, nevertheless, trusting in his mercy, endeavour to inquire and examine how that great variety and diversity of the world may appear to be consistent with the whole rationale of righteousness. I say 'rationale', of course, in a general sense; for it is the mark of an ignorant person to seek, and of a foolish person to give, the particular rationale for each being.

---

[16] Perhaps Eph. 4:9: 'In saying "he ascended", what does it mean but that he descended to the lower [parts] of the earth' (κατέβη εἰς τὰ κατώτερα [μέρη] τῆς γῆς); 'parts' is lacking in the manuscript traditions but regularly supplied in modern editions and translations.

[17] Col. 1:16.   [18] John 1:1–3.   [19] Ps. 103:24.

[20] Cf. 1 Cor. 1:30.   [21] Cf. Matt. 7:7.

2.9.5. When, then, we say that this world was arranged in that variety in which, as we have explained above, it was created by God, the God whom we say is both good and just and most equitable, there are numerous individuals (especially those coming from the schools of Marcion, and Valentinus, and Basilides, who assert that the natures of souls are diverse) who are accustomed to object: how is it consistent with the justice of God in creating the world that to some he would assign a habitation in the heavens, and not only bestow upon them a better habitation, but also would grant them a higher and more glorious rank, that he would favour some with a 'principality', others with 'powers', that he would confer on yet others 'dominions',[22] that he would present to some the most honourable seats in the heavenly courts, that some would shine more brilliantly and glitter with a starry splendour, for *The glory of the sun is one, another the glory of the moon, another the glory of the stars, for star differs from star in glory*;[23] and, to sum it up briefly, if the Creator God lacks neither the will for, nor the power to effect, a good and perfect work, what reason can there be that, in creating rational natures, that is, those of whose existence he is himself the cause, he should make some of a higher degree and others of second or of third or of many still inferior and worse degrees? Then they object regarding those who dwell upon earth, that a happier lot befalls some by birth, as for example the one begotten of Abraham and born of the promise,[24] the other also, of Isaac and Rebecca, who, while still in the womb, supplants his brother and is said, before he is born, to be loved by God;[25] and, generally, this very fact—that one person is born among the Hebrews, with whom he finds instruction in the divine Law, another among the Greeks, themselves also wise and a people of no small learning, and again another among the Ethiopians, who are accustomed to feed upon human flesh, others among the Scythians, with whom parricide is practised as if by law, or amongst the Taurians, where strangers are sacrificed.[26] They thus ask us: if this great diversity and these various and diverse conditions of birth, in which the faculty of free will has no place (for one does not choose for oneself either where or with whom or in what condition one is born), if then, they say, this is not caused by a diversity in the natures of souls, that is, a soul of an evil nature is destined for an evil nation and a good one for a good nation, what alternative remains than that these things must be supposed to be the result of accidence and chance? And if that be admitted, then it will no longer be believed that the world was made by God or administered by his providence, and consequently it would seem that no judgement of God upon the deeds of each is to be expected.[27] In this

---

[22] Cf. Col. 1:16.   [23] 1 Cor. 15:41.
[24] Cf. Gen. 12:2, 17:16; Rom. 9:8–9; Gal. 4:23.
[25] Cf. Gen. 25:21–6; Rom. 9:10–13.
[26] Cf. Euripides, *Iph. taur.*; similar lists occur in Origen, *Cels.* 5.27, 34.
[27] Cf. Origen, *Princ.* 2.5.2.

matter, what is clearly the truth of things is for him alone to know *who searches out all things, even the depths of God.*[28]

2.9.6. We however, although but human, that we might not feed the insolence of the heretics by being silent, will give to their objections such answers as are able to occur to us, according to our ability, as follows. We have frequently shown in the above, by the declarations we were able to quote from the divine Scriptures, that God, the Creator of the universe, is good and righteous and almighty. When, *in the beginning,*[29] he created those beings that he desired to create, that is, rational beings, he had no other reason for creating them other than himself, that is, his own goodness. As, then, he himself, in whom was neither variation nor change nor inability, was the cause of all those things which were to be created, he created all whom he created equal and alike, since there was in himself no ground for variety and diversity. But since these rational creatures, as we have frequently shown and will nevertheless show yet again in the proper place,[30] were endowed with the faculty of free will, this freedom of will either incited each one to progress by the imitation of God or drew him to defection through negligence.[31] And this, as we have already said before, is the cause of the diversity among rational creatures, drawing its origin not from the will or judgement of the Creator, but from the freedom of the individual will. But God, to whom it forthwith seemed just to arrange his creatures according to merit, drew these diversities of intellects into the harmony of one world, that with these diverse vessels or souls or intellects he might adorn, as it were, one house, in which there ought to be *not only vessels of gold and of silver, but also of wood and of clay, and, indeed, some unto honour and others unto dishonour.*[32] And these are the causes, in my opinion, why this world has assumed its diversity, while divine providence arranges each individual according to the variety of their movements or of their intellects and purposes. On this account, the Creator will neither appear unjust, when, according to the antecedent causes, he distributes to each one according to his merit; nor will the happiness or unhappiness of each one's birth, or whatever be the condition that falls to him, be deemed accidental; nor will it be believed that there are different creators and diverse natures of souls.

2.9.7. But even holy Scripture does not appear to me to be altogether silent on the rationale of this mystery, as when the Apostle Paul, discussing Esau and Jacob, says: *For when they were not yet born and had done nothing either good*

---

[28] 1 Cor. 2:10.   [29] Gen. 1:1.
[30] Cf. Origen, *Princ.* 1.5.3; 1.7.2; 1.8.3; 2.1.2; 3.1.2–6.
[31] Compare with Origen's statement above, *Princ.* 2.9.2 and 1.5.5 (and the material cited there in n.39). On the imitation of God, see also *Princ.* 3.6.1; 4.4.4.
[32] 2 Tim. 2:20.

or evil, that the decree, made by the election of God, might continue, not from works but from him who called, it was said 'The elder shall serve the younger', as it is written, 'Jacob I loved, but Esau I hated.'[33] And after that, he answers himself and says, *What then shall we say? Is there injustice with God?*[34] And that he might supply us with an opportunity for inquiring into these matters and ascertaining how these things do not happen without reason, he answers himself and says, *By no means!* For the same question, it seems to me, which is raised regarding Jacob and Esau may also hold for all heavenly beings and for earthly creatures and even for those of the lower regions; and likewise, it seems to me, that just as he there says, *For when they were not yet born and had done nothing either good or evil*, so too it can be said about all the rest: 'When they were not yet created, and had done nothing either good or evil, that the decree of God, according to election, might stand, then (as some think) some things were created heavenly, others earthly, and others again of the lower regions, not from works (as they think), but from him who called. What then shall we say, if these things be thus? Is there unrighteousness with God? By no means!' Therefore, just as when the Scriptures are carefully examined regarding Jacob and Esau it is found that there is no unrighteousness with God, that it might be said, before they were born or had done anything in this life, that *the elder shall serve the younger*, and as it is found not to be unrighteous that even in the womb Jacob supplanted his brother, if we suppose him to be worthily beloved by God by the merits from a preceding life so as to be worthy of being preferred to his brother, so also with regard to the heavenly creatures, if we note that diversity was not the original state of the creature, but that, from antecedent causes, a different office of service was prepared by the Creator for each one in proportion to the degree of merit, on this ground, indeed, that each one, in that it has been created by God as an intellect or rational spirit, has gained for itself, according to the movements of his intellect and the affections of his soul, greater or lesser merit, and has become either lovable or even hateful to God; while, nevertheless, some of those who are of higher merit[35] are ordained to suffer with others, for fitting out the state of the world and to offer service to those below them, that by this they may also themselves be participants in the forbearance of the Creator, according to what the Apostle himself said, *For the creature was subject to futility, not willingly, but by reason of him who subjected it in hoped.*[36]

---

[33] Rom. 9:11–13; Gen. 25:23; Mal. 1:2–3. Cf. Origen, *Princ.* 1.7.4.

[34] Rom. 9:14.

[35] Note how 'merit' is used here positively, rather than in a negative context of a fall, and correlated to service for others. See above, *Princ.* 2.9.2, and, earlier, *Princ.* 1.5.5 and the material cited there in n.39.

[36] Rom. 8:20.

Observing, then, this sentiment, which the Apostle said when speaking of the birth of Esau and Jacob, *Is there injustice with God? By no means!,* I think it right that this same sentiment should be observed in the case of all creatures, since, as we have said above, the justice of the Creator ought to be visible in everything. And this, it seems to me, will only be shown with real clarity, if each one, whether of the heavens or earth or below the earth, may be said to have the causes of diversity in himself, preceding his bodily birth. For all things were created by the Word of God and by his Wisdom, and were set in order through his Righteousness. And by the grace of his compassion he provides for all and exhorts all to be cured, by whatever remedies they may and incites them to salvation.[37]

2.9.8. As, then, there is no doubt that at the day of judgement the good will be separated from the bad, and the righteous from the unrighteous, and each one will be assigned, by the judgement of God, to that place of which his merits have made him worthy—as we shall show, God willing, in what follows—so also, I think, some such thing has also already happened previously. For God must be believed to do and to arrange all things and at all times by [his] judgement. This is what the Apostle teaches when he says, *In a great house there are not only vessels of gold and of silver, but also of wood and of earth, and some unto honour and some unto dishonour*; and those words which he adds, saying that, *if anyone purifies himself, he will be a vessel unto honour, sanctified and useful to the master, prepared for every good work,*[38] undoubtedly point out this, that whoever *purifies himself* when placed in this life, will be *prepared for every good work* in the future, but whoever does not purify himself will be, according to the amount of his impurity, a *vessel unto dishonour,* that is, unworthy. In this way, therefore, there can be understood to have previously been rational vessels, whether purified or less purified, that is, which had purified themselves or had not, and each vessel [can be understood] to have received from this, according to the measure of its purity or impurity, a place or region or condition in which to be born or some service to discharge in this world; God, providing for all these to the smallest detail by the power of his Wisdom and discerning by the management of his judgement, arranges all things in a most equitable retribution, to the extent that each one, according to its merits, ought to be assisted or taken care of. Herein is assuredly demonstrated the complete rationale of equity, while the inequality of circumstances preserves the equality of retribution for merit. But he alone, along with his only-begotten Word and Wisdom and the Holy Spirit, knows with truth and clarity the reasons for the merits in each case.

---

[37] Cf. Origen, *Hom. Jer.* 6.2.   [38] 2 Tim. 2:20–1.

II: The Church's Preaching

The Judgement

2.10.1.[1] But since our discourse has reminded us of the judgement to come and of the retribution and punishment of sinners, in accordance with the things threatened by holy Scripture and contained in the ecclesiastical preaching—that at the time of judgement, *eternal fire* and *outer darkness* and a *prison* and a *furnace* and other similar things to these have been prepared for sinners[2]—let us also see what ought to be thought about these points.

But that these subjects may be arrived at in proper order, it seems to me that a discussion on the resurrection must be begun, that we may know what it is that shall come either to punishment or to rest and blessedness; we have argued about this more fully in other books also, which we have written on the resurrection,[3] and have shown what were our views about it. But now also, for the sake of the logical order of our treatise, it will not seem out of place to repeat a few points from them, especially since some are offended by the ecclesiastical faith, as if what we believe about the resurrection is silly and altogether foolish, especially the heretics, who, I think, must be answered in this way. If they admit that there is a resurrection of the dead, let them answer us: what is it that died, if not a body?[4] There will therefore be a resurrection of the body. Let them next say if they think that we are to make use of the body or not. I think that, with the Apostle Paul saying that *It is sown an animated body, it will rise a spiritual body,*[5] they cannot deny that a body rises, or that we make use of a body in the resurrection. What then? If it is certain that we are to make use of bodies, and if those bodies which have fallen are proclaimed to rise again (for to rise again cannot be properly said except of that which has previously fallen), it is, on this account, a matter of doubt to no one that they rise again, that we may be clothed with them once more at the resurrection. The one thing, therefore, is bound up with the other. For if bodies rise again, without doubt they rise as clothing for us; and if it is necessary, as it certainly is necessary, for

---

[1] The manuscripts give as the title 'On the Resurrection and the Judgement', and for *Princ.* 2.11, 'On the Promises'. After mentioning 'the soul' (treated in *Princ.* 2.8, see also the footnote appended to title of *Princ.* 2.9), Photius lists, as the remaining topics of *Princ.* 2: 'about resurrection, about punishment, about promises' (περὶ ἀναστάσεως, περὶ κολάσεως, περὶ ἐπαγγελιῶν). However, as the introductory lines of *Princ.* 2.10.1 indicate, the discussion of the resurrection in *Princ.* 2.10.1–3 is meant as a preliminary to the subject of the judgement (and punishments), dealt with in the remainder of the chapter. As *Princ.* 2.11 deals with 'the promises', both 2.10 and 2.11 in fact deal with what happens in the resurrection, and so it seems better to give 2.10 the title of 'The Judgement'. Crouzel and Simonetti here give the title 'On the Resurrection' and the title 'On the Judgement' at *Princ.* 2.10.4.

[2] Cf. Matt. 25:41; 8:12; 1 Pet. 3:19; Matt. 13:42.

[3] A *Treatise on the Resurrection*, in two volumes, was written by Origen before *Princ.* (Eusebius, *Hist. eccl.* 6.24); fragments from this are preserved by Pamphilus in his *Apology* (113, 128, 130, 132, 134), and by Methodius of Olympus in his work *On the Resurrection*, according to Photius, *Bibl.* 234.

[4] Cf. Tertullian, *Res.* 17–27.   [5] 1 Cor. 15:44.

us to be in bodies, we ought to be in no other bodies than our own. But if it is true that they rise again and they rise as *spiritual,* there is no doubt that they are said to rise from the dead, having cast away corruption and having laid aside mortality; otherwise it will appear vain and superfluous for anyone to rise from the dead [only] in order to die again. And this, finally, may be understood more clearly in this way, if one carefully observes what are the qualities of an *animated body,* which, when sown in the earth, regains the quality of a *spiritual body.* For it is from *the animated body* that the very power and grace of the resurrection draws out the *spiritual body,* when it transforms it from dishonour to glory.

2.10.2. Since the heretics see themselves as persons of great learning and wisdom, we shall ask them whether every body has some form, that is, is fashioned in some shape. And if they shall say there is a body which is not fashioned in some shape, they will be seen to be the most ignorant and foolish of all. For no one, except one who is an utter stranger to all learning, will deny this. But if, according to what is logical, they say that every body is fashioned in some definite shape, we shall ask them whether they are able to demonstrate and describe to us the shape of a spiritual body; which they certainly will in no way be able to do. We shall ask of them, moreover, about the differences of those who rise again. How will they show that saying to be true, that *There is one flesh of birds, another of fish; there are heavenly bodies and earthly bodies, but the glory of the heavenly is one, and the glory of the earthly another; the glory of the sun is one, another the glory of the moon, another the glory of the stars, for star differs from star in glory: thus it is with the resurrection of the dead?*[6] Let them show us, then, the differences in the glory of those who rise again following that gradation of heavenly bodies, and if by any chance they have tried to think out a principle in accordance with the differences in heavenly bodies, we will ask of them that they assign the differences in the resurrection by comparison with earthly bodies. We, however, understand the matter in this way: that the Apostle, wishing to describe how great are the differences among those who rise again in glory, that is, of the saints, took up a comparison with the heavenly bodies, saying, *the glory of the sun is one, another the glory of the moon, another the glory of the stars.* And wishing, on the other hand, to teach us the differences among those who come to the resurrection without being purified in this life, that is, sinners, he took an example from earthly things, saying, *there is one flesh of birds, another of fish.* For heavenly things are worthily compared to the saints, earthly things to sinners. These things are said in opposition to those who deny the resurrection of the dead, that is, the resurrection of bodies.

---

[6] 1 Cor. 15:39–42. Cf. Origen, *Res.* 2 (in Pamphilus, *Apol.* 134).

2.10.3. We now direct our discussion towards some of our own, who, either from poverty of mind or lack of instruction, introduce a very low and abject idea of the resurrection of the body.[7] We ask them in what manner they understand the *animated body,* which is transformed by the grace of the resurrection, and the *spiritual body,* and how they think that what is *sown in weakness* will be *raised in power,* and what is *sown in dishonour* will *rise in glory,* and what *is sown in corruption* will be transformed into *incorruption?* If, indeed, they believe the Apostle—that the body, when rising in glory and power and incorruptibility, has already become *spiritual*—it seems absurd and contrary to his meaning to say that it can again be entangled in the passions of flesh and blood, when the Apostle says most clearly, *Flesh and blood shall not inherit the kingdom of God, neither shall corruption inherit incorruption.*[8] But how do they take that passage, where the Apostle says that *We shall all be transformed?*[9] This transformation, according to that order of which we have spoken above, is certainly to be looked for; in it, undoubtedly, it is fitting for us to hope for something worthy of divine grace; this we believe will take place in the same sequence in which the Apostle describes the sowing in the ground of a *bare grain of wheat or some other kind,* to which *God gives a body as it pleases him,* after the grain of wheat has first died.[10] For in the same way our bodies also must be supposed to fall into the earth like a grain, in which is implanted that principle which holds together the bodily substance, so that although the bodies die and are corrupted and dispersed, yet by the Word of God that very principle, which is always preserved in the substance of the body, raises them up from the earth and refashions and restores them, just as the power, which exists in the grain of wheat, after its corruption and death, restores and refashions the grain into a body with stalk and ear.[11] And so also, to those who shall deserve to attain an inheritance in the kingdom of heaven, that principle of the body's refashioning, which we have mentioned before, by the command of God refashions out of the *earthly* and *animated body* a *spiritual body,* able to inhabit the heavens; while to those who may be of inferior merit or more abject still, or even of the lowest condition and thrust aside, will be given a body of

[7] No doubt referring to Papias, who is cited favourably by Irenaeus, *Haer.* 5.33.3–4, but criticized by Eusebius, *Hist. eccl.* 3.39.12–13, for his vivid millenarian depiction of the resurrection: 'I suppose he got these ideas through a misunderstanding of the apostolic accounts, not perceiving that the things said by them were spoken mystically in figures. For he appears to have been of very limited understanding, as one can see from his discourses.'

[8] 1 Cor. 15:50. On the spiritual quality of the body in the resurrection, see Origen, *Princ.* 3.6.4–6; and also *Or.* 26.6; *Mart.* 47; *Cels.* 5.19. Irenaeus, *Haer.* 5.9–14, responds to his opponents' use of this Pauline verse by pointing out that while flesh and blood cannot inherit the kingdom, they are nevertheless inherited *by* the Spirit in the kingdom; see also Tertullian, *Res.* 5–10, 48–51.

[9] 1 Cor. 15:51.

[10] 1 Cor. 15:36–8. Cf. Origen, *Cels.* 5.18; 5.23; *Res.* 2 (in Pamphilus, *Apol.* 130).

[11] Cf. Origen, *Cels.* 5.18, 19; 7.32.

glory and dignity corresponding to the dignity of the life and soul of each, in such a way, however, that even for those who are destined to *eternal fire* or to *punishments*,[12] the body which rises again is, through the very transformation of the resurrection, so incorruptible that it cannot be corrupted and dissolved even by punishments.[13]

2.10.4. If, then, such be the quality of the body which will arise from the dead, let us now see what the threat of *eternal fire* signifies.[14] Now we find in the prophet Isaiah that the fire by which each one is punished is described as his own; for he says, *Walk in the light of your fire and in the flame which you have kindled for yourself.*[15] It seems to be indicated, by these words, that every sinner kindles for himself the flame of his own fire, and is not plunged into some fire which has already been kindled by another or existed before himself.[16] The food and material of this fire are our sins, which are called, by the Apostle Paul, *wood and hay and straw.*[17] And I think that just as in the body an excess of nourishment and a detrimental kind and quantity of foods gives rise to fevers, and the fevers are also diverse either in kind or duration, according to the degree in which accumulated intemperateness supplies material and fuel for the fevers (the quality of this material, gathered together from diverse intemperateness, is the cause either of a more acute or more lingering disease), so also, when the soul has gathered together a multitude of evil works and an excess of sins in itself, at a suitable time all that assembly of evils boils up to punishment and is set aflame to chastisements; at which time, the intellect itself, or the conscience, bringing to memory by divine power all those things, the impressions and forms of which it had stamped in itself when sinning,[18] will see exposed before its eyes a history, as it were, of its evil deeds, of every single act it had done, whether foul or shameful, and had even impiously committed; then the conscience itself is agitated and pierced by its own stings and becomes its own accuser and witness. And this, I think, is what the Apostle Paul meant when he says, *While their thoughts mutually accuse or perhaps excuse them in the day when God will judge the secrets of human beings, according to my Gospel, by Jesus Christ.*[19] From which it is understood that, in what concerns the substance of the soul, certain torments are produced from the hurtful affections of the sins themselves.

---

[12] Cf. Matt. 25:41, 46.
[13] Koetschau suspects that Rufinus has here omitted some further discussion of the resurrectional body, and suggests that it should be completed by the teaching of the tenth anathema of the Second Council of Constantinople, which he places in his critical apparatus; the text of this anathema is included in the Appendix as item no. 16.
[14] Matt. 25:41.   [15] Isa. 50:11.
[16] Cf. Origen, *Comm. Rom.* 2.6; *Hom. Lev.* 9.8.   [17] 1 Cor. 3:12.
[18] Cf. Origen, *Comm. Rom.* 2.10; *Hom. Jer.* 16.10; *Hom. Ps. 38*, 2.2 (PG 12, 1402–4); *Or.* 28.5.
[19] Rom. 2:15–16.

2.10.5. And that the understanding of this matter may not appear too difficult, one can consider the result of those faults of the passions which often befall souls—as when a soul is burnt up by the flame of love, or tormented by zeal or envy, or agitated by the madness of anger, or consumed by the immensity of sorrow—how some, finding the excess of these evils unbearable, have deemed it more tolerable to submit to death than to endure perpetually torment of such a kind. You will indeed ask whether for those who have been entangled in those evils arising from the faults mentioned above, and have not been able, while existing in this life, to procure any amelioration for themselves, and have in this way departed this world, it would suffice for their punishment that they be tormented by the hurtful affections remaining in them, that is, the anger, the fury, the madness, the sorrow, whose deadly poison was in this life assuaged by no healing remedy; or whether, when these affections have been transformed, they will be tormented by the stings of a general punishment?

Now I think that another species of punishment may be understood, because, just as when the limbs of the body are loosened and torn away from their mutual connections we feel a torment of intense pain produced, so also when the soul is found outside the order and connection and harmony in which it was created by God for good action and useful experience, and not to harmonize with itself in the connection of its rational movements,[20] it must be supposed to bear the chastisement and torment of its own dissension and to feel the punishments of its own instability and disorder. But when the soul, thus dissolved and rent asunder, has been tried by the application of rational fire, it is undoubtedly reinforced in the consolidation and re-establishment of its structure.

2.10.6. There are also many other things that are hidden from us, which are known to him alone who is the Physician of our souls. For if, because of the ills that we have brought upon ourselves through food and drink, we occasionally take, for the health of the body, the necessary cure of harsher and more bitter medicine, and sometimes even, if the character of the sickness demands it, we need the rigor of the knife and the severity of an amputation, and if the virulence of the disease surpasses even these remedies, as the last resort the illness is burnt out by fire, how much more is it to be understood that God our Physician, desiring to wash away the ills of our souls, which they had contracted through a variety of sins and crimes, should employ penalties of this sort, and even apply the punishment of fire to those who have lost their soul's health?[21]

---

[20] On the harmony of the soul, see Plato, *Resp.* 3.410cd; 9.591d; *SVF* 3.121; Philo, *Deus* 24; Clement of Alexandria, *Strom.* 4.4.18.

[21] On the remedial and therapeutic value of pain, see Origen, *Princ.* 1.6.3; 2.5.3.

Images of this are also found in the holy Scriptures. Thus, in Deuteronomy the divine Word threatens sinners that they are to be punished with fevers and colds and jaundice, and tormented with feebleness of eyes and derangement of mind and paralysis and blindness and weakness of kidneys.[22] If, then, anyone, at leisure, will gather together out of the whole of Scripture every mention of suffering which, in the threats to sinners, are called by the names of bodily afflictions, he will find that either the ills or the punishments of souls are figuratively indicated through them. This is so that we might understand that in the same way in which physicians apply remedies to the sick in order that through treatment they might recover, so also God deals towards those who have lapsed and fallen. There is a proof of this in that passage in which, through the prophet Jeremiah, God's *cup of fury* is commanded *to be set before all nations* that *they may drink it and become mad and vomit;* in saying this, it is threatened that if anyone refuses to drink, he shall not be cleansed.[23] From which it must be understood that the fury of the vengeance of God advances the purification of souls. That even the punishment said to be inflicted by fire is understood to be applied as an aid is taught by Isaiah, who speaks of Israel in this way, *The Lord will wash away the filth of the sons and daughters of Zion and shall purge away the blood from their midst by a spirit of judgement and a spirit of burning.*[24] Of the Chaldeans he speaks thus, *You have coals of fire: sit upon them! They will be a help to you;*[25] and in other places he says, *The Lord will sanctify them in burning fire;*[26] and in Malachi, the prophet speaks thus: *The Lord, sitting, will kindle his people like gold and silver; he will kindle and purify and smelt the purified sons of Judah.*[27]

2.10.7. And also that passage, mentioned in the Gospel, about the unjust stewards who are said to be *cut asunder* and *their portion placed with the unfaithful,*[28] as if that portion, which was not their own, were to be sent elsewhere, undoubtedly indicates some kind of punishment for those, it seems to me, whose spirit is shown as separated from their soul. For if this Spirit is of divine nature, that is, is understood to be the Holy Spirit, we shall take this passage to be said of the gift of the Holy Spirit; that when, whether by baptism or by the grace of the Spirit *a word of wisdom* or *a word of knowledge*[29] or of any other gift has been bestowed upon someone and not rightly administered, that is, either buried in the earth or tied up in a napkin,[30] the gift of the Spirit

---

22 Deut. 28:22, 28, 29.
23 Jer. 31:1–2, 13–15 (Heb. 25:15–16, 27–9); similarly in Origen, *Comm. ser. Matt.* 95.
24 Isa. 4:4. Cf. Origen, *Hom. Jer.* 2.2; *Hom. Luc.* 14.3.
25 Isa. 47:14–15. Cited also in Origen, *Princ.* 2.5.3; *Cels.* 5.15; 6.56.
26 Isa. 66:16–17.
27 Mal. 3:3. Cf. Origen, *Or.* 29.15, where he also cites Mal. 3:2 together with Isa. 4:4.
28 Luke 12:46.   29 1 Cor. 12:8.   30 Cf. Matt. 25:25; Luke 19:20.

will certainly be withdrawn from his soul, and the portion that remains, that is, the substance of the soul, will be placed with the unfaithful, being divided off and separated from that Spirit with whom, by *joining itself to the Lord*, it should have been *one Spirit*.[31] But if this is not understood of the Spirit of God, but of the nature of the soul itself, then that, which was made *in the image and likeness* of God,[32] will be called its better part, whereas the other part is that which was assumed, after its fall through free will, against the nature of its original condition and purity; this part, being the friend and beloved of the material body is punished with the lot of the unfaithful. This division may also be understood in a third sense: that, as each of the faithful, even if the least in the Church, is said to be attended by an angel,[33] who is declared by the Saviour to *always behold the face of God the Father*,[34] and this angel of God, who was certainly one with him over whom he was set, is said to be taken away from him if he by disobedience becomes unworthy, then that *portion* of him, that is, the *portion* of his human nature, being torn away from the divine part, is assigned a place *with the unfaithful*,[35] because it has not faithfully observed the warnings of the angel allotted to it by God.

2.10.8. But the *outer darkness*,[36] in my opinion, is to be understood not as a place with a dark atmosphere without any light, but rather as of those who, being immersed in the darkness of profound ignorance,[37] have become alien to every glimmer of reason or understanding. It must also be considered whether perhaps this expression does not also mean that just as the saints will receive those bodies, in which they have lived in holiness and purity in the habitations of this life, luminous and glorious after the resurrection, so also the wicked, who in this life have loved the darkness of error and the night of ignorance, may be clothed with dark and black bodies after the resurrection, so that the very fog of ignorance, which in this world had taken possession of their minds within them, may appear in the future as the garment of their outward body.[38] One should think similarly about the *prison*.[39] Let these remarks made as briefly as possible suffice for the moment, that order of our discourse might in the meantime be preserved.

---

[31] 1 Cor. 6:17.   [32] Cf. Gen. 1:26.

[33] On 'guardian angels', see Origen, *Princ.* 1.8.1 and the material cited in n.5 there.

[34] Matt. 18:10. According to Origen, *Hom. Isa.* 4.1, to see the face of God is to know the principles of divine realities, that is, the reasons and principles of the works of God. See also Origen, *Princ.* 2.11.7.

[35] Luke 12:46.   [36] Matt. 8:12 etc.   [37] Cf. Origen, *Comm. Jo.* 2.133–6.

[38] Cf. 1 Pet. 3:19. Koetschau here adds a passage from Jerome, *Ep.* 124.7.2 (ed. Hilberg 3, 104.25–105.2), and, after the following sentence, a passage made up of sentences from the *De Sectis* attributed to Leontius (PG 81.1, 1265) and from Justinian's *Ep. ad Menam* (ed. Schwartz, p. 205.9–10), numbering it as Fragment 25; these texts are included in the Appendix as item no. 17.

[39] 1 Pet. 3:19.

The Promises

2.11.1. Let us now see briefly what must be thought regarding the promises. It is certain that no animated being can be wholly inactive and immobile, but eagerly delights in moving in all kinds of ways and in being perpetually active and in willing something; and I think it is clear that this nature is in all animated beings. Much more, then, is it necessary for a rational animal, that is, a human being, always to be in some movement or action. And if he forgets himself and is ignorant of what befits him, his whole purpose moves around bodily enjoyments and in all his movements he is occupied with the desires and lusts of the body; but if he be one who strives to care or provide for the common good, then he exerts himself either by working in service of the state or by obeying the magistrates or whatever else may seem clearly to be of common benefit. And if, now, any one is such that he understands that there is something better than those things that seem bodily, and can diligently bestow his labour upon wisdom and knowledge, then he will undoubtedly direct all his activity towards endeavours of that kind, that he may, by inquiring into the truth, know the causes and reasons of things. As, therefore, in this life one person judges that the highest good is the pleasure of the body, another to serve for the common good, and another to devote attention to study and learning, so let us inquire whether in that life, which is the true one, which is said to be *hidden with Christ in God*,[1] that is, in that eternal life, there will be for us some such order or condition of living.[2]

2.11.2. Certain persons, then, rejecting the labour of thinking and following the superficial view of the letter of the law, or yielding, rather, in some way to their own desires and lusts, being disciples of the letter alone, reckon that the promises of the future are to be looked for in the pleasure and luxury of the body; and especially because of this they desire to have again, after the resurrection, flesh of such a kind that never lacks the ability to eat and drink and to do all things that pertain to flesh and blood, not following the teaching of the Apostle Paul regarding the resurrection of a *spiritual body*.[3] And consequently they say that there will be contracts of marriages and procreation of children even after the resurrection, picturing for themselves the rebuilding of the earthly city of Jerusalem,[4] with precious stones laid down for its foundations and its walls constructed of jasper and its battlements adorned with crystal; that it will have an outer wall composed of different precious stones, namely,

---

[1] Col. 3:3.
[2] On 'true life', see Origen, *Comm. Jo.* 1.181–2; 2.155–7; 13.140; *Comm. Matt.* 16.28; *Comm. Rom.* 6.14; *Hom. Num.* 19.4; *Sel. Ps.* 26.1 (PG 12, 1276).
[3] 1 Cor. 15:44. Origen is referring again to 'millenarians' such as Papias; cf. *Princ.* 2.10.3, n.7.
[4] A position developed by Irenaeus, *Haer.* 5.34.4–35.2. Cf. Justin Martyr, *Dial.* 81.

jasper and sapphire and chalcedony and emerald and carnelian and onyx and chrysolite and chrysophrase and jacinth and amethyst.[5] Then, also, they think that *foreigners* are to be given to them as the servants of their pleasure, whom they will have as *ploughmen or vinedressers* and as *wall-builders*,[6] by whom their ruined and fallen city may be raised up again; and they think that they will receive the *wealth of the nations* to consume and that they will have control over their riches, that even the camels of Midian and Gaiphar will come and bring to them *gold and incense and precious stones*.[7] And they think to confirm this by the authority of the prophets, from those promises which are written about Jerusalem; where it is also said that *They who serve God shall eat and drink, but sinners shall hunger and thirst*, and that *The righteous shall be joyful but the wicked will be possessed by confusion*.[8] And from the New Testament, they quote the saying of the Saviour, in which he makes a promise to his disciples about the gladness produced by wine, saying, *I shall not drink of this, until I drink of it anew with you in my Father's kingdom*.[9] They add, moreover, that statement in which the Saviour calls those blessed who now *hunger and thirst*, promising them that *they shall be satisfied*;[10] and many other illustrations are adduced by them from the Scriptures, the meaning of which they do not perceive [because they] must be understood figuratively or spiritually. Then, again, after the fashion of the form of things in this life, and according to the grades of dignities or ranks or the degrees of authorities in this world, they reckon they are to be kings and princes, like those earthly ones are, obviously because of that saying in the Gospel, *You shall have authority over five cities*.[11] And, to speak briefly, they desire that all things, which are looked for in the promises, should be similar, in every respect, with the fashion of things in this life, that is, that what is should be again. Such then are the thoughts of those who believe indeed in Christ, but, understanding the divine Scriptures in a sort of Judaistic sense, draw from them nothing worthy of the divine promises.

2.11.3. Those, however, who accept the interpretation of Scriptures in accordance with the sense of the apostles, do indeed hope that the saints will eat, but that they will eat *the bread of life*,[12] which nourishes the soul with the food of truth and wisdom, and enlightens the intellect, and causes it to drink from the cup of divine Wisdom, just as the divine Scripture says, *Wisdom has prepared her table, she has slaughtered her victims, she has mixed her wine in the bowl, and she cries with a loud voice: 'Turn to me and eat the bread which I have*

---

[5] Cf. Rev. 21:10–21; Isa. 54:12; Ezek. 28:13.   [6] Isa. 61:10, 60:5.
[7] Isa. 61:6; 60:5–6.   [8] Isa. 65:13–14.   [9] Matt. 26:49.
[10] Matt. 5:6; Luke 6:21.   [11] Luke 19:19. Cf. Jer. 18:25; Origen, *Hom. Num.* 11.4.
[12] John 6:35. Cf. Origen, *Comm. Jo.* 20.406; *Comm. Matt.* 14.6; *Comm. Cant.* 1 (GCS 8, p. 104); *Cels.* 1.48; *Hom. Lev.* 16.5.

prepared for you, and drink the wine which I have mixed for you.[13] By this food
of Wisdom, the intellect, being nourished to a whole and perfect state, as the
human being was made in the beginning, is restored to the *image and likeness
of God,*[14] so that even though a certain person may have departed from this life
insufficiently instructed, yet if he bears the report of approved works, he will
be capable of being instructed in that Jerusalem, the city of saints, that is, of
being taught and being formed, and being made a *living stone,* a stone *elect and
precious,*[15] because he has borne with fortitude and constancy the trials of life
and the struggles of piety; and will come there to a truer and clearer knowledge of that which has here already been spoken beforehand, that *the human
being shall not live by bread alone, but by every word that proceeds from the
mouth of God.*[16] Moreover, the princes and rulers must be understood to be
those who both govern those of lower rank and instruct and teach them and
establish them in things divine.

2.11.4. But if these considerations should appear scarcely able to inspire a
worthy desire in intellects hoping in literal promises, resuming our discussion
a little further let us examine how that desire for the reality of things is natural
to us and implanted in our soul, so that we may at last be able to describe, as it
were, the very forms of the *bread of life* and the quality of that *wine* and the
characteristics of the *principalities* according to the spiritual interpretation.
Just as, therefore, in those arts which are usually accomplished manually, the
design—the why or what quality or for what purpose something is made—
remains indeed in the intellect, while the actuality is unfolded by the aid of the
work of our hands, so also in those works of God, which were created by him,
it must be held that the design and meaning of those things which we see done
by him remains in secret. And just as, when our eye sees the things made by an
artist, the intellect, if it perceives something made exceptionally skilfully,
immediately burns to know of what nature it is or how or for what purpose it
was made, so also, in a much greater degree, and in one that is beyond all comparison, does the intellect burn with an inexpressible desire to know the reason of those things which we see done by God. This desire, this love, we believe,
has undoubtedly been implanted in us by God; and as the eye naturally seeks
light and vision, and our body naturally desires food and drink, so our intellect
bears an appropriate and natural desire for knowing the truth of God and to
learn the causes of things. Now we have received this desire from God, not that
it should not or could not ever be satisfied; otherwise the *love of truth*[17] would

---

[13] Prov. 9:2–5. For Christ, the Wisdom of God, as the fruit of the vine, see Origen, *Comm. Jo.*
1.205–8; *Hom. Cant.* 2.7; *Comm. Cant.* 3 (GCS 8, p. 200); *Hom. Lev.* 7.1–2.
[14] Gen. 1:26.   [15] 1 Pet. 2:4–6. Cf. Origen, *Cels.* 8.19; *Hom. Ex.* 13.3.
[16] Matt. 4:4; cf. Deut. 8:3.   [17] 2 Thess. 2:10.

appear to have been implanted in our intellects by God the Creator with no purpose, if the possession of its desire is never accomplished. Whence also, even in this life, those who devote themselves with great labour to the studies of piety and religion, although they obtain only some small fragments from the numerous and immense treasures of divine knowledge, yet, by this very fact—that they occupy their understanding and intellect with these things and surpass themselves in the eager desire—they receive much advantage from this fact itself, for they turn their intellects to the study and love of searching for the truth and make themselves fitter for receiving the instruction to come; just as, when someone would paint an image, if he first with a light pencil trace a sketch of the shape to come and prepare the marks ready for the superimposition of the features, undoubtedly, by the outline now laid down through the sketch, the canvas is found to be more ready for the reception of the real colours, [so it will be with us] if only that sketch and outline may be traced *on the tablets of our hearts*[18] by the pencil of our Lord Jesus Christ. And therefore, perhaps, it is said, *To everyone who has shall be given and be added.*[19] From which it is clear that to those who have, in this life, a kind of outline of truth and knowledge, shall be added the beauty of the perfect image in the future.[20]

2.11.5. Such, I think, was the *desire* indicated by him who said, *I am hard pressed between the two, having a desire to depart and be with Christ, which is far better,*[21] knowing that when he should have returned to Christ he would know more clearly the reasons for all things which are done upon earth, that is, regarding the human being or the soul of the human being or the intellect, or whichever of these constitutes the human being, what is *the guiding Spirit, the Spirit who works,* and *the Spirit of life,*[22] or what is the grace of the Holy Spirit which is given to the faithful.[23] Then he will also understand what Israel signifies,[24] or what the diversity of the nations and what the twelve tribes of Israel mean and what the individual people of each tribe [signify].[25] Then he will also understand the reason for the priests and the Levites and the different

---

[18] 2 Cor. 3:3.   [19] Matt. 25:29. Cf. Origen, *Comm. ser. Matt.* 69.

[20] Cf. Origen, *Hom. Ps. 36,* 5.1 (PG 12, 1359–60).

[21] Phil. 1:23. Cf. Origen, *Princ.* 1.7.5.

[22] Ps. 50:14; Eph. 2:2, and 1 Cor. 12:6, 11; Rom. 8:2, 11; and 1 Cor. 15:45.

[23] Cf. Origen, *Princ.* 1.3.5. In the remainder of this chapter, Origen expounds in a typically apocalyptic fashion those things that human beings will come to know when returning to Christ. Many of the items he mentions are treated elsewhere in *Princ.* or his other works. For this theme more generally, see M. E. Stone, 'List of Revealed Things in the Apocalyptic Literature', in F. M. Cross et al., eds., *Magnalia Dei* (New York, 1976), 414–52.

[24] Cf. Origen, *Princ.* 4.3.12. All aspects of the history of Israel upon earth are, for Origen, types of the heavenly Israel. Cf. Origen, *Princ.* 4.3.7; *Hom. Ex.* 1.2; *Hom. Lev.* 13.4; *Hom. Num.* 1.3; 3.3; *Cels.* 7.29.

[25] Cf. Num. 1, 26. Cf. Origen, *Princ.* 4.3.7–8.

priestly orders,[26] whose type was in Moses,[27] and will learn, too, what is the true meaning of the jubilees and the weeks of years with God;[28] and he will also see the reasons for the feast days and the holy days,[29] and will perceive the causes of all the sacrifices and purifications;[30] he will observe what is the reason for the purification from leprosy and the different kinds of leprosy,[31] and for the purification of those who suffer an emission of seed;[32] he will come to know, moreover, about the good powers, what they are, their greatness and qualities, and of those also of the opposite kind,[33] and what is the affection of the former towards human beings and the contentious jealousy of the latter;[34] he will perceive also the principle of souls and the diversity of animals, whether of those that live in the water or of birds or of beasts, and what is the cause why each genus is divided into so many species, and what intention of the Creator, or what meaning of his Wisdom, is concealed in each individual thing. He will also come to know the reason why certain powers are associated with certain roots or herbs,[35] and why, on the other hand, they are absent from others; and what is the reason for the apostate angels,[36] and for what cause they are able to flatter in some things those who do not despise them with complete faith, and to exist for the purpose of error and deception.[37] He will also learn the judgement of divine providence upon each individual thing;[38] about things that happen to human beings, that they happen not by chance or by accident, but by a reason so carefully considered, so lofty, that it does not overlook even the number of *hairs on the heads*, not only of the saints but probably of all human beings, the scope of which providence extends even to the *two sparrows* sold for a denarius,[39] whether the sparrows there are understood spiritually or literally. For now, in the meantime, [the judgement of divine providence] is still sought out; but then and there it will forthwith be seen clearly.[40]

2.11.6. From all this it must be reckoned that not a little time may pass meanwhile, until the reason merely of those things which come to pass on earth may be shown to the worthy and deserving after their departure from life, that by the knowledge of it all and by grace full of knowledge, they may enjoy an

---

[26] Cf. Num. 3, 4, 8, 18. Cf. Philo, *Alleg. Int.* 3.82; *Det.* 132–4; *Spec.* 2.120–2; Clement of Alexandria, *Strom.* 3.11.72; 4.25.157; 5.6.32–3; Origen, *Hom. Num.* 3.2; *Hom. Lev.* 2.3–4; 3.1; 6.3–6; 7.1.

[27] For Moses, see esp. Origen, *Hom. Exod.* and *Hom. Num.*

[28] Cf. Lev. 25. Cf. Origen, *Comm. Matt.* 15.32; *Or.* 27.13–16.   [29] Cf. Lev. 23.

[30] Cf. Lev. 1–7, 11–16. Cf. Origen, *Hom. Lev.* 3, 4, 5, 9.

[31] Cf. Lev. 13–14. Cf. Origen, *Hom. Lev.* 8.5–11.   [32] Cf. Lev. 15:13–18.

[33] Cf. 1 Cor. 12:10. Origen, *Princ.* 1.5.1–2; 1.6.2; 1.8.1.

[34] Cf. Origen, *Princ.* 3.2.1–3.   [35] Cf. Wis. 7:20; Origen, *Hom. Luc.* 21.6.

[36] Cf. Origen, *Princ.* 3.1.12; *Hom. Ezech.* 9.5.

[37] Cf. Origen, *Princ.* 3.2–3; *Hom. Ezech.* 6.8.   [38] Cf. Origen, *Princ.* 2.1.2.

[39] Matt. 10:29–30. Cf. Origen, *Mart.* 34; *Or.* 11.5; *Cels.* 8.70; *Hom. Luc.* 32.3.

[40] Cf. 2 Cor. 13:12.

unspeakable joy. Then, next, if that air which is between heaven and earth is not devoid of animated and rationally animated beings—as the Apostle said, *In which you once walked, following the course of this world, following the prince of the power of the air, the spirit who is now at work in the sons of disobedience,*[41] and again he says, *We shall be caught up in the clouds to meet Christ in the air, and so we shall always be with the Lord*[42]—it must be supposed, then, that the saints will remain there for some time, until they learn the reason of the two-fold mode of the arrangement of those things that happen in the air. When I say 'twofold mode', I mean, for example, when we were upon earth, we saw either animals or trees, and perceived the differences among them, and also the very great diversity among human beings; yet, although we saw these, we did not understand the reasons for them, but this alone was suggested to us from the diversity which we saw, that we should search out and examine for what reason these things were either created diverse or were arranged diversely, and that a zeal and love for knowledge of this kind be conceived upon earth, the knowledge and understanding of which will be granted after our departure, if indeed things turn out as desired; when, therefore, we shall have fully comprehended the reason, then we shall understand in a twofold manner what we saw on earth. Some such thing, then, must be said about the abode in the air. I think that the saints who depart from this life will remain in some place situated upon the earth, which the divine Scripture calls *paradise*,[43] as if in some place of instruction and, so to speak, an auditorium or school for souls, in which they may be instructed regarding all things which they had seen on earth and may also receive some information regarding things that are to follow in the future, just as when placed in this life they had received some indications of future events, *through a mirror, in enigmas,* indeed, yet comprehended *in part*,[44] which are revealed more clearly and luminously to the saints in their proper place and time. If anyone indeed is *pure in heart*[45] and more clear in intellect and more practised in understanding, he will make quicker progress and speedily ascend to a place of the air,[46] and will reach the kingdom of heaven, through each of those *stages*,[47] so to speak, which the Greeks have termed 'spheres', that is, 'globes', but which the divine Scripture calls *heavens;* in each of these he will first observe the things that are done there, and, second, he will come to know the reason why they are done: and thus he will pass in order through each stage, following him *who has passed into the heavens, Jesus the Son of God*,[48] who has said, *I will that where I am, they may also be*

---

[41] Eph. 2:2.   [42] 2 Thess. 4:17.   [43] Gen. 2:8; Luke 23:43.

[44] 1 Cor. 13:12.   [45] Matt. 5:9.

[46] Cf. Plato, *Phaedr.* 246–7; *Tim.* 42a–b; *3 Bar.*; *Ascen. Isa.*; Origen, *Cels.* 6.21–4.

[47] The Latin word *mansiones* clearly translates the μοναί of John 14:2, cited below, which in this context is most appropriately translated as 'stages' rather than the more familiar 'dwelling-places'.

[48] Heb. 4:14.

with me.[49] He also alludes to this diversity of places, when he says, *There are many stages with my Father.*[50] He is himself everywhere,[51] however, and traverses all things; we are no longer to understand him in those narrow limits, in which he came to be amongst us for our sake, that is, not in that circumscribed condition which he had when placed among human beings upon earth in our body, by which he might be thought of as enclosed in some one place.

2.11.7. When, then, for example, the saints shall have reached the heavenly places, then they will clearly see the natures of the stars one by one, and will understand whether they are animated or something else.[52] And they will understand also the other reasons for the works of God, which he will himself reveal to them. For now he will show to them, as to sons,[53] the causes of things and the power of his creation, teaching them why that star was placed in that particular position in the heavens and why it is separated from another by so great an intervening space; for example, if it had been nearer, what would have come about from this, or if it had been further, what would have happened; or, if this star had been larger than that, how the universe would not have remained the same, but everything would have been changed into another form. And when they have finished going through all those matters pertaining to the reason of the stars and their circulations in the heavens, they will come to those things which are unseen[54] or to those whose names alone we have as yet heard, and to things which are *invisible*,[55] which, the Apostle Paul has taught, are many, although what they are or what difference there may be among them, we are not able even to conjecture with our feeble intellect.[56] And so,[57] the rational being, growing through each step, not as it grew in this life in flesh and body and soul but enlarged in intelligence and understanding, is advanced as an intellect already perfected to perfect knowledge, no longer impeded by those fleshly senses, but being enlarged by intellectual increase and beholding, always purely and, so to speak, *face to face,*[58] the cause of things, it thus attains perfection, firstly, that by which it ascends, and, secondly, that by which it remains, having, as the food upon which it feasts, the contemplation and

---

[49] John 17:24.

[50] John 14:2. On the translation as 'stages', see n.47 above. Cf. Origen, *Hom. Jes. Nav.* 10.1; 23.4; *Hom. Num.* 27.2.

[51] Cf. Origen, *Princ.* 2.1.3; *Comm. Jo.* 6.188–90.

[52] Cf. Origen, *Princ.* Pr.10; 1.7.2–5.   [53] Cf. Origen, *Comm. Jo.* 1.92–3.

[54] 2 Cor. 4:18.   [55] Rom. 1:20; Col. 1:16.

[56] Cf. Origen, *Princ.* 4.1.7; *Comm. Jo.* 6.241; 10.283–4.

[57] Cf. Jerome, *Ep.* 124.7.3 (ed. Hilberg 3, 105.3–10): 'And, at the end of the second volume, discussing our final perfection, he says: when we have progressed so far that we are no longer flesh and bodies, and perhaps not even souls, but intellect and understanding, coming to perfection, not blinded by any cloud of disturbing passions, we shall see rational and spiritual substances *face to face*.'

[58] 1 Cor. 13:12. Cf. Origen, *Princ.* 1.4.1 and the material cited there in n.74.

understanding of things and the reasons for their causes. For just as in this bodily life of ours, we first grew bodily into that which we now are, in the first years a sufficiency of food supplying us with the means of increase, but after the stature has been attained by growth to its measure, we use food no longer that we might grow, but that we might live and might remain in life by it, so also, I think the intellect, when it has reached perfection, still feeds on appropriate and suitable food in such a measure that it ought neither to lack anything or to be in excess. And this food, in every respect, must be understood to be the contemplation and understanding of God, having measures appropriate and suitable to this nature, which was made and created; it is appropriate that every one of those beginning to see God, that is, to understand him through *purity of heart*,[59] observe these measures.

[59] Matt. 5:8. Cf. Origen, *Comm. Matt.* 18.5; *Or.* 27.13.

Rufinus' Preface to Book Three

The two previous books of *On First Principles* I translated, not only being urged on by you but even being constrained by you, during the forty days of Lent. But since in those days you, my devout brother Macarius, were living nearby and had more leisure, so I also worked harder; whereas I have been slower in interpreting these two latter books, seeing as you visited me, from the outermost and furthest parts of the city, to urge me on less frequently. Now, if you remember what I warned about in my former preface—that certain persons would be angry if they did not hear us speak some evil of Origen—that immediately followed, as, I think, you found out. But if those demons who incite the tongues of human beings to speak evil were so incensed by that work, in which he not as yet fully laid bare their secrets, what, do you think, will happen to this, in which he has revealed all their dark and hidden ways, by which they creep into the hearts of human beings and deceive weak and fragile souls? You will immediately see all things thrown into confusion, seditions stirred up, clamours raised throughout the whole city, and him, who endeavoured to dispel the diabolical darkness of ignorance by the evangelical lamp, summoned to condemnation. Let such things, however, be weighed lightly by him who desires to be trained in divine instruction, preserving the rule of the Catholic faith.

I must mention this, however, that, as we did in the former books, so in these we have taken care not to translate such passages as appear to be contrary to the rest of Origen's teaching and to our faith, but to omit them as being interpolations and forgeries of others. If he appeared to have uttered any novelties about rational beings, since the chief point of the faith does not consist in this, for the sake of knowledge and exercise (since perhaps by necessity we must reply to certain heresies in such a manner) I have neither omitted them in these nor in the preceding books, except when perhaps he wished to repeat in the subsequent books what he had already said in those previous ones and, for the sake of brevity, I thought it convenient to cut out some of these repetitions. If anyone, however, reads these passages with a desire to advance in knowledge and not to raise objections, he will do better if he choose to have them expounded to him by experts. For it is absurd to have the fictitious songs of the poets and the ridiculous fables of comedies expounded by grammarians, while anyone thinks he can learn without a master or an interpreter those things which are spoken either of God or of the heavenly powers and of the whole universe, in which every distorted error either of pagan philosophers or of heretics is refuted; thus it comes about that human beings would rather rashly and ignorantly condemn things that are difficult and obscure than learn by study and diligence.

Free Will

3.1.1.[1] *[Latin]* Some such opinions, we believe, are to be held regarding the divine promises, when we direct our understanding to the contemplation of that eternal and never-ending age and contemplate its ineffable joy and blessedness. But since the ecclesiastical preaching includes a belief in a future righteous judgement of God, which belief summons and persuades human beings to live in a good and blessed manner and to avoid sin in every way, and as by this it is undoubtedly indicated that it is within our power to devote ourselves either to a life worthy of praise or one worthy of blame, I therefore think it necessary to discuss also a few points regarding the freedom of our will, seeing as this question has been treated by very many writers in no insignificant a manner. But that we may more easily understand what freedom of the will is, let us inquire what the nature of this will and desire may signify.

1: On Free Will

3.1.2. *[Latin]* Of all things that move, some have the causes of their movements within themselves, while others receive them from without; for example, all things

---

[1] For Origen, *Princ.* 3.1, we also have the Greek text (translated below) from the *Philocalia*. As will be clear, Rufinus has not infrequently extended the text in his translation; those places where it is likely that the *Philocalia* has either omitted a passage or abridged it are noted.

On Self-Determination

3.1.1.[1] *[Greek]* Since in the ecclesiastical preaching there is included the doctrine of the righteous judgement of God, which, when believed to be true, summons those who hear it to live well and to avoid sin in every way, clearly acknowledging that things worthy of praise and blame are within our own power, come and let us discuss separately a few points regarding self-determination, a problem that is one of the most necessary importance. And that we may understand what self-determination is, it is necessary to unfold the meaning of it, in order that, this being made clear, that which is sought may be posed precisely.

---

[1] The Greek text of Origen, *Princ.* 3.1, has been preserved for us by its inclusion, as chapter 21, in the *Philocalia*, a compendium of passages from Origen made by Basil of Caesarea and Gregory of Nazianzus; there it bears the title: 'Concerning self-determination and an explanation and interpretation of those scriptural passages which seem to deny it, from the third book of On First Principles.' The numeration of the paragraphs in the editions and translations of the *Philocalia* differ slightly from those given here, which are aligned to the text of *Princ.*

which are without life—such as stones, and pieces of wood, and whatever things are of this kind, which are held together solely by the constitution of their material substance or bodies—are moved only from without. That view, which regards it as movement when bodies dissolve in corruption, must be excluded for now, for it contributes nothing to our present purpose. Other things, again, have the cause of movement in themselves, such as animals and trees and all things that are held together by natural life or by the soul; among which some think that even the veins of metals are to be counted; and fire, also, is supposed to be self-moving and perhaps even springs of water. Of those things which have the cause of their movements within themselves, some are said to be moved *of* themselves, others *by* themselves: and they are thus divided because those which are moved *of* themselves are alive but are not, however, animated beings, while animated beings move *by* themselves when there comes to them an image, that is, a sort of desire or incitement, which stimulates them to be moved or roused towards something.[2] Then again, in certain animated beings there is such an image, that is, a desire or feeling, which by a kind of natural instinct stimulates and drives them to an ordered and complex movement; just as we see spiders doing, when they are roused by an image, that is, a sort of wish and desire for weaving, to the task of weaving in a most orderly manner, some natural movement undoubtedly stimulating the impulse to work of this kind; nor is this same animal found to possess any other feeling besides the natural desire of weaving, just as the bee for fashioning honey-combs and gathering, as they say, aerial honey.

[2] For the Stoic background to Origen's comments, see *SVF* 3.40; Philo, *Alleg. Int.* 1.30; *Deus* 41–4; Clement, *Strom.* 2.20.110–11. See also the material referred to in *Princ.* 2.8.1, n.3.

3.1.2. *[Greek]* Of things that move, some have the cause of their movement within themselves, while others are only moved from without. Thus, portable things, such as pieces of wood and stone and all matter held together by its constitution alone, are only moved from without. Let the view that calls the flux of bodies 'motion' be set aside for now, since there is no need of this for our purpose. But animals and plants, and generally whatever is held together by nature and soul, have the cause of movement in themselves; among these, they say, are included even metals; besides these, fire also is self-moved and perhaps also springs of water. But of those things having the cause of movement within themselves, some, they say, are moved *of* themselves, others *by* themselves: inanimate beings *of* themselves, animated beings *by* themselves. And animated beings are moved by themselves, when there arises an image, inciting an impulse. And, again, in certain animals images arise inciting an impulse, the imaginative nature moving the impulse in an orderly manner; as in the spider,

3.1.3. *[Latin]* But while a rational animal has in itself these natural movements, it has moreover, to a greater extent than other animals, the power of reason, by which it is able to judge and discern between the natural movements, disapproving of and rejecting some and approving of and accepting others, so that by the judgement of this reason the movements of human beings may be directed and governed towards a commendable life. From this it follows that, since the nature of this reason which is in the human being has within itself the power of distinguishing between good and evil, and, when he has determined, there is also in him the faculty of choosing what he has approved, he may rightly be deemed praiseworthy when choosing what is good and blameworthy when following that which is base or wicked. This indeed must in no way escape our notice, that in some dumb animals there is found a more regulated movement than in other animals, such as in hunting dogs or war horses, so that they appear to some to be moved by a kind of rational sense. But it must be believed that this is not so much of reason as of some instinctive and natural movement, abundantly bestowed for purposes of this kind. But, as we began to say, with this being the case for the rational animal, some things may happen to us human beings from without and, presenting themselves to our sight or hearing or any of our other senses, may arouse and stimulate us to good movements or the contrary, which movements, because they come to us from without, it is not in our power to ensure that they neither happen nor occur; but to judge and determine how we ought to use them, when they happen, is a matter and act of nothing other than that reason which is in us, that is, our own judgement. By the judgement of this reason we use the stimuli that come to us from without for whatever purpose

the image of weaving arises and the impulse to weaving follows, its imaginative nature inciting it in an orderly manner to this task, with the insect being entrusted with nothing beyond its imaginative nature; and in the bee [there is the impulse] to make a honeycomb.

3.1.3. *[Greek]* The rational animal, however, in addition to its imaginative nature, also has reason, which judges the images, rejecting some and accepting others, so that the animal may be led in accordance with them. Therefore, since there are, in the nature of reason, means to contemplate both the good and the shameful—following which, contemplating the good and the shameful, we choose the good but avoid the shameful—we are praiseworthy when devoting ourselves to the practice of the good, but blameworthy in the opposite case. One must not fail to note, however, that the greater part of the nature assigned to all [rational beings] is, in the case of animals, of a certain amount, that reason itself may approve, directing by its bidding our natural movements either to the good or the contrary.

3.1.4. *[Latin]* But if anyone should say that those things which strike from without, arousing our movements, are such that it is not possible to resist them, whether they incite us to good or to evil, let the one who holds this turn his attention for a little while to himself, and carefully examine his own movements, and see if he does not find that, when the enticement of any desire strikes him, nothing is accomplished until the assent of the soul is gained and the bidding of the mind indulges the wicked suggestion; just as if an appeal were seen to be made from two parties on certain plausible grounds to a judge residing within the tribunals of our heart, in order that when the grounds have first been set forth the determination to act may be brought forth from the judgement of reason. To give an example, if to a man who has determined to live continently and chastely and to keep himself from all intercourse with women, a woman should happen to appear, inciting and alluring him to act against his purpose, that woman is not a cause or necessity of his transgressing, since he is certainly able by remembering his resolution to bridle the incitements of lust and by the stern admonitions of virtue to restrain the pleasures of the allurement that solicits him, so that, all desire for indulgence being driven away, the firmness and constancy of his determination may endure. Finally, if allurements of this kind

some more, some less; so that the action of hunting dogs and war horses comes close, if I may speak thus, to the rational faculty. To fall under one of those causes from without, which incites such or such an image, is admittedly not one of those things that are within our power; but to determine to use what has happened either in this way or that is the work of nothing other than the reason which is in us, either activating us, from its promptings, to the impulse inciting us to what is good and befitting, or turning us aside to the opposite.

3.1.4. *[Greek]* But if someone says that that which comes from without is such that it is impossible to resist it, whatever it might be, let him turn his attention to his own affections and movements [and see] whether the approval and assent and inclination of the controlling faculty towards some action is not on account of some specious attractions. To take an example, a woman who has appeared before a man, determined to be chaste and to keep himself from intercourse, and who has incited him to act contrary to his purpose, is not the complete cause of the abandonment of his purpose; for being entirely delighted with the titillation and allure of the pleasure, neither wishing to resist it nor to strengthen his determination, he commits the licentious act. But someone else, on the

present themselves to men of greater learning, who have been strengthened by divine training, remembering at once who they are, recalling to mind what had recently been their meditation and in which they had been instructed, and fortifying themselves by the support of a holier teaching, they reject and repel every allurement of the incitement and drive away the opposing lusts by the interposition of the reason implanted within them.

3.1.5. *[Latin]* Since, then, it is established by a sort of natural evidence that these things are so, is it not specious to refer the causes of our actions back to those things which happen to us from without, and to remove the blame from ourselves, in whom the entire cause lies, that is, to say that we are like pieces of wood or stones, which have no movement in themselves, but suffer the causes of their movements from without? It is, indeed, neither true nor becoming for this to be said, but it is contrived for this purpose only, that the freedom of the will may be denied; unless we suppose that freedom of will can stand just like that, or that nothing occurring to us from without can incite us to good or evil. And if anyone were to refer the causes of our faults to the natural intemperance of the body, this is shown to be contrary to the rationale of all instruction. For how many do we see who have previously lived incontinently and intemperately and have been captives of luxury and lust, yet if perchance they are aroused by the word of teaching and instruction to that which is better there

other hand, when the same things have happened to him, having received more instruction and disciplined himself, the titillations and enticements do occur, but his reason, as being strengthened to a higher degree and trained by practice and confirmed towards the good by [right] doctrines, or near to being confirmed, repels the enticements and weakens the desire.

3.1.5. *[Greek]* To accuse things from without for what thus happens to us and to absolve ourselves from blame, by declaring that we are like pieces of wood and stones dragged about by those that move them from without, is neither true nor reasonable, but is the argument of someone wishing to give a false account of self-determination. For if we were to ask such a one what self-determination was, he would say it is that when I propose something, nothing from without opposes, inciting me to the contrary. Again, to blame our bare natural constitution is contrary to the evidence, for formative discourse takes hold of the most intemperate and savage, if they will follow the exhortation, and transforms them, so that the alteration and transformation for the better is very great, the most licentious people often becoming better than those who formerly did not seem to be such by nature, and the most savage changing to such

takes place so great a change that from being immoderate and foul they are converted to being sober and most chaste, and from being fierce and savage to being exceedingly mild and gentle? So also, on the other hand, we see in the case of others, quiet and honest people who have associated with disturbed and foul persons, *good manners corrupted by bad company*,[3] and they are made such as those who lack nothing in wickedness; and this sometimes happens to men of mature age, so that such have lived more continently in youth than when more advanced age has granted the opportunity for a freer life. The result of our reasoning, therefore, shows that those things which happen from without are not within our power; but that to use well or badly those things which do happen, by that reason which is within us, distinguishing and determining how these things ought to be used, is within our power.

3.1.6. *[Latin]* But that we may confirm, by the authority of the Scriptures, those things which the results of reasoning have shown, that is, that it is our doing whether to live rightly or not, and we are not compelled either by those causes which happen from without or, as some think, by the pressure of fate,

---

[3] 1 Cor. 15:33.

---

a degree of gentleness, so that those who were never at any time savage in this way appear to be savage in comparison with the one who has changed into gentleness. And we see others, most stable and honourable, through perversion to lower ways being driven from their solemnity and honour, so as to change into a state of licentiousness, often beginning their licentiousness in middle age and plunging into disorder after the period of youth—which, as regards its nature, is unstable—has passed. Reason, therefore, demonstrates that things from without are not within our power, but to use them in this way or otherwise—having received reason as a judge and investigator of the manner in which we ought to meet those things that come from without—this is our doing.

3.1.6. *[Greek]* Now, that it is our doing to live in a good manner, and that God asks this of us, not as something coming about from him nor any other, nor, as some think, from fate, but as our own work, the prophet Micah will bear witness, saying, *Has it been told to you, O human being, what is good, or what the Lord seeks from you, but to do judgement and to love mercy and to be ready to walk with the Lord your God?* Moses also, *I have set before your face the way of life and the way of death; choose what is good and walk in it.* Isaiah too, *If you are willing and listen to me, you shall eat the good things of the land; but if you*

the prophet Micah will bear witness, saying these words, *Has it been told to you, O human being, what is good or what the Lord seeks from you, but to do judgement and to love mercy and to be ready to walk with the Lord your God?*[4] And Moses speaks thus, *I have set before your face the way of life and the way of death; choose what is good and walk in it.*[5] And Isaiah says, *If you are willing and listen to me, you shall eat the good things of the land; but if you are not willing nor listen to me, the sword will consume you; for the mouth of the Lord has spoken these things,*[6] and in the Psalms it is written, *If my people had heard me, and Israel had walked in my ways, I would have humbled her enemies to nothing,*[7] by which he shows that it was in the power of the people *<to hear and> to walk* in the ways of God.

And also when the Saviour says, *I say to you, resist not one who is evil,*[8] and, *Whoever shall be angry with his brother shall be liable to judgement,*[9] and, *Whoever shall look at a woman to lust after her, has already committed adultery with her in his heart,*[10] and when he gives any other commandments, what else does he indicate but that it is in our power to observe what is commanded, and

---

[4] Micah 6:8.　　　[5] Deut. 30:15, 19.　　　[6] Isa. 1:19–20.
[7] Ps. 80:14–15.　　　[8] Matt. 5:39.　　　[9] Matt. 5:22.　　　[10] Matt. 5:28.

---

are not willing nor listen to me, the sword will consume you; for the mouth of the Lord has spoken these things. And in the Psalms, *If my people had heard me, and Israel had walked in my ways, I would have humbled their enemies to nothing and laid my hand upon those that afflict them,* as being in the power of the people *to hear and to walk* in the ways of God.

The Saviour also, saying, *But I say to you, resist not one who is evil,* and, *Whoever shall be angry with his brother shall be liable to judgement,* and, *Whoever shall look at a woman to lust [after her], he has already committed adultery in his heart,* and if he gives any other commandment he says that it is within our power to keep what is enjoined and that we shall reasonably be *liable to judgement* for transgressing them. And hence he says, *Everyone who hears these my words and does them is like a wise man, who built his house upon a rock,* and so on, *while he who hears and does not do them is like a foolish man who built his house upon the sand,* and the rest. And when he says *to those at his right hand, 'Come unto me, you blessed of my Father',* and the rest, *'for I was hungry and you gave me to eat; I was thirsty, and you gave me to drink',* it is exceedingly clear that he gives the promises as to those who are worthy of being praised, and, on the contrary, to the others as being blameworthy compared to the former, he says, *Depart, you cursed, unto everlasting fire.*

that for this reason we are rightly rendered *liable for judgement* if we transgress that which we are certainly able to keep? And hence he himself also says, *Everyone who hears these my words and does them is like a wise man, who built his house upon a rock,* and the rest, and he says, *He who hears these things and does not do them, is like a foolish man, who built his house upon the sand,* and the rest.[11] And even that which he says *to those at his right hand, 'Come unto me, all you blessed of my Father',* and the rest, *'for I was hungry and you gave me to eat; I was thirsty and you gave me to drink',*[12] clearly shows that it depended upon themselves, whether they should be those worthy of praise, for keeping the commandments and receiving what was promised, or those worthy of censure, who deserved to hear or receive the opposite, to whom it was said, *Depart, you cursed, into everlasting fire.*[13]

Let us see how the Apostle Paul also addresses us as having power over our will and as having within ourselves the causes either of our salvation or destruction; he says, *Or do you despise the riches of his goodness and forbearance and long suffering, not knowing that the goodness of God leads you to repentance? But by your hard and impenitent heart you are treasuring up wrath for yourself in the day of wrath and of the revelation of the just judgement of God, who will render to every one according to his works: to those who, by patience in doing good, seek for glory and honour and incorruptibility, eternal life; but to those who are factious and obey not the truth, but obey iniquity, wrath and anger. There will be tribulation and distress upon every human soul working evil, the Jew first and also the Greek; but glory and honour and peace for every one*

---

[11] Matt. 7:24, 26.   [12] Matt. 25:34, 35.   [13] Matt. 25:41.

Let us see how Paul addresses us as having self-determination and as being ourselves the cause of destruction or salvation: he says, *Or do you despise the riches of his goodness and forbearance and long-suffering, not knowing that the goodness of God leads you to repentance? But by your hard and impenitent heart you are treasuring up wrath for yourself in the day of wrath and of the revelation and the just judgement of God, who will render to every one according to his works; to those who, by patience in doing good, seek for glory and honour and incorruptibility, eternal life; but to those who are factious and obey not the truth, but obey iniquity, wrath and anger; there will be tribulation and distress upon every human soul working evil, the Jew first and also the Greek; but glory and honour and peace for everyone working good, the Jew first and also the Greek.* There are, indeed, ten thousand passages in the Scriptures which with the utmost clarity establish the existence of self-determination.

working good, the Jew first and also the Greek.[14] You will find many other, even innumerable, passages in the holy Scriptures which clearly show that we have the power of free will. Otherwise it would be a contradiction for us to be given commandments, by the observing of which we may be saved or by transgressing we may be condemned, if the power of observing them is not in us.

2: Difficult Passages in Scripture

3.1.7. *[Latin]* But since there are found in the divine Scriptures themselves certain words so set down that the opposite of this may seem to be possibly understood from them, let us, bringing them forward and discussing them according to the rule of piety, offer an explanation of them, so that, from those few passages which we now expound, the solution of other similar sayings, by which the power of the will seems to be excluded, may become clear. So, then, those sayings which are spoken by God about Pharaoh trouble a great many, for he says frequently, *I will harden Pharaoh's heart.*[15] For if he is hardened by God and through being hardened sins, the cause of the sin is not himself. And if this is so, it will appear that Pharaoh does not possess freedom of will, and it will consequently be maintained, by this example, that neither do others who perish have the cause of perdition in the freedom of their own will. That, also, which is written in Ezekiel, when he says, *I will take away their stony hearts and will give them fleshly ones, that they may walk in my precepts and keep my*

---

[14] Rom. 2:4–10.   [15] Exod. 4:21; 7:3.

3.1.7. *[Greek]* But since certain texts from both the Old and the New [Testaments] tend to the opposite conclusion, that is, that it is not within our power either to keep the commandments and to be saved or to transgress them and to be lost, come, let us also bring some of them forward and consider their explanation, in order that, from the cases we have brought forward, by their similarity, someone, picking out for himself every text seeming to destroy self-determination, may inspect aspects regarding their explanation. Now many have been troubled by the passages concerning Pharaoh, regarding whom God declared repeatedly, *I will harden Pharaoh's heart.* For if he is hardened by God, and through being hardened sins, he is not in himself the cause of sin; and if so, neither does Pharaoh possess self-determination. And someone will say that, in a similar way, those who perish neither have self-determination nor perish of themselves. The saying also in Ezekiel, *I will take away their stony* ordinances,[16] disturbs some, because it seems to be given by God both *to walk in his mandates and to keep his prescriptions,* if, indeed, he takes away that *stony heart* which impedes keeping the commandments and bestows and implants a better and more perceptible heart, which now is called *fleshly.*

Let us also consider what is the nature of that answer which the Lord and Saviour, in the Gospel, gives to those who asked of him *why he spoke to the multitude in parables*; for he says, *That seeing they may not see and hearing they may not hear and not understand, lest they should be converted and it be forgiven them.*[17] And that also which was said by the Apostle Paul, that, *It is not of him that wills nor of him that runs, but of God who has mercy,*[18] and, in another place, *Both to will and to work are of God;*[19] and again, in another place, *Therefore he has mercy upon whom he wills, and he hardens whom he will. You will say to me then: 'Why does he still find fault? For who can resist his will?' O human being, who are you to answer back to God? Will what is moulded say to the one who moulded it: 'Why did you make me thus?' Has not the potter power over the clay, to make out of the same lump one vessel unto honour and another unto dishonour?*[20] These and similar statements seem to have no small ability to deter many from believing that everyone is held to have the freedom of his own will, but makes it seem that it depends on the will of God whether one is either saved or lost.

---

[16] Ezek. 11:19–20.   [17] Mark 4:12. Cf. Isa. 6:9; Acts 28:26.
[18] Rom. 9:16.   [19] Phil. 2:13.   [20] Rom. 9:18–21.

---

hearts and will give them fleshly ones, that they may walk in my precepts and keep my ordinances, disturbs some, as suggesting that God gives the ability *to walk in the commandments and to keep the ordinances* by the removal of the obstacle, *the stony heart,* and implanting the better *fleshly* one.

Let us also look at the passage in the Gospel, at what the Saviour answers to those asking *why he speaks to the multitude in parables; That,* he says, *seeing they may not see, and hearing they may hear and not understand, lest they should be converted and it be forgiven them.* And also the saying by Paul, *It is not of him that wills nor of him that runs, but of God who has mercy*; and, in another place, *Both to will and to work are of God*; and, in another place, *Therefore he has mercy upon whom he wills, and hardens whom he wills. You will say to me then, 'Why does he still find fault? For who can resist his will?'* [*The persuasion is from him who calls,* not from us.[2]] *O human being, who are you to answer back to God?* [And again,] *Will what is moulded say to the one who moulded it: 'Why did you make me thus?' Has not the potter power over the*

---

[2] Gal. 5:8. This quotation is not in Rufinus' translation; it is likely an interpolation.

I will harden Pharaoh's heart[21]

3.1.8. *[Latin]* Let us begin, therefore, with what was said to Pharaoh, who is said to have been *hardened* by God, that he might not let the people go; and, with it, the word of the Apostle will also be considered, who says, *Therefore he has mercy upon whom he wills, and he hardens whom he wills.* For it is principally upon these that the heretics rely, when they say that it is not in our power whether we will be saved, but that the nature of souls is such that they in any case either perish or are saved, and that in no way can a soul which is of an evil nature become good nor one which is of a good nature become evil. So they say that Pharaoh, also, since he was of a lost nature, was therefore hardened by God, who hardens those who are of an earthy nature, but has mercy on those who are of a spiritual nature. Let us see, then, what is the meaning of what they assert, and let us, in the first place, ask them to tell us whether they maintain that Pharaoh was of an earthy nature, which they term 'lost.' They will undoubtedly reply: 'An earthy one.' If, then, he was of an earthy nature, he was, with his nature opposing this, altogether unable to believe in God or to obey him. But if this condition was his by nature, what further need was there for his heart to be *hardened* by God, and this not once but several times, unless it was indeed possible for him to yield to persuasion? Nor could anyone be said to be hardened by another, except him who of himself was not hard. And if he were not hard of himself, it follows that neither was he of an earthy nature, but of such

---

[21] On this passage, see also Origen, *Philoc.* 27; *Sel. Exod.* (PG 12, 281c); *Hom. Exod.* 3.3; 4.1–7; 6.9; *Or.* 29.16; *Comm. Rom.* 7.16.

clay, to make out of the same lump one vessel unto honour and another unto dishonour? These passages are sufficient of themselves to trouble the multitude, as suggesting that the human being does not have self-determination, but that it is God who saves and destroys whom he wills.

3.1.8. *[Greek]* Let us begin, then, with what is said about Pharaoh as being *hardened* by God so that he might not send away the people; together with which will also be examined the apostolic saying, *Therefore he has mercy upon whom he wills, and hardens whom he wills.* Since some of the heterodox use these passages, practically also destroying self-determination themselves by introducing natures which are lost, incapable of being saved, and other natures which are saved, unable to be lost—they say that Pharaoh, being of a lost nature, is on this account hardened by God, who has mercy upon the spiritual but hardens the earthy—come, let us now see what they mean. We shall ask them if Pharaoh was of an earthy nature. When they answer, we shall say that he who is of an earthy nature is completely disobedient to God; but if disobedient, what need is there for his heart to be *hardened,* and that not once but

a kind that he might give way when amazed by signs and mighty works. But he was necessary to God, in order that, for the salvation of the many, God might demonstrate his power in him while he resists greatly and struggles against the will of God, and by this his heart is said to be *hardened*.

Let what has been said first be [our argument] against them, by which their assertion may be overturned, insofar as they think that Pharaoh was lost by nature. And let us also deal in a similar way against them regarding that which was said by the Apostle Paul. For who does God harden, according to your view? Those, really, you say are of a lost nature? Am I to believe they would have done something else if they had not been hardened? If, indeed, they come to perdition from being hardened, they no longer perish naturally but by accident. Then, in next place, upon whom, tell us, does God show mercy? On those, really, who are to be saved? And in what respect do they need a second act of mercy, those who are once for all saved by nature and come naturally to blessedness, unless it is shown even from their case that, because it was possible for them to perish, they therefore obtain mercy so that they, by this, do not perish but come to salvation and possess the kingdom of the devout. Let this be said, then, against those who by fabricated fables introduce good or evil natures, that is, earthy or spiritual, by which, as they say, each one is either saved or lost.

frequently? Unless, perhaps, it was possible for him to obey, and he certainly would have obeyed if not earthy when put to shame by the wonders and signs, but God needs him to be more disobedient in order to demonstrate his mighty deeds for the salvation of the many, and therefore *hardens* his heart.

These things have been said against them first, to overthrow their supposition that Pharaoh was of a lost nature. The same [argument] must also be addressed to them concerning the saying by the apostle. Whom does God harden? The lost? Because they would obey if they were not hardened? Or those who will be saved, since they are not of a lost nature? Upon whom does he have mercy? Is it upon those who will be saved? And how is there need of a second mercy for those who have once for all been fashioned for salvation and who by their nature are certain to become blessed? Unless, perhaps, since they are capable of being lost if they do not obtain mercy, they obtain mercy in order that they may not receive that of which they are capable, that is, to be lost, but may be in the position of those who are saved. This is our answer to such people.

3.1.9. *[Latin]* We must reply to those who would have the God of the Law to be only just and not also good: how do they suppose the heart of Pharaoh to have been *hardened* by God—by doing or foreseeing what? For the view and conception of God must be noted, that he is, according to us, both just and good, but according to them only just. And let them show us how a God, whom they themselves admit to be just, acts justly in causing the heart of a human being to be hardened, such that from this very hardening he may sin and be lost; and how the justice of God may be defended in this case, if God himself is the cause of perdition for those whom thereafter he, with the authority of a judge, condemns on the grounds that they were hard and unbelieving. Why, also, does he blame him, saying, *But since you will not let my people go, behold, I will kill all the firstborn in Egypt, even your firstborn,*[22] and whatever else that is written as said by God through Moses to Pharaoh? For it is necessary for everyone who believes the things recounted in the Scriptures to be true, and desires to show the God of the Law and the Prophets to be just, to give an explanation for all these things and show how absolutely nothing in them diminishes the justice of God, since although they deny that he is good, they nevertheless admit that the judge and the creator of the world is just. There is, however, another way to answer those who assert that the creator of the world is a wicked being, that is, the devil.

[22] Exod. 4:23; 12:12.

3.1.9. *[Greek]* But to those who think they understand the term *hardened,* we must address the question: what do they mean by saying that God in his work hardens the heart, and what is his purpose in doing this? They must maintain a conception of God who is just and good, according to sound teaching; if they will not, let it be conceded to them for the moment that he is only just; and let them show how the good and just, or only the just, God appears just in hardening the heart of him who, on account of being hardened, is lost, and how the just God becomes the cause of the loss and disobedience of those who are punished by him on account of their being hardened and being disobedient. And why does he find fault with him, saying, *You will not let my people go. Behold, I will kill all the firstborn in Egypt, even your firstborn,* and whatever else that is written as said by God through Moses to Pharaoh? For one who believes that the Scriptures are true and that God is just must necessarily, if he is honest, endeavour to show how God, in using such expressions, may be clearly understood to be just. If, however, anyone should stand, denouncing with uncovered head[3] that the Creator is inclined towards evil, we should need other arguments for him.

[3] Cf. Plato, *Phaedrus,* 243b.

3.1.10. *[Latin]* But since we acknowledge that the God who spoke through Moses is not only just, but also good, let us inquire carefully how it befits one who is just and good to be said *to harden the heart of Pharaoh*. Let us see whether, perhaps, following the Apostle Paul, we are able to solve the difficulty by the help of certain examples and illustrations, if we can show that by one and the same act God *has mercy on one but hardens another*, not working or willing that he who is hardened should be hardened, but that while he exercises his kindness and forbearance, the heart of those who treat his kindness and forbearance with contempt and insolence is hardened, while the punishment of their crimes is deferred, whereas those who receive his kindness and forbearance as an opportunity for their repentance and correction obtain mercy. To show more clearly what we mean, let us take the illustration used by the Apostle Paul in the Epistle to the Hebrews, where he says, *For the land which has drunk the rain which frequently falls upon it and brings forth vegetation useful to those for whom it is cultivated receives a blessing from God; but that which bears thorns and thistles is rejected and close to being cursed, whose end is to be burned.*[23] Therefore, from those words of Paul which we have quoted, it is clearly shown that by one and the same act of God—that by which he bestows rain upon the earth—one piece of ground, when carefully cultivated, brings forth good fruit, but another, when neglected and uncultivated, produces thorns and thistles. And if, speaking as it were in the character of the rain, one were to say, 'It was I, the rain, who made the good fruits, and it was I who made

---

[23] Heb. 6:7–8. For the images that follow here and in *Princ.* 3.1.11, using the action of rain and the sun respectively, see Matt. 5:45: 'He makes his sun rise on the evil and on the good, and he sends rain on the just and the unjust.'

3.1.10. *[Greek]* But since they claim to hold him as just, and we as both good as well as just, let us consider how the good and just God could *harden the heart of Pharaoh*. See then whether, through an example used by the Apostle in [the Epistle] to the Hebrews, we are able to establish how by one act God *has mercy upon one, but hardens another*, not intending to harden, but [acting] with a good purpose, upon which the hardening follows on account of the underlying element of evil, the evil present in such people, so that he is said to harden the one who is hardened. It says, *The earth which has drunk the rain which falls upon it and brings forth vegetation useful to those for whom it is cultivated, receives a blessing from God; but that which bears thorns and thistles is rejected and close to being cursed, whose end is to be burned.* As regards the rain, then, there is one act; and there being one act as

the thorns and thistles, however hard the saying might seem, it is nevertheless said truthfully; for unless the rain had fallen, neither fruits nor thorns nor thistles would spring up, whereas after the coming of showers the earth produces both from out of itself. But, although the earth has produced buds of both kinds by the beneficial action of the showers, it is not to the rain, however, that the diversity of buds is properly to be attributed, but the blame for an evil crop will justly fall upon those who, when they are able to break the ground by frequent ploughing, and to turn over the solid clods with heavy hoes, and to cut away and root out all useless roots of harmful weeds, and, with all the labour and toil that such cultivation demands, to clear and till the fields for the coming rains, have nevertheless neglected to do this, and who accordingly will reap the most appropriate fruit of their sloth, thorns and thistles; in this way, then, it happens that the goodness and impartiality of the rain comes upon the whole earth equally, yet by one and the same operation of the showers that land which has been cultivated yields, as a blessing, fruits useful to the diligent and careful cultivators, while that which, by the sloth of its cultivators, has become hardened, sprouts only thorns and thistles. Let us, therefore, take those signs and mighty works, which were done by God, as showers furnished by him from above; and the purposes and desires of human beings must be taken as the earth, whether uncultivated or cultivated, which is of one nature, as is every soil compared to another, yet not in one and the same state of cultivation. From which it follows that the will of each person is either hardened by the mighty and wonderful works of God, if it is untrained and uncultivated and barbarous, so that it becomes even more savage and thorny, or it becomes more pliant and yields itself up with the whole mind into obedience, if it be cleared from vices and cultivated.

regards the rain, the earth which is cultivated bears fruit, while that which is neglected and barren bears thorns. It might seem outrageous for the giver of rain to say 'I produced the fruits and the thorns that are in the earth,' but even if outrageous, it is true; for had there been no rain, there would have been neither fruits nor thorns; but having fallen in due time and measure, both were produced. *The earth which has drunk the rain which frequently falls upon it, bearing thorns and thistles is rejected and close to being cursed.* The blessing, then, of the rain comes also upon the inferior earth, but the underlying element, being uncared for and uncultivated, yielded thorns and thistles. In this way, then, the wonders done by God are, as it were, the rain, while the differing human wills are, as it were, the cultivated and the neglected earth, both being, as earth, of one nature.

3.1.11. *[Latin]* But to prove the point more clearly, it will not be superfluous to employ another illustration: for example, if one were to say that it is the sun which binds and loosens, when loosening and binding are opposites. Now it is not false to say that, by one and the same power of its heat, the sun loosens up wax yet dries out and binds together mud; not that its power works one way upon mud and another way upon wax, but that the qualities of mud and of wax are different, although according to nature they are one thing, because both are of the earth.[24] In this way, then, one and the same action of God, which was worked through Moses in signs and mighty acts, made known, on the one hand, the hardness of Pharaoh, which he had conceived in the intensity of his wickedness, and proclaimed, on the other hand, the obedience of those other Egyptians, who were mingled among the Israelites and are reported to have departed from Egypt along with them. Regarding what is written, that the heart of Pharaoh was gradually being softened, so that on one occasion he said, *You shall not go far; you shall go a three days' journey, but leave your wives and your children and your cattle,*[25] and any other passages according to which he seems to yield gradually to the signs and mighty works, what else is indicated by these except that the power of the signs and wonders had some effect on him, though not as much was wrought as ought to have been? For if the

---

[24] Although Rufinus appears to have extended various passages in comparison with what we have in the *Philocalia,* such as the extended agricultural comparison in the preceding paragraph *(Princ.* 3.1.10, with reminiscences of Virgil), Simonetti and Crouzel (SC 269, p. 29, n.53c) suggest that the technical nature of this clause ('not that its power…both are of the earth') make it unlikely that it is due to Rufinus alone, but have no explanation for why the *Philocalia* should have dropped it.

[25] Cf. Exod. 8:28, 27; 10:9, 11.

3.1.11. *[Greek]* Just as if the sun, uttering a voice, said, 'I melt and dry out', melting and drying out being opposites, it would not speak falsely regarding the subject matter, as wax is melted and clay dried out by the same heat, so also the same act, which occurred through Moses, proved the hardening of Pharaoh on account of his wickedness and the persuasibility of the mixed Egyptians who departed together with the Hebrews. And the succinctly recorded comment that the heart of Pharaoh was, as it were, softened, when he said, *You shall not go far; you shall go a three days' journey, but leave your wives,* and whatever else he said, yielding slightly to the wonders, makes it clear that the signs had some effect even upon him, but did not have their full effect. Yet even this would not have happened if, as is supposed by the multitude, the saying, *I will harden the heart of Pharaoh,* was wrought by him, that is, by God.

hardening were of such a kind as many reckon, he would certainly not be found acquiescing even a few times.

It will not appear absurd, I think, to explain the tropological or figurative character of the language of him who wrote about the *hardening*, even from common usage. For often kindly masters are wont to say to their slaves, who, through the great forbearance and gentleness of their masters, have become insolent and reprobate: 'It was I who have made you like this; I have spoiled you; it is my forbearance that has made you good for nothing; I am the cause of your hard and worthless character, because I did not punish you at once for every single fault according to your deserts.' It is necessary to take note of the tropological or figurative character of the language, and so come to understand the force of the expression, and not find fault with a word whose inner meaning we have not carefully examined. Finally, the Apostle Paul, clearly treating of such things, says to him who remained in his sins, *Do you disdain the riches of his goodness and forbearance and long-suffering, not knowing that the goodness of God leads you to repentance? But by your hard and impenitent heart you are treasuring up wrath for yourself in the day of wrath and the revelation of the just judgement of God.*[26] Let us, then, take these words of the Apostle to him who is in sin and convert the very same expressions to be said of Pharaoh, and see if you will not find it spoken appropriately of him, since, *by* his *hard and impenitent heart* he is *treasuring up* and storing away *wrath* for himself *in the day of wrath*, because of the fact that his hardness could never

---

[26] Rom. 2:4–5.

And it is not absurd to tone down such expressions even from our customary speech, for kind masters often say to their slaves, spoiled by kindness and forbearance, 'I have made you bad' and 'I am the cause of these grave sins in you.' It is necessary to attend to the character and the force of what is said, and not misrepresent it through failing to hear the meaning of the expression. Paul, at any rate, having clearly examined these points, says to the sinner, *Or do you disdain the riches of his goodness and forbearance and long-suffering, not knowing that the goodness of God leads you to repentance? But by your hard and impenitent heart you are treasuring up wrath for yourself in the day of wrath and the revelation and the just judgement of God.* Let what the Apostle says to the sinner be addressed to Pharaoh, and then it will be understood to be entirely appropriate that these things are declared to him, *by your hard and impenitent heart you are treasuring wrath up for yourself*, as his hardness would not have

have been thus made known and come to be exposed unless signs and wonders of such number and magnificence had been in attendance.

3.1.12. *[Latin]* But if the proofs we have adduced seem less than complete, and the apostolic illustration insufficiently warranted, let us also add the witness of prophetic authority and see what the prophets proclaim about those who at first, indeed, living righteously, have deserved to receive very many proofs of the goodness of God, but afterwards have fallen, as human beings do, into sin. A prophet, identifying himself with them, says, *Why, O Lord, did you make us stray from your way? And why have you hardened our hearts so that we would not fear your name? Turn back on account of your slaves, on account of the tribes of your inheritance, that we may obtain as an inheritance a little of your holy mountain.*[27] Jeremiah also speaks in the same way: *O Lord, you have misled us, and we were misled; you have held fast and have prevailed.*[28] The saying, then, *Why, O Lord, have you hardened our heart so that we would not fear your name?*, said by those who prayed for mercy, is certainly to be taken in a moral or figurative sense, as if one were to say: 'Why have you spared us so long and did not requite us when we sinned, but abandoned us, so that our wickedness might increase and our license for sinning be extended when punishment ceased?' In this way, a horse, if it does not continually feel the spur of its rider and have its mouth chafed by a rough bridle, becomes hardened. In this way, a young boy, if not constantly disciplined by whipping, will become an insolent youth and ready to fall headlong into vice. God, accordingly, abandons and neglects those whom he has judged undeserving of chastisement. *For the Lord chastens and punishes those whom he loves, and scourges every son*

---

[27] Isa. 63: 17–18.   [28] Jer. 20:7. Cf. Origen, *Hom. Jer.* 19.15.

---

thus been proved nor made manifest unless the signs had been performed, or if they had been wrought but not so many or so great.

3.1.12. *[Greek]* But since such narratives are hard to believe and are considered to be forced, let us see from the prophetic words also, what those say who have experienced the great kindness of God and have {not} lived well, but have afterwards sinned. *Why, O Lord, did you make us stray from your way? Why have you hardened our heart, not to fear your name? Turn back on account of your slaves, on account of the tribes of your inheritance, that we may obtain as an inheritance a little of your holy mountain.* And in Jeremiah: *You have misled me, O Lord, and I was misled; you were stronger and have prevailed.* For the

whom he receives.[29] From which it must be supposed that those to be received into the rank and affection of sons are they who have deserved to be scourged and chastened by the Lord, in order that through endurance of trials and tribulations they also may be able to say, *Who shall separate us from the love of God which is in Christ Jesus? Shall tribulation or distress or famine or nakedness or peril or sword?*[30] For through all these is each one's resolve manifested and exhibited, and the firmness of perseverance made known, not so much to God, who *knows all things before they happen,*[31] as to the rational and heavenly powers, who have been allotted to be, as it were, assistants and ministers of God in the procurement of human salvation. But those who do not yet offer themselves to God with such constancy and affection, and who are not yet ready, when entering into the service of God, to prepare their souls for trial, are said to be abandoned by God, that is, not to be chastened, since they are not ready for chastisement, their treatment or healing being undoubtedly postponed to a later time. These indeed do not know what they will obtain from God, unless they first come to the desire of obtaining a benefit; which will only happen in this way, if one first comes to a knowledge of oneself and perceives what is lacking from oneself and understands from whom one should or can seek what is lacking. For he who does not first understand his infirmity or sickness, does not know to seek a physician;[32] or at any rate, having recovered his health, he will not be grateful to the physician if he did not first recognize the danger of his sickness.[33] And so, if one has not first learned

---

[29] Prov. 3:12; Heb. 12:6. This quotation and the next do not appear in the *Philocalia,* though they certainly are in the character of Origen; Schnitzer *(Origenes,* 179) suggested that there is a lacuna here in the *Philocalia,* and Koetschau (p. cxxxiv) that Rufinus might have taken a passage from another work of Origen.
[30] Rom. 8:35.   [31] Sus. Θ 42.   [32] Cf. Matt. 9:12.
[33] For other uses of medicinal imagery, see Origen, *Princ.* 2.7.3; 2.10.6; 3.1.13, 15.

---

statement, *Why have you hardened our heart, not to fear your name?*, said by those begging to receive mercy, said in character, means this: 'Why have you spared us for so long, not visiting us because of our sins, but abandoning us until our transgressions have grown so great?' He abandons most people by not punishing them, in order that, from the things within our power, the character of each may be tested and the better ones may become manifest from the trial applied, while the others, not escaping notice—not from God (for *he knows all things before they come to be*), but from the rational beings and from themselves—may later come upon the way of healing, for they would not have known the benefit if they had not condemned themselves; and this is beneficial to each, that he perceive his own particularity and the grace of God. For

the defects of his soul and the wickedness of his sins, and exposed this by confession with his own lips, he cannot be cleansed and absolved, lest he be unaware that what he possesses has been granted to him by grace and should think of the divine liberality as his own good; which idea would undoubtedly generate arrogance of soul and pride, and once again become the cause of his ruin.[34] It must be understood that this was the case with the devil, who believed that the primacy which he had then, when he was blameless, was his own and not given to him by God; and thus was fulfilled in him that statement which says that *everyone who exalts himself shall be humbled.*[35] Whence it seems to me that the divine mysteries were *concealed from the prudent and the wise* (so that, as Scripture says, *no flesh might glory before the presence of God*[36]) *and revealed to babes,*[37] to those, that is to say, who, after they have become infants and babes, that is, who have returned to the humility and simplicity of infants, then make progress, and when they reach perfection remember that they have obtained blessedness not, indeed, by their own virtues, but by the grace and mercy of God.

3.1.13. *[Latin]* It is, therefore, by the judgement of God that one who deserves to be abandoned is abandoned, while over some sinners God has forbearance,

---

[34] Cf. Origen, *Princ.* 1.5.5; *Hom. Num.* 12.4; *Hom. Judic.* 3.1; *Hom. Ezech.* 9; *Comm. Ps.* 4 (= *Philoc.* 26.7).
[35] Luke 14:11, 18:14.   [36] 1 Cor. 1:29.   [37] Luke 10:21.

one who does not perceive his own weakness and the grace of God, if he receive a benefit, without having made a trial of himself nor having condemned himself, will imagine that what is bestowed upon him by the grace of heaven is his own good work. And this produces conceit and pride, and will be the cause of a downfall; which, we think, also happened to the devil, who attributed to himself the superiority which he had when he was blameless. *For everyone who exalts himself shall be humbled, as everyone who humbles himself shall be exalted.* And consider whether on this account the divine things *have been concealed from the wise and prudent* (so that, as the Apostle says, *no flesh might glory before the presence of God*) *and revealed to babes,* to those who, after childhood, have come to better things and who remember that it is not from their own effort so much as by the unspeakable bounty [of God] that they have reached the heights of blessedness.

3.1.13. *[Greek]* That the one who is abandoned is abandoned by divine judgement and that God is long-suffering with certain sinners is not without reason, not, however, without a definite reason. For this very fact, that he is forbearing, makes for their advantage, since the soul, for whose healing and oversight he acts, is immortal; and, as something immortal and everlasting, it is not, even if not quickly cared for, excluded from salvation, which is postponed to more appropriate times. It is, moreover, perhaps expedient for those who have been more deeply infected with the poison of wickedness to obtain salvation slowly. Just as physicians, when they could quickly cover over the scars of wounds, occasionally conceal and defer the cure for the present, with a view to a better and sounder health, since they know that it is preferable to cause a delay in cases of swellings caused by wounds and to allow the malignant humours to flow for a while, rather than to hasten to a superficial cure and, by covering it, to shut up in the veins the poison of the morbid tumour, which, when cut off from its usual outlets, will undoubtedly creep into the inner parts of the limbs and penetrate to the vitals of the entrails themselves, so as to bring about no longer mere disease in the body but the loss of life; so also, in like manner, God, who knows the secret things of the heart and foreknows the future, through great forbearance allows certain things to happen, which, coming from without upon human beings, provoke the passions and vices which are concealed within to come out and proceed into the light, so that by these means those may be cleansed and saved who through great negligence and carelessness have admitted within themselves the roots and seeds of sin, which having been driven outwards and brought to the surface may in a way be vomited out and dispersed. And so, even if someone seems to be afflicted with

but because, with regard to the immortality of the soul and the limitless age, it will be for their advantage that they not be too quickly assisted to salvation, but be slowly led to it after experiencing many evils. Just as physicians, though able to heal a patient quickly, when they suspect that hidden poison exists in the body do the reverse of healing, doing this because they wish to heal the patient more surely, deeming it better to retain the patient in inflammation and sickness so that he may regain his health more securely than that he should seem to regain strength quickly but later relapse and the hasty cure prove to be temporary, in the same way, God also, knowing the secret things of the heart and foreknowing the things to come, through his long-suffering perhaps forbears, and while drawing out the hidden evil by means of things that happen from without, so as to cleanse the one who through carelessness has received the seeds of sin, in order that having vomited them out when they come to the surface, even though he may have been greatly immersed in evil deeds, he may later on, attaining to purification after his wickedness, be renewed. For God deals with souls not with reference, let me say, to the fifty years of the present

very serious evils, suffering convulsions in all his limbs, he may yet at some point be able to cease and desist and to reach satiety of evils and so, after many troubles, to be restored to his [proper] state.[38] For God deals with souls not merely with reference to this time of our life, which is concluded in sixty or a few more years, but with reference to an everlasting and eternal age, as he himself is eternal and immortal, exercising his providence over immortal souls. For he made the rational being, which he fashioned in his own *image and likeness*,[39] incorruptible, and therefore the soul, which is immortal, is not excluded by the brevity of the time of our present life from the divine healing and remedies.

3.1.14. *[Latin]* But let us also take from the Gospels illustrations of those things we have been speaking about, where a certain rock is mentioned, having on it a little and shallow earth, in which, when a seed falls, it is said to spring up quickly, but after it has sprung up, because it did not cast its roots deeply, *when the sun arises* what has sprung up is said to *be scorched and to wither* away.[40] Now this rock without a doubt stands for the human soul, hardened through its own negligence[41] and made stony by its wickedness. For no one has a *stony heart* created by God, but the heart of each one is said to become stony through his own wickedness and disobedience. Just as if,

---

[38] Cf. Origen, *Princ.* 3.1.17; 3.4.3; *Or.* 29.13.
[39] Gen. 1:26. Cf. Origen, *Princ.* 1.1.7; 3.6.1; 4.4.9-10; *Cels.* 3.40; *Comm. Matt.* 17.27; *Mart.* 47.
[40] Matt. 13:3–9; Mark 4:3–10; Luke 8:4–8.
[41] On 'negligence', see also Origen, *Princ.* 1.4.1 and the material cited in n.73 there.

---

life, but with reference to the limitless age, for he made the intellectual being incorruptible and akin to himself, and the rational soul is not excluded from healing, as [it might seem] in this present life.

3.1.14. *[Greek]* Come now, and let us use the following image from the Gospel. There is a certain rock, with a little surface soil, on which, if seeds fall, they sprout up quickly, but when sprouted, because *they have no root, when the sun arose they are scorched and wither away*. Now this rock is a human soul, hardened on account of its carelessness and made stone through its evil; for no one has a *stony heart* created by God, but it becomes such from wickedness. Just as, then, if someone were to reproach the farmer for not sowing the seed upon the rocky ground sooner, when he saw the other rocky ground receiving the seed and flowering, the farmer would reply, 'I sow this ground more slowly, laying down seeds that might be able to endure, the slower way being better for

therefore, one were to blame the farmer for not casting his seed more quickly upon rocky ground, because he sees that seed cast upon other rocky ground was quickly springing up, the farmer would certainly say in reply: 'I sow this earth more slowly for this reason, that it may retain the seed which it has received; for it is better for earth like this to be sown somewhat slowly, lest perhaps the crop should spring up too rapidly, and coming from the very top of a shallow soil, should not be able to withstand the rays of the sun' (would he not now acknowledge the reason and the skill of the farmer and approve as rationally done what had formerly seemed to him irrational?); in the same way, therefore, God, the most skilled farmer of his entire creation, conceals and defers, undoubtedly to another time, those things which seem to us ought to obtain health sooner, in order that not the outside, but rather the inside, may be cured. But if someone were to pose this question to us, 'Why do certain seeds even fall upon rocky ground, that is, on a hard and stony soul?', we must reply to this that even this does not happen without the arrangement of divine providence, since, unless by this means the condemnation which follows heed-lessness in hearing and wickedness in examination became known, it would certainly not be known what benefit there would be by being trained in an orderly fashion. And hence it happens that the soul comes to know its faults and blames itself, and, consequently, keeps and submits itself to cultivation, that is, it sees for itself that its faults must first be removed and then it must come to instruction in wisdom.

Since, therefore, just as souls are innumerable, so also are their manners and purposes and diverse individual movements, and inclinations and impulses, the variety of which the human mind is in no way able to consider; and

this ground and more secure than that which receives the seed more quickly but more superficially,' and we would be persuaded that the farmer spoke reasonably and acted skilfully, so also, the great farmer of all nature postpones the benefit which might have been deemed premature, so that it may not prove superficial. But it is likely that someone may object to us about this, 'why do some seeds fall upon the soul having superficial soil, being as it were a rock?' In response to this one must say that it was better for this soul, desiring better things too precipitously and not by the way leading to them, to obtain what it desired, in order that, condemning itself for this, it might thereafter have patience to receive over a long period the cultivation that accords with nature.

For souls are, as one may say, innumerable, and their dispositions are innumerable, so many as are also the movements and purposes and inclinations and impulses, of which there is only one most excellent administrator, who understands both the seasons and the appropriate aids and the paths and

therefore to God alone must be left the skill and the power and the knowledge needed for an arrangement of this kind, as he alone is able to know the remedy for each and to measure out the time for its healing.[42] He, then, who alone, as we said, recognizes the ways of individual mortals, knows by what way he ought to lead Pharaoh, *that through him his name might be named in all the earth,*[43] having previously chastised him by many blows and then leading him on to be drowned in the sea. It must certainly not be supposed that in this drowning the providence of God towards Pharaoh came to an end; for it must not be supposed that, because he was drowned, he immediately perished substantially. *For in the hand of God are both we and our words, and all understanding and skill in crafts,*[44] as Scripture declares. But these points we have discussed according to our ability, treating that chapter of Scripture in which it says that *God hardened the heart of Pharaoh,* and concerning the saying, *He has mercy upon whom he wills, and he hardens whom he will.*[45]

I will take away their stony heart
3.1.15. *[Latin]* Let us now look at those passages of Ezekiel where he says, *I will take away the stony heart from them and I will put in them a fleshly heart, that they may walk in my ordinances and keep my statutes.*[46] For if God, when he wills, *takes away a stony heart and puts in a fleshly heart,* so that his precepts may be observed and his commandments be kept, then it will appear that it is

---

[42] Cf. Origen, *Princ.* 2.3.2; *Hom. Jer.* 18.6.
[43] Exod. 9:16; Rom. 9:17.   [44] Wis. 7:16.   [45] Exod. 10:20; Rom. 9:18.
[46] Ezek. 11:19–20.

---

the ways, the God and Father of all, who knows how he guides even Pharaoh by means of great events and by drowning in the sea, at which his dispensation for Pharaoh does not end, for he was not destroyed when drowned: *For in the hand of God are both we and our words, and all understanding and skill in crafts.* This, then, sufficiently provides a defence of the texts: *Pharaoh's heart was hardened,* and, *He has mercy upon whom he wills and hardens whom he wills.*

3.1.15. *[Greek]* Let us also look at the passage in Ezekiel where he says: *I will take away the stony hearts from them and will put in them fleshly hearts, that they may walk in my ordinances and keep my statutes.* For if God, when he wills, *takes away the stony hearts and implants fleshly hearts,* so that his statutes are kept and his commandments are observed, then it is not in our power to put away wickedness. For the *taking away of stony hearts* is nothing other than the putting away of the evil, by which one is hardened, from whom God wills;

not in our power to put away wickedness (for the *taking away of a stony heart* seems to be nothing else than the removal of the wickedness, by which one is hardened, from whomsoever God wills), nor that the insertion of a *fleshly heart*, so that the precepts of God may be walked in and his commandments kept, is anything other than becoming obedient and not resisting the truth and performing works of virtue. If, then, God promises to do this, and before he *takes away the stony heart* we are unable to remove it from ourselves, it follows that it is not in our power to cast out wickedness, but in God's. And again, if it is not in our doing to form a *fleshly heart* within ourselves, but the work of God alone, then to live virtuously will not be our work, but it will in everything seem to be a work of the grace of God.

Such assertions are made by those who wish to prove from the authority of Scripture that nothing lies within our own power. To them we reply that these passages ought not to be understood in such a manner, but rather as if an ignorant and untaught person, becoming aware of the disgrace of his ignorance, should, driven either by the exhortation of another or by the desire to emulate those who are wise, hand himself over to one by whom he is confident that he will be carefully trained and ably instructed, so that if he, who formerly had grown hard in ignorance, entrusts himself, as we have said, with full purpose of mind to a master and promises to be obedient in all things, the master, seeing clearly the resolution of his determination, will appropriately promise to take away from him all ignorance and to implant knowledge; not that he promises to do this with the disciple refusing or resisting his efforts, but only on his offering and binding himself to obedience in all things. So also the divine Word promises to those who draw near to him, that the *stony heart* will be

and the engendering of a *fleshly heart*, so that one may walk in the ordinances of God and keep his commandments, what else is it than to become yielding and not opposed to the truth and able to practise the virtues? But if God promises to do this, and, before he *takes away the stony hearts*, we do not lay them aside, it is clear that it is not within our power to put away evil; and if we do not do anything that the *fleshly heart* may be engendered within us, but it is the work of God, to live virtuously will not be our work, but wholly divine grace.

These things one will assert, who, from the bare letters, would destroy our power over ourselves. But we shall answer that these words ought to be understood as saying that, just as someone who happens to be ignorant or uneducated, on perceiving his own flaws, whether by an exhortation from a teacher or otherwise from himself, should give himself over to the one who he thinks is able to guide him in learning and virtue, and, on giving himself over, the teacher promises to take away his ignorance and to implant learning, not as if his having brought himself to be healed contributed nothing to his being educated and removed, not indeed from those who do not listen to him, but from those who receive the precepts of his teaching, just as in the Gospels we find the sick approaching the Saviour, asking that they might receive health, and thus at last be cured. When, for example, the blind are healed and see, it is, assuredly, inasmuch as they certainly made supplication to the Saviour and believed that they could be healed by him, a work of those who were healed; but inasmuch as sight was restored to them, it is a work of the Saviour. So also, in this way does the divine Word promise that instruction will be bestowed by *taking away the stony heart,* that is, by removing wickedness, so that, through this, they will be able to *walk in the* divine *precepts and keep the commandments* of the law.

That seeing they may see and not see
3.1.16. *[Latin]* And after this, there is placed before us that passage from the Gospel, where the Saviour said, *For this reason I speak in parables to those that are outside, that seeing they may see and not see, and hearing they may hear and not understand, lest they should be turned and be forgiven.*[47] Regarding this, our opponent will say: 'If those who hear more clearly are in every respect

[47] Mark 4:11–12; Matt. 13:13; Luke 8:10; cf. Isa. 6:9–10; Acts 28:26.

escaping his ignorance, but as promising to improve the one who desires it, so, in the same way, the divine Word promises, to those who draw near, to take away the wickedness, which it calls a *stony heart,* not from those who are unwilling, but from those who offer themselves to the Physician of the sick; just as in the Gospels the sick are found coming to the Saviour and asking for a cure and are healed. And, so to speak, *to give sight to the blind*[4] is, with respect to the request of those believing themselves able to be healed, a work of the sufferers, but with respect to the restoration of sight, it is the work of our Saviour. Thus, then, does the Word of God promise to implant knowledge in those who approach, *taking away a stony* and a hard *heart,* which is wickedness, so that one *may walk <in> the* divine *commandments and keep the* divine *statutes.*

3.1.16. *[Greek]* After this, there was the passage from the Gospel, where the Saviour said, *For this reason I speak in parables to those who are outside, that seeing they may not see, and hearing they may not understand, lest they should be turned and it be forgiven them.* Now our opponent will say, 'If, on hearing clearer words some do assuredly turn, and having thus turned so as to become

[4] Matt. 11:5.

corrected and turned, and turned in such a way as to be worthy to receive remission of sins, yet it is not in their own power to hear the word clearly, but is in the power of the teacher to teach more openly and clearly, yet the teacher says that he does not proclaim to them the word clearly for this reason, lest they should hear and understand and be turned and be saved, then to be saved is certainly not dependent upon themselves. And if this is so, we will have no free will either with respect to salvation or destruction.' Now, if it were not for what was said in addition, *lest they should be turned and be forgiven*, one might be more inclined to answer that we would say that the Saviour did not wish those, whom he foresaw would not become good, to understand the mysteries of the kingdom of heaven, and for this reason *he spoke to them in parables.* But now, with the addition, *lest they should be turned and be forgiven,* the explanation is made more difficult.

And in the first place we must note what defence this passage holds against those heretics who are accustomed to hunt out in the Old Testament expressions which may seem to them, as they understand them, to describe some severe and inhuman quality of God the Creator, as when he is described as being moved by desire, or however they are wont to call it, for vengeance or punishment, from which they deny the existence of goodness in the Creator;

worthy of forgiveness of sins, and the hearing of clearer words doesn't depend on them but on the one teaching, and he does not declare it to them more clearly for this reason, lest they should see and understand, then to be saved does not depend upon them; and if so, we do not have self-determination as regards salvation and destruction.' There is a plausible defence against this, if there were not added, *lest they should be turned and it be forgiven them,* that is, that the Saviour did not wish those who would not become good and virtuous to understand the deeper mysteries and therefore *spoke to them in parables.* But now, there being found, *lest they should turn and it be forgiven them,* the defence is more difficult.

In the first place, then, the passage must be noted for its bearing upon the heterodox, who hunt out such passages from the Old Testament where is revealed, as they make so bold to assert, the cruelty of the Creator or his revengeful and punitive disposition, or whatever they wish to call such a quality, towards the wicked, only in order that they might claim that goodness does not exist in the Creator; and who do not deal similarly, nor even candidly, with the New [Testament], but pass over statements closely resembling those they consider to be censurable from the Old. For clearly, and according to the Gospel, the Saviour is shown, as they themselves claim, by his former words, for they do not pass judgement on the Gospels with the same mind and feeling, nor do they observe whether any such statements, as those they condemn and censure in the Old Testament, are found in the Gospels. For clearly in this chapter the Saviour is shown, as they themselves say, to not speak clearly for this reason, that human beings may not be turned and, when turned, receive remission of sins. Now assuredly if these words be understood according to the mere letter, it will contain nothing less than those passages in the Old Testament which are censured. But if this statement, as it is found thus placed in the New Testament, seems, even to them, to need an explanation, it will necessarily follow that those also which they censure in the Old Testament may be cleared by a similar explanation, so that by such means what is written in both Testaments may be proved to be of one and the same God. But let us turn, as best we can, to the question posed.

3.1.17. *[Latin]* We said before, when discussing the case of Pharaoh, that sometimes to be cured quickly does not yield good results, especially if the disease, being shut up in the internal organs, rages more fiercely. Whence God, who knows secret things and *knows all things before they come to be*,[48] in his great goodness delays the healing of such persons and defers the remedy to a more distant time, so that, so to speak, he heals them by not healing them, lest a premature healing should render them incurable. It is therefore possible that, in the case of those to whom the word of our Lord and Saviour was addressed

[48] Sus. Θ 42.

not speaking clearly, for this reason, that human beings might not turn and, when turned, become worthy of remission of sins, which, of itself, is in no way less than those passages from the Old Testament which are criticized. And if they seek a defence for the Gospel, they must be asked whether they are not acting censurably, dealing differently with similar problems, and not taking offence regarding the New Testament but seeking a defence, while attacking the Old for similar statements, which ought to be defended similarly to those from the New. From these considerations, we shall force them, on account of their resemblances, to regard all as the writings of the one God. Come, then, and let us provide, to the best of our ability, a defence in the matter before us.

3.1.17. *[Greek]* We also said, when examining the case of Pharaoh, that sometimes being healed rapidly is not for the advantage of those who are healed, if, after falling of themselves into difficulties, they should be easily relieved of the conditions into which they had fallen; for thinking little of the evil, as something easily cured, by not being on their guard against falling into it they will

as being *outside*,[49] he saw, by *searching out the hearts and kidneys*,[50] that they were not yet able to receive the teaching in clearer language, and covered faith in a deeper mystery by veiled speech, lest perhaps being rapidly turned and healed, that is, having quickly received the remission of their sins, they should again easily fall back into the same disease of sin, which they had found could be healed without any difficulty. And if this should happen, no one can doubt that the punishment is doubled and the amount of wickedness increased, since not only are the sins, which seemed to be forgiven, repeated, but even the court of virtue is desecrated when trodden by those of a deceitful and corrupted mind, full of hidden wickedness within. And what remedy can there ever be for those who, after the impure and filthy food of wickedness, have tasted the pleasantness of virtue and received its sweetness into their mouths, and have then yet again turned themselves to the poisonous and deadly food of iniquity?[51] And who doubts that it is better for such to be delayed and to be abandoned for a period, in order that if some day they should happen to have had their fill of wickedness and be able to shudder at the filth with which they are now delighted, then the Word of God may at last be fittingly revealed to them, so that *what is holy is not given to dogs nor are pearls cast before swine, which will trample them under foot,*[52] and, moreover, turning around, interrupt and assault those who have preached the Word of God to them? These, then, are those who are said to be *outside,* undoubtedly by comparison with those

---

[49] Mark 4:11.   [50] Ps. 7:10. Cf. Origen, *Or.* 8.2.
[51] Cf. Heb. 6:4–8; 10:26–31.   [52] Matt. 7:6.

come to be in it a second time. Therefore, concerning such as these, the eternal God, the one who knows the hidden things, who *knows all things before they come to be*, in accordance with his goodness delays the more speedy assistance, and, so to speak, helps them by not helping, this being to their advantage. It is probable, then, that *those who are outside*, of whom we are speaking, having been seen by the Saviour, according to the passage before us, not to be steady in their turning, if they should hear more clearly what was said, were disposed by the Lord so as not to hear more clearly the deeper points, lest, perhaps, after turning quickly and being healed by obtaining forgiveness, they should think little of the wounds of their wickedness as being slight and easily healed, and should fall quickly again into them. Perhaps, also, suffering punishment for the former sins, which they committed against virtue when they had forsaken her, they had not yet fulfilled the proper time, being themselves abandoned by the divine oversight, and being filled ever more with their own evils, whose seeds they had sown, to be called, afterwards, to a more steadfast repentance, so that they do not fall quickly again into the sins into which they had formerly

who are *inside* and hear the Word of God with greater clarity.[53] Those, however, who are *outside* do hear the Word, although covered by parables and overshadowed by proverbs.[54] But there are others, besides those who are *outside,* who are called 'Tyrians', who do not hear at all; even, indeed, with the Saviour knowing that *They would have repented long ago, sitting in sackcloth and ashes, if the mighty works had been done among them which were done among others,*[55] they nevertheless do not hear, not even those things which those who are *outside* hear. I believe this is because the rank in wickedness of such was far inferior and worse than that of those who are said to be *outside,* that is, not far from those who are *inside* and who deserved to hear the Word, although in parables, and perhaps their cure was arranged for that time, when *it will be more tolerable for them on the day of judgement,*[56] than for those before whom had been done the mighty works, which are written, so that in this way, being relieved at last from the weight of their sins, they may more easily and more enduringly enter upon the way of salvation.

But this is a point about which I wish to remind those who read these pages, that with topics of such difficulty and obscurity we use our utmost endeavour,

---

[53] Cf. Mark 4:11; 1 Cor. 5:12–13.
[54] Cf. Origen, *Dial.* 15; *Cels.* 2.64; 3.21; 3.46; 6.6; *Comm. Matt.* 10.1, 4; 11.4; *Frag. Prov.* (PG 13, 21).
[55] Matt. 11:21; Luke 10:13.   [56] Matt. 11:22

fallen when mocking the value of noble things and abandoning themselves to worse things. These then, who are said to be *outside* (clearly in comparison with those *inside*), not being very far from those *inside*, while those who are *inside* hear clearly, they hear unclearly, because they are spoken to *in parables*; but yet they do hear. Others, again, of *those who are outside*, who are called 'Tyrians', although it was foreknown that *they would have repented long ago, sitting in sackcloth and ashes,* had the Saviour drawn near their borders, they do not even hear what those *outside* heard, likely being much further from being worthy than those *outside*, in order that in another season, after it has been *more tolerable for them* than for those who did not receive the word, among whom he mentioned the Tyrians, they may, on hearing the word at an opportune time, repent more steadfastly.[5]

But observe whether, besides our investigation, we do not also strive to maintain piety in every way towards God and his Christ, endeavouring in every way to defend, in matters of such importance and difficulty, the manifold providence of God providing for the immortal soul. If, indeed, someone

---

[5] Matt. 11:21–2.

not so much that we might argue out clearly the solutions of the questions (for everyone will do this as the Spirit gives him to speak), but that we might maintain, by the most cautious assertions, the rule of piety in this, that we strive to show that the providence of God justly governs all things and rules immortal souls with the most equitable economy according to the merits and motives of each; the present economy is not confined within the life of this age, but a previous state of merit always furnishes the cause of the state that is to come, and thus by the immortal and eternal management of divine providence the immortal souls are brought to the summit of perfection. If, however, someone were to counter what we said—that the word of preaching was purposely put aside by certain very depraved and wicked persons; that the word was preached to those who are, in comparison, preferred over the Tyrians, who were certainly despised; whereby their wickedness was increased and their condemnation made more severe by the fact that those who heard the word did not believe it—it would seem we must answer in this way: God, who knows the minds of all, foreknowing the complaints against his providence—especially from those who say, 'How could we believe when we neither saw those things which others saw, nor heard those things which were preached to others? So far are we from blame, since those to whom the word was announced and the signs manifested made no delay at all, but, amazed at the very power of the miracles, came to believe'—wishing to denounce excuses for complaints of this

should ask concerning those who were reproached, why seeing wonders and hearing divine words they were not benefitted, while the Tyrians would have repented if such had things had been done and spoken amongst them, and should ask, saying, 'Why, then, did the Saviour proclaim such to these people, to their own hurt, that their sin might be accounted heavier?', one must say to him that he who understands the dispositions of all those who find fault with his providence—on the ground that they did not believe because it was not given to them by [his providence] to see what it granted others to behold and it did not arrange for them to hear the things that others heard to their profit— wishing to prove that their defence is not reasonable, [his providence] gives them the things which they who blame his administration asked for; in order that, after receiving them, being convicted nonetheless of the greatest impiety for not having even then surrendered themselves to be benefitted, they may cease from such audacity, and having been made free on this very point they may learn that God sometimes, in doing good to some, lingers and delays, not granting to see and to hear such things that, when seen and heard, would prove the sin of those who do not believe, after such great and wonderful things, to be heavier and grievous.

sort and to show that it was not a delay of divine providence, but the will of each human mind, that was the cause of its ruin, [he] bestowed the grace of his blessings even upon the unworthy and unbelieving, *that every mouth may be stopped,*[57] and that the human mind might know that the failure was wholly on its part and none on the part of God, and that, at the same time, it may understand that he, who has despised the divine blessings bestowed upon him, is condemned more severely than him who has not deserved to obtain them or hear of them at all, and recognize that this is a mark of divine compassion and his most equitable economy, that it sometimes delays giving certain people the opportunity either to see something or to hear the mysteries of divine power, lest once the power of the miracles has been seen and the mysteries of his wisdom have been known and heard, if they should despise and neglect them, they would be punished with a severer chastisement for their impiety.

It is not of him that wills...
3.1.18. *[Latin]* Let us now look at the saying, *It is not of him that wills nor of him that runs, but of God who has mercy.*[58] For our opponents say: 'If *it is not of him that wills nor of him that runs,* but that one is saved upon whom God has mercy, it is not in our power that we should be saved. For our nature is such as to be able to be saved or not to be saved, or else it surely depends solely upon the will of him who, if he will, shows mercy and saves'. Let us first ask of

[57] Rom. 3:19.   [58] Rom. 9:16.

3.1.18. *[Greek]* Let us next look at the words, *It is not then of him that wills, nor of him that runs, but of God who has mercy.* Those who attack it say, 'If *it is not of him that wills, nor of him that runs, but of God who has mercy,* to be saved is not from what is in our power, but is from the constitution received from the one who has constituted us such or from the purpose of him who is merciful when he pleases'. One must ask this of them: Is it good or bad to will good things? And is it praiseworthy or blameworthy to run desiring to reach the goal in the drive for good things? And if they should say blameworthy, they would be answering contrary to the evidence, since the saints will and run, and clearly in this do <nothing> blameworthy; but if they should say that it is good to will good things and to run towards good things, we shall ask them how a lost nature wills better things; for it would be like a bad tree producing good fruit, if to will better things is good. They will say, thirdly, that to will the good and to run after the good is one of the things that are indifferent, neither honourable nor wicked. To this one must say that if to will the good and to run after the good is something indifferent, then the opposite of this, that is, to will

them this: is it good or evil to will good things? And is it laudable or culpable for one who runs to hasten so that he arrives at the goal of the good? And if they should say that it is culpable, they would clearly be mad; for all the saints both will good things and run towards good things, and they are certainly not culpable. What is the case, then, if he who is not saved is of an evil nature yet wills good things and runs towards good things, but does not find good things? For they say that *A bad tree does not bring forth good fruit,*[59] whereas it is a good fruit to will good things; and how is the fruit of a bad tree good? But if they should say that to will good things and to run towards good things is something indifferent, that is, neither good nor bad, we shall reply to them: if it is something indifferent to will good things and to run after good things, then that which is opposite to this will also be indifferent, that is, to desire evil things and to run towards evil things; but it is certain that it is not indifferent to will evil things and to run towards evil things, but something that is clearly evil: it is established, therefore, that it is not something indifferent to desire good things and to run towards good things, but good.

3.1.19. *[Latin]* Having then rebutted these objections with this answer, let us hasten now to the explanation of the subject of inquiry itself, in which it says, *It is not of him that wills nor of him that runs, but of God who has mercy.* In the Book of Psalms, in the Songs of Ascents, which are attributed to Solomon, it is

---

[59] Matt. 7:18. Cf. Origen, *Princ.* 1.8.2; 2.5.4.

---

the evil and to run towards the evil, is indifferent. But to will the evil and to run after the evil is not something indifferent; therefore it is not indifferent to will the good and to run after the good.

3.1.19. *[Greek]* Such, then, is the defence which, I think, we can offer regarding the statement, *It is not of him that wills nor of him that runs, but of God who has mercy.* Solomon says in the Book of Psalms (for the Song of Ascents, from which we will quote the words, is his): *Unless the Lord builds the house, those who build it labour in vain; unless the Lord guards the city, the guard stayed awake in vain,* not dissuading us from building nor teaching us not to keep awake in order to guard the city in our soul, but showing us that what is built without God and does not receive a guard from him is built in vain and watched to no purpose, since God may reasonably be entitled 'Lord of the building', and the Master of the universe 'Ruler of the guard of the city'. Just as, then, if we were to say that the building is not the work of the builder but of God, and that it is not from the successful effort of the guard but of *the God* written thus, *Unless the Lord builds the house, those who build it laboured in vain; unless the Lord guards the city, the guard stayed awake in vain.*[60] By these words he does not indeed indicate that we ought to stop building or staying awake for the care of that city which is within us; but what he points out is this, that whatever is built without God and whatever is guarded without God, is built in vain and guarded to no purpose. For in all things that are well built and well preserved, the Lord is held to be the author of the building or of its safe-keeping. Just as, for example, if we were to see some magnificent work and massive structure of a splendid building, erected with architectural beauty, would we not justly and deservedly say that this was not constructed by human power but by divine help and might? By this, however, it will not be meant that the labour and industry of human effort had ceased and effected nothing at all. Or again, suppose we were to see some city surrounded by a harsh blockade of the enemy, with threatening machines brought against the walls, and a pressing attack made by ramparts, weapons, fire, and all the instruments of war by means of which destruction is prepared; if the enemy were repelled and put to flight, we would properly and deservedly say that deliverance was granted to the liberated city by God, yet we would not mean by this, however, that the sentinel's vigils, the young men's readiness, and the guards' vigilance had been lacking. The Apostle, therefore, must also be understood to have spoken in a similar way, since the human will alone is not sufficient for the accomplishment

---

[60] Ps. 126:1. Cf. Origen, *Comm. Ps.* 4 (= *Philoc.* 26.7).

who is over all[6] that such a city did not suffer from its enemies, we should not err, it being understood that something had been done on the part of human beings, but the great deed being thankfully offered to the accomplishes,[7] God, so also, since human willing is not sufficient to attain the end, nor is the running of those who are, as it were, athletes, sufficient to gain *the prize of the upward call of God in Christ Jesus* (for with God's assistance these things are accomplished), it is well said that *it is not of him that wills nor of him that runs, but of God who has mercy.* As if it were also said, with regard to farming, what is actually written: *I planted, Apollos watered, but God gave the growth. So then neither he who plants nor he who waters is anything, but God who gave the growth,* and we could not piously say that the production of full crops was the work of the farmer or the work of him that watered, but the work of God, so also, our own perfection does not come to pass with our doing nothing, yet is

---

[6] Rom. 9:5.   [7] Heb. 12:2.

of salvation, nor is the running of a mortal fit for attaining things heavenly and for obtaining *the prize of the upward call of God in Christ Jesus,*[61] unless this good will of ours itself and our ready purpose, and whatever diligence there may be within us, is aided or fortified by divine assistance. And therefore the Apostle said, most consequentially, that *it is not of him that wills nor of him that runs, but of God who has mercy,* just as if we were to say of agriculture that which is actually written, *I planted, Apollos watered, but God gave the growth. So then neither he who plants nor he who waters is anything, but God who gave the growth.*[62] Just as, therefore, when a field has brought good and rich crops to perfect maturity, no one could piously and coherently say that the farmer made those fruits, but will acknowledge that they had been produced by God, so also is our own perfection brought about not by us being inactive and idle, nor, on the other hand, is its consummation attributed to us, but to God, who effects the greater part of it. So also, when a ship has overcome the dangers of the sea, although the result has been achieved by the exercise of the great labour of the sailors and by all the skill of navigation, and by diligence and industry of the captain, the favourable breezes of the winds and the signs of the stars being carefully noted, when, after being tossed by the waves and wearied by the billows it has at last reached the harbour in safety, no one in a right mind would ascribe the safety of the ship to anything apart from the mercy of God. Not even the sailors or the captain would dare to say, 'I have

[61] Phil. 3:14.   [62] 1 Cor. 3:6–7.

not completed from ourselves, but God works the greater part of it. And that this assertion may be more clearly believed, we shall take an illustration from the art of navigation. For when compared with the blowing of the winds and the mildness of the air and the light of the stars, all cooperating for the preservation of those who sail, what proportion should one say that the art of navigation has contributed to returning the ship back to harbour? Even the sailors themselves, through piety, do not often venture to assert that they have saved the ship, but offer all to God; not that they have done nothing, but that what comes about from providence is very much in excess of what comes about from their art. And in the case of our salvation, what is done by God is very much in excess of what results from what is in our power. Therefore, I think, it is said that, *It is not of him who wills nor of him who runs, but of God who has mercy.* For if one must take the saying, *It is not of him who wills nor of him who runs, but of God who has mercy,* as they suppose, the commandments are superfluous, and it is in vain that Paul himself blames some for having fallen

saved the ship, but they refer it all to the mercy of God; not that they feel that they have contributed no skill or labour to the ship being safe, but because they know that, while the labour was from them, the safety of the ship was furnished by God. So also in the race of our life, the expended labour and diligence and industry depends upon us, but salvation, the fruit of our labour, is to be hoped for from God. Otherwise, if God demands nothing of our work, the commandments will certainly seem to be superfluous; in vain, also, does Paul himself blame some for having fallen from the truth and praise others for abiding in the faith; to no purpose does he hand down certain precepts and directions to the churches; in vain also do we ourselves either will or run towards the good. But it is certain that these things are not done in vain, and it is certain that neither do the apostles give instructions in vain, nor does the Lord give laws with no purpose. It remains, then, that we claim rather that the heretics make a calumny of these good declarations in vain.

away and approves of others for remaining steadfast, and enacts laws for the churches; it is useless for us to devote ourselves to willing better things, yet indeed not also to running.[8] But it is not in vain that Paul gives such advice and censures some and approves of others, nor in vain that we give ourselves to willing better things and to press on to things that are excellent. They have therefore not understood well the meaning of the passage.

---

[8] Although the MSS uniformly read 'yet indeed not also to run' (οὐχὶ δέ γε καὶ τρέχειν, the γε being omitted by two MSS), every editor since Delarue has emended this to, 'it is also in vain [to try] to run' (εἰκῇ δὲ καὶ ἐπὶ τὸ τρέχειν, with the exception of Görgemanns and Karpp, who while placing the text between obeli yet translate it as others) to produce a series of four rhetorical absurdities (the commandments are superfluous; so too are Paul's words and actions; it is useless for us to try to will better things; it is also useless to try to run towards better things). Yet it is possible to take the latter two as correlated: it is useless to will better things (which we all do), and yet not also make an effort towards them. In this way, there would be three implicit affirmations: the commandments have been given, to be kept; Paul does indeed apportion blame and approval, and lays down laws expecting them to be kept; and not only do we all desire salvation, but those who are sincere also run towards it; yet nevertheless what makes all of this effective is the mercy of God.

To will and to do are of God

3.1.20. *[Latin]* After this there followed that subject of inquiry, that, *To will and to do are of God.*[63] They say: 'If *to will is of God and to do is of God,* then whether we will or act well or evil, it is *of God;* if this is so, then we do not have free will.' To this we must answer that the statement of the Apostle does not say that to will evil things is of God or that to will good things is of God, nor that to do good things or evil things is of God, but he speaks generally, that *to will and to do are of God.* For just as we have from God this very fact, that we are human beings, that we breathe, that we move, so also we have from God that we have the power of willing; just as if we were to say that the fact that we move is from God, or that each of our members performs its function and moves is from God. It must certainly not be understood from this that because the hand moves, for example, to hit unjustly or to steal, the act is from God, but only that it moves is from God; it is our part to direct those movements, the movement being from God, either to good or to evil. And therefore what the Apostle says is that we receive from God the power of volition, but that it is we who use the will either for good or evil desires. We must think similarly of the outcomes.

[63] Phil. 2:13.

3.1.20. *[Greek]* Besides these, there is the passage, *To will and to do are of God.* Now some say, 'If *to will is of God and to do is of God,* then even if we will evilly and act evilly, these come to us *from God;* and if so, we do not have self-determination. But again, when we will better things and do deeds that are excellent, since *to will and to do are from God,* it is not we who have done the more excellent deeds, but we seemed to do so, while it was God who bestowed them; so that even in this case we do not have self-determination.' In reply, one must say that the language of the Apostle does not say that to will evil things is of God, or that to will good things is of God, nor likewise to do better things or worse things, but that to will in general and to do in general. For as we have it from God to be living beings and to be human beings, so also we have the facility of willing in general, as I said, and the facility of movement in general. And just as, being living beings we have the facility of movement, and, for instance, can move these members, the hands or the feet, yet we could not rightly say that we have from God the specific facility of movement to strike or to destroy or to take away another's goods, but that we have received from him the generic faculty of movement, while we use the facility of movement for better or worse purposes, so also we have received from God the facility of doing, as being living creatures, and received the ability to will from the Creator, while we employ the facility of willing either for the noblest purposes or the opposite, and likewise the facility of doing.

Therefore he has mercy on whom he wills

3.1.21. *[Latin]* But with respect to what the Apostle said—*Therefore he has mercy upon whom he wills and hardens whom he will. You will say to me then: 'Why does he still find fault? For who can resist his will?' O human being, who are you to answer back to God? Will what is moulded say to its moulder: 'Why have you made me thus?' Has not the potter power over the clay, to make out of the same lump one vessel unto honour and another unto dishonour?*[64]—someone will perhaps say: 'If, just *as the potter makes from the same lump some vessels unto honour and others unto dishonour,* so also God creates some for salvation and others for destruction, then it is not in our power either to be saved or to be destroyed; by which it seems that we do not possess free will.' We must reply to those who thus understand these words: is it possible that the Apostle could contradict himself? And if this cannot be imagined of the Apostle, how, according to them, will it seem just for him to blame those who committed fornication in Corinth, or those who had fallen away and *did not show repentance for the acts of immodesty and fornication and impurity which they had committed?*[65] How also does he praise those who acted rightly, like the house of Onesiphorus, saying: *May the Lord grant mercy to the house of Onesiphorus, for he often refreshed me and was not ashamed of my chain, but when he had arrived in Rome he searched for me eagerly and found me. May the Lord grant*

---

[64] Rom. 9:18–21.   [65] 2 Cor. 12:21; cf. 1 Cor. 5:1–5.

3.1.21. *[Greek]* Moreover, the apostolic saying will seem to tend to the position that we are not self-determining, where, objecting to himself, he says: *Therefore he has mercy upon whom he wills and hardens whom he wills. You will say to me then, 'Why does he still find fault? For who can resist his will?' O human being, who are you to answer back to its moulder, 'Why have you made me thus?' Will what is moulded say to its moulder, 'Why have you made me thus?' Has not the potter power over the clay, to make out of the same lump one vessel unto honour and another unto dishonour?* Someone will say: 'If, just as *the potter makes from the same lump some vessels unto honour and some unto dishonour,* so also God makes some unto salvation and others unto destruction, then to be saved or destroyed does not depend upon ourselves, nor are we self-determining.' We must ask the one using these passages thus, whether it is possible to conceive of the Apostle as contradicting himself? I do not think that anyone would dare to say so. If, then, the Apostle does not utter contradictions, how can he, according to the one who takes the passage thus, reasonably lay blame, censuring the one in Corinth who had committed fornication or those who had fallen away *and have not repented of the licentiousness and impurity which they have committed*?

him to find mercy from the Lord on that day.[66] *It is not consistent* with apostolic solemnity to blame him who is worthy of blame, that is, who has sinned, and to praise him who is worthy of praise for his good works, and then, on the other hand, as if it was in no one's power to do any good or evil, to say that it was the Creator's doing that everyone should act well or evilly, seeing that he makes *one vessel unto honour and another unto dishonour.* And how can he add that statement, *We must all stand before the judgement seat of Christ, so that each one of us may receive good or evil according to what he has done in the body?*[67] For what good reward will be conferred on him who could not do evil, being formed by the Creator for this very end? Or what punishment will rightly be inflicted upon him who by the creative act of his maker was not able to do good? Then, finally, how is there not a contradiction between this assertion and what he said elsewhere, *In a great house there are not only vessels of gold and silver, but also of wood and of earth, and some unto honour and some unto dishonour. If anyone therefore purges himself from these, he will be a vessel unto honour, sanctified and useful to the master, prepared for every good work.*[68] He, accordingly, who purges himself is made a *vessel unto honour,* while he who has disdained to purge himself from his impurities becomes a *vessel unto dishonour.* From such declarations, in my opinion, it is in no way possible for the

---

[66] 2 Tim. 1:16–18.   [67] 2 Cor. 5:10.
[68] 1 Tim. 2:20–1. The connection between this text and Rom. 9:18–21 is also made in Origen, *Comm. Rom.* 7.17. See also *Princ.* 2.9.8.

And how can he bless those whom he praises as having done well, as he does the house of Onesiphorus, saying: *May the Lord grant mercy to the house of Onesiphorus, for he often refreshed me and was not ashamed of my chain, but when he had arrived in Rome, he searched for me eagerly and found me. May the Lord grant him to find mercy from the Lord in that day?* It is not consistent for the same apostle to blame the sinner as worthy of censure and to approve him as having done well, and again, on the other hand, to assert, as if nothing was within our power, that it is from a cause within the Creator that *one vessel was formed unto honour and another unto dishonour.* And how is it correct that, *We must all stand before the judgement seat of Christ, so that each one may receive either good or bad according to what he has done in the body,* if those who have done evil have come to this kind of conduct through having been created *vessels of dishonour,* and if those who have lived virtuously have done good by being created from the beginning for this purpose and became *vessels of honour?* And again, how does what is said elsewhere not conflict with the position which they have drawn from those words we have quoted, that it is from a cause within the Creator that a *vessel* is either in *honour* or *dishonour*; that is:

cause of our actions to be referred to the Creator. For God the Creator makes certain *vessels unto honour,* and makes other *vessels unto dishonour;* but it is that *vessel,* which has purged itself from all impurities, which he makes a *vessel unto honour,* while that which has stained itself with the filth of vices, he makes a *vessel unto dishonour.* The conclusion from this, therefore, is that the cause of the former actions of each one precedes, and each one, according to his merits, is made by God either a *vessel unto honour* or *dishonour.* Thus each *vessel* has, from itself, provided the Maker with the causes and occasions for its being formed by the Creator *unto honour* or *unto dishonour.*

3.1.22. *[Latin]* But[69] if this assertion seems to be just—as it certainly is just and in harmony with all piety—that from antecedent causes each *vessel* is prepared by God either *unto honour* or *dishonour,* it does not seem absurd, when we are discussing antecedent causes in the same order and by the same method, to think in the same manner regarding souls, that this is the reason why Jacob was loved even before he was born into this world and Esau hated while he was still held within the womb of his mother.

---

[69] Cf. Jerome, Ep. 124.8.1 (ed. Hilberg 3, 105.11–19): 'In the third book these errors are contained: if we once admit that it is from antecedent causes that one vessel is made *unto honour* and another *unto dishonour,* why do we not return to the mystery of the soul and understand that, because of what it did of old, in one it is loved and in another it is hated, in Jacob's case before he became a supplanter and in Esau's case before his heel was grasped by his brother?' See also Origen, *Princ.* 1.7.4; 2.8.3; 2.9.7; *Comm. Rom.* 7.17.

In a great house there are not only vessels of gold and silver, but also of wood and of earth, and some unto honour and some unto dishonour. If anyone therefore purges himself from these, he will be a vessel unto honour, sanctified and useful to the master, prepared for every good work? For if the one who purges himself becomes a *vessel unto honour,* and the one who negligently remains unpurged becomes a *vessel unto dishonour,* then, as far as these words are concerned, the Creator is not at all the cause. For the Creator makes *vessels of honour* and *vessels of dishonour,* not from the beginning, according to his foreknowledge, since he does not, according to it, condemn or justify beforehand; but [he makes] *vessels of honour* those who purged themselves and *vessels of dishonour* those who negligently remained unpurged; so that it is from causes older than the fashioning of *vessels unto honour and unto dishonour* that one came to be *unto honour* and another *unto dishonour.*

3.1.22. *[Greek]* But if we once admit that there are certain older causes in the fashioning of the *vessel unto honour* and the *vessel unto dishonour,* what absurdity is there, returning to the subject of the soul, <in recognizing> that the older

But also, that saying, that *from the same lump a vessel* is formed both *unto honour and dishonour,* will not be able to constrain us, for we assert that there is one nature of all rational souls, just as *one lump of clay* is described as being subject to the potter. Seeing, then, that the nature of rational creatures is one, out of it God, as the potter out of the *one lump,* created and formed, according[70] to the antecedent causes of merit, *some unto honour and others unto dishonour.* But, regarding the language of the Apostle, when he said, as if chiding, *O human being, who are you to answer back to God?,* I think that this is what he means by this, that such a censure does not refer to any believer who lives rightly and justly and who has confidence in God, that is, to such a one as was Moses, of whom Scripture says that *Moses spoke and God answered him with a voice,*[71] and as God answered Moses, so also does the saint answer God. But the one who is an unbeliever and loses confidence in answering God, because of the unworthiness of his life and conduct, and who inquires into these matters not so as to learn and make progress, but to dispute and resist, and to speak more plainly, one of such a kind who can say those things, which the Apostle indicates, saying, '*Why does he still find fault? For who can resist his will?'*—to such a one may that censure rightly be directed: *O human being, who*

---

[70] Cf. Jerome, *Ep.* 124.8.2 (ed. Hilberg 3, 105.19–21): 'And again: the merits of antecedent causes precede the fact that some souls are made *unto honour* and some to *dishonour.'*

[71] Exod. 19:19. On Moses as representing the highest degree of ascent in this life, see Origen, *Hom. Num.* 22.3; *Cels.* 1.19; *Hom. Ps. 36,* 4.1.

---

causes of Jacob being loved and Esau being hated occurred with Jacob before his embodiment and with Esau before he came to be in the womb of Rebecca?

But at the same time, it is clearly shown that, as regards the underlying nature, just as there is one clay which is subject to the potter, from which *lump* come *vessels unto honour* and *unto dishonour,* so also, there being one nature of every soul subject to God and, so to speak, *one lump* of rational beings, certain older causes have made some to be *unto honour* and others *unto dishonour.* But if the language of the Apostle rebukes, saying, *O human being, who are you to answer back to God?,* perhaps it teaches that the one who has boldness towards God, and is faithful, and has lived virtuously, would not hear: *Who are you to answer back to God?* Such a one was Moses; for *Moses spoke and God answered him with a voice*; and as God answers Moses, so also does a saint answer God. But one not possessing this boldness, clearly being lost or investigating these matters not with a love of learning but with a love of contention and on this account saying, *Why does he still find fault? For who can resist his will?,* such a one would be worthy of the rebuke which says, *O human being, who are you to answer back to God?*

are you to answer back to God? This censure, therefore, is not addressed to the faithful and saints, but to the unbelievers and impious.

3.1.23. *[Latin]* But to those who bring in diverse natures of souls, and drag this saying of the Apostle to the support of their teaching, we must reply in this way:[72] if they agree with what the Apostle says, that out of *one lump* are those made *unto honour* and those made *unto dishonour,* whom they call those of a saved and of a lost nature, then there will no longer be different natures of souls, but one nature for all. And if they admit that the one and the same potter undoubtedly designates the one Creator, there will not be different creators either, of those who are saved or of those who are destroyed. Now, sensibly, let them choose whether they will have the passage be understood as speaking of a good God, who creates those who are evil and lost, or of one who is not good, who creates those who are good and prepared for honour. For the necessity of giving an answer will wrench out of them one of these two alternatives. But following our assertion, that it is from antecedent causes that God, we say, makes *vessels* either *unto honour* or *dishonour,* the proof of the justice of God

---

[72] Simonetti and Crouzel suggest that the more fully developed argument in what follows, compared to the *Philocalia,* should be taken as Rufinus' fidelity to the original text of Origen, which the *Philocalia* here abridges.

3.1.23. *[Greek]* But to those who introduce [diverse] natures and who make use of this saying, one must say the following. If they preserve the point that those who are lost and those who are saved are from *one lump,* and that the Creator of those who are saved is the Creator also of those who are lost, and if he who creates not only spiritual but also earthly natures (for this follows their argument) is good, it is nevertheless possible for one who, from certain former righteous deeds, has become now a *vessel of honour,* but has not been doing similar things nor such as befits a *vessel of honour,* to become in another age a *vessel of dishonour*; as, on the other hand, it is possible for one who, on account of things older than this life, became here a *vessel of dishonour,* to become, when corrected in *the new creation,*[9] *a vessel of honour, sanctified and useful to the master, prepared for every good work.* And perhaps those who are now Israelites, not having lived worthily of their nobility, will be cast out from their race, being changed from *vessels of honour* into a *vessel of dishonour*; while many of the present Egyptians and Idumaeans who have come near to Israel, when they shall have borne more fruit, *shall enter into the Church of the Lord,*

---

[9] Gal. 6:15.

is in no way curtailed. For[73] it is possible that one *vessel,* which, from previous causes was made *unto honour* in this world, if it acts negligently, may become, according to the merits of its conduct, a *vessel unto dishonour* in another age; just as, on the other hand, if one, from antecedent causes, was formed by the Creator as a *vessel unto dishonour* in this life, and has amended his ways and purged himself from all vices and filth, he may, in the new age, be made *a vessel unto honour, sanctified and useful to the master, prepared for every good work.*[74] Finally, those who were formed by God to be Israelites in this age, and who have lived a life unworthy of the nobility of their birth and have fallen away from all the grandeur of their race, will, because of their unbelief, be changed in the age to come as it were from *vessels of honour* into *vessels of dishonor;* and, on the other hand, many who in this life were counted among the Egyptian or Idumaean vessels, having accepted the faith and practice of the Israelites and having done the works of Israelites, having *entered the Church of*

[73] Cf. Jerome, *Ep.* 124.8.3 (ed. Hilberg 3, 105.22–106.5): 'And in the same place: but according to us a vessel which was made, from antecedent merits, *unto honour,* if the work it has done is not worthy of its name, will be made a vessel *unto dishonour* in another age, and in reverse a vessel which, from a previous fault, has accepted the name of *dishonour* will, if it has willed to be corrected in this present life, become in the new creation a vessel *sanctified and useful to the master, prepared for every good work.'*

[74] 1 Tim. 2:21.

no longer being accounted Egyptians and Idumaeans, but becoming Israelites; so that, according to this view, through their [diverse] purposes some advance from worse things to better ones, while other fall from better things to worse ones; some again are preserved in good things or ascend from good things to better ones, while others remain in wicked things, or, as their wickedness flows on, from wicked become worse.

3.1.24. *[Greek]* But since the Apostle in one place does not pretend that becoming *a vessel unto honour* or *a vessel unto dishonour* depends on God, but attributes the whole back to us, saying, *If anyone therefore purges himself from these, he will be a vessel unto honour, sanctified and useful to the master, prepared for every good work,* and elsewhere does not pretend that it is within our power, but appears to attribute the whole to God, saying, *The potter has power over the clay, to make out of the same lump one vessel unto honour and another unto dishonour,* and as his statements are not contradictory, one must reconcile both and draw out from both a single complete account: neither is what is within our power apart from the skill of God; nor does the skill of God force us to make progress unless we ourselves contribute something to the good

the Lord shall exist as *vessels of honour* in *the revelation of the sons of God.*[75] Therefore it is more agreeable to the rule of piety that we should believe that every rational being, according to his purpose and conduct, is sometimes turned from evil things to good ones and sometimes falls away from good things to evil ones; that some abide in good things, and others even advance to what is better and always ascend to higher things, until they reach the highest level of all; while others remain in evil things or, if the wickedness in them begins to spread itself further, they advance to a worse condition and sink to the lowest depth of wickedness.

Whence[76] also we must suppose that it is possible for some, who at first indeed began with small sins, to be so immersed in wickedness and to go to such lengths of evil that, in the measure of wickedness, they are equal even to the opposing powers; and, on the other hand, if, through many severe punishments and most bitter chastisements, they are able at some future point to recover their senses and attempt gradually to find healing for their wounds, they may, with wickedness ceasing, be restored to the good. From which we reckon that, since the soul, as we have frequently said, is immortal and eternal, it is possible that, in the many and endless periods in the immeasurable and different ages, it may descend from the highest good to the lowest evil or be restored from the lowest evil to the highest good.[77]

---

[75] Deut. 23:7–8; Rom. 8:19. Cf. Origen, *Hom. Num.* 11.7.

[76] Cf. Jerome, *Ep.* 124.8.4–5 (ed. Hilberg 3, 106.5–21): 'And he immediately adds: I think that certain human beings, beginning with small faults, are able to arrive at such wickedness, if they have not willed to turn to better things and through repentance correct their sins, that they become opposing forces; and, in reverse, that hostile and contrary powers may, through the course of much time, apply such medicine to their wounds and check the flow of their former offences that they may cross over to the place of the good. As we have often said, in those countless and unceasing ages, in which the soul subsists and lives, some of them sink down towards the worse, until they hold the lowest place of wickedness, while some progress, such that they come, from the lowest level of wickedness, to the perfect and highest virtue.'

[77] In *Princ.* 2.3.3 the perpetual instability of rational creatures is discussed as a hypothesis; elsewhere, e.g. *Princ.* 3.6.3–6, Origen affirms a final unity when God will be 'all in all'. See also Origen, *Comm. Rom.* 5.10.

---

outcome; nor does what is within our power, apart from the skill of God and from the use of what is within our power with regard to virtue, make us become *unto honour* or *unto dishonour*; nor does what is within the power of God by itself fashion someone *unto honour* or *unto dishonour*, unless he has our purposes as a ground of difference, as it inclines either to better things or to worse things. And let these observations which we have elaborated on the subject of self-determination suffice.

3.1.24. *[Latin]* Now, since the words of the Apostle, in what he says regarding *vessels of honour* or *dishonour,* that, *if anyone purge himself, he will be a vessel unto honour, sanctified and useful to the master, prepared for every good work,*[78] seem to put nothing in the power of God, but all in ourselves, whereas in those [words] in which he says *The potter has power over the clay, to make out of the same lump one vessel unto honour and another unto dishonour,*[79] the whole seems to refer to God, these two statements cannot be taken as contradictory, but the meaning of each must be brought together into one, and a single sense must be drawn from both; that is, that neither should we suppose that those things which are in the power of our will can be done without the assistance of God, nor should we imagine that those things which are in the hand of God are brought to completion without our acts and endeavours and purpose. Indeed, we do not have it in the power of our will either to will or to do anything without being obliged to recognize that this very power by which we are able to will or to do was given to us by God, following the distinction which we spoke about above. Yet, on the other hand, when God forms *vessels,* some *unto honour* and others *unto dishonour*, it is to be supposed that he has, as grounds for honour or dishonour, our wills and purposes and merits, as a sort of matter from which he may form each one of us *unto honour* or *unto dishonour,* for the very movement of the soul and the purpose of the intellect of itself suggests to him, who is not unaware of the heart and the thoughts of the mind, whether his *vessel* ought to be formed *unto honour* or *unto dishonour*. But let these points suffice, which we have discussed as best we could, regarding questions concerning the freedom of the will.

[78] 1 Tim. 2:21.   [79] Rom. 9:21.

The Opposing Powers

3.2.1.[1] We must now see how, according to Scripture, the opposing powers, or the devil himself, are engaged in struggle against the human race, inciting and instigating them to sin. First, a serpent is described in Genesis as having seduced Eve;[2] regarding this serpent, in the *Ascension of Moses*, a little work which the Apostle Jude mentions in his Epistle, the archangel Michael, when disputing with the devil regarding the body of Moses, says that the serpent was inspired by the devil to become the cause of the transgression of Adam and Eve.[3] This also is inquired about by some: who the angel is that speaks from heaven to Abraham, saying, *Now I know that you fear God, and for my sake you have not spared your beloved son.*[4] For clearly it is an angel that is described, who says that he then knew that Abraham feared God and had not spared his beloved son, as Scripture says, but he did not state that it was for the sake of God, but for his sake, that is, for the sake of him who said these things. We must also investigate who that one is, of whom it is said in Exodus, that he wished to kill Moses because he was departing from Egypt.[5] And also, later, who it is who is called the destroying angel,[6] and, as well, who it is who in Leviticus is described as *Apopompeus* (that is, *Averter*), of whom Scripture speaks thus, *One lot for the Lord and one lot for Apopompeus* (that is *Averter*).[7] Moreover, in the first book of Reigns, an evil spirit is said to throttle Saul.[8] And in the third book, Michaiah the prophet says, *I saw the God of Israel sitting on his throne, and all the host of heaven stood near him, on his right and on his left. And the Lord said, 'Who will entice Ahab, king of Israel, that he will go up and fall at Ramoth-Gilead?' And one spoke this way, and another spoke that way. And a spirit came forward and stood before the Lord and said, 'I will entice him.' And the Lord said to him, 'By what means?' And he said, 'I will go forth and be a lying spirit in the mouth of all his prophets.'*[9] *And he said, 'You will entice him and indeed you will prevail. Go, therefore, and do so'. And now the Lord has put*

---

[1] According to Photius, *Bibl.* 8 (ed. Henry 1, 4a12–13), *Princ.* 3, after dealing with free will, discusses 'how the devil and hostile powers, according to the Scriptures, wage war against the human race' (πῶς ὁ διάβολος καὶ αἱ ἀντικείμεναι δυνάμεις κατὰ τὰς γραφὰς στρατεύονται τῷ ἀνθρωπίνῳ γένει).

[2] Gen. 3:1–6.

[3] Cf. Jude 9. The *Ascension of Moses* (or the *Assumption of Moses*) is now lost; for its relation to the *Testament of Moses*, see James H. Charlesworth, *The Old Testament Pseudepigrapha*, vol. 2 (Garden City, NY: Doubleday, 1985), 925.

[4] Gen. 22:12.　　　[5] Cf. Exod. 4:24.

[6] Cf. Exod. 12:23. In *Hom. Num.* 3.4, the angel who struck down the firstborn of the Egyptians is identified with Christ himself; in *Cels.* 6.43 it is identified with Satan.

[7] Lev. 16:8. Cf. Origen, *Cels.* 6.43; *Hom. Lev.* 9.4.

[8] Cf. 1 Rgns 16:14. See also 1 Sam. 18:10, a verse not in the LXX, but one known to Origen as evidenced by the *Hexapla* (ed. Field, 1.519).

[9] Cf. Origen, *Comm. Jo.* 20.256–67, esp. 258–61.

a lying spirit in the mouth of all these your prophets; and the Lord has spoken evil against you.[10] It is clearly shown from this that a certain spirit, by his own will and purpose, chose to deceive and to work a lie, and that God makes use of this spirit for the death of Ahab, who deserved to suffer this. In the first book of Supplements, also, it is said, *The devil raised up Satan in Israel and incited David to number the people.*[11] In the Psalms an evil angel is said to oppress certain people.[12] In Ecclesiastes, also, Solomon says, *If the spirit of one holding authority rise up against you, do not leave your place, for healing will restrain many transgressions.*[13] In Zechariah we read that the devil stood at the right hand of Jesus and opposed him.[14] Isaiah says that the sword of the Lord arises against the dragon, the crooked serpent.[15] And what shall I say of Ezekiel, prophesying most clearly in the second vision to the prince of Tyre about an opposing power, who also says that the dragon dwells in the rivers of Egypt?[16] And as for the entire book written about Job, what else does it contain but an account of the devil, seeking for power to be given to him over all that Job possesses, and over his sons, and even over his own body? He is conquered, however, by Job's patience. In that book the Lord, by his answers, has taught a great deal about the power of that dragon which opposes us. These, for the present, are the statements from the Old Testament, as far as we are able to call them to memory at the moment, concerning the opposing powers, which are either named in Scripture or said to oppose the human race, and [are] afterwards punished.

Let us also look to the New Testament, where Satan approaches the Saviour, tempting him;[17] and where evil spirits and unclean demons, which had taken possession of many, were expelled by the Saviour from the bodies of the sufferers, who are said to have been set free by him.[18] Judas, also, when the devil had already put it into his heart to betray Christ, afterwards received Satan wholly into himself; for it is written that *after the morsel, Satan entered into him.*[19] And the Apostle Paul teaches us that we ought *not to give place to the devil, but put on,* he says, *the armour of God, that you may be able to resist the wiles of the devil,* pointing out that the saints *wrestle not against flesh and blood, but against the principalities, against the authorities, against the rulers of the darkness of this world, against spiritual hosts of wickedness in the heavenly places.*[20] Further, he says that the Saviour was crucified by the principalities of this world, who are brought down, whose wisdom also, he says, he does not speak.[21]

---

[10] 3 Rgns 22:19–23.   [11] 1 Suppl. 21:1, conflated with 3 Rgns 11:14.
[12] Cf. Ps. 34:5–6.   [13] Eccl. 10:4.
[14] Cf. Zech. 3:1. In the Greek of the LXX 'Joshua' is 'Jesus'.
[15] Cf. Isa. 27:1. Cf. Origen, *Princ.* 2.8.3.   [16] Cf. Ezek. 29:3. Cf. Origen, *Princ.* 1.5.4.
[17] Cf. Matt. 4:1–11; Mark 1:13; Luke 4:1–13.   [18] Cf. Mark 1:23–8; 32–4, etc.
[19] John 13:2, 27.   [20] Eph. 4:27; 6:11–12.   [21] Cf. 1 Cor. 2:6–8.

Through all these passages, therefore, the divine Scripture teaches us that there are certain invisible enemies, fighting against us, and warns us that we ought to arm ourselves against them. From this, also, the simpler ones of those who believe in the Lord Christ suppose that every sin which human beings have committed results from the persistent efforts of the opposing powers upon the minds of transgressors, because in this invisible struggle these powers are found to be superior; but that if, for example, there were no devil, no human being would transgress.

3.2.2. We, however, examining the rationale of things more carefully, do not at all hold this to be so, by considering those acts which clearly arise from bodily necessity. Must one indeed suppose that the devil is the cause of our being hungry or thirsty? There is no one, I think, who would venture to maintain that! If, then, he is not the cause of our being hungry and thirsty, what of that condition when the age of an individual has reached the period of virility and this has aroused the stimulations of the natural heat? It undoubtedly follows that, as the devil is not the cause of our being hungry and thirsty, so neither is he the cause of that impulse which is naturally aroused at the age of maturity, that is the desire yearning for sexual intercourse. It is certain that this impulse is by no means always aroused by the devil, such that it should be supposed that, if the devil did not exist, bodies would not have the desire for intercourse of that kind. Then again, let us consider—if, as we have shown above, food is desired by human beings, not from [the prompting of] the devil, but by a kind of natural instinct—whether it could happen that, if there were no devil, human experience could employ such restraint in the partaking of food that it never exceeds due measure at all, that is, [that human beings would] never take otherwise than the occasion required or more than reason allowed, so that it would never happen that human beings go astray in observing due measure and moderation of their food. I do not, indeed, think that, even if there were no incitement aroused by the devil, this could be observed by human beings—that no one, in partaking of food, exceed due measure and restraint—before they had learned to do so from long practice and experience. What, then, is the result? In the case of eating and drinking it was possible for us to go astray even apart from the instigation of the devil, if we happened to be found being less continent or less diligent; in the case of moderating the yearning for sexual union or the natural desires, is it to be supposed that we should not be affected in a similar way? I reckon that the same train of reasoning can be understood in the case of other natural movements, as of covetousness, or of anger, or of sorrow, or of all those generally which through the vice of intemperance exceed the natural measure of moderation.

The principle, therefore, is clear that, just as in good things, the human intention alone is, of itself, incapable of the accomplishment of any good (for everything is brought to perfection by divine assistance[22]), so also in opposite things, we receive certain beginnings and, as it were, seeds of sin from those things that we naturally have for our use; but, when we have indulged them beyond what is sufficient and have not resisted the first movements towards intemperance, then the hostile power, seizing the opportunity of this first transgression, incites and presses hard in every way, striving to extend sins more profusely—we human beings providing the occasions and beginnings of sins, while hostile powers spread them far and wide, and, if possible, beyond any limit.[23] Thus, when human beings first desire money a little, then their greed increases as the vice grows, the fall into avarice finally takes place. After this, when blindness of mind has succeeded passion, and with the hostile powers prompting and urging vehemently, money is no longer desired but stolen and acquired by force or even by the shedding of human blood. Finally, a sure proof of the fact that these enormities of vices come from the demons may easily be seen from this, that those who are driven either by immoderate love or uncontrollable anger or excessive sorrow do not suffer less than those who are vexed bodily by demons. For it is related in certain histories that some have fallen into insanity from love, others from anger, not a few from sorrow or excessive joy; I think that this happens because those opposing powers, that is, those demons, having been given a place in their minds, already laid open by intemperance, have taken complete possession of their intelligence, especially when no glory of virtue has roused them to resistance.

3.2.3. That there are certain sins, however, which do not come from the opposing powers but take their beginnings from the natural movements of the body is clearly stated by the Apostle Paul in the place where he says, *The flesh lusts against the spirit and the spirit against the flesh; these oppose one another, so that you cannot do that which you would.*[24] If, then, the flesh lusts against the spirit and the spirit against the flesh, we occasionally have *to wrestle against flesh and blood,*[25] that is, when we are human beings and *walking according to the flesh,*[26] and when we cannot be tempted with temptations greater than human, when it is said of us, that *no temptation has seized you except what is human. But God is faithful; he will not let you be tempted beyond that of which you are capable.*[27] For just as those who preside over the games do not allow those who come to the games to enter the competitions against each other either indiscriminately or by chance, but, after they have inspected them by a

---

[22] Cf. Origen, *Princ.* 3.1.19.

[23] Cf. Origen, *Princ.* 3.2.4; *Comm. Jo.* 20.176–84, 378–80; *Comm. Matt.* 12.40; 13.23; *Hom. Num.* 20.3.

[24] Gal. 5:17. In *Frag. Eph.* 33, a propos of Eph. 6:12, Origen seems to attribute to the adverse powers even the temptations which arise from flesh and blood.

[25] Eph. 6:12.   [26] 1 Cor. 3:4; 2 Cor. 10:2.   [27] 1 Cor. 10:13.

careful examination of either size or age, pairing most equitably this one with that and that one with this, for example, boys with boys and men with men, who are suited to one another by closeness in age or strength; so also must it be understood of divine providence, which arranges all who descend into the struggles of this human life with the most just measure, according to the character of each individual's strength, which is known only to him who alone beholds the hearts of human beings, so that one fights against a flesh of one kind, another against another kind; one for so long a time, another for so long; one is incited by the flesh to this or that, another to something else; one struggles against this or that hostile power, another against two or three at once, or now against one and now again against another, and at one particular time against one and at another against another; or after certain acts one fights against certain powers, after other acts against other powers. For consider whether some such arrangement is not indicated by that which the Apostle says, *God is faithful; he will not let you be tempted beyond that of which you are capable,* that is, because each one is tempted in proportion to the amount or possibility of his strength.[28]

However, although we have said that by the just judgement of God everyone is tempted in proportion to the amount of his strength, it is not to be supposed that therefore he who is tempted ought to be victorious in every case; just as neither will he who contends in the games, even though he is paired with an opponent of equal measure, nevertheless be able to be victorious in every case. Yet, unless the strength of the combatants are equal, the victor's palm will not justly be won, nor will the vanquished be justly blamed; for this reason, God indeed allows us to be tempted, but not beyond that of which we are capable, for we are tempted in proportion to our strength. Nor is it written, however, that in temptation he will also make a way out from bearing it, but a way out so that we might be able to bear it; that is, he gives us the ability to bear it. But whether we apply this power that he has given us strenuously or slothfully depends upon ourselves. There is no doubt that in every temptation we have the strength to bear it, if only we use to the full the strength granted to us. For to possess the strength of conquering is not the same thing as to conquer, as the Apostle himself has shown in very careful language, saying, *God will give a way out, that you may be able to bear it,*[29] not that you will bear it. For many do not bear it, but are conquered in temptation. It is not given by God that we will bear it (otherwise there would appear to be no struggle), but that we may be able *to bear it.*

---

[28] For other examples of such confidence, see Origen, *Hom. Lev.* 16.6; *Hom. Jes. Nav.* 4.1; *Cels.* 8.27; *Or.* 29.

[29] 1 Cor. 10:13.

But this strength, which is given to us that we may be able to conquer, we employ, according to the faculty of free will, either strenuously and we conquer, or slothfully and we are defeated. For if it were given to us so completely that we would be superior in every case, and in no way be defeated, what reason would remain for struggling to one who is not able to be overcome? Or what merit is there in the palm of victory, when the ability to conquer is removed from the opponent? But if the possibility of conquering is bestowed equally upon us all, while how to use this possibility is within our own power, that is, either strenuously or slothfully, then justly will the conquered be censured and the palm given to the victorious. From these considerations, then, which have been discussed to the best of our power, I think that it is clearly evident that there are certain transgressions that we commit quite apart from the urging of wicked powers, and others which are aroused to excess and immoderation at their instigation. From this it follows for us now to inquire how those opposing powers produce these incitements within us.

3.2.4. We find that thoughts which proceed out of the heart[30] (whether a memory of things we have done or a contemplation of any thing and cause whatsoever), sometimes proceed from ourselves, and sometimes are aroused by the opposing powers, and occasionally are also implanted by God or by the holy angels.[31] This might perhaps appear to be incredible unless it be proved by testimonies from the divine Scripture. That, therefore, a thought may arise within ourselves, is testified by David in the Psalms, saying, *The thought of a human being will acknowledge you, and a remnant of thought shall hold a day of festival to you.*[32] That it may also happen from the opposing powers, is testified by Solomon in the book of Ecclesiastes, in this way, *If the spirit of one holding authority rise up against you, leave not your place, for healing will restrain great offences.*[33] And the Apostle Paul will bear testimony to the same point, saying, *Casting down thoughts and every high thing that exalts itself against the knowledge of Christ.*[34] That it might be due to God is no less testified by David in the Psalms, in this way, *Blessed is the man whose help is from you, O Lord; ascents are in his heart.*[35] And the Apostle says that *God put it in the heart of Titus.*[36] That some thoughts are suggested to human hearts either by good or evil angels is shown both by the angel that accompanied Tobias[37] and by the word

---

[30] Cf. Matt. 15:18–19. Origen equates the biblical term 'heart' with the Platonic term 'mind' (νοῦς) and with the Stoic 'guiding principle' (ἡγεμονικόν); for the former, see *Princ.* 1.1.9; *Frag. Jo.* 13 (GCS 4, p. 495); *Cels.* 6.69; for the latter, see *Or.* 29.2; *Hom. Jer.* 5.15; *Comm. Cant.* 1 (GCS 8, p. 93).

[31] On 'guardian angels', see also Origen, *Princ.* 1.8.1 (and the material cited in n.5 there); 2.10.7.

[32] Ps. 75:11.   [33] Eccl. 10:4.

[34] 2 Cor. 10:4–5, which has 'God' rather than 'Christ'.

[35] Ps. 83:6.   [36] 2 Cor. 8:16.   [37] Cf. Tobit 5:5ff.

of the prophet, saying, *And the angel who was speaking in me answered;*[38] and the book of *The Shepherd* asserts the same thing, teaching that two angels accompany each human being, and that whenever good thoughts arise in our hearts it says they are suggested by the good angel, but when of a contrary kind it says it is the instigation of the evil angel.[39] The same is asserted by Barnabas in his Epistle, where he says there are two ways, one of light and one of darkness, over which he says certain angels preside: the angels of God over the way of light, and the angels of Satan over the way of darkness.[40] It must be understood, however, that nothing else happens to us as a result of the things suggested to our heart, whether good or bad, but a mere agitation and incitement arousing us either to good or to evil. For it is possible for us, when an evil power has begun to incite us to evil, to cast away from us the wicked suggestions and to resist the base enticements and to do nothing at all worthy of blame; and, on the other hand it is possible that, when a divine power arouses us to better things, we do not follow it, our faculty of free will being preserved in both cases.

We were saying, in the above, that certain memories of either good or evil actions were suggested to us, either by divine providence or by the opposing powers; just as it is shown in the book of Esther, when Artaxerxes had not remembered the benefits rendered by that righteous man Mordecai, and, when worn out by sleepless nights, the idea had arisen in his mind by God to request that the memorial of the great deeds in the records be brought; being reminded by them of the benefits rendered by Mordecai, he ordered his enemy Haman to be hanged, and he granted splendid honours to Mordecai and safety to the whole race of saints from the impending danger.[41] On the other hand, it must be supposed that it was the power of the devil that suggested to the minds of the high priests and scribes what they said when coming before Pilate, 'Sir, we *remember that the deceiver said, while he was yet alive, that after three days I will rise again.*'[42] And, when Judas had the idea about betraying the Saviour, it did not come solely from the wickedness of his mind, for Scripture testifies that *The devil put it into his heart to betray him.*[43] And therefore Solomon rightly gave a precept, saying, *Keep your heart with all vigilance;*[44] and the Apostle Paul, <when> he says, *We must pay closer attention to what we hear, lest perhaps we drift* away,[45] and when he says, *Give no place to the devil,*[46] shows by that injunction that through certain acts or a kind of sloth of the mind a place is given to the devil, so that once he has entered into our heart he either takes possession of us or at least pollutes the soul, if he was not able to

---

[38] Zech. 1:14.   [39] Hermas, *Mand.* 6.2.   [40] *Barn.* 18.
[41] Cf. Esther 6–8.   [42] Matt. 27:63.   [43] John 13:2.
[44] Prov. 4:23.   [45] Heb. 2:1.   [46] Eph. 4:27.

take complete possession of it, by throwing his flaming darts at us,[47] with which we are sometimes wounded with a wound that penetrates deeply, and at other times we are merely inflamed. Seldom indeed and only by a few persons are these flaming darts quenched, so as not to find a place for a wound, that is, when one has been covered by the most secure and most robust shield of faith.[48] What is said in the Epistle to the Ephesians—*We wrestle not against flesh and blood, but against the principalities, against the authorities, against the rulers of the darkness of this world, against spiritual hosts of wickedness in the heavenly places*[49]—must be understood such that 'we' means I, Paul, and you Ephesians and whoever does *not wrestle against flesh and blood*'; for such the struggle is *against principalities and authorities, against the rulers of the darkness of this world*, not as it was for the Corinthians, whose struggle was still *against flesh and blood* and whom no temptation had seized, except what is human.[50]

3.2.5. It must not be supposed, however, that each person struggles against all these powers. For it would be impossible, I think, for any human being, even if he were a saint, to carry on a contest against them all at the same time. If indeed in some way that were to happen, which is certainly not possible, it would be impossible for human nature to bear it without being completely overwhelmed. Just as, for example, if fifty soldiers were to say that a battle was about to take place between them and fifty other soldiers, it would not thus be understood that one of them was going to fight against fifty, yet each of them would rightly say that 'our battle is against fifty', all against all; so also what the Apostle said is to be heard in this way, that all the athletes and soldiers of Christ are engaged in a wrestling-match and struggle against all the powers which have been enumerated; that all will engage in the struggle, but individuals against individuals, or at least according to the determination of God, who is the just president of the contest. For I think that human nature has definite limits, although there is a Paul of whom it is said, <*He is a chosen vessel of mine,*>[51] or a Peter, against whom the gates of hell do not prevail,[52] or a Moses, the *friend* of God,[53] for none of these could sustain the whole crowd of these opposing powers at once without destruction to himself, unless indeed there was working in him the power of him alone who said, *Be of good cheer, I have overcome the world.*[54] Because of this Paul could say with confidence, *I can do all things in him who strengthens me,*[55] and again, *I worked harder than them all, yet not I, but the grace of God in me.*[56]

---

[47] Cf. Eph. 6:16.   [48] Cf. Eph. 6:16.   [49] Eph. 6:12.
[50] Cf. 1 Cor. 10.13. Cf. Origen, *Fr.Eph.* 33 (on 6:12): 'I think *against flesh and blood* refers to those temptations he calls *human*.'
[51] Acts 9:15.   [52] Matt. 16:18.   [53] Exod. 33:11.   [54] John 16:33.
[55] Phil. 4:13.   [56] 1 Cor. 15:10.

On account, then, of this power, which is certainly not human, working and speaking in him, Paul could say, *I am sure that neither death, nor life, nor angels, nor principalities, nor authorities, nor things present, nor things to come, nor strength, nor height, nor depth, nor any other creature, will be able to separate us from the love of God which is in Christ Jesus our Lord.*[57] For human nature by itself alone is not able, I think, to maintain the struggle against angels and the heights and the depth and any other creature; but when it has sensed the Lord to be present and dwelling within, with confidence in divine assistance it will say, *The Lord is my illumination and my Saviour; whom shall I fear? The Lord is the protector of my life; of whom shall I be afraid? When evildoers would approach me, to devour my flesh, those who afflict me, my enemies, they became weak and fell. Though an army be arrayed against me, my heart shall not fear; though war rise up against me, in this I hope.*[58]

From this I think that perhaps a human being would never be able by himself to conquer an opposing power, unless he had the benefit of divine assistance. Hence also the angel is said to have wrestled with Jacob. We understand the passage in this way, that it is not the same thing for the angel to have wrestled with Jacob and to have wrestled against Jacob; but the angel, who was present with him for the sake of his salvation, and who, after learning of his progress, gave him the additional name of Israel, wrestled together with him, that is, he was with him in the contest and assists him in the struggle, for there was undoubtedly another angel against whom he was fighting and against whom his struggle was being waged.[59] And, indeed, Paul did not tell us that we wrestle with principalities or with authorities, but *against principalities and against authorities.*[60] Thus, if Jacob wrestled, it was undoubtedly against some one of those powers which Paul enumerates as opposing and launching attacks on the human race and especially the saints. Therefore, finally, Scripture says of him that he was wrestling with an angel and was strengthened with God,[61] so that the struggle is sustained by the assistance of the angel, but the palm of accomplishment leads the conqueror to God.

3.2.6. Nor, indeed, should it be supposed that struggles of this kind are carried on by means of bodily strength or the arts of the wrestling school, but the fight is of spirit against spirit, in the same way that Paul asserts that our present

---

[57] Rom. 8:38–9.   [58] Ps. 26:1–3. Cf. Origen, *Comm. Rom.* 7.12.
[59] Cf. Gen. 32:22–30. See also *Sel. Gen.* 32:24 (PG 12, 128): 'Who else is he who is called both human and God, who wrestles and struggles with Jacob, but he who in many places and many ways spoke to the fathers, the sacred Word of God, called both Lord and God, who also, blessing Jacob, called him Israel?' (*Τίς δ' ἂν ἄλλος εἴη ὁ λεγόμενος ἄνθρωπος ὁμοῦ καὶ θεός, συμπαλαίων καὶ συναγωνιζόμενος τῷ Ἰακώβ, ἢ ὁ πολυμερ ῶ ς καὶ πολυτρόπος λαλήσας τοῖ ς πατράσιν ἱερὸς τοῦ θεοῦ λόγος, κύριος καὶ θεὸς χρηματίζων, ὃς καὶ εὐλογήσας τὸν Ἰακώβ , Ἰσραὴλ αὐτὸν ὠνόμασεν.*)
[60] Eph. 6:12.   [61] Cf. Gen. 32:24, 28.

struggle is *against principalities and authorities and the rulers of the darkness of this world.*[62] This kind of struggle is to be understood thus: when losses and dangers, reproaches and accusations are raised up against us, the opposing powers do not do this that we should only suffer these things, but that by means of them we should be aroused either to great anger or excessive sorrow or to the depths of despair, or indeed, what is more serious, that, we should be induced, when wearied and overcome by these nuisances, to make complaints against God, as if he were not administering human life justly and equitably; [they do this] so that by these efforts we may become weakened in faith or give up hope or be driven to abandon the truth of the teachings and be persuaded to think something impious about God. For some such things are written regarding Job, when the devil had requested of God to be given power over his goods. By this we are also taught that it is not by any accidental attacks that we are assailed, if ever such losses of property should strike us, nor is it by chance if any one of us is taken captive or that our houses fall into ruins, in which those who are dear to us are crushed to death;[63] in all these circumstances, every one of the believers ought to say that *you would have no power over me, unless it were given to you from above.*[64] For observe that the house of Job would not have fallen upon his sons unless the devil had first received power against them; nor would the horsemen have made a raid in three columns, that they might seize his camels or oxen and other cattle, unless they had been instigated to that by that spirit to whom they had delivered themselves up as servants by their obedience to his will. Nor would that which appeared to be fire, or has been supposed to be a lightning flash, have fallen upon Job's sheep, until the devil had said to God, *Have you not put a fence around all that is without and within his house and around all the rest of his property? But now put forth your hand and touch all that he has, [and see] if indeed he blesses you to your face!*[65]

3.2.7. From all these considerations it is shown that all those events that happen in this world, which are considered indifferent, whether they be sorrowful or are of any other kind, are brought about neither by God nor yet without him; not only does he not prevent those wicked and opposing powers who wish to wreak such events, but he even permits them to do so,[66] although only on certain occasions and to certain persons, just as it is said about Job himself that for a certain time he was ordained to fall under the power of others and his house to be plundered by iniquitous people. Therefore the divine Scripture teaches us to accept all that happens to us as sent by God, knowing that nothing happens without God. That such is the case, that is, that nothing happens

---

[62] Eph. 6:12.   [63] Cf. Job 1:6–19.   [64] John 19:11.
[65] Job 1:10–11.   [66] Cf. Origen, *Hom. Jes. Nav.* 15.5.

without God, how can we doubt, when our Lord and Saviour clearly proclaims and says, *Are not two sparrows sold for a penny, and not one of them shall fall to the ground without your Father who is in heaven?*[67]

But necessity has led us into a lengthy digression on the subject of the struggle waged by the hostile powers against human beings, while also discussing those more sorrowful events which happen to the human race, that is, the trials of this life—just as Job says, *Is not the whole of human life upon earth a trial?*[68]— so that the way in which they occur, and how one should piously think about them, might be clearly shown. Now let us consider how human beings fall away into the sin of false knowledge, and with what purpose the opposing powers are also wont to stir up conflict against us regarding such things.

3.3.1.[69] Wishing to teach us some great and hidden truth concerning knowledge and wisdom, the holy Apostle says in the First Epistle to the Corinthians, *We speak wisdom among the perfect, yet not the wisdom of this world nor of the rulers of this world, who are coming to nought; but we speak the wisdom of God in a mystery, the hidden wisdom which God foreordained before the world unto our glory, which none of the rulers of this world knew. For had they known it, they would not have crucified the Lord of glory.*[70] In this passage, wishing to show the different kinds of wisdom, he describes one as *the wisdom of this world,* one as the wisdom *of the rulers of this world,* and another as the *wisdom of God.*[71] But when he uses the expression, wisdom *of the rulers of this world,* I do not think that he means some one wisdom common to all rulers of this world, but he seems to me to indicate a particular wisdom for each individual ruler. And again, when he says, *we speak the wisdom of God in a mystery, the hidden wisdom, which God foreordained before the world unto our glory*, it must be asked whether he means that this wisdom of God, which has been hidden and has not been made known to the sons of men in other times and generations as it has now been revealed to his holy apostles and prophets, is the same as that wisdom of God which existed before the coming of the Saviour, by means of which Solomon became wise, yet compared to which the saying of

---

[67] Matt. 10:29. Cf. Origen, *Princ.* 2.11.5.   [68] Job 7:1.

[69] Only two manuscripts (B and C) have, before the 'Now' of the previous sentence, the title 'That there is a difference between the wisdom of God and the wisdom of this world and the wisdom of the rulers of this world, or, how one might be entrapped through that wisdom which is of the rulers of the world'. Merlin inserted the title 'On the Threefold Wisdom' at this point, and he has been followed by all editors (and the translation of Butterworth) with the exception of Fernandez. As Origen has just noted, however, although turning to the question of knowledge, the subject remains the work of the opposing powers, as the first sentence of *Princ.* 3.3.2 indicates, and remains so until the conclusion of *Princ.* 3.3.6, as the final sentence there makes clear.

[70] 1 Cor. 2:6–8.

[71] The same distinction is made, on the basis of the same texts, in Origen, *Comm. Cant.* 1 (GcS 8, p. 100).

the Saviour himself proclaims that what the Saviour teaches is greater than Solomon, when he says, *And behold [someone] greater <than> Solomon is here*,[72] by which it is shown that those who were taught by the Saviour were taught something more than what Solomon knew. If one were to say that the Saviour did indeed know more, but did not however impart more to others than did Solomon, how will this agree and be reckoned as consistently said with what he says in the following passage, *The queen of the south will arise at the judgement and condemn the men of this generation, because she came from the ends of the earth to hear the wisdom of Solomon, and behold, [someone] greater than Solomon is here?*[73] There is, therefore, a *wisdom of this world*, and probably also a wisdom belonging to each individual *ruler of this world*. But as for the wisdom of the one God, we believe that to be indicated which was at work in a lesser degree in those of ancient and former times, but was more fully and more clearly revealed through Christ. We shall, however, investigate the wisdom of God in the proper place.[74]

3.3.2. But now, since our task is to treat of the opposing powers, how they stir up those struggles by means of which false knowledge is implanted in the minds of human beings and souls are led astray, while they suppose that they have discovered wisdom, I think it necessary to discern and distinguish between that which is *the wisdom of this world* and that of *the rulers of this world*, that by doing so we may be able to discover who are the fathers of this wisdom, or indeed of these kinds of wisdom. I think, therefore, as we said above, that *the wisdom of this world* is a different one than those varieties of wisdom which belong to *the rulers of this world*, and that by this wisdom there appears to be understood and comprehended those things which belong to this world. This wisdom, however, possesses in itself nothing by which it is able to perceive anything of divinity, or of the cause of the world, or of any higher matters whatsoever, or of the principles of a good and blessed life, but is such, for example, that it is wholly concerned with the arts of poetry or grammar or rhetoric or geometry or music, with which medicine perhaps should also be counted. In all these subjects *the wisdom of this world* must be supposed to be present.[75] We understand the wisdom of *the rulers of this world*, on the other hand, to be what they call the secret and hidden philosophy of the Egyptians, and the astrology of the Chaldeans and Indians, who profess knowledge of high things,[76] and also the manifold and diverse opinions of the Greeks about divinity. Accordingly, we find in the holy Scriptures that there are rulers over

---

[72] Matt. 12:42.   [73] Ibid.   [74] Cf. Origen, *Princ.* 4.3.14.

[75] In *Hom. Num.* 18.3, a propos of Sir. 1:1 ('All wisdom is from God') and other texts, Origen ascribes the origin of human wisdom, knowledge, crafts, and arts to God. See also Gregory Thaumaturgus, *pan. Or.* 8 on the range of topics taught by Origen.

[76] Cf. Origen, *Comm. Gen.* 3 (= *Philoc.* 23).

individual nations, as we read in Daniel that there was *a ruler of the kingdom of Persia* and another *ruler of the kingdom of the Greeks*,[77] who, as is clearly shown by the sense of the passage itself, are not human beings but certain powers. In the prophet Ezekiel also *the ruler of Tyre* is most clearly shown to be a kind of spiritual power.[78] When these, then, and other similar rulers of this world, each possessing his own wisdom and building up his own teachings and diverse opinions, beheld our Lord and Saviour professing and proclaiming that he had come into the world for this purpose, that all the teachings, whatever they may be, of *knowledge falsely so called*[79] might be destroyed, not knowing who was concealed within, they immediately lay in ambush for him; for, *the kings of the earth set themselves and the rulers assembled together, against the Lord and against his Christ*.[80] But their snares became known and the plots they had contrived against the Son of God were understood when they *crucified the Lord of glory*; therefore the Apostle says, *We speak wisdom among the perfect, yet not the wisdom of this world nor of the rulers of this world, who are coming to nought, which none of the rulers of this world knew. For had they known it, they would not have crucified the Lord of glory*.[81]

3.3.3. It must indeed be examined whether those wisdoms of the rulers of this world, with which they endeavour to infect human beings, are forced upon human beings by the opposing powers with the desire of ensnaring and injuring them, or whether they are offered only as a result of error, that is, not with a view to injuring human beings, but because the rulers of this world themselves think these things to be true and therefore desire to teach others things that they themselves hold to be true, which, I think, is more likely. Just as, for example, certain Greek authors or the leaders of each of the schools, when they have first themselves accepted the error of false teaching instead of the truth and have determined in themselves that such is the truth, they then strive to persuade others of that which they assessed of themselves to be true, so also, it must be supposed, the rulers of this world act, certain spiritual powers having been assigned the rule over certain nations in this world and who are, on this account, termed *rulers of this world*.

There are also, besides these rulers, certain special forces of this world, that is, certain spiritual powers, working certain works, which they have themselves, through the freedom of their will, chosen to effect, among whom are those spirits who work the wisdom of this world: for example, there is a particular force or power which inspires poetry, another geometry, and in the same way they animate each of the arts and disciplines of this kind. Moreover,

---

[77] Dan. 10: 13, 20. Origen, *Princ.* 1.5.2, and n.16 there.
[78] Cf. Ezek. 28. Origen, *Princ.* 1.5.4.   [79] 1 Tim. 6:20.
[80] Ps. 2:2.   [81] 1 Cor. 2:6–8, omitting a couple of phrases.

many of the Greek writers have been of the opinion that the art of poetry cannot exist without madness, which also is why it is often recorded in their histories that those whom they call poets were suddenly filled with a kind of spirit of madness. And what is to be said also of those whom they call diviners, from whom, by the work of those demons who have charge over them, oracles are given in artfully constructed verses? But those also, whom they call magi or malevolent, have often, by invoking demons over boys still young in years, made them recite poems in verse to the wonder and amazement of all. These effects must be supposed to be brought about in the following way: just as holy and immaculate souls, when they have devoted themselves to God with all affection and all purity and have kept themselves apart from all contact with demons and purified themselves by lengthy abstinence and have been steeped in pious and religious training, acquire thereby participation in divinity and become worthy of the grace of prophecy and of the other divine gifts, so also, it is to be supposed that those who show themselves appropriate subjects for the opposing powers, that is, those who adopt a form of activity, life, and purpose agreeable to them, receive their inspiration and become participators in their wisdom and teaching. The result of this is that they are filled with the workings of those powers to whose service they have already subjected themselves.

3.3.4. Concerning those, indeed, who teach otherwise regarding Christ than is supported by the rule of the Scriptures, it is not an idle task to ascertain whether it is with treacherous purpose that the opposing powers, exerting themselves against the faith of Christ, have devised certain fabulous and simultaneously impious doctrines, or whether even they, on hearing the word of Christ and being able neither to cast it out from the hidden depths of their conscience nor to retain it pure and holy, have introduced, by means of vessels convenient for them and, so to speak, through their prophets, various errors contrary to the rule of Christian truth. It is, rather, to be supposed that apostate and exiled powers who have departed from God—either by the very wickedness of their mind and will or by their jealousy of those for whom there is prepared, once they have learned the truth, an ascent to the same rank from which the powers have fallen—did invent these errors and delusions of false doctrine in order to hinder progress of that kind.

It is therefore clearly demonstrated by many proofs that the human soul, while it is in the body, is able to accept different energies, that is, works from a variety of spirits either good or evil; and there is a twofold mode of work of the evil spirits: that is, either they take complete and entire possession of the mind, so that they allow those whom they possess to understand or think nothing at all, as for instance those popularly called 'possessed', whom we see to be demented and insane, such as those who are related in the Gospel to have been healed by the Saviour; or they deprave the soul, while it still thinks and understands, by the hostile suggestion of various thoughts and evil persuasions, of which Judas is an example, being incited to the act of betrayal by the devil's insertion of the thought, as Scripture declares, saying, *the devil had already put it into the heart of Judas to betray him.*[82] On the other hand, someone receives the energy and work of a good spirit when he is moved and incited to good and inspired towards heavenly or divine things; just as the holy angels of God himself worked in the prophets, arousing and exhorting them by holy suggestions towards better things, yet, indeed, such that it remained within the will and judgement of the person, whether he was willing or unwilling to follow the encouragement to heavenly and divine things. Whence also from this clear distinction it is discerned when it is that the soul is moved by the presence of a better spirit, that is, if it encounter no disturbance or aberration of mind whatever from the impending inspiration nor lose the free judgement of its will; just as, for example, were all, whether prophets or apostles, who ministered to the divine oracles without any disturbance of mind. We have already shown by previous examples, when we made mention of Mordecai and Artaxerxes, that by the suggestions of a good spirit the human memory is aroused to the recollection of better things.[83]

3.3.5. This[84] also, I think, must next be investigated: the grounds why the human soul is influenced at one time by good spirits and at another time by evil spirits. I suspect the grounds of such a matter to be something even older than this bodily birth, as John shows by leaping and rejoicing in his mother's womb when the voice of the salutation of Mary reached the ears of his mother Elizabeth,[85] and as the prophet Jeremiah declares, who *before he was formed in his mother's belly* was known by God and *before he came forth from the womb* was sanctified by him and while yet a boy received the grace of prophecy.[86] And again, on the other hand, it is clearly shown that some are possessed by adverse spirits right from the very beginning of their years, that is, some are

---

[82] John 13:2.   [83] Cf. Origen, *Princ.* 3.2.4.

[84] Cf. Jerome, *Ep.* 124.8.6–7 (ed. Hilberg 3, 106.23–107.9): 'And in the same book: but this also must be investigated, why the human soul is moved in different directions, at one time by these powers, at another time by others. And he supposes some, before they come into bodies, to have previous merits, such as is the case of John, rejoicing in his mother's womb when, at the voice of Mary's greeting, Elizabeth confessed herself to be unworthy of conversing with her. And he immediately adds: on the other hand, little boys, hardly weaned, are possessed by evil spirits, and diviners and soothsayers are inspired to such a degree that some are even possessed by a prophetic demon from their earliest years; that these should be abandoned from the providence of God, when they have done nothing such that they should rightly bear madness of this kind, cannot be maintained by one who holds that nothing happens apart from God and that all things are governed by his justice.'

[85] Cf. Luke 1:41–4. Cf. Origen, *Princ.* 1.7.4; *Hom. Luc.* 7–9.   [86] Jer. 1:5–6.

born with their demon,[87] while others the testimony of histories declare to have practised divination from childhood, and yet others from their earliest years have been subject to the demon they call 'Python,'[88] that is, the spirit of ventriloquism.[89] To all these instances, those who maintain that everything in this world is governed by the providence of God, as also our faith holds, as it seems to me, can give no other answer, so as to show divine providence exempt from any reproach of injustice, than say there were certain antecedent grounds by which souls, before they were born in the body, contracted a certain amount of guilt in their thoughts and movements, in respect of which they have been deemed worthy by divine providence to suffer these things.[90] For the soul is always in possession of free will, when in the body and when out of the body; and freedom of will always moves either towards good or evil; nor can the rational sense, that is, the intellect or the soul, ever exist without some movement, either good or evil. It is probable that these movements furnish grounds for merit even before they do anything in this world, so that in accordance with these grounds or merits they are arranged by divine providence immediately upon their birth, indeed even before birth, so to speak, to endure either good or evil.

3.3.6. These things, then, are to be said in regard to those events which appear to befall human beings, either immediately from their birth or even before they emerge into this light. In regard, however, to suggestions made by diverse spirits to the soul, that is, to the thoughts of human beings, and which arouse them to good or to its opposite, even in such a case there must sometimes be supposed to exist certain grounds prior to bodily birth. But sometimes the mind, being vigilant and casting away from itself whatever is evil, calls to itself the aid of the good spirits; or, on the contrary, being negligent and slothful, when it is less cautious, it makes room for those spirits which, like robbers lying secretly on the path, contrive to rush into the human minds whenever they see a place made for them by sloth, just as the Apostle Peter says that *Your adversary the devil prowls around like a roaring lion, seeking whom he may devour.*[91] Because of this, our heart must be guarded with all carefulness day and night, and no place be given to the devil,[92] but everything must be done such that the ministers of God (those spirits, that is, who were sent to minister

---

[87] Cf. Mark 7:25, 9:17, etc.   [88] Cf. Acts 16:16.

[89] This is the LXX way of speaking of 'divination'; ἐγγαστρίμυθος is translated by Margaret M. Mitchell, in other works, as 'belly-myther'. Cf. 'Patristic Rhetoric on Allegory: Origen and Eustathius put 1 Samuel 28 on Trial', *JR* 85 (2005), 414–45.

[90] Cf. Origen, *Princ.* 1.7.4, and the material cited in the notes there.

[91] 1 Pet. 5:8. On vigilance, see Origen, *Comm. Jo.* 20.176–81; *Hom. Jes. Nav.* 16.5; *Hom. Gen.* 9.3; for negligence, see *Princ.* 1.4.1; 1.6.2; 2.9.2.

[92] Cf. Eph. 4:27.

to those who are called to the inheritance of salvation[93]) may find a place within us and be delighted to enter into the guest-chamber of our soul and, dwelling within us, that is, in our heart, may guide us with better counsels, if indeed they shall find the habitation of our heart adorned by the cultivation of virtue and holiness.

But let these points, expounded by us according to our strength, suffice regarding those powers which are opposed to the human race.

---

[93] Cf. Heb. 1:14.

On Human Temptations

3.4.1.[1] And now, I think, we must not pass over in silence the subject of human temptations,[2] which are engendered sometimes from *flesh and blood*,[3] or from *the shrewdness of flesh* and blood, which is said to be *hostile to God*,[4] after having already spoken about the temptations which are said to be more than human, that is, which we maintain *against principalities and authorities and against the rulers of the darkness of this world and spiritual hosts of wickedness in the heavenly places*,[5] and with those which afflict us against wicked spirits and unclean demons. In this matter, I suppose logically it must be inquired whether there is in us, that is, in human beings who are composed of soul and body and vital spirit,[6] something else besides, which has its own stimulus and movement inciting towards evil, just as the question is wont to be raised by some in this way: whether two souls, as it were, should be said to be in us, the one more divine and heavenly, the other inferior;[7] or whether, from the very fact that we adhere to bodies (which bodies are, according to their own proper nature, dead and utterly lifeless, since it is from us, that is, from our souls, that the material body is vivified, since it is assuredly contrary and hostile to the spirit[8]) we are drawn and incited to those evils which are pleasing to the body; or whether, thirdly, as some of the Greeks have supposed, our soul, although it is one in substance, nevertheless consists of several elements, that is, one element of it is called rational and another irrational, and that which is called irrational is again divided into the two affections of desire and anger.[9] We have found, then, that each of the three opinions we have stated regarding the soul is held by some. Of them, however, that one, which we said

---

[1] Some manuscripts have here, as a title, the following, 'Whether what is said by some is true, that each individual has two souls'; others have this as part of the text. This chapter division and title is adopted by Koetschau (and Butterworth in his translation), and followed by Crouzel and Simonetti, and Görgemanns and Karpp, and, in parenthesis by Fernandez. While this is indeed a topic of discussion from *Princ.* 3.4.2 on, it is nevertheless clear that Origen is continuing his discussion of the struggles facing human beings: having dealt with the conflicts resulting from the opposing forces in *Princ.* 3.2–3, he now turns to the temptations arising from human nature. Thus, taking the express statement of Origen in the first sentence, I have followed the earlier editions which had the heading 'On Human Temptations', either after the previous sentence but one (Merlin) or at this point (Delarue).

[2] Cf. 1 Cor. 10:13.   [3] Eph. 6:12.

[4] Rom. 8:7: τὸ φρόνημα τῆς σαρκὸς ἔχθρα εἰς θεόν. Cf. Gen. 3:1, where the serpent is described as φρονιμώτατος.

[5] Eph. 6:12.   [6] Cf. Wis. 15:11; 1 Thess. 5:23.

[7] According to Porphyry, Numenius spoke of two souls in the human being, a rational one and a non-rational one (Stobaeus, 1.350.25–351.1), as did various disciples of Basilides (cf. Clement *Exc.* 50; *Strom.* 2.20.112–14), and Tatian, *Or.* 12; see also Tertullian, *An.* 10, and Clement, *Strom.* 6.16.135–6.

[8] Cf. Rom. 8:6, 10; Gal. 5:17; John 6:63.   [9] Cf. Plato, *Resp.* 4.436a–441c; *Tim.* 42a.

was entertained by certain Greek philosophers, that the soul is tripartite, I do not see to be strongly confirmed by the authority of the divine Scriptures; whereas with respect to the remaining two, a certain number of passages may be found in the divine writings which seem capable of being applied.

3.4.2. Of these opinions, let us first discuss that which some are accustomed to construct, that there is in us a good and heavenly soul, and another earthly and inferior, and that the one which is better is implanted from heaven, such as was that which, while Jacob was still in the womb set against Esau, gave the prize of victory in supplanting his brother, and which, in the case of Jeremiah, was sanctified from the womb, and in that of John was filled by the Holy Spirit from the womb.[10] But that soul, which they call inferior, they say is sown together with the body from the bodily seed,[11] whence they deny that it can live or subsist apart from the body, on account of which they say that it is frequently termed the flesh. For the saying, *The flesh lusts against the spirit,*[12] they take not to be spoken of the flesh, but of this soul, which is properly the soul of the flesh. But they also endeavour, moreover, to corroborate from this what is written thus in Leviticus, *The soul of all flesh is its blood.*[13] For from the fact that the blood, being diffused throughout the flesh, provides life to the flesh, they claim that this soul, which is said to be *the soul of all flesh,* resides in the blood. And the same thing that is spoken about by [the statement], *The flesh wars against the spirit and the spirit against the flesh,*[14] and the saying, *The soul of all flesh is its blood,*[15] is, they claim, termed by another name as *the shrewdness of the flesh,*[16] as it is a kind of material spirit which is not subject to the law of God, nor can it be subject, since it has earthly wishes and bodily desires. It is about this that they suppose the Apostle to be speaking when he said, *But I see another law in my members, warring against the law of my mind and bringing me into captivity to the law of sin which is in my members.*[17]

But if one were to object to them that these words were spoken of the nature of the body, which according to the property of its nature is indeed dead, but is said to possess a *mind* or a *shrewdness* that is *hostile to God* or which *wars against the spirit,*[18] in the same way as if one were to say that the flesh itself has a voice which should cry out against being hungry or thirsty or cold, or against suffering any discomfort arising whatsoever, whether from excess or deficiency, they would endeavour to resolve and combat this objection by showing that there were many other passions of the soul which in no way derive their origin from the flesh and yet against which the spirit struggles, such as ambition,

---

[10] Cf. Gen. 25:22–6; Jer. 1:5; Luke 1:41. Origen, *Princ.* 1.7.4 (and the material cited in the notes there); 2.9.7; 3.1.22; 3.3.5.

[11] Cf. Tertullian, *An.* 27; 36; Clement, *Exc.* 50; 55.   [12] Gal. 5:17.

[13] Lev. 17:14. Cf. Origen, *Or.* 29.2; *Dial.* 16.   [14] Gal. 5:17.   [15] Lev. 17:14.

[16] Rom. 8:7.   [17] Rom. 7:23.   [18] Rom. 8:7; Gal. 5:17.

avarice, jealousy, envy, pride, and others like them; and seeing that the mind or spirit of the human being is in conflict with these, they would lay down as the cause of all such evils nothing other than this bodily soul, as it were, which we have spoken of above and which is generated by the transmission of seed. They are also accustomed to bring forward, in support of their assertion, the testimony of the Apostle, where he says, *Now the works of the flesh are clear, which are these: fornication, impurity, licentiousness, idolatry, sorcery, enmity, strife, jealousy, anger, dispute, dissension, heresy, envying, drunkenness, revelling, and the like;*[19] they claim that not all these derive their origin from the habits or the pleasures of the flesh, such that all these movements are to be reckoned to be of that substance which does not have a soul, that is, the flesh. Moreover, that statement which he makes, *For consider your calling, brethren, how not many among you were wise according to the flesh,*[20] would seem to point to this, that there appears to be a certain proper fleshly and material wisdom, the wisdom according to the spirit being another, and that the former cannot indeed be called 'wisdom' unless there be a soul of the flesh which would be wise in respect of what is called *the shrewdness of the flesh.*[21] And in addition to these passages, they also add this, if *the flesh wars against the spirit and the spirit against the flesh, so that we may not do the things that we would,*[22] what things are these of which he says *that we may not do the things we would?* It is certain, they say, that it does not mean the things of the spirit, for the will of the spirit is not forbidden; but neither does it mean the things of the flesh, since if it does not have a soul of its own, it undoubtedly will not have a will; it remains, then, that it means the will of this soul, which is able to have a will of its own, which is certainly opposed to the will of the spirit. And if this is so, it is established that the will of this soul is something intermediate between the flesh and the spirit,[23] undoubtedly serving and obeying one of the two, whichever it has chosen to obey; and when it yields itself to the pleasures of the flesh, it makes human beings fleshly, but when it joins itself to the spirit it makes the human being to be *in the spirit* and to be called, on this account, *spiritual.* It seems to be this that the Apostle indicates when he says, *But you are not in the flesh but in the spirit.*[24]

It must be ascertained what exactly is this will itself, intermediate between flesh and spirit, besides that which is said to be of the flesh or of the spirit. For it is certainly held that everything said to be of the spirit is the will of the spirit and everything called *works of the flesh* is the will of the flesh.[25] What then, besides these, is that will of the soul, which is named separately, which will the Apostle wishes us not to do when he says, *So that you may not do that which*

---

[19] Gal. 5:19–21.   [20] 1 Cor. 1:26.   [21] Rom. 8:7.   [22] Gal. 5:17.
[23] Cf. Origen, *Princ.* 2.8.4; *Comm. Jo.* 32.218; *Comm. Rom.* 1.18; *Hom. Lev.* 2.2.
[24] Rom. 8:9.   [25] Cf. Gal. 5:19, 22.

you would?[26] By this it would seem to be indicated that it ought to adhere to neither of these two, that is, neither to the flesh nor to the spirit. But someone may say that, just as it is better for the soul to do its own will than that of the flesh, so also it is better for it to do the will of the spirit than its own will. How, then, does the Apostle say, *So that you may not do that which you would*? Because in that contest, which is waged between flesh and spirit, the spirit is by no means certain of victory, for it is clear that in many cases the flesh prevails.

3.4.3. But since we have entered upon a very deep discussion, in which it is necessary to analyse every single point which may be advanced, let us see whether at this point some such conclusion may not perhaps be determined: that just as it is better for the soul to follow the spirit at the time when the spirit has conquered the flesh, so also, even though it would seem to be worse for it to follow the flesh, when the flesh is warring against the spirit and desiring to call the soul to itself, it may nevertheless perhaps appear more advantageous for the soul to be mastered by the flesh than to abide in the sphere of its own will.[27] Since, as long as it remains in the sphere of its will, then is the time when it is said to be *neither hot nor cold*,[28] but continuing in a sort of luke-warm condition it will find conversion a slow and somewhat difficult process; but if it adheres to the flesh, then, at some time it will be satiated and filled with those very evils which it suffers from the vices of the flesh, and wearied, as it were, by the heavy burdens of luxury and lust, it may more easily and rapidly be converted from the squalor of material things to a desire for heavenly things and to spiritual grace.[29] And the Apostle must be supposed to have said, therefore, that *the spirit wars against the flesh and the flesh against the spirit, so that we may not do that which we would*[30] (those things, undoubtedly, which are designated as apart from the will of the spirit and apart from the will of the flesh), meaning, if we were to say it in other words, that it is better for a human being to be either in a condition of virtue or in a condition of wickedness than in neither of these; but that the soul, before it converts to the spirit and is made one with it, while it adheres to the body and thinks of fleshly things, appears to be neither in a good condition nor in a clearly wicked one, but to be, if I may so speak, like an animal. It is better, however, if it be possible, for it to be rendered spiritual by adhering to the spirit; but, if this is not possible, it is more expedient to follow even the wickedness of the flesh than, fixed in the sphere of its own will, to hold the position of an irrational animal.

We have treated these points, wishing to discuss every single opinion, at greater length than we intended, that those views might not be supposed to

---

[26] Gal 5:17.   [27] Cf. Origen, *Hom. Luc.* 17.3.   [28] Rev. 3:15.
[29] Cf. Origen, *Princ.* 1.3.8 (and the material cited in n.71 there); 3.1.13, 17.
[30] Gal. 5:17.

have escaped us that are commonly advanced by those who inquire whether there is in us any other soul besides this heavenly and rational one, which is naturally opposed to that one and is called either the flesh or the wisdom of the flesh or the soul of the flesh.

3.4.4. Let us now see what answer is usually given to these statements by those who maintain that there is in us a single movement and a single life of one and the same soul, whose salvation or destruction is ascribed to itself according to its own actions. And let us first see of what kind the passions of the mind are, which we suffer whenever we feel within ourselves as if we are being dragged in different directions, when there arises a certain conflict of thoughts in our hearts and certain images are suggested to us, by which we are inclined now this way and now that, and by which we are at one time reproved and another time we are ourselves approved.[31] It is nothing remarkable, however, if we say that wicked spirits have a varying and self-conflicting and self-discordant judgement, since such is found to be the case with all human beings whenever deliberation about an uncertain matter is brought to council and consideration and consultation is given as to what should be chosen as better and more advantageous. It is therefore not surprising that if two images occur to someone in turn and suggest opposite things, they should drag the mind in different directions. For example, if someone is led by reflection to faith and fear of God, it cannot then be said that *The flesh wars against the spirit*; but while it is uncertain about what is true and advantageous, the mind is dragged in diverse directions. So also, when it is supposed that the flesh incites someone to lust, while a better counsel opposes this sort of incitement, it must not be supposed that there is one life that opposes another, but that [the conflict is due to] the nature of the body, which longs to empty out and exhaust the places filled with seminal fluid; just as it must neither be supposed that it is any opposing power or the life of another soul which excites thirst in us and incites us to drink or which causes us to become hungry and drives us to food. But just as these things are desired or expunged through the natural movements of the body, so also the moisture of the natural seed, collecting from time to time in its proper places, strives to be expelled and discharged, which is so far from never happening without the impulse of some external excitement that sometimes it is even wont to be emitted spontaneously.

When, therefore, it is said that *the flesh wars against the spirit*, they must understand the passage thus: that the use or the needs or the delights of the flesh, inciting a human being, draw and lead him away from divine and spiritual things. For, being drawn away because of the needs of the body, we are not allowed to be at leisure for things divine and profitable for eternity; just as, on

---

[31] Cf. Rom. 2:15.

the other hand, when the soul has leisure for divine and spiritual things and, being united with the Spirit of God, it is said to war against the flesh, for it does not allow itself to become relaxed through indulgences and to be swayed by the pleasures in which it naturally delights. In this way they take the saying, *The shrewdness of the flesh is hostile to God*,[32] not that the flesh really has a soul or a wisdom of its own, but just as we are accustomed to say improperly that the earth is thirsty and wants to drink water (where we indeed say 'want', yet employ the word not properly but improperly, just as if we were to say again that this house wants to be rebuilt and many other similar expressions), so also must *the shrewdness of the flesh* be understood or the saying that *flesh wars against the spirit*. They are accustomed to add to these the saying, *The voice of your brother's blood cries out to me from the ground*.[33] For what cries out to the Lord is not properly the blood itself that was shed, but the blood is improperly said to cry out when vengeance is demanded from God upon him who shed the blood. That also which the Apostle said, *I see another law in my members*,[34] they understand in this way, as if he had said that the one who wishes to devote himself to the Word of God is, because of the bodily needs and functions that are like a sort of law in the body, distracted and divided and impeded, lest by devoting himself more attentively to the *Wisdom of God*[35] he should be able to behold the divine mysteries.

3.4.5. With regard, however, to the fact that *heresies and envyings and strifes* and other vices are described as being among the *works of the flesh*,[36] they understand in this way, that the soul—when rendered grosser in feeling from yielding itself to the passions of the body, being weighed down by the mass of its vices, and being sensitive to nothing refined or spiritual—is said to be made flesh and takes its name from that in which it exercises the greater part of its endeavour and purpose. They also pose this further question: 'Who will be found, or who will be said to be the creator of this evil mind, which is called the mind of the flesh?' For they maintain that it is to be believed that there is no other creator of the soul and flesh than God. But it would certainly seem absurd if we should say that the good God created anything in his own creation that is hostile to himself. If, then, it is written that *The shrewdness of the flesh is hostile to God,* and if it is said that this is a result of creation, then it will appear that God himself has made a nature hostile to himself, which cannot be subject to him nor to his law,[37] at least if it is assumed that it is an animate being about which these things are said. But if this is accepted, in what way will it appear to differ from those who say that different natures of souls are created, which are by nature either to be saved or to be destroyed? This is

---

[32] Rom. 8:7.   [33] Gen. 4:10.   [34] Rom. 7:23.
[35] 1 Cor. 1:21, 24.   [36] Gal. 5:19–20.   [37] Cf. Rom. 8:7.

satisfactory indeed to heretics alone, who, not able to defend the justice of God by pious reasoning, compose impious inventions such as this.

We have, then, brought into the open, as best we can, in the person of each of the theories, what might be said in the manner of discussion by each teaching; let the one who reads choose from them which is more to be embraced by reason.[38]

---

[38] Conclusions are likewise left to the reader at *Princ.* 1.6.4; 1.7.1; 2.3.7.

That the World Began in Time and Expects an End

3.5.1.[1] Now, after these matters, since one of the ecclesiastical doctrines is held pre-eminently, in accordance with the assurance of our historical narratives—that this world was made and began at a definite time and, in accordance with the consummation of the age known to all, is to be dissolved because it is corruptible—it does not seem absurd to repeat again a few points regarding this. And, indeed, insofar as it concerns the assurance of the Scriptures, the discussion about this seems very easy. For, in fact, even the heretics, although divided on many other matters, yet on this point seem to be at one in submitting to the authority of Scripture.

Concerning, then, the creation of the world, what other book of Scripture is more able to instruct us than that which was written by Moses regarding its origin? This account may well contain certain deeper matters than the historical narrative appears to reveal and may contain a spiritual meaning in many passages and employ the letter as a kind of veil[2] for mystical and profound matters, yet nevertheless the language of the narrator certainly indicates this, that at a definite time all visible things were created. And with regard to the consummation of the world, Jacob is the first to indicate this, when he testifies to his sons, saying, *Gather together to me, sons of Jacob, that I may tell you what shall be in the last days* or *after the last days.*[3] If, then, there are *last days* or an *after the last days,* it is necessary that the days, which had begun, must cease. David also says, *The heavens shall perish, but you will endure, and they will all become old like a garment; like clothing will you change them, and they will be changed; but you are the same, and your years will not fail.*[4] Our Lord and Saviour, indeed, when he says, *He who created them in the beginning, made them male and female,*[5] himself bears witness that the world was made; and again when he says that *Heaven and earth will pass away, but my words will not pass away,*[6] he points out that they are corruptible and coming to an end. The Apostle, moreover, saying, *The creation was subjected to futility, not willingly, but by the one who subjected it in hope, because the creation itself will also be set free from the bondage of corruption into the glorious liberty of the children of God,*[7] clearly announces the end of the world, as also he does when he says,

---

[1] According to Photius, *Bibl.* 8 (ed. Henry 1, 4a13–14), the final part of *Princ.* 3 shows 'that the world, beginning in time, is originated and corruptible' (ὅτι γενητὸς ὁ κόσμος καὶ φθαρτὸς ἀπὸ χρόνου ἀρξάμενος); that Origen intends to write both about the beginning and about the end of the world is made clear in the opening lines.

[2] Cf. 2 Cor. 3:14.   [3] Gen. 49:1.

[4] Ps. 101:27–8. Origen puts these verses together with 1 Cor. 7:31, cited below, in *Princ.* 1.6.4.

[5] Matt. 19:4.   [6] Matt. 24:35.

[7] Rom. 8:20–1. Cf. Origen, *Princ.* 1.7.5.

The form of this world passes away.[8] Yet in that expression which he uses, that *the creation was subjected to futility*, he also points to its beginning. For if the creation was subjected to futility on account of a certain hope, it was certainly subjected from a cause, and if it was from a cause, it is necessary that it began; for without any beginning the creation could not be subjected to futility and hope to be *set free from the bondage of corruption*, if it had not begun to be subjected to corruption. But if anyone searches at leisure, he will find numerous other such sayings in the divine Scriptures, in which the world is said both to have a beginning and to hope for an end.

3.5.2. If, however, there is anyone who would in this matter oppose either the authority or the credibility of our Scriptures, we would ask of him whether he would say that God can comprehend all things or that he cannot?[9] Now, to say that he cannot is clearly impious. If, then, as is necessary, he answers that he can comprehend all things, it follows from this very fact—that they can be comprehended—that they are understood to have a beginning and an end. For that which is altogether without any beginning cannot be comprehended at all. However far understanding may extend, so far is the ability of comprehending withdrawn and deferred without end when there is held to be no beginning.

3.5.3. But they are wont to object, saying, 'If the world began in time, what was God doing before the world began? For it is at once impious and absurd to say that the nature of God is inactive and immobile, or to suppose that goodness at one time did not do good and omnipotence at one time did not exercise its power.'[10] Such is the objection they are accustomed to make when we say that this world began at a definite time and when we count the years of its age according to the assurance of Scripture.[11] I do not think that any of the heretics can easily give an answer, in accordance with the logic of their own teaching, to these questions. Yet we can give a logical answer in accordance with the rule of piety, by saying that God did not begin to work for the first time when

---

[8] 1 Cor. 7:31.

[9] Cf. Origen, *Princ.* 2.9.1. The word 'to comprehend' (*compraehendere*, no doubt translating χωρε ἦν) has the double meaning of 'to understand' and 'to contain'.

[10] Cf. Origen, *Princ.* 1.2.10; 1.4.3–5.

[11] As was done, for instance, by Origen's contemporary, and correspondent, Julius Africanus, fragments of whose works remain (PG 12, 63–94); he is mentioned by Eusebius, *Hist. eccl.* 6.31; Jerome, *Vir. ill.* 63; and Photius, *Bibl.* 34. It was a project undertaken by many others, from Josephus, in his *Jewish Antiquities,* to early Christian apologists, such as Tatian and Theophilus, to Eusebius, whose chronologies were edited by Jerome.

he made this visible world, but that[12] just as after its dissolution there will be another world, so also we believe others to have existed before this one was. And both of these claims will be confirmed by the authority of the divine Scripture. For Isaiah teaches that there will be another world after this one, saying, *There will be a new heaven and a new earth, which I will cause to remain in my sight, says the Lord.*[13] And Ecclesiastes shows that there were others even before this world, saying, *What is that which came to be? The very thing that shall be. And what is that which has been created? The very thing that is to be created; and there is nothing new at all under the sun. If one should speak and say, See, this is new!'; it has already been in the worlds which were before us.*[14] By these testimonies it is established at the same time both that there were prior worlds and that there will be others hereafter. It must not be supposed, however, that several worlds existed at once, but that after this one another will exist in its turn, about which it is not now necessary to repeat each point, since we have already done this above.[15]

3.5.4. This point, certainly, I think, is not to be passed by idly, that the holy Scriptures have named the creation of the world by a new and particular name, terming it the καταβολή of the world (which has been very improperly translated into Latin as *constitutio*; for in Greek καταβολή signifies rather *deicere*, that is, to cast downwards), which, as we have said, is improperly rendered into Latin by the *constitutio* of the world; just as in the Gospel according to John, when the Saviour says, *And there will be tribulation in those days, such as has not been since the constitution of the world* (here καταβολή is rendered *constitutio*, which is to be understood as explained above).[16] The Apostle, also, has used the same word in the Epistle to the Ephesians, when he says, *Who has chosen us before the foundation of the world*[17] (here also the *constitutio* of the

---

[12] Cf. Jerome *Ep.* 124.9.1–2 (ed. Hilberg 3, 107.10–26): 'Again, of the world: we hold, he says, that before this world there was another and after it another will exist. Would you learn that after the dissolution of this world another will come to be? Listen to Isaiah, saying, *There will be a new heaven and a new earth, which I will make to remain in my sight.* Would you know that before the fabrication of this work, other worlds existed in the past? Listen to Ecclesiastes: *What is that which came to be? The very thing that shall be. And what is that which has been created? The very thing that is to be created; and there is nothing new at all under the sun. If one should speak and say, "See this is new!"; it has already been in the ages which were before us.* This testimony bears witness not only to the past, but also to the future worlds, not all existing side by side at the same time, but one after another.'

[13] Isa. 66:22.   [14] Eccl. 1:9–10.   [15] Cf. Origen, *Princ.* 2.3.1–6.

[16] The passage is not from John, but Matt. 24:21, which in fact uses the word αρχή (*initio*); καταβολή (*constitutio*) occurs in John 17:24 (and Matt. 25:34). It is possible that this (misattributed and mistaken) illustration was added by Rufinus, who has also added many explanatory comments in the preceding sentences. On the 'foundation' as a 'throwing-down', see esp. Origen, *Comm. Jo.* 19.149 and Jerome, *Comm. Eph.* 1.4 (especially when he reports what 'another says', presumably Origen).

[17] Eph. 1:4.

world translates καταβολή, understood in the same meaning as we interpreted it above). It seems worthwhile, therefore, to inquire what is indicated by this new term. And[18] I am of the opinion that as the end and the consummation of the saints will be in those [worlds] that are *not seen* and eternal,[19] it must be supposed, from a contemplation of that very end, as we have frequently pointed out above, that rational creatures have also had a similar beginning.[20] And if they had a beginning such as the end for which they hope, they were undoubtedly from the beginning in those [worlds] that are *not seen* and *eternal*. And if this is so, then there has been a descent from the higher conditions to the lower, not only on the part of those souls who have by the variety of their own movements deserved it, but also on that of those who, to serve the whole world, were brought down from the higher and invisible conditions to these lower and visible ones, even against their will.[21] *Because the creation was subjected to futility, not willingly, but by the one who subjected it in hope,*[22] so that both the sun and the moon and the stars and the angels of God might fulfil an obedient service for the world; and for those souls which, because of their excessive spiritual defects needed these denser and more solid bodies, and because of those for whom this was necessary, this visible world was founded. From this, therefore, a descent of everyone alike would seem to be indicated by the meaning of the word, that is, of καταβολή. The whole creation indeed entertains the hope of freedom, of being *set free from the bondage of corruption* when *the children of God,*[23] who either fell away or were scattered abroad, shall be gathered together into one, or[24] when they shall have fulfilled their other duties in this world, which are known to

---

[18] Cf. Jerome, *Ep.* 124.9.3–5 (ed. Hilberg 3, 107.27–108.19): 'And immediately he adds: I think it must be understood that there is above a heavenly dwelling place and true rest, in which rational creatures used to abide before they descended to these lower regions and travelled from invisible to visible places, and where, before they were cast down to earth and needed solid bodies, they enjoyed a primeval blessedness. Whence God the creator made for them bodies appropriate for their lowly surroundings and has fashioned this visible world and sent ministers into the world for the salvation and correction of those who have fallen; of these ministers some have held assigned positions and were obedient to the necessities of the world, while others assiduously performed the duties laid upon them at the various times which the artificer God knows. To the former class belong the sun and the moon and the stars, which are called by the Apostle *the creation*, and these have been given their place in the higher regions. This *creation* has been *subjected to futility* by being clothed in dense bodies and made visible to sight. And yet it *was subjected to futility not willingly, but according to the will of him who subjected it in hope.*'

[19] 2 Cor. 4:18. Cf. Plato, *Tim.* 28; Philo, *Opif.* 12.

[20] Cf. Origen, *Princ.* 1.6.2; 2.1.1.

[21] Note how again Origen differentiates between those who descend due to their own faults and others who descend to serve. Cf. *Princ.* 1.5.5 (and the material cited in n.39 there); 1.7.5; 2.9.7; *Comm. Jo.* 1.98–100; 2.175–92; *Hom. Ezech.* 1.1–5.

[22] Rom. 8:20.   [23] Rom. 8:21.

[24] Cf. Jerome *Ep.* 124.9.6 (ed. Hilberg 3, 108.19–22): 'And again: but others in their various places and times, which the Artificer alone knows, undertake the governance of the world, whom we believe to be his angels.'

God alone, the Artificer of all things. It must be supposed that the world was created of such a kind and of such a size as to be able to contain all those souls which were appointed to be trained in this world, and also those powers which were prepared to attend, to serve, and to assist them. For it is proved by many assertions that all rational creatures are of one nature; on which ground alone can the justice of God in all his arrangements concerning them be defended, when everyone has within himself the reasons he has been placed in this or that rank of life.

3.5.5. This[25] arrangement of God, therefore, which he appointed afterwards, when he had already from the beginning of the world foreseen the reasons and causes both of those who, because of spiritual defect, deserved to enter into bodies, and of those who were carried away by their desire for visible things, and also of those who, either willingly or unwillingly, were compelled by him who subjected the same in hope to perform services for those who had fallen into that condition—not understanding [this arrangement] nor perceiving that this variety of arrangement has been founded by God as a result of prior causes arising from free will, they have supposed that everything that happens in this world is directed either by chance movement or by a fateful necessity, and that nothing is within the power of our will. Consequently they have not been able to show that the providence of God is blameless.

3.5.6. But just as we have said that all souls who have dwelt in this world have been in need of many ministers or rulers or assistants, so, in the last times, when the end of the world is already imminent and the whole human race was verging upon the final destruction, and not only those who were governed by others but also those to whom the care of governing had been committed had become infirm, it was no longer such assistance nor protectors like these that were needed, but the aid of the Author and Creator himself was required, which restores the discipline, which had been corrupted and profaned, of obeying to the one and of ruling to the other. And therefore the only-begotten Son of God, who was the Word and the Wisdom of the Father, when he was with the Father in that *glory* which he had *before the world was*,[26] *emptied himself and taking the form of a servant became obedient even unto death*,[27] that he might teach obedience to those who could not otherwise than by obedience obtain salvation; he restored also the corrupted laws of ruling and

---

[25] Cf. Jerome, *Ep.* 124.9.7 (ed. Hilberg 3, 108.22–109.4): 'And a little further on: this order of things and the entire world is ruled by the providence of God, such that while some powers fall quickly from the higher realms, others gradually glide down to earth; some descend of their own free will, others are thrown down unwillingly; some freely undertake the task of lending a hand to those who are falling, while others are unpleasantly constrained and continue in their allotted tasks for a certain period.'

[26] John 17:5.   [27] Phil. 2:7–8.

reigning in that he *subdues all enemies under his feet,*[28] and by the fact that he must reign until he puts all enemies under his feet and *destroys the last enemy, death,*[29] he teaches the rulers themselves the art of ruling. As he had come, then, to restore the discipline not only of ruling and reigning, but also of obeying, as we have said, fulfilling in himself first what he desired to be fulfilled by others, becoming obedient to the Father not only unto the death of the cross but also in the consummation of the age, by embracing in himself all whom he subjects to the Father and who come to salvation through him, he himself, with them and in them, is also said to be subject to the Father, when *all things subsist in him* and he is *the head* of all things, and *in him is the fullness* of those attaining salvation.[30] This, therefore, is what the Apostle says of him, *When all things have been subject to him, then shall the Son himself also be subject to him who put all things under him, that God may be all in all.*[31]

3.5.7. Indeed I know not how the heretics, not understanding the meaning of the Apostle contained in these words, calumniate the term 'subjection' in regard to the Son; if the propriety of the title is sought, it may easily be found by its opposite. For if to be subject is not good, it follows that the opposite is good, that is, not to be in subjection. Now the language of the Apostle, as they would have it, appears to demonstrate this when it says, *When all things have been subject to him, then shall the Son himself also be subject to him who put all things under him,*[32] as if he, who is now not subjected to the Father, will then be subjected, when the Father has first subjected all things to him. But I am astonished how it can be understood this way—that he who, while all things are not yet subjected to him, is not himself subjected; then, when all things have been subjected to him, when he is king over all and holds power over the universe, they should then suppose him to be made subject, although he was not subjected before—not understanding that the subjection of Christ to the Father shows the blessedness of our perfection and announces the victory of the work undertaken by him,[33] since he offers to the Father not only the summit of ruling and reigning, which he has amended throughout the whole creation, but also the laws, corrected and renewed, of the obedience and subjection due from the human race. If, then, that subjection, by which the Son is said to be subject to the Father, is good and salvific, it is very logically and coherently concluded that the subjection also of enemies, which is said of the Son of God, is to be understood as something salvific and useful; so that, just as when the Son is said to be subjected to the Father, the perfect restoration of the whole

---

[28] 1 Cor. 15:27.   [29] 1 Cor. 15:26.
[30] Col. 1:17, 18; 2:9.   [31] 1 Cor. 15:28.   [32] 1 Cor. 15:28.
[33] Cf. Origen, *Hom. Lev.* 7.2: 'As long as I am not subjected to the Father, neither is he said to be *subjected* to the Father. Not that he himself is in need of subjection before the Father but for me, in whom he has not yet completed his work, he is said not to be subjected, for, as we read, *we are the body of Christ and members in part*' (1 Cor. 12:27).

creation is announced, so also when the enemies are said to be subjected to the Son of God, the salvation of the subjected and the restoration of the lost is understood in that.

3.5.8. But this subjection, however, will be accomplished in certain ways and disciplines and periods of time; that is, the whole world is not brought into subjection to God by some necessity nor subdued by force, but by word, by reason, by teaching, by exhortation to better things, by the best instruction, and by threatenings, merited and appropriate, which will justly impend over those who despise the care and health of their salvation or benefit.[34] For even we human beings, in training either slaves or children, while they are incapable of reason because of their young age, restrain them by threats and fear; but when they have acquired an understanding of what is good and beneficial and honourable, the fear of the lash being over, persuaded by word and reason, they acquiesce in everything that is good.

But how,[35] with the freedom of will in all rational creatures preserved, each one ought to be arranged—that is, those whom, as if already prepared and capable, the Word of God both finds and instructs; and those whom he puts off to a later time; and those from whom he is utterly concealed and arranges himself to be far from their hearing; and again those whom, despising the Word of God revealed and preached to them, being afflicted with certain corrections and chastisements, he presses into salvation and whose conversion is as it were demanded and extorted; and those to whom he even provides certain opportunities of salvation, so that sometimes, with faith evoked even by an answer alone, someone has obtained an assured salvation;[36] and those to whom these things happen from causes or certain occasions, while perceiving inwardly this in them, or beholding the movements of their will, divine Wisdom arranges all these things—is known to God alone[37] and to his only-begotten Son, through whom all things were created and restored, and to the Holy Spirit, through whom all things are sanctified, *who proceeds from the Father*,[38] to whom be glory unto the eternal ages. Amen.[39]

---

[34] Cf. Origen, *Princ.* 1.2.10.

[35] Cf. Jerome, *Ep.* 124.9.8 (ed. Hilberg 3, 109.4–18): 'And again: from which it follows that because of these various movements various worlds are created, and after this one, in which we dwell, there will be another world quite unlike it. And no one is able to arrange the merits of those who in diverse degrees fall or rise, or the rewards for virtue or the punishments for sin, both in the present and in the future, and at every time both past and [...] in prior times, and can bring everything once again to a single end, except God the Creator of all, who knows the reasons why he allows some to perform their own will and to sink gradually from the higher realms to the lowest, while others he begins to visit and to draw back gradually, as if giving them a hand, to their former state and to place them once more on high.'

[36] Perhaps Luke 18:41–2. Cf. Origen, *Comm. Rom.* 3.9.

[37] Cf. Origen, *Princ.* 2.9.8.   [38] John 15:26. Cf. Origen, *Princ.* 1.2.13, and n.66 there.

[39] Only here and at *Princ.* 4.1.7 does Origen end with a doxology and an 'Amen'. *Princ.* 4.3.14 ends with a doxology, but no 'Amen'.

The Consummation

3.6.1.[1] We have already discussed, to the best of our ability in the preceding pages, the subject of the end and the consummation of all things, so far as the authority of the divine Scripture allowed; this we deem sufficient for instruction, being now reminded of a few more points, since the order of the inquiry has brought us back to the subject. The highest good, then, towards which every rational being hastens, which is also called the end of all things, is defined even by many among the philosophers in this way, that 'The highest good is to become as far as possible like God.'[2] But this is not so much a discovery of theirs as, I think, taken by them from the divine books.[3] For Moses, before all others, points to it when he describes the first creation of the human being, saying, *And God said, 'Let us make the human being in our image and likeness'.* Then he adds afterwards: *And God made the human being, in the image of God he made him; male and female he made them and he blessed them.*[4] The fact that he said, *in the image of God he made him* and was silent about the *likeness,* indicates nothing else except that the human being obtained the dignity of the *image* in his first creation, but the perfection of the *likeness* was reserved for him at the consummation; that is, that he might acquire it for himself by the exercise of his own diligence in the imitation of God, so that while the possibility of attaining perfection was given to him in the beginning through the dignity of the *image,* he should in the end, through the accomplishment of the works, complete in himself the perfected *likeness.*[5] Now the Apostle John more openly and clearly determines this to be the case, when speaking thus: *Little children, we do not yet know what we shall be; but when he is revealed to us* (speaking, no doubt, of the Saviour), *we shall be like him.*[6] By this he points out with utmost certainty both the end of all things, which he says was still unknown to him, and also the hoped-for likeness to God, which will be conferred in proportion to the perfection of merits. The Lord himself, in the Gospel, also points out that these same things will not only come to pass, but will come about by his own intercession, when he saw fit to make this request

---

[1] Photius, *Bibl.* 8 (ed. Henry 1, 4a15), gives 'On the End' (περί τέλους), but as the first item of *Princ.* 4.

[2] Plato, *Theat.* 176b.

[3] A claim similarly made by Justin, *1 Apol.* 59–60; Tatian, *Or.* 31–41, esp. 40; Theophilus of Antioch, *Autol.* 1.14; 3.23; Clement, *Strom.* 1.17.87; 1.22.150; 5.14, esp. 92; 6.2.27.5; and in other places by Origen: *Comm. Cant.* Prol. (GCS 8, p. 75); 1 (GCS 8, p. 141); *Cels.* 1.15; 6.19; 7.30.

[4] Gen. 1:26–8.

[5] The distinction between 'image' and 'likeness' had already been made by Irenaeus, who, however, refers the first to the body (*Haer.* 5.6.1) and the second to the possession of the Spirit, and by Clement, in a manner similar to Origen, *Prot.* 10.98.4; *Strom.* 2.22.131; 6.97.2. Origen returns to this theme frequently, e.g. *Cels.* 4.30; *Comm. Rom.* 4.5; *Or.* 27.2; *Hom. Ezech.* 13.2.

[6] 1 John 3:2. Origen connects this verse to Gen. 1:26–8 also in *Hom. Ezech.* 13.2; see also *Hom. Exod.* 6.5.

of the Father for his disciples, saying, *Father, I will that where I am these also may be with me;* and, *as I and you are one, so also may they be one in us.*[7] In this the likeness itself already seems, if we may so say, to advance, and from being similar to become one,[8] for the reason, no doubt, that in the consummation or end *God is all and in all.*[9]

In this context,[10] the question is asked by some whether the condition of bodily nature, however much cleansed to purity and rendered completely spiritual, does not seem to offer an obstruction towards the dignity of the likeness and to the property of unity, for it does not seem possible that a being who is in a body can either be said to be like the divine nature, which is in any case principally bodiless, or be described truly and rightly as one with it, especially as the truth of our faith teaches that the fact that the Son is *one* with the Father must be referred to the property of nature.

3.6.2. When,[11] then, it is promised that in the end *God is all and in all*, it is not to be supposed, as is fitting, that animals, either cattle or beasts, come to that end, lest it should be implied that God is even in animals, either cattle or beasts; neither will pieces of wood or stones, lest it should be said that God is in them also. So also it is not to be supposed that anything wicked comes to that end, lest when it is said that *God is in all* he should be said to be even in some vessels of wickedness. For although we say that *God* is even now everywhere and *in all*, for the reason that nothing can be empty of God, we do not, however, say that he is now *all* in those in whom he is. Hence it must be examined more carefully what that condition is which marks the perfection of blessedness and the end of things, where *God* is said not only *to be in all*, but *God* is said even *to be all*. Let us inquire, then, what is this *all* which *God shall be in all*.

3.6.3. I reckon that this expression, where *God* is said *to be all in all,* also means that he is all in each individual person. And he will be *all* in each indi-

---

[7] John 17: 24, 21.

[8] On unity as a sign of perfection, see also Origen, *Or.* 21.2; 27.8; *Fragm. Comm. Jo.* 5 (=*Philoc.* 5).

[9] 1 Cor. 15:28.

[10] At this point Koetschau places in his apparatus, as indicating the real content of this paragraph, a passage from Jerome, *Ep.* 124.8[9].9 (ed. Hilberg 3, 109.19–110.1), the eleventh anathema of the Second Council of Constantinople, and a sentence from Theophilus of Alexandria, *Ep. Synod.* (= Jerome, *Ep.* 92.2 [ed. Hilberg 2, 149.12–14]), and refers back to *Princ.* 2.3.2. Following this paragraph, Koetschau inserts into his text two paragraphs from Jerome, *Ep.* 124.8[9].10–12 (ed. Hilberg 3, 110.1–111.5). This material is included in the Appendix as item no. 18.

[11] Cf. Justinian, *Ep. ad Menam* (ed. Schwartz, 211.29–212.2), an extract said to be from *Princ.* 3 and numbered by Koetschau as Fragment 27: 'When God is said to become *all in all,* just as we cannot include evil, when God becomes *all in all,* nor irrational animals, lest God should come to be in evil and in irrational animals, nor soulless beings, lest God be in them, when he becomes *all,* so also neither can we include bodies, which are in their own nature soulless.'

vidual in such a way that everything which the rational mind, when cleansed from all the dregs of the vices and utterly swept clean of every cloud of wickedness, can sense or understand or think will be all God; it will no longer sense anything else apart from God; it will think God, see God, hold God; God will be the mode and measure of its every movement; and thus *God* will be *all* to it:[12] for there will no longer be any distinction between good and evil, since evil nowhere exists (for *God*, to whom evil never approaches, is *all* things to it), nor will one, who is always in the good and to whom *God* is *all*, desire any longer to eat from *the tree of the knowledge of good and evil*.[13] When,[14] then, the end has been renewed to the beginning and the departure of things joined to their entrance, that condition will be restored which rational beings then had, when they did not need to eat of the tree of the knowledge of good and evil, so that to them, with all perception of wickedness having been removed and having been cleansed, to be sound and pure, he who is alone the one good *God* himself becomes *all*, and he himself becomes *all* not in a few things or in many, but *in all*, when indeed there is nowhere death, nowhere *the sting of death*,[15] nowhere any evil; then, truly, *God will be all in all*. But some suppose that this perfection and blessedness of rational beings only remains in that condition we have described above—that is, that all things should possess God and God should be all things to them—if union with bodily nature in no way at all prevents them. Otherwise, if any intermingling with material substance were introduced, they reckon that the glory of the highest blessedness would be impeded. Concerning this subject, those things that had occurred to us have been more fully investigated and analysed in the preceding pages.

3.6.4. But now, since we find mention by the Apostle Paul of a *spiritual body*, let us inquire, to the best of our ability, how we also ought to think of this. As far, then, as our understanding can grasp it, we consider the quality of a spiritual body to be such as befits being inhabited not only by all holy and perfect souls, but also by that *whole creation* which will be *set free from the slavery of corruption*.[16] Regarding this body, the Apostle has also said that *We have a house not made by hand, eternal in the heavens*,[17] that is, in the mansions of the blessed. From this statement, then, we can form a conjecture of what great purity, of what great refinement, and of what great glory is the quality of that

---

[12] This is similar to the way that Origen describes the soul of Christ, in *Princ.* 2.6.6, 'which, like iron in the fire, was placed in the Word forever, in Wisdom forever, in God forever, is God in all that it does, feels, and understands'.

[13] Gen. 2:17.

[14] Koetschau here places in his apparatus a passage from Jerome, *Ep.* 124.10.1–4 (111.6–112.9) as representing the full scope of what Origen originally wrote and Rufinus omitted; it is included in the Appendix as item no. 19.

[15] 1 Cor. 15:56.   [16] Cf. Rom. 8:21.   [17] 2 Cor. 5:1.

body, if we make a comparison of it with those which now, although they are bodies celestial and most splendid, are yet made by hand and visible. But of that body it is said that it is *a house not made with hands but eternal in the heavens.* Since, then, *things seen are temporal, but those not seen are eternal,*[18] all those bodies which we see, either on earth or in the heavens, and which are able to be seen, and have been made by hand and are not eternal, are very greatly surpassed in glory by that which is neither visible nor made by hand but is eternal. From this comparison, it may be conjectured how great is the beauty, how great the splendour, and how great the brilliance of a spiritual body, and how true is that saying, that *eye has not seen nor ear heard nor has it entered into the heart of a human being what God has prepared for those who love him.*[19] It ought not to be doubted, however, that the nature of this body of ours may, by the will of God who made it such, be brought, by the Creator, to that quality characterizing the exceptionally refined and pure and splendid body, according as the condition of things shall require and the merits of the rational being shall demand. Finally, when the world needed variety and diversity, matter offered itself with all docility throughout the diverse appearances and species of things to the Maker, as to its Lord and Creator, that he might bring forth from it the diverse forms of heavenly and earthly things.[20] But when things have begun to hasten towards that end, *that they all may be one* as the Father is one with the Son,[21] it may rationally be understood that where all are one, there will no longer be any diversity.[22]

3.6.5. It is on this account, moreover, that *the last enemy,* who is called *death,* is said to be *destroyed,*[23] that there may no longer be any sadness when there is no death, nor diversity when there is no enemy. The destruction of the last enemy, indeed, is to be understood in this way, not that its substance, which was made by God, shall perish, but that the hostile purpose and will which proceeded not from God but from itself shall disappear. It is destroyed, therefore, not in the sense that it shall not be, but that it shall not be an enemy and death. For nothing is impossible to the Almighty,[24] nor is anything beyond healing by its Maker, for it was on this account that he made all things, that they might exist;[25] and those things which were made that they might exist cannot not exist. Because of this, they will undergo change and variation, so as to occupy a better or worse position in accordance with their merits;[26] but

---

[18] 2 Cor. 4:18.   [19] 1 Cor. 2:9.

[20] Cf. Origen, *Princ.* 2.1.2, 4.   [21] John 17:22.

[22] Koetschau suggests supplementing this last sentence by placing in his apparatus anathemas 12, 13, 14, 15 of the Second Council of Constantinople; they are included in the Appendix as item no. 20.

[23] 1 Cor. 15:26.   [24] Cf. Job 42:2; Matt. 19:26.   [25] Cf. Wis. 1:14.

[26] Cf. Origen, *Princ.* 2.1.2; 3.6.3.

things which were made by God, that they might exist and abide, cannot undergo a destruction of substance. For those things which, in the opinion of the common people, are believed to perish, the rule of faith or truth alike accepts that they have not perished. Finally, our flesh is considered by the uneducated and unbelievers to be so destroyed after death, such that it is believed to have no remnant at all of its former substance. We, however, who believe in its resurrection, understand that a change only is effected in it by death, but that its substance certainly abides and that by the will of its Creator, at the appointed time, it is restored to life again and that once again a change is effected in it, so that what at first was flesh, *of the earth, earthy,*[27] was then dissolved by death and again made *ashes and earth*[28] (for *earth you are,* it says, *and to the earth you will go*[29]), is raised again from the earth and afterwards shall, as the merits of the indwelling soul will have required, advance to the glory of a *spiritual body.*[30]

3.6.6. Into this condition, then, it must be supposed that this entire bodily substance of ours will be brought when all things will be restored, when they shall be one, and when *God shall be all in all.* It must be understood, however, that this shall happen not suddenly, but gradually and by degrees, during the passing of infinite and immeasurable ages,[31] with the improvement and correction being accomplished slowly and by degrees, some hastening on in advance and tending towards perfection by a quicker route,[32] and others following behind at a close distance, with others far behind: and so, through the many and innumerable ranks of those making progress and being reconciled, from enmity, to God, until *the last enemy,* which is called *death,* is reached, so that it too may be *destroyed* and no longer be an enemy.[33]

When, therefore, all rational souls have been restored to a condition like this, then also the nature of this body of ours will be brought into the glory of a *spiritual body.*[34] For just as in the case of rational natures, we do not see one kind which has lived in dishonour on account of sin and another kind which has been invited to blessedness because of its merits, but we see the same, who were formerly sinful, then later being converted and reconciled to God, being recalled to blessedness, so also, with respect to the nature of the body, it must be understood that there is not one body which we now make use of in lowliness and corruption and weakness, and that it will be a different one which we shall use in incorruption and power and glory, but that this same body, having cast off the weaknesses in which it now exists, will be transformed in glory,

---

[27] 1 Cor. 15:47.   [28] Gen. 18:27.   [29] Gen. 3:19.
[30] 1 Cor. 15:44.   [31] Cf. Origen, *Princ.* 1.6.2–3; 3.1.23.
[32] Cf. Origen, *Princ.* 2.11.6; 3.1.17.   [33] Cf. 1 Cor. 15:26. Origen, *Princ.* 3.6.5.
[34] 1 Cor. 15:44.

being rendered spiritual, so that what was a vessel of dishonour may, when cleansed, become a vessel of honour and an abode of blessedness.[35] And in this condition also, it must be believed, will it abide forever and unchangeably by the will of the Creator, of which we are made certain by the declaration of the Apostle, saying, *We have a house, not made by hand, eternal in the heavens.*[36]

For the faith of the Church does not accept the view of certain Greek philosophers, that there is besides the body, which is composed of four elements, another fifth body, which is entirely other than and different from our present body,[37] since neither can anyone produce from holy Scripture the slightest suspicion of this, nor does any rational inference from the facts of the case allow it to be accepted, especially when the holy Apostle clearly specifies that no new bodies shall be given to those who rise from the dead, but that they shall receive these very ones, which they had while living, transformed from an inferior to a better condition. For he says, *It is sown an animated body, it will rise a spiritual body,* and, *it is sown in corruption, it will rise in incorruption; it is sown in weakness, it will rise in power; it is sown in lowliness, it will rise in glory.*[38] Just as, therefore, there is a kind of progress for the human being, so that although he is first an *animated* human being and does not understand things that are of the Spirit of God, by means of instruction he comes to be rendered *spiritual* and *judges all things, but is himself not judged by anyone,*[39] so also regarding the state of the body, it must be supposed that this very body which now, because of its service to the soul, is called *animated,* will, through a certain progress—when the soul, united to God, shall have been made *one spirit* with him,[40] the body even then serving, as it were, the spirit—attain a spiritual state and quality, especially since, as we have often pointed out, bodily nature was so made by the Creator as to pass easily into whatever condition he should wish or the circumstances should require.

3.6.7. This whole argument, then, presupposes this, that God created two universal natures: a visible, that is, a bodily nature, and an invisible nature, which is bodiless.[41] These two natures each undergo different changes. That invisible one, which is also rational, is changed in mind and purpose, because it is endowed with freedom of will, and on this account is sometimes found in the good, and other times in the opposite. But this bodily one undergoes a substantial change, so that, in whatever he wishes to undertake or to fashion or to rework, the Artificer of all things, God, has the service of this matter in every

---

[35] Cf. Origen, *Princ.* 3.1.21–4.   [36] 2 Cor. 5:1.

[37] The fifth element referred to here is probably Aristotle's 'aether', discussed in his lost work *On Philosophy*; see Cicero, *Acad.* 1.7.26; Origen, *Princ.* 1.6.4; *Comm. Jo.* 13.126; *Cels.* 4.60.

[38] 1 Cor. 15:42–4.   [39] 1 Cor. 2:14–15.   [40] 1 Cor. 6:17.

[41] Cf. Origen, *Comm. Rom.* 8.11; *Hom. Gen.* 1.2; on the necessary connection between these two realities, see *Princ.* 1.7.1; 2.2.2; 4.4.8.

way, so that he can transform and apply it in whatever forms and species he desires, as the merits of things require. The prophet evidently points to this when he says *God who makes and transforms all things.*[42]

3.6.8. And now this point must be investigated, whether, when *God shall be all in all,*[43] in the consummation of all things, the whole of bodily nature will consist of one species,[44] and the whole quality of body will be only that which will shine in that indescribable glory which, it must be believed, will be the property of the spiritual body. For if we rightly take the passage, which Moses writes in the beginning of his book, saying, *In the beginning God created the heaven and the earth,*[45] to be the beginning of all creation, it is appropriate for the end and consummation of all things to be recalled to this beginning, that is, that that heaven and that earth may be a dwelling and a resting-place for the pious, so that the saints and the meek may first obtain an inheritance in that land,[46] since this is what the Law and the Prophets and the Gospel teach. In that earth, I think, there exist those true and living forms of those observances which Moses handed down under the *shadow* of the Law.[47] For it is said of them that *they serve a copy and a shadow of the heavenly things,*[48] that is to say, those who served under the Law. Moreover, to Moses himself, it was said, *See that you make all things according to the form and likeness that has been shown to you on the mountain.*[49] From this it appears to me that, just as on this earth the Law was a sort of pedagogue to those who were duty bound to be led by it to Christ,[50] being trained and instructed by it, so that they might more easily, after the ordinances of the Law, be able to receive the more perfect ordinances of Christ, so also that other earth,[51] when it receives all the saints, first imbues and educates them in the ordinances of the true and everlasting Law, that they may more easily bear those perfect ordinances of heaven to which nothing can ever be added; in which there will truly be that which is called the *eternal Gospel* and that testament ever new, which shall never grow old.[52]

3.6.9. In this way, then, it is thought to be in the consummation and restoration of all things, that those gradually making progress and ascending in order and measure shall arrive first at that other earth and the training that is in it, in which they may be prepared for those better ordinances, to which

---

[42] Amos 5:8.   [43] 1 Cor. 15:28.   [44] Cf. Origen, *Princ.* 3.6.4.

[45] Gen. 1:1, alluding to the distinction he makes (in *Princ.* 2.3.6–7, see also *Sel. Ps. 36, 2,* cited in n.62 there) between the earth of Gen. 1:1 and the 'dry land' also called 'earth' in Gen. 1:10.

[46] Cf. Deut. 4:38; Ps. 36:11; Matt. 5:4; Heb. 4:9. Cf. *Princ.* 2.3.7.

[47] Heb. 10:1.   [48] Heb. 8:5.

[49] Exod. 25:40. Cf. Origen, *Hom. Exod.* 9.2.

[50] Cf. Gal. 3:24.   [51] See n.45 above.

[52] Cf. Rev. 14:6; Heb. 8:13, 9:15, 12:24. On the 'eternal Gospel', see also Origen, *Princ.* 4.3.13; *Hom. Lev.* 4.10.

nothing can ever be added. For after *the stewards and guardians*,[53] the Lord Christ, who is king of all, will himself assume the kingdom; that is, after [their] training in the holy virtues, he himself will instruct those who are capable of receiving him in respect of his being Wisdom,[54] reigning in them until he subjects them to the Father, who has subjected all things to himself; that is,[55] when they shall have been rendered capable of God, then *God will be* to them *all in all*. Then, therefore, it follows that even bodily nature will receive that highest condition to which nothing more can ever be added.

Having discussed to this point the principle of bodily nature, or of the spiritual body, we leave it to the decision of the reader to determine which of the two he decides to be better.[56] For our part, we here bring the third book to an end.

---

[53] Gal. 4:2. Cf. Origen, *Princ.* 2.11.3.   [54] Cf. Origen, *Princ.* 1.2.1, 9–12.

[55] Cf. Jerome *Ep.* 124.10.5–6 (ed. Hilberg 3, 112.12–20): 'And after a very long discussion, in which he says that all bodily nature must be changed into spiritual and subtle bodies and that all substance must be converted into one body most pure and brighter than all splendour and of such a quality as the human mind cannot conceive, at the end he concludes: And God shall be *all in all*, so that the whole of bodily nature shall be reduced into that substance which is superior to all, that is to say, into the divine nature, than which nothing is better.'

[56] Origen addresses his readers also in *Princ.* 1.6.3; 2.3.7; 2.8.4, 5.

PART THREE: THE INSPIRED SCRIPTURES

That the Scriptures are Divinely Inspired

4.1.1.[1] *[Latin]* But, since it is not sufficient, in discussing topics so great and important, to leave the conclusion of the matter to human opinion and common conceptions[2] and, so to speak, to pronounce on things invisible as if visible, we must also adduce, for the proof of what we have said, the testimonies of the divine Scriptures. And that these testimonies may possess an assured and indubitable conviction, both regarding what we have to say and what we have already said, it seems necessary first to show that the Scriptures themselves are divine, that is, inspired by the Spirit of God. We shall, therefore, as briefly as we can, establish even this point, by offering from the divine Scriptures themselves passages that can suitably make an impression upon us, that is, first from Moses, the lawgiver of the Hebrew nation, and [then] from the words of Jesus Christ, the author and leader of the Christian religion and teaching.

---

[1] Photius, *Bibl.* 8 (ed. Henry 1, 4a15–16), speaks of *Princ.* 4 as treating (besides 'Concerning the End', which we have as *Princ.* 3.6) 'that the Scriptures are divine; finally, how the Scriptures ought to be read and understood' (ὅτι θεῖ αι αἱ γραφαί· τέλος ὅπως δεῖ ἀναγινώσκειν καὶ νοεῖν τὰς γραφάς). For *Princ.* 4.1–3, we also have the Greek text (set below) from the *Philocalia*. As will be clear, Rufinus has not infrequently extended the text in his translation; those places where it is likely that the *Philocalia* has either omitted a passage or abridged it are noted.

[2] The 'common conceptions' (κοιναὶ ἔννοιαι) were widely appealed to in ancient philosophy, either as 'innate ideas' or commonly held positions, to which appeal could be made before developing an argument. See also Origen, *Cels.* 1.4; 3.40; 8.52.

On the Divine Inspiration of the Divine Scriptures

4.1.1.[1] *[Greek]* Since, in investigating matters of such importance, not being satisfied with the common conceptions and the evidence of things that are seen, adducing in addition, for the manifest proof of our assertions, testimonies from what are believed by us to be divine writings, both from that which is called the Old Testament and that which is called the New, we endeavour by reason to confirm our faith, and, as we have not yet spoken of the Scriptures as divine, come and let us treat of a few points regarding them, as in an epitome, laying out for this purpose the reasons that move us [to regard

---

[1] The full title given at the beginning of *Philocalia* 1 is: 'Concerning the divine inspiration of the divine Scripture and how it is to be read and understood; what is the reason for the obscurity in it and for what is impossible or irrational in some cases when taken according to what is said'; this heading covers *Princ.* 4.1–3, which is then followed by extracts from *Hom. Jer.* 39, *Comm. Ps.* 50, and *Hom. Lev.* 5. The paragraph divisions of this lengthy extract from *Princ.* 4.1–3 in editions and translations of the *Philocalia* are numbered continuously.

For although there have been very many lawgivers among the Greeks and Barbarians, and also countless teachers and philosophers professing that they declare the truth, we remember no lawgiver who was able to instil in the minds of foreign nations a certain desire and eagerness such that they adopted his laws willingly or defended them with every effort of mind.[3] No one, then, has been able to introduce and implant what seemed to himself the truth not only among many foreign nations but even among a single nation, in such a way that knowledge of and belief in this should extend to all. And yet it cannot be doubted that the lawgivers would have wished their laws to be observed by all human beings, if it were possible, while the teachers would have wished that what appeared to themselves to be the truth should become known to all. But knowing that they were altogether incapable of this, and that they did not possess such power as would summon foreign nations to the observance of their laws and teaching, they did not dare to attempt or to try this at all, lest an ineffective and futile effort at this should brand them as foolhardy. And yet throughout the whole world, throughout the whole of Greece and every foreign nation, there are innumerable and immeasurable people who have abandoned their ancestral laws and those whom they had reckoned gods, and handed themselves over to the observance of the Law of Moses and to the discipleship and worship of Christ, and this despite the fact that an intense hatred has been incited against them by those who worship idols, such that they are frequently subjected by them to tortures and sometimes even led to death; yet they nevertheless embrace and guard, with all affection, the word of Christ's teaching.[4]

---

[3] This, and what follows, is a major theme throughout Origen's *Contra Celsum*, e.g. 1.27; 1.64; 3.51, etc.
[4] Cf. *Cels.* 1.27.

them] as divine writings. And first of all, <before> making use of the words in the writings themselves and the things set forth in them, one must treat these points regarding Moses and Jesus Christ, the lawgiver of the Hebrews and the author of the saving doctrines of Christianity.

For although there have been very many lawgivers among the Greeks and Barbarians, and teachers who proclaimed doctrines declaring the truth, we have no record of a lawgiver able to instil zeal for the acceptance of his words among the other nations; although a great apparatus of supposed logical demonstration has been brought forward by those professing to philosophize about truth, no one has been able to impress upon diverse nations what was deemed by him the truth, or even upon any credible number of persons in a single nation. And yet not only would the lawgivers have wished to enforce

4.1.2. *[Latin]* And one can see how in a short time this religion has increased, making progress through the punishment and death of its worshippers, and also by the plundering of their goods and every kind of torture endured by them. And this is especially wonderful since its teachers themselves are neither very skilful nor very numerous; yet this word is *preached in all the world,*[5] so that *Greeks and barbarians, wise and foolish,*[6] adopt the Christian religion. From which there is no doubt that it is not by human strength or assistance that the word of Christ Jesus comes to prevail, with all force and conviction, in the minds and hearts of all. Moreover, that this was foretold by him and confirmed by his divine utterances is clear, as when he says, *You shall be brought before governors and rulers for my sake, for a testimony to them and to the nations,*[7] and also, *This Gospel will be preached to all nations,*[8] and again, *Many will say to me on that day: 'Lord, Lord, have we not eaten and drunk in your name, and in your name cast out demons?' And I will say to them: 'Depart from*

---

[5] Matt. 24:14; cf. Ps. 18:5.   [6] Rom. 1:14.   [7] Matt. 10:18.
[8] Matt. 24:14. This quotation is not in the *Philocalia;* Koetschau and Bardy (*Recherches,* 43–4) held that it belongs to the original text of Origen, but dropped out from the *Philocalia* due to the same words ('the nations') concluding this and the previous quotation. But, as Simonetti and Crouzel (SC 269, p. 156, n.13–13a) point out, Rufinus omits this second quotation from his translation of this passage in Pamphilus *Apol.* 84.

those laws which appeared to be good, if possible, upon the whole race of human beings, but the teachers also would have wished that what they imagined to be the truth should have spread throughout the world. But being unable to summon those of other languages and from many nations to the observance of [their] laws and the acceptance of [their] teachings, they did not at all attempt to do this, considering, not unwisely, the impossibility of such a result happening for them. Yet every land, Greek and barbarian, throughout our world, contains thousands of devotees, who have abandoned ancestral laws and those reckoned to be gods for the observance of the laws of Moses and the discipline of the words of Jesus Christ, even though those who adhere to the Law of Moses are hated by the worshippers of idols, and those who accept the word of Jesus Christ in addition to being hated are in danger of death.

4.1.2. *[Greek]* And if we consider how in a very few years, although those professing Christianity are persecuted, and some of them are put to death on this account, while others suffer the loss of their possessions, yet the word has been able, despite there not being many teachers, *to be preached everywhere*

me, you workers of iniquity; I never knew you.[9] If these sayings, indeed, had been thus uttered by him, and yet those things foretold had not come to fulfilment, they might perhaps hardly appear to be true and not to possess any authority. But now, when the things foretold by him do indeed come into effect, and since they were foretold with such power and authority, he is most clearly shown to be truly God who, having become human, has delivered the saving commandments to human beings.

4.1.3. *[Latin]* But what, then, is to be said of this, that the prophets had foretold beforehand of him that *Rulers will not cease from Judah, nor leaders from his loins, until he should come, for whom it is reserved,* that is, the kingdom, *and until the expectation of the nations shall come?*[10] For it is most abundantly evident from history itself and from what is clearly seen at the present day that from the times of Christ onwards kings have not existed among the Jews. Moreover, all those ceremonies of the Jews, of which they made such a great deal of boasting and in which they exulted, whether regarding the adornment of the temple or the ornaments of the altar, and all those priestly head-bands and the robes of the high priests, were all destroyed together. For the prophecy has been fulfilled which said, *For the children of Israel will sit for many days without a king, without a ruler; there will be no sacrifice nor altar nor priesthood nor oracles.*[11]

---

[9] Matt. 7:22–3.
[10] Gen. 49:10. See also Heb. 7:14; Rev. 5:5; Justin, *1 Apol.* 32; *Dial.* 52; Irenaeus, *Haer.* 4.10.2; *Dem.* 57; Tertullian, *Marc.* 4.40.6; Clement, *Paed.* 1.6.47.3; Origen, *Comm. Jo.* 1.143; 13.154; *Hom. Jer.* 9.1.
[11] Hos. 3:4.

---

throughout the world, so that *Greeks and barbarians, wise and foolish*, have submitted themselves to the worship of God through Jesus, we shall not hesitate to say that the matter is more than human, Jesus having taught with all authority and persuasiveness that his word should prevail;[2] so that one may reasonably regard as oracles those utterances of his, such as, *You shall be brought before governors and rulers for my sake, for a testimony to them and to the nations,* and, *Many will say to me on that day: Lord, Lord, have we not eaten in your name and drunk in your name and cast out demons in your name?' And I will say to them: 'Depart from me, you workers of iniquity; I never knew you.'* That he uttered these words speaking in vain, so that they were not true, was perhaps possible; but when what was said with so much authority has come to pass, it shows that God, having truly become human, delivered to human beings the doctrines of salvation.

---

[2] Cf. Mark 13:31.

We use these testimonies, then, against those who seem to assert that what is said by Jacob in Genesis is said of Judah and say that there remains to this day a prince from the race of Judah, that is, he who is the prince of their nation, whom they call 'the Patriarch,' and that neither can there fail [a ruler] of his seed, who will remain until the arrival of that Christ as they picture him to themselves. But if what the prophet says is true, *The children of Israel will sit for many days without king, without ruler; there will be no sacrifice nor altar nor priesthood,* and if, indeed, from the time when the temple was overthrown, no sacrifices are offered, nor is an altar found, nor does a priesthood exist, then it is most certain that *rulers* have *ceased from Judah,* as it is written, *and a leader from his loins,* [*when*] *he came, for whom it is reserved.* It is established, then, that *he came, for whom it is reserved,* and in whom also is *the expectation of the nations.* This is clearly seen to have been fulfilled in the multitude of those who, from different nations, have believed through Christ in God.

4.1.3. *[Greek]* What need is there to mention also [how] Christ was foretold, that then those called '*rulers' would cease from Judah and leaders from his loins, when he should come for whom it is reserved,*[3] the kingdom clearly, *and the expectation of the nations should sojourn?* For it is abundantly clear from the history and from what is seen today that from the times of Jesus there were no longer those who were called kings of the Jews, all those Jewish institutions in which they prided themselves having been destroyed, I mean those relating to the temple and the altar and the performance of worship and the robes of the high priest. For the prophecy was fulfilled which said, *The children of Israel will sit for many days, there being neither king nor ruler, neither sacrifice, nor altar, nor priesthood, nor oracles.*

And these sayings we use in response to those who, in being perplexed by what was said in Genesis by Jacob to Judah, assert that the Ethnarch, being of the race of Judah, rules the people, and that those of his seed will not cease until the sojourn of Christ, as they imagine him. For if *The children of Israel will sit many days, there being neither king nor ruler, neither sacrifice nor altar nor priesthood nor oracles,* [and] from the point when the temple was razed to the ground there is neither sacrifice nor altar nor priesthood, it is clear that *a ruler has ceased from Judah and a leader from his loins.* And since the prophecy says, *A ruler would not cease from Judah nor a leader from his loins until there should come the things reserved for him,* it is clear that *he has arrived to whom*

---

[3] On the difference between the way this verse is cited here and below, see Justin, *Dial.* 120; he asserts that the reading 'when he should come for whom it is reserved' is that of the Seventy, while 'until there should come the things reserved for him' is the Jewish one.

4.1.4. *[Latin]* In the song in Deuteronomy, also, it is indicated through prophecy that, on account of the sins of the former people, there will be an election of a foolish nation, none other certainly than that which has come to pass through Christ. For it says this, *They have provoked me with their idols, and I will drive them to jealousy; I will enrage them with a foolish nation.*[12] It is therefore evident enough to perceive how the Hebrews, who are said to have *provoked God with those which are no gods* and to have *enraged him with their idols,* have *themselves* also *been enraged in jealousy* by means of the *foolish nation,* which God chose through the arrival of Christ Jesus and his disciples. For the Apostle speaks in this way, *For consider your calling, brethren, that not many among you were wise according to the flesh, not many mighty, not many noble; but God chose the foolish things of the world and those which are not, that he might destroy the things which formerly* were.[13] Therefore, *Israel according to the flesh,* for such is it called by the Apostle, should not glory: Let *no flesh,* I say, *glory in the presence of* God![14]

---

[12] Deut. 32:21. Cf. Justin, *Dial.* 119; Irenaeus, *Dem.* 95; Tertullian, *Marc.* 4.36.1; Clement, *Strom.* 2.9.43.1.
[13] 1 Cor. 1:26–8.   [14] 1 Cor. 10:18; 1:29.

---

it is reserved, the expectation of the nations. And this is clear from the multitude of the nations who have believed, through Christ, in God.

4.1.4. *[Greek]* And in the song of Deuteronomy the future election of foolish nations on account of the sins of the former people is prophetically made known, which has come to pass through none other than Jesus. *For,* it says, *they made me jealous with what is no god, they enraged me with their idols; so I will make them jealous with what is no nation, and enrage them with a foolish nation.* Now it is possible to understand very clearly in what manner the Hebrews, who are said to have *made God jealous with what is no god* and to have *enraged him by their idols, have been enraged to jealousy by what is no nation, by a foolish nation,* which God chose through the sojourn of Christ Jesus and his disciples. *We see, then, our calling, that not many were wise after the flesh, not many mighty, not many noble; but God chose the foolish things of the world, in order to shame the wise, and God chose the low and the despised, even things that are not, in order to bring to naught things that formerly were,* and *so that Israel according to the flesh* (which is called by the Apostle *flesh*) *should not boast in the presence of God.*

4.1.5. *[Latin]* What is to be said, moreover, regarding those prophecies regarding Christ in the Psalms, especially in that one which is entitled *A Song for the Beloved,* in which it is said that his *tongue is the pen of a scribe swiftly writing, fairer than the children of human beings,* that *grace was poured on his lips?*[15] Now, a proof that *grace was poured on his lips* is this, that although the time of his teaching was brief (for he taught for but a year and some months[16]), the whole world, nevertheless, has been filled with his teaching and faith in his religion. There has arisen *in his days righteousness and an abundance of peace,* abiding even to the end, which end is called *the taking away of the moon;* and *he has dominion from sea to sea and from the river to the ends of the earth.*[17] A sign was also given to the house of David. *For a virgin has conceived in the womb and born Emmanuel, which is interpreted 'God with us'.*[18] There is also

[15] Ps. 44:1–3.
[16] As maintained by the Valentinians, according to Irenaeus, *Haer.* 1.3.3, and Clement, *Strom.* 1.21.145.3. Irenaeus himself, *Haer.* 2.22.3–6, on the basis of the question 'You are not yet fifty years old, and yet you have seen Abraham' (John 8:57) and a tradition going back to the elders in Asia, concluded that Christ must have reached at least forty years old. In *Hom. Luc.* 32.5, Origen accepts that it might have been one year; but in *Comm. ser. Matt.* 40 and *Cels.* 2.12, he also accepts a three-year period.
[17] Ps. 71:7–8.
[18] Isa. 7:14; Matt. 1:23. See *Cels.* 1.34–5 for Origen's comments on the difference between παρθένος, as found in the LXX, and νεᾶ νις, as found in other versions. See also Justin, *Dial.* 66; Irenaeus, *Haer.* 3.21; Tertullian, *Adv. Jud.* 9.

4.1.5. *[Greek]* And what need is there to speak about the prophecies regarding Christ in the Psalms, there being a certain ode with the superscription *For the Beloved,* whose *tongue* is said to be *the pen of a swift writer; fairer in beauty than the sons of men,* since *grace was poured upon his lips?* A proof that *grace was poured upon his lips* is that although the period of his teaching was short (for he taught for about a year and a few months) the world has been filled with his teaching and the religion that came through him. For, *In his days righteousness has arisen and an abundance of peace* abiding until the consummation, which is called *the taking away of the moon;* and he remains *having dominion from sea to sea and from the rivers to the ends of the earth.* And a *sign has been given to the house of David: for the virgin [did bear and] conceived and bore a son, and his name is Emmanuel, which is God with us.* Also fulfilled is, as the same prophet says, *God is with us; Understand, you nations, and be defeated; you who are strong, be defeated.* For we have been defeated and vanquished, we who have been captured from the nations by the grace of his word. But even the

fulfilled that which the same prophet says, *God is with us. Understand, you nations, and be defeated.*[19] For we have been conquered and overcome, we who are of the nations and who are as it were the spoils of his victory, who have bowed our necks to his grace. Even the place of his birth was foretold in the prophet Micah, saying, *And you, Bethlehem, land of Judah, are by no means least among the leaders of Judah; for from you shall come a leader, who shall rule my people Israel.*[20] And, also, the weeks of years until Christ the leader, which the prophet Daniel had foretold, has been fulfilled.[21] He is, moreover, at hand, who was foretold by Job, *who is about to destroy the great beast,*[22] who also gave to his familiar disciples *the power to tread upon serpents and scorpions and over all the power of the enemy*, without being harmed in any way by them.[23] But if anyone will consider the journeys of the apostles of Christ throughout each place, in which, sent by him, they preached the Gospel, he will find both that what they ventured to undertake is beyond human and also that it is from God that they were able to accomplish what they had ventured. If we consider how human beings, when hearing that a new teaching is being introduced by these [apostles], were able to receive them, or rather, when often desiring to bring them to destruction, were prevented by some divine power that was present with them, we will find that nothing in this matter was effected by human strength, but the whole by divine power and providence, *signs and wonders,*[24] manifest beyond all doubt, bearing witness to their word and teaching.

---

[19] Isa. 8:8–9.
[20] Matt. 2:6; cf. Micah 5:2. Cf. Justin, *1 Apol.* 34; *Dial.* 78; Irenaeus, *Dem.* 63; Tertullian, *Adv. Jud.* 13.2; Origen, *Cels.* 1.51.
[21] Dan. 9:24. Rufinus omits 'seventy'. On this passage, see also Tertullian, *Adv. Jud.* 8.2; Clement, *Strom.* 1.21.125; Origen, *Comm. ser. Matt.* 40.
[22] Job 3:8.   [23] Luke 10:19.   [24] Cf. Acts 5:12; Heb. 2:4.

---

place of his birth has been foretold in Micah: *For you, Bethlehem,* he says, *in the land of Judah, are by no means least among the rulers of Judah; for from you shall come a ruler who will shepherd my people Israel.* And the *seventy weeks* until Christ the ruler, according to Daniel, were fulfilled. And he came, the one who, according to Job, *has subdued the great beast* and *has given* to his genuine disciples *authority to tread upon serpents and scorpions and over all power of the enemy*, without being harmed by them in any way. Let anyone also consider the universal sojourn of the apostles sent by Jesus to announce the Gospel, and he will see both that the daring venture was not human and that the command was divine. And if we examine how human beings, on hearing new teachings and strange words, accepted these men, being defeated, in their

4.1.6. *[Latin]* These points having briefly been demonstrated, that is, regarding the divinity of Jesus Christ and the fulfilment of all that was prophesied regarding him, I reckon that it has also been proved at the same time that the Scriptures themselves, which have prophesied about him, were divinely inspired, those which had either foretold his advent or the power of his teaching or the gathering in of all the nations. To which must also be added that the divine character and the divine inspiration both of the predictions of the Prophets and the Law of Moses have been most clearly brought to light and proved from the point that Christ arrived in this world. For before those things which were foretold by them were fulfilled, although they were true and inspired by God, they nevertheless could not be shown to be true because they were not yet proved to have been fulfilled; but the arrival of Christ proclaimed what had been said to be true and divinely inspired, whereas before it would certainly have been held doubtful whether the accomplishment of those things which had been foretold would be fulfilled.[25] Moreover, if anyone consider the

---

[25] Cf. Irenaeus, *Haer.* 4.26.1; Clement, *Strom.* 4.21.134; Origen, *Comm. Jo.* 1.32–6; 13.305–6; 19.28; *Frag. Luc.* 251.

desire to plot against them, by some divine power watching over them, we will not disbelieve that they even wrought miracles, *God bearing witness* to their words *by signs and wonders and various miracles.*

4.1.6. *[Greek]* In demonstrating, in summary fashion, the divinity of Jesus and using the prophetic words regarding him, we simultaneously demonstrate that the writings prophesying him are divinely inspired and that the words announcing his sojourn and teaching were spoken with all power and authority and on this account they have prevailed for the election from the nations. It must also be said that the inspiration of the prophetic words and the spiritual character of the Law of Moses shone forth with the sojourn of Jesus. For it was not at all possible to bring forward clear arguments concerning the inspiration of the ancient Scriptures before the sojourn of Christ; but the sojourning of Jesus led those who might have suspected the Law and the Prophets not to be divine to the clear conviction that they were composed by heavenly grace. One who reads the prophetic words with care and attention, experiencing from the act of reading itself a trace of divine inspiration, will be persuaded, through the things he experiences, that the words believed by us to be of God are not

prophetic sayings with all the diligence and reverence they deserve, it is certain that, in the very act, while he reads and carefully scrutinizes, his mind and senses having been touched by a divine breath, he will recognize what he reads to be not human utterances but the words of God; and in himself he will discern that these books have been composed not by human skill, nor mortal eloquence, but, if I may so speak, in a style that is divine. The splendour of Christ's arrival, therefore, illuminating the Law of Moses with the brightness of truth, has taken away that veil which had covered the letter and disclosed, for everyone who believes in him, all the good things which were concealed, buried within.[26]

4.1.7. [*Latin*] It is, however, a considerably laborious matter to recount how and when every instance of what the prophets of old foretold has been fulfilled, so as to appear by this to confirm those who are in doubt; although it is possible for everyone who wishes to become more thoroughly acquainted with these things to gather proofs in abundance from the books of the truth themselves. But if the sense, which is beyond human beings, does not appear to present itself immediately, on the first sight of the letter, to those who are less versed in the divine disciplines, it is not at all surprising, because divine things are conveyed to human beings in a somewhat more obscure manner and are the more hidden in proportion as one is either unbelieving or unworthy. For[27] although

---

[26] Cf. 2 Cor. 3:15–16; Heb. 10:1.
[27] Simonetti and Crouzel (SC 269, p. 164, n.41–41a) suggest that, although the following sentences are much more developed and bold than what is found in the *Philocalia*, they are certainly in the spirit of Origen, and that the *Philocalia* probably abridges this passage out of prudence.

---

compositions of human beings. And the light contained in the Law of Moses, but hidden by a veil, shone forth at the sojourn of Jesus, when the veil was taken away and the good things, of which the letter had a shadow, came gradually to be known.

4.1.7. [*Greek*] It would be a huge task to recount now the most ancient prophecies regarding each future event, in order that the doubter, being impressed by them as divine and putting aside every hesitation and distraction, may devote himself with his whole soul to the words of God. But if the supra-human [sense] of the meanings of every part of the writings does not seem to present itself to the uninstructed, no wonder; for, with respect to the works of that providence which embraces the whole world, some appear most clearly to be works of providence, while others are concealed in such a way as to seem to furnish ground for

it is certain that all things that exist or take place in this world are arranged by the providence of God, there are some things which clearly enough appear to have been disposed by the government of providence, but others are unfolded so obscurely and incomprehensibly that the design of divine providence regarding them is completely concealed, so that occasionally some things are not believed by some to belong to providence, because the design, by which the works of divine providence are arranged with certain ineffable art, is hidden from them, although this design is not equally concealed from all. For even among human beings themselves, it is pondered upon less by one and more by another; whoever is an inhabitant of heaven knows more than every human being who is upon earth. And the design of bodies is clear in one way, that of trees in another way, that of animals in yet another way, but that of souls is concealed in yet another way; and the manner in which the diverse movements of rational minds are arranged by divine providence eludes to a greater degree human beings, and even, I think, in no small degree the angels. But just as divine providence is not refuted, especially for those who are certain of its existence, because its workings and arrangements cannot be comprehended by human minds, so also neither will the divine inspiration of holy Scripture, which extends throughout its entire body, be believed to be non-existent because the weakness of our understanding is not able to trace out the obscure and hidden meaning in each single word, for the treasure of divine wisdom is hidden in the paltry and inelegant vessels of words, as the Apostle also points out, saying, *We have this treasure in earthen vessels, so that the strength of divine*

disbelief in that God who orders all things with unspeakable skill and power. For the skilful plan of the providential ruler is not so evident in matters upon the earth as it is with the sun and moon and stars, and not so clear in matters regarding human events as it is with the souls and bodies of animals, where the purpose and the reason of the impulses and the mental images and the nature of animals, and the structure of their bodies, are accurately discovered by those who attend to these things. But just as providence is not annulled, by those who have once for all accepted it rightly, on account of those things which are not understood, so neither is the divinity of Scripture, which extends to it all, annulled because our weakness cannot in every expression approach the hidden splendour of the teachings concealed in poor and humble language. *For we have a treasure in earthen vessels, so that the transcendent power of God might shine forth* and not be thought to be from us human beings. For if it had been the hackneyed methods of demonstration used by human beings, laid up in books,

power might shine out the more,[28] when no taint of human eloquence is mingled with the truth of the doctrines.[29] For if our books enticed human beings to believe because they were composed either by rhetorical art or by philosophical skilfulness, then undoubtedly our *faith* would be considered to be based upon the art of words or *upon human wisdom* and not *upon the power of God.*[30] But now it is well known to all that this *word of preaching* has been so accepted by multitudes throughout almost the whole world that they have understood that they believed *not in persuasive words of wisdom but in the demonstration of the Spirit and of power.*[31] On this account, being led by a heavenly, or rather more than heavenly, power to faith and belief, for this reason, that is, that we may worship the sole Creator of all things, our God, let us also endeavour to strive earnestly, that *leaving behind the teaching of the first principles of Christ,* which are but the elementary principles of knowledge, *we may press on to perfection,*[32] in order that that wisdom, which is delivered to the perfect, may also be delivered to us.[33] For such does he, to whom was entrusted the preaching of this wisdom, promise, saying, *Yet we speak wisdom among the perfect, but not the wisdom of this world, nor of the rulers of this world, who will be destroyed.*[34] By this he shows that this wisdom of ours, so far as concerns the beauty of language,

---

[28] 2 Cor. 4:7.
[29] For the divine power at work through the 'paltry and inelegant' words of Scripture, see the various passages drawn from *Cels.* in Origen, *Philoc.* 15.
[30] Cf. 1 Cor. 2:5.   [31] 1 Cor. 2:4.   [32] Heb. 6:1.
[33] Cf. Origen, *Comm. Jo.* 1.42–6; 2.21–31; 13.26–39; *Frag. Jo.* 63 (GCS 4, pp. 531–2); *Dial.* 15; *Frag. Prov.* 1.6 (PG 13, 20); *Comm. Matt.* 10.4; 12.30–3; 16.8; *Hom. Gen.* 7.4; *Hom. Ex.* 12.4; *Hom. Lev.* 4.6. See also Clement, *Strom.* 2.6.25–31; 2.9.45; 5.1.2.4–5; 5.1.1–13; 5.4.19–26; 7.3.13.
[34] 1 Cor. 2:6.

---

that had prevailed over human beings, our *faith* might reasonably be supposed to rest *upon the wisdom of human beings* and not *upon the power of God;* but now, for one lifting up their eyes, it is clear that *the word and the preaching* have prevailed among the multitude *not in persuasive words of wisdom but in the dem-onstration of the Spirit and of power.* Therefore, since a celestial or super-celestial power compels us to worship only the one who created us, let us endeavour, *leaving behind the teaching of the first principle of Christ,* that is, of the elements, *to press on to perfection,* in order that the wisdom spoken to the perfect may be spoken to us also. For he who acquired wisdom promises *to speak it among the perfect,* but another wisdom besides *the wisdom of this age and the wisdom of the rulers of this age, which is being destroyed.* And this wisdom will be stamped upon us distinctly, *according to the revelation of the mystery which was kept secret through times eternal, but now made manifest through the prophetic scriptures* and *the appearance of our Lord and Saviour Jesus Christ,* to whom be glory for all ages. Amen.

has nothing in common with the wisdom of this world. This wisdom, then, will be inscribed more clearly and perfectly in our hearts, if it is made known to us *according to the revelation of the mystery which has been hidden from eternity but is now manifest through the prophetic Scriptures,* and *through the arrival of our Lord and Saviour Jesus Christ,*[35] to whom is the glory unto eternal ages. Amen.[36]

---

[35] Rom. 16:25–7 and 2 Tim. 1:10 (cf. 1 Tim. 6:14); Origen frequently combines these verses, e.g. *Comm. Jo.* 6.25; 13.101; 13.306; *Cels.* 2.4; 3.61.

[36] Here, and at the end of *Princ.* 3.5.8 are the only two places where Origen concludes with a doxology and 'Amen'; in *Princ.* 4.3.14 he concludes with a doxology but no 'Amen'.

How One Must Read and Understand the Scriptures

4.2.1.[1] *[Latin]* These points, then, being briefly noted, concerning the fact that the divine Scriptures are inspired by the Holy Spirit, it seems necessary also to explain this: in what way certain people, not reading or understanding them correctly, have given themselves over into many errors, inasmuch as the way that ought to be followed for the understanding of the divine writings is unknown to many. For the Jews, through their hardness of heart, and because they wish to appear wise in their own sight, have not believed in our Lord and Saviour, supposing that those things which were prophesied of him ought to be understood according to the letter, that is, that he ought, perceptibly and visibly, to *proclaim release to the captives,* and that he ought at first to build a city such as they think *the city of God* truly to be, and at the same time to *cut off the chariots of Ephraim and the horse from Jerusalem,* but also to *eat butter and honey in order to choose the good before he should know to bring forth evil;* they also think that it has been prophesied that at the arrival of Christ, *the wolf,*

---

[1] The Latin manuscripts, and previous editions following them, have, for *Princ.* 4.2, 'Many, not understanding the Scriptures in a spiritual sense and interpreting badly have fallen into heresy' and for *Princ.* 4.3, 'Illustrations from Scripture of the method in which Scripture should be understood'. However, as *Princ.* 4.2 deals not only with misunderstandings, but, from *Princ.* 4.2.4 onwards, how to read and understand Scripture, and as *Princ.* 4.3 continues the same subject by giving illustrations exemplifying such a reading, I have followed Photius (see note to title of *Princ.* 4.1) in taking *Princ.* 4.2–3 as a single chapter with the title given by Photius.

How the Divine Scripture is to be Read and Understood

4.2.1. *[Greek]* After having spoken, as in summary, about the inspiration of the divine Scriptures, it is necessary to proceed to the manner of reading and understanding them, since many errors have occurred from the fact that the way by which the holy readings ought to be examined has not been discovered by the multitude. For the hard-hearted and ignorant of the people of the circumcision have not believed in our Saviour, thinking they follow the language of the prophecies regarding him, and not seeing him visibly *proclaiming release to the captives,* nor building up what they consider to be truly a *city of God,* nor *cutting off the chariots from Ephraim and the horse from Jerusalem,* nor *eating butter and honey, and before knowing or preferring evil, choosing the good;* and thinking it was prophesied that the *wolf,* the four-footed animal, was *to feed with the lamb and the leopard to lie down with the kid, the calf and the bull and the lion to feed together, being led by a little child, and the ox and the bear to pasture together, their young ones growing up together, and the lion to eat straw*

that four-footed animal, *is to feed with the lambs, and the leopard is to lie down with the kids, and the calf and the bull are to feed together with the lions and to be led to the pasture by a little child, and the ox and the bear are to lie down together in the green fields, and their young ones are to be fed together, and the lions are to stand at the stalls with the oxen and be fed on straw.*[2] Therefore, seeing that of all these things, which were prophesied of him and in which they believed that the signs of the arrival of Christ were especially to be observed, none was enacted in history, they refused to accept the presence of our Lord Jesus Christ; or rather, indeed, contrary to all propriety and justice, that is, contrary to the faith of prophecy, they nailed him to the cross for taking upon himself the name of Christ. Then, again, the heretics, reading what is written in the Law, *A fire has been kindled from my anger,*[3] and, *I am a jealous God, repaying the sins of the fathers upon the children unto the third and fourth generation,*[4] and, *I regret that I anointed Saul to be king,*[5] and, *I am God, who makes peace and creates evil,*[6] and again, *There is no evil in the city which the Lord has not done,*[7] and, *Evils came down from the Lord upon the gates of Jerusalem,*[8] and, *An evil spirit from God throttled Saul,*[9] and reading many other passages of Scripture similar to these they did not dare to say that these are not Scriptures

---

[2] Cf. Isa. 61:1; Ezek. 48:15–35; Ps. 45:5; Zech. 9:10; Isa. 7:15; Isa. 11:6–7.
[3] Deut. 32:22; Jer. 15:14.   [4] Exod. 20:5.   [5] 1 Rgns 15:11.
[6] Isa. 45:7.   [7] Amos 3:6.   [8] Micah 1:12.
[9] 1 Rgns 16:14. See also 1 Sam. 18:10, a verse not in the LXX, but one known to Origen, as evidenced by the *Hexapla* (ed. Fields, 1.519).

like the ox—seeing none of these things visibly happening in the sojourn of him believed by us to be Christ, they did not accept our Lord Jesus, but they crucified him as having improperly called himself Christ. While those from the heretical sects reading this, *A fire has been kindled from my anger,* and, *I am a jealous God, repaying the sins of the fathers upon the children unto the third or fourth generation,* and *I regret that I anointed Saul to be king,* and, *I am God, who makes peace and creates evil,* and, amongst others, *There is no evil in the city which the Lord has not done,* and again, *Evils came down from the Lord upon the gates of Jerusalem,* and, *An evil spirit from God throttled Saul,* and numberless other passages like these, have not dared to disbelieve that these are Scriptures of God, but believing them to be of the creator, whom the Jews worship, they thought that, as the creator was imperfect and not good, the Saviour had sojourned announcing a more perfect God, who they say is not the creator, motivated in various ways regarding this; and once fallen away

of God, but they supposed them, however, to be of that creator God whom the Jews worshipped and whom they esteemed should be believed to be merely just and not also good; but that when the Saviour had come, he proclaimed to us a more perfect God, whom they say is not the creator of the world, yet being divided with different opinions about him, since having once fallen away from the faith in God the Creator, who is the God of all, they have given themselves over to various fictions and fables, imagining certain things and saying that some things are visible and made by a certain one, but other things are invisible and created by another, just as the fancy and vanity of their own minds suggest to them. Yet also not a few of the more simple of those who appear to be enclosed within the faith of the Church esteem that there is no greater than the creator God, holding in this a correct and sound belief, but believe such things about him as would not be believed even of the most unjust and savage of human beings.[10]

4.2.2. *[Latin]* Now, the reason for the false apprehension of all these points by those whom we have mentioned above is nothing other than this, that holy Scripture is not understood by them according to its spiritual sense, but according to the sound of the letter. On this account we shall endeavour, according to

---

[10] Cf. Origen, *Princ.* 2.10.3 for a similar comment regarding the impoverished understanding of the resurrection by some believers. See also Origen, *Princ.* 1.1.1; 2.11.2; *Comm. Rom.* 1.19; *Hom. Lev.* 16.4; *Hom. Num.* 22.1. On the question of punishments, see Origen, *Princ.* 2.5.2.

from the Creator who is the only uncreated God, they have given themselves up to fictions, mythologizing for themselves hypotheses according to which they suppose that there are some things that are seen and certain others which are not seen, which their own souls have idolized. However, even the more simple of those who claim to be of the Church have supposed that there is none greater than the Creator, doing so soundly; but they suppose such things about him that would not be supposed of the most savage and unjust human being.

4.2.2. *[Greek]* The reason, in all the cases mentioned, for the false beliefs and impious or ignorant assertions about God appears to be nothing else than Scripture not being understood according to its spiritual sense, but taken as regarding the bare letter. Therefore, for those who are persuaded that the

our moderate understanding, to demonstrate for those who believe the holy Scriptures to be composed not by merely human words, but written by the inspiration of the Holy Spirit and handed down and entrusted to us by the will of God the Father through his only-begotten Son Jesus Christ, what appears to us to be the right way of understanding [the Scriptures], as we observe that rule and discipline which, delivered to his apostles by Jesus Christ, they handed down in succession to their posterity, the teachers of the heavenly Church.[11]

Now, that there are certain mystical economies indicated through the holy Scriptures, everyone, I think, even the most simple of believers, admits. But what these are or of what kind they are, one who is of right mind and not plagued by the vice of boasting will reverently acknowledge himself to be ignorant. For if anyone, for example, were to ask us about the daughters of Lot, who seem to have had unlawful intercourse with their father,[12] or about the two wives of Abraham,[13] or of the two sisters who were married to Jacob,[14] or

---

[11] On the 'rule' and 'succession' or 'tradition', see Origen, *Princ.* Pr.2 and the material cited in the notes there.

[12] Cf. Gen. 19:30–6; Origen, *Hom. Gen.* 5.5. In *Cels.* 4.45, Origen gives a different interpretation of this passage, similar to Philo, *QG* 4.56, and Irenaeus, *Haer.* 4.31, who is reporting the exegesis of a presbyter before him, almost certainly Polycarp.

[13] Cf. Gen. 16; Gal. 4:24.   [14] Cf. Gen. 29:21–30.

---

sacred books are not compositions of human beings, but that they were composed and have come down to us from the inspiration of the Holy Spirit by the will of the Father of all through Jesus Christ, one must indicate the apparent ways [of understanding Scripture followed] by those who keep the rule of the heavenly Church of Jesus Christ through succession from the apostles.

Now, that there are certain mystical economies made known through the holy Scriptures all, even the most simple of those adhering to the Word, have believed; but what these are, sensible and modest people confess that they do not know. If, for instance, one were to be perplexed about the intercourse of Lot with his daughters, and about the two wives of Abraham, the two sisters married to Jacob, and the two handmaids who bore children by him, they can say nothing except that these are mysteries not understood by us. But when [the passage about] the preparation of the tabernacle is read, persuaded that what is written is a type, they seek to attach what they can to each detail mentioned about the tabernacle; not erring insofar as they are persuaded that the tabernacle is a type of something, but insofar as they rightly attach the word of Scripture to something specific, of which the tabernacle is a type, they sometimes fall short. And they

of the two handmaids who increased the number of his sons,[15] what else can be answered than that they are certain mysteries and forms of spiritual things, but that it is unknown by us of what kind they are? When, also, we read about the construction of the tabernacle, we hold it as sure that the things that are written are figures of certain hidden things;[16] however, I reckon that it is very difficult, not to say impossible, to apply to them their appropriate standards and to uncover and discuss each separate detail. But that, as I have said, that description is full of mysteries does not escape even the most common mind. And all those narratives, which appear to be composed about marriages or about the begetting of children or about different kinds of battles or about any other narratives whatever, what else can they be believed to be, except the forms and figures of hidden and sacred things? But either because human beings make little effort to exercise their minds, or because, before they learn, they think that they already know, the consequence is that they never begin to know; on the other hand, if neither zeal nor a master is lacking, and if these things are examined as divine, not as if human—that is, in a religious and pious manner, and [as mysteries] which are hoped will be opened by revelation of God, at least in most cases, since to human sense they are exceedingly difficult and obscure—then, perhaps, one who thus seeks will find what it is proper to find.

4.2.3. *[Latin]* But perhaps this difficulty is supposed to exist only in the prophetic words, seeing that it is certain to all that the prophetic style is always strewn with figures and enigmas,[17] what, then, [do we find] when coming to

---

[15] Cf. Gen. 30:1–13.
[16] Cf. Exod. 25–31. See also Philo, *Mos.* 2.89–94; *QE* 2.68; Clement, *Strom.* 5.6; *Exc.* 27; Origen, *Hom. Exod.* 9.
[17] Cf. Prov. 1:6. Used also in Origen, *Comm. Jo.* 2.173; *Cels.* 3.45; 7.10.

---

declare that every account, which is thought to speak about marriage or childbearing or wars, or any other narratives that are accepted by the multitude, are types; but regarding the detail of each case, partly because their disposition is not fully trained, partly because of rashness, and sometimes, even if someone is well trained and deliberate, because the discovery of these things is excessively difficult for human beings, the rationale of each detail regarding these types is not altogether clearly articulated.

4.2.3. *[Greek]* And what is the need to speak about the prophecies, which we all know to be filled with enigmatic and dark sayings? Even if we come to the Gospels, the precise sense of these also, as being *the mind of Christ,* requires the

the Gospels? Is there not hidden even there an inner sense, as being *the mind of the Lord*, which is revealed by that grace alone which he had received, who said, *But we have the mind of Christ, that we might know the gifts bestowed upon us by God, which also we speak, not in the words of the teaching of human wisdom but in the teaching of the Spirit?*[18] And, again, if someone were to read the things revealed to John, how would he not be amazed at the great obscurity of the ineffable mysteries contained therein? In these, it is clearly understood, even by those who are not able to understand what is concealed in them, that something is nevertheless concealed. And also the epistles of the Apostles, which to some seem to be plainer, are they not filled with meanings so profound that by means of them, as through some small receptacle, the brightness of immeasurable light seems to be poured into those who are able to understand the meaning of divine wisdom? Therefore, since these things are so and there are many who go astray on this path, I do not think that anyone can without danger lightly claim to know or understand those things for which, in order that they might be opened up, *the key of knowledge* is necessary, which key is said by the Saviour to be with those skilled in the law.[19] At this point, although by a certain digression, I think it should be asked of those who say that before the arrival of the Saviour there was no truth among those who were occupied with the law, how it could be said by our Lord Jesus Christ that the *keys of knowledge* were with those, who had the books of the law and the prophets in their hands. For the Lord spoke thus: *Woe unto you, teachers of the law, for you have taken away the key of knowledge: you did not enter yourselves, and you hindered those wishing to enter.*[20]

---

[18] 1 Cor. 2:16, 12–13.   [19] Luke 11:52. Cf. Origen, *Sel. Ps. 1* (PG 12, 1077); *Philoc.* 2.2.
[20] Luke 11:52.

---

grace that was given to him who said, *We have the mind of Christ, that we might know the gifts bestowed upon us by God; which also we speak, not in words taught by human wisdom but in those taught by the Spirit.* And who, on reading the revelations made to John, would not be struck with amazement at the obscurity of the unspeakable mysteries, evident even to one who does not understand what is written? And to whom of those skilled in investigating words would the epistles of the apostles seem to be plain and easily understood, since there are in them thousands of passages providing, as if through a lattice, a narrow opening to the greatest and deepest thoughts? Therefore, this being the case, and with countless people falling into error, it is not without danger when reading to profess lightly to understand things that need *the key of knowledge*, which the Saviour says is with the lawyers; and those who will not allow that the truth was

4.2.4. *[Latin]* But, as we began to say, the way that seems to us to be correct for understanding the Scriptures and investigating their sense, we consider to be of the following kind, just as we are indeed taught by Scripture itself how we ought to think of it. We find some such observation regarding the divine Scriptures prescribed by Solomon in Proverbs. *And you,* he says, *represent these things for yourself thrice, in counsel and knowledge, so that you may answer the words of truth to those who have asked you.*[21] Each one, therefore, ought to represent in his own soul the sense of the divine letters thrice; that is, in order that the more simple may be edified from, if I may speak thus, the very body of Scripture (for such do we term that common and narratival sense); while if some have begun to make considerable progress and are able to perceive something more, they may be edified from the very soul of Scripture; and those who are perfect and resemble those of whom the Apostle says, *We speak wisdom among the perfect, yet a wisdom not of this world nor of the rulers of this world, who will be brought to nought; but we speak the wisdom of God, hidden in a mystery, which God has foreordained before the ages for our glory,*[22] such as these may be edified from that *spiritual law* which has *a shadow of the good things to come,*[23] as if from the Spirit. Just as the human being, therefore, is said to consist of body and soul and spirit, so also does holy Scripture, which has been granted by the divine bounty for human salvation.

---

[21] Prov. 22:20–1. Cf. Origen, *Hom. Num.* 9.7. In *Hom. Gen.* 2.6, Origen proposes a threefold interpretation a propos of Gen. 6:16. For the analogy with the human being, see Origen, *Hom. Lev.* 5.1; *Sel. Lev.* (PG 12, 421 = *Philoc.* 1.30). See also Philo, *Migr.* 93; *Contempl.* 78; Clement, *Strom.* 6.15.132.
[22] 1 Cor. 2:6–7.   [23] Rom. 7:14; Heb. 10:1.

---

with these before the sojourn of Christ, let them explain how *the key of knowledge* was said by our Lord Jesus Christ to be with those who, as they allege, did not have the books containing the secrets of knowledge and perfect mysteries. For the passage is thus: *Woe to you lawyers, for you have taken away the key of knowledge; you did not enter yourselves, and you hindered those who were entering.*

4.2.4. *[Greek]* The way, then, as it appears to us, in which we ought to deal with the Scriptures and gather their sense, is such as the following, which has been traced out from the writings themselves. We find something such as this enjoined by Solomon in Proverbs regarding the divine teachings of the writings: *You are to register them thrice in counsel and knowledge, to answer words of truth to those who challenge you.* It is, therefore, necessary to register in one's

This we see indicated also in the book of *The Shepherd*, which seems to be despised by some, where Hermas is commanded to 'write two books', and afterwards, 'to announce to the presbyters of the Church what he learned from the Spirit'. For it is written in these words: 'And you', he says, 'will write two books and you will give one to Clement and one to Grapte. And let Grapte admonish the widows and orphans, and let Clement send throughout all the cities, which are abroad, while you shall announce to the presbyters of the Church.'[24] Grapte, therefore, who is commanded to admonish the orphans and widows, is the bare understanding of the letter itself, by which the young souls are admonished, who have not yet deserved to have God as Father, and on that account are termed orphans. The widows, in turn, are those who have departed from the wicked husband to whom they had been united contrary to the law, but remain widows because they have not yet advanced to the point of being united to the heavenly bridegroom. But Clement is ordered to send what was said to those who are already departing from the letter into 'the cities which are abroad', as if he meant to those souls who, being built up by these means, have begun to be above the cares of the body and the desires of the flesh. And what he had learnt from the Holy Spirit, he himself is commanded to announce, not by letters nor by a book, but by the living voice, to the presbyters of the Church of Christ, that is, to those who, by their capacity for receiving spiritual teaching, possess a mature mind of wisdom.

[24] Hermas, *Vis.* 2.4.3. Hermas is also cited in Origen, *Princ.* Pr.4 and 1.3.3.

own soul the senses of the sacred writings thrice: so that the simple may be edified from the flesh, as it were, of Scripture, for so we designate the obvious interpretation; while one who has ascended a certain measure may be edified from the soul, as it were; and the person who is perfect and like those spoken of by the Apostle—*We speak wisdom among the perfect, a wisdom not of this age nor of the rulers of this age, who are being brought to nought; but we speak the wisdom of God hidden in a mystery, which God foreordained before the ages unto our glory*—[may be edified] from *the spiritual law, having a shadow of the good things to come*. Just as the human being consists of body and soul and spirit, in the same way so also does Scripture, arranged by God to be given for the salvation of human beings.

On this account we also explain in this way that passage in the book, *The Shepherd*, which is despised by some, where Hermas is commanded to 'write two books', and after doing so 'to announce to the presbyters of the church'

4.2.5. *[Latin]* This point indeed is not to be disregarded, that there are certain passages in Scripture in which what we have called 'the body', that is, the sequence of the narratival meaning, is not always found, as we shall demonstrate in the following pages; and there are places where what we have called 'the soul' or 'the spirit' are alone to be understood. I think that this is indicated in the Gospels, when *six jars* are said to be set down *for the purification of the Jews, each containing two or three firkins,*[25] by which, as I have said, the evangelical word seems to indicate those who are called by the Apostle *Jews in secret*[26] because they are purified by the word of Scripture, receiving indeed sometimes *two firkins,* that is accepting the meaning of the soul and of the spirit, as we have said above, and sometimes even *three,* when the reading is also able to preserve, for edification, the bodily meaning, which is that of the narrative. And *six jars* are appropriately mentioned regarding those who are being purified while placed in this world. For we read that in six days (which is a perfect number[27]) the world and all things in it were finished.

---

[25] John 2:6; a 'firkin' is a unit of liquid volume (usually 9 gallons); this archaic term is used so as to retain the reference to 'two' or 'three'.

[26] Rom. 2:29. Cf. Origen, *Princ.* 4.3.6; *Comm. Jo.* 1.1; 1.259; 13.103; *Frag. Jo.* 8 and 114 (GCS 4, pp. 489–90, 557–8); *Hom. Jer.* 12.13.

[27] Cf. *Comm. Jo.* 28.1: 'Those who investigate the nature of numbers have said that six is the first perfect number, being equal to its own parts, both from the combination of what is doubled from the unity, one and two, which is three, a prime number, and the doubling of the number arrived at, now I mean from the two, for when the two has been multiplied by the three it makes six' (Preuschen indicates this as follows: $6 = (1+2) \times 2$ or $6 = 1+2+3$). See also Philo, *Opif.* 3.13: 'If we start with 1 it [i.e. 6] is the first perfect number, being equal to the product of its factors [i.e. $1 \times 2 \times 3$] as well as made up of the sum of them [i.e. $1+2+3$], its half being 3, its third part being 2, its sixth part 1.'

---

what he learnt 'from the Spirit'. The wording is this: 'You will write two books, and give one to Clement and one to Grapte. And let Grapte admonish the widows and the orphans, and let Clement send to the cities abroad, while you shall announce to the presbyters of the church.' Grapte, who admonishes the widows and the orphans, is the mere letter, admonishing the young souls who are not yet able to be enrolled with God as Father and therefore called 'orphans', admonishing also those who no longer associate with the unlawful bridegroom, but remain 'widows' because they have not yet become worthy of the Bridegroom. But Clement, who has already risen above the letter, is said to send the sayings 'to the cities abroad', as if we were to say the 'souls' who are outside bodily and lower thoughts; while the disciple of the Spirit himself is commanded to announce, no longer by letters, but by living words, to the presbyters of the whole Church of God, who have grown grey through wisdom.

4.2.6. *[Latin]* How great the usefulness is in this first, what we have called the narratival, sense is witnessed by the entire multitude of believers, who believe quite faithfully and simply; nor does it need much argument, because it is openly manifest to all. But of that sense, which we have spoken above as being the soul, as it were, of Scripture, the Apostle Paul has given us numerous examples, as for example in the First Epistle to the Corinthians. *For it is written,* he says, *you shall not muzzle the ox when it is treading out the grain.* And, then, when explaining how this precept ought to be understood, he adds, saying, *Is it for the ox that God is concerned? Or does he speak altogether for our sake? It was written for our sake, so that he who ploughs ought to plough in hope and he who threshes in hope of partaking.*[28] Moreover, very many other similar passages of the Law, which are explained in this way, impart great instruction to those who hear them.

[28] 1 Cor. 9:9–10; Deut. 25:4. Cf. Origen, *Cels.* 4.49.

4.2.5. *[Greek]* But since there are certain passages which do not at all contain the bodily sense, as we will show in the following, there are places where it is necessary to seek only the soul and the spirit, as it were, of the Scriptures. And perhaps on this account the *jars,* as we read in the Gospel according to John, are said *to be placed for the purification of the Jews, containing two or three firkins each*; the language alludes to those who [are called] by the Apostle *Jews in secret,* as these are purified by the word of the Scriptures, which contain, in some cases, *two firkins,* that is, so to speak, the psychical and the spiritual principle, and sometimes *three,* since some have, in addition to those already mentioned, the bodily one also, which is capable of edifying. And there are rightly *six jars,* for those being purified in the world, which came to be in six days, the perfect number.

4.2.6. *[Greek]* That there is benefit to be had from the first interpretation, which in this respect is profitable, the multitude of genuine and simple believers bears witness; while of that explanation referring to the soul, an illustration is provided by Paul in the first [Epistle] to the Corinthians: *For it is written,* he says, *you shall not muzzle the ox when it is treading out the grain.* Then, explaining this precept, he adds: *Is it for the ox that God is concerned? Or does he speak altogether for our sake? It was written for our sake, so that he who ploughs ought to plough in hope and he who threshes in the hope of partaking.* And most of the interpretations in circulation, being adapted to the multitude and edifying those unable to understand the higher meanings, have somewhat the same character.

But a spiritual interpretation is like this: when one is able to show of what *heavenly realities they,* who are Jews *according to the flesh, serve the patterns and shadow,* and of what *good things to come the Law has a shadow,*[29] and any other such expressions which may be found in holy Scripture; or when it is asked what is that *wisdom hidden in a mystery, which God foreordained before the world for our glory, which none of the rulers of this world knew;*[30] or that which the same Apostle says, when he employs certain illustrations from Exodus or Numbers and affirms that *these things happened to them in a figure, but they were written for our sake, upon whom the ends of the ages has come,*[31] and offers us an opportunity for understanding, so that we can perceive of what those things that happened to them were figures, when he says, *For they drank of that spiritual rock that followed them, and that rock was Christ.*[32] In another epistle, also, he mentions that command, which was enjoined upon Moses, regarding the tabernacle, *You shall make,* he says, *all things according to the figure which was shown to you on the mountain.*[33] And writing to the Galatians and as if reproaching some who seem to themselves to read the Law, yet do not understand it, because they are unaware that there are allegories in what is written, he says to them in a certain tone of rebuke: *Tell me, you who*

---

[29] Heb. 8:5; 1 Cor. 10:18; Heb. 10:1.
[30] 2 Cor. 2:7–8.   [31] 1 Cor. 10:11.
[32] 1 Cor. 10:4. Cf. Origen, *Hom. Exod.* 11.2.
[33] Heb. 8:5; Exod. 25:40. Cf. Origen, *Princ.* 4.2.2, and the material cited there in n.16.

But spiritual interpretation is for one who is able to show of what *heavenly realities* the Jews *according to the flesh serve the pattern and shadow,* and *of what good things to come the Law has a shadow.* And, generally speaking, according to the apostolic promise one must seek everywhere *the wisdom hidden in a mystery, which God foreordained before the ages for the glory* of the righteous, *which none of the rulers of this age knew.* The same Apostle says somewhere, after mentioning certain passages from Exodus and Numbers, that *these things happened to them figuratively, but they were written on our account, upon whom the ends of the ages has come.* And he offers an opportunity for ascertaining of what things these were types, when he says, *For they drank of that spiritual rock that followed them, and that rock was Christ.* And, when sketching out the various matters pertaining to the tabernacle in another epistle, he makes use of this: *You shall make all things according to the figure which was shown to you on the mountain.* Moreover, in the Epistle to the Galatians, as if reproaching those who think they read the Law and yet do not understand it, judging that those who do not think that there are allegories in

desire to be under the Law, do you not hear the Law? For it is written that Abraham had two sons, one by a slave, the other by a free woman. But he who was born of the slave was born according to the flesh; while he of the free woman, according to the promise. These things are allegorical; for these are the two covenants, and the rest.[34] Here this point must be noted, how carefully the Apostle said, *You who desire to be under the Law,* and did not say 'who are under the Law, *do you not hear the Law?*' *Do you hear,* that is, do you understand and know? And, again, in the Epistle to the Colossians, briefly summing up and condensing the sense of the whole Law, he says, *Let no one, therefore, judge you in matters of meat or drink or holy days or a new moon or a sabbath, which are a shadow of things to come.*[35] Writing to the Hebrews, also, and discussing those who are of the circumcision, he says, *They serve a pattern and shadow of heavenly things.*[36] Now, probably, through these examples no doubt will appear regarding the five books of Moses for those who accept the writings of the Apostle as divine sayings. But should they ask, regarding the rest of the narrative, whether the events related therein may also be said to have *happened in a figure*[37] to those about whom it is written, we have noted that even this has been stated in the Epistle to the Romans, where the Apostle cites an example from the third book of Reigns, which says, *I have left for myself seven thousand men who have not bowed the knee to Baal.*[38] This Paul takes as spoken figuratively of those who are called Israelites *according to election,*[39] in order to show the arrival of Christ to have been beneficial not only to the Gentiles, but also that very many of the race of Israel are called to salvation.

---

[34] Gal. 4:21–4. Cf. Origen, *Hom. Num.* 11.1.   [35] Col. 2:16–17.   [36] Heb. 8:5.
[37] 1 Cor. 10:11.   [38] Rom. 11:4; cf. 3 Rgns 19:18.   [39] Rom. 11:5.

what is written do not understand it, he says, *Tell me, you who desire to be under the Law, do you not hear the Law? For it is written that Abraham had two sons, one by a slave and the other by a free woman. But he who was of the slave was born according to the flesh, but he who was of the free woman, according to the promise. These things are allegorical; for these are the two covenants,* and the rest. One must observe carefully each thing said by him, for he says, *You who desire to be under the Law,* not 'you who are under the Law', and, *do you not hear the Law? To hear* is taken to mean 'to understand' and 'to know'. And in the Epistle to the Colossians, briefly abridging the intent of the whole legislation, he says, *Let no one, therefore, judge you in matters of meat or drink or with*

4.2.7. *[Latin]* These things being so, we shall sketch out the manner in which holy Scripture is to be understood by us on these several points, using what may occur to us by way of illustration and example, in the first instance repeating and pointing out that the Holy Spirit, who by the providence and will of God through the power of his only-begotten *Word*, who *was in the beginning God with God*,[40] enlightened the ministers of the truth, the prophets and apostles,[41] to know the mysteries of those things or causes which take place among human beings or with respect to human beings. And by human beings I now mean souls that are placed in bodies.[42] These mysteries, which were made known and revealed to them through the Spirit, they portrayed figuratively, as if narrating certain human deeds or handing down certain legal observances and precepts; so that not anyone who wished might have them placed under his feet as something to be trampled upon,[43] but that one who had devoted himself to studies of this kind, with all chastity and sobriety and nights of

---

[40] John 1:1.
[41] Koetschau, followed by other editors, suspects a lacuna at this point, suggesting something like 'wished above all to form them'.
[42] Cf. Origen, *Cels.* 7.38.   [43] Cf. Matt. 7:6.

---

regard to a festival or a new moon or a Sabbath, which are a shadow of things to come. And again, in that to the Hebrews, discussing those who are of the circumcision, he writes, *They serve a pattern and shadow of heavenly things.* Now it is probable that, from these illustrations, those who have once for all accepted the Apostle as a divine man will have no doubt regarding the five books ascribed to Moses; but regarding the rest of the history, they wish to learn whether those things also *happened figuratively.* One must note the quotation in [the Epistle] to the Romans, *I have left for myself seven thousand men who have not bowed the knee to Baal,* occurring in the third book of Reigns: Paul has taken it on the part of the Israelites *according to election,* for not only were the nations benefitted by the sojourn of Christ, but also some from the divine race.

4.2.7. *[Greek]* These things being so, one must outline what seems to us the characteristics of the intellectual apprehension of the Scriptures. And in first place, it must be pointed out that the aim of the Spirit, who, by the providence of God through *the Word in the beginning with God*, illumines the ministers of the truth, the prophets and apostles, was pre-eminently concerned with the unspeakable mysteries regarding the affairs of human beings (and by human beings I now mean souls making use of bodies) in order that one who is watching, might perhaps through these means be able to trace out the sense of the Spirit of God hidden in profundity and concealed by an ordinary narrative style, pointing in another direction, and that thus he might become an associate in the Spirit's knowledge and a partaker in the divine counsel, because the soul cannot come to the perfection of knowledge otherwise than by being inspired with the truth of divine wisdom. Therefore, it is [the teaching] about God, that is about the Father and the Son and the Holy Spirit, which is primarily described by these men, filled with the divine Spirit; then, [the teaching] of the mysteries relating to the Son of God—how *the Word became flesh* and for what reason he went even to the point of *assuming the form of a servant*[44]— have been made known, as we have said, by those filled with the divine Spirit. It next followed, necessarily, that they should instruct the race of mortals by divine teaching concerning rational creatures, both heavenly and earthly, the more blessed ones and the lowlier ones, and also concerning the difference among souls and how these differences arose; and then what this world is, and why it was made, and also why it is that wickedness is so widespread and terrible over the world, and whether it is only upon this earth or in some other places as well, it was necessary for us to learn from the divine teaching.

---

[44] John 1:14; Phil. 2:7.

---

capable of being taught may, by *searching out* and devoting himself *to the deep things* of the sense of the words,[1] become a participant in all the doctrines of the Spirit's counsel. And in matters regarding souls, who cannot otherwise attain perfection apart from the rich and wise truth about God, the [doctrines] concerning God and his only-begotten Son are necessarily ranked as primordial— of what nature he is, and in what manner he is the Son of God, and what are the reasons he descends to human flesh and completely assumes the human being, and what also is his activity and to whom and when it is exercised. Necessarily also the subject of kindred beings and other rational beings, both those more divine and those fallen from blessedness, together with the reasons for their fall, should be included in the accounts of the divine teaching, and also that of the difference between souls, and whence these differences came about, and what is the world and why it exists, and again whence evil came to be so widespread and terrible upon the earth, and whether it is not upon the earth only but also elsewhere—[all this] it is necessary that we should learn.

---

[1] 1 Cor. 2:10.

4.2.8. *[Latin]* Thus, while it was the intention of the Holy Spirit to enlighten those holy souls, who had devoted themselves to the service of the truth, about these and similar matters, there was, in second place, this aim, namely—for the sake of those who either could not or would not give themselves up to this labour and toil so that they might deserve to be taught and come to know things of such value—to wrap up and conceal, as we have said before, in ordinary language, under the cover of some history and narrative of visible things, hidden mysteries. There is, therefore, introduced the narrative of visible creation, and the creation and formation of the first human being,[45] and then the offspring which followed from him in succession; some of the actions done by the righteous amongst them are recounted, and occasionally also certain of their transgressions are mentioned, inasmuch as they were human; and then also a number of things done shamelessly and wickedly by the impious are described. In a wonderful manner, also, the account of battles is presented, and the alternation, now of the conquerors, now of the conquered, is described, by which certain ineffable mysteries are made known to those who know how to examine statements of that kind. But also, by the marvellous teaching of Wisdom, the law of truth is implanted and prophesied in the writings of the Law, each of which are woven by the divine art of Wisdom as a kind of covering and veil of the spiritual meanings; and this is what we have called the body of holy Scripture, so that even through this, which we have called the covering of the letter, woven by the art of Wisdom, very many may be edified and progress, who otherwise could not.

---

[45] The 'creation' and 'formation' refers, respectively, to Gen. 1 and 2; a distinction also made by Philo. See also, Origen, *Comm. Jo.* 20.182 (cited in *Princ.* 2.2.2, n.20) and the discussion in the introduction, section 3.

4.2.8. *[Greek]* While these and similar subjects were placed before the Spirit, who enlightens the souls of the holy ministers of the truth, there was a second aim for the sake of those unable to bear the toil of investigating matters of such importance, [that is,] to conceal the doctrine regarding the previously mentioned items in words expressing an account containing a report about the visible works of creation, and the creation of the human being, and the successive descendants of the first human beings until they became numerous, and other narratives reporting the acts of the righteous and the sins occasionally committed by the same, as being human, and deeds of wickedness and licentiousness and greed done by the lawless and impious. And what is most striking is that by the narratives of wars and of conquerors and conquered certain ineffable [mysteries] are indicated to those able to examine them. And even more wonderful still, the laws of truth are prophesied through the written legislation, all these having been recorded in a series with a power truly

4.2.9. *[Latin]* But since, if, in every detail of this covering, that is of the history <and> of the Law, the sequence had been kept and the order preserved, we would, possessing a continuous series of meaning, certainly not believe that there is anything else contained within the holy Scriptures except what was indicated on the surface, for this reason divine Wisdom took care that certain *stumbling-blocks* or interruptions of the narratival sense should occur, by inserting into the midst certain *impossibilities and incongruities*,[46] so that the very interruption of the narrative might make the reader pause, as if by casting certain obstacles before him, on account of which he might refuse to proceed along the path of the ordinary sense and, by excluding and debarring us, it might recall us to the beginning of another way, in order that, by entering upon a narrow path,[47] it might unfold, as a loftier and more sublime road, the immense breadth of divine knowledge. We must also know this, that, as the principle object of the Holy Spirit is to preserve the coherence of the spiritual sense, either in those things which ought to be done or in those things which have already been performed, whenever he found things, done according in history, capable of being adapted to a spiritual meaning, he composed a texture of both kinds in a single style of narrative, always concealing the secret

---

[46] Cf. Rom. 8:3; 9:33; 14:3.   [47] Cf. Matt. 7:13.

---

appropriate to the wisdom of God. For it was intended to make even the covering of the spiritual aspects, I mean the bodily part of Scripture, not profitless in many respects, but able to improve the multitude as far as they receive it.

4.2.9. *[Greek]* But since, if the usefulness of the legislation and the sequence and the beauty of the narrative were clearly evident from the outset throughout, we would not have believed that any other meaning could be understood in the Scriptures besides the obvious, the Word of God has arranged that certain *stumbling blocks*, as it were, and *obstacles and impossibilities* be inserted into the midst of the Law and the narrative, in order that we may not be drawn away completely by the sheer attractiveness of the language and so we either completely reject the teachings, learning nothing worthy of God, or, not moving away from the letter, we learn nothing more divine. It is also necessary to know that, the principal aim being to announce the connection amongst spiritual events, both those that have happened and those to be done, wherever the Word found that things that have happened according to the narrative could be harmonized with these mystical events, he made use of them, concealing from the multitude the deeper sense; but wherever in the account the action of certain people here, recorded for the sake of the more mystical meanings, did not follow the sequence of intellectual realities, the Scripture interwove in the narrative something that did not happen, sometimes what could not happen, and sometimes what could happen but did

sense more deeply; but where the narrative of deeds done could not be made appropriate to the spiritual coherence, he sometimes inserted certain things which either less likely happened or could not have happened at all, and sometimes things which might happen, but however did not; sometimes he does this with a few words, which, according to their bodily sense, do not seem able to preserve the truth, at other times by inserting many words, which is principally found to happen in the legislative material, where there are many things which are manifestly useful among the bodily precepts, but also a considerable number in which no principle of utility appears at all, and sometimes even impossibilities are decreed. Now the Holy Spirit took care of all this, as we have said, in order that, when those things on the surface can be neither true nor useful, we should be recalled to the search for that truth demanding a loftier and more diligent examination, and should eagerly search for a sense worthy of God in the Scriptures that we believe to be inspired by God. Nor was it only with those Scriptures that were written up to the arrival of Christ that the Holy Spirit took care of these things, but, as being one and the same Spirit and proceeding from the one God, he has acted in the same way in the Gospels and [the writings of] the apostles.[48] For even those narratives, which he inspired through them, were not woven together without the art of that Wisdom of his, the nature of which we have explained above. And so in them also he has mingled not a few things by which, interrupting and breaking up the historical order of the narrative, he might turn about and recall the attention of the reader, by the impossibility of the case, towards an examination of the inner sense.

[48] Cf. Origen, *Comm. Jo.* 10.18–20.

not, and occasionally a few words are inserted which are not true according to the bodily sense, and occasionally a greater number. A similar practice is also to be noticed in regard to the legislation, in which is often to be found what is useful in itself, appropriate to the times of the legislation; sometimes, however, no good reason is apparent. And at other times, even impossibilities are legislated for the sake of the more skilful and inquisitive, in order that, giving themselves to the toil of investigating what is written, they may gain a sound conviction concerning the necessity of seeking in such instances a meaning worthy of God. The Spirit arranged these things not only regarding the [Scriptures composed] prior to the advent [of Christ], but, as being the same Spirit and from the one God, he has done the same with the Gospels and [the writings] of the apostles, for neither is the narrative of these completely unmixed, there being things interwoven according to the bodily sense which did not happen; nor do the legislation and the commandments therein entirely exhibit what is reasonable.

4.3.1.[49] *[Latin]* But that what we say may be acknowledged from the matter itself, let us now consider the actual passages of Scripture. For to whom, possessed of understanding, I ask, will it seem a reasonable statement that the first day and the second and the third, in which are also mentioned both evening and morning, existed without sun and moon and stars, and the first day without even a sky?[50] And who is found so foolish as to suppose that *God,* as a human gardener, planted trees *in paradise, in Eden towards the east,* and planted *a tree of life* in it, that is, a visible and palpable tree of wood, so that anyone eating of this tree with bodily teeth would gain life, and again eating of another tree would lay hold of the knowledge of *good and evil?*[51] And again when God is said to *walk in paradise in the afternoon* and Adam to *hide himself behind a tree,*[52] no one, I reckon, really doubts that these things are related by Scripture figuratively, so that certain mystical truths are indicated through them. And *Cain going out from the presence of God* clearly stirs a careful reader such that he will seek what *the presence of God* is and how one can *go out* from it.[53] But that we do not extend the work we have in hand beyond its due limits, it is very easy for anyone who wishes to gather out of holy Scripture things which are recorded as having been done but which are not, however, appropriately and reasonably believed to have been done in history. This kind of writing is illustrated sufficiently and abundantly even in the Gospel books, as

[49] The Latin manuscripts have here the title 'Illustrations from Scripture of the method in which Scripture should be understood', but see note to *Princ.* 4.2.1.

[50] Or 'heaven' (*caelo*); cf. Gen. 1:5–13.

[51] Gen. 2:8–9.   [52] Gen. 3:8.

[53] Gen. 4:16. On the 'presence' or 'face' of God, see Origen, *Princ.* 2.10.7; *Hom. Isa.* 4.1.

4.3.1. *[Greek]* For who possessed of understanding will suppose that the first and the second and the third day, evening and morning, happened without a sun and moon and stars? And that the first day was as it were also without a sky? And who is so foolish as to suppose that *God,* after the manner of a human farmer, *planted a paradise in Eden towards the east,* and placed in it a visible and perceptible *tree of life,* so that one tasting of the fruit by bodily teeth would obtain life, and again that one could partake of *good and evil* by chewing what was received from the tree there? And if God is said to *walk in the paradise in the afternoon,* and Adam *to hide himself behind the tree,* I do not think that anyone doubts that these figuratively indicate, through apparent narratives

when the devil is said to have placed Jesus *on a high mountain,* that he might from there show him *all the kingdoms of the world and their glory.*[54] How will this appear to have possibly been done according to the letter, either that Jesus should have been led by the devil onto a high mountain, or that the devil should have shown to his fleshly eyes, as if they were lying below or adjacent to one mountain, all the kingdoms of the world, that is, the kingdoms of the Persians and Scythians and Indians, and, also, how their kings were glorified by human beings? And anyone who has read carefully will find in the Gospels many other instances similar to this, from which he will note that in those narratives, which appear to be recorded according to the letter, there are inserted and interwoven things which are not accepted as history but which may hold a spiritual meaning.[55]

4.3.2. *[Latin]* Moreover, similar things are found in the passages containing the commandments. For in the Law it was commanded by Moses that every male who has not been circumcised on the eighth day is to be destroyed, which is most illogical, since it would certainly be proper, if the Law was delivered to be observed according to the narrative, to command that the parents who did

---

[54] Cf. Matt. 4:8.   [55] Cf. Origen, *Comm. Jo.* 10.18–20.

---

and through things that did not happen bodily, certain mysteries. Moreover, *Cain,* also, *going out from the presence of God,* clearly appears to thoughtful people to move the reader to inquire <what> is *the presence of God* and *going out* from it. And what need is there to say more, as those who are not altogether blind can collect countless examples of a similar kind, recorded as having occurred, but which did not take place according to the letter? But even the Gospels are full of the same kind of passages, [as, for example,] the devil leading Jesus up *to a high mountain* in order to show him from there *the kingdoms of all the world and their glory.* For who is there among those who do not read such passages carelessly who would not condemn those who suppose that with the eye of the flesh—which requires a great height that what lies below and adjacent may be seen—the kingdoms of the Persians and the Scythians and the Indians and the Parthians, and the way in which their kings were glorified by human beings, were seen? The careful reader will observe innumerable other passages like these in the Gospels so that he will be convinced that with the narratives of things which happened according to the letter are interwoven others, which did not occur.

4.3.2. *[Greek]* And if we come to the legislation of Moses, many of the laws exhibit the irrationality and others the impossibility as regards the observance

not circumcise their sons be punished, or else those who were bringing up the infants; but as it is Scripture says, *The uncircumcised male, that is, who shall not have been circumcised, shall be cut off from his people.*[56] And if the impossibilities of the Law should be investigated, we find an animal called the *goat-stag,*[57] which cannot possibly exist, but which, along with the clean animals, Moses commands to be eaten, and a *griffin,* which no one has ever recorded or has heard of as having come into human hands, but which the lawgiver forbids to be eaten.[58] Concerning the celebrated observance of the Sabbath, he speaks thus: *You shall sit, every one in your dwellings; no one shall move from his place on the Sabbath day.*[59] It is certainly impossible for this to be observed according to the letter; for no human being can sit for the whole day so as not to move from the place in which he sat down. Regarding each one of these points, those who are of the circumcision, and whoever would have it that in the holy Scripture nothing more is to be understood than what is indicated by the letter, reckon that no inquiry need be made concerning the *goat-stag* and the *griffin* and the *vulture,* but they make up certain empty and frivolous fables, drawing from I know not what traditions about the Sabbath, claiming that each one's place is calculated as inside two thousand cubits.[60] Others, again, among whom is Dositheus the Samaritan,[61] censure expositions of this kind, but

---

[56] Gen. 17:14.   [57] Deut. 14:5.   [58] Lev. 11:13; Deut. 14:12.
[59] Exod. 16:5.   [60] Cf. Num. 35:5.
[61] On Dositheus, see Origen, *Comm. Jo.* 13.162; *Cels.* 1.57; 6.11; *Comm. ser. Matt.* 33; *Hom Luc.* 25.4; Ps. Clement, *Recogn.* 2.8; Epiphanius, *Pan.* 13.

---

itself. Examples of the irrational are these: the prohibition to eat *vultures,*[2] as no one, not even in the direst famines, was ever driven by need to turn to this animal; and, *uncircumcised eight day old infants* are ordered *to be destroyed from their kin,* it being necessary, if what is legislated regarding them is really something [meant] according to the letter, that their fathers or those by whom they were being cared for should be ordered to be put to death. But as it is, Scripture says: *Every uncircumcised male, who shall not be circumcised on the eighth day shall be destroyed from among his kin.* And if one wishes to see the impossibilities that are legislated, let us observe that the *goat-stag,* which Moses commands us to offer as a clean offering, is an animal of the class of things that cannot exist, while a *griffin,* which is not recorded ever to have come into human hands, the lawgiver forbids to be eaten. Moreover, for one who is scrupulous, the famous [injunction about the] Sabbath—*You shall sit, every one in your dwellings; no one shall go out from his place on the seventh*

---

[2] Cf. Lev. 11:14.

themselves decree something even more ridiculous, that everyone, in whatever posture or place or position he is found on the Sabbath day, must remain
thus until the evening; that is, if he is sitting, he should sit the whole day, or if
reclining, then he should recline the whole day. Moreover, the saying, *Do not
bear a burden on the Sabbath day*,[62] seems to me an impossibility. From these
words, the teachers of the Jews have sunk into endless fables, as the holy
Apostle says,[63] saying that it is not to be counted a *burden* if someone wears
shoes without nails, but it is a *burden* if someone wears galoshes with nails; and
they consider it a *burden* if someone carries something on one shoulder, but if
on both, they deny it is a *burden*.

4.3.3. *[Latin]* If we now seek for similar statements in the Gospels, how will it
not appear absurd if that saying, *Salute no one on the road*,[64] is taken according
to the letter? Yet the more simple folk reckon that this is what our Saviour
prescribed for the apostles. How also can it appear possible for that order to be

---

[62] Jer. 17:21.　　　[63] Cf. 1 Tim. 1:4.　　　[64] Luke 10:4.

---

day—is impossible to be kept according to the letter, for no one living is able to
sit for the whole day and not move from a sitting position. Therefore, those
who are of the circumcision and all who desire that nothing more than the
actual wording is signified, do not investigate at all such matters as *the goat-
stag* and *griffin* and *vulture*, while on others they sophistically trifle with words,
bringing in insipid traditions, as, for example, with regard to the Sabbath, saying each one's place is two thousand cubits, while others, among whom is
Dositheus the Samaritan, condemning such an interpretation, think that in
whatever position someone is found on the day of the Sabbath, he is to remain
until the evening. Moreover, the commandment, *Do not bear a burden on the
day of the Sabbath*, is impossible, and therefore the Jewish teachers have
entered into interminable arguments, saying that a shoe of such a kind was a
burden, but not one of another kind, and that a sandal having nails was one,
but not one that was without nails, and similarly that what was borne upon one
shoulder was, but not that which was carried on both.

4.3.3. *[Greek]* If we also, coming to the Gospel, seek similar examples, what
could be more irrational than this, *Salute no one on the road*, which simple
people think the Saviour enjoined on the apostles? But speaking of *the right*

observed that one should not possess two coats nor shoes, especially in those countries where the winter bitterness is exacerbated by icy frost?[65] And also this, that when one is struck on the right cheek, he is ordered to present the left as well,[66] since everyone who strikes with the right hand will strike the left [cheek]? But this precept also, which is written in the Gospel, must be counted among the impossibilities, that *If the right eye offend you, let it be plucked out;*[67] since, even if we were to suppose that this was spoken of eyes of flesh, how will it seem appropriate that, when both eyes see, the blame of the offence should be attributed to one [only], and that the right one? Or who will be held free of the greatest crime, that of laying hands upon oneself? But perhaps the epistles of the Apostle Paul will seem free of these things? Yet this is what he says: *Was anyone circumcised when he was called? Let him not draw forward the fore-skin.*[68] This expression, in the first place, if one considers it carefully, does not seem to be said with reference to the subjects that he had in hand, for his discourse provided precepts regarding marriage and chastity, and in such a context mention of this would certainly seem to be superfluous. In the second place, what harm is done if, for the sake of avoiding that indecency, which comes from circumcision, someone were able to draw forward the foreskin? In third place, it is certain that that is in every way impossible.

---

[65] Cf. Matt. 10:10.   [66] Cf. Matt. 5:39.
[67] Matt. 5:29; 18:9. Cf. Origen, *Comm. Matt.* 15.2.   [68] 1 Cor. 7:18.

---

cheek being struck is most incredible, since everyone who strikes, unless he suffers from some unnatural defect, strikes the left cheek with his right hand. And it is impossible to accept [the precept] from the Gospel about *the right eye that offends*, for, while we grant the possibility of someone *being offended* by the faculty of sight, how, when there are two eyes that see, should the blame be laid upon the right eye? And who, condemning himself for having looked *at a woman to lust [after her]*, and attributing the blame to the *right eye* alone, would rationally *throw it away*? The Apostle, moreover, legislates, saying, *Was anyone circumcised when he was called? Let him not draw forward the foreskin.* In the first place, anyone who wishes can see that he says these things apart from the discussion set before him; for how, when legislating about marriage and purity, will it not appear that they have been introduced at random? And, second, who will say that a man does wrong who attempts to pull forward the foreskin, if it is possible, in view of the disgrace that is considered by many to attach to circumcision?

4.3.4. *[Latin]* All these things have been mentioned by us that we might show that the aim of the Holy Spirit, who deigned to bestow upon us the divine Scriptures, is not that we would be able to be edified by the letter alone or by it in every case—which we know to be frequently impossible and not itself sufficient; that is, not only irrational things but even impossible ones are occasionally described by it—but that we might understand that certain things were interwoven in this visible narrative which, when considered and understood in their inner meaning, provide a law beneficial to human beings and worthy of God. But that no one should suspect us of saying that, because we suspect that some of the scriptural history did not happen, we think that none of it happened, or that, because we have said that some of the precepts of the Law cannot be observed according to the letter in those cases in which either reason or the possibility of the case does not permit this, then none of them stand according to the letter, or that those things which were written of the Saviour are not even to be thought of as having been accomplished perceptibly, or that his precepts ought not to be obeyed according to the letter—it must be answered, therefore, that we are clearly resolved that the truth of history can and ought to be preserved in the majority of cases. For who can deny that Abraham was buried in the double cave at Hebron, together with Isaac and

4.3.4. *[Greek]* We have mentioned all these instances in order to show that the aim of that divine power which bestowed on us the sacred Scriptures is that we should not accept what is presented by the letter alone, such things sometimes being not true with regard to the letter but actually irrational and impossible, and that certain things are interwoven with the narratives of things that happened and with the legislation that is useful according to the letter. But that no one may suppose that we assert that, with respect to it all, none of the narratives actually happened, because a certain part did not, and that none of the legislation is to be observed according to the letter, because a certain part is irrational or impossible according to the letter, or that what is written about the Saviour is not true on the perceptible level, or that no legislation of his or commandment is to be kept, it must be said that regarding certain things it is perfectly clear to us that the [detail] of the narrative is true, as that Abraham was buried in the double cave in Hebron, and also Isaac and Jacob, and the wives of each of them, and that Shechem was given as a portion to Joseph, and that Jerusalem is the metropolis of Judea, in which the temple of God was built by Solomon, and innumerable other statements. For the passages that are true on the level of the narrative are much more numerous than those which are woven with a purely spiritual meaning. And again, who would not say that the

Jacob and each of their wives?[69] Or who doubts that Shechem was in the portion given to Joseph?[70] Or that Jerusalem is the chief city of Judea, in which the temple of God was built by Solomon, and countless other things? For there are many more passages which stand firm according to history than those which contain a purely spiritual sense. Then again, who would not affirm that the commandment that was prescribed, *Honour your father and mother, that it may be well with you,*[71] is sufficient even without any spiritual meaning and its observance necessary, especially when Paul has also confirmed the command by repeating it in the same words?[72] And what ought to be said concerning the saying, *You shall not commit adultery, you shall not kill, you shall not steal, you shall not bear false witness,* and others of this kind?[73] Now with respect to those things commanded in the Gospels, there can be no doubt that very many of them are to be observed according to the letter, as when he says, *But I say to you, do not swear at all,*[74] and also when he says, *Whoever looks upon a woman to lust after her, has already committed adultery in his heart,*[75] and those things enjoined by Paul, *admonish the unruly, encourage the fainthearted, support the weak, be patient towards all,*[76] and very many others.

---

[69] Cf. Gen. 23:2, 9, 19; 25:9–10; 49:29–32; 50:13.   [70] Cf. Gen. 48:22; Josh. 24:32.
[71] Exod. 20:12.   [72] Cf. Eph. 6:2–3.   [73] Exod. 20:13–15.
[74] Matt. 5:34.   [75] Matt. 5:28.   [76] 1 Thess. 5:14.

---

command which says, *Honour your father and mother, that it may be well with you,* is useful apart from any higher reference and ought to be observed, the Apostle Paul also having quoted these very same words? And what need is there to mention the following: *You shall not kill, you shall not commit adultery, you shall not steal, you shall not bear false witness*? And again, there are commandments written in the Gospel that need no inquiry whether they are to be observed according to the letter or not, such as that which says, *But I say to you, whosoever is angry with his brother* and the rest;[3] and, *But I say to you, do not swear at all.* And the word from the Apostle must be kept: *Admonish the unruly, encourage the fainthearted, support the weak, be patient to all,* even if it is possible for the more ambitious to preserve each one of them, without setting aside the commandment according to the letter, [as] *the depths of the wisdom of God.*[4]

---

[3] Matt. 5:22.   [4] Cf. Rom. 11:33; 1 Cor. 2:10.

4.3.5. *[Latin]* Nevertheless if someone reads attentively I have no doubt that in very many cases he will be uncertain whether this or that narrative can be held to be true according to the letter or not true, and whether this or that precept ought to be observed according to the letter or not.[77] Because of this, great effort and labour are to be exercised, so that each reader may with all reverence understand that he is dealing with divine, and not human, words that are placed in the holy books. As we see it, therefore, the way of understanding the holy Scriptures which ought, rightly and consistently, to be observed, is believed by us to be of this kind.

---

[77] The Latin text omits a sizeable passage at this point (corresponding to 'Therefore one who reads…to be impossible' in the *Philocalia* text); an omission which has received various assessment (Butterworth, p. 296, n.2, suggesting 'probably because he [Rufinus] could not understand it'). However, as Simonetti and Crouzel (SC 269, p. 204, n.30–30a) point out, the first words in Greek of the omitted passage are διὰ τοῦ τo, and the first word of the text where the Latin resumes is διόπερ, the latter being translated *propter quod*, which is also the natural translation for the former. As such, it is most likely that Rufinus did indeed translate the passage, but that it was subsequently dropped by scribes due to the dittography.

4.3.5. *[Greek]* Nevertheless, the precise reader will be torn regarding certain points, being unable to show without lengthy investigation whether the supposed narrative happened according to the letter or not, and whether the letter of the legislation is to be observed or not. Therefore one who reads in an exact manner must, observing the Saviour's injunction which says *Search the Scriptures*,[5] carefully ascertain where the meaning according to the letter is true and where it is impossible, and as far as possible trace out, by means of similar expressions, the sense, scattered throughout Scripture, of that which is impossible according to the letter. When, then, as will be clear to those who read, the connection taken according to the letter is impossible, yet the principal [sense] is not impossible but even true, one must endeavour to grasp the whole sense, which spiritually connects the account of things impossible according to the letter to things not only not impossible but even true according to the narrative, with as many things as did not happen according to the letter being taken allegorically. For our position is that with respect to the whole of the divine Scripture all of it has a spiritual meaning, but not all of it has a bodily meaning, for there are many places where the bodily is proved to be impossible. And therefore great attention must be given by the careful reader to the divine books, as being divine writings; the manner of understanding of which seems to us to be such as follows:

[5] John 5:39.

4.3.6. *[Latin]* The divine writings declare that a certain nation on earth was chosen by God, which they call by several names: for sometimes the nation as a whole is called Israel, and sometimes Jacob, and, in particular, when the nation was divided into two parts by Jeroboam son of Nebat,[78] and the ten tribes, which were formed under him, were called Israel, and the other two, with which were included the tribe of Levi and the one which was descended from the royal race of David, was called Judah. The entire country, which was inhabited by this race, which it had received from God, was called Judea, in which the metropolis was Jerusalem; and it is called 'metropolis' as being a kind of mother of many cities, the names of which cities you will find frequently mentioned here and there in the other divine books, but which are

---

[78] Cf. 3 Rgns 12.

4.3.6. *[Greek]* The accounts relate that God chose a certain nation upon the earth, which they call by many names. For the nation as a whole is called Israel, and is also spoken of as Jacob. When it was divided in the times of Jeroboam the son of Nebat, the ten tribes said to be subject to him were named Israel, the remaining two together with the tribe of Levi, being ruled over by those of the seed of David, were named Judah. And the entire country which those of this nation inhabited, being given to them by God, is called Judah, the metropolis of which is Jerusalem, as, clearly, the 'mother-city' of many cities, the names of which lie scattered about in many places elsewhere, but are listed together in the book of Jesus the son of Nave.[6] Such, then, being the case, the Apostle, elevating our power of discernment, says somewhere, *Behold, Israel according to the flesh,* as if there is an Israel according to the spirit. And in another place he says, *For it is not the children of the flesh that are the children of God, for not all who are descended from Israel belong to Israel.*[7] And, *Neither is he a Jew who is one in the open, nor is that circumcision which is in the open, in the flesh; but he is a Jew who is one in secret, and circumcision is of the heart, in spirit not in letter.*[8] For if the determination of being a Jew depends upon what is *in secret,* it must be understood that, just as there is a race of bodily Jews, so also there is a race of those who are Jews *in secret,* the soul having acquired this nobility according to certain ineffable reasons. There are, moreover, many prophecies that make predictions concerning Israel and Judah, describing things that are going to befall them. And, indeed, do not such great promises written about on their behalf, inasmuch as they are impoverished in language and offer nothing elevated and worthy of a promise of God, need a mystical interpretation? If, then, the promises are spiritual, announced through things perceptible, those also to whom the promises are made are not bodily.

---

[6] Cf. Joshua 13–21.   [7] Rom. 9:8, 6.   [8] Rom. 2:28–9.

gathered together in a single catalogue in the book of Jesus the son of Nave.[79] These things, therefore, being so, the holy Apostle, desiring somehow to elevate and raise our understanding above the earth, says in a certain place, *Behold, Israel according to the flesh*.[80] By this he certainly indicates that there is another Israel, which is not according to the flesh, but according to the spirit. And again, in another passage, he says, *For not all who are descended from Israel belong to Israel*.[81]

---

[79] Cf. Joshua 13–21. In the Greek of the LXX 'Joshua' is 'Jesus'.　　[80] 1 Cor. 10:18.

[81] Rom. 9:6. From this point to the end of *Princ.* 4.3.8, the Latin text omits a great deal that has been preserved in the *Philocalia*. Although various suggestions have been made for why Rufinus would omit this passage, such as that Rufinus thought it unnecessary or repetitive, shocking, or did not understand it, none of them are really convincing: it is not more daring in its exegesis than other passages of the work and it does indeed contain ideas (such as the relation between Adam and Christ, Eve and Mary) that are not found elsewhere in this work, nor are they unorthodox. Neither can it be the result of dittography, as with the omitted passage in *Princ.* 4.3.5. Simonetti and Crouzel (SC 269, pp. 208–9, n.36–36a) conclude that the only plausible hypothesis is that a leaf of the ms with which Rufinus was working had already dropped out before reaching him, and that he then adapts the first sentence of *Princ.* 4.3.8 to tie it back to the quotation with which his ms had concluded *Princ.* 4.3.6.

4.3.7. *[Greek]* And, so that we do not linger on the topic of the *Jew who is one in secret* and that of *the inner human being*,[9] the Israelite, this being sufficient for those not lacking acumen, we return to our subject and say that Jacob was the father of the twelve patriarchs, and they of the rulers of the people, and these again of the rest of the Israelites. So, then, the bodily Israelites have reference to the rulers of the people, and the rulers of the people to the patriarchs, and the patriarchs to Jacob and those still higher up; the spiritual Israelites, on the other hand, of whom the bodily were a type, are they not from the clans, the clans having come from the tribes, and the tribes from some one individual having a birth not of a bodily kind but of the better kind,[10] he too being born from Isaac, and he being descended from Abraham, all referring back up to Adam, whom the Apostle says is Christ?[11] For the beginning of every lineage

---

[9] Cf. Rom. 7:22; 2 Cor. 4:16; Eph. 3:16.

[10] Alluding clearly to Jacob, whose birth is described in Gen. 25:21–6; see also Origen, *Hom. Gen.* 12. On the two names, Jacob and Israel, see Origen, *Hom. Gen.* 15.4; *Hom. Num.* 15.2–4; 16.5–7; 17.3–4; 18.4. 'Jacob represents those who are perfect in their deeds and works, while Israel stands for those who are zealous in their pursuit of wisdom and knowledge' (*Hom. Num.* 17.4).

[11] Origen makes a similar assertion in *Comm. Jo.* 1.108: 'And perhaps for this reason, he is not only the *firstborn of all creation* [Col. 1:15], but also Adam, [which] means "human being". And because he is Adam, Paul says, *The last Adam has become a life-giving spirit*' [1 Cor. 15:45]. See also *Cels.* 4.40. Perhaps in the background of *Princ.* 4.3.7 is the contrast between the genealogies of Matthew (1:1–17), where 'the genesis of Jesus' (Matt. 1:1, 18) is described in a descending line from Abraham, and that of Luke (3:23–38), which traces the genealogy backwards or upwards to Adam the son of God; the first genealogy describes the descent of Israel according to the flesh, the second the descent (or ascent) of the spiritual Israel.

4.3.8. *[Latin]* Being, therefore, taught by him that there is one Israel according to the flesh, and another according to the Spirit, when the Saviour says that *I am not sent but to the lost sheep of the house of Israel,*[82] we do not take these words as do those who savour earthly things, that is, the Ebionites, who even by their very name are called 'poor' (for 'Ebion' means 'poor' in Hebrew),[83] but we understand that there is a race of souls, which is named 'Israel', as is indicated by the interpretation of the name itself:[84] for 'Israel' is interpreted as 'the intellect seeing God' or 'the human being seeing God'. The Apostle, again, reveals things such as this about Jerusalem, that the *Jerusalem which is above is free, she is our mother.*[85] And in another of his epistles he says, *But you have come to Mount Zion and to the city of the living God, the heavenly Jerusalem, and to a multitude of angels praising together and to the assembly of the firstborn who are enrolled in the heavens.*[86] If, then, there are certain souls in this world

---

[82] Matt. 15:24.
[83] On the 'Ebionites', see Irenaeus, *Haer.* 1.26.2; 4.33.4; Tertullian, *Carn. Chr.* 14.5; 18.1; Origen, *Cels.* 2.1; 5.61; 5.65; *Hom. Jer.* 19.2; *Comm. Matt.* 11.12; Eusebius, *Hist. eccl.* 3.27; 5.8.10; 6.17.
[84] On the name 'Israel', see Origen, *Hom. Num.* 11.4; see also *Princ.* 2.11.5 and the material cited in n.24 there.
[85] Gal. 4:26.   [86] Heb. 12:22–3. Cf. Origen, *Hom. Lev.* 1.3; *Hom. Num.* 3.3; *Hom. Luc.* 7.8.

as [referring] to the God of all began lower down from Christ, who is next to the God and Father of all, being thus the father of every soul, as Adam is the father of all human beings. And if Eve is touched on by Paul as referring to the Church, it is not surprising—Cain being born of Eve and all after him having reference to Eve—to have here types of the Church, since they were all born from the Church in a pre-eminent sense.

4.3.8. *[Greek]* Now, if the statements made by us regarding Israel and its tribes and clans are convincing, when the Saviour says, *I was not sent but to the lost sheep of the house of Israel,* we do not take these words as the poor-minded Ebionites do, named because of their poverty of mind ('ebion' is the Hebrew word for the poor), so as to suppose that Christ came principally to the Israelites after the flesh. *For it is not the children of the flesh that are the children of God.*[12] Again, the Apostle teaches such things about Jerusalem, that, *The Jerusalem above is free, she is our mother.* And, in another epistle, *But you have come to Mount Zion and to the city of the living God, to the heavenly Jerusalem, and to a multitude of angels in festal gathering and the church of the firstborn who are enrolled in the heavens.* If, then, Israel consists in a race of souls, and Jerusalem is a city in heaven, it follows that the cities of Israel have for their mother-city the Jerusalem in the heavens and consequently so for all Judea.

---

[12] Rom. 9:8.

who are called Israel, and a city in heaven which is named Jerusalem, it follows that those cities, which are said to be of the nation of Israel, have the heavenly Jerusalem as their metropolis, and, in accordance with these things, we should understand it as referring to the whole of Judea, of which we reckon even the prophets have spoken in certain mystical narratives, whatever they prophesied either regarding Judea or Jerusalem or whenever the sacred narratives declare that this or that invasion had befallen Judea or Jerusalem.[87] Whatever, then, is either narrated or prophesied of Jerusalem we ought, if we hear the words of Paul as Christ speaking in him,[88] to understand, in accordance with his mind, to have been said of that city, which he calls the heavenly Jerusalem, and of all those places or cities, which are said to be cities of the holy land, of which Jerusalem is the metropolis. For it must be supposed that it is from these very cities that the Saviour, wishing to raise us to a higher level of understanding, promises to those who have managed well the money entrusted to them by him, that they are to have power *over ten or over five cities.*[89]

4.3.9. *[Latin]* If, then, the prophecies which were prophesied concerning Judea and Jerusalem and Israel and Judah and Jacob, when they are not understood

---

[87] See especially Origen, *Hom. Num.* and *Hom. Jes. Nav.* In *Hom. Num.* 28.2, Origen comments, 'Concerning these names very many secrets and cryptic statements are contained in the books which bear the name of Enoch. But since these books do not appear to have any recognized authority with the Hebrews, we will for the present postpone citing examples from the things that are identified in them.'
[88] Cf. 2 Cor. 13:3.
[89] Cf. Luke 19:17–19. Origen, *Hom. Num.* 11.4; *Hom. Jes. Nav.* 23.4.

Whatever, therefore, is prophesied of Jerusalem and said about her, if we hear from [Paul] as from God[13] and as one speaking wisdom, one must understand that the Scriptures are reporting about the heavenly city and the whole territory included within the cities of the holy land. Perhaps it is to these cities that the Saviour refers us, when to those approved for their good administration of the pounds he gives authority over *ten or five cities.*

4.3.9. *[Greek]* If, therefore, when we do not take them in a fleshly sense, the prophecies relating to Judea and relating to Jerusalem and Israel and Judah and Jacob suggest some such mysteries, it should follow that the prophecies also concerning Egypt and the Egyptians, and Babylon and the Babylonians,

---

[13] Cf. 1 Thess. 2:13; 2 Cor. 13:3. All the manuscripts have 'if we hear from God as from God'; all editors and translators have chosen to amend to 'from Paul'.

by us in a fleshly manner, signify certain divine mysteries, it certainly follows
that those prophecies also which were prophesied either concerning Egypt and
the Egyptians, or Babylon and the Babylonians, and Sidon and the Sidonians,
are not to be understood as prophesied of that Egypt which is situated on
earth, or Babylon or Tyre or Sidon.[90] Nor can those which the prophet Ezekiel
prophesied about Pharaoh, king of Egypt, apply to any human being who
may have appeared to reign in Egypt, as the context of the reading itself clearly
indicates.[91] Similarly, the things said of the prince of Tyre cannot be understood
as said of any human being or king of Tyre;[92] and also how could we possibly
accept as said of a human being those things which are said of Nebuchadnezzar
in many passages of Scripture, and especially in Isaiah? For one who is said
to have *fallen from heaven* or who was *the morning star,* or who *arose in the
morning,* is not a human being.[93] Moreover, those statements which are given
in Ezekiel concerning Egypt—such as that it is to be *desolated for forty years,*
so that the *footstep of human beings* should not be found in it, and that it shall
be assaulted so greatly that throughout the whole land human blood should
rise to the knees[94]—I do not know that anyone possessing understanding
could refer this to that land of Egypt which adjoins Ethiopia.

[90] For interpretations of Egypt and Babylon, see Origen, *Hom. Gen.* 15.5; *Hom. Num.* 11.4;
Hom. Ezech. 11.4; 12.2–3; 13; *Comm. Matt.* 12.1.
[91] Cf. Ezek. 29:1–9.   [92] Cf. Ezek. 28; Origen, *Princ.* 1.5.4.
[93] Isa. 14:12. Cf. Origen, *Princ.* 1.5.5.   [94] Cf. Ezek. 29:11–12; 30:7, 10–12; 32:5–6, 12–13, 15.

Tyre and the Tyrians, Sidon and the Sidonians, and the rest of the nations, are
prophesied not only regarding these bodily Egyptians and Babylonians and
Tyrians and Sidonians. For if there are spiritual Israelites, it follows that there
are also spiritual Egyptians and Babylonians. For what is said in Ezekiel about
Pharaoh, king of Egypt, does not fit at all what is said regarding a human being
who was the ruler or will be the ruler of Egypt, as will be clear to those who
carefully examine it. Similarly, what is said about the ruler of Tyre cannot be
understood of any particular human being ruling Tyre. And what is said in
many places and especially in Isaiah about Nebuchadnezzar, how is it possible
to take them as of that man? For Nebuchadnezzar, the human being, neither
fell from heaven, nor was he *the morning star,* nor did he *arise* upon the earth
in the morning. Nor indeed would anyone of understanding take what is said
in Ezekiel about Egypt—that *it shall be desolated for forty years,* so that *the
footstep of a human being* should not be found there, and that at some time it
will be so ravaged by war that there shall be blood up to the knees throughout

But[95] let us see whether it may not be understood more fittingly in this way, that, just as there is a heavenly Jerusalem and Judea, and undoubtedly a nation which inhabits it, which is named Israel, so also it is possible that there are certain regions near to these places which appear to be named Egypt or Babylon or Tyre or Sidon, and that the princes of these places and the souls, if there are any who dwell in them, may be called Egyptians and Babylonians and Tyrians and Sidonians; from whom, also, according to that mode of life which they have there, a kind of captivity would seem to have taken place, by which the inhabitants of Judea are said to have descended into Babylon or Egypt from better and higher places, or to have been scattered among the other nations.

4.3.10. *[Latin]* For[96] perhaps, just as those who, departing from this world by that common death, are arranged according to their actions and merits, as they have been deemed worthy, some in the place which is called the 'lower regions', others in *the bosom of Abraham*,[97] and throughout various places and *stages*,[98] so also from those places, as if dying there, if one may so speak, they descend from the upper regions to this lower one. For that lower region, to which the souls of those who die here are led away, is, I believe, on account of this

---

[95] That this paragraph was omitted by the compilers of the *Philocalia*, rather than added by Rufinus, is indicated by the words, placed between *Princ.* 4.3.8 and 4.3.9, 'and after other things' (καὶ μεθ' ἔτερα).

[96] Cf. Jerome, *Ep.* 124.11.1 (ed. Hilberg 3, 112.21–113.3): 'And, in the fourth book, which is the last of his work, he inserts these sentences which must be condemned by the churches of Christ: And perhaps, just as those who die in this world by the separation of flesh and soul obtain diverse positions in the world below according to the difference of their works, so also, those who die in the administration of the heavenly Jerusalem, so to speak, descend to the lower regions of our world, so that they hold diverse positions on earth by the quality of their merits.'

[97] Luke 16:22.

[98] As in *Princ.* 2.11.6, the Latin word *mansiones* clearly translates the μοναί of John 14:2, and, as in *Princ.* 2.11.6, is best translated 'stages'; for the 'stages' of the Israelites, see Origen, *Hom. Num.* 27.2; *Hom. Jes. Nav.* 10.1; 23.4.

---

the whole land—as about that Egypt lying beside the Ethiopians whose bodies are blackened by the sun.

4.3.10. *[Greek]* Perhaps, just as those who on earth, dying that common death, are arranged according to the deeds done here, if they are judged deserving of the place called Hades, to obtain different places according to the proportion of their sins, so also those dying there, so to speak, descend into this Hades, being judged deserving of different abodes, better or worse, throughout all this distinction, called the 'lower Hades' by Scripture, as it says in the Psalms, *You have delivered my soul from the lower Hades.*[99] Everyone, therefore, of those who descend to earth is arranged, in accordance with his merits or with the position that he had had there, to be born in this world in a particular place or nation or walk of life or infirmity, or to be begotten from parents who are religious, or not, so that it may sometimes happen that an Israelite descends among the Scythians and a poor Egyptian is brought down to Judea.[100] Nevertheless, our Saviour came *to gather the lost sheep of the house of Israel;*[101] and as very many of the Israelites did not assent to his teaching, those who were of the Gentiles were called. From this, it would seem to follow that the prophecies, which were uttered concerning the particular nations, ought rather to be referred to the souls and to their different heavenly stages.[102] Moreover, the narratives of the events which are said to have happened either to the nation of Israel or to Jerusalem or Judea, when assailed by this or that nation, are to be examined and investigated, so that, [as] in very many cases they cannot be held to have happened in a bodily sense, [we may see] in what way they are more appropriate to those nations of souls who dwell in that heaven which is said to pass away, or who may be supposed to dwell there even now.[103]

4.3.11. *[Latin]* If, now, anyone demand from us clear and sufficiently manifest declarations on these matters from the holy Scriptures, it must be answered that [the design] of the Holy Spirit was rather to conceal and to cover them

---

[99] Ps. 85:13.
[100] Cf. Plato, *Resp.* 3.414e–15c, the 'noble lie', where a golden parent may sometimes have a silver son, or vice versa.
[101] Matt. 15:24.   [102] John 14:2.
[103] Koetschau places a passage from Jerome, *Ep.* 124.11.2 (ed. Hilberg 3, 113.3–20) at this point; the text is given in the Appendix as item no. 21.

earthly space, and to be from this or that lineage; so that it is possible sometimes for an Israelite to fall among Scythians and an Egyptian to descend into Judea. Nevertheless, the Saviour came to gather *the lost sheep of the house of Israel*; and since many from Israel have not yielded to his teaching, those from the nations are also called.

4.3.11. *[Greek]* These things, as we suppose, have been concealed in the narratives. For *the kingdom of heaven is like a treasure hidden in the field, which someone found and hid, and then in his joy he goes and sells all that he has and*

deeply in those passages which seem to be a narrative of deeds done, in which they are said to descend into Egypt or be carried captive to Babylon, or when, in these countries, some are said to be brought to extreme humiliation and to be put under bondage to masters, while others, in these very countries of their captivity, were held as famous and illustrious, so that they occupied positions of power and leadership and were set to rule over the people; all these things, as we have said, are buried, hidden, and covered, in the narratives of the holy Scriptures, for, *the kingdom of heaven is like a treasure hidden in a field, which, when a human being finds it, he hides it, and in his joy goes and sells all that he has and buys the field*.[104] Consider carefully whether in this there is not indicated that the very soil and surface, so to speak, of Scripture, that is, its reading according to the letter, is the field, filled and flowering with all kinds of plants; while that deeper and more profound spiritual sense is that very *hidden treasure of wisdom and knowledge*,[105] which the Holy Spirit, by Isaiah, calls *the dark and invisible and hidden treasures*,[106] which, for them to be found, requires the help of God, who alone is able to *break in pieces the doors of bronze*, by which they are enclosed and hidden, and *break the iron bolts* and *bars*,[107] by which is prevented the way of arriving at all those things which are written and concealed in Genesis concerning the different kinds of souls, and

---

[104] Matt. 13:44. Cf. Origen, *Comm. Matt.* 13.14; see also Irenaeus, *Haer.* 4.26.1.
[105] Col. 2:3.   [106] Isa. 45:3.   [107] Isa. 45:2.

---

buys that field. Let us consider whether the apparent and superficial and surface aspect of Scripture is not the field as a whole, full of all kinds of plants, while the things lying in it and not seen by all, but as if buried under the visible plants, are *the hidden treasures of wisdom and knowledge*, which the Spirit through Isaiah calls *dark and invisible and hidden*, needing, for them to be found, God, who alone is able *to break in pieces the doors of bronze* that hide them and *to break the iron bars* that are upon the gates, in order that all the points in Genesis about various real kinds and, as it were, seeds of souls, near to Israel or afar off, may be discovered; and the descent into Egypt of the seventy souls, that there they become *as the stars of heaven in multitude*. But since not all who are of them are *the light of the world* (*for not all who are descended from Israel belong to Israel*), from seventy they become as *the innumerable sand beside the sea shore*.

the seeds and generations which either have a close connection to Israel or are widely separated from his progeny, as well as what is that descent of seventy souls into Egypt, which seventy souls became in Egypt *as the stars of heaven in multitude.*[108] But, as not all who are from these are a light of this world,[109] *For not all who are descended from Israel belong to Israel,*[110] the descendants from these seventy souls become *as the sand that is by the mouth of the sea, innumerable.*[111]

4.3.12. *[Latin]* This descent of the holy fathers into Egypt, that is, into this world, will be seen to have been granted by the providence of God for the illumination of others and for the instruction of the human race, so that through them other souls might be aided by this illumination.[112] *For to them first were granted the oracles of God,*[113] because theirs is the only race that was said to see God; for the name Israel, when translated, means this.[114] And it follows at once that what comes next ought to be adapted and interpreted in accordance with this principle:[115] that Egypt is scourged with ten plagues in order to allow the people of God to depart,[116] or those things which happen to the people in the desert,[117] or that from the contributions from all the people the tabernacle is constructed,[118] or the priestly vestment is woven,[119] or whatever is said of the vessels of ministry,[120] because truly, as it is written, they contain within them the shadow and form of heavenly things. For Paul clearly says of them that *they serve a shadow and pattern of heavenly things.*[121] There is, moreover, contained in this same Law an account of the precepts and institutions by which one is to live in the holy land.[122] Threats, too, are held against those who shall transgress the Law; and also those different kinds of purification are delivered for those who need purification, as being frequently polluted, that by means of these they may arrive at that one purification, after which it is not permitted to be polluted.[123]

---

[108] Cf. Gen. 10; 11; 25; 36; 46. For the quotation, Deut. 10:22; cf. Gen. 22:17.
[109] Cf. Matt. 5:14.   [110] Rom. 9:6.   [111] Heb. 11:12; cf. Gen. 32:12.
[112] Cf. Origen, *Princ.* 1.7.5; 2.9.7; 3.5.4; *Hom. Ezech.* 1.1–5; *Comm. Jo.* 2.175–92.
[113] Rom. 3:2.   [114] Cf. Origen, *Princ.* 4.3.8.
[115] The points that follow are also mentioned in Origen, *Princ.* 2.11.5; for the plagues, see *Hom. Exod.* 4; the tabernacle, *Hom. Exod.* 9; the priestly vestments, *Hom. Lev.* 6; the purifications, *Hom. Lev.* 8.
[116] Cf. Exod. 7–12.   [117] Cf. Exod. 19ff.   [118] Cf. Exod. 25ff.
[119] Cf. Exod. 28.   [120] Cf. Exod. 30:17ff.   [121] Heb. 8:5.
[122] On this holy land, see Origen, *Princ.* 3.6.8–9, and for its distinction from the 'dry land' of Gen. 1:10, see *Princ.* 2.3.6–7.
[123] Cf. Heb. 6:4–6; 10:26–31.

Moreover, a census is taken of the people themselves, though not all;[124] for the childlike souls are not yet of an age to be numbered by the divine command, nor are the souls who cannot become *the head* of another but are themselves *subject* to others as to a head, which Scripture names *women*, who certainly are not included in that census ordered by God, for they alone who are called *men* are numbered;[125] by this it is clearly shown that they could not be numbered separately, but that they were to be included among those called men.[126] Those,[127] however, who are prepared to go forth to the Israelite battles, who are able to fight against those *enemies and adversaries* whom the Father subjects to the Son *sitting at his right hand*, that he may *destroy every principality and power*, belong especially to the sacred number,[128] that, by these numbers of his soldiers, who as fighting for God do not *take part in worldly affairs*,[129] he may overturn the kingdom of his adversary, [and] by whom *the shields of faith* are borne and the darts of wisdom are brandished, and among whom *the helmet* of *the hope of salvation* gleams and *the breastplate of love* guards the breast filled with the love of God.[130] Such soldiers seem to me to be indicated, and to be prepared for wars of this kind, in those who are ordered in the divine books to be numbered by the command of God. But far more illustrious and more perfect than these are shown to be those of whom even *the hairs on the head* are said to be numbered.[131] Those, however, who were punished for their sins, whose bodies fell in the wilderness, appear to bear resemblance to those who had indeed made no little progress, yet have not been able to attain the goal of perfection for various reasons, because they are said to have murmured or to have worshipped idols or to have committed fornication or to have done some other such thing which the mind ought not even to conceive.[132]

I do not reckon that even the following is devoid of some mystical meaning, that certain of the people, possessing large flocks and many animals, go and seize beforehand a suitable region for pasture and the feeding of their flocks, which was the first of all the places that the right hand of the Israelites had secured by war. Requesting this place from Moses, they are placed apart,

---

[124]   Cf. Num. 1–4; 26. See also Origen, *Hom. Num.* 1.1; 4.1.

[125]   On the distinction that Origen makes between male and female, see *Hom. Gen.* 1.15; 4.4; 5.2; 8.10; *Hom. Exod.* 2.2; *Sel. Exod.* 23.17 (PG 12, 296d). In *Hom. Num.* 11.7, Origen comments, 'According to the spiritual understanding, however, this is to be related not to the distinction of sex, but that of souls'; see also *Hom. Jes. Nav.* 9.9.

[126]   Num. 1:2–3 etc.; 1 Cor. 11:3; Eph. 5:22–3.

[127]   Koetschau places a passage from Jerome, *Ep.* 124.11.4 (ed. Hilberg 3, 113.25–114.6), in his critical apparatus as paralleling the following sentence; Butterworth suggests that it should be inserted after the words 'the kingdom of his adversary' later in this sentence. The text is included in the Appendix as item no. 22.

[128]   Eph. 1:20–2; 1 Cor. 15:24–7.   [129]   2 Tim. 2:4.   [130]   Eph. 6:14–17; 1 Thess. 5:8.

[131]   Matt. 10:30. Cf. Origen, *Princ.* 2.11.5; *Dial.* 22.

[132]   Cf. Num. 11, 14, 16, 21, 25; Exod. 32; 1 Cor. 10:5–10; Heb. 3:17.

beyond the running waters of the Jordan and set apart from the occupation of the holy land.[133] And this Jordan might seem, according to the form of heavenly things, to water and flood the thirsty souls and minds adjacent to it.[134] In this context, even this point does not seem idle, that Moses indeed hears from God those things which are described in the law of Leviticus, while in Deuteronomy it is the people who are made the hearers of Moses and who learn from him things that they could not hear from God. This is why, as a second law, it is called Deuteronomy, a point that to some will seem to indicate that when the first law which was given through Moses had come to an end, so a second legislation seems to have been delineated, which was specially delivered by Moses to Jesus[135] his successor, who is certainly believed to preserve a type of our Saviour, by whose second law, that is, the precepts of the Gospel, all things are brought to perfection.[136]

4.3.13. *[Latin]* But it is to be seen, however, whether perhaps this deeper meaning may not seem to be indicated: that, just as in Deuteronomy the legislation is disclosed more clearly and distinctly than in those which were first written, so also, from the arrival of the Saviour which he fulfilled in humility, when he assumed *the form of a servant,*[137] that more splendid and more glorious second coming in the glory of his Father may be pointed out,[138] and in it the types of Deuteronomy may be fulfilled, when in the kingdom of heaven all the saints will live according to the laws of the *eternal Gospel;*[139] and[140] just as in his coming now he has fulfilled that Law which has *a shadow of good things to come,*[141] so also by that glorious arrival the shadows of this arrival will be fulfilled and brought to perfection. For the prophet has spoken of it thus: *The breath of our face, Christ the Lord, of whom we have said that under his shadow we shall live among the nations,*[142] that is, when he will more fittingly transfer all the saints from the temporal Gospel to *the eternal Gospel,* following that which John, in the Apocalypse, designates as *the eternal Gospel.*[143]

---

[133] Cf. Origen, *Hom. Num.* 26.3–4.

[134] On Jordan as a symbol of baptism, see Origen, *Comm. Jo.* 6.222–32; *Hom. Jes. Nav.* 4.

[135] In the Greek of the LXX 'Joshua' is 'Jesus'.

[136] For Joshua/Jesus as a type of Jesus Christ, see *Barn.* 12.8–10; Justin, *Dial.* 113, 132; Clement, *Paed.* 1.7.60; Tertullian, *Marc.* 3.16.3–4; Origen, *Hom. Num.* 28.2, and *Hom. Jes. Nav. passim.*

[137] Phil. 2:7.   [138] Cf. Matt. 16:27.

[139] Rev. 14:6. Cf. Origen, *Princ.* 3.6.8; *Hom. Lev.* 4.10.

[140] Koetschau cites Jerome *Ep.* 124.12 (ed. Hilberg 3, 114.7–115.8) in his critical apparatus as paralleling the remainder of this paragraph; the last sentence of the extract from Jerome is paralleled by a sentence in Justinian, *Ep. ad Menam* (ed. Schwartz, 213.3–7), said to be from *Princ.* 4 and numbered by Koetschau as Fragment 30. These texts are included in the Appendix as item no. 23. Fernandez inserts the passage from Justinian into the text at the end of *Princ.* 4.3.13.

[141] Heb. 10:1.   [142] Lam. 4:20.   [143] Rev. 14:6.

4.3.14. *[Latin]* But let it be sufficient for us in all these matters to conform our mind to the rule of piety[144] and to think of the words of the Holy Spirit in this way, that the text shines not because composed according to the eloquence of human fragility, but because, as it is written, *all the glory of the King is within,*[145] and the treasure of divine meanings is contained enclosed within the frail vessel of the common letter.[146] And, furthermore, if a more curious reader were to seek for an explanation of the details, let him come and hear, along with ourselves, how the Apostle Paul, scrutinizing, by the Holy Spirit who searches even the deep things of God,[147] *the depths of the* divine *wisdom and knowledge,*[148] and yet, however, not having the strength to come to the end and, so to speak, to an intimate knowledge, exclaims in despair and amazement and says, *O the depths of the riches of the knowledge and wisdom of God!*[149] And that it was from despair of attaining a perfect understanding that he uttered this, listen to him *saying, How unsearchable are the judgements of God and his ways past understanding!*[150] For he did not say that it is difficult for the *judgements* of God to be searched out, but that they cannot be searched out at all; he did not say that it is difficult for his ways to be traced out, but that they cannot be traced out. For however far one may advance in the search and make progress by intense study, assisted even by the grace of God and an enlightened mind, he will not be able to arrive at the final goal of those things that are investigated. Nor can any mind, which is created, have the possibility to comprehend everything, but as soon as it has discovered a small piece of the things which it seeks, it again sees others which are to be sought; and even if it arrives at these, it will again see many others succeeding them that must be examined.[151] Because of this, therefore, the most wise Solomon, beholding by wisdom the nature of things, says, *I said, I will become wise; and wisdom herself was removed far from me, further than it was; and a profound depth, who shall find it?*[152] Isaiah also—knowing that the beginnings of things could not be discovered by a mortal nature, and not even by those natures which, although more divine than human, were nevertheless themselves either created or formed; knowing, then, that by none of these could either the beginning or end be found—says, *Tell me the former things which have been, and we will know that you are gods; or announce what the last things are, and then we will see that you are gods.*[153] For my Hebrew teacher also used to teach thus: that as the beginning or end of all things could not be comprehended by anyone except only the Lord Jesus Christ and the Holy Spirit, Isaiah, speaking in the form of a vision, spoke of there being only two seraphim, who with two wings cover the face of God, and

---

[144] On the 'rule', see Origen, *Princ.* Pr.2 and the material cited in n.7 there.
[145] Ps. 44:14.   [146] Cf. 2 Cor. 4:7.   [147] Cf. 1 Cor. 2:10.   [148] Cf. Rom. 11:33.
[149] Rom. 11:33.   [150] Ibid.   [151] Cf. Origen, *Princ.* 2.3.7; *Hom. Num.* 17.4.
[152] Eccl. 7:23–4.   [153] Isa. 41:22–3.

with two his feet, and with two they fly, calling one to the other and saying, *Holy, holy, holy is the Lord God of Sabaoth, the whole earth is full of your glory*.[154] Therefore, as the seraphim alone have both their wings over the face of God and over his feet, it may be ventured to declare that neither the armies of holy angels, nor the holy thrones, nor the dominions, nor the principalities, nor the powers are able to understand fully the beginning of all things and the ends of the universe.[155] But it is to be understood that those holy spirits and powers, enumerated here, are closest to those very beginnings and attain to a height which the others are not able to follow; and yet whatever it is that these powers have learned through the revelation of the Son of God and from the Holy Spirit, and they will be able to understand a great deal and the higher ones much more than the lower ones, nevertheless it is impossible for them to comprehend all things, since it is written, *The most part of the works of God are in secret*.[156] And therefore it is to be desired that everyone, according to his strength, should always *stretch out to those things that are ahead, forgetting the things that are behind*,[157] both to better works and also to a clearer understanding and knowledge, through Jesus Christ our Saviour, to whom is glory unto the ages.

4.3.15. *[Latin]* Let everyone, then, who cares for truth be little concerned about names and words, since in every nation different usages of words prevail; but let him attend, rather, to that which is signified rather than the nature of the words by which it is signified, especially in matters of such importance and difficulty;[158] just as, for example, when it is inquired whether there is any substance in which neither colour nor form nor touch nor magnitude is to be understood to be visible to the mind alone, which anyone names as he pleases; for the Greeks call such ἀσώματον, that is 'bodiless', while the divine Scriptures name it 'invisible',[159] for Paul declares that God is invisible, for he says that Christ is *the image of the invisible God*, and again he says that *all things were created* through Christ, *visible and invisible*.[160] By this it is declared that there are, even among created things, certain substances that are, by their property, invisible. But these, although they are not themselves bodily, nevertheless make use of bodies, while they themselves are better than any bodily substance.[161] But that substance of the Trinity, which is the beginning and cause of all things, from which are all things and through which are all things and in

---

[154] Isa. 6:2–3. Cf. Origen, *Princ.* 1.3.4, and the material cited in n.28 there.

[155] Cf. Origen, *Comm. Cant.* 2 (GCS 8, p. 186); *Cels.* 6.62; *Mart.* 13.

[156] Sir. 16:21.   [157] Phil. 3:13.

[158] Unlike proper names, which Origen holds are intimately connected with their bearer: see *Cels.* 1.24–5; 5.45–6; *Hom. Jes. Nav.* 23.4.

[159] Cf. Origen, *Princ.* Pr.8–9; 1.7.1.   [160] Col. 1:15–16.

[161] Cf. Origen, *Princ.* 1.7.1; 2.2.2; *Cels.* 6.71; 7.32.

which are all things,[162] is believed to be neither a body nor in a body, but is wholly bodiless.[163]

Let it suffice to have spoken briefly on these points, although by digression because of the nature of the subject, in order to show that there are certain things the significance of which cannot be adequately explained at all by any words of human language, but which are made clear more through simple apprehension than by any properties of words. Under this rule must be brought also the understanding of the divine writings, so that what is said may not be assessed by the lowliness of the language, but by the divinity of the Holy Spirit, who inspired them to be written.

---

[162] Cf. Rom. 11:36.   [163] Cf. Origen, *Princ.* 1.6.4; 2.2.2.

Recapitulation

4.4.1.[1] It[2] is now time, having traversed to the best of our ability the matters discussed above, to recapitulate, for the sake of bringing to mind what we have said in different places, the particular points, and first of all to repeat those concerning the Father and the Son and the Holy Spirit.

As God the Father is in<di>visible and inseparable from the Son, it is not by emanation from him, as some suppose, that the Son is generated. For if the Son is an emanation of the Father, and it is said that 'emanation signifies such a generation as is customary in the case of the progeny of animals or human beings, then both he who emitted and he who is emitted are necessarily bodies.[3] For we do not say, as the heretics suppose, that some part of God was changed into the Son, nor that the Son was procreated by the Father from no substance at all, that is, outside his own substance, so that there was a 'when' when the Son was not; but, putting away all bodily senses, we say that the Word and Wisdom was begotten from the invisible and bodiless God apart from any bodily passion, as an act of will proceeds from the intellect.[4] Nor will it seem absurd, seeing that he is called the *Son of love*,[5] if in this way he is also regarded as Son of his will.[6] Moreover, John also indicates that *God is light*,[7] and Paul also declares that the Son is the *brightness* of eternal *light*.[8] As *light*, then, could never exist without *brightness*, so neither can the Son be understood without the Father, for he is called *the express figure of his substance*[9] and the Word and Wisdom. How, then, can it be said that there was a 'when' when the Son was not?[10] For that is nothing other than to say that there was a 'when' when Truth was not, a 'when' when Wisdom was not, a 'when' when Life was not, although in all these respects the substance of God the Father is perfectly accounted. For these things cannot be severed from him or ever separated from his substance.

---

[1] The title in the Latin manuscripts is: 'Recapitulation [given as a transliteration of the Greek word] concerning the Father and the Son and the Holy Spirit and of other matters discussed above.'

[2] Cf. Eusebius, *C. Marc.* 1.4 (Klostermann, 21.16–22), numbered by Koetschau as Fragment 31: 'It is now time, taking up our discussion concerning the Father and the Son and the Holy Spirit, to go through a few points of the things previously left aside. In regard to the Father, as he is indivisible and undivided, he becomes the Father of the Son not by emitting him, as some think. For if the Son is an emanation of the Father, and an offspring from him, of the same kind as the offspring of animals, then by necessity both the one emitting and the emanation are, of necessity, bodies.' The opening sentence of this chapter, as preserved in Pamphilus' *Apology for Origen*, 104, also speaks of picking up matters previously left aside: 'Since the matters that we have discussed concerning the Father and the Son and the Holy Spirit have been traversed, it is time to recapitulate a few matters that we have left on the side.'

[3] Cf. Origen, *Princ.* 1.2.6.   [4] Cf. Origen, *Princ.* 1.2.6; 1.2.9.   [5] Col. 1:13.

[6] Koetschau, and Fernandez likewise, here inserts a passage from Justinian, *Ep. ad Menam* (ed. Schwartz, 209.12–15), which is said to be from *Princ.* 4 and numbered by Koetschau as Fragment 32, and a passage from Athanasius, *De decr. Nic. Syn.* 27.2 (ed. Opitz, 23.23–30), numbered as Fragment 33. Both texts are included in the Appendix as item no. 24.

[7] 1 John 1:5.   [8] Cf. Heb. 1:3.   [9] Heb. 1:3.

[10] Cf. Origen, *Princ.* 1.2.9; *Comm. Rom.* 1.5; *Fr. Heb.* 1.8; and also the passage cited by Athanasius in *De decr. Nic. Syn.* 27.2 (in the Appendix as item no. 24[b]).

Although they are said to be, by our understanding, many, nevertheless in reality and substance they are one, and in them is *the fullness of divinity.*[11]

But this expression which we say—that there never was a 'when' when he was not—is to be heard with a reservation. For these very words, that is, 'when' or 'never', bear the signification of a temporal vocabulary; whereas those things said of the Father and the Son and the Holy Spirit are to be understood as transcending all time and all ages and all eternity. For it is the Trinity alone which exceeds all comprehension of understanding, not only temporal but even eternal. Other things, however, which are external to the Trinity, are to be measured by ages and periods of times.

No one, therefore, should rationally suppose that the Son of God, inasmuch as *the Word is God* and *was in the beginning with God,*[12] is contained in any place;[13] nor yet inasmuch as he is Wisdom, or inasmuch as he is Truth, or inasmuch as he is Life or Righteousness or Sanctification or Redemption: for all these do not need a place to be able to act or to operate, but each of them is to be understood as referring to those who participate in his power and operation.

4.4.2. Now if anyone were to say that, through those who are partakers of the Word of God, or of his Wisdom or Truth or Life,[14] the Word and Wisdom itself appeared to be in a place, it must be answered that there is no doubt that Christ, inasmuch as he is the Word or Wisdom or all other things, was in Paul, according to what Paul said, *Do you seek a proof of him who speaks in me, Christ?,*[15] and again, *I no longer live but Christ lives in me.*[16] Since, then, he was in Paul, who will doubt that he was in a similar manner in Peter and in John and in each of the saints, and not only those who are on earth, but also those who are in heaven? For it is absurd to say that Christ was in Peter and in Paul, but that he was not in Michael the archangel and in Gabriel. And from this it is clearly demonstrated that the divinity of the Son of God was not shut up in some place; otherwise it would have been in it only and not in another; but that while, in accordance with the majesty of bodiless nature, it is confined to no place, in no place, on the other hand, is it understood to be absent. But this is understood to be the only difference: that although he is in different beings as we have said, in Peter or Paul or Michael or Gabriel, he is not, however, in all beings in a similar manner. For he is more fully and more clearly and, if I may so speak, more openly in archangels than in other holy men. This is clear

---

[11] Col. 2:9. On the multiplicity of 'aspects' in the one Christ, see Origen, *Princ.* 1.2.1; *Comm. Jo.* 1.119. Following this sentence, Koetschau inserts a passage from Athanasius, *De decr. Nic. Syn.* 27.3 (Opitz, 23.30–24.3) and numbered it as Fragment 34; it is included in the Appendix as item no. 25.

[12] Cf. John 1:1.

[13] Cf. Origen, *Comm. Jo.* 20.152–9; *Cels.* 4.5; 5.12; *Or.* 32.2; see also Clement, *Strom.* 7.2.5.

[14] Cf. Origen, *Princ.* 1.2.3; 1.3.6, 8; *Comm. Jo.* 2.20–33; *Comm. Rom.* 8.2.

[15] 2 Cor. 13:3.   [16] Gal. 2:20.

from the following point, that when the saints reach the height of perfection they are said to be made like or equal to the angels, according to the evangelical statement.[17] From this it is certain that Christ is in each one to such a degree as the measure of his merits allows.[18]

4.4.3. Having, then, briefly restated these points regarding the Trinity, it follows that we next recall equally that *all things* are said to *have been created* by the Son, *things which are in heaven and which are on earth, visible and invisible, whether thrones or dominions or principalities or powers; all things were created through him and for him, and he is before all things and all these hold together in him, who is the head.*[19] John also agrees with this when in the Gospel he says that *All things were made by him and without him was not anything made.*[20] And David, pointing to the entire mystery of the Trinity in the creation of the universe, says, *By the Word of the Lord the heavens were made and all their host by the Spirit of his mouth.*[21]

After these points, we shall appropriately make mention of the bodily arrival and incarnation of the only-begotten Son of God, in whom it is not to be supposed that all the majesty of his divinity is confined within the limits of a tiny body, so that the whole of the Word of God and his Wisdom and substantial Truth and Life was either separated from the Father or forced and confined within the tininess of that body, and is not considered to be working anywhere else; but the careful confession of piety ought to be between the two, so that neither is it believed that anything of divinity was lacking in Christ, nor is it supposed that there took place any separation at all from the substance of the Father, which is everywhere. For some such thing is indicated by John the Baptist, when, with Jesus bodily absent, he said to the multitude, *Among you stands one whom you do not know, who comes after me, the thong of whose sandal I am not worthy to unloose.*[22] For it certainly could not be said of one who, as far as pertains to bodily presence, was absent, that he stood among them, between whom he was not bodily present.[23] Thus it is shown that the Son of God was both wholly present in the body and also wholly present elsewhere.

4.4.4. Let no one, however, suppose from this that we affirmed that some portion of the divinity of the Son of God was in Christ, while the remaining portion was elsewhere or everywhere, which may be thought by those who are ignorant of the nature of a bodiless and invisible essence. For it is impossible to speak of a part of what is bodiless or to make any division; but he is in all things and through all things and above all things, in the way that we have

---

[17] Cf. Matt. 22:30; Luke 20:36; Origen, *Comm. Matt.* 17.30.   [18] Cf. Origen, *Princ.* 1.3.6.
[19] Col. 1:16–18.   [20] John 1:3.   [21] Ps. 33:6.   [22] John 1:26–7.
[23] Cf. Origen, *Comm. Jo.* 2.215; 6.154, 189, 257; see also *Hom. Num.* 3.2.

spoken of above,[24] that is, in the way in which he is to be understood as Wisdom or Word or Life or Truth, by which mode of understanding all idea of confinement in a particular place is without doubt excluded. The Son of God, therefore, for the sake of the salvation of the human race, wanting to appear to human beings and to sojourn among them, assumed not only a human body, as some suppose, but also a soul,[25] in its nature indeed like our souls, but in intention and power like himself and such as is able to accomplish all the desires and arrangements of the Word and Wisdom.[26] Now, that he had a soul the Saviour himself most clearly shows in the Gospels, saying, *No one takes my soul from me, but I lay it down of myself. I have the power to lay it down and I have the power to take it up again,* and again, *My soul is sorrowful even unto death,* and again, *Now is my soul troubled.*[27] The[28] *sorrowful* and *troubled soul* must not be understood to be the Word of God, since with the authority of divinity he says, *I have the power to lay down my soul.* Nor, however, do we say that the Son of God was in that soul, as he was in the soul of Paul or Peter and the other saints, in whom we believe Christ spoke, as in Paul.[29] But, of all these it must be thought, as Scripture says, *No one is clean from filth, not even if his life lasted but one day.*[30] But this soul, which was in Jesus, *before it knew evil, chose the good,* and because *it loved righteousness and hated iniquity, therefore God anointed it with the oil of gladness above its fellows.*[31] It is anointed, then, with *the oil of gladness* when it was united with the Word of God in an unblemished union and thereby alone of all souls it became incapable of sin, because it was well and fully capable [of receiving] the Son of God; and therefore it was made one with him[32] and is addressed by his titles and called Jesus Christ, through whom all things are said to have been made.[33]

---

[24] Cf. Origen, *Princ.* 4.4.2–3.   [25] Cf. Origen, *Princ.* 2.6; 2.8.2–4.

[26] Koetschau suspects an omission here, placing in his critical apparatus a sentence from Justinian, *Ep. ad Menam* (ed. Schwartz, 198.31-3), numbering it as Fragment 35; the text is included in the Appendix as item no. 26.

[27] John 10:18; Matt. 26:38 *et par.;* John 12:27.

[28] Cf. Theophilus of Alexandria as quoted by Theodoret of Cyrus, *Eran.* Dialogue 2, florilegia 58 (ed. Ettlinger, 172.18–22), a passage numbered as Fragment 36 by Koetschau: 'The *troubled* and *sorrowful soul* is not, of course, the Only-begotten and First-born of all creation. For the God Word, himself the Son, as being stronger than the soul, says, *I have the power to lay it down and the power to take it up.*' This passage is also found in the Latin translation of Theophilus *Ep. pasch.* 2 (i.e. Jerome, *Ep.* 98.16.3 [ed. Hilberg 2, 200.23–201.1]).

[29] Cf. 2 Cor. 13:3. See also Origen, *Comm. Jo.* 6.42; 28.54.

[30] Job 14:4–5. Cf. Origen, *Comm. Jo.* 20.335; *Hom. Num.* 3.2; *Hom. Luc.* 19.1; *Comm. Rom.* 5.4.

[31] Isa. 7:15–16; Ps. 44:8.

[32] Here Koetschau places, as Fragment 37, a passage from Theodoret of Cyrus, *Eran.* Dialogue 2, florilegia 58 (ed. Ettlinger, 178.5–6), which is paralleled by Theophilus of Alexandria, *Ep. pasch.* 2 (= Jerome, *Ep.* 98.16.1 [Hilberg 2.200.10–11]); these texts are included in the Appendix as item no. 27.

[33] Cf. John 1:3; Col. 1:16.

It was of this soul, since it had received into itself the whole Wisdom of God, and the Truth and the Life, that, I reckon, the Apostle spoke when he said that *Your life is hidden with Christ in God; but when Christ, our life, shall appear, then you shall appear with him in glory.*[34] For who else is meant to be understood by this Christ, who is said to be hidden in God and afterwards to appear, except him who is related to have been *anointed with the oil of gladness,* that is, to have been filled substantially with God, in whom he is now said to be hidden? For this reason Christ is put forward as an example to all believers, because just as he always, even *before he knew evil* at all, *chose the good* and *loved righteousness* and *hated iniquity,* and therefore *God anointed him with the oil of gladness,* so also each one ought, after a lapse or transgression, to cleanse himself from the blemishes by the example put forward, and, having him as the guide of the journey proceed along the arduous path of virtue, that so, perchance by this means, as far as is possible we may, by the imitation of him, *be made partakers of divine nature,*[35] as it is written that, *He who says that he believes in Christ ought himself to walk just as he walked.*[36] This Word, then, and this Wisdom, by the imitation of whom we are said to be either wise or rational, becomes all things to all, that he might gain all, and to the weak he becomes weak, that he might gain the weak,[37] and because he is made weak, therefore it is said of him, *Though he was crucified in weakness, yet he lives by the power of God.*[38] Finally, to the Corinthians who were weak, Paul *determines to know nothing among them except Jesus Christ and him crucified.*[39]

4.4.5. Some, indeed, want the statement—even that which the Apostle says, *Who, being in the form of God, thought it not robbery to be equal with God, but emptied himself, taking the form of a servant*[40]—to be seen as applying to the soul itself, at the moment it assumes a body from Mary, since he undoubtedly restored it to the form of God by means of better examples and precepts, and recalled it to that fullness of which he had emptied himself.

Just as by participation in the Son of God one is adopted among the sons, and by participation in the Wisdom in God one is rendered wise, so also by participation in the Holy Spirit one is rendered holy and spiritual.[41] For this is one and the same thing as to receive participation in the Holy Spirit, who is of

---

[34] Col. 3:3–4. Cf. Origen, *Princ.* 2.6.7.

[35] 2 Pet. 1:4.   [36] 1 John 2:6.   [37] Cf. 1 Cor. 9:22.   [38] 2 Cor. 13:4.

[39] 1 Cor. 2:2. Koetschau places the following material in his critical apparatus to supplement this paragraph: Anathema 7 of the Second Council of Constantinople; Anathema 4 of Justinian; Jerome, *Apol.* 2.12; and Theophilus of Alexandria, *Ep. synod.* (= Jerome, *Ep.* 92.4.3 [ed. Hilberg 2, 152.15–23]). These texts are all included in the Appendix as item no. 28.

[40] Phil. 2:6–7.

[41] For participation in the Son, see Origen, *Hom. Jer.* 9.4; in Wisdom, *Princ.* 1.2.4; 1.3.8; in the Spirit, *Princ.* 1.1.3; 1.3.8; 1.7.2–4.

the Father and the Son, since the nature of the Trinity is one and bodiless. And what we have said regarding the participation of the soul is to be understood of the angels and heavenly powers in a similar way as that of the souls, since every rational creature needs a participation in the Trinity.

Moreover, regarding the plan of this visible world, since the very important question is often raised about how the world is constituted, we have spoken in the above to the best of our ability,[42] for the sake of those who are accustomed to examine the basis of belief in our religion, and also for those who stir up heretical arguments against us and who are accustomed to bring up frequently the word 'matter', which even they themselves have not yet been able to understand; regarding this I think it necessary to make mention now, even if briefly.

4.4.6. In the first place, it must be known that we have, up to the present time, nowhere found in the canonical[43] Scriptures the word 'matter' itself used for that substance which is said to underlie bodies. For what Isaiah says—*And he shall devour ὕλη*, that is, matter, *like hay*,[44] speaking of those who were appointed for punishment—used 'matter' instead of 'sins'. And even if the word 'matter' happens to be written in any other place, it will never be found, so I reckon, to signify that which we now seek, unless perhaps in the Wisdom which is said to be of Solomon, which is, in any case, a book not held in authority by all.[45] Nevertheless, we do find it written there, in this way: *For your all-powerful hand*, it says, *that created the world out of formless matter, was not at a loss to send out on them a multitude of bears or fierce lions.*[46] Very many, indeed, reckon that the matter of things itself is signified in that which is written in the beginning of Genesis by Moses, *In the beginning God made the heaven and the earth; and the earth was invisible and unordered;*[47] for by this *invisible and unordered earth*, Moses seems to them to indicate nothing else but unformed matter. But if this is truly matter, it is evident then that the first principles of bodies are not incapable of change. For those who posited atoms—either those which cannot be divided into parts, or those which are divided into equal parts, or any one element as the first principles of bodily things—were not able to place among the first principles the word 'matter', that

---

[42] Cf. Origen, *Princ.* 2.1–3.

[43] This expression is not used by Origen in any extant Greek text, and presumably comes from Rufinus.

[44] Isa. 10:17.

[45] Though nevertheless used extensively by Origen in *Princ.* 1.2.9–13; and cited as 'the divine word' (ὁ θεῖος λόγος) in *Cels.* 3.72.

[46] Wis. 11:17.   [47] Gen. 1:1.

is, that which primarily signifies matter.[48] Nor, if they think matter lies beneath every body, as a substance convertible or changeable or divisible throughout all its parts, will they think it lies beneath, according to its own proper character, without qualities. With them we agree, we who in every way deny that matter should be spoken of as 'unbegotten' or 'uncreated', in conformity with what we have shown as far as we were able in the preceding pages,[49] when we pointed out that from water and earth and air and heat, different kinds of fruit are produced by different kinds of trees; or when we showed that fire, air, water, and earth are alternately changed into one another, and that one element is resolved into another by a sort of mutual relationship; and also when we proved that the substance of the flesh comes from the food either of human beings or animals or that the moisture of the natural seed was converted into solid flesh and bones. All of which are a proof that bodily substance is changeable and may pass from one quality into any others.

4.4.7. Nevertheless this must be known, that a substance never exists without a quality, but, in understanding alone, that which underlies bodies and is capable of receiving a quality is demarcated as matter. Some, indeed, wanting to investigate these subjects more profoundly, have ventured to assert that bodily nature is nothing other than qualities. For if hardness and softness, heat and cold, wetness and dryness, are qualities, and when these or all other such things are taken away nothing is conceived to lie beneath, then all things will appear to be qualities. And so those who assert this have endeavoured to maintain that, since all who say that matter was uncreated will allow that qualities were created by God, it may in this way be shown that even according to them matter is not uncreated, if indeed qualities are everything, and these are declared by all without contradiction to have been made by God. Those, however, who want to show that qualities are added from without to a certain underlying matter, make use of illustrations of this kind: for example, Paul undoubtedly is either silent or speaks or watches or sleeps or maintains a certain attitude of body, for he either sits or stands or lies down. For these are accidents of a human being, without which they are scarcely ever found. However, our mind clearly does not define a human being by any of these things; but through them we think of him and consider him in such a way that we do not at all take into account the idea of his condition, either that in which he watches or sleeps or talks or is silent, or other conditions which necessarily happen to a human being. Just as, therefore, one can consider Paul as existing

---

[48] For an account of such teachings, see Aristotle, *Metaph.* 1.3–4 (983a24–985b23).
[49] Cf. Origen, *Princ.* 2.1.4.

without all these things that are capable of happening, so also will he be able to understand that which lies beneath without qualities. When our mind, therefore, having put away every quality from its conception, gazes upon the point, so to speak, of that which lies beneath alone, and clings to that, without in the least looking at the hardness or softness or heat or cold or wetness or dryness of the substance, then, by this somewhat artificial process of thought, it will appear to behold matter stripped of all these qualities.

4.4.8. But perhaps someone may ask whether we can obtain any grounds for such an understanding of this subject from Scripture. It seems to me that some such view is indicated in the Psalms, when it is said by the prophet, *My eyes have seen your imperfection.*[50] In this verse, the mind of the Prophet, examining with more piercing insight the first principles of things and distinguishing, in mind and reason alone, between matter and its qualities, perceived the imperfection of God, which is certainly understood to be perfected by the addition of qualities. Moreover, Enoch also in his book speaks as follows: 'I walked even to imperfection',[51] which, I reckon, may be understood in a similar manner, namely, that the mind of the Prophet, examining and discussing every single visible thing, walked until it arrived at that first principle in which it beheld imperfect matter without qualities; for it is written in the same book, with Enoch himself speaking, 'I beheld the whole of matter.'[52] This is assuredly understood thus, that he has seen all the divisions of matter which have, from one, been broken off into each species, that is, of human beings or of animals or of the sky or of the sun or of everything that is in this world.

Then, after these points, we proved to the best of our ability in the above pages,[53] that all things which exist were made by God, and that there is nothing that is not made except the nature of the Father and the Son and the Holy Spirit; and that God, who is by nature good, wanting to have those whom he might benefit and who might rejoice in receiving his benefits, made creatures worthy of himself, that is, who were capable of receiving him worthily, whom also, he says, he begot as sons.[54] He made all things, moreover, *by number and*

---

[50] Cf. Ps. 138:16: 'Your eyes beheld my unwrought state [τὸ ἀκατέργαστόν μου]'; Hilary (*Trac. in Ps. 138,* 32; CSEL 22.766ff) also renders this as *imperfectum* and *inoperatum*.

[51] 1 Enoch 21:1 (GCS 5, p. 50.4), which uses the word ἀκατασκεύαστος, no doubt taken from Gen. 1:2. Origen also cites Enoch in *Princ.* 1.3.3, and also in *Hom. Num.* 28.2; *Comm. Jo.* 6.217; *Cels.* 5.54, where he states that it is not generally held to be divine by the churches.

[52] Cf. 1 Enoch 19:3 (GCS 5, p. 48.18f), which speaks of Enoch seeing the 'extremities of all things' (πέρατα πάντων). The text is found in Clement of Alexandria, *Ecl. proph.* 2.1 (Stählin, 3.137.16–17): καὶ εἶδον τὰς ὕλας πάσας. Cf. 2 Enoch 40:1.

[53] Cf. Origen, *Princ.* 1.3.3; 1.4.3–4; 1.7.1.   [54] Cf. Isa. 1:2. Origen, *Princ.* 4.4.5.

measure,[55] for to God there is nothing without end or without measure.[56] For by his power he comprehends all things, and he himself is not comprehended by the intellect of any created being. For that nature is known to itself alone. For the Father alone knows the Son, and the Son alone knows the Father,[57] and the Holy Spirit alone *searches out even the deep things of God.*[58]

Every created thing, therefore, is distinguished by him as being within a certain number or measurement, that is, number for rational beings or measure for bodily matter; since, then, as it was necessary for intellectual beings to make use of bodies, and this nature is shown to be changeable and convertible by the very condition of its being created (for what was not and began to be, by this very circumstance is shown to be of a mutable nature, and therefore it has goodness or wickedness not as a substantial property but as an accident), since, then, as we have said, rational nature was mutable and convertible, so that it made use of a different bodily covering of this or that kind, according to its merits, it was necessary that just as God foreknew there would be variations of souls or spiritual powers, so he should also create a bodily nature which might be changed, by the will of the Creator, by an alteration of qualities, into everything that the case required. And it is necessary that this must last as long as those endure who need it for a covering; for there will always be rational beings who need a bodily covering, and there will always be a bodily nature, whose coverings must necessarily be used by rational creatures,[59] unless someone reckons that he is able to prove by any argument that a rational being can lead a life without a body at all. But how difficult, if not almost impossible, this is for our understanding, we have shown in discussing the particular points in the above.

4.4.9. It will not appear, I think, contrary to this work of ours if we also revisit, as briefly as we can, the immortality of rational beings.[60] Everyone who partakes

---

[55] Wis. 11:20. See also Origen, *Comm. Jo.* 6.295; 32.184.

[56] Koetschau (and Fernandez similarly) inserts here, as Fragment 38, a passage from Justinian, *Ep. ad Menam* (ed. Schwartz, 209.8–10); he places a passage from Jerome, *Ep.* 124.13.1–2 (ed. Hilberg 3, 115.9–19), in his critical apparatus as representing a fuller version of what Rufinus translated by the following sentence ('For by his power ... created being'); then, after that sentence, he inserts, as Fragment 39, a passage from Justinian, *Ep. ad Menam* (ed. Schwartz, 209.19–23), and includes a parallel passage from Jerome, *Ep.* 124.13.2–3 (ed. Hilberg 3, 115.19–116.4), in his critical apparatus. All these texts are included in the Appendix as item no. 29.

[57] Cf. John 10:15; 17:25.   [58] 1 Cor. 2:10.

[59] Koetschau suggests that the remaining lines of this paragraph are paralleled by a more extensive passage from Jerome, *Ep.* 124.14.1 (Hilberg 3, 116.5–17), which he puts in his critical apparatus; the last lines of this passage from Jerome are paralleled by a passage from Justinian, *Ep. ad Menam* (ed. Schwartz, 212.16–19), said to come from *Princ.* 4 and which Koetschau places within the text as Fragment 40. Similarly Fernandez. These texts are included in the Appendix as item no. 30.

[60] The immortality of rational beings, intellects, was alluded to in *Princ.* 2.8.3, and a propos of the resurrection in 2.3.2; 3.6.4; but it has not been stated explicitly for it now to be 'revisited'.

of anything is without doubt of one substance and one nature with one who is a partaker of the same thing. So, for example, all eyes partake of light, and therefore all eyes which partake of light are of one nature; yet, although every eye partakes of light, as one sees more clearly and another more dimly, every eye does not equally partake of light. And again, every faculty of hearing receives voice or sound, and therefore every faculty of hearing is of one nature; but, according to the condition of purity and clarity of the faculty of hearing, each one hears more quickly or slowly. Let us now pass from these examples pertaining to the senses to the contemplation of things intellectual.

Every[61] intellect that partakes of intellectual light ought, without doubt, to be of one nature with every intellect that partakes in a similar manner of intellectual light. If then the heavenly powers receive a share of intellectual light, that is, of the divine nature, because they partake of wisdom and sanctification, and the human soul receives a share of the same light and wisdom, then they will be of one nature and of one substance with each other. But the heavenly powers are incorruptible and immortal; undoubtedly the substance of the human soul will also be incorruptible and immortal. And not only so, but since the nature of the Father and the Son and the Holy Spirit, of whose intellectual light alone the universal creation obtains a share, is incorruptible and eternal, it is absolutely consistent and necessary that every substance which obtains a share of that eternal nature should remain forever, both incorruptible and eternal, so that the eternity of divine goodness may be understood in this respect as well, that those who obtain its benefits are also eternal. But just as, in the illustrations, a diversity in the perception of light was preserved, when the gaze of the beholder was described as duller or more acute, so also a diversity of participation in the Father and the Son and the Holy Spirit is to be preserved, in accordance with the application of the understanding and the capacity of the intellect.[62]

---

[61] Cf. Jerome, *Ep.* 124.14.2–4 (ed. Hilberg 3, 116.17–117.7): 'And so we should not think that the impiety of these quotations was too little, at the end of the same volume he adds that all rational natures—that is, the Father and the Son and the Holy Spirit, angels, authorities, dominions, and the other powers, and even the human being himself in virtue of the dignity of the soul—are of one substance. God, he says, and his only-begotten Son and the Holy Spirit, are conscious of an intellectual and rational nature; the angels and the authorities and the other powers also; *the inner human being,* who was made *in the image and likeness of God,* likewise. From which it is concluded that God and they are in some way of one substance. He adds this one phrase, "in some way", so as to escape the charge of sacrilege; and so he, who in another place will not allow the Son and the Holy Spirit to be of the substance with the Father, lest he should seem to be dividing the divinity into parts, bestows the nature of the omnipotent God upon angels and human beings.'

[62] Cf. Origen, *Princ.* 1.3.6; 2.6.3; 4.4.2.

On the other hand, let us consider if it would not even seem impious to say that the intellect, which is capable of receiving God, should receive the destruction of its substance; as if the very fact that it is able to understand and perceive God were not able to suffice for its perpetuity, especially since, even if, through negligence, the intellect falls away from the pure and complete reception of God into itself,[63] it nevertheless always contains within itself some seeds, as it were, of being restored and recalled to a better understanding, when *the inner human being,* who is also called the 'rational' human being, is *renewed according to the image and likeness* of God who created him.[64] And therefore the prophet says, *All the ends of the earth shall remember and turn to the Lord, and all the families of the nations shall worship before him.*[65]

4.4.10. If anyone indeed dares to ascribe substantial corruption to him who was made *according to the image and likeness* of God, then, I think, this impious charge extends even to the Son of God himself, for he is called in Scripture *the image of God.*[66] Or one who holds this would certainly impugn the authority of Scripture, which says that the human being was made *in the image* of God; and in him the marks of the divine image are manifestly discerned not through the form of his body,[67] which goes to corruption, but through the prudence of his mind, justice, moderation, virtue, wisdom, discipline, in sum through the whole band of virtues, which exist in God essentially and which may exist in the human being through diligence and the imitation of God, just as the Lord points out in the Gospel, saying, *Be merciful as your Father is merciful* and, *Be perfect, as your Father is perfect.*[68] From this it is clearly shown that in God all these virtues exist forever and they can never come to him or depart from him, while with human beings they are acquired slowly and one by one. From this also they are seen to have a kind of kinship,[69] through this, to God; and since God knows all things, and nothing of intellectual things can escape his notice (for God the Father alone, and his only-begotten Son and the Holy Spirit, not only possesses a knowledge of those things which he has created, but also of himself[70]), it is possible that a rational intellect also, advancing from small things to great, and from things visible to things invisible, may attain to a more perfect understanding. For it is placed in the body, and of necessity advances from things perceptible to the senses, which are bodily, to things that are not

---

[63] Cf. Origen, *Princ.* 1.4.1 and the materials cited in n.71 and n.73 there.

[64] Gen. 1.26; 2 Cor. 4:16.   [65] Ps. 22:28.   [66] Col. 1:15.

[67] As in Irenaeus, *Haer.* 5.6.1. Melito of Sardis is perhaps also in view here; see Origen, *Sel. Gen.* 1:26 (PG 12, 93).

[68] Luke 6:36; Matt. 5:48. Cf. Origen, *Princ.* 3.6.1, and the material cited in n.5 there.

[69] Cf. Origen, *Princ.* 1.1.7.

[70] Cf. Origen, *Princ.* 2.6.1; *Hom. Isa.* 1.2; 4.1; *Cels.* 6.17; *Com. Rom.* 8.13.

perceptible to the senses, which are bodiless and intellectual. But lest what was said, that things intellectual are not perceptible to the senses, seem inappropriate, we will utilize, as an example, the statement of Solomon, who says, *You will find also a divine sense.*[71] By this he shows that those things which are intellectual are to be sought out not by means of a bodily sense, but by a certain other, which he calls *divine.*

It is with this sense that we must look upon each of those rational beings which we have spoken about above; and with this sense that those words which we speak must be heard and those which we write must be considered. For the divine nature knows even those silent thoughts which we turn around inside ourselves. And concerning those points about which we have spoken, or others which follow on from them, we must think in accordance with the pattern we have laid out above.[72]

---

[71] Prov. 2:5. Cf. Origen, *Princ.* 1.1.9.   [72] Cf. 2 Tim. 1:13.

Appendix
Koetschau's Fragments

As noted in the introduction, Koetschau was convinced that the 'Origenist' teaching condemned in the sixth century was an accurate representation of Origen's own thought, and so, taking his lead from Rufinus' own admission in his Preface to the translation of *On First Principles* that he had omitted various passages, Koetschau felt justified in adding to that translation various passages alleged by others to come from the work, reports of the work, and, indeed, composite passages produced from diverse later sources, so as to 'restore' the original text. This Appendix contains those passages so inserted into the text of *On First Principles,* together with a few that Koetschau placed in his critical apparatus. In some cases, the texts are from more recent editions than those used by Koetschau, in which case I have noted any variants.

1: PASSAGE INSERTED INTO *PRINC.* 1.1.8.

Jerome, **Jo. Hier.** *7 (PL 23, 360):*

For as it is incongruous to say that the Son can see the Father, so it is unfitting to hold that the Holy Spirit can see the Son.

2: PASSAGE INSERTED INTO *PRINC.* 1.2.6, AS FRAGMENT 4.

Justinian, **Ep. ad Menam** *(ed. Schwartz, 209.25–7), said to be from* **Princ.** *1:*

We, therefore, having been made according to the image, have the Son, the prototype, as the truth of the good things imprinted in us; and what we are to him, such is he to the Father, the truth.

3: PASSAGES IN CRITICAL APPARATUS TO COMPENSATE FOR SUSPECTED OMISSION AT END OF *PRINC.* 1.2.6.

[a] Jerome, **Ep.** *124.2.1 (ed. Hilberg 3, 97.14–17):*

God the Father is light incomprehensible; Christ compared with the Father is but a minute brightness, although to us by reason of our weakness he seems to be a great one.

[b] Theophilus of Alexandria, **Ep. Synod.** *(= Jerome,* **Ep. 92.2.1;**
ed. Hilberg, 2, 149.2–3):

As much as Paul and Peter differ from the Saviour, so much is the Saviour less than the Father.

4: PASSAGE INSERTED INTO *PRINC.* 1.2.13, AS FRAGMENT 6.

Justinian, *Ep.* ad *Menam (ed. Schwartz, 210.1–6), said to be from* **Princ. 1:**

Thus, then, I think that in the case of the Saviour it would be right for it to be said that he is *the image of the goodness of God*,[1] but not goodness itself. And perhaps also the Son is good, but yet not good simply, and that just as *he is the image of the invisible God*[2] and, in this respect, God, but not the one of whom Christ himself says *that they may know you the only true God*,[3] so also he is *the image of the goodness*, but not, as the Father, invariably good.

Cf. Jerome, Ep. 124.2.2 (ed. Hilberg 3, 97.20–3), placed in critical apparatus:

God the Father he calls good and of perfect goodness; the Son is not good, but is a kind of breath and image of goodness, so that he is not called good absolutely, but with an addition, such as 'the good shepherd', and so on.

5: PASSAGES INSERTED INTO *PRINC.* 1.3.3, AS FRAGMENT 7.

Fernandez would place this sentence in parallel with the first sentence of the third paragraph of Princ. *1.2.6.*

Justinian, **Ep.** ad **Menam** *(ed. Schwartz, 210.9–10):*

Following the same reasoning, we are persuaded therefore that everything whatsoever except the Father and God of the universe is created.

From the preceding sentence from Justinian's letter (given below), Koetschau takes the words 'ministering animals' and inserts them into the body of the text following the sentence given above.

Justinian, **Ep.** ad **Menam** *(ed. Schwartz, 210.7–9):*

That he called the Holy Spirit a created being along with the Son and included them in the number of the other created beings, and accordingly he calls them 'ministering animals', from the fourth [*em. Koe.* first] book of the volume *On First Principles*.

---

[1] Wis. 7:26.   [2] Col. 1:15.   [3] John 17:3.

6: PASSAGE INSERTED INTO *PRINC.* 1.3.5, AS FRAGMENT 9.

***Justinian,* Ep. ad Menam** *(ed. Schwartz, 208.26–32), said to be from* **Princ. 1:**

The God and Father, holding all things together, is superior to every being, giving to each, from his own, to be whatever it is; the Son, being less than the Father, is superior to rational creatures alone, for he is second to the Father; and the Holy Spirit is still less, dwelling with the holy ones alone. So that in this way the power of the Father is greater than the Son and the Holy Spirit, and that of the Son is greater than the Holy Spirit, and again the power of the Holy Spirit differs greatly from other holy beings.

The following texts are given in the critical apparatus.

[a] Jerome, **Ep.** *124.2.3 (ed. Hilberg 3, 98.1–6):*

The Son is inferior to the Father, inasmuch as he is second from him, and the Holy Spirit, who dwells in the saints, is inferior to the Son, so also in the same way the power of the Father is greater than the Son and the Holy Spirit; and the power of the Son is greater than the Holy Spirit, and, so too, that of the Holy Spirit is greater than the power of the other things called holy.

[b] Theophilus of Alexandria **Ep. pasch.** *(= Jerome,* **Ep.** *98.13; ed. Hilberg, 2, 196.26–7):*

He says that the Holy Spirit does not work with things that are inanimate nor extends to things irrational.

7: PASSAGES INSERTED AT END OF *PRINC.* 1.4.1.

[a] Jerome, **Jo. Hier.** *16 (PL 23, 368):*

[…whether the doctrine of Origen is true, who said that:] all rational creatures, incorporeal and invisible, if they become negligent, gradually sink to a lower level and, according to the character of the places to which they descend, take to themselves bodies—for example, first, ethereal bodies and then aerial—and when they reach the vicinity of the earth they are enclosed in grosser bodies, and last of all tied to human bodies.

[b] Jerome, **Ep.** *124.3.1 (ed. Hilberg 3, 98.7–12):*

[Then when he comes to rational creatures and says that the fall through negligence is into earthly bodies, he adds even this:] It is of great negligence and sloth to descend and empty oneself so greatly that, approaching the vices of the irrational beasts of burden, it can be bound to a gross body.

Cf. Jerome, Jo. Hier. *19 (PL 23, 370), placed in critical apparatus:*

Origen, by way of Jacob's ladder, taught that rational creatures gradually descend to the lowest level, that is, to flesh and blood.

8: PASSAGES INSERTED AT *PRINC.* 1.7.4.

[a] Jerome, Ep. 124.4.1 (ed. Hilberg 3, 99.22–7):

The sun also and the moon and the rest of the stars are animated; indeed, just as we human beings, because of certain sins, have been enveloped in bodies which are gross and heavy, so also the lights of heaven have received bodies of one sort or another, to provide more or less light, and demons, for greater offences, have been clothed with aerial bodies.

[b] Justinian, Ep. ad Menam (ed. Schwartz, 212.20–3), said to come from Princ. 1 and numbered by Koetschau as Fragment 13:

I think that it is possible to demonstrate that the soul of the sun is older than its covering [serving as] the body, by reasoning from a comparison of the human being with it and from the Scriptures.

9: PASSAGE INSERTED INTO *PRINC.* 1.7.5.

Jerome, Ep. 124.4.1–3 (ed. Hilberg 3, 100.2–17):

[That no one may suppose that what I say are my own thoughts, I shall give his actual words:] At the end and consummation of the world, when souls and rational creatures shall have been released from their bars and prisons by the Lord, some of them will move slowly on account of their sluggishness, while others will speed along in quick flight because of their assiduity. And as all have free will and of their own accord can acquire virtue or vice, the former will be in a much worse condition than they are now, while the latter will arrive at a better state; for diverse movement and various wills will receive diverse states in either direction, that is, angels may become humans or demons, and, in reverse, humans or angels may come from them.

10: PASSAGE INSERTED AFTER *PRINC.* 1.8.1, AS FRAGMENT 15.

This is a composite passage, made up of the following pieces:

[a] *Antipater of Bostra*, apud *John of Damascus*, Sacra Parallela (*PG 96:501d*)
[b] *Leontius of Byzantium*, De Sectis *10.5 (PG 86.1:1264–5)*
[c] *Epiphanius*, Pan. 64.4.6 (*ed.* Holl 2, 411.4–412.1)
[d] *Antipater of Bostra*, apud *John of Damascus*, Sacra Parallela (*PG 96:504a and 505c); sentence constructed by putting five words from 505c into a sentence in 504a (divisions marked by |)*
[e] *Theophilus of Alexandria*, Ep. Synod. (*=Jerome, Ep. 92.3; ed. Hilberg 2, 149.27–150.3)*
[f] *Antipater of Bostra*, apud *John of Damascus*, Sacra Parallela (*PG 96:504a*)

[g] *Antipater of Bostra*, apud *John of Damascus*, Sacra Parallela *(PG 96:504c)*

[h] *Antipater of Bostra*, apud *John of Damascus*, Sacra Parallela *(PG 96:504c, 505b, division marked by |)*

[a] God did not begin to create intellects *** [b] Before the ages all intellects were pure, both daemons and souls and angels, ministering to God and doing his commandments. But the devil, being one of them, since he possessed free will desired to oppose God, and God drove him away. With him apostatized all the other powers. Some, sinning greatly, became daemons; others, less, became angels; others, still less, became archangels; and thus each in turn received according to their own sin. But there remained some souls, who had not sinned so greatly as to become daemons, nor, on the other hand, so lightly, as to become angels. Therefore God made the present world and bound the soul to the body as a punishment. For *God is no respecter of persons*,[4] that, all these being of one nature (for all immortal beings are rational), he should make some daemons, some souls, and some angels; rather it is clear that, punishing each one according to its sin, he made one a daemon, another a soul, and yet another an angel. For if this were not so—that souls pre-exist—why do we find some newborn babies blind, when they have not sinned, while others are born having no affliction? But it is clear that certain sins pre-exist the souls, as a result of which each receives according to merit. [c] They are sent away from God as punishment; such that they receive their first judgement here; therefore the body is called a frame, because the soul is framed in the body.

[d] But when they had apostatized from their former blessedness, because of the sin of the first which had occurred in them, | becoming bodies, they were allotted to various ranks | and from intellects they became angels *** [e] Just as the daemons, attending the altars of the Gentiles, used to feed on the fumes of the sacrifices, so also the angels—being allured by the blood of the victims, which Israel sacrificed as images of spiritual things, and by the smoke of incense—used to dwell by the altars and were nourished by food of this sort. [f] But when they apostatized, according to the New Scripture, from the unity of God, they obtained as their portion to rule and have dominion over those falling further still, and *being sent forth to serve, for the sake of those who are to inherit salvation*,[5] though they had fallen away from this and were in need of the one who would lead [them] back, *** [g] not wishing to command them to return to their original perfect blessedness, for being commanded they would be *mighty in power*, according to the prophet, *to do his word and to hear the voice of his words*;[6] and the witness of the Spirit cannot lie. *** [h] They were zealous for the sake of those who had lost *the good seed* sown by the Lord,[7] and they sought to be entrusted by the Lord with the restoration of these, although they themselves had cast away the purity of their first seed. | But if they become *mighty in power*[8] to do the will of God, and seek the destruction of the wicked, this indicates that it is because of their goodwill towards the divine that they stand before God and serve him and are at his right hand.

---

4 Acts 10:34.   5 Heb. 1:14.   6 Ps. 102:20.
7 Cf. Matt. 13:24ff.   8 1 Macc. 8:1; 1 Suppl. 12:31.

11: PASSAGE INSERTED INTO *PRINC.* 1.8.3, AS FRAGMENT 16.

Antipater of Bostra apud ***John of Damascus,*** Sacra Parallela *(PG 96, 505):*

But the devil, it has been shown, was not created such, but fell into this by his own wickedness; it is clear, therefore, that they also came into this by their own virtue.

12: PASSAGE INSERTED IN *PRINC.* 1.8.4, AS FRAGMENT 17A.

This is a composite passage, made up of the following pieces:

[a] *Gregory of Nyssa*, anim. et res. *(PG 44:112c)*
[b] *Gregory of Nyssa*, hom. opif. 28 *(PG 44:229b)*
[c] *Gregory of Nyssa*, anim. et res. *(PG 44:112c–113a)*
[d] *Gregory of Nyssa*, anim. et res. *(PG 44:113cd)*
[e] *Gregory of Nyssa*, hom. opif. 28 *(PG 44:232bc)*

[a] Certain nations of souls are laid aside somewhere, in a realm of their own, living comparably to the life in the body; they spin around, in the subtlety and mobility of their natures, with the rotation of the universe. [b] Set before them there are the examples of evil and of virtue; and while the soul continues remaining in the good, it remains without experience of conjunction with the body. [c] But, losing their wings, through some inclination towards evil, the souls come to be in bodies, first in human beings, then, after that, because of their association with the beasts of the passions, after passing out of human life, they become animals, and from which they sink even as far as this, the insensate natural life: so that what is subtle and mobile by nature, that is the soul, first becomes heavy and weighed down, coming to dwell in human bodies because of evil; thereupon, its power of reason being extinguished, it takes up life in irrational animals; thereupon, with even this gift of the senses being withdrawn, it takes in exchange this insensate life of plants; from this it rises again through the same steps, and is restored to its heavenly place. [d] Growing wings through virtue here below, <souls> soar aloft; but there, their wings falling off because of evil, falling to the ground, they become earthbound, commingled with the density of material nature.

[e] For if the soul, being torn away, by some evil, from the more exalted realm, and after (as they say) having once tasted of corporeal life, again becomes a human being; and life in the flesh is acknowledged to be wholly impassioned compared to the eternal and incorporeal life; it necessarily follows that that which comes to be in such a life, in which the occasions of sin are more numerous, also comes into the midst of greater evil and is rendered more impassioned than before. A passion of the human soul is a similarity to the irrational; the soul, being assimilated to this, descends to an animal nature; and once it has set out on its way through wickedness, it never ceases its advance towards evil, not even when in an irrational state; for the standing still of evil is the beginning of the impulse towards virtue; but in irrational creatures there is no virtue; therefore, of necessity, the soul will continually be changed for the worse, always proceeding to what is more dishonourable, and always finding out what is worse than the nature in which it is; and just as the sensible nature is lower than the rational, so too there is a fall from this into the insensate.

13: PASSAGE INSERTED INTO *PRINC.* 1.8.4, AS FRAGMENT 17B.

Justinian, **Ep. ad Menam** *(ed. Schwartz, 211.19–23), said to be from* **Princ.** *2:*

With the soul falling away from the good and inclining towards the evil, and coming to be ever more in this state, if it doesn't turn back it becomes bestial by its folly and brutish by its wickedness. [And after a little] and it is carried towards becoming irrational and towards, so to speak, the watery life; and perhaps as befits its evil fall towards the worse, it is clothed with the body of this or that animal.

14: PASSAGE INSERTED IN *PRINC.* 2.8.3, AS FRAGMENT 22.

Epiphanius, **Pan.** *64.4.7–8 (ed. Holl 2, 412.5–11):*

[He says] when the prophet says, *Before I was humbled, I went wrong,*[9] the saying, he claims, is from the soul itself, as it went wrong in heaven on high before it was humbled in the body; and when he says, *Turn unto your rest, O soul,*[10] it means that he who has been manly down here in good deeds turns to the rest on high on account of the uprightness of his conduct.

Cf. Jerome, Jo. Hier. *7 (PL 23, 360), placed in critical apparatus:*

According to which, souls are bound in this body as in a prison, and that before the human being was made in paradise, they dwelt among the rational creatures in the heavens. Whence, afterwards, in order to console itself, the soul says in the Psalms, *Before I was humbled, I went wrong,* and, *Turn unto your rest, O soul,* and *Bring my soul out of prison,*[11] and other similar utterances.

15: PASSAGES INSERTED AT END OF *PRINC.* 2.8.3.

[a] Anathemas 2 to 6a of the Second Council of Constantinople, 553 (ACO 4.1, 248), with an extra sentence, following anathema 4, taken from Justinian, Ep. ad Menam (ed. Schwartz, 202.13–14); these are given as Fragment 23a:[12]

2: [If anyone says that] the production of all rational beings resulted in incorporeal and material intellects without number or name, such that there was a henad of them all in identity of substance and power and activity and in union with and knowledge of God the Word, but that they arrived at satiety of divine contemplation and turned to what is worse, according to the proportion of the inclination of each to this, and that they took more subtle or denser bodies and were allotted names, as among the heavenly powers there is a difference of names just as there is also of bodies, and thence some became and were named cherubim, others seraphim, others

---

[9] Ps. 119:67.   [10] Ps. 116:7.   [11] Ps. 114:7; 141:8.
[12] Koetschau does concede that these texts are 'nicht wörtliches'.

principalities, and powers or dominions, thrones, angels, and whatever heavenly orders there are, [let him be anathema.]

3: [If anyone says that] the sun and the moon and the stars, being themselves of the same henad of rational beings, became what they are through turning towards what is worse, [let him be anathema.]

4: [If anyone says that] the rational beings who grew cold in divine love were bound to our more dense bodies and were named human beings, while those who had reached the lowest point of evil were bound to cold and dark bodies and are called demons and *spiritual hosts of wickedness*,[13] [let him be anathema.]

Justinian: <Therefore> the soul received its body on account of previous sins, by way of punishment or retribution.

5: [If anyone says that] the state of the soul comes from the angelic and archangelic state, and the demonic and human from that of the soul, and from that of the human come angels and demons again, and that each order of the heavenly powers is constituted either entirely from those below or from those above or from those above and those below [let him be anathema.]

6a: [If anyone says that] the race of demons displays a double origin, being compounded both from human souls and from superior spirits who had descended to this, but that from the whole henad of rational beings one intellect remained in unmoved divine love and contemplation, which, becoming Christ and king of all rational beings, produced the whole of corporeal nature, heaven and earth and what is in between [...let him be anathema.]

[b] Justinian Ep. ad Menam *(ed. Schwartz, 190.19–24):*

[And that] those rational beings who sinned, and on that account fell from the state in which they were, according to the proportion of their own sins, were enveloped in bodies as retribution; and when they are purified they rise again in the state in which they formerly were, completely putting away the bodies. And, again, a second time or a third or many times they are thrown into different bodies for retribution. It must be supposed that different worlds also were constituted and will be constituted, some in the past and some in the future.

[c] Justinian Ep. ad Menam *(ed. Schwartz, 212.5–8), said to come from* Princ. *2, and numbered by Koetschau as Fragment 23b:*

Along with the falling away and the cooling from life in the Spirit came what is now called 'soul,' which is also capable of an ascent to the state in which it was *in the*

---

[13] Eph. 6:12.

beginning.[14] This I think is spoken of by the prophet in the verse, *Turn unto your rest, O my soul;*[15] so that this becomes wholly intellect.

[d] Jerome, Ep. 124.6.5–6 (ed. Hilberg 3, 104.2–16):

Intellect, that is, mind, when it fell was made soul, and soul in its turn provided with virtues will become intellect. This we can find by considering the soul of Esau, who was condemned to a worse life for ancient sins. And in regard to celestial beings, it must be inquired how the soul of the sun, or whatever it ought to be called, began to exist not at the time that the world was made, but before it entered that shining and burning body. Let us also think similarly for the moon and the stars, that although they have been compelled unwillingly to be *subject to vanity*,[16] as a result of antecedent causes, yet it is in the hope of future reward that they do not their own will, but that of the Creator, by whom they have been apportioned to these duties.

16: PASSAGE PLACED IN CRITICAL APPARATUS TO SUPPLEMENT PERCEIVED OMISSION AT END OF *PRINC.* 2.10.3.

Anathema 10 of the Second Council of Constantinople, 553 (ACO 4.1, 249):

[If anyone says] that the Lord's body after the resurrection was ethereal and spherical in form, and that such shall be the bodies of others after the resurrection, and that, with the Lord himself laying aside his own body and all likewise [thereafter], the nature of bodies will pass into non-existence, [let him be anathema.]

17: PASSAGES INSERTED AT END OF *PRINC.* 2.10.8.

[a] Jerome, Ep. 124.7.2 (ed. Hilberg 3,104.25–105.2):

Perhaps, however, the gloom and darkness should be taken to mean this coarse and earthly body, through which, at the consummation of this world, each one that must pass into another world will receive the beginnings of birth.

[b] After a short intervening sentence, the following composite passage is inserted, as Fragment 25:

[i]   De Sectis *attributed to Leontius (PG 81.1, 1265)*
[ii] *Justinian Ep.* ad Menam *(ed. Schwartz, 205.8–10)*

[i] There is a resurrection of the dead and there is punishment, but not everlasting. For when the body is punished the soul is gradually purified, and so is restored back to the primordial rank.

---

[14] Gen. 1:1; John 1:1.   [15] Ps. 116:7.   [16] Rom. 8.20.

[ii] The punishment of all wicked human beings, and for demons, has an end, and both the wicked and demons shall be restored to their former rank.

18: PASSAGES RELATED TO FINAL PARAGRAPH OF *PRINC.* 3.6.1.

[a] Jerome, Ep. 124.8[9].9 (ed. Hilberg 3, 109.19–110.1), in Koetschau's critical apparatus:

[And when he begins a discussion on the end, he produced this:] since, as we have frequently said before, a new beginning arises from an end, it must be asked whether there will be bodies then or whether, when they have been brought to nothing, we will live without any bodies, and whether it is to be believed that the life of incorporeal beings is incorporeal, such as we know God to be. Now there is no doubt that if all bodies, which are called by the apostle *things visible*, belong to this sensible world, the life of incorporeal beings will be incorporeal.

[b] Anathema 11 of the Second Council of Constantinople, 553 (ACO 4.1, 249), in Koetschau's critical apparatus:

[If anyone says that] the coming judgement signifies the total destruction of bodies and that the end of the story will be an immaterial nature, and that in the future nothing that is material will exist but only pure intellect, [let him be anathema].

[c] Theophilus of Alexandria, Ep. Synod. (= Jerome, Ep. 92.2.2; ed. Hilberg 2, 149.12–14) in Koetschau's critical apparatus:

[He said that] after many ages our bodies gradually return into nothingness and dissolve into a tenuous breath...

[d] Jerome, Ep. 124.8[9].10–12 (ed. Hilberg 3, 110.1–111.5), inserted into text at end of Princ. 3.6.1:

That also which was said by the same apostle, *The whole creation will be set free from the bondage of corruption into the liberty of the glory of the sons of God,*[17] we understand in such a way as to say that the first creation of rational beings was also incorporeal; it is now in bondage to corruption, because it is also clothed with bodies, for wherever there are bodies, corruption immediately follows; but afterwards *it will be set free from the bondage of corruption,* when it has received *the glory* of the Son *of God* and when *God shall be all in all.*[18]

[And in the same place] And that the end of all things is incorporeal we believe because of that statement in our Saviour's prayer, in which he says, *That as I and you are one, so may they also be one in us.*[19] For we ought to know what God is and what the Saviour will be in the end, and how the likeness of the Father and the Son has been promised to the saints, so that as the Father and the Son are one in themselves, so too the saints may be one in them. For either the God of the universe must be supposed to

---

[17] Rom. 8:21.   [18] 1 Cor. 15:28.   [19] John 17:21.

be clothed with a body and, as we are with flesh, enveloped with some sort of matter, so that the likeness of the life of God may in the end be assimilated by the saints, or, if this is unseemly—as it most certainly is for those who desire, even in the smallest degree, to think of the majesty of God and to apprehend the glory of his unbegotten and all-transcendent nature—we are compelled to accept one of two alternatives: either despair of ever attaining the likeness of God, if we are always to have bodies, or, if there is promised to us the blessedness of the same life of God, then we must live in the same condition in which God lives.

19: PASSAGE PLACED IN CRITICAL APPARATUS AS PARALLELING *PRINC.* 3.6.3.

Jerome, Ep. 124.10.1–4 (ed. Hilberg 3, 111.6–112.5):

[And again, when arguing for a variety of worlds, and maintaining that angels may become demons and demons angels or human beings, or that, on the contrary, human beings may become demons and any being may become any other, at the end he confirms that such is his opinion:] there is no doubt that after certain intervals of time matter will exist again and bodies will be created and a different world constructed in conformity with the varying wills of rational beings, who, after being perfected in blessedness at the end of all things, gradually falling to lower levels have accepted evil to such an extent that they have been turned into the opposite, for they were unwilling to preserve their first state and to retain their blessedness incorrupt. Nor must one be ignorant of this, that many rational beings preserve their first state to the second and third and fourth world, and give no ground for change in their condition; others deteriorate so little that they appear to have lost scarcely anything; while some have to be hurled in complete ruin into the lowest abyss. And God, the dispenser of all things, alone knows how to use each class, according to their merit and opportunity and motives, in the constitution of worlds, and by whom the courses of the world are initiated and sustained, so that one who has surpassed everyone in wickedness and has reduced himself to the level of the earth may, in another world which will be constructed later, become a devil, *the beginning of something moulded by the Lord, to be mocked by the angels,*[20] who have lost their original virtue.

20: PASSAGES PLACED IN CRITICAL APPARATUS TO SUPPLEMENT THE END OF *PRINC.* 3.6.4.

Anathemas 12 ,14 ,15 of the Second Council of Constantinople, 553 (ACO 4.1,249) (Koetschau refers to these as the Anathemas of 543 rather than 553, and mentions Anathema 13, saying that it is 'similar' to 12, but does not reproduce its text):

12: [If anyone says that] the heavenly powers and all human beings and the devil and *the spirits of wickedness*[21] are united to God the Word in just the same way as the intel-

---

[20] Job 40:19, LXX.　　[21] Eph. 6:12.

lect which is called by them Christ and which *is in the form of God and emptied itself,* as they assert, and that the kingdom of Christ will have an end, [let him be anathema].

14: [If anyone says] that there will be one henad of all rational beings, when the hypostases and numbers are annihilated together with bodies, and that knowledge about rational beings will be accompanied by the destruction of the world and the setting aside of bodies and the abolition of names, and there will be identity of knowledge just as of hypostases, and that in this mythical restoration there will be only naked intellects [just as there were in the pre-existence blathered about by them, let him be anathema].

15: [If anyone says] that the way of life of the intellects will be identical to the earlier one when they had not yet descended or fallen, so that the beginning is identical to the end and the end is the measure of the beginning [let him be anathema].

21: PASSAGE PLACED AT THE END OF 4.3.10.

Jerome, Ep. *124.11.2 (ed. Hilberg 3, 113.3–20):*

[And again:] And since we have compared the souls who pass from this world to the infernal regions to those souls who, by a kind of death, come from the heights of heaven to our dwelling places, it must be thoughtfully inquired whether we might make this same claim even regarding the birth of every single soul, so that just as souls that are born on this earth of ours would either come from the lower world, by desiring better things, to a higher place again and assume a human body, or else descend to us from better places, so also those places, which are above in the firmament, may be occupied by some souls who have advanced from our seats to better things, and by others, who, while having fallen from the heavenly places to the firmament, yet have not sinned enough to be thrust into the lower places in which we dwell.

22: PASSAGE PLACED IN CRITICAL APPARATUS AS SUPPLEMENTING *PRINC.* 4.3.12.

Jerome, Ep. *124.11.4 (ed. Hilberg 3, 113.25–114.6):*

[And not content with this argument, he says] at the end of all things, when we shall have returned to the heavenly Jerusalem, wars of hostile powers will rise against the people of God, so that their power will not be idle, but be exercised in battles and gain firmness, which they cannot do, unless they had first resisted their adversaries, who are overcome, as we read in the book of Numbers, by reason and order and by skill in fighting.

23: PASSAGES RELATING TO *PRINC.* 4.3.13.

[a] Jerome, Ep. 124.12 (ed. Hilberg 3, 114.7–115.8), placed in critical apparatus as supplementing Princ. *4.3.13:*

[And when he has said that, according to the Apocalypse of John, *the eternal Gospel,*[22] which shall exist in the heavens, is as far superior to our Gospel as the preaching of Christ is to the mysteries of the old law, he goes to the extreme length of inferring (which is sacrilegious even to think) that Christ will also suffer in the air and in the realms above for the salvation of the demons. And although he does not actually say so, nevertheless it must be understood to follow logically, that just as he was made human being for the sake of humans, to set human beings free, so also for the salvation of the demons God will be made what they are, for whose liberation he is then to come. Lest we be thought to have added our own interpretation, we must give his very own words:] For just as he fulfilled the shadow of the Law through the shadow of the Gospel, so also, because all law is a pattern and shadow of the heavenly ceremonies, it must be carefully inquired whether we ought not to understand rightly even the heavenly <law> and the ceremonies of the heavenly worship not to possess completeness, but to need the truth of the Gospel which in the Apocalypse of John is called *the eternal Gospel*, in comparison, that is, with this Gospel of ours, which is temporal and was preached in a world and an age that shall pass away. But if we wish to continue our inquiries as far as the passion of the Lord <and> Saviour, although it is an audacious and impetuous thing to seek for his passion in the heavens, nevertheless if there are *spiritual forces of wickedness in the heavens,*[23] and if we are not ashamed to confess that the Lord was crucified in order to destroy those whom he destroyed through his passion, why should we fear to suspect that something similar may happen in the heavenly realms at the consummation of the ages, that the nations of all realms may be saved by his passion?

[b] Justinian, Ep. ad Menam (ed. Schwartz, 213.3–7), said to come from Princ. *4 and numbered by Koetschau as Fragment 30, paralleling the last sentence, said to be Origen's own words, in passage from Jerome above; inserted into text at end of* Princ. *4.3.13:*

But if we continue our inquiries as far as the passion, to seek for this in the heavenly places will seem a bold thing to do. Yet if there are *spiritual forces of wickedness* in the heavenly places, consider whether, just as we are not ashamed to confess that he was crucified here in order to destroy those whom he destroyed through his suffering, so also we should not fear to allow that a similar event also happens there and in what follows, until the consummation of the whole age.

[22] Rev. 14:6.   [23] Eph. 6:12.

24: TWO PASSAGES INSERTED IN *PRINC.* 4.4.1.

[a] Justinian (ed. Schwartz, 209.12–15), said to be from **Princ. 4** and numbered by Koetschau as Fragment 32:

Now this Son was begotten of the Father's will, for *he is the image of the invisible God,*[24] and the *effulgence of his glory, the impress of his substance,*[25] *the firstborn of all creation,*[26] a thing created, Wisdom. For Wisdom herself says, *God created me, the beginning of his ways for his works.*[27]

[b] Athanasius, **De decr. Nic. syn.** 27.2 (ed. Opitz, 23.23–30), numbered by Koetschau as Fragment 33:

If he is *the image of the invisible God,*[28] he is an invisible image; and I dare to add, that as he is a likeness of the Father, there is never a 'when' when he was not. For when did God, who according to John is called light (for *God is light*[29]), not have *the effulgence of his* own *glory,*[30] such that some daring person might assign a beginning to the existence of the Son, before which he was not? And when did the image of the ineffable and unnameable and unutterable being of the Father, his impress,[31] the Word who knows the Father, not exist? Let the one who dares to say 'there was a "when" when he was not' understand that he asserts that once Wisdom also was not and Word was not and Life was not.

25: PASSAGE INSERTED IN *PRINC.* 4.4.1, AS FRAGMENT 34.

Athanasius, **De decr. Nic. syn.** 27.3 (ed. Opitz, 23.30–24.3):

But it is not proper nor free of danger if, because of our weakness, we deprive God, as far as in us lies, of the only-begotten Word, eternally coexisting with him, the Wisdom in which he rejoiced;[32] for in this way he would be understood as not eternally rejoicing.

26: PASSAGE PLACED IN CRITICAL APPARATUS AT *PRINC.* 4.4.4, AS FRAGMENT 35.

Justinian, **Ep. ad Menam** (ed. Schwartz, 198.31–3):

[Origen, blaspheming, said that] the soul of the Lord pre-existed, and that the God Word was united to it before he took flesh from the Virgin.

---

[24] Col. 1:15.   [25] Heb. 1:3.   [26] Col. 1:15.   [27] Prov. 8:22.
[28] Col. 1:15.   [29] 1 John 1:5.   [30] Heb. 1:3.
[31] Heb. 1:3.   [32] Cf. Prov. 8:30–1.

27: PASSAGE INSERTED IN *PRINC.* 4.4.4, AS FRAGMENT 37.

Theodoret of Cyrus, **Eran.** *Dialogue 2, florilegia 58 (ed. Ettlinger, 178.5–6):*

…as the Father and the Son *are one*,[33] so also the soul of the Son and the Son are one… Cf. Theophilus of Alexandria, *Ep. pasch.* 2 (= Jerome, *Ep.* 98.16.1; ed. Hilberg 2, 200.10–11]):

Indeed, if, just as the Father and the Son *are one*,[34] so also the soul of the Son and the Son himself are one, the Father and the soul of the Saviour will be one, and so the soul itself is able to say, *He who sees me sees the Father.*[35]

28: PASSAGES PLACED IN CRITICAL APPARATUS, AS SUPPLEMENTING *PRINC.* 4.4.5.

[a] Anathema 7 of the Second Council of Constantinople, 553[36] *(ACO 4.1,249):*

[If anyone says] that Christ, said to be *in the form of God* and united to the God Word before all the ages, in the last days *emptied himself*[37] into what is human, took pity, as they put it, upon the various falls of those of the same henad, and, wishing to lead them back up, he passed through everything and took on different bodies and obtained various names, becoming all things to all, among angels an angel, among powers a power, and among other orders or classes of rational beings took on appropriately the form of each, then, like us, partook of flesh and blood and became for human beings a human being, [if anyone says this and does not profess that the God Word emptied himself and became a human being, let him be anathema].

[b] Anathema 4 of Justinian, **Ep. ad Menam** *(ed. Schwartz, 213.22–4):*

[If anyone says or has it that] the Word of God has become like all the heavenly orders, having become a cherub for the cherubim, a seraph for seraphim, and become likened to every one of the powers above [let him be anathema].

[c] Jerome, **Ruf.** *2.12 (ed. Lardet, 46.6–9):*

[I reckon among the many bad things said by Origen, these to be especially heretical:…] the soul of the Saviour existed before it was born of Mary and that it was this *which was in the form of God and thought it not robbery to be equal to God but emptied itself, taking the form of a servant.*[38]

---

[33] John 10:30.   [34] John 10:30.   [35] John 14:9, 12:45.
[36] Koetschau misattributes this canon to the Synod of 543.
[37] Phil. 2:6–7.   [38] Phil. 2:6–7.

[d] Theophilus of Alexandria, **Ep. synod.** *(= Jerome, Ep. 92.4.3; ed. Hilberg 2, 152.15–23):*

[Besides, in the books *On First Principles*, he even tries to persuade us that the living Word of God did not assume a body, for he writes, contrary to the statement of the apostle, that] *he who, in the form of God, was equal to God*, was not the Word of God, but a soul descended from the heavenly region and *emptying itself* of the form of its eternal majesty assumed a human body.[39] [In saying this he most clearly contradicts John who writes, *And the Word was made flesh*.[40] Nor is it to be believed that it was the soul of the Saviour and not the Word of God who possessed *the form* of and *equality* with the Father's majesty.]

29: PASSAGES RELATED TO *PRINC.* 4.4.8.

[a] Justinian, **Ep. ad Menam** *(ed. Schwartz, 209.8–10), said to be from* **Princ. 4**, *numbered by Koetschau as Fragment 38, and inserted into* **Princ. 4.4.8**:

Let no one stumble at the saying, if we put limits even to the power of God. For to encompass things that are endless is by nature an impossibility. But when once the things which God himself grasps have been bounded, necessity suffices as a boundary to the amount that has been bounded.

[b] Jerome, Ep. 124.13.1–2 (ed. Hilberg 3, 115.9–19), placed in critical apparatus as representing a fuller version of what Rufinus translated by the following sentence ('For by his power . . . created being'):

[And again he blasphemes against the Son by speaking thus:] for if the Son knows the Father, it would seem that by the fact that he knows the Father he is able to comprehend the Father, as if we were to say that the mind of a craftsman knows the measure of his craft. Nor can we doubt that if *the Father is in* the Son,[41] he is also comprehended by him in whom he is.

But if we mean that kind of comprehension by which one comprehends someone not only by understanding and wisdom, but holds them under authority and power, then we cannot say that the Son comprehends the Father.

[c] Justinian, **Ep. ad Menam** *(ed. Schwartz, 209.19–23), said to be from* **Princ. 4**, *numbered by Koetschau as Fragment 39, and inserted into* **Princ. 4.4.8** *one sentence after [a] above:*

[But if] the Father comprehends all things and the Son is among all things, it is clear that he also comprehends the Son. But someone else will inquire whether it is true that God being known by himself is similar to his being known by the only-begotten, and he will declare that the saying, *My Father who sent me is greater than I*,[42] is true in every

---

[39] Phil. 2:6–7.   [40] John 1:14.   [41] Cf. John 14:11.   [42] John 14:24, 28.

respect, so that the Father is great even in knowing, and is known more clearly and more perfectly by himself than by the Son.

[d] Jerome, Ep.124.13.2–3 (ed. Hilberg 3,115.19–116.4), placed by Koetschau in his critical apparatus as parallel to [c]:

[The Father, however, comprehends all things, but among all things is the Son, and therefore he comprehends the Son. And that we may know the reasons why the Father comprehends the Son, whereas the Son is not able to comprehend the Father, he adds these words:] the careful reader will inquire whether the Father is known by himself in the same way as he is known by the Son; and knowing what is written, *The Father who sent me is greater than I,* he will affirm it to be true in every respect, so that he will say that even in his knowledge the Father is greater than the Son, being more perfectly and more clearly known by himself than by the Son.

30: PASSAGE PLACED IN CRITICAL APPARATUS AS SUPPLEMENTING *PRINC.* 4.4.8.

Jerome, Ep. 124.14.1 (ed. Hilberg 3,116.5–17):

[By this passage also he is proved to hold the transmigration of souls and the annihilation of bodies:] if anyone can show that an incorporeal and rational being, when deprived of a body, can live by itself, and that it is in a worse condition when clothed with a body and in a better condition when it lays it aside, then there is no doubt that bodies do not subsist primordially, but are now made at intervals on account of the various movements of rational creatures, in order to clothe those who need it, and, in reverse, when these have been amended from the degradation of their falls to a better condition, the bodies are dissolved into nothing and this succession of changes continues for ever.

The last lines of this passage from Jerome are paralleled by a passage from Justinian, Ep. ad Menam *(ed. Schwartz, 212.16–19), which Koetschau places in the text as Fragment 40:* Necessarily the nature of bodies is not primordial, but is caused to subsist at intervals on account of certain falls that happen with rational beings who need bodies; and, again, when the restoration is perfectly accomplished, they are dissolved into nothing, so that this happens for ever.

Bibliography

Classical authors whose works are readily found in the Loeb Classical Library series or other standard series are not given here.

OT Apocryphal texts, unless otherwise indicated, are cited as found in James H. Charlesworth, *The Old TestamentPseudepigrapha* (Garden City, NY: Doubleday, 1985), 2 vols.

Editions and Translations of Origen: *On First Principles*

Butterworth, G. W., *Origen: On First Principles* (London: SPCK, 1936).

Crombie, Frederick, *On First Principles*, Ante-Nicene Christian Library (Edinburgh: T. & T. Clark, 1869); reprinted in ANF 4.

Crouzel, Henri, and Manlio Simonetti, *Origène: Traité des Principes*, SC 252, 253, 268, 269, 312 (Paris: Cerf, 1978, 1980, 1984).

Delarue, Charles, *Origenis opera omnia*, vol. 1 (Paris, 1733); reprinted in PG 11.

Fernandez, Samuel, *Orígenes: Sobre Los Principios*, Fuentes Patrísticas 27 (Madrid: Ciudad Nueva, 2015).

Görgemanns, Herwig, and Heinrich Karpp, *Origenes vier Bücher von den Prinzipien* (Darmstadt, 1976; 3rd edn 1992).

Harl, Marguerite, Gilles Dorival, and Alain Le Boulluec, *Origène. Traité des Principes (Peri Archon)*, Études Augustiniennes (Paris, 1976).

Koetschau, Paul, *De principiis*, Origenes Werke 5, GCS (Leipzig: Hinrichs, 1913).

Merlin, J., *Operum Origenis Adamantii*, vol. 4 (Paris, 1512).

Redepenning, *Origenes: De principiis* (Leipzig, 1836).

Rius-Camps, J., *Orígenes: Tractat dels Principis* (Barcelona, 1998).

Schnitzer, Karl Frank, *Origenes über die Grundlehren der Glaubenswissenschaft: Wiederherstellungsversuch* (Stuttgart: Imle u. Krauß, 1935).

Simonetti, Manlio, *I Principi di Origene*, Classici delle religioni (Turin, 1968).

Editions and Translations of Origen, *The Philocalia*

Harl, Marguerite, *Origène: Philocalie 1–20: Sur les Écritures;* together with Nicholas de Lange, ed. and trans. *La Lettre à Africanus sur l'histoire de Suzanne*, SC 302 (Paris: Cerf, 1983).

Junod, Éric, *Origène: Philocalie 21–27: Sur le libre arbitre*, SC 226 (Paris: Cerf, 1976).

Lewis, George, *The Philocalia of Origen* (Edinburgh: T. & T. Clark, 1911).

Robinson, Joseph Armitage, *The Philocalia of Origen: The Text Revised with a Critical Introduction and Indices* (Cambridge: Cambridge University Press, 1893).

Tarin, Io, *Origenis Philocalia* (Paris, 1619).

Editions and Translations of Other Works of Origen

Hexapla. Ed. Frederick Field, *Origenis Hexaplorum*, 2 vols. (Oxford: Clarendon, 1875).

Homilies on Genesis. Ed. W. A. Baehrens, GCS 29, Origenes Werke 6 (Leipzig: Hinrichs, 1920); ed. and French trans., L. Doutreleau, SC 7 (Paris: Cerf, 1976); Eng. trans. Ronald E. Heine, FC 71 (Washington, DC: Catholic University of America, 1981).

Selecta on Genesis. PG 12, 91–146.

Homilies on Exodus. Ed. W. A. Baehrens, GCS 29, Origenes Werke 6 (Leipzig: Hinrichs, 1920); ed. and French trans. M. Borret SC 321 (Paris: Cerf, 1985); Eng. trans. Ronald E. Heine, FC 71 (Washington, DC: Catholic University of America, 1981).

Selecta on Exodus. PG 12, 281–97.

Homilies on Leviticus. Ed. W. A. Baehrens, GCS 29, Origenes Werke 6 (Leipzig: Hinrichs, 1920); ed. and French trans. M. Borret, SC 286–7 (Paris: Cerf, 1981); Eng. trans. Gary Wayne Barkley, FC 83 (Washington, DC: Catholic University of America, 1990).

Selecta on Leviticus. PG 12, 395–405.

Homilies on Numbers. Ed. W. A. Baehrens, GCS 30, Origenes Werke 7 (Leipzig: Hinrichs, 1921); ed. and French trans. L. Doutreleau, SC 415, 442 (Paris: Cerf, 1996, 1999); Eng. trans. Thomas P. Scheck, Ancient Christian Texts (Downers Grove, IL: IVP Academic, 2009).

Homilies on Joshua. Ed. W. A. Baehrens, GCS 30, Origenes Werke 7 (Leipzig: Hinrichs, 1921); ed. and French trans. A. Jaubert, SC 71 (Paris: Cerf, 1960); Eng. trans. Barbara J. Bruce, ed. by Cynthia White, FC 105 (Washington, DC: Catholic University of America, 2002).

Homilies on Judges. Ed. W. A. Baehrens, GCS 30, Origenes Werke 7 (Leipzig: Hinrichs, 1921); ed. and French trans. P. Messié et al., SC 389 (Paris: Cerf, 1993); Eng. trans. Elizabeth Ann Dively Lauro, FC 119 (Washington, DC: Catholic University of America, 2010).

Homily on 1 Kings (1 Samuel) 28. Ed. W. A. Baehrens, GCS 33, Origenes Werke 8 (Leipzig: Hinrichs, 1925); ed. and French trans. P. and M. Nautin, SC 328 (Paris: Cerf, 1986); Eng. trans. Thomas P. Scheck, ACW 62 (New York, NY: Newman Press, 2010).

Homilies on the Psalms. Ed. Lorenzo Perrone, GCS ns 19, Origenes Werke 13 (Berlin: De Gruyter, 2015); Ed. and French trans. H. Crouzel and G. Dorival, *Homélies sur les Psaumes 36 à 38*, SC 411 (Paris: Cerf, 1995); ed. and French trans. *La chaîne palestinienne sur psaume 118* (Origène et al.), M. Harl and G. Dorival, SC 189–90 (Paris: Cerf, 1972).

Selecta on the Psalms. PG 12, 1053–1686.

Fragments on Proverbs. PG 13, 17–34.

Commentary and Homilies on Song of Songs. Ed. W. A. Baehrens, GCS 33, Origenes Werke 8 (Leipzig: Hinrichs, 1925); ed. and French trans. L. Brésard et al., SC 375–6 (Paris: Cerf, 1991–2); Eng. trans. R. P. Lawson, ACW 26 (New York, NY–Mahwah, NJ: Newman Press, 1956).

Homilies on Isaiah. Ed. W. A. Baehrens, GCS 33, Origenes Werke 8 (Leipzig: Hinrichs, 1925); Eng. trans. Thomas P. Scheck, ACW 68 (Washington, DC: Catholic University of America Press, 2015).

Homilies on Jeremiah. Ed. Erich Klostermann, rev. P. Nautin, GCS 6, Origenes Werke 3, 2nd edn (Berlin, 1983); ed. and French trans. P. Nautin et al., SC 232, 238 (Paris: Cerf, 1976, 1977); Eng. trans. John Clark Smith, FC 97 (Washington, DC: Catholic University of America Press, 1998).

Fragments on Lamentations. Ed. Erich Klostermann, rev. P. Nautin, GCS 6, Origenes Werke 3, 2nd edn (Berlin, 1983).

Homilies on Ezekiel. Ed. W. A. Baehrens, GCS 33, Origenes Werke 8 (Leipzig: Hinrichs, 1925); ed. and French trans. M. Borret, SC 352 (Paris: Cerf, 1989); Eng. trans. Thomas P. Scheck, ACW 62 (New York, NY: Newman Press, 2010).

Selecta on Ezekiel. PG 13, 767–825.

Commentary on Matthew. Ed. Erich Klostermann and Ernst Benz, GCS 40, Origenes Werke 10, two parts (Leipzig: Hinrichs Verlag, 1935, 1937); ed. and French trans. of books 10–11, R. Girod, SC 162 (Paris: Cerf, 1970); partial Eng. trans. in ANF 10.

Series of Commentaries on Matthew. Ed. Erich Klostermann and Ernst Benz, 2nd edn rev. U. Treu, GCS 38, Origenes Werke 11 (Berlin: Akademie Verlag, 1976).

Homilies on Luke. Ed. M. Rauer, GCS 49, Origenes Werke 9, rev. edn (Berlin: Akademie, 1959); ed. and French trans. H. Crouzel et al., SC 87 (Paris: Cerf, 1962); Eng. trans. Joseph T. Lienhard FC 94 (Washington, DC: Catholic University of America, 1996).

Fragments on Luke. Ed. M. Rauer, GCS 49, Origenes Werke 9, rev. edn (Berlin: Akademie, 1959).

Commentary on John. Ed. Erwin Preuschen, GCS 10, Origenes Werke 4 (Leipzig, Hinrichs, 1903); ed. and French trans. C. Blanc, SC 120, 157, 222, 290, 385 (Paris: Cerf, 1966, 1970, 1975, 1982, 1992); English trans. R. E. Heine, FC 80, 89 (Washington, DC: Catholic University of America, 1989, 1993).

Fragments on John. Ed. Erwin Preuschen, GCS 10, Origenes Werke 4 (Leipzig, Hinrichs, 1903).

Commentary on Romans. Ed. C. P. Hammond Bammel, Vetus Latina: Die Rest der alt-lateinischen Bibel. Aus der Geschichte der Lateinischen Bibel 16, 33, 34 (Freiburg im Breisgau: Herder, 1990, 1997, 1998); Eng. trans. Thomas P. Scheck, FC 103, 104 (Washington, DC: Catholic University of America, 2001, 2002).

Commentary on Romans; Greek Fragments. Ed. A. Ramsbotham, 'The Commentary of Origen on the Epistle to the Romans', *JTS* 13 (1912), 209–24, 357–68; *JTS* 14 (1913), 10–22.

Commentary on 1 Corinthians, Fragments. C. Jenkins, 'Origen on 1 Corinthians', *JTS* 9 (1908), 231–47, 353–72, 500–514; *JTS* 10 (1909), 29–51.

Commentary on Ephesians, Fragments. Ed. J. A. F. Gregg, 'The Commentary of Origen upon the Epistle to the Ephesians', *JTS* 3 (1902), 233–44, 398–420, 554–76; Eng. trans. R. E. Heine, *The Commentaries of Origen and Jerome on St. Paul's Epistle to the Ephesians,* OECS (Oxford: Oxford University Press, 2002).

Commentary on Titus, Fragments. PG 14, 1303–6.

Commentary on Philemon, Fragments. PG 14, 1305–8.

Against Celsus. Ed. Paul Koetschau, GCS 2 and 3, Origenes Werke 1 and 2 (Leipzig, Hinrichs, 1899); ed. and French trans. M. Borret, SC 132, 136, 147, 150, 227 (Paris: Cerf, 1967, 1968, 1969, 1976); Eng. trans. H. Chadwick (Cambridge: Cambridge University Press, 1953).

On Prayer. Ed. Paul Koetschau, GCS 3, Origenes Werke 2 (Leipzig, Hinrichs, 1899); Eng. trans. Alistair Stewart-Sykes, *Tertullian, Cyprian, Origen: On the Lord's Prayer,* PPS (Crestwood, NY: St Vladimir's Seminary Press, 2004).

Exhortation to Martyrdom. Ed. Paul Koetschau, GCS 2, Origenes Werke 1 (Leipzig, Hinrichs, 1899); Eng. trans. Rowan A. Greer, *Origen: An Exhortation to Martyrdom, Prayer and Selected Works,* Classics of Western Spirituality (New York, NY: Paulist Press, 1979).

Dialogue with Heraclides. Ed. Jean Scherer, *Entretien d'Origène avec Héraclide et les évêques ses collègues sur le Père, le Fils, et l'âme,* Publications de la Société Fouad I de Papyrologie, Textes et Documents 9 (Cairo: Institut Français d'Archéologie Orientale, 1949); ed. and French trans. Jean Scherer, SC 67 (Paris: Cerf, 1960); Eng. trans. Robert J. Daly, ACW 54 (New York, NY–Mahwah, NJ: Paulist Press, 1992).

On Pascha. Ed. and French trans. O. Guéraud and P. Nautin, *Origène: Sur la Pâque: Traité inédit publié d'après un papyrus de Toura,* Christianisme Antique 2 (Paris: Beauchesne, 1979); ed. and German trans. Bernd Witte, *Die Schrift des Origenes 'Über das Passa': Textausgabe und Kommentar* (Altenberge: Oros Verlag, 1993); Eng. trans. Robert J. Daly, ACW 54 (New York, NY: Paulist Press, 1992).

Editions and Translations of Ancient Texts

Acts of the Council of Constantinople (553). ACO 4.1. Eng. trans. R. Price, *The Acts of the Council of Constantinople of 553 with Related Texts on the Three Chapters Controversy,* Translated Texts for Historians 51, 2 vols. (Liverpool: Liverpool University Press, 2009).

Alcinous, *Epitome. Didaskalikos. Enseignement des doctrines de Platon,* ed. J. Whittaker (Paris: Belles Lettres, 1990); Eng. trans. J. Dillon, *The Handbook of Platonism* (Oxford: Clarendon, 1993).

Alexander of Aphrodisias, *On Mixture.* Ed. I. Bruns, *Alexandri Aphrodisiensis praeter commentaria scripta minora,* Commentaria in Aristotelem Graeca, suppl. 2.2 (Berlin: Reimer, 1892).

Aristotle, *Posterior Analytics.* Trans. with commentary by Jonathan Barnes, 2nd edn, Clarendon Aristotle Series (Oxford: Clarendon, 1993).

Athanasius, *On the Council of Nicaea* (also known as *On the Decrees of the Council of Nicaea).* Ed. H. G. Opitz, *Athanasius Werke,* vol. 2, pt. 1 (Berlin: De Gruyter, 1935–41), 1–45. Trans. in NPNF 4.

Athanasius, *On the Incarnation.* Trans John Behr, *On the Incarnation: Saint Athanasius,* PPS (Crestwood, NY: St Vladimir's Seminary Press, 2011).

Athenagoras, *Legatio* and *On the Resurrection,* ed. and trans. W. R. Schoedel, OECT (Oxford: Clarendon, 1972).

Pseudo-Augustine, *On the Incarnation and the Deity of Christ to Januarius,* ed. Lukas J. Dorbauer, CSEL 99 (Vienna: Verlag der Österreichen Akademie der Wissenschaften, 2011).

Barnabas, *The Epistle of Barnabas,* ed. and trans. K. Lake, LCL Apostolic Fathers, 1 (Cambridge, MA: Harvard University Press, 1985).

Clement of Alexandria, *Paedagogue,* ed. O. Stählin, 3rd edn, rev. U. Treu, GCS 12 (Berlin: Akademie Verlag, 1972); trans. in ANF 2.

Clement of Alexandria, *Protrepticus,* ed. O. Stählin, 3rd edn, rev. U. Treu, GCS 12 (Berlin: Akademie Verlag, 1972).

Clement of Alexandria, *Stromata. Stromata I–VI,*ed. O. Stählin, 3rd edn, rev. L. Früchtel, GCS 52 (Berlin: Akademie Verlag, 1972); trans. in ANF 2; *Stromata VII, VIII,* ed. O. Stählin, 2nd edn rev. L. Früchtel and U. Treu, GCS 17 (Berlin: Akademie Verlag, 1970); trans. in ANF 2.

Clement of Alexandria, *Excerpta ex Theodoto,* ed. O. Stählin, 2nd edn rev. L. Früchtel and U. Treu, GCS 17 (Berlin: Akademie Verlag, 1970); trans. in ANF 2.

Clement of Alexandria, *Eclogae Propheticae.* Ed. O. Stählin, 2nd edn, rev. L. Früchtel and U. Treu, GCS 17 (Berlin: Akademie Verlag, 1970); trans. in ANF 2.

Clement of Rome, *First Epistle,* ed. and Eng. trans. Bart D. Ehrman, LCL 24, The Apostolic Fathers (Cambridge, MA: Harvard University Press, 2003).

Pseudo-Clement, *Recognitions.* PG 1; Eng. trans. in ANF 8.

Cyril of Alexandria, *First Letter to Succensus,* ed. and trans. Lionel R. Wickham, *Cyril of Alexandria, Select Letters,* OECT (Oxford: Clarendon, 1983).

The Epistle to Diognetus, ed. and Eng. trans. Clayton N. Jefford, OAP (Oxford: Oxford University Press, 2013).

The First Book of Enoch, ed. Johannes Flemming and Ludwig Radermacher, GCS 5 (Leipzig: Hinrichs, 1901); Eng. trans. George W. E. Nickelsburg and James C. Vanderkam (Minneapolis, MN: Augsburg, 2004).

Epiphanius, *Panarion,* ed. K. Holl: Epiphanius I, *Ancoratus, Panarion* (heresies 1–33), GCS 25 (Leipzig: Hinrichs Verlag, 1915); Epiphanius II, *Panarion* (heresies 34–64), rev. J. Dummer, GCS 31 (Berlin: Akademie Verlag, 1980); Epiphanius III, *Panarion* (heresies 65–80), rev. J. Dummer, GCS 37 (Berlin: Akademie Verlag, 1985). Selective Eng. trans. P. R. Amidon, *The Panarion of Epiphanius of Salamis: Selected Passages* (Oxford: Oxford University Press, 1990).

Eusebius of Caesarea, *Historia ecclesiastica,* ed. and trans. K. Lake, LCL, 2 vols. (Cambridge, MA: Harvard University Press, 1989).

Eusebius of Caesarea, *Ecclesiastical Theology* and *Against Marcellus,* ed. E. Klostermann, 3rd edn, rev. G. C. Hansen, *Eusebius Werke, 4: Gegen Marcell, Über die kirchliche Theologie, Die Fragmente Marcells,* GCS 14 (Berlin: Akademie Verlag, 1972).

Gregory of Nyssa, *Against Eunomius 1,* ed. W. Jaeger, *Contra Eunomium libri,* GNO 1 (Leiden: Brill, 2002 [1921, 1960]). Trans. Stuart Hall in L. F. Mateo-Seco and J. I. Bastero, *El 'Contra Eunomium'* (Pamplona: Universidad de Navarra, 1988); trans. also in NPNF 5.

Gregory of Nyssa, *Against Eunomius 3,* ed. W. Jaeger, *Contra Eunomium libri,* GNO 2 (Leiden: Brill, 2002 [1921, 1960]); trans. Stuart Hall available at http://theo.kuleuven. be/page/translations (accessed 23 December 2015); trans. also in NPNF 5, where *Eun.* 3.3 is counted as *Eun.* 5, and only divided by chapters, not sections. Trans. in NPNF 5, 35–314. (Note that the numeration of the books of *Eun.* in NPNF differs from that of GNO.)

Gregory of Nyssa, *Antirrheticus against Apollinarius,* ed. F. Müller, in W. Jaeger ed., *Opera dogmatica minora,* GNO 3.1 (Leiden: Brill, 1958), 131–233. Trans. Robin Orton, FC 131 (Washington, DC: Catholic University of America, 2015).

Gregory Thaumaturgus, *Oration of Thanksgiving,* ed. and French trans. H. Crouzel, *Remerciement à Origène de Grégoire le Thaumaturge suivi de la lettre d'Origène à*

Grégoire, SC 148 (Paris: Cerf, 1969); Eng. trans. in ANF 6; W. C. Metcalfe, *Gregory Thaumaturgus: Origen the Teacher* (London and New York, NY: SPCK, 1907).

Hermas, *The Shepherd,* ed. and trans. K. Lake, LCL Apostolic Fathers, 2 (Cambridge, MA: Harvard University Press, 1976).

Corpus Hermeticum, ed. Arthur Darby Nock and André-Jean Festugière, Collections des Universités de France (Paris: Les Belles Lettres, 1945–54).

Hilary of Poitiers, *Tractates on the Psalms.* CSEL 22 (Vienna and Prague: Tempsky & Leipzig: Freytag, 1891).

Ignatius of Antioch, *Letters,* ed. and trans. Alistair Stewart (Crestwood, NY: St. Vladimir's Seminary Press, 2013).

Irenaeus of Lyons, *Against the Heresies: Haer.* 1–3 ed. and French trans. A. Rousseau and L. Doutreleau, SC 263–4, 293–4, 210–11 (Paris: Cerf, 1979, 1982, 1974); *Haer.* 4 ed. and French trans. A. Rousseau, B. Hemmerdinger, L. Doutreleau, and C. Mercier, SC 100 (Paris: Cerf, 1965); *Haer.* 5 ed. and French trans. A. Rousseau, L. Doutreleau, and C. Mercier SC 152–3 (Paris: Cerf, 1969); Eng. trans. ANF 1; *Haer.* 1, D. J. Unger, rev. J. J. Dillon, ACW 55 (New York, NY: Paulist Press, 1992); *Haer.* 2, ACW 65 (New York, NY: Paulist Press, 2012); *Haer.* 3, D. J. Unger, rev. Irenaeus M. C. Steenberg, ACW 64 (New York, NY: Newman Press, 2012).

Irenaeus of Lyons, *Demonstration of the Apostolic Preaching,* ed. and Eng. trans. K. Ter-Mekerttschian, and S. G. Wilson, with Prince Maxe of Saxony, French trans. J. Barthoulot, PO 12.5 (Paris, 1917; repr. Turnhout: Brepols, 1989); ed. and French trans. A. Rousseau, SC 406 (Paris: Cerf, 1995); Eng. trans. J. Behr (New York, NY: Saint Vladimir's Seminary Press, 1997).

Ascension of Isaiah, ed. E. Norelli, CCSA 8 (Leuven: Brepols, 1995): Eng. trans. M. A. Knibb in James H. Charlesworth, *The Old Testament Pseudepigrapha* (Garden City, NY: Doubleday, 1985), vol. 2, 143–76; and trans. R. H. Charles, rev. J. M. T. Barton in H. F. D. Sparks, *Apocryphal Old Testament* (Oxford: Clarendon Press, 1984).

Jerome, *Epistles.* Ed. I. Hilberg, CSEL 54, 55, 56 (Vienna: Tempsky & Leipzig: Freytag, 1910, 1912, 1918); Eng. trans. of selected letters in NPNF Series 2, vol. 6.

Jerome, *Apology Against Rufinus,* ed. P. Lardet, CCSL 79. Eng. trans. in NPNF Series 2, vol. 3.

Jerome, *On Famous Men.* PL 33.601–720; trans. in NPNF, Series 2, vol. 3.

Jerome, *Against John of Jerusalem.* PL 23.

Jerome, *Commentary on Isaiah,* ed. M. Adriaen, CCSL 73–73A (Turnholt: Brepols, 1963); Eng. trans. Thomas Scheck, ACW 68 (New York, NY: Paulist Press, 2015).

John of Damascus, *Sacra Parallela.* PG 96.

John of Scythopolis. *Scholia on Dionysius the Areopagite's Ecclesiastical Hierarchy.* PG 4; Eng. trans. Paul Rorem and John C. Lamoreaux, *John of Scythopolis and the Dionysian Corpus: Annotating the Areopagite,* OECS (Oxford: Oxford University Press, 1998).

Julius Africanus, *Fragments of Five Books on Chronography.* PG 10, 63–94.

Justin Martyr, *First and Second Apologies,* ed. and Eng. trans. Denis Minns and Paul Parvis, *Justin, Philosopher and Martyr: Apologies,* OECT (Oxford: Oxford University Press, 2009).

Justin Martyr, *Dialogue with Trypho,* ed. M. Marcovich, *Iustini martyris dialogus cum Tryphone,* PTS 47 (Berlin, New York, NY: De Gruyter, 1997); trans. in ANF 1.

Justinian, *Epistle to Menas,* ed. E. Schwartz, ACO 3, 189–214.

Leontius Scholasticus, *De sectis.* PG 86A.1193–1268.

Nicholas Cabasilas, *Life in Christ*, ed. and French trans. M.-H. Congourdeau, SC 361 (Paris: Cerf, 1990); Eng. trans. C. J. deCatanzaro (Crestwood, NY: St Vladimir's Seminary Press, 1974).

Pamphilus of Caesarea, *Apology for Origen,* ed. and trans. R. Amacker and E. Junod, SC 464, 465 (Paris: Cerf, 2002); Eng. trans. Thomas P. Scheck, FC 120 (Washington, DC: Catholic University of America, 2010).

Photius, *Bibliotheca*, ed. and French trans. R. Henry, 8 vols. (Paris: Belles Lettres, 1959–77); trans. (to chap. 145) J. H. Freese (London: SPCK, 1920).

Porphyry, *Commentary on Aristotle's Categories,* ed. A. Busse, *Porphyrii isagoge et in Aristotelis categorias commentarium,* Commentaria in Aristotelem Graeca, 4.1 (Berlin: Reimer, 1887).

Ptolemy, *Letter to Flora.* Text from Epiphanius, *Panarion* 33.3–7. *Ptolémée: Lettre à Flora,* ed. and trans. G. Quispel, SC 24 bis (Paris: Cerf, 1966); Eng. trans. in P. R. Amidon, *The Panarion of Epiphanius of Salamis: Selected Passages* (Oxford: Oxford University Press, 1990), 119–23, and in R. Grant, *Second-Century Christianity: A Collection of Fragments* (London: SPCK, 1946), 30–7.

Rufinus, *On the Falsification of the Books of Origen,* ed. and trans. R. Amacker and E. Junod, SC 464, 465 (Paris: Cerf, 2002); Eng. trans. Thomas P. Scheck, FC 120 (Washington, DC: Catholic University of America, 2010).

Rufinus, *Apology against Jerome,* ed. Manlio Simonetti, CCSL 20. Eng. trans. in NPNF, Series 2, vol. 3.

Rufinus (Palestine), *On Faith.* PL 21.

Stobaeus, ed. C. Wachsmuth and O. Hense, *Ioannis Stobaei Anthologium,* vols. 1–4 (Berlin: Weidmann, 1884–1912).

Stoicorum Veterum Fragmenta, ed. J. von Arnim (Leipzig: Teubner, 1903–24).

Tatian, *Oration to the Greeks,* ed. and trans. M. Whittaker, OECT (Oxford: Clarendon, 1982).

Tertullian, *Against Marcion,* ed. and trans. E. Evans, OECT (Oxford: Clarendon Press, 1972).

Tertullian, *Against Praxeas,* ed. and trans. E. Evans (London: SPCK, 1948).

Tertullian, *On the Resurrection,* ed. and trans. E. Evans (London: SPCK, 1960).

Tertullian, *Prescription against the Heresies,* ed. R. F. Refoulé, SC 46 (Paris: Cerf, 1957).

Tertullian, *Apology,* ed. and trans. T. R. Glover and Gerald H. Rendall, LCL 250 (Cambridge, MA, Harvard University Press, 1931).

Tertullian, *On the Incarnation of Christ (Carne Christi),* ed. E. Evans (London: SPCK, 1956).

Tertullian, *On the Soul,* ed. J. H. Waszink (Amsterdam: Mülenhoff, 1947); Eng. trans. in ANF 3.

Tertullian, *Against the Jews,* ed. H. Tränkle (Wiesbaden: Steiner, 1964); Eng. trans. in ANF 3.

Theodoret of Cyrus, *Eranistes,* ed. Gerard H. Ettlinger (Oxford: Oxford University Press, 1975).

Theophilus of Antioch, *To Autolycus,* ed. and trans. R. M. Grant, OECT (Oxford: Clarendon, 1970).

Secondary Material

Albright, William, *Yahweh and the Gods of Canaan: A Historical Analysis of Two Contrasting Faiths* (Garden City, NY: Doubleday, 1968).

Alexandre, Monique, 'Le statut des questions concernant la matière dans le *Peri Archon*', in Crouzel et al., eds., *Origeniana*, 63–81.

Ashton, John, *Understanding the Fourth Gospel*, new edn (Oxford: Oxford University Press, 2007).

Bardy, Gustave, 'Les citations bibliques d'Origène dans le *De Principiis*', *RB* 28 (1919), 106–35.

Bardy, Gustave, 'Le texte du *Peri Archon* d'Origène et Justinien', *RSR* 10 (1920), 224–52.

Bardy, Gustave, *Recherches sur l'histoire du texte et des versions latines du* De Principiis *d'Origène*, Mémoires et Travaux des Facultés catholiques de Lille, 25 (Paris: Édouard Champion, 1923).

Behr, John, *Asceticism and Anthropology in Irenaeus and Clement*, OECS (Oxford: Oxford University Press, 2000).

Behr, John, *The Way to Nicaea*, Formation of Christian Theology, 1 (Crestwood, NY: St Vladimir's Seminary Press, 2001).

Behr, John, *The Nicene Faith*, Formation of Christian Theology, 2 (Crestwood, NY: St Vladimir's Seminary Press, 2004).

Behr, John, *The Mystery of Christ: Life in Death* (Crestwood, NY: St Vladimir's Seminary Press, 2006).

Behr, John, *The Case against Diodore and Theodore: Texts and their Contexts*, OECT (Oxford: Oxford University Press, 2011).

Behr, John, *Irenaeus of Lyons*, CTIC (Oxford: Oxford University Press, 2013).

Behr, John, *Becoming Human: Meditations on Christian Anthropology in Word and Image* (Crestwood, NY: St Vladimir's Seminary Press, 2013).

Bostock, G., 'The Sources of Origen's Doctrine of Pre-Existence', in L. Lies, ed., *Origeniana Quarta*, 259–64.

Brightman, F. E., *Eastern Liturgies* (Oxford: Clarendon Press, 1896).

Broek, R. van den, 'The Christian School of Alexandria', in J. W. Drijvers and A. A. MacDonald, eds., *Centers of Learning and Location in Pre-Modern Europe and the Near East* (Leiden: Brill, 1995), 39–47.

Buchinger, Harald, *Pascha bei Origenes*, Innsbrucker theologische Studien, 64 (Innsbruck: Tyrolia, 2005).

Chadwick, Henry, *Early Christian Thought and the Classical Tradition* (Oxford: Clarendon, 1966).

Clark, Elizabeth A., *The Origenist Controversy: The Cultural Construction of an Early Christian Debate* (Princeton, NJ: Princeton University Press, 1992).

Collins, John J., *The Apocalyptic Imagination: An Introduction to the Jewish Matrix of Christianity*, 2nd edn (Grand Rapids, MI: Eerdmans, 1998).

Cramer, J. A., *Catenae Graecorum Patrum in Novem Testamentum*, vol. 4, *In Epistolam S. Pauli ad Romanos* (Oxford, 1844).

Crouzel, Henri, *Bibliographie critique d'Origène*, Instrumenta Patristica 8 (Steenbrugge: Abbatia s. Petri, 1971).

Crouzel, Henri, 'Comparaisons précises entre les fragments du *Peri Archon* selon la *Philocalie* et la traduction de Rufin', in Crouzel et al., eds., *Origeniana*,113–21.

Crouzel, Henri, 'Qu'a voulu faire Origène en composant le *Traité des Principes*', *BLE* 76 (1975), 161–86, 241–60.

Crouzel, Henri, *Bibliographie critique d'Origène*, Supplement 1, Instrumenta Patristica 8a (Steenbrugge: Abbatia s. Petri, 1982).

Crouzel, Henri, 'Les condamnations subies par Origène et sa doctrine', in W. A. Bienert and U. Kühneweg, eds., *Origeniana Septima* (Leuven: Peeters, 1999), 311–15.

Crouzel, Henri, *Origen*, trans. A. S. Worrall (Edinburgh: T&T Clark, 1989 [French edition, 1985]).

Crouzel, Henri, Gennaro Lomiento, and Joseph Rius-Camps, eds., *Origeniana: Premier colloque international des études origéniennes (Monserrat, 18–21 septembre 1973)*, Quaderni di 'Vetera Christianorum', 21 (Bari: Istituto di Letteratura Cristiana Antica-Università di Bari, 1975).

Daley, Brian E., 'What did Origenism Mean in the Sixth Century', in G. Dorival and A. Le Boulluec, eds., *Origeniana Sexta*, 627–38.

Daley, Brian E., 'Origen's *De Principiis*: A Guide to the Principles of Christian Scriptural Interpretation', in John Petruccione, ed., *Nova et Vetera: Patristic Studies in Honor of Patrick Halton* (Washington, DC: Catholic University of America Press, 1998), 3–21.

Davis, Joshua B., and Douglas Harink, *Apocalyptic and the Future of Theology: With and Beyond J. Louis Martyn* (Eugene, OR: Cascade, 2012).

Dechow, Jon F., 'The Heresy Charges against Origen', in L. Lies, ed., *Origeniana Quarta*, 112–22.

Dechow, Jon F., *Dogma and Mysticism in Early Christianity: Epiphanius of Cyprus and the Legacy of Origen*, NAPS Monograph Series, 13 (Macon, GA: Mercer University Press, 1988).

Dorival, Gilles, 'Remarque sur la forme du *Peri Archon*', in Crouzel et al., eds., *Origeniana*, 33–45.

Dorival, Gilles, 'Nouvelles remarques sur la forme du *Traité des Principes*', *RAug* 22 (1987), 67–108.

Dorival, G. and A. Le Boulluec, *Origeniana Sexta* (Leuven: Peeters, 1995).

Edwards, Mark Julian, *Origen Against Plato*, Ashgate Studies in Philosophy and Theology in Late Antiquity (Aldershot: Ashgate, 2002).

Eliot, T. S., *Collected Poems 1909–1962* (Orlando: Harcourt, 1963).

Festugière, André-Jean, *La révélation d'Hermès Trismégiste*, Études Bibliques, 4 vols. (Paris: Cabalda, 1944–54).

Fuhrman, Manfred, *Das systematische Lehrbuch: Ein Beitrag zur Geschichte der Wissenschaften in der Antike* (Göttingen: Vandenhoeck and Ruprecht, 1960).

Gasparro, Giulia Sfameni, *Origene e la tradizione origeniana in Occidente: letture storico-religiose*, Biblioteca di scienze religiose (Libreria Ateneo salesiano) 142 (Rome: LAS, 1998).

Graham, Susan L., 'Structure and Purpose of Irenaeus' *Epideixis*', *StP* 36 (Leuven: Peeters, 2001), 210–21.

Grant, Robert M., 'Eusebius and his Lives of Origen', in *Forma Futuri: Studi in Onore del Cardinale Michele Pellegrino* (Turin: Bottega d'Erasmo, 1975), 635–49.

Guillaumont, Antoine, *Les 'Képhalia gnostica' d'Évagre le Pontique et l'histoire de l'origénisme chez les Grecs et chez les Syriens,* Patristica Sorbonensia, 5 (Paris: Seuil, 1962).

Hamburger, Jeffrey F., *St. John the Divine: The Deified Evangelist in Medieval Art and Theology* (Berkeley, CA: University of California Press, 2002).

Harl, Marguerite, 'Recherches sur le περὶ ἀρχῶν d'Origène en vue d'une nouvelle édition: La division en chapitres', *StP* 3, TU 78 (Berlin, 1961), 57–67.

Harl, Marguerite, 'Structure et coherénce du *Peri Archôn*', in Crouzel et al., eds., *Origeniana,* 11–32.

Harl, Marguerite, 'La préexistence des âmes dans l'oeuvre d'Origène', in Lothar Lies, ed., *Origeniana Quarta,* 238–58.

Hay, David M., *Glory at the Right Hand: Psalm 110 in Early Christianity,* SBL Monograph Series, 18 (Nashville, TN: Abingdon, 1973).

Heine, Ronald E., *The Commentaries of Origen and Jerome on St Paul's Epistles to the Ephesians,* OECS (Oxford: Oxford University Press, 2002).

Heine, Ronald E., *Origen: Scholarship in Service of the Church,* CTIC (Oxford: Oxford University Press, 2010).

Hoek, Annewies van den, 'The Catechetical School of Early Christian Alexandria and Its Philonic Heritage', *HTR* 90 (1997), 59–87.

Holl, Karl, 'Die Zeitfolge des ersten origenistischen Streits' (1916), reprinted in idem, *Gesammelte Aufsätze zur Kirchengeschichte. II Der Osten* (Tübingen: J.C.B. Mohr [Paul Siebeck], 1928), 310–50.

Hombergen, D., *The Second Origenist Controversy: A New Perspective on Cyril of Scythopolis' Monastic Biographies as Historical Sources for Sixth-Century Origenism,* Studia Anselmiana, 132 (Rome: S. Anselmo, 2001).

Huby, P., and G. Neals, eds., *The Criterion of Truth* (Liverpool: Liverpool University Press, 1989).

Hurtado, Larry, *One God, One Lord: Early Christian Devotion and Ancient Jewish Monotheism* (Philadelphia, PA: Fortress Press, 1988).

Hurtado, Larry, *Lord Jesus Christ: Devotion to Jesus in Earliest Christianity* (Grand Rapids, MI: Eerdmans, 2003).

Jonas, Hans, 'Origenes' *ΠΕΡΙ ΑΡΧΩΝ:* Ein System patristischer Gnosis', *Theologische Zeitschrift* 4 (1948), 101–19.

Junod, Éric, 'Que savons-nous des "Scholies" [*ΣΧΟΛΙΑ ΣΗΜΕΙΩΣΕΙΣ*] d'Origène', in G. Dorival and A. Le Boulluec, *Origeniana Sexta,* 133–49.

Kannengiesser, Charles, 'Origen, Systematician in *De Principus*', in R. J. Daly, ed., *Origeniana Quinta* (Leuven: University Press–Peeters, 1992), 395–405.

Kannengiesser, Charles, and W. L. Petersen, eds., *Origen of Alexandria: His World and His Legacy* (Notre Dame, IN: University of Notre Dame Press, 1988).

Kettler, Franz Heinrich, *Der ursprüngliche Sinn der Dogmatik des Origenes,* Beiheft 31 zur *ZNTW* (Berlin, 1966).

Koch, Hal, *Pronoia und Paideusis. Studien über Origenes und sein Verhältnis zum Platonismus* (Berlin: De Gruyter, 1932).

Kübel, Paul, 'Zum Aufbau von Origenes De Principiis', *VC* 25 (1971), 31–9.

Kuschel , Karl-Josef, *Born Before All Time? The Dispute over Christ's Origin* (New York, NY: Crossroad, 1992).

Lauro, Elizabeth Ann Dively, *The Soul and the Spirit of Scripture Within Origen's Exegesis*, The Bible in Ancient Christianity (Atlanta, GA: Society of Biblical Literature, 2010).

Le Boulluec, A., 'La place de la polémique antignostique dans le *Peri Archon*', in Crouzel et al., eds., *Origeniana*, 47–61.

Ledegang, F., *Mysterium Ecclesiae: Images of the Church and Its Members in Origen*, Bibliotheca Ephemeridum Theologicarum Lovaniensium, 156 (Leuven: Leuven University Press–Peeters, 2001).

Lied, Sverre Elgvin, 'Participation in Heavenly Worship: The Pre-Nicene Growth of a Concept' (PhD thesis, Stavanger: VID Specialized University, 2016).

Lies, Lothar, ed., *Origeniana Quarta* (Innsbruck: Tyrolia Verlag, 1987).

Lies, Lothar, *Origenes' Peri Archon: Eine undogmatische Dogmatik: Einführung und Erläuterung* (Darmstadt: Wissenschaftliche Buchgesellschaft, 1992).

Long, A. A., and D. N. Sedley, *The Hellenistic Philosophers*, vol. 1, *Translations of the Principal Sources, with Philosophical Commentary;* vol. 2, *Greek and Latin Texts with Notes and Bibliography* (Cambridge: Cambridge University Press, 1987).

Lubac, Henri de, *History and Spirit: The Understanding of Scripture according to Origen*, trans. Anne Englund Nash (San Francisco, CA: Ignatius Press, 2007 [1950]).

Martens, Peter W., *Origen and Scripture: The Contours of the Exegetical Life*, OECS (Oxford: Oxford Christian Studies, 2012).

Martyn, J. Louis, *History and Theology in the Fourth Gospel*, 3rd edn (Louisville, KY: Westminster John Knox Press, 2003 [1968]).

Martyn, J. Louis, *Theological Issues in the Letters of Paul*, Studies of the New Testament and its World (Edinburgh: T & T Clark, 1997).

McCabe, Herbert 'The Involvement of God', *New Blackfriars* (November 1985), reprinted in idem, *God Matters* (London: Geoffrey Chapman, 1987; Continuum, 2012), 39–51.

McGuckin, John Anthony, 'Structural Design and Apologetic Intent in Origen's *Commentary on John*', in G. Dorival and A. Le Boulluec, eds., *Origeniana Sexta*, 441–57.

McGuckin, John Anthony, ed., *The Westminster Handbook to Origen* (Louisville, KY: Westminster John Knox Press, 2004).

McLynn, Neil, 'What was the *Philocalia* of Origen?', *Meddelanden från Collegium Patristicum Lundense* 19 (2004), 32–43.

Miller, Patrick D., 'The Divine World and the Human World', chapter 1 in *idem, Genesis 1–11: Studies in Structure and Theme*, Journal for the Study of the Old Testament Supplement 8 (Sheffield: JSOT Press, 1978), 9–26.

Miller, Patrick D., 'The Sovereignty of God', in Doug Miller, ed., *The Hermeneutical Quest* (Allison Park, PA: Pickwick, 1986), 129–44.

Mitchell, Margaret M., 'Patristic Rhetoric on Allegory: Origen and Eustathius put 1 Samuel 28 on Trial', *JR* 85 (2005), 414–45.

Mullen, E. Theodore, *The Assembly of Gods: The Divine Council and Early Hebrew Literature*, Harvard Semitic Monographs, 24 (Chico, CA: Scholars Press, 1986).

Müller, Karl, 'Kritische Beiträge', *Sitzungsberichte der deutschen Akademie der Wissenschaften zu Berlin*, II (1919), 616–31 ('Zu den Auszügen des Hieronymus, Ad Avitum, aus des Origenes *Peri Archon*', 616–29; 'Über die angeblichen Auszüge Gregors von Nyssa aus *Peri Archon*', 630–1).

Nautin, Pierre, *Origène: Sa vie et son oeuvre*, Christianisme Antique 1 (Paris: Beauchesne, 1977).

Norden, Eduard, 'Die Composition und Litteraturgattung der horazischen Epistula ad Pisones', *Hermes* 40 (1905), 481–528.

Ramelli, Ilaria, and David Konstan, *Terms for Eternity: Aiônios and Aïdios in Classical and Christian Texts* (Piscataway, NJ: Gorgias Press, 2011).

Rist, J. M., 'The Greek and Latin Texts of the Discussion on Free Will in *De Principiis*, Book III', in Crouzel et al., eds., *Origeniana*, 97–111.

Rius-Camps, J., 'La suerte final de la naturaleza corpórea según el *Peri Archon* de Origenes', *StP* 14, TU 117 (Berlin: Akademie, 1976), 167–79.

Rombs, Ronnie, 'A Note on the Status of Origen's *De Principiis* in English', *VC* 61 (2007), 21–9.

Rowland, Christopher, *The Open Heaven: A Study of Apocalyptic in Judaism and Early Christianity* (New York, NY: Crossroad, 1982).

Schofield, M., M. Burnyeat, and J. Barnes, eds., *Doubt and Dogmatism: Studies in Hellenistic Epistemology* (Oxford: Oxford University Press, 1980).

Segal, Alan F., *Two Powers in Heaven: Early Rabbinic Reports about Christianity and Gnosticism,* Studies in Late Antiquity (Leiden: Brill, 1977; reprinted Waco, TX: Baylor University Press, 2012).

Simonetti, Manlio, 'Osservazioni sulla struttura del *De Principiis* di Origene', *Rivista di filologia e d'istruzione classica,* n.s. 40 (1962), 273–90, 372–93.

Smith, Mark S., *The Early History of God: Yahweh and the Other Deities in Ancient Israel* (San Francisco, CA: Harper, 1990).

Sommer, Benjamin D., *The Bodies of God and the World of Ancient Israel* (Cambridge: Cambridge University Press, 2009).

Spinks, Bryan D., *The Sanctus in the Eucharistic Prayer* (Cambridge: Cambridge University Press, 1991).

Steidle, Basilius, 'Neue Untersuchungen zu Origenes Περὶ Ἀρχῶν', *ZNTW* 40 (1941), 236–43.

Stewart, Alistair C., *The Original Bishops: Office and Order in the First Christian Communities* (Grand Rapids, MI: Baker Academic, 2014).

Stone, Michael E., 'List of Revealed Things in the Apocalyptic Literature', in Frank Moore Cross et al., eds., *Magnalia Dei: The Mighty Acts of God* (New York, NY, 1976), 414–52.

Striker, G., 'Κριτήριον τῆς ἀληθείας', *Nachrichten der Akademie der Wissenschaften in Göttingen,* Phil.-hist. Kl. (1974), 2:47–110.

Sumner, Paul B., 'Visions of the Divine Council in the Hebrew Bible' (PhD thesis, Malibu, CA: Pepperdine University, 1991), available at http://www.hebrew-streams. org/works/hebrew/council.html (accessed 19 December 2015).

Taft, Robert, 'The Interpolation of the Sanctus into the Anaphora: When and Where? A review of the Dossier', *OCP* 57 (1991), 281–308; 58 (1992), 83–121.

Torjesen, Karen Jo, *Hermeneutical Procedure and Theological Method in Origen's Exegesis* (Berlin: De Gruyter, 1986).

Torjesen, Karen Jo, 'Hermeneutics and Soteriology in Origen's *Peri Archon*', *StP* 21 (Leuven: Peeters, 1989), 333–48.

Tzamalikos, P., *The Concept of Time in Origen* (Bern: Peter Lang, 1991).

Tzamalikos, P., *Origen: Philosophy of History and Eschatology*, Supplements to *VC*, 85 (Leiden: Brill, 2007).

Widdicombe, Peter, *The Fatherhood of God from Origen to Athanasius* (Oxford: Clarendon, 1994).

Wiegel, James B., 'The Trinitarian Structure of Irenaeus' *Demonstration of the Apostolic Preaching*', SVTQ 58.1 (2014), 113–39.

Wilken, Robert L., 'Alexandria: A School for Training in Virtue', in P. Henry, ed., *Schools of Thought in the Christian Tradition* (Philadelphia, PA: Fortress Press, 1984), 15–30.

Williams, Rowan, *Arius: History and Tradition*, 2nd edn (London: SCM Press, 2001 [1987]).

Williams, Rowan, 'Damnosa haereditas: Pamphilus' *Apology* and the Reputation of Origen', in H. C. Brennecke, E. L. Grasmück, and C. Markschies, eds., *Logos: Festschrift für Luise Abramowski zum 8 Juli 1993* (Berlin: De Gruyter, 1993), 151–69.

Williams, Rowan, 'Origen: Between Orthodoxy and Heresy', in W. A. Bienert and U. Kühneweg, *Origeniana Septima* (Leuven: Peeters, 1999), 3–14.

Worp, K. A., and K. Treu, 'Origenes' *De Principiis* III 1, 6–8 in einem Amsterdamer Papyrus', *Zeitschrift für Papyrologie und Epigrafik* 350 (1979), 43–7.

Young, Frances M., *Biblical Exegesis and the Formation of Christian Culture* (Cambridge: Cambridge University Press, 1997).

Index of Ancient Sources

Where texts are not divided into books and chapters, reference is given to the page number of the edition cited in the bibliography.

IV Other Ancient Texts

Index of Modern Authors Cited